Canadian Professional Meat Cutting

A textbook for
Industry Practitioners
and those interested in a career in
The Meat Industry

www.meatforce.ca
info@meatforce.ca

Written by Daniel Westgeest and edited by Kenneth Jakes for the CPMCA

Tellwell Talent
www.tellwell.ca

ISBN
978-0-2288-0191-7 (Hardcover)
978-0-2288-0190-0 (Paperback)

Acknowledgements

Consumer demand and Industry needs are the driving force behind the education of those seeking a career in meat cutting. It is exactly these types of concerns as expressed with food handling, safety, origin and knowledge of products that make it imperative those working with food need acquire nationally recognized training certification. This textbook is designed to supplement, aid and guide the reader toward that end - nationally recognized training certification.

The CPMCA acknowledges the outstanding contributions of both Daniel Westgeest and Kenneth Jakes for their hard work, commitment, and perseverance in bringing this textbook to publication. Also, a special thanks goes out to Jakes & Associates Meat Industry Specialists, for the over 500 unmarked images and graphics used throughout this text.

This textbook was made possible by the following contributors:

PROJECT TEAM:

Daniel Westgeest	*Writer, Researcher, Editor, Consultant & Subject Matter Expert*
Kenneth Jakes	*Project Manager, Editor, Consultant & Subject Matter Specialist*
Tellwell Talent	*Publishers, Editing & Design*

PRINCIPAL FUNDING PARTNERS:

Alberta Agriculture & Forestry (AF)	*Project Principal Funding Partner*
Canadian Professional Meat Cutters Association	*Joint Funding partner*

ADDITIONAL FUNDING & RESOURCE CONTRIBUTORS:

Saskatchewan Polytechnic, Prince Albert, Saskatchewan	*www.saskpolytech.ca*
TRU, Faculty of Adventure, Culinary Arts & Tourism, Kamloops BC	*www.tru.ca*
Malabar Super Spice Company, Ontario	*www.malabarsuperspice.com*
Canada Beef, Alberta	*www.canadabeef.ca*
Canada Pork International, Ontario	*www.canadapork.com*
Stuffer's Supply Company, Langley BC	*www.stuffers.com*

RESOURCE CONTRIBUTORS:

Alberta Sheep Breeders Association	*www.albertasheepbreeders.ca*
Andrew Snucins Photographer, Kamloops BC	*www.andrewsnucins.ca*
Angela MacEachem Graphic Design, Alberta	*instgram: angela_maceachem_photography*
Archives Canada	*www.archivescanada.ca*
Biro USA	*www.birosaw.com*
Bunzl Canada & USA	*www.bunzlpd.com*
Canadian Beef Grading Agency	*www.beefgradingagency.ca*
Canadian Bison Association	*www.canadianbison.ca*
Canadian Blonde d'Aquitaine Association	*www.canadianblondeassociation.ca*
Canadian Charolais Association	*www.charolais.ca*
Canadian Encyclopedia, The	*http://www.thecanadianencyclopedia.ca*
Canadian Limousin Association	*www.limousin.com*
Canadian Poultry & Egg Processor Council	*www.cpepc.ca*
Canadian Professional Meat Cutters Association	*www.meatforce.ca*
Canadian Swine Breeder Association	*www.canswine.ca*
City of Toronto Archives	*www.toronto.ca*
Columbia Products, USA	*www.columbiasinks.com*
Costco, Canada	*www.costco.ca*
Diversey, USA	*www.diversey.com*
Dreamstime stock images	*www.dreamstime.com*
F.Dick, Germany	*www.dick.de*
FG Deli Group, Langley BC	
Fisherman's Market, Kamloops BC	*www.thefishersmarket.ca*
Gelbvieh, Tasmania	*www.gelbvieh-tasmania.com*
Guardian Equipment, USA	*www.gesafety.com*
I-Stock by Getty images	*www.istockphoto.com*
J- Springs Ranch, Pinantan BC	*www.jayspringslamb.ca*
Jakes & Associates, Meat Industry Specialists	*www.jakesandassociates.wordpress.com*
Jarvis Industries Canada Ltd	*www.jarviscanada.com*
Just Manufacturing, USA	*www.justmfg.com*
Ketchum Manufacturing Inc., Ontario	*www.ketchum.ca*

KLVM – Provincial Harvesting plant, Cherry Creek BC   www.klvm.ca

Mairi Budreau, Publishing & Design, Kamloops BC   www.budreau.ca

Master Lock, Canada   www.masterlock.com

NAIT Professional Meat Cutting & Processing Program, Alberta   www.nait.ca

Newell Brands, USA   www.newellbrands.com

Raven Ridge Farms, Barriere BC   www.growravenridge.com

Save on Foods, Kamloops BC   www.saveonfoods.com

Stuffers Supply Company, Langley BC   www.stuffers.com

Summit Gourmet Meats, Kamloops BC   www.summitgourmetmeats.com

Sun-Gold Specialty meats, Innisfail, Alberta   www.sungoldmeats.com

TRU, micro-biology and Human Resources, Kamloops BC   www.tru.ca

TRU, Retail Meat Processing Program, Kamloops BC   www.tru.ca/culinary-arts/meatcutter

Two Rivers specialty meats, North Vancouver BC   www.tworiversmeats.ca

Uni-Pac Packaging Products Ltd   www.unipac.ca

Western Hog Exchange, Alberta   www.westernhogexchange.com

Daniel Westgeest

The popular adage, "variety is the spice of life," aptly describes retired Professional Meatcutting and Merchandising Chair Daniel Westgeest's pursuit of lifelong learning. A seasoned professional now working as an independent consultant with more than 50 years of experience in retail, wholesale and educational sectors of the meat industry, Daniel is constantly expanding his repertoire of knowledge. His educational background includes:

- A Certificate in Retail Meatcutting from NAIT
- A Bachelor of Education Degree from the University of Alberta
- A Certificate in Computer Network Administrator from NAIT
- A Culinary Arts Diploma from NAIT
- An Alberta qualified Journeyman Cook designation

Daniel is a founding member of the Canadian Professional Meat Cutters Association (CPMCA) having served in the capacity of Vice President, Secretary Treasurer, and a voting member. He also collaborated with industry and educational representatives at the request of the Canadian Food Industry Council in the development of Retail Meatcutting Occupational Standards.

Under Daniel's guidance, NAIT's Professional Meatcutting and Merchandising Program has become a recognized leader in Western Canada, offering students hands-on experience and top quality instruction, including:

- Complete instruction on fundamentals of meat fabrication and related theory courses
- In-house production of smoked and cured products

- Product display, marketing, merchandising and customer service experience in both Industry and NAIT's popular Retail Meat Store
- Workshops and demonstrations for industry, special interest groups, career fairs and continuing education programs

As a former instructor, administrator, educator and subject matter expert, Daniel was commissioned by the Canada Professional Meat Cutters Association (CPMCA) to write the Canadian Professional Meat Cutting textbook for industry practitioners and those interested in a career in the meat industry.

Daniel strongly believes in the unlimited opportunities offered in the meat industry, including emerging niche markets such as product development, artisanal products and, organic and naturally raised products, as well as other educational opportunities.

Kenneth Jakes

Kenneth Jakes is a retired Coordinator/Instructor of the Retail Meat Processing Program at Thompson Rivers University (TRU). He is the principal consultant for Jakes & Associates, meat industry consulting specialists with over 50 years of experience in retail, wholesale and educational sectors of the meat industry. Kenneth's educational/training background includes:

- trade certification in New Zealand (N.Z.)
- trade certification in British Columbia (B.C.)
- British Columbia Instructors Diploma (B.C.I.D.)

TRU's Retail Meat Processing Program became the leading meat training center in the province of British Columbia thanks to Kenneth's hard work and dedication to excellence. Kenneth's experience in New Zealand, Australia, China and Canada compliments his career in the meat industry, adding tribute to his development of the TRU meat training program. As a subject matter expert, Kenneth expanded the TRU's meat training program to include the following:

- Sausage formulation and processing
- Processing of hams, bacon and jerky
- Custom game processing
- Business math courses
- Level I and II apprenticeship courses
- A retail meat store
- Industry representation on Program Advisory Board
- Securing industry sponsored student awards and bursaries

In addition to Kenneth's educational contributions to the meat industry, he was an active member of numerous boards and committees such as:

- Thompson Rivers University BC Cattle Industry Research team under Dr. John Church for the Cattle Industry Research Advisory Committee (CIRAC)
- Canadian Professional Meat Cutters Association (CPMCA)
- Past president and founding member of CPMCA
- Current secretary / treasurer of CPMCA
- TRU School of Tourism Leadership team.
- BC Meat Cutters Apprenticeship Task Group for examination re-development
- Canadian Food Inspection Agency's (CFIA) Fair Labeling Program and Private Industry consultant

Kenneth believes strongly in lifelong learning and the long-term benefits of continuing education through active apprenticeship training and journeymen certification, both provincially and on a national level within the Canadian meat industry. Upon retirement Kenneth was commissioned by the CPMCA as Project Manager in the development of a hardcover full colour textbook complete with images and graphics for the Canadian meat industry. As contributing subject matter expert and co-editor, Kenneth's responsibility was to oversee the entire project including planning, funding, sourcing resources, publishing and distribution.

Contents

Chapter 8: Poultry   *373–410*

Chapter 9: Seafood

Chapter 10: Charcuterie   *465–590*

Chapter 12: Harvesting   *649–716*

Preface

This hardcover edition of the Professional Meat Cutting Textbook for Canadian meat cutters reflects the changing needs of the meat industry in Canada. The core material focuses on the essentials of our industry and related sectors. The idea behind this book is to offer a comprehensive understanding of meats and meat-cutting techniques used to merchandise and market meat cuts and associated products to and for Canadian consumers, with an eye on food safety, food production and governing regulations.

The nature of government regulations surrounding food is constantly changing to meet new arising issues and discoveries. This means it is impossible to guarantee definitive accuracy of the material contained in this book in that regard. The authors therefore do not assume any responsibility for omissions, errors, misprinting or ambiguity contained within this publication and shall not be held liable in any degree for any loss or injury caused by such omissions, errors, misprinting or ambiguity presented herein.

Although this book presents a lot of widely used and accepted information regarding the meat industry in Canada, it is no substitute for experience. Common to the observant participant are the major roles played by demographics, dietary requirements/restrictions and seasonal fluctuations our industry caters to in our towns, cities and principalities across this vast nation of ours. Different areas of our country have different styles, different cuts or unique products and different market demands. What is practised in one province may not be practised in another; however, the basics are all derived from domestic species and common methodologies used in obtaining the intended outcome – a safe saleable product. Consequently, this book is dedicated to serving that need.

Goals of the Organization

The Canadian Professional Meat Cutters Association (CPMCA) came about when a group of individuals got together to share ideas and literature they developed for teaching and training students of meat-cutting programs offered across the country. Member participation, through a continuous interchange of ideas and information, developed various educational mediums of which one was a training manual. These educational mediums were then offered and are available for use and to be of assistance to those members in the meat industry who have looked to meet the challenges of today's Canadian market.

In addition, the CPMCA became and is active, networking with other national and regional associations such as local producing, processing and marketing boards, municipal, provincial and federal governing bodies and related associations. This network system provides membership with opportunity for professional dialogue and exchange of industry data and practices.

Though the CPMCA originally began providing learning materials for both entry-level learners and industry practitioners, it now also manages a website. This website is designed for use by the meat industry. The site offers links to the industry, training institutions that offer entry-level programs, news about apprenticeship training and where it's offered, job and career opportunities and a blog for posting trends and emerging ideas threaded throughout the industry. For more information, we encourage you to visit the website: www.meatforce.ca

Chapter 1

Introduction to the Meat Industry

This chapter covers the dawn of the meat industry in Canada starting with meat processing and the industrialization of the meat packing industry beginning in the late 1800s. Our history covers the major packinghouse players of the time, their contribution to the international and domestic markets, their impact on the workforce and the role our independent butcher shops had serving the local populace.

As the meat industry developed and progressed in their advancement so did concerns of food safety and inspection. Our history shows the establishment of meat inspection along with public health concerns regarding food safety for export, which eventually cleared the path toward domestic food safety concerns and inspection.

Introduction to the Meat Industry

Overview

Canada's slaughtering and meat-processing sector comprises livestock slaughter and carcass dressing, secondary processors that manufacture and package meat products for retail sale, and purveyors that prepare portion-ready cuts for hotel, restaurant and institutional food service. Products include fresh, chilled or frozen meats and edible offal (i.e. organ meats); cured meats; fresh and cooked sausage; canned meat preparations; animal oils and fats; and products such as bone and meat meal. Meat processing is one of Canada's largest single manufacturing industries and the largest employer in the food-manufacturing group. It was among the earliest food industries to develop mass production technologies geared toward international markets.

History

PRE-INDUSTRIAL MEAT PROCESSING TO 1870

Meat processing has always been among Canada's most regulated industries. The Superior Council of New France established regulations in 1706 to control the sale of meat in different seasons and required butchers to advise a colonial official prior to the slaughter of an animal. Inspection was required to ensure that the animal was healthy and that its meat would be fit for sale. By 1805, Lower Canada regulated beef and pork packing with legislation specifying the weight and quality of meat cuts, the quality of the barrels in which they were packed, and the amount of preservative required.

In the early 19th century, most meat originated with farm slaughter and village butchers, but meat-packing for export was becoming significant. Production scales increased as butchers sold fresh meat for domestic consumers and packed cured meat products for overseas markets. During the winter months, hogs were slaughtered, the carcasses were dressed and pork was cured and packed in barrels filled with brine. F.W. Fearman began operations in Hamilton, Ontario, in 1852 and continues to operate in nearby Burlington. Despite changes in ownership, it is Canada's oldest pork processor. William Davies — whose company was a precursor of Canada Packers — began business in Toronto in 1854. In 1874, Davies built Canada's first large-scale hog slaughtering facility in Toronto's east end.

From 1911 William Davies Company store
Courtesy: City of Toronto Archives

INDUSTRIALIZATION OF MEAT-PACKING, 1870–1930

Development of industrial meat-packing in the American Midwest during the 1870s influenced meat processing in Canada. A growing railway network enabled the procurement of unprecedented volumes of livestock from a vast hinterland and the distribution of chilled meat to an extensive market aboard refrigerated railcars. The scale of production increased and packing plants came to employ a semi-skilled, largely immigrant labour force. Unlike traditional butcher shops, packing plants had a finely graduated division of labour that allowed each meat cutter to specialize in a single task as a carcass moved along an overhead rail. Inaugurated in Chicago, the industrial meat-packing model was followed in other metropolitan centres of the Midwest such as St. Louis, and at a smaller scale in Toronto and Winnipeg.

Driven by buoyant markets for cured "Wiltshire sides" of pork in Britain, the Canadian industry grew rapidly from 1880 to 1890. As meat processing industrialized, hundreds of small butcheries were absorbed by larger enterprises seeking international markets for their meat exports. By the turn of the century, meat processing establishments were among the largest employers in Canada's food and beverage industry and sales of cured pork products became a significant part of Canada's agro-food exports.

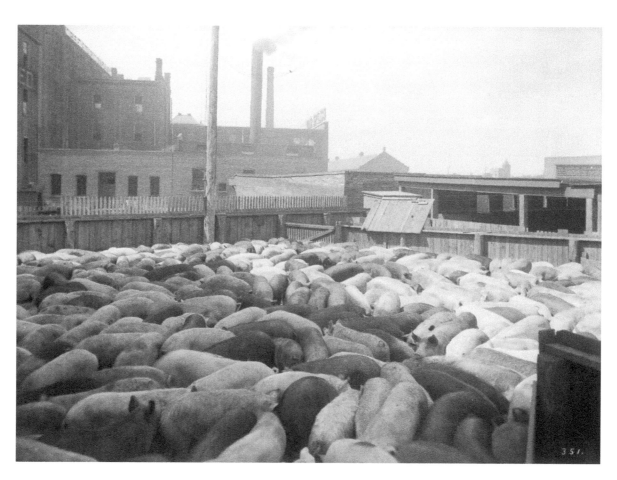

1920's Hogs in the William Davies Company pens
Courtesy William James Topley / Library Archives, Canada.

1920's Inside the slaughterhouse; William Davies Company in Toronto, Canada. (2 sides of pork)
Courtesy: William James Topley / Library and Archives.

Patrick Burns, Alberta's most famous "cattle king," founded his cattle and meat-packing empire by supplying beef to railway gangs and the mining and lumber camps of Western Canada's resource periphery in the 1880s and 1890s. In 1890, he established his first substantial slaughterhouse, in Calgary. Called P. Burns & Co. (later Burns Foods), it became Western Canada's largest meat-packing company.

In the east, the Harris Abattoir was established in Toronto in 1896. With a slaughter capacity of 500 cattle per week, the Harris Abattoir was a bold innovation. It specialized in cattle slaughter at a time when most industrial meat-packers focused on pork. Unlike P. Burns & Co., it was intended primarily to export chilled sides of beef for the British market.

Influenced by calls for meat inspection in the United States — which were spurred by reactions to Upton Sinclair's 1906 novel, *The Jungle*, which exposed unsanitary practices at packing houses — J. G. Rutherford, veterinary director general and later livestock commissioner for Canada, was instrumental in drafting the *Meat and Canned Foods Act*, Canada's first federal meat inspection legislation. From 1907, federal sanitation standards required ante-mortem and post-mortem veterinary inspection of all animals whose meat was intended for export or shipment across provincial borders.

THE BIG THREE, 1930–1980

Meat processing grew rapidly during the First World War. At that time, Sir Joseph Flavelle came to epitomize the many meat-packing industrialists who earned windfall profits through their home-front participation in the war effort. However, the industry was left with surplus capacity in the 1920s, prompting several large American meat-packers to withdraw from the Canadian market and the creation of Canada Packers — the merging of William Davies, Gunns Limited, and the Harris Abattoir.

By 1930, a new and more concentrated corporate structure emerged that would dominate the red meat industry (mainly pork and beef) for nearly 50 years. The Big Three integrated meat-packers (Canada Packers, Burns Foods, and Swift Canadian) slaughtered all species and processed their carcasses into a full line of fresh and processed meat products in packing plants from Charlottetown, PE, to Victoria, BC. Most of these plants were organized by the United Packinghouse Workers of America during the Second World War, and a system of pattern bargaining was developed that brought meat-packing wages well above the manufacturing average.

In terms of white meat, consumption began to grow substantially in the 1950s, leading to large-scale broiler processing. This shift was prompted by advances in genetics and in poultry nutrition science.

Livestock processors have relatively low profit margins, usually between one and two per cent of sales. Meat-packing profits depend on large-scale production in which the full value of animal by-products are salvaged in order to attain the sales volume required to earn an acceptable rate of return.

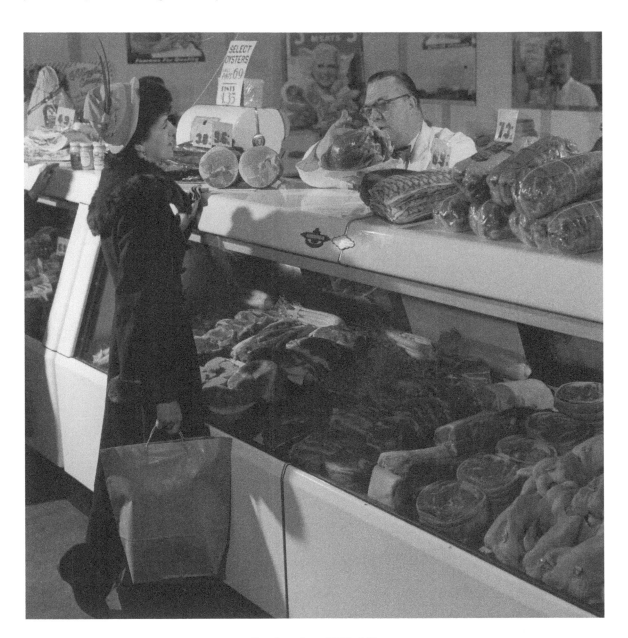

Butcher shop 1950-60's
Two Women customers purchasing meat from a butcher. ca.
Courtesy: Library and Archives Canada.

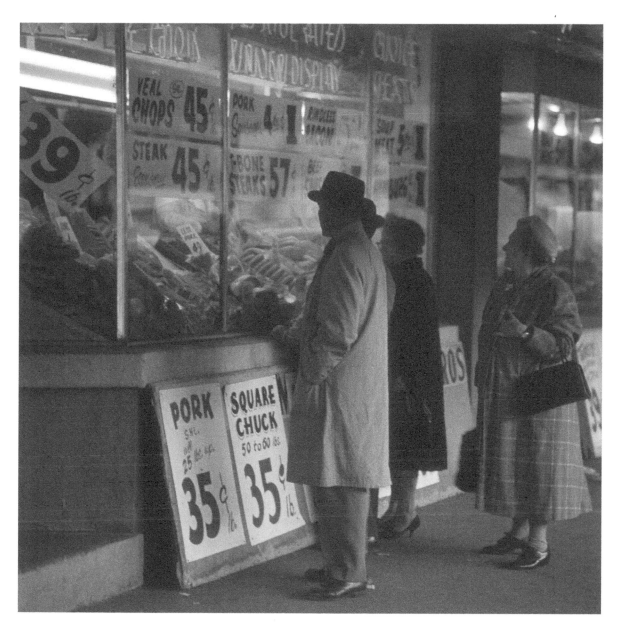

The display window of a Butcher's shop in the Farmers Market, Ottawa – 1961.
Courtesy: Library and Archives Canada.

MEAT PROCESSING TODAY, 1980–PRESENT

The Big Three meat packers domination of the market was restructured in the 1980s as domestic beef consumption fell and competition from American packers intensified. The Big Three withdrew from fresh beef and, through a complex series of mergers, many of their operations came under the control of Maple Leaf Foods (controlled by McCain Capital Corporation and West Face Capital Inc.), which is still the leading hog processor in Manitoba. Olymel (controlled by La Coop Fédérée) has become Québec and Alberta's leading pork processor with nine pork and hog processing plants in Québec, one in Red Deer, Alberta, and one in Cornwall, Ontario. Beef processing is dominated by three large plants: Cargill Foods operates in High River, Alberta, and Guelph, Ontario; Lakeside Packers in Brooks, Alberta, is operated by JBS Canada, part of a Brazil-based multinational that was reputed to be the world's largest processor of fresh beef and pork in 2014.

Chicken production is distributed across all provinces in approximate proportion to the consumer market and due to Canada's system of supply management. State-of-the-art poultry plants that slaughter and process up to 25,000 broiler chickens per hour account for the majority share of poultry meat output. Among the largest processing companies are: Lilydale Foods (Alberta, Saskatchewan and British Columbia), Maple Leaf Poultry (Ontario and Alberta), Maple Lodge Farms (Ontario, New Brunswick and Nova Scotia), Olymel (Québec and Ontario) and Sunrise Poultry (British Columbia, Alberta, Ontario and Manitoba). Most poultry processors operate their own egg hatcheries that sell chicks to producers who then sell the finished birds back to the processors on a live-weight basis.

Large-scale meat processing plants increasingly specialize in just one sex, age and species of livestock and in a narrow range of meat products. However, a small but growing market segment asserts a preference for locally produced and certified organic meats that originate with livestock that are produced in less confined settings and are typically processed by small-scale, provincially-inspected plants and sold at a premium at local farmer's markets and specialty food stores.

INTERNATIONAL TRADE

From its inception in the 19th century, the meat processing industry has been a significant exporter. Led by pork and beef, meat and meat preparations are among Canada's highest value agro-food exports. Since the US embargo on Canadian beef was lifted in 2005, those exports have accounted for about half of total production. The United States, Mexico, Japan, China, Hong Kong and Russia are the most important global importers of Canadian beef and pork, while Canadian chicken products are exported mainly to the United States and Asian destinations such as Taiwan and the Philippines.

FOOD SAFETY AND MEAT INSPECTION

Federally inspected plants account for over 90 per cent of all animals slaughtered in Canada. Since 1997, the Canadian Food Inspection Agency (CFIA) has been responsible for verifying that the meat and poultry products leaving federally-inspected establishments are safe and wholesome. Federal inspection is required for establishments that distribute their product across provincial lines. Each province is responsible for food safety in plants that supply intra-provincial markets. Despite this relatively stringent regulatory environment, meat processors are subject to occasional episodes of contamination by pathogens such as listeria, E. coli and salmonella. Prion disease — manifest in cattle as bovine spongiform encephalopathy (BSE) — was first discovered in a Canadian-born cow in May 2003. Since that time, 17 further cases of BSE have been discovered, the most recent in February 2011. The disease may be spread by consuming brain, spinal cord, and other "specified risk materials" from infected animals. For that reason, packing house procedures are stringently regulated to ensure that such by-products do not enter the food chain for human or animal consumption.

Federally inspected red-meat processing firms are represented nationally by the Canadian Meat Council in Ottawa. The Canadian Poultry and Egg Processors Council speaks for the processors of chickens, turkeys and table eggs. A significant proportion of the red-meat-processing labour force is unionized and represented by the United Food and Commercial Workers.

Chapter 2

Professionalism

Studies have shown that a significant percentage of food related illnesses are attributed to poor sanitation and food hygiene, including poor personal hygiene and contamination of equipment. This chapter emphasizes the co-operative approach between government and industry servicing consumers of food, the important role sanitation has within the industry, as well as the personal hygiene habits of those handling food products designated for the consumer market.

This chapter introduces basic microbiology and food related illness information, industry proven sanitation practices while promoting good personal hygiene, the proper storage and handling of food and cleaning supplies, as well as pathogenic organisms common to our industry. The principal thing to note about this chapter is that the content is not static. An effective sanitation program is one that responds to the dynamics of its environment, is proactive and recognizes emerging food safety risks.

Professionalism

Introduction

CO-OPERATIVE APPROACH BETWEEN INDUSTRY AND GOVERNMENT

Professionalism is characterized as being competent or skilled in an activity such as meat cutting or working within a specific sector of the meat industry for personal gain or livelihood. For the most part, being professional is more than just knowing your craft. It's about engaging all aspects associated with the craft. So here we start with the most important, our attitude toward sanitation and personal hygiene.

As a worker in the meat industry you will note that processes and methods of food preparation and service change, and new problems arise which further complicate the already difficult task of food protection. The public must be assured that operations and techniques are such that food is protected at all times from contaminants and infective agents. Although these facts are well known, food continues to be the source of many human illnesses.

Because food is a source of illness, Canadian public health authorities at all levels of government have created extensive food control regulations and provide staff of qualified personnel to check the quality of food from its source to the customer. In the face of this expert assistance, it is alarming that many operators in the food industry still do not fully comprehend the danger involved in handling food or the methods of successfully meeting sanitary requirements.

The industry and public health authorities both have important roles to play in helping to ensure that only safe food and drink are offered to the millions who patronize Canada's large and important food preparation and food service industries. Government efforts alone are not enough. Operators have a moral and legal obligation to protect the health of customers and ensure that only safe food is available.

ECONOMIC IMPACT

The total amount of food-borne illness in Canada is not known since reporting is neither complete nor accurate, but it is reported by Health Canada that the most recent average yearly estimates for food-borne illness due to known and unknown causes are:

Known causes of 30 food-borne bacteria, parasites and viruses:

- 1.6 million illnesses (40% of food-borne illnesses)
- 4,000 hospitalizations (34% of food-borne hospitalizations)
- 105 deaths (44% of food-borne deaths)

Unknown causes:

- 2.4 million illnesses (60%)
- 7,600 hospitalizations (66%)
- 133 deaths (56%)

Hospital emergency room scene
©istock.com / credit to uchar

This means that every year, a total of about 4 million (1 in 8) Canadians are affected by a food-borne illness. Of these there are about:

- 11,600 hospitalizations
- 238 deaths

Reflecting on these average estimates of Food-borne illnesses we see they result in considerable suffering by customers and can mean ruined vacations or even death. The negative publicity associated with food poisoning outbreaks has ruined many operators and cost many more hundreds of thousands of dollars in associated costs. Some of the problems with an outbreak are loss of customers and sales, loss of prestige and reputation, legal suits resulting in legal and court fees, increased insurance premiums, lowered employee morale and professional embarrassment. In addition, the cost to the health care system in terms of laboratory analysis, investigation time, physician time and hospital care is tremendous.

The public expects to be served clean, safe and healthy food. It's the responsibility of those in the food industry to ensure that food is indeed clean and safe for consumption; after all, it is their customers that keep them in business. If any food outlet wishes to remain in business, it must have the public's confidence. Proper sanitation practices and procedures can help bring about that confidence thereby becoming a promotional feature. To assist the food industry in their sanitary practices and procedures, there are the Public Health Act and Food Regulation Act, two pieces of legislation governing food operations. Also to be considered is the role of the Canadian Food Inspection Agency (CFIA) and other municipal and provincial governing bodies.

What the food industry needs, and what our governing regulations point to, is a well-designed "sanitation program" to control pathogenic microorganisms. The difficulty in selling and promoting a sanitation program is that the results of such a program are not easily determined in immediate terms of profits and loss; and that's why we still have food related illnesses making front page news. The food industry can, however, attach some monetary value to these facts.

Strategic planning in implementing an effective sanitation program realizes the following three results:

a) Less product contamination by spoilage organisms, which cause surface discolouration, shrinkage, deterioration and a shorter shelf life.

b) Higher efficiency of equipment and workers. Clean equipment is easier to maintain and requires less effort in the maintenance process. Less equipment down time saves money on time and labour.

c) Easier cleaning and disinfecting. Neglect means more effort is needed in elevating standards. When equipment and facilities are well maintained, they are easier to clean and keep clean.

These three results relate to savings, whereas possible closures due to public and employee health risks could amount to costs in insurance premiums, payroll, lost sales and potential lab, hospital, doctor and legal costs. Sanitation practices and procedures are important and necessary to the food industry. Money is saved through management of such practices and procedures.

CONSUMER EXPECTATIONS

Operators in the food industry cannot afford to ignore sanitation standards from an aesthetic viewpoint either. The public's expectations of quality and cleanliness are very high. In fact studies have shown that cleanliness and food quality rank as two of the more important criteria when choosing a food preparation or service outlet. Establishments are judged based on customer observation and experience. In order to stay competitive, it is essential that premises, equipment and facilities be maintained in excellent condition. An establishment with superior food handling techniques may be judged negatively if the service area is shabby and carelessly maintained.

Most important, however, are those unobservable conditions that are of a direct public health concern. The areas that contribute most directly to the incidents of food-borne disease and which receive the most emphasis in the *Guide to Food Safety* put out by the CFIA include: the facilities, the food itself, the personal habits of employees, the manner in which food preparation, storage and serving are carried out, and most critically, the cooling, heating and holding of foods.

EFFECTIVE USE OF SANITATION

To obtain maximum benefit from the *Guide to Food Safety*, operators are urged to utilize the information it provides in a constant assessment of their operations. The guide can be an invaluable tool in programs of self-inspection and staff training, practices, which are essential to sanitary food operators. This guide can also be used to achieve a common ground of understanding and cooperation when dealing with public health authorities.

Education of employees in the food industry is probably the most effective method of obtaining compliance with the sanitation standards. Most municipalities offer training in food handling, with programs such as FOODSAFE or a food handler's certificate (www.foodsafe.ca). Food industry employees should have a basic knowledge of food-borne diseases and their modes of transmission, and they should be thoroughly acquainted with requirements of the food service operation laws and regulations governing the handling of food. Further, they should be made to realize the dangers involved in working when they are ill or have infected sores or wounds, and they should have a full appreciation of the importance of good personal hygiene.

Sanitation: The Basics

Rules around personal hygiene and sanitary food handling are not written and implemented to make work difficult. There are good reasons behind establishing regulations for the handling, storage and sale of food. Paramount is the safety of those who consume food. Here we present practical and theoretical methodologies used to ensure food safety for those employed in the food industry as well as those who consume the food our industry produces and distributes.

DEVELOPMENT OF LEGAL MEASURES

Since Pasteur's discovery of the "infinitely small," bacteriologists and chemists have discovered ways of breaking the chain of infectious contacts. A sound basis now exists for control of sanitary conditions in food plants, food service, food processing and food outlets. These days, legal measures not known in earlier days are widely accepted by producers and the public alike as necessary for general safety and security.

HEALTH AND SANITATION REGULATORY DEPARTMENTS

In Canada various departments and different levels of government share responsibilities for maintaining the health of the public, including:

Federal:

- Health Canada
- Agriculture and Agri-Food Canada
- Fisheries and Oceans Canada
- Canadian Food Inspection Agency, etc.

Provincial:

- Ministries of Agriculture and/ or Forestry
- Provincial Health Services (under Resources)

Municipal:

- Administered collaboratively with Federal and Provincial Agencies

In recent years the three levels of government have been working collaboratively in coordinating activities related to food inspection. The areas of responsibilities for public health service for each department or level of government are clearly differentiated. Two or more levels may have authority in the same area. The resulting regulations are intended to ensure optimum protection for the public.

Food safety involves a complex collaboration between governments and industry at all levels. As in all provinces, food safety is regulated by both provincial and federal legislation. Generally speaking, provincial regulation relates to hygiene requirements, whereas federal legislation covers specific food safety requirements such as food additives, process controls, allergens, composition and labelling requirements.

It is recommended that participants in our industry become familiar with provincial regulations concerning their region, and this can be obtained via the web by searching for food safety legislation in the area where they preside. For example, a search for food legislation in Ontario produces a link to Ontario's Public Health Standards' page.

OBJECTIVES OF REGULATORY DEPARTMENTS.

These groups focus attention on the importance of

a) increasing knowledge in sanitation through research, and
b) distributing that knowledge through education.

Activities extend from research on such practical problems as dishwashing, detergents, sanitizing agents and swab testing to the establishment of testing laboratories where products in the sanitary field can be examined and approved or rejected.

Educational projects include personnel training, legalized inspection in commercial eating places (carried out by Health Inspectors) and other contributions, which emphasize a positive approach to health and sanitation rather than a negative approach with emphasis on disease.

Prevention of Contamination

PERSONAL HYGIENE

The cleanliness, health and habits of food industry personnel are important because people frequently serve as the host or carrier for disease organisms, which are so readily spread through food. These organisms are frequent especially on our hands as well as the face, hair, in our mouths, noses and intestinal tracts. Trays or other containers such as meat tubs, cutting and processing boards, dishes, utensils and food will be easily contaminated by an employee's hands and/or clothing. This is known as **cross-contamination,** defined as the transfer of hazardous substances, mainly microorganisms, to food from either another food or another food surface such as but not limited to equipment, worktables or hands, etc.

It is essential to safe food preparation and service that all food handlers be aware of this potential danger and manage their activities accordingly.

PRINCIPLES OF GOOD PRACTICE FOR PERSONAL HYGIENE

Important factors in the control of food-borne infection are the personal hygiene habits of each food industry employee. Therefore, each employee should be aware of the need for personal cleanliness and good hygienic habits as well as have adequate training to put this knowledge into practice.

1. Sneeze or cough into disposable paper towels or into your armpit in an emergency. Wash hands immediately!

2. Avoid scratching, picking at the face or putting fingers in hair, mouth or nose; ignorance of the harm such unsanitary habits may cause may be overcome by providing workers with the knowledge of what pathogenic microorganisms are and how they may be spread.

3. Tools such as ladles, lifters, tongs, scoops or protective vinyl gloves should be used instead of hands wherever possible. Where needed, consideration should be given to the use of disposable utensils.
   - Nibbling or sampling of food with utensils or fingers is not permitted because of the potential danger of direct mouth-to-food contamination.

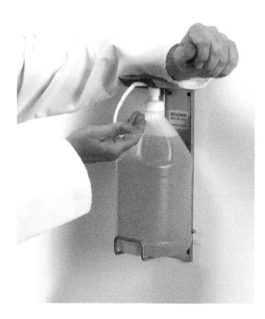

Utilize good peer supervision to encourage sanitary habits to replace careless habits until the former become normal habits.
Credit: Bunzl Processor Division/Koch Supplies

4. Personal cleanliness
   - Bathe or shower daily
   - Use of non-offensive deodorant or antiperspirant
   - Employees should not brush teeth or hair, apply cosmetics, or change clothing in food preparation or service areas.
   - Avoid spilling, dripping, or splashing food soil on their clothing.
   - Keep their hands and nails free from soil.

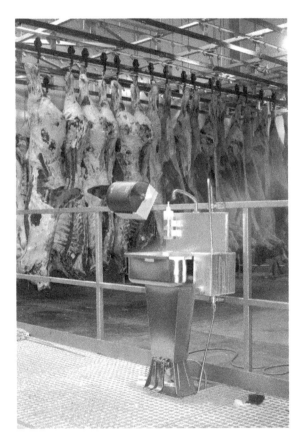

Hand wash & Knife sanitizer unit in a beef plant
Credit: Canada beef

   - Hands and arms should be washed prior to starting work, and as frequently as is necessary after handling objects or surfaces which could cross-contaminate food.
   - Hands should be washed before returning to work after using the toilet facilities, after meal and smoke breaks, coughing or sneezing, handling raw foods and before handling potentially hazardous food.
   - Spitting is prohibited.

- Smoking and the use of tobacco are strictly prohibited in all food processing facilities because of potential danger of direct mouth-to-food contamination.

5. Employers should provide
   - Hand washing basins in working areas, with hot water, dispensed soap and single-use drying devices,
   - Lockers or the equivalent for holding personal clothing and belongings.

Hand wash stations at a Processing plant
Credit: Canada beef

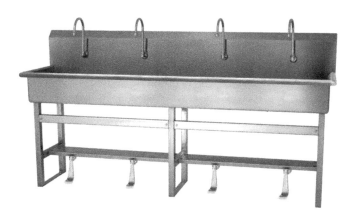

Hands free multi-wash station
Credit: Columbia Equipment Sani lav USA Model # 58F1

Hands free single valve wash station
Credit: Columbia Equipment Sani lav USA Model # 531FS

6. Hair and facial hair
   - Hair should be clean and suitably controlled or covered.
   - Hairnets are required in many sectors of the meat industry as well as in some retail operations.
   - Beards are not recommended, but if present must be totally covered with a beard net when working in a meat outlet.

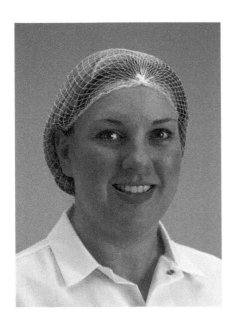

Hair net
Credit: Bunzl Processor Division/Koch Supplies

Beard net guard
Credit: Bunzl Processor Division/Koch Supplies

7. Cuts, abrasions and burns
   - All wounds must be assessed for further medical attention, dressed and the incident documented.
   - If the employee is able to continue work the wound must be cleaned and bandaged immediately.
   - Bandages and band aids must be of the waterproof type and be in a bright non-meat colour i.e., blue or yellow.
   - A hand or finger wound already bandaged can also be covered with a disposable glove if approved by your health and safety officer.
   - Wound dressings and gloves must be changed frequently once they are too soiled or damaged.

8. Protective and work clothing
   - Material should be clean and comfortable, of a material suited to the purpose, and laundered daily.
   - The wearing of street clothing in food handling areas should be discouraged.
   - Working apparel should not be worn outside of the food service establishment.
   - Sweaters should not be worn over a working uniform unless they are a part of the uniform.
   - Comfortable shoes of a smooth, readily cleanable type (preferably leather), with soles of a non-porous, non-absorptive should be worn.

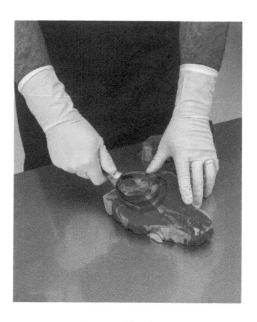

Disposable gloves
Credit: Bunzl Processor Division/Koch Supplies

Food service workers in a Supermarket
Credit: Save on Foods

Note: Body jewellery has a known habit of dislodging itself as the body most often rejects facial and tongue jewellery, and so the jewellery eventually comes loose posing a health hazard. It is also worth noting that eventually all food processing and distributing establishments will have to impose **HACCP** (Hazard Analysis Critical Control Points) regulations, something that has become part of the cost of doing business. HACCP regulations clearly disallow food handlers in federal and provincially approved processing and distributing establishments from wearing body or facial jewellery; however, it does not as yet apply to all retail food outlets or food service outlets, as these to date are free to make their own judgment based on the nature of their business.

Employees shall be encouraged to report illnesses, particularly those involving digestive upset and infections, to management. Such persons, while afflicted, should not work in areas or in a capacity in which there is likelihood of contaminating food contact surfaces or food. It is a public health requirement that when a food industry worker is suffering from a communicable disease, it be reported to a designated public health officer in the jurisdiction. Teachers and food service managers are responsible for reporting such diseases.

Microbiology and Food-Borne Illness

Basic Microbiology is the study of small living things commonly known as microorganisms or "germs." These microorganisms are so small they cannot be seen with the unaided eye but can be seen with a microscope. The smallest microorganisms are viruses that require a magnification of a million times before they can be seen. Bacteria are small microorganisms that can be seen when magnified one thousand times. Yeasts or fungi are larger microorganisms that can be seen when magnified four hundred times.

Microorganisms are responsible for food contamination. Certain microorganisms cause food spoilage resulting in off-odours, off-flavours, or changes in food textures and colour. Others do not alter the appearance, odour or taste, but are capable of causing food-borne illness. These microorganisms are known as pathogens. Most microorganisms require certain environmental conditions for growth and reproduction: food (particularly protein), warmth, moisture and time.

Some bacteria require oxygen to grow and some do not. Others grow in either environment, with or without oxygen. Bacteria that require oxygen are known to be aerobic and are found to reproduce on surfaces where air is present. Bacteria that do not require oxygen are known to be anaerobic and grow in the absence of air as with canned or sealed products. Bacteria that grow in either environment, with or without air, are known to be facultative.

Bacterial contamination can occur at any time meat is cut. Each time meat is cut; the two surfaces are essentially inoculated. Further contamination from cutting boards, chutes, knives and conveyor belts adds additional bacteria to the product. Temperature is the only barrier that can be imposed on fresh meats. The short shelf life of fresh meats necessitates adequate sanitation, excellent temperature control and rapid distribution. Microbial growth takes place in four stages: Lag phase, Log phase, Stationary phase and Death phase.

Lag phase is the point at which the microbes are getting adjusted to their new environment. However, there is no lag if the cells to be used for the inoculums were grown in the same medium under the same environment. It is at this point that proper sanitation practices and temperature control have the most influence on retarding bacterial growth.

Log phase (logarithmic) represents that period of time at which cell division is maintained at a constant and maximum rate under the environmental conditions present.

Stationary phase is when the number of viable microorganisms remain constant.

Death phase refers to the decline in microbial activity and occurs when the microorganisms begin to self-destruct due to autolytic enzymes that degrade the cell envelope.

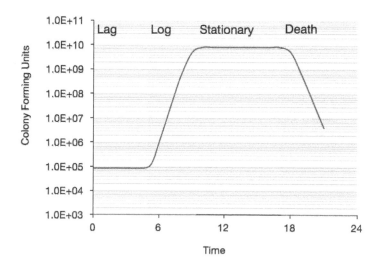

Lag, log and Death Phase graph
Credit: Dr J. Van Hamme, Microbiology, TRU

BACTERIA

The microorganisms of most concern to food service operators are bacteria, which can be destroyed by sufficient heat over an adequate period of time, or growth can be slowed or stopped by refrigeration. But at temperatures greater than 4°C and less than 60°C, known as the **danger zone,** bacteria can flourish and multiply to enormous numbers. At optimum growth temperatures of 35° to 40°C they can double in number every 10 to 20 minutes. This could result in 100 bacteria multiplying to more than one million in three and a half hours. For this reason, potentially hazardous foods such as milk, eggs, fish and meats should never be kept within the danger zone.

Bacteria may be carried by water, in draughts of air and also as "hitch-hikers" via the human body, insects, rodents, in and on food (milk, fruits and vegetables) and food equipment.

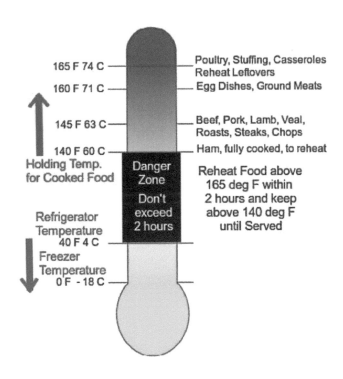

Danger zone food safety temperature chart
Credit: Dr. John Anderson

Note: For further details on Bacterial growth & Safe Meat Handling see the thermometer guides, appendix pages 746-747.

VIRUSES

Viruses are the smallest form of microorganisms. They only grow and reproduce inside living cells. Some viruses cause food-borne infections such as hepatitis.

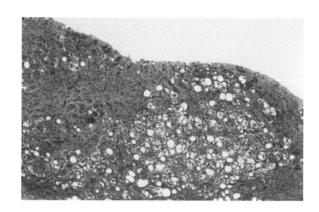

Chronic Hepatitis & Cirrhosis of the liver
©istock.com / credit to OGphoto

PARASITES

Microorganisms which are dependent on a living host for growth and reproduction are called parasites. Parasites can exist in the form of single-celled animals (e.g., Protozoa) or multi-celled animals (e.g. tape worms). Trichinosis is probably the best-known parasitic disease. Parasitic larvae occur in the muscles of infected pigs. If uncooked pork is eaten, it is almost certain that the larvae will develop into small round worms in that person's intestines. These cause a gastro-intestinal illness resulting in fever, muscular pain and general weakness. Later these worms migrate into the muscles of the patient to form cysts and cause muscle spasms.

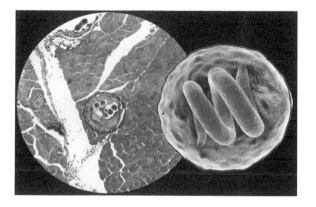

Trichinosis worm enlarged
©istock.com / credit to Dr. Microbe

Good Bacteria – Mould on Cheeses
©istock.com / credit to destillat

MOULDS

Moulds are multi-cellular microorganisms which are often visible to the naked eye as fuzzy or powdery patches. They can exist at almost any storage temperature under almost any condition. Foods most susceptible to mould are meat, fruits, bread and cheese. Some moulds produce harmful toxins.

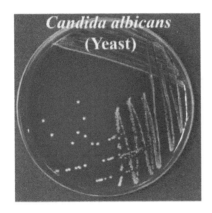

Yeast growing on a petri dish
Credit: Thompson Rivers University
Microbiology: Dr. Soumya Ghosh, Timothy Crowe
and Kamal Grewal-Choudhury

YEASTS

Yeasts are single celled organisms, which also require food (particularly carbohydrates) and moisture for growth. They can grow at refrigeration temperatures as well as room temperatures. Yeast contaminations can be identified by "slimy" or powdery film, cloudy sediment in liquids or the presence of gas bubbles. Yeast most often grows on fruit, jam, syrups, processed meats, cottage cheese and yogurt.

TRANSMISSION OF BACTERIA

Direct Transmission of Bacteria from Person to Food to Person

The food handler (or carrier) contaminates by
- respiratory tract, through
- coughing,
- sneezing,
- open sores and cuts,
- from intestinal tract through hands soiled with feces.
  - To - Prepared Food
  - To - Customer

INDIRECT TRANSMISSION OF BACTERIA FROM AGENTS TO FOOD TO PERSON

Through agents of transmission, food is contaminated by

- sewage,
- polluted water,
- rodents,
- insects such as flies & roaches,
- contaminated equipment & utensils.
    - To - Prepared Food
    - To - Consumer

CONTROL OF TRANSMISSION OF INFECTIOUS DISEASE

Since the food industry employee is a possible source of pathogens, which readily grow in food and which can result in the spread of disease to the public, it is important that all food industry personnel be free of communicable disease. Food handlers who have infectious diseases or infected cuts or sores should be excluded from handling food or food service equipment.

ALLERGENS

We know how bacteria are transmitted, how they grow, the conditions that best suit their appetite, but there is another illness not associated with bacteria as much as it is with our immune system. Allergens have come to play an important part of our health concerns, and here too we need to mention a caution regarding the handling of materials that are not potentially hazardous to the greater populace but do have an affect on some.

An allergen is a substance that causes an allergic reaction. They affect some people more than others and to a greater or lesser degree. Allergens are not pathogenic but do cause considerable discomfort to those affected by them. People with allergens are known to be allergic to a specific substance. Becoming more common is an allergy to gluten. Other allergens are eggs, milk, mustard, nuts, seafood and soy, etc.

The CFIA website has more detailed information on allergens (www.inspection.gc.ca/eng/ and in the search bar type allergens).

Food-Borne Disease

Diseases carried by food can fall under one of the following three categories:

FOOD-BORNE INFECTION.

Caused by food contaminated with pathogenic bacteria, parasites, and viruses.

- Food is ingested, and bacterial growth of organisms occurs in the intestines.
- Results: **Infection** of the body (e.g., Salmonellosis, Trichinosis, Hepatitis A).

    or

- Production of **Toxins** - (e.g., Clostridium Perfringens) - commonly found on raw meat and poultry known as gastroenteritis, caused by a toxin produced by bacteria growing on food that has been prepared or stored improperly.

FOOD-BORNE INTOXICATION *BACTERIAL.*

Caused by food contaminated with pathogenic bacteria e.g., Escherichia coli (E. coli) bacteria, which normally live in the intestines of people and animals. Most E. coli is harmless and actually is an important part of a healthy human intestinal tract. However, some E. coli are pathogenic, meaning they can cause illness either in the form of diarrhea or illness outside of the intestinal tract.

- Bacteria grow on food and toxins are produced.
- Food with toxins is ingested.
- Results: **Intoxication** (e.g., Staphylococcal intoxication - Botulism).

FOOD-BORNE INTOXICATION *CHEMICAL.*

Caused by food contaminated with toxic chemicals either deliberately (e.g., excess sodium nitrite) or accidentally (e.g., pesticides, rodenticides or cleaning compounds).

- Food containing chemicals is ingested.
- Results: Chemical **Intoxication.**

CATEGORIES OF BACTERIA

Harmless: This is the largest group of bacteria. Members of this group live in air, water and in our bodies (especially in the intestines) as well as on our bodies. These bacteria neither cause harm nor are they beneficial to humans.

Beneficial: These bacteria live all about us and carry on activities, which are of a definite value to our lives. The making and aging of cheese, production of fruit juices and vinegar, fermentation of tobacco,[1] aging beef, tanning hides,[2] and fermentation of alcohol for liquor are all examples of beneficial uses of bacteria. These bacteria are also necessary for the proper functioning of the digestive organs.

Harmful: These are the bacteria that produce disease. Many sorts of fermentation caused by bacteria are harmful, for example, milk turns sour and butter becomes rancid when certain bacteria are allowed to grow in them. Bacterial action also causes many other foods to spoil; the growth and multiplication of bacteria in bakery goods may cause serious poisoning. Botulism poisoning may occur in canned goods when bacteria produces gases and causes cans to bulge, and Salmonella poisoning is often caused by bacteria in meats, more commonly in poultry.

Good bacteria – Mould on dry aged sausage
©istock.com / credit to joakimbkk

Good bacteria – Mould on dry aged beef loins
©istock.com / credit to Night And Day Images

1   Tobacco - bacteria invade the moist leaves and cause fermentation resulting in a fine flavor.

2   Tanning of Hides - silos bacteria attack the hide to make it more pliable.

Bad Bacteria – Mould on fruit
©istock.com / credit to maerzkind

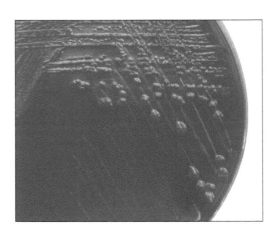

E-coli growing on a petri dish
©istock.com / credit to chfonk

Bacteria that cause disease (pathogens) live inside plants, animals and man. They live and grow in the soft tissues, blood and bones of animals or in the stems of fruit and plants. The bacteria live on muscles, blood and other tissues such as the large intestine were e-coli can develop. and some give off poisonous wastes. The damage to the tissues and the poisons sent into the blood stream cause disease. Bacteria cause many diseases of man and animals such as scarlet fever, whooping cough, tetanus, diphtheria, pneumonia, tuberculosis, typhoid fever, syphilis, leprosy, meningitis, plague and anthrax. Bacteria also affect plants, causing cabbage black rot, leaf spots, fire blight and many other plant diseases.

For more on bacteria and food related illnesses associated with certain types of bacteria, viruses, parasites, mould and yeasts, you can visit the Health Canada website (www.hc-sc.gc.ca/index-eng.php). Under "Food and Nutrition" you will find an extensive menu of topic selections related to food safety.

Cleaners, Disinfectants and Sanitizers

The removal of dirt or debris from utensils, floors, fixtures and fittings cannot, in most cases, be effected adequately with just the use of hot water. In very few cases is water alone satisfactory. Some form of cleaning agent has to be used. A detergent is a cleaning agent, which, by physical or chemical action, loosens the meat protein and fats and renders them soluble to be dispersed in the water.

The selection of a detergent or cleaning agent for any particular purpose requires some knowledge of the type of action that is required and of the range of cleaning products that are available. Not every detergent is suitable for every cleansing operation, and there is no one detergent that is ideal for all cleansing operations.

A disinfectant is an antimicrobial agent that is applied to the surface of non-living objects to destroy microorganisms that are living on the objects. A sanitizer is a substance or preparation for killing germs, designed for use especially on food processing equipment. In the meat shop, extra care must be exercised in selecting cleaners, disinfectants and sanitizers as none of these should be toxic to human beings.

All cleaning agents used must comply with the Canadian Environmental Protection Act, which was legislated into action in 1999. It is an act respecting pollution prevention and the protection of the environment and human health in order to contribute to sustainable development, ensuring the safe and effective use of biotechnology.

Health Canada has approved the sale of disinfectants for food premises that contain chlorine compounds (e.g., bleach), peroxide and peroxyacid mixtures, carboxylic acids, quaternary ammonium compounds, acid anionic and iodine compounds for use on food contact surfaces. Disinfectants for use in food premises must have a drug identification number (DIN) and must meet criteria, including those regarding antimicrobial efficacy, stipulated in the Health Canada's Guidance Document: Disinfectant Drugs. Products are evaluated by the Therapeutic Products Directorate (TPD) of Health Canada. Not all disinfectants are appropriate for use on food contact surfaces (e.g., toxic residues may be left). Product labels specify the intended or appropriate use of the disinfectant and should be read before use (Safety Data Sheet) - (SDS). Food contact sanitizers are regulated by the Bureau of Chemical Safety (BCS), Food Directorate and Health Canada. The BCS determines the maximum residue levels that remain on food products after use and, if acceptable, the CFIA issues a No Objection Letter for these products. Only food contact sanitizers that have disinfectant claims (such as bactericidal, virucidal) require a DIN.

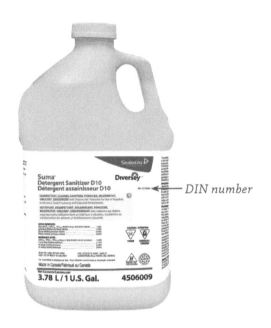

— DIN number

Meat industry Sanitizer and Din #
Credit: Diversey, USA

You can discover more of this information on the Public Services and Procurement Canada website in the Permitted Substances Lists under the topic section titled, "Permitted Substances Lists for Cleaners, Disinfectants and Sanitizers." There you will find outlined the types of cleaners, disinfectants and sanitizers permitted along with usage ratios (ppm) etc.

HOUSEKEEPING AND GENERAL MAINTENANCE

It is essential that meat production equipment and facilities be maintained on a regular basis, not only for sanitary reasons but to remain efficient. A strictly followed schedule of maintenance will help ensure safe food and prevent equipment malfunction. Essential elements of maintenance include:

1. All areas within and adjacent to the meat production operation. These areas are to be kept neat, visibly clean and free from litter and garbage. Normal passageways or work aisles should not be allowed to accumulate waste of any kind; a definite area shall be designated and kept for this purpose. Miscellaneous articles not used in the operation of meat production should be excluded from the premises. Meat products must be stored in designated meat storage areas only.

SUMA D10 DETERGENT SANITIZER

HMIS		NFPA	Personal protective equipment
Health	3	3	
Flammability	0	0	
Physical Hazard / Instability	0	0	

Version Number: 3

Preparation date: 2016-10-12

1. PRODUCT AND COMPANY IDENTIFICATION

Product name: SUMA D10 DETERGENT SANITIZER

SDS #: MS0127166
Product Code: 4506009
Recommended use: Disinfectant - Sanitizer. This product is intended to be diluted prior to use.

Manufacturer, importer, supplier:

US Headquarters
Diversey, Inc.
P.O. Box 19747
Charlotte, NC 28219-0747
Phone: 1-888-352-2249
SDS Internet Address: https://sds.sealedair.com

Canadian Headquarters
Diversey, Inc. - Canada
3755 Laird Road
Mississauga, Ontario L5L 0B3
Phone: 1-800-668-7171

Emergency telephone number: 1-800-851-7145; 1-651-917-6133 (Int'l)

2. HAZARDS IDENTIFICATION

EMERGENCY OVERVIEW
DANGER. CORROSIVE. CAUSES SKIN AND EYE BURNS. HARMFUL OR FATAL IF SWALLOWED.

Principal routes of exposure: Eye contact. Skin contact. Inhalation. Ingestion.
Eye contact: Corrosive. Causes permanent eye damage, including blindness.
Skin contact: Corrosive. Causes permanent damage.
Inhalation: May cause irritation and corrosive effects to nose, throat and respiratory tract.
Ingestion: Corrosive. Causes burns to mouth, throat and stomach.

3. COMPOSITION/INFORMATION ON INGREDIENTS

Ingredient(s)	CAS #	Weight %	LD50 Oral - Rat (mg/kg)	LD50 Dermal - Rabbit	LC50 Inhalation - Rat
Di-n-alkyl dimethyl ammonium chloride	68424-95-3	1 - 5%	238	Not available	Not available
n-alkyl dimethyl benzyl ammonium chloride	68424-85-1	1 - 5%	304.5	Not available	Not available
Ethyl alcohol	64-17-5	0.1 - 1.5 %	7060	Not available	=124.7 mg/L (4 h)

4. FIRST AID MEASURES

Eye contact: Immediately flush eyes with running water for 15-20 minutes, keeping eyelids open. Get medical attention immediately.
Skin contact: Immediately flush with plenty of water for 15-20 minutes. Get medical attention immediately.
Inhalation: If breathing is affected, remove to fresh air. Get medical attention immediately.
Ingestion: If swallowed, rinse mouth. Give a cupful of water or milk. THEN IMMEDIATELY CONTACT A

SUMA D10 DETERGENT SANITIZER

1 of 4

Safety Data Sheet (SDS)
Credit: Diversey, USA

Commercial mop bucket.
Credit: Newell – Rubbermaid
products, USA

2. Mops and mop buckets, brushes and brooms should be made of materials that can be easily sanitized. These tools should be stored separately from meat production and storage areas in a place that is well ventilated.

3. Dirt or refuse shall be removed from under fixtures, in corners and in hard-to-reach places.

4. Wet cleaning mops shall incorporate the use of separate buckets for washing and rinsing. Where possible, servicing is to be done at a janitor's sink.

5. Normal floor or wall cleaning operations should not be carried out during meat preparation or service periods. Except for emergencies, such cleaning should be done after closing or prior to opening.

6. Portable spray units may be used to disinfect surfaces that have been cleaned, providing food is removed from area being sprayed. The use of aerosol pressure sprays for sanitizing has limited effectiveness and should not replace regular sanitizing procedures except to supplement or to reach areas where normal sanitizing procedures cannot satisfactorily function.

7. Washrooms should be kept clean by regular maintenance, with special attention to thorough cleaning with bactericidal detergent for urinals, toilets, toilet seats, door handles, floors and basins. Washrooms must be provided at all times with soap and single use towels or other services for use in hand drying, providing necessary waste receptacles.

8. Live animals are not permitted in food storage, preparation or service areas.

CLEANING AND SANITIZING

General Guidelines: The fact that food is so easily contaminated makes it imperative that all equipment and utensils, particularly those which come in contact with meats and food, be regularly cleaned and sanitized.

Effective cleaning and sanitizing requires that visible soil be removed and microorganisms, which are invisible, be destroyed. To prevent dangerous contamination of food from food contact surfaces, utensils and equipment, an efficient cleaning and disinfectant program must be carried out on a regular schedule, utilizing effective materials. A sanitary maintenance schedule should be developed for all cleaning operations and each piece of equipment in the establishment.

The schedule should be in the form of a chart and should include a comprehensive list of what is to be cleaned, when to clean, how to clean, what to use to clean, how to keep it clean or store it until used, who is to clean and any precautions to be taken when cleaning.

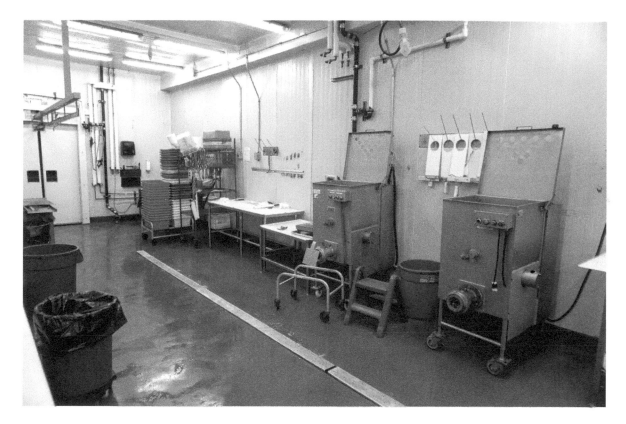

Well maintained establishments
Credit: Two Rivers Specialty Meats

Points to be considered:

1. All food contact surfaces used in the preparation, service, display or storage of meat and food, exclusive of cooking surfaces should be cleaned after each use. Surfaces that do not contact food should be cleaned at regularly scheduled intervals, the frequency of cleaning to be regulated by location of equipment, use and need.

2. Cooking, processing and cutting surfaces used at intervals throughout the day should be scraped and cleaned on completion of each use.

3. Equipment should be cleaned and sanitized as often as is necessary to maintain the surfaces in a sanitary condition.

4. Safety guards or shields which are removable should be removed to permit thorough cleaning and sanitizing of rotating cutting parts such as meat saw and slicer blades.

5. Infrequently used or stored equipment or utensils should be cleaned and sanitized before being used.

6. Detergents and abrasive residues should be removed by rinsing from food contact surfaces before food is placed on the surface.

7. Wipes should be single use, disposable or of some material that can be easily rinsed in hot water and sanitized in an approved manner. Such wipes should be maintained for surface wiping purposes only and stored in a sanitizing solution.

8. Food contact surfaces should be sanitized after cleaning. If after it has been cleaned and the food contact surface is again contaminated by any means, it should be re-cleaned and sanitized before being used.

9. Special care should be directed to the cleaning and sanitizing of cutting and chopping boards and especially meat slicers. Cutting boards and blocks should be resurfaced or replaced as necessary. Cutting boards need to be elevated after cleaning and sanitizing to ensure that the sanitizer dries off completely.

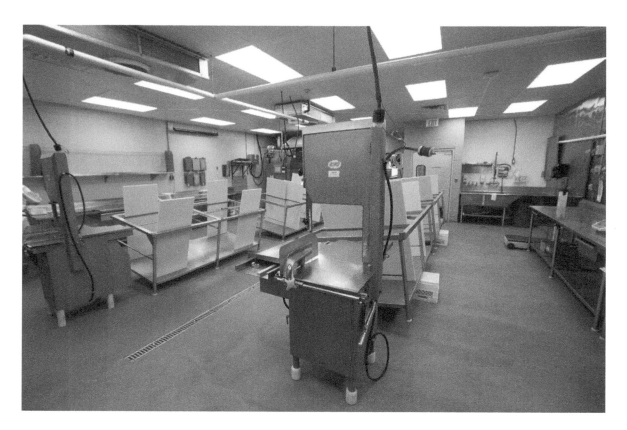

Credit: TRU Retail Meat Processing Program.

Note: the cutting tables & boards are positioned to enable proper drainage & air drying according to good sanitation practices & procedures as per point 9 on page 40.

10. Equipment and utensils used for continuous preparation or service should be sanitized at scheduled intervals according to their type and use. Utensils and equipment when sanitized should be drained dry and then stored in a clean place to prevent recontamination.

11. After cleansing and sanitizing, utensils should be kept in such a place and manner as to prevent contamination and should be handled in a sanitary manner.

12. All hand and power tools should be cleaned and sanitized according to manufacturer's specifications and instruction. Important to those instructions are the removable components of each device and the cleaning and sanitizing thereof.

MANUAL WASHING:

1. Where cleaning and sanitizing is carried out manually, it should be done in a three-compartment sink. Except where specifically exempt, all sinks used for washing and sanitizing equipment and utensils manually should be of a size, length, width and depth to allow for complete immersion of articles to be washed and should be supplied with a drain outlet and water hot enough (60 degrees c) to meet the requirements of this section.

2. Adequate space should be provided for holding soiled utensils; this should be separated from areas used for stacking and holding clean utensils.

3. Shelving and sinks with drain boards should be of non-corrodible metal, (stainless steel) suitably constructed to withstand the weight without buckling and sloped for self-drainage.

Dishwashing: The 3-step (compartment) procedure for washing meat processing equipment is as follows:

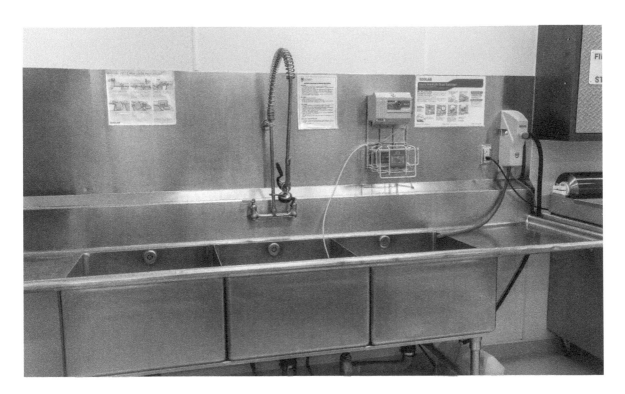

3 compartment sink
Credit: NAIT Professional Meat Cutting & Merchandising Program

1. Sort, scrape and pre-rinse utensils.

2. **First Compartment:**

   Wash utensils in clean hot water 60°C with an efficient detergent in concentrations recommended by the manufacturer. This is for the removal of soil from utensils. Change wash water frequently.

3. **Second Compartment:**

   Rinse before sanitizing, since any remaining detergent or soil must be removed before the sanitizing agent can perform effectively. Clean hot water at 60°C is to be used. Change rinse water frequently.

4. **Third Compartment:**

   Recommendation is to refer to the type of sanitizing solution, the direction it provides and the application it is intended for whether or not it be used for food equipment or other applications.

   Important to you and the establishment is that the use of sanitizer complies with regulations governing food handling, production and storage.

5. Utensils should be examined. Recycle any found unclean and dispose of any found damaged.

6. Allow utensils to air dry.

7. A two-compartment sink may be used in certain circumstances for the washing of large equipment, where washing and rinsing can be done effectively in the first sink. The second sink is used for sanitizing.

Two compartment sink.
Credit: Just Manufacturing

8. Equipment too large to be immersed shall be sprayed or rinsed with live steam or a sanitizing solution at twice the concentration noted above.

** IMPORTANT **

Unless your establishment has an automated dispenser for sanitizing solutions, when using chemical sanitizing agents, litmus colour coded test papers are required to check that proper strengths are used or to check manufacturer's recommendations for usage.

Meat Processing area washing and sanitizing spray system.

Foam cleaning a sink

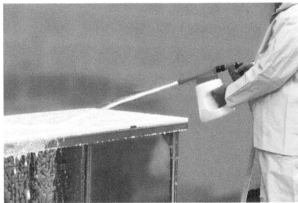

Foam cleaning a Cutting table. This practice needs to be followed by hand brush scrubbing prior to rinsing.

Rinsing a cutting table after foaming and scrubbing

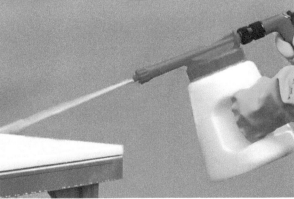

Spray sanitizing a cutting table. Then elevate table or cutting boards to drain and air dry.

Credit: Bunzl Processor Division/Koch Supplies

Sanitation for Multiple Departments

In addition to general guidelines for various departments where food is exposed, some departments require specific instructions on control procedures.

Meat Departments are areas that are used for the storage, preparation, production, sales and servicing of meat products. It may be sufficient to follow general guidelines in meat departments; however, special care should be taken to keep separate the different types of meats and meat products so as to prevent possible cross contamination. Ideally, it is now recommended that equipment used should be cleaned and sanitized between each change of product so as to ensure food safety.

The foods in the meat departments most frequently involved in food-borne illness are poultry and chopped meats (prepared or ground).

Major sources of contamination in meat departments are:

Cutting team in operation
Credit: Two Rivers Specialty Meats

- humans: by hands, coughs, sneezes and hair;
- Cross contamination from different types of meats;
- dirty aprons and wiping cloths;
- improperly sanitized equipment, cutting boards, tables, utensils, scales, etc.;
- improper refrigeration temperatures or poor storage practices.

The organisms most likely to cause or activate food-borne illness in the meat department are

1. **Salmonella,**

2. **Staphylococcus,**

3. **Escherichia Coli (e-coli),**

4. **Clostridium Perfringens,**

5. **Listeria Monocytogenes.**

Red Meats: The retail case life of red meats (beef, bison, venison, pork and lamb, etc.), is usually limited to two to three days due to the development of undesirable surface discolouration. This reduction in colour acceptability is related to the growth of bacteria on the meat surface. The retailer can improve the quality of red meats by reducing the number of bacteria initially contaminating the meat and by controlling the growth of organisms which are present. Although the application of a rigorous program of sanitation will reduce the initial bacteria count on the meat equipment surfaces, the retailer has no control over the sanitary conditions of the wholesaler or shipper of the product. Due to the nature of the product, the bacterial contamination of the product is relatively high before it reaches the retailer. Bacterial contamination is then spread via contact with knives, saws, tables, meat cutters and meat handlers. As the product is fabricated, the spread of bacteria and growth of organisms contaminates all other products that come in contact with the contaminated product, item or person.

Responsibility rests with the retailer to keep his environment as clean as possible to retard the growth of bacteria on working surfaces and on the hands and garments of the product handlers.

The nature of the retail display environment is such that the product is exposed to a wide range of temperatures. This alone is enough to cause the bacteria count to increase. Temperature controls then become of utmost importance. The retailer must be able to provide the customer with a product that when taken home will last a period of time and still maintain that fresh quality look.

Fresh red meats displayed in illuminated self-serve and service cases allow the customer a view of the product prior to purchase. Bacteria contamination on the meat surface produces undesirable odours, slime and surface discolouration, making the product unacceptable for the consumer. If the volume of the outlet is not sufficient to turn meat over rapidly, the retailer's loss can be high.

Losses due to bacteria spoilage can be responsible for thousands of dollars of lost revenue for a single retail outlet. In view of this, methods for controlling these losses are of prime importance to the retailer. It has been shown that the implementation of a rigid sanitation program can result in extended counter life of the product and provide economic benefit to the retailer.

The following points will prove useful in maintaining sanitation and extremely beneficial in preventing the growth or multiplication of bacteria.

1. Keep all cutting rooms and working surfaces dry.

2. Cloths should not be used for removing bone dust from cuts of meat.

3. Refrigeration temperatures should be checked three times daily. Recommended cooler and freezer temperature figures and defrost cycle temperatures should be prominently displayed on the appropriate unit doors. This will enable personnel to determine whether cooler and freezer are running correctly.

4. Fat and bone containers should be cleaned and sanitized daily.

5. Where in use, roller hooks and "S" hooks should be cleaned and sanitized after each use.

6. Cutting room doors should be kept closed whenever possible.

7. There is a rapid build-up of bacterial action on dirty equipment, which is not in use. All equipment not being used should be cleaned before and after storage.

8. A regular cleaning schedule should be prepared and kept prominently displayed. A daily follow up on the cleaning schedule should be maintained.

9. All cleaning equipment should be stored away from the meat cutting area.

10. Fit all garbage containers with lids.

11. An area should be designated for storage of protective clothing; dryness is essential.

12. The sanitary condition and temperatures of vehicles delivering product to your establishment should be checked. Use only good quality thermometers which give correct readings (not approximations)

13. All bulk meats delivered in carcass, quarters, primal or sub-primal units should be wrapped appropriately when delivered on pallets.

    A periodic temperature check should be made on carcass, quarters, primal, or sub-primal units to ensure proper holding temperatures from plant to truck and truck to customer.

Charcuterie

1. For products fabricated for retail sales, only use properly inspected meat materials.

2. Inspect all products prior to processing for bone chips, cartilage or other hard items or foreign objects contained in the product.

3. Carefully check restrictions or maximum usage guidelines when using non-meat ingredients.

4. Don't use spoiled or rotten materials.

5. Keep all product containers clean, sanitized and cold.

6. **Lock out** all machinery before cleaning.

Lock out hasp – 420
Credit: Master lock Canada

A Lock out notice
Credit: Master lock Canada

7. Clean all machine and work surfaces before use.

8. Clean all tools daily.

9. Clean smokehouses every week.

10. Clean floors and walls daily.

11. Clean drains and sinks daily.

12. Use proper storage procedures (First in First Out).

13. Don't sell product with expired Best Before Date.

14. Maintain good personal health and hygiene.

15. Adhere to manufacturer's safety rules for assembly and disassembly of all equipment and machinery.

16. Adhere to Food Safe program standards.

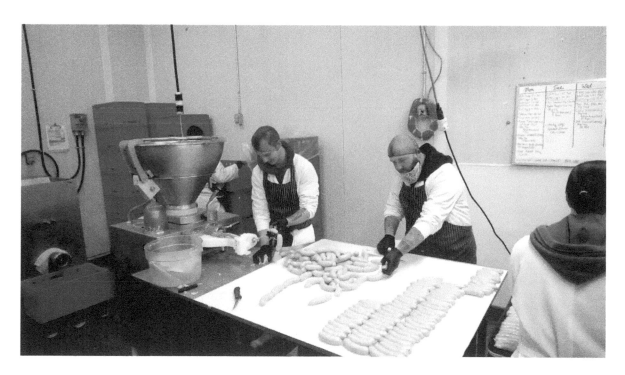

Sausage Manufacturing in operation
Credit: Two Rivers Specialty Meats

Deli departments offer for sale many products and these products may be end products such as ham, pastrami, turkey loaf, etc., or a combination of many food items as with prepared and cooked items like salads, party platters, lasagna, cabbage rolls, etc. These products, by their nature, are handled frequently and many are subjected to various temperatures used for cooking, storage and display. Temperatures must therefore be regulated carefully. In addition to standard procedures:

Deli department
Credit: Save on Foods

- prepared foods should be rapidly refrigerated and cooled between cooking and storage or use, to prevent and discourage the growth of harmful bacteria.
- cooked products should be stored in shallow pans to allow the food to cool evenly and quickly.
- special care should be taken to keep separate products in display, holding and preparation areas to avoid contamination or cross- contamination.
- hand contact with food should be avoided to prevent contamination. Disposable protective hygienic gloves should be worn to handle food.

- product should not be put or left on unclean or un-sanitized surfaces. Waxed butcher paper or other approved material should be between the product and the contact surface as a disposable shroud.
- cutting blocks or surfaces should be sanitized after use with each product.
- before they are used, all canned goods, bottles and containers should be checked for dents, holes, rust, and swells which may indicate damaged or contaminated product.
- any and all canned, bottled or vacuum packed products found to have holes, rust, dents or swells should not be used as they are most likely already contaminated. They should be returned to their source of origin or discarded.
- over-aged or outdated foods should be discarded as they may contain unacceptable bacteria counts.
- no food product should be held out or left in the temperature ranges between 4° to 60° C for more than two hours.

Foods in the deli department that are most likely to cause food-borne illnesses are:

- cooked ham
- cooked beef,
- cooked poultry,
- stews,
- gravies,
- salads: potato, poultry, ham, fish, macaroni, egg, etc.,
- salami,
- bread pudding,
- smoked fish,
- vacuum packed foods of low acidity (such as sliced ham, etc.).

Major sources of contamination in the deli department consist of the following:

- humans: hand contact, coughing, sneezing, hair
- cross-contamination among different products such as raw meats, fish and carrots
- improperly cleaned and sanitized equipment such as cutting blocks and surfaces, cutting and slicing machines, storage trays, soaker pad containers, utensils, scales and storage areas

- cooked foods not properly cooled or stored
- over exposure to incorrect (unsafe) temperatures
- vacuum packaged products (leakers), canned foods with pinholes, dents, rust and swells

The organisms found in the deli department that are most likely to cause food-borne illnesses are

1. **Salmonella,**

2. **Staphylococcus,**

3. **Clostridium Perfringens,**

4. **Clostridium Botulinum.**

Fish departments offer live, fresh, and frozen fish and value added fish products. A fish department can be a wholesome addition to the store as long as it is properly staffed with knowledgeable people familiar with the products being offered for sale and familiar with sanitary practices used in the handling of fish and fish products. The very nature of fish lends itself to odour and flavour problems if handled incorrectly, left unchecked or in the hands of un-trained personnel.

It is not necessarily sufficient to follow general guidelines in any specific department. Special care should always be taken in the rotation of products and storage of products to assure freshness. Keep different types of fish separate, and clean and sanitize utensils and equipment between uses on different species and products such as live, fresh, or frozen.

It should also be noted that the care of live fish is important, in particular the condition of the tank in which they live. These tanks should be cleaned regularly and the water changed as often as necessary to ensure the safety and well-being of the fish.

The foods in the fish department most frequently involved in food-borne illnesses are: shellfish, cooked fish and smoked fish. Major sources of contamination in the fish department are:

Fish Market & staff
Credit: Fisherman's Market

- **humans:** hand contact, coughing, sneezing, hair;
- cross contamination among different types of seafood;
- dirty aprons and wiping cloths;
- improper refrigeration temperatures.

The organisms that are most likely to cause food-borne illnesses in fish departments are:

1. **Listeria Monocytogenes,**

2. **Salmonella,**

3. **Staphylococcus,**

4. **Clostridium Perfringens,**

5. **Clostridium Botulinum.**

Receiving and Storage

Proper handling and storage are two of the most vital processes undertaken by staff once meat orders arrive at their point of sale. Because foodborne illnesses have not been fully eradicated yet, and food storage is often subject to human error, rigid procedures need to be followed to ensure that all products arriving for sale are checked, refrigerated immediately, and stored correctly. Poor food-handling and storage procedures can prove to be disastrous to a food service company and to customers alike.

Because in Canada some form of food-borne illness affects an estimated 4 million people annually we need to consider the economic impact on our industry. Here are some examples of what can happen if a food poisoning outbreak occurs due to mishandling or poor storage procedures:

- Loss of customers and sales
- Illness and even death of clients
- Loss of prestige and reputation
- Costly legal and court costs
- Increased insurance premiums
- Lower employee morale
- Professional embarrassment
- Increased cost to the health care system, such as laboratory analysis, physician time, and hospital care
- CFIA investigation time and possible consequences if charged

RECEIVING PROCEDURES

Safe food handling begins before the delivery truck arrives; it begins with the selection of reputable suppliers, those known to have clean facilities and sound food handling practices. Besides keeping the receiving area clean and well lit, here are several steps to ensure that meat products are handled in a timely and safe manner once they arrive:

- Check to see that the order matches the invoice (number of boxes, etc., and list of product names; have driver and receiver sign off).
- Ensure all packages are still sealed and not damaged.
- Check the temperature of the delivery truck storage area (was it cold on arrival?).
- Sort and move all the meat products immediately to their correct storage coolers.
- Ensure fish, meats, and poultry are kept as far apart as possible and fish containers are kept sealed until ready to use.

- Check cooler temperatures daily and record data according to health department regulations.
- Ensure cooler and freezer doors are kept closed at all times.
- Immediately report any unusual temperature fluctuations to your employer.

Receiving area
Credit: TRU Retail Meat Processing Program

STORAGE PROCEDURES

Meat should be packaged appropriately to prevent drying out, spoilage, or **freezer burn**. Whole sub-primal cuts are often vacuum packed as soon as they are removed from the carcass and will have a long shelf life when kept in the original vacuum packaging. Cut meat products for retail use should be wrapped in permeable film on trays or vacuum packaged after portioning. Cut meat products for food service use may be vacuum packed after cutting or stored in food-grade containers, wrapped appropriately, and stored according to food safety standards. Products for frozen storage should be vacuum packed or wrapped tightly in freezer paper to prevent freezer burn.

Coolers should be maintained at 0°C to 2°C. This is considered the safest temperature to hold meats and maintain flavour and moisture. Water freezes at 0°C; however, meat freezes at about -2°C.

Today the most common cooling units are the blower coil type, in which cool air is circulated via coils and fans from a ceiling-mounted unit that draws air from the floor up through the cold coils and then drives air back into the cooler area. Floor areas of the cooler must be free of containers that may impede the airflow. This means that all food containers and boxes must be elevated above floor level.

For most modern coolers, the **humidity** levels are built into the system and are maintained automatically. For example, lean beef is made up of approximately 70% moisture to optimize its flavour, sales appeal, and value. Moisture content in the air is expressed as relative humidity and is measured as a percentage. To maintain the moisture in meats, coolers need to maintain a humidity level of approximately 75% to 80%. If the moisture level drops below 70%, shrinkage will occur. However, if the humidity level is too high, moisture will condense onto the meat and appear on the walls of the cooler, creating an excellent medium for bacteria growth and sooner-than-normal meat spoilage.

Product in an aging cooler
Credit: Two Rivers Specialty Meats

Carcass lambs hanging in a cooler
Credit: Two Rivers Specialty Meats

Beef long loins and carcass lambs in a cooler
Credit: Two River Specialty meats

Modern meat coolers and freezers also have a built in defrost cycle, which is usually timed to activate in the early morning hours when there is less traffic in and out of the units. This important cycle is designed to melt away ice buildup on the blower coils (as they operate at below freezing temperatures) into a drain system. This part of the cycle takes about 20 to 60 minutes. Meat freezer temperatures should be maintained at approximately -23°C to -29°C.

Product containers in a walk-in freezer
©istock.com / credit to Lebazele

Freezer storage at a Supermarket
Credit: Save on Foods

HANDLING PROCEDURES

Once processing begins, the following steps must be taken to reduce any additional contamination of the product:

- Do not allow product in any kind of box or container to come into contact with any cutting or work surface or the floors.
- Ensure that all processing tables and cutting boards are already cleaned and sanitized.
- Ensure surfaces are dry with no residue of any **sanitizer** on them (remember that most sanitizers are toxic while wet).
- Maintain separate cutting and processing boards for different species, especially fish, chicken, and pork.
- Clean and sanitize boards immediately after use and elevate to air dry as quickly as possible.
- Have separate cutting boards for cooked meat slicing.
- Thoroughly clean and sanitize meat slicers and tenderizers between uses for different species and between cooked and raw products. These slicing tools and machines pose a very real risk for **cross contamination** and are always subject to scrutiny by health inspectors.
- If possible, process different species and cooked and raw products on different days. This helps minimize risk of cross-contamination in processing areas, tools, and machines that are used for a variety of products.

PROCEDURES WHICH APPLY TO ALL DEPARTMENTS

Many steps for preventing and controlling the growth and spread of micro organisms in any food service or food preparation outlet, retail or wholesale, are the same for all of the food service industry. These include:

1. Maintaining proper temperatures for storage and display of food to discourage the growth of microorganisms.

2. Separating different foods to prevent cross-contamination. Beef, pork, lamb, chicken and fish are all considered to be different foods.

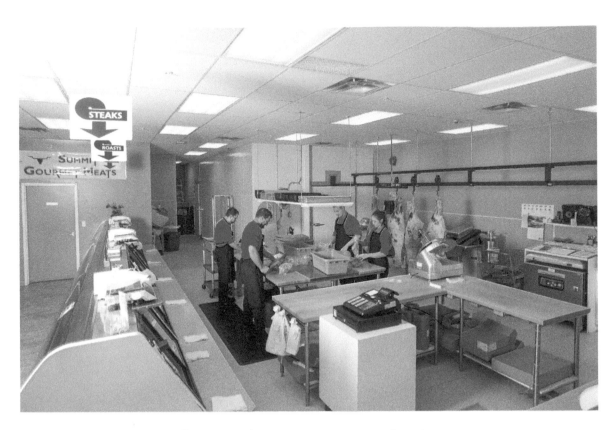

A well maintained meat store processing and service area.
Credit: Summit Gourmet Meats

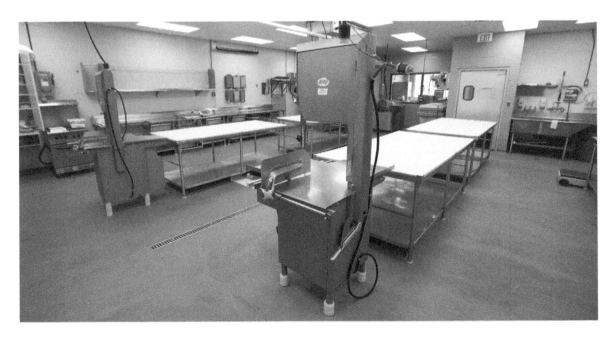

A well maintained retail production, processing area.
Credit: TRU, Retail Meat Processing Program

Pathogenic Organisms Common to our Industry

Bacteria are minute, unicellular, plant-like organisms that differ from plants in that they lack chlorophyll (green pigment or colouring matter) and they reproduce by binary fission (when a cell reaches maturity it merely separates into two cells by forming a wall through the middle).

Bacteria live on animal tissue (live or dead), causing a variety of processes and conditions that affect the tissue of the products, such as decay, discolouration, and in some cases disease. Bacteria will multiply faster on dead tissue than on live tissue, owing to fewer preventative measures. The materials in which and on which bacteria reproduce the fastest are meat soils and meat juices, both of which are found in abundance in any meat department. Cooling will retard the reproduction of bacteria to an extent. For example, the generation time (the time it takes to double the number) of bacteria is twenty hours at $0°$ C but only 6 hours at $4°$ C. Therefore, an increase of 8 degrees allows bacteria to double their numbers approximately three times faster.

One function of bacteria is to break down (decompose) organic matter. The greater the number of bacteria, the faster decomposition will occur. It is in the range of $16°$ to $38°$ C that bacteria reach maximum efficiency. At this temperature their reproduction is extremely rapid, the decaying action now takes the form of toxins which are highly poisonous to humans and to which food poisoning can be attributed.

When meat in the form of carcasses, quarters, primal, sub-primal cuts, block ready, knife ready, or counter ready meats and prepackaged meats are received from the packers and distributors the core of the product is relatively free from bacteria. With respect to raw materials it is during the handling and processing stage that bacteria are introduced, and this occurs mostly during cutting procedures. With packaged or prepackaged items bacteria can be introduced through mishandling of products.

The three factors allow for the bacterial reproduction that cause discolouration of meat are: warmth (temperature), food (meat and meat juices), and air. In order to embark on a program that prevents or minimizes the discolouration, an indication of spoilage, it is advisable to address the three factors separately. Since raw meat is most vulnerable to contamination during processing, it is obvious that effective programs of sanitation should be observed in the cutting room. To begin with, as a rule, keep perishable products out of the temperature danger zone.

BACTERIAL SHAPE CLASSIFICATION

Bacteria may be classified into three main classes according to shape:

a) Bacilli (bacillus, singular) - rod shaped organisms.
b) Cocci (coccus, singular) - rod shaped or spherical organisms.
c) Spirilla (spirillum, singular) - small, comma shaped or spiralled organisms, which are motile.

Bacteria, like humans, require nutrients to grow. They can be reproduced or cultured in water to which appropriate nutrients have been added, usually in the dissolved form. The aqueous solution containing such necessary nutrients is called a culture medium (media, plural).

FOOD-BORNE ILLNESS: AN ABSTRACT OF TERMS

Definition: Food-borne illness (acute gastroenteritis) is caused by the presence in the intestines (gastrointestinal tract) of microbial pathogens which multiply profusely in the food, or by poisons released by micro organisms into the food, or by the accidental addition of chemicals to foods.

Causes: Food infections are caused by the ingestion of food contaminated with harmful bacteria. When harmful bacteria are ingested in large quantities, the human body cannot fight them effectively. The bacteria multiply in the intestines and produce the symptoms of gastroenteritis (food-borne illness). Food-borne illnesses caused by these large intakes of harmful reproducing bacteria are known as a food-borne infection.

Food Intoxication: Ingested food contaminated with harmful bacteria may cause another type of food-borne illness known as food poisoning. In this type, primarily toxins produced by the harmful bacteria and then released from the bacteria into the food itself cause the symptoms. The toxins produced are highly poisonous thus the term food poisoning. Food poisoning or food-borne illness related to food toxins produced from bacteria is known as food intoxication.

MAJOR CAUSES OF FOOD-BORNE ILLNESS

In brief, these are the bacteria substances/sources that are the main causes of food-borne illness associated with meat processing and retail operations.

- Staphylococcus
- Clostridium Perfringens
- Salmonella
- Clostridium Botulinum
- Escherichia Coli
- Listeria Monocytogenes

Staphylococcus intoxication: The main contributing source of Staphylococcus intoxication is the human body via the food handler. The incubation time is short, usually two to six hours. The duration of the illness caused by Staphylococcus is one to two days.

The most important principles for control of this microorganism are sound hygienic and applied sanitation practices especially frequent hand washing.

Clostridium Perfringens intoxication and/or infection: Clostridium Perfringens are mainly found on meat sources especially when cooked and allowed to cool slowly. The incubation time ranges from eight to twenty hours. The duration of illness caused by Clostridium Perfringens is one day.

The most important principles for controls of this microorganism are temperature control and properly applied personal hygiene practices, especially frequent hand washing.

Salmonella infection: The main contributing source of Salmonella is more often than not traced to improperly prepared poultry or the cross contamination thereof. The incubation time is twelve to twenty-four hours. The duration of illness caused by the most common strains of Salmonella is two to three days.

The most important principles for control of the microorganism are temperature control and sound personal hygienic practices.

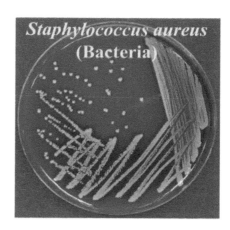

Staphylococcus growing on a petri dish
Credit: TRU Micro-biology-Dr. Soumya Ghosh,
Timothy Crowe and Kamal Grewal-Choudhury

Does Chicken contain Salmonella bacteria? One reason that a lot of chicken may have harboured salmonella is likely because of a processing procedure used by many kill plants till resent times. The process was as follows: After the chickens were stunned, bled, de-feathered with head and feet removed, they were cooled off in huge stainless steel water vats. It is during this procedure that those chicken containing the salmonella organism contaminate the water and distribute it to all chicken cooling off in the same water. It did not take long for the water to become saturated with this common organism. However, most slaughter plants today have replaced the water-cooling baths with ice or air cool drying methods in an attempt to control the spread of bacteria. Air or ice cooled chickens can be stored longer for periods of up to 8 days in proper refrigeration of 1 degree Celsius or 34 degrees

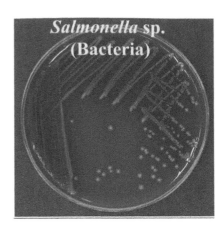

Salmonella growing on a petri dish
Credit: TRU Micro-biology-Dr. Soumya Ghosh,
Timothy Crowe and Kamal Grewal-Choudhury

Fahrenheit; whereas fresh chicken chilled using the huge water vat system have a two to three day shelf life.

More Poultry concerns: Avian influenza is a contagious viral infection caused by the influenza virus Type "A", which can affect several species of food producing birds (chickens, turkeys, quails, guinea fowl, etc.), as well as pet birds and wild birds.

Avian influenza viruses can be classified into two categories, low pathogenic avian influenza and high pathogenic avian influenza, each based on the severity of the illness caused in birds, with high pathogenic avian influenza causing the greatest number of deaths in birds. Most avian influenza viruses are low pathogenic and typically cause little or no clinical signs in infected birds. However, some low pathogenic viruses are capable of mutating into high pathogenic viruses. There are many influenza subtypes, two of which include

H5 and H7. Historically, only H5 and H7 subtypes are known to have become high pathogenic in avian species.

Diagnosis of avian influenza may be made on the basis of clinical signs and events leading to the disease. However, since the signs and course of avian influenza are similar to other diseases, laboratory diagnosis is essential.

Domestically, the virus can spread to birds through contact with infected poultry and poultry products, and through manure and litter containing high concentrations of the virus, for example through contaminated clothing and footwear, vehicles and equipment, and feed and water, thus the importance of good effective sanitation programs. However, wild birds, especially waterfowl, are natural carriers of the influenza viruses - yet show no clinical signs - and can be responsible for the primary introduction of infection into domestic poultry. But from a consumer point of view the real concern questions whether or not avian influenza is transmissible to humans.

Avian influenza viruses, such as H5 virus present in Asia, may, on rare occasions, cause disease in humans. Human transmission has occurred to people having prolonged contact with heavily contaminated environments. Human to human transmission of avian influenza is extremely limited.

For more on avian influenza visit the CFIA website: inspection.gc.ca and under the menu bar selection "Animals" click on "Terrestrial Animals" then on the left side choose "Diseases or visit the Health Canada Website: http://www.phac-aspc. gc.ca under infectious diseases.

Clostridium Botulinum intoxication (botulism): Botulism is most likely to be found in vacuum-packed foods of low acidity. The incubation time is twelve to thirty-six hours. The duration of the illness is very long and it is sometimes fatal. Recovery may take several months.

To control outbreaks of botulism, procure only properly prepared foods. Always check vacuum packed and canned products for any signs of abnormality such as swelling, rust, or punctures.

Escherichia coli intoxication: E. coli intoxication is most likely to occur through transmission of the organism from the feces of humans and other animals or from intestines or intestinal contents during slaughtering or evisceration of animals. The incubation time ranges from 18 hours to about 4 days, depending on the strain of E. coli involved.

The most important principles for control of this organism are temperature control and sound hygienic and applied sanitation practices and especially frequent hand washing.

Hamburger Disease: There have been outbreaks of E.Coli also known as "hamburger

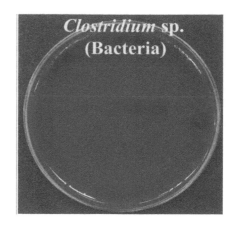

Clostridium growing on a petri dish
Credit: TRU Micro-biology-Dr. Soumya Ghosh, Timothy Crowe and Kamal Grewal-Choudhury

E-coli growing on a petri dish
©istock.com / credit to Scharvik

disease" which occurs when minced/ground meat becomes contaminated with the bacteria. In recent years large meat plants have had to make recalls of ground product shipped to major retailers. Thanks to their diligence this product was removed from stores avoiding any potential food related hazard to the general public.

Fecal contamination is most evident during the slaughtering process when the hide (most often soiled with fecal matter) and viscera (the intestinal tract containing feces) are removed. As the hide is removed it can flick undetected particles of feces onto the hot flesh of the animal and during

evisceration the inside rounds on the hips of the animal where the pelvis is split open can also be contaminated.

Note: Cargill's High River Plant in Alberta took a progressive approach to reducing e-coli contamination by installing a carcass hide wash system prior to removal of the hide.

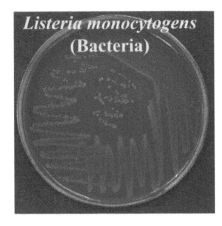

Listeria Moncytogenes growing on a petri dish Credit: TRU Micro-biology-Dr. Soumya Ghosh, Timothy Crowe and Kamal Grewal-Choudhury

Listeria Monocytogenes infection: Listeria has been found in soil and water and some animals, including poultry and cattle. It has been associated with such foods as raw milk, cheeses made from raw milk, raw vegetables, fermented raw sausage meats, raw and cooked poultry, raw meats of all types, and raw and smoked fish. Listeria bacteria can grow at zero degrees Celsius. It survives both aerobic and anaerobic conditions and has been found to survive on equipment in hard to clean places.

Best method of control for Listeria is temperature (refrigeration), cleanliness, and product utilization (FIFO).

HACCP

Hazard Analysis Critical Control Point (HACCP) is an approach to food safety that is systematic and preventive. It is recommended by the Codex Alimentarius Commission, the United Nations international standards organization for food safety. HACCP is used by most countries around the world. It has been in use since the 1960s. HACCP goes beyond inspecting finished food products. It helps to find, correct and prevent hazards throughout the production process. These include physical, chemical and biological hazards.

HACCP is both a system and an association which oversees, monitors and helps implement, through its established regulations, safe food handling from a raw state to finished product. This organization is one of international acclaim. The main intent of HACCP is to ensure the safety of food from pathogenic micro-organisms. According to our research HACCP revolves around the following principles:

- Assess hazards and risks associated with growing, harvesting raw materials and ingredients, processing, manufacturing, distribution, marketing, preparation and consumption of food.
- Determine the critical control point required for controlling the identified hazards.
- Establish the critical limits that must be met at each critical control point.
- Establish procedures to monitor the critical control point.
- Establish corrective action to be taken when there is a deviation identified by monitoring a critical control point.
- Establish and practice effective record-keeping systems that document the HACCP plan.
- Establish procedures for verification that the HACCP system is working correctly.

The direction HACCP's principles point to in the food industry makes it crucial that management develop effective sanitation practices and procedures (a sanitation program) for the area over which they have responsibility. To do this they must analyze the way in which they handle food and identify the potential hazards of their food handling. Potential hazards are practices or procedures that place the food at risk of contamination, thereby encouraging the onslaught of food related illnesses. Managers having identified these hazardous areas, known as critical control points of their food operation establishment, can then implement effective strategies to minimize or eliminate potential hazard(s) to the food they handle. To do so they must take charge to oversee and activate a strategic plan designed to control these critical points of their food handling operation.

Any sanitation program developed under the auspices of those strategies prescribed above should be able to meet the requirements of HACCP. The construction of HACCP is to ensure food safety at each stage of its handling rather than the final product. Implementation of HACCP principles and philosophies transfer the responsibility of sanitary practices and procedures in the food industry to both management and staff. In other words, under the HACCP umbrella, industry regulates itself, as HACCP is industry driven and industry monitored. Therefore it becomes the industry's responsibility to police itself and to design HACCP programs suited to their operations.

HACCP is the standard for the food industry. The generic code for quality products is established in the International Standards Organization (ISO). The specific code for the food industry is established under the HACCP program. The HACCP program being specific to the food industry and food industry standards, allies itself directly under the broad scope of the ISO.

SUMMARY

Management with the assistance of their food-handling employees should design a sanitation program suited to the needs of their operation. The sanitary processes and procedures in the handling of food for consumption by the paying public are no less important than the processing process of the product itself. A good sanitation program ensures efficiency in the daily operations of a food-handling establishment.

The food industry is such that complete sterilization of food and its handling is virtually impossible, in that it is not economically feasible. The industry can, however, make every effort to safeguard the food that they handle. In the prevention of food related illnesses, cleaning and corrective measures must be frequent. It's essential therefore to have a cleaning schedule that designates assigned duties for specific tasks pertaining to the sanitary operation of the food facility.

Food sanitation is a subject where "too much attention" cannot be given in the safe handling of food. Sanitation is one of the most important operations in any food handling facility and involves more detail than the food processing itself. The practitioner must be knowledgeable in all facets of its application. This would of course include three important operational practices.

1. Good Personal Hygiene

2. Temperature Control

3. Sanitation Practices & Procedures

This equates to a safer longer lasting saleable product, eliminating additional cost factors through efficiency of workers and the work place via a viable, effective and feasible sanitation program.

TERMS FOR REVIEW

Aerobic	Disinfectant	Microbiology
Allergen	Facultative	Pathogenic
Anaerobic	Food-borne Infection	Pathogens
Cross Contamination	Food-borne Intoxication	Professionalism
Danger Zone	Lag Phase	Sanitizer
Death Phase	Log Phase	

1. Why do we need extensive food control measures, (regulations) and what is their purpose?

2. Discuss the economic impact food-borne illness has on the Canadian public; cost of health care, lost time, and the loss of potential earnings both corporately and individually.

3. List the temperatures of the safe zone?

4. Why should we not leave perishable items in the danger zone?

5. Why concern ourselves with cleaning worktables between applications of cutting fish, chicken or red meats?

6. How is bacteria transmitted?

7. What is a virus?

8. Should an employee who has an infectious disease be working in the food industry? Why or why not?

9. Define HACCP.

10. What are the objectives of regulatory departments?

11. Are all bacteria harmful to humans? Explain your answer.

12. Should the food industry, in particular the meat industry, be concerned about allergens? Explain your answer.

Chapter 3

Equipment

As we know, tools are an extension of the hand and nothing is more important to the successful manipulation of tools than the safety of our appendages. In this chapter we explore the various tools and equipment of the trade, their usage, safety and lockout features, and operational practices. Important to know is the purpose of equipment and our attention to particular potential hazards equipment poses to the untrained or inattentive worker.

The chapter introduces you to more common types of equipment used in the meat industry but not all equipment available to the industry. A comprehensive list of meat industry equipment with illustrations would make a textbook of its own.

Here as elsewhere we note that the content of this chapter is no substitute for demonstration and training by a qualified instructor in the use and maintenance of equipment listed herein. As with the use of any tool, practice is required to develop safe and efficient operational skills.

Equipment

Occupational Health & Safety

Before we delve into the topic of equipment, we have a responsibility to bring to your attention the subject of occupational health and safety. Occupational health and safety also commonly referred to as OHS, is a multidisciplinary field concerned with the occupation, health, and safety or welfare of people at work. OHS programs are not new to the workplace as history records efforts to improve workplace standards as early as the 1800s. Today we have both federal and provincial legislation guarding and enforcing workplace standards that all employers must adhere to. However, the legislation is clear that OHS is not just the employer's responsibility; it is also the responsibility of employees. All employees should know exactly what is expected of them in health and safety terms.

Although work provides us many economic benefits, there are work hazards that risk the health and safety of people at work. Risks are as varied as occupations. They include but are not limited to chemicals, biological agents, physical factors, ergonomic conditions, allergens and a complex range of safety issues surrounding the use and maintenance of equipment. Personal protective equipment can help protect against many of these risks or hazards but none as effective as occupational health and safety education and training. Each employee should have the ability and competence training can provide to engage in the work activities of a craft or occupation successfully. The ability and competence training can provide complements the worker's responsibility, the use of reasonable conscientious judgment while following safe work procedures in the performance of required duties.

Every place of employment should have an OHS program designed to foster a health and safety work environment. A health and safety program is a definite plan of action designed to prevent accidents and occupational diseases. Some form of a program is required under occupational health and safety legislation in most Canadian jurisdictions. A health and safety program must include the elements required by the health and safety legislation as a minimum. Because organizations differ, a program developed for one organization cannot necessarily be expected to meet the needs of another. The meat industry has many sectors, and so OHS programs may vary from one organization to another meeting the needs of specific sectors of the industry.

In our industry equipment is used for ripping, tearing, cutting, and cooking, etc. Therefore a worker needs to be cognizant of what is being ripped, torn, cut or cooked and have the required ability and competence to perform assigned duties. This means having the physical attributes needed, using personal protection and safety equipment as required by the employer, following safe work procedures, reporting injury immediately, recognizing and reporting unsafe conditions and participating in making the workplace a safer environment for all participants.

Canadian Human Rights Act

EXCEPTIONS:

> Section 15 (1)
> It is not a discriminatory practice if (a)
> any refusal, exclusion, expulsion, suspension or preference in relation to any
> employment is established by an employer to be based on a bona fide occupational
> requirement.

What this means is those persons working in the industry are hired based on their ability to perform the duties required of them in applying their craft. Therefore workers with physical or mental impairment cannot be assigned to work where such impairment endangers themselves or others.

OHS also states that no employee shall enter or remain or be permitted to remain on the premises of any place of employment while his ability to work is so affected by alcohol, a drug or other substances that endanger his health or safety or that of any other person; and no person shall engage in any improper activity or behaviour that might create or constitute a hazard to himself or any other worker. Improper activity or behaviour includes:

- Horseplay-scuffling
- Fighting, practical jokes
- Unnecessary running
- Unnecessary jumping
- Similar conduct

Statistics say that 95% of all accidents can be avoided. Only when people are thinking constantly of their own safety and the safety of others will they work safely.

For more on OHS visit the Canadian Centre for Occupational Health and Safety website or visit your local jurisdiction.

Hand Tools

Equipment plays a major role in the fabrication of meat cuts and meat items; however, the most sophisticated equipment does not necessarily assure an excellent outcome with respect to the end product, for quality depends mainly on the skill of the person operating the equipment. As long as the equipment is in good working order and the user is in possession of the appropriate skills needed to operate that equipment then a usable product can be expected or produced.

Definition: Hand and Power Tools are devices used as an extension of the hand. In the Meat Industry they are such tools used in the day-to-day operation of the department.

The definition means we use tools specifically designed to make the type of work we do easier. The tools of the industry have advantages and disadvantages. The advantages have already been implied, ease of production resulting in saving time. The disadvantage to the unskilled, inattentive or careless user is that these tools are dangerous. Bandsaws are designed to cut bone and flesh cleanly and quickly. This equipment does not distinguish between meats of the trade and the user's appendages.

Accidents are usually caused by:

1. Inattention
2. Using the wrong tool for the job
3. Using tools in poor condition
4. Using tools improperly
5. Leaving tools where they may contribute to an accident
6. Not knowing, or simply
7. Not caring

Safety is essential in the meat industry. Every meat cutter must be careful that the job is consistently done only one way, "the right way and the safe way."

To ensure the safety of the workplace, regulations are enforced under the Canada Occupational Health and Safety Regulations (www.justice.gc.ca).

CARE AND USE OF HAND TOOLS

This section describes the tools and equipment used in the meat cutting industry and the safety factors involved in their use. Cutting tools, particularly knives, are stressed since these are most frequently involved with hand injuries. Hands are the most valued instrument of any trades person. The loss of thumbs or index fingers can be devastating. Try working using only the last three fingers of one hand and you will immediately get the point.

Listed here are some of the Hand Tools and aids used in meat cutting operations:

- Bone dust remover
- Block or table scrapper
- Cleaver
- Dry stones
- Electric sharpening Stones
- Handsaws
- Knives
- Oil stones
- Packer's hooks
- Roller rails and hooks
- Steels
- Stitching needles
- String (twine)
- Stuffing Horns
- Tree or chuck hooks
- Water stones
- Wire hook or "S" hooks

Sharpening oil stone & knives
Credit:Bunzl Processor Division/Koch Supplies

Sharpening wet stone – 360 grit
Credit: Friedr. Dick

Knife angle set guide with 1000 grit wetting stone
Credit: Friedr. Dick

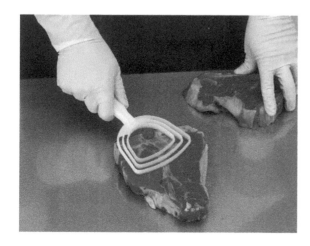

Bone dust remover
Credit: Bunzl Processor Division/Koch Supplies

Block or Table scraper
Credit: Bunzl Processor Division/Koch Supplies

Small sharpening machine
Credit: Friedr. Dick

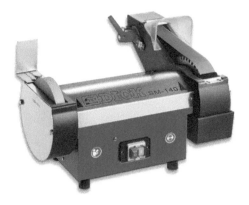

Water-cooled Belt & stone sharpening machine
Credit: Friedr. Dick

Precision water-cooled knife sharpener with
magnetic knife holder and buffing wheel
Credit: Friedr. Dick

Universal water-cooled grinder for knives, cutter
blades, cleavers & serrated edged knives
Credit: Friedr. Dick

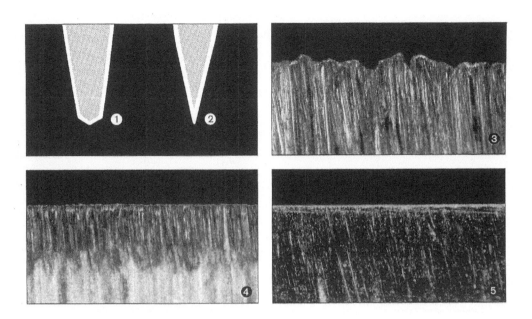

1. Dull edge prior to sharpening, 2. Edge after sharpening process, 3. Secondary edge after grinding,
4. Primary cutting edge, 5. Polished Primary edge
Credit: Friedr. Dick

General Safety Rules

1. Keep floors clean and dry.
2. Keep suitable fire-fighting equipment on hand and functional.
3. Apply basic safety rules for lifting heavy products.
4. Keep first-aid box stocked with necessary products for rendering first aid to anyone injured.
5. Keep phone numbers for fire and hospital by the telephone.
6. Record all injuries no matter how slight.
7. Walk; do not slide across floor areas.
8. Wear sensible or industry approved footwear with safety toecaps.
9. Keep your mind on your work. People who daydream have accidents.
10. Keep sleeves of uniform rolled up during operation of power saw.
11. Don't try to carry too heavy a load. Know your limitations and use proper lifting techniques for rail hung and boxed meat products.
12. Clean as you go, keeping the work area free of debris and clutter.
13. Use an approved stepladder to access high storage shelves.

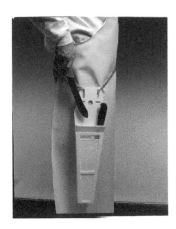

Scabbard for two knives both long or short blades
Credit: Bunzl Processor Division/ Koch Supplies

Scabbard for three or four short blades
Credit: Friedr. Dick

Wall mounted magnetic knife holder.
Credit: Bunzl Processor Division/Koch Supplies

Safety Checklist For Knives & Sharp Tools

1. Keep all knives sharp; less pressure is needed to cut with a sharp knife and there's less chance of it slipping.
2. Keep knives in your personal scabbard when not in use.
3. **Never** grab for a falling knife; let it fall.
4. If you don't have a scabbard, return knives to storage place when not in use.
5. Do not throw or pretend to throw a knife.
6. Do not stick knives in cuts of meat and leave them there.
7. Do not test the blade of the knife by running the thumb along its edge.
8. Do not clean fingernails with a boning knife.
9. Keep handles of knives (and other hand tools) free from grease build-up.
10. Do not carry knives in your hands (or other hand tools) when loaded down with meat.
11. Do not walk around with a knife pointed outwards.
12. When washing knives or any other sharp-edged tool, do not immerse them in water where they cannot be seen.
13. Do not "bury" knives or any other sharp-edged tool under piles of meat when working on the block.
14. Hold bladed hand tools with a firm grip so that no part of the hand comes in contact with the sharp edge.

15. Smooth and round off the back edge or shoulder of new knives.
16. Do not leave knives stuck in meat blocks, tables, boxes or product.
17. Use the right knife for the right job – a boning knife for removing bones and a steak knife for cutting steaks; and there is to be absolutely no horseplay with knives.
18. Use knives that have a hand-formed safety grip handle.
19. Use hand and body protection such as mesh gloves and aprons, armguards when provided or consider purchasing your own.

Chain mail apron
Credit: Bunzl Processor Division/Koch Supplies

HexArmor – Arm guard
Credit: Bunzl Processor Division/Koch Supplies

Kevlar glove
Credit: Bunzl Processor Division/Koch Supplies

Chain mail gloves
Credit: Bunzl Processor Division/Koch Supplies

Chain mail glove
Credit: Friedr. Dick

Chain mail glove with long cuff
Credit: Friedr. Dick

TYPES OF KNIVES

Widths and lengths of meat cutting knives vary, but there are some common sizes in use. Cutting knives or steak knives are usually 30 cm in length with scimitar-shaped blades and made of stainless steel.

One theory has it that one should use a knife with a razor shape blade no longer than 20 cm to avoid undue aggravation to the worker's wrist. However, the most common length of steak knife in Canada seems to be 25 cm especially in supermarkets.

A good-quality knife will have a longer life and hold the edge longer than a cheaper knife. Boning knives should be fairly rigid but flexible enough to bend slightly and spring back. The blades are usually 15 cm long with blade widths varying from 12 mm to 19 mm, according to the preference of the user.

Boning knives can be straight or curved, flexible or rigid. Flexible curved boning knives are very popular for use in supermarket style cutting, where a lot of trimming of steaks is common. However, they do not last as long as the rigid straight boning knives used in heavy production. The beginner may find this knife more difficult to learn to use. Rigid straight boning knives are used or preferred for breaking rail hung beef and for prolonged periods of heavy boning. Both knives can be used in similar situations depending on personal preference.

Curved boning knife, flexible blade

Boning knife, straight & narrow blade

Boning knife, straight & wide blade

Butcher's knife, narrow curved blade

Butcher's knife, Cimitar curved steak knife

Butcher's knife, Curved wide blade

Credit: Friedr. Dick

Some meat cutters own a variety of knives and take great pride in their tools, but the two knives mentioned above will usually suffice to perform any function in a retail outlet. It is recommended that students obtain a pair of good-quality knives and keep them as their own particular tools. They will become good friends and a person works a little better with familiar tools. The knives should be in a scabbard and worn on the meat cutter's hip.

Handles on all meat cutting knives should be shaped to fit the hand's grip. Straight type handles tend to allow the user's hand to slip down along the blade during use, particularly if the hands are greasy. Most suppliers of butcher knives will recommend only handles with a moulded formed safety handgrip.

To get maximum production from knives, keep them separated from other tools so that they will not be dulled or nicked. A good blade needs only occasional sharpening, but it should always be steeled before using. Well-kept tools add to a meat cutter's confidence.

While using a knife, the index finger or the ball of the thumb will often rest on the back of the blade about one inch past the handle. This is an extremely sharp edge which with very little pressure will puncture the flesh with a wide cut. The edges of the back of the blade can be filed down and rounded off with the butcher steel to eliminate this hazard.

STEELS

There are various types of steels on the market, ranging from ribbed steels with a file-type finish to those with a mirror-type finish. Steels come in different lengths, 25, 30, 35 cm. etc. Width and shapes of steels also differ greatly.

Most steels have magnetic tips that enable the user to set the edge of the knife more accurately to the tip of the steel before beginning the steeling action.

Steels should not be used for any other purpose than for which they are designed. Using them for levers for breaking box-binding material will only damage the smooth surface, which may then score and damage the fine cutting edge of a knife.

When not in use, keep the steel in a designated place preferably through a steel ring attached by a short length of either plastic or stainless steel chain to your scabbard waist chain on the opposite hip to your knives.

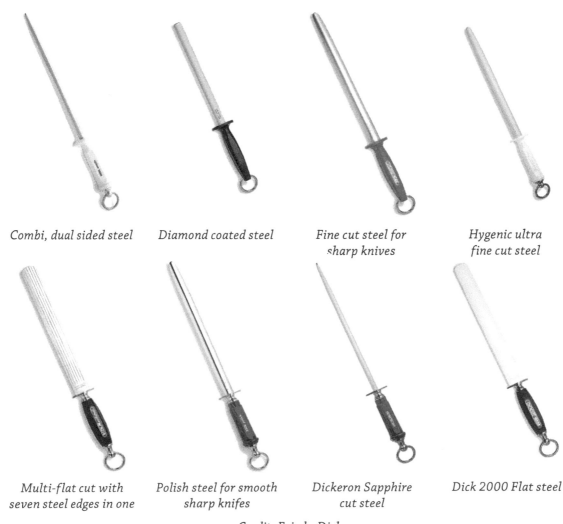

Combi, dual sided steel   *Diamond coated steel*   *Fine cut steel for sharp knives*   *Hygenic ultra fine cut steel*

Multi-flat cut with seven steel edges in one   *Polish steel for smooth sharp knifes*   *Dickeron Sapphire cut steel*   *Dick 2000 Flat steel*

Credit: Friedr. Dick

Steeling guide for straightening & smoothing knife edges, bench mounted
Credit: Bunzl Processor Division/Koch Supplies

Steeling guide, handheld
Credit: Bunzl Processor Division/Koch Supplies

Knives that have been sharpened and have a razor edge must be steeled carefully. It is important to set the knife's original sharpened bevel angle (the primary edge or the final edge that is ground in with the fine sharpening stone) at the same angle on the steel. Steeling is then done with very careful but steady strokes until the edge is smooth and sharp (three to four strokes each side of the blade).

The steel is used to only true the blade of a sharp knife and keep the edge in perfect condition. Although there is a technique to handling the steel, it is easily mastered with practice. However, steeling guides both handheld and table mounted are often used in commercial operations.

It is a popular misconception that the steel is used to sharpen the knife. Some meat cutters use a coarse or rougher edged steel to put an edge on a knife; however, this is usually only a quick fix procedure that eventually produces an even duller knife in the long-term. This method of steeling requires a lot of vigorous steeling to produce an even moderate edge on a knife.

STITCHING NEEDLES

These are used in conjunction with meat cutter's twine to insert stitches for tying meat muscles together or holding flat pieces of meat that have been rolled and stuffed together. Their use is minimal in most retail outlets today.

Keep in a safe place when not in use as for all sharp or pointed tools.

Stitching needles
Credit: TRU retail meat processing program

HANDSAWS

Although the handsaw or meat cutting saw is still used in breaking hinds in some retail outlets, its use in modern meat markets is declining with the increasing availability of primal and sub-primal cuts, block-ready beef, knife and counter ready meats and pre-processed pork. Most handsaws in retail outlets are supplied by contracting companies that periodically service them and provide the number of saw blades needed between servicing. Handsaws still require careful attention. The blade should be removed during cleanup to eliminate the build-up of meat deposits around the handle and blade guides.

When replacing a blade, the teeth set of the saw edge should always point in a forward direction so that the cutting takes place on the forward stroke. When starting a cut, rest the ball of the free thumb lightly on the back of the blade to inhibit any jumping or skipping of the saw, which

Meat handsaw
Credit: Bunzl Processor Division/Koch Supplies

could result in injury to the back of the hand holding the product. When the blade has penetrated deeply enough to eliminate this danger, the thumb can be removed. Utilize the whole length of the saw blade with long strokes to conserve the operator's energy in cases of long periods of use. The saw will have a tendency to travel off at an angle during the cutting procedure. This is usually due to too much force being applied by the operator or to the blade being blunt. When blades are blunt and need to be replaced, we recommend they be stored clean in a dry place. Stored blades should be coated in a light spray of mineral oil to protect the metal from rusting.

Handsaw Safety Checklist

- ✓ **Remove the Blade** with saw blade directed toward the floor to avoid hitting someone should the blade eject too quickly.
- ✓ Don't try to cut too rapidly so as to avoid catching your knuckles on protruding bones.
- ✓ Hang or store the saw in a designated safe place when not in use.

CLEAVERS

This particular piece of meat cutting equipment is quickly becoming obsolete as the advent of block, knife and counter ready meats take over. These days the power saw has replaced the cleaver. The use of the cleaver is usually restricted to family meat cutting operations that cut and process meat by hand. The cleaver, which seems an unwieldy tool to the beginner, can only be mastered through continuous use.

Meat and bone cleaver
Credit: Friedr. Dick

The cutting edge of the blade need not be as razor sharp like a knife but must be keen enough so as not to splinter the material being cut or chopped. The bevel put on the blade should be no more than 30 mm from the edge, and because the edge must withstand violent force, the angle of the bevel is very severe, usually about 24°. This will produce an edge, which will last for weeks. Most cleavers have a hole drilled in the corner above the tip, which can be used for hanging the tool.

A cleaver should only be used on a wooden cutting block because it will cause severe damage to other tabletops. If used negligently, it can also damage the surface of a wooden block. This makes scraping extremely difficult when cleaning the block. The experienced operator applies only enough force to cut the product; however, this skill comes only with experience.

The blade of a cleaver will pit and discolour very quickly, particularly if not in continuous use. A light spray coat of mineral oil helps keep it in good appearance. The blade should have the same cleaning attention as knives.

Cleaver Safety Checklist

- ✓ Don't try to catch a falling cleaver.
- ✓ Jump clear if you drop a cleaver to avoid injuries to your feet.
- ✓ Store in a safe place when not in use.
- ✓ Do not use a cleaver for cutting box bindings or as a hammer.

Meat Rail & Hooks

Meat rails and meat rail hooks are not found in markets that use only block-ready beef or knife and counter ready meats but are still in use in other independent outlets.

Roller Hooks are used in conjunction with the roller rail, come in two sizes - short and long. The short-shanked hooks are usually used to hang hindquarters of beef for transport to and storage in the meat coolers. The long-shanked hooks are for the front quarters. The two designs keep the meat product from trailing on the floor areas and minimize the energy needed for handling.

The roller hooks will only remain free-running if given adequate attention. Periodically they should be steam-cleaned and lubricated with food safe oil. This will serve a dual function: ensure good mobility and also inhibit corrosion, which could result from the relatively moist conditions in most meat coolers. Hooks should be stored near the receiving area on a support rail, which will keep them above floor level.

When receiving products where roller hooks are needed, it is recommended the receiver wear a safety hard hat for protection. Hooks usually weigh approximately 3 kg each and can cause considerable injury. A loose hook should never be left on a meat rail unless it is being held by the receiver or weighted down with other loose hooks. Should it be necessary to lift a quarter of

beef from a roller hook, always attempt to have one person pulling down firmly on the roller hook while the other person does the lifting. This prevents the roller hook from lifting off the rail and hitting the lifter's head.

Rail roller hook
Credit: Bunzl Processor Division/Koch Supplies

The meat rails are suspended from the ceiling or from beams and are secured with struts that are hooked or bolted onto the rail. These allow the roller hook to be utilized only on the correct side. If the hooks are placed on the rails incorrectly, they will be violently stopped by the struts.

Rail roller hooks racked for use on a stable hanging rack
Credit: TRU retail meat processing program

Roller Hook Safety Checklist

✓ Before pushing product away that is hung on roller hooks, ensure that meat rail gates are safely closed to ensure safe passage of the product.

✓ Hang roller hooks on correct side of rail and store empty hooks away in the designated receiving area.

✓ Keep roller hook wheels in good condition and running freely.

✓ Wear hard hats when roller hooks are in use.

✓ Check ends of hooks to ensure they are suitably bent for safe hanging of product.

✓ Use two persons when removing product from the rail, one to hold the hook firmly downwards and the other to lift the product.

✓ Never leave empty roller hooks on the meat rails.

MEAT RAILS

1. Ensure that all meat rail gates are safely tripped into place to provide smooth and safe passage of product.
2. Replace rusted or corroded rails.
3. Ensure rails are engineered and structurally designed to withstand the maximum weight expected to be used on them.
4. Keep switches in good condition.
5. Supply rail ends with positive end stops.
6. Don't push rail-hung product without first observing that the area ahead of you is clear.
7. Don't try to push too much product. Work with a partner to share the workload.
8. Never push product along the rail rapidly and unattended so as not to knock someone over.

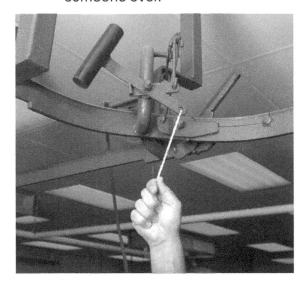 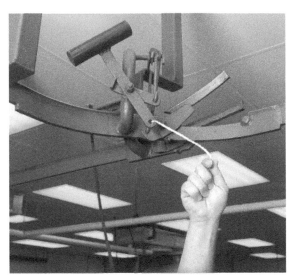

Meat rail gate switches
Credit: TRU retail meat processing program

TREE HOOK OR CHUCK HOOK

Tree hooks are now mostly found to be in use in independent markets. They are of varying lengths, constructed from a 50 mm by 17 mm piece of mild steel, galvanized or tinned against corrosion. At intervals along the metal strip, a small but strong hook is attached. The whole unit is usually suspended from a small roller hook and used for hanging or transporting large amounts of primal or sub-primal cuts.

Chuck Hook Safety Checklist

✓ Care should be taken if these hooks are hanging around unloaded, as it is quite easy to become impaled on one of the many protruding spikes.

WIRE HOOKS OR "S" HOOKS

These are the most frequently used hooks in retail outlets. Today they are constructed mainly of stainless steel or mild steel, which is tinned or galvanized against corrosion. Constructed to hang relatively light pieces of meat, these hooks are capable of supporting only a limited load and when stressed beyond that, will open up to release the product being hung. This usually results in a product becoming contaminated from falling onto the work floor. Any meat cut, scratched or pierced by "S" hooks should receive particular attention owing to the lack of cleaning these hooks usually receive in most retail outlets.

Hooks should be cleaned after each use in hot water and detergent solution, rinsed in a hot water and sanitizer solution and left to air dry. Hooks should be stored in an appropriate container in the cooler or in a refrigerated working area.

Some operators when hanging more than one meat product on a hook will employ the use of needle and twine in making a loop of string through the product. In the trade this used to be termed a "gallus" - meaning suspender. Meat cutter's twine is usually strong enough for this purpose. A gallus will reduce the number of hooks needed.

Meat tree 8 hook
Credit: Bunzl Processor Division/Koch Supplies

Meat tree staggered/offset hook
Credit: Bunzl Processor Division/Koch Supplies

Meat S hooks
Credit: Friedr. Dick

Meat Hook Safety Checklist

✓ Do not overload the master hook.

FOOT HOOKS OR PACKER HOOKS

These are mild steel, heavily constructed hooks, usually about 0.6 and 0.3 meters in length. They have a hook on each end and can be used in conjunction with the roller assembly to hang larger amounts of small products on one roller hook or are sometimes still used to hang front quarters of beef onto short shank roller hooks.

Packer Hook Safety Checklist

✓ Never leave packer hooks on the meat rail or attached to a roller hook. This situation could be the cause of serious eye, head or throat injuries to other staff moving through the area.
✓ Store in a safe place immediately after use.

TWINE (STRING)

This material is specifically designed for use with food and in particular for tying and holding product into desirable shapes. Twine comes in both nylon and cotton form. It also comes in different colours. The cotton is easier to use and can be purchased in different thickness to suit delicate needs such as the tying of game birds or London Broils.

Particular attention should be paid to cleaning string holding boxes or cans, so they do not become a reservoir for scraps of meat, fat or other debris.

Butcher's twine & holder
Credit: Bunzl Processor Division/Koch Supplies

Twine Safety Checklist

✓ Don't leave loose end of string lying about and keep them off the floors.
✓ Roll up the ball of string after use to avoid someone's feet becoming tangled in it.

STUFFING HORNS

Stuffing horns come in different sizes. Smaller horns are made of plastic and larger horns are made of stainless steel. The purpose of these horns is to net products by covering the opening of the horn with a netting and then stuffing the product through the horn and out with the netting.

Plastic stuffing horn.
Credit: Canada Beef

Horn Safety Checklist

   ✓ On plastic horns check for cracks as they may interfere with the netting.
   ✓ On stainless horns check for bent edges that may cause net tearing.

Power Tools

The safe operation of power tools, particularly power saws and grinding machines, cannot be adequately covered on paper. Therefore individual practical lessons must be provided on these machines during orientation and training.

In this section, we will briefly discuss the safety related practices for the most common pieces of power equipment used in meat and sausage manufacturing departments:

- Bowl Cutters
- Brine Injectors (manual/automatic)
- Meat Grinders and Mixer Grinders
- Meat Slicers (both automatic and manual)
- Power Saws
- Sausage Clipper
- Sausage Mixer
- Sausage Stuffer
- Smokehouses
- Tenderizing Machines
- Vacuum Packing Machines
- Vacuum Tumbler

✓ Make sure that plugs and leads are in tip-top condition.

✓ Make sure that the lead and plug are suitable for grounding the appliance.

✓ Always pull out the plug before cleaning the equipment and lock out power control panel.

✓ If no individual plug is available, make sure all operators know where the main switch is located.

✓ Keep areas around electrical equipment free from water.

✓ After each business day, remove plugs or switch off all unnecessary equipment.

✓ Make sure that adequate lighting prevails in work areas.

✓ Make sure that light globe protectors are present on lights in coolers.

✓ Make sure that lighting switches are in good condition.

✓ Make sure all electrical outlets have waterproof covers.

THE POWER SAW

If industry trends continue to focus on knife and counter ready meats, the use of the power saw or bandsaw may become obsolete in some major chain store operations. For most, the importance of this machine is really not appreciated until it is out of operation. Poor maintenance, misuse and power failures are factors contributing to its immobilization. It is imperative therefore that this piece of equipment be given the best possible attention, owing to its enormous contribution to the production workload.

Although power meat saws in most retail outlets are serviced by contracting companies, the following information will acquaint the power meat saw user with the common sense care the machine requires to get the best results.

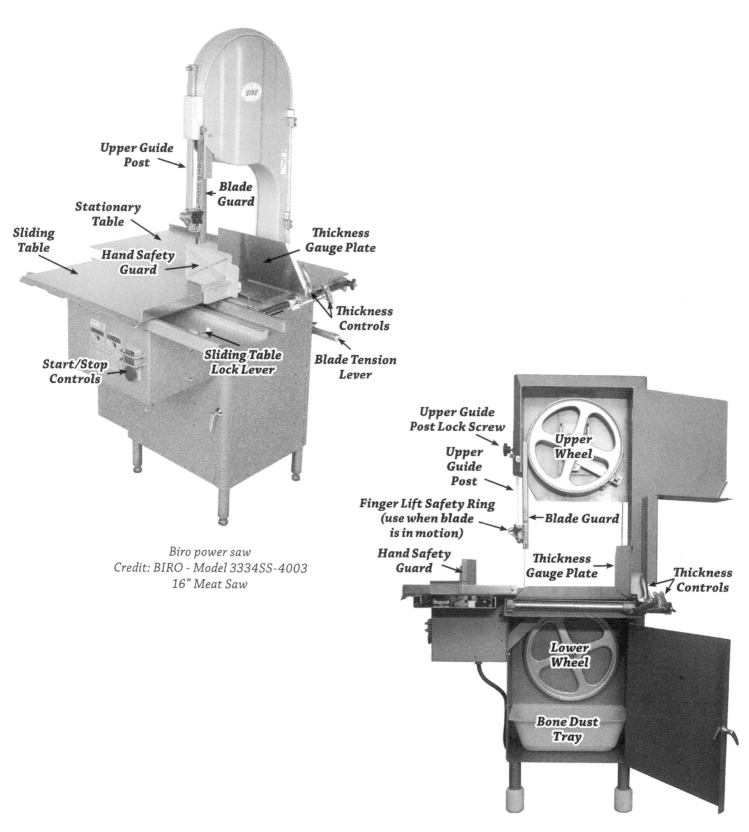

Upper Guide
Post

Blade
Guard

Stationary
Table

Sliding
Table

Hand Safety
Guard

Thickness
Gauge Plate

Thickness
Controls

Start/Stop
Controls

Sliding Table
Lock Lever

Blade Tension
Lever

Biro power saw
Credit: BIRO - Model 3334SS-4003
16" Meat Saw

Upper Guide
Post Lock Screw

Upper Wheel

Upper
Guide
Post

Finger Lift Safety Ring
(use when blade
is in motion)

Blade Guard

Hand Safety
Guard

Thickness
Gauge Plate

Thickness
Controls

Lower
Wheel

Bone Dust
Tray

Biro power saw
Credit: TRU Retail Meat
processing program

Troubleshooting Band Saw Cutting Problems

When a band saw blade cuts crookedly, too frequently the blade is blamed. Most likely it is the result of damage to the delicate, sharp teeth of the saw caused by poor adjustment of the guides, lack of blade tension or other careless operation of the machine. Observing the following simple precautions can prevent crooked cutting and other cutting problems.

Adjust the Blade to the Correct Tension

If a band saw blade is to run true, it must be adjusted to the correct tension - not too much or it will be apt to snap under strain, not too little or it will probably run crooked in the cut. For this very important reason, most power saws have a tension indicator while others have tension limits. Consult the instruction book supplied by the manufacturer. Blade tension requires a check-up every time a blade is replaced.

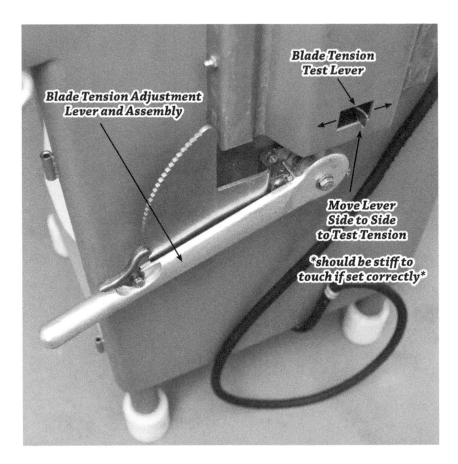

Biro power saw blade tension lever assembly
Credit: TRU-Retail Meat Processing Program

Maintain the Tension Devices Regularly

Tension adjustment differs somewhat on each power saw, but all are based on the principle of moving the blade pulleys (upper and lower wheels) further apart to tighten the blade. These moving parts must be kept clean and well lubricated. This is especially true of machines where the whole upper wheel-housing portion lifts up and down on channels, or where upper pulley support slides are employed. Such channels or slides are apt to gum up unless frequently cleaned and oiled.

An important part of tension devices is the tension spring. This tension spring acts as a sort of shock absorber and has a vital role in straight cutting. If it becomes weakened, is pressed down too flat or is not kept clean, it will not give properly under the pressure added by actual cutting. The following are blade checkpoints:

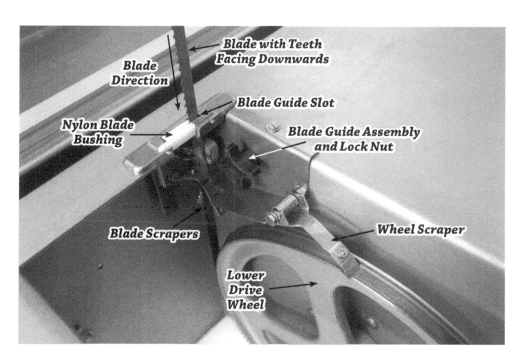

Biro power saw Left blade guide & wheel scraper assembly
Credit: TRU-Retail Meat Processing Program

1. Check the Blade Guides for wear. A good blade may be ruined in the first few turns of the pulleys wheels.
2. Keep the product table in good working shape to avoid wear on bearings.
3. Check the product for metal tag staples prior to cutting to avoid blade damage.
4. Run the meat through carefully to avoid hitting the back of the running blade.
5. Keep Pulleys (upper and lower wheels) clean and aligned to help prevent the blade jumping off.

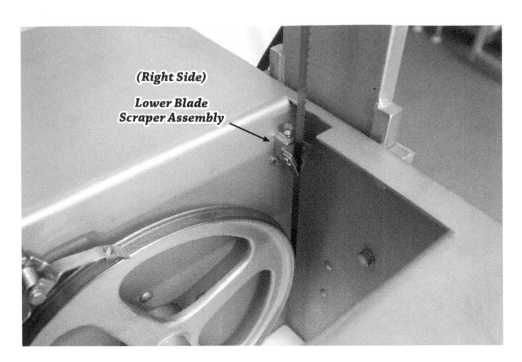

Biro power saw right blade guide assembly
Credit: TRU-Retail Meat Processing Program

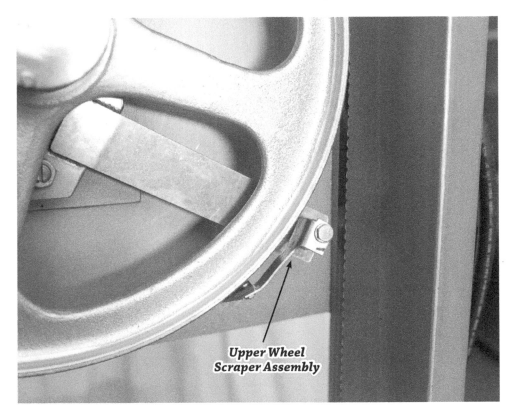

Biro power saw upper wheel scraper assembly
Credit: TRU-Retail Meat Processing Program

6. Control speed when feeding meat to avoid overworking the blade and causing breakage.
7. Clean blade saw slots to avoid overheating the moving blade. To protect the bearings, never wash the upper pulley wheel by submerging it in water. If pulley wheel groves become smooth from wear, replace them.
8. Make sure pulleys (upper and lower wheels) are aligned.
9. Rough handling usually causes permanently twisted blades: by forcing product through the blade too quickly or machine misalignment or incorrect blade installation.

Power Saw Maintenance Checklist

✓ **Remember to Lock out the device before checking machine parts.**
✓ Saw teeth - Are they pointing down? If not, turn the blade inside out to reverse their direction.
✓ Head assembly - Is it clean? Has it been oiled?
✓ All other parts of tension mechanism, including tension spring - Are they clean and well lubricated?
✓ Blade guides - Are they worn, properly adjusted and are slots clean?
✓ Tracking of blade - Do teeth clear guides and scrapers? Turn upper and lower wheels (pulleys) by hand and check.
✓ Blade back-up - If roller type, does it turn freely? Is it adjusted to the proper distance from back of blade? For carbide bar type, replace if slotted.
✓ Upper guide post - Does it give proper support to blade, or is it worn?
✓ Moveable meat table - Are bearings worn enough to prevent straight cutting?
✓ Meat gauge plate - Does it give cut proper support?
✓ Metal tags/staples - Have they been removed from meat?
✓ Pulleys (upper and lower wheels) - Are they clean? Are they correctly lined up? Are bearings worn?
✓ Tension of blade - Check indicator.

The High Cost of Dull Blades

• The continued use of a blade that has become dulled is not only dangerous but heats up the product reducing the shelf life and causes excessive wear on guides.

Power Saw Safety Checklist

- ✓ Lockout power saw before checking, disassembling and/or cleaning.
- ✓ No talking by or to the power saw operator while it is in operation.
- ✓ No horseplay in the vicinity of the power saw.
- ✓ Always pull down the upper blade guard to expose minimum blade when operating.
- ✓ Make sure that a "fence guide" and "pusher plate" (safety guards) is available and is used for those jobs where the fingers could come too close to the blade.
- ✓ Whenever possible, locate saw out of traffic and away from swinging doors.
- ✓ Keep floor areas clear of slip or trip hazards.
- ✓ Learn the correct method of coiling a band saw blade.

Lock out sign
Credit: Master Lock Canada

Lock out hasp

Lock out hasp in action
Credit: Master Lock Canada

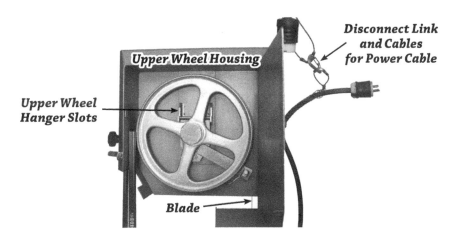

Power cable disconnect
Credit: CPMCA image collection

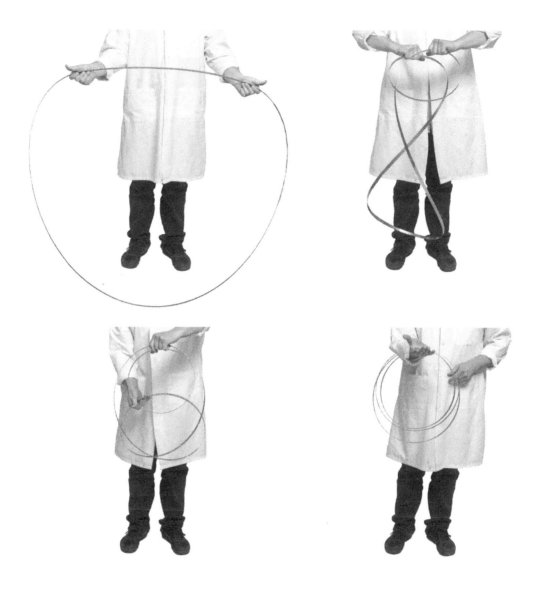

Folding a saw blade

✓ When operating the saw with the thickness gauge in a fixed position, always face the gauge plate!

✓ Feed the meat through with the right hand and take the slice away with the left hand.

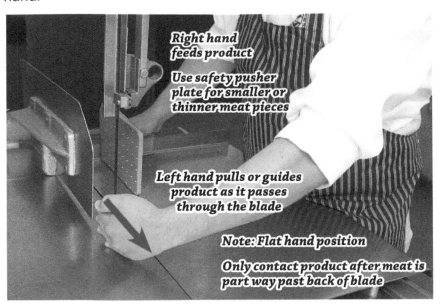

Saw operator in proper work position
Credit: TRU retail meat processing program

Saw operator using correct hand & body position
Credit: TRU Retail Meat Processing Program

- ✓ Never twist the blade while operating the saw.
- ✓ Never leave the machine running when it is **not** in use.
- ✓ Do not become careless in operation. The machine has many guards but not one is accident-proof.
- ✓ Become familiar with the normal running sound of the machine - unusual noises may mean abnormal running.

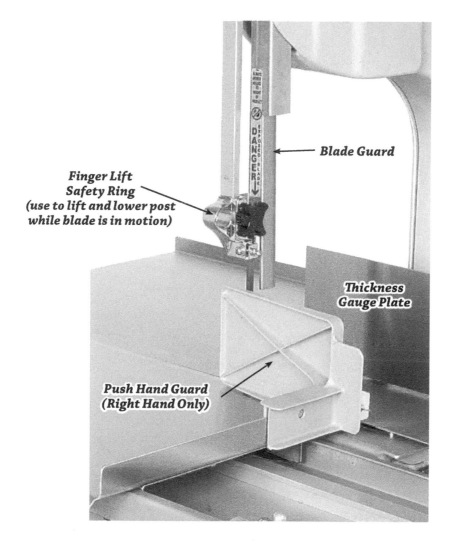

Upper guide safety post
Credit: TRU Retail Meat Processing Program

Bright, clean-cut, appetizing ground meat can come only from a machine operating in perfect condition. Any one of a number of small faults can cause the meat to lose its attractive appearance or spoil quickly. The maintenance described here requires little effort and will help in assuring a high-quality product.

The meat grinder is a very important piece of equipment in the retail operation. If the meat grinder turns well, clean trimmings of meat turn into an appetizing and appealing product with excellent profit returns. However, too many meat cutters do not appreciate the value of correct handling and operation of this piece of equipment and as a result are faced with many problems. Approximately 8% to 12% of the beef tonnage in an average meat market can be realized in some form of ground product. Therefore, the welfare and correct handling of any grinding equipment is of paramount importance.

Most meat grinders are designed for speedy dismantling and are made of materials, which are stain and corrosion proof. However, this does not mean that further cleaning is not needed or that sanitation can be relaxed. Replacement parts for the machine are expensive and may have to be ordered from outside the local area. Should a vital part become unusable, the machine could be out of use for a significant period of time until a replacement part has been acquired. Look after the machine and be aware of parts which are wearing so that they may be ordered well in advance of a breakdown.

Recommendations for Grinding Meat Products:

1. Take the meat directly from the cooler to the meat grinder.
2. If possible, operate the machine in the cooler.
3. Store moveable parts in the cooler when not in use.
4. Use the correct plate and knife for the job.
5. Make sure the knife is clean and sharp.
6. Never run the grinder dry (without product in the throat).
7. Lubricate the cutting knife & plate with a food grade mineral oil prior to use.
8. Do not over tighten the adjusting ring head with a lever.
9. Do not put any material other than meat into the throat.
10. Clean the knife and plate frequently (some companies advocate cleaning after each use).

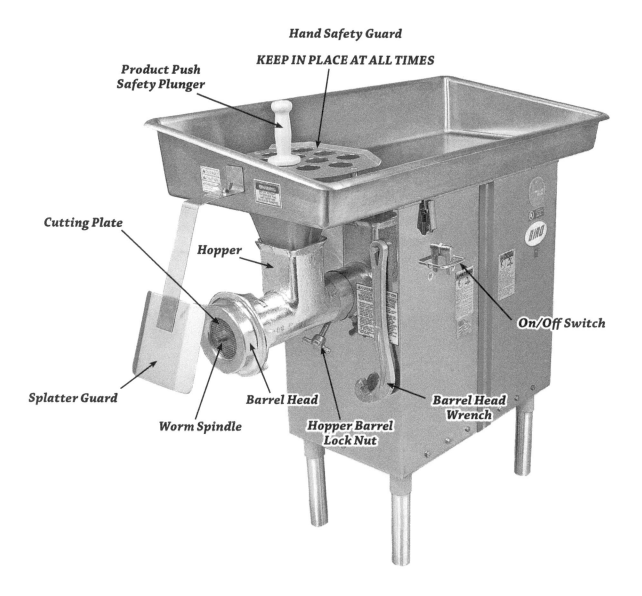

Hand Safety Guard

KEEP IN PLACE AT ALL TIMES

Product Push Safety Plunger

Cutting Plate

Hopper

On/Off Switch

Splatter Guard

Barrel Head

Worm Spindle

Hopper Barrel Lock Nut

Barrel Head Wrench

Biro standard manual meat grinder
Credit: BIRO - Model # 346-SS Meat Grinder

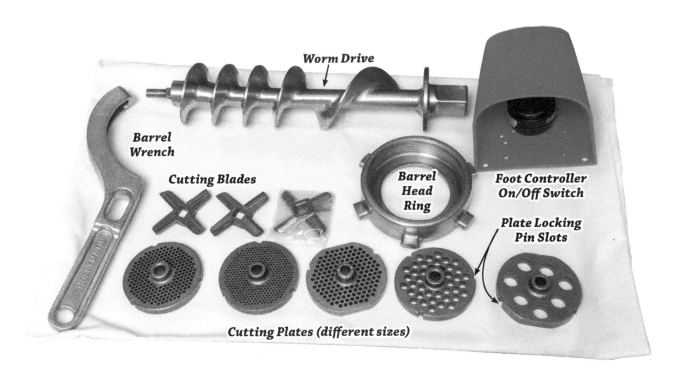

Worm Drive

Barrel
Wrench

Cutting Blades

Barrel
Head
Ring

Foot Controller
On/Off Switch

Plate Locking
Pin Slots

Cutting Plates (different sizes)

Credit: NAIT Professional Meat Cutting & Merchandising Program

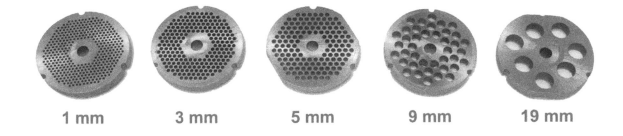

1 mm   3 mm   5 mm   9 mm   19 mm

Clean Threads

Clean the threads on both the cylinder and adjusting ring. To ensure the plate and knife will bear properly; keep these threads free of meat accumulation or rust. Worn threads will allow the adjusting ring to work loose and the plate to lose contact with the knife.

Clean Cutting Plates

There are different sized cutting plates. The diameter of the holes allows different types of grind. In retail outlets, usually only two are used: fine and coarse.

If the grinder knife fails to make complete contact with the plate even for an instant, a glaze of sinew or collagen may spread over the surface of the cutting plate, covering the holes so that further satisfactory cutting cannot be accomplished until the cutting plate is scraped clean. Sinews wound around the hub of the knife also will interfere with its action.

Lubricate Parts

Lubricate the plate and knife with a food safe mineral oil after each cleaning to avoid rusting.

Correct Cutting Plate Position

Most machines have two flat sides on the cutting plate to hold it in position. The cutting plate must extend slightly beyond the cylinder to come in contact with the knife but not so far that the flat sides become ineffective in holding the cutting plate in place.

Other grinders may have holding pins just inside the cylinder's barrel shaped head that line up with the grooves on the plate. The cutting plate won't go into position unless the grooves and pins are lined up accurately.

Keep the Drive Shaft Stud in Good Condition

The square stud on the end of the worm drives the knife and also acts as a front bearing for the worm. When the driving square is excessively worn, it can cause knife breakage. A worn stud may permit sinews to work through the cutting plate hub and get into the ground meat.

Biro standard manual meat grinder
Credit: BIRO - Model # 346-SS Meat Grinder

The safety plate on the hopper of the grinder has holes made to prohibit the entry of the hands. On these machines a plastic or wooden plunger or feed stomper is used to clear any blockages that may occur in the throat of the machine.

Handle the worm, cylinder and throat and other parts with care as most are made of heavy cast and break easily. The thick end of the worm fits into a receiver on the electric motor at the rear of the machine's throat that feeds the worm (auger). The thin spindle on the opposite end is what the knife and cutting plate fit onto.

The Hopper

Both older and newer machines have hoppers. The older machines have open hoppers with a slotted safety plate covering the throat while the newer machines (called mixer grinders) have closed covers.

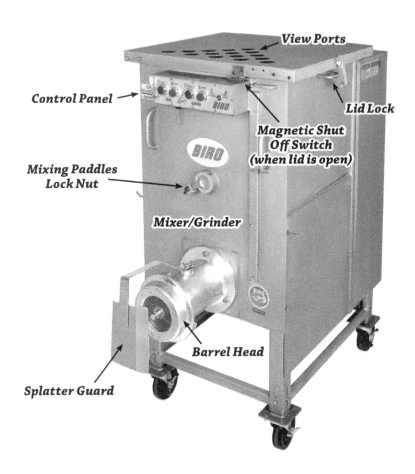

View Ports

Control Panel

Lid Lock

Magnetic Shut
Off Switch
(when lid is open)

Mixing Paddles
Lock Nut

Mixer/Grinder

Barrel Head

Splatter Guard

Biro mixer/grinder –
Credit: Biro model AFMG-52 Mixer gGrinder

Biro mini mixer/ grinder
Credit: BIRO - Mini 22 - Mixer Grinder

The closed style hoppers are self-feeding. The mixing arm turns the meat toward the worm, where it is trapped and fed through the cutting plate. Most closed hoppers are top feed, meaning they have a lid that closes over top of them and indirectly controls the amount you can put into them. These lids are usually tied into a magnetic safety switch that turns the grinder off when opened or forced open in the case of overloading.

Grinding Machine Safety Checklist

- ✓ **Lock out** grinder before checking, disassembling or cleaning.
- ✓ Keep the feed-opening guards in place at all times.
- ✓ Only use a proper plastic feed plunger to maneuver product through the throat of the machine.
- ✓ Keep a suitable stand or tub trolley nearby for resting trim bowls on during grinding.
- ✓ Only one person need operate the grinder at one time.

THE TENDERIZING MACHINE

What do smart operators and merchandisers do with lean trimmings and hindquarter hip cuts? They drop them through a tenderizer. The disc-type knives, which make up the roller blade, cut the tendons and other tough fibres, producing tender, juicy steaks.

Most tenderizing machines have a see-through plastic cover, which also acts as a safety device. It must be kept in place during operation and will automatically switch off the machine if raised. A safety chute beneath the guard keeps hands a safe distance from the tenderizing knives.

As with most food processing equipment, the meat-tenderizing machine is made of easy cleaning stainless steel. The combs, which guide the meat between the rollers, prevent any significant accumulation of meat between the knives; however, the entire roller blade assembly should be lifted out for cleaning after use.

Lock out sign
Credit: Master Lock Canada

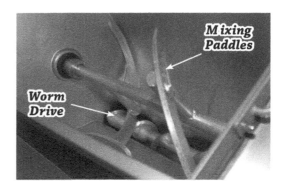

Mixer Grinder worm and mixing paddles
Credit: Jakes & Associates

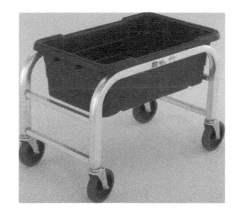

Meat grinder trolley & tub
Credit: Bunzl Processor Division/Koch Supplies

Tenderizing Machine Safety Checklist

✓ **Lock out** before checking, disassembling and/or cleaning.

✓ Do not operate a machine which has no safety cover.

✓ Do not put fingers near the cutters underneath the machine while in operation.

✓ Do not attempt to remove meat blocking the cutters while power is on.

Lock out sign
Credit: Master Lock Canada

✓ Handle the roller cutters carefully during cleaning. If dropped, the roller knives will bend or break easily.

Meat tenderizer
Credit: BIRO - Model Pro -9 Tenderizer

Tenderizer cradle with product
Credit: BIRO - Model Pro-9 Series-Standard
Knitting / Tenderizer Cradle Assembly

Biro strip cutter
Credit: BIRO - Model Pro-9 Series Optional Strip
Cutting Assembly

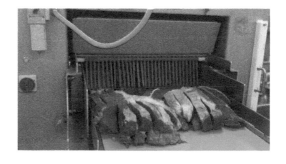

Whole muscle Needle tenderizer
Credit: Costco

Whole muscle Steak cutting machine
Credit: Costco

AUTOMATIC MEAT CHOPPERS/CUTTERS/SLICERS/ NEEDLERS/CUBING EQUIPMENT:

There is meat equipment designed for an explicit function such as the cutting of stir-fry meats, the cubing of steak, the chopping of pork chops, the slicing of strip-loins or the tenderizing by needling etc. This equipment comes in various sizes and their function is volume specific. This type of equipment is found mostly in larger meat processing or retail establishments that produce counter ready meats in sizable proportions.

An example would be a scanner/slicer of boneless products such as boneless pork loins, strip-loins etc., used by high volume establishments that wholesale products to retail outlets that sell counter ready meats. The product is placed on a conveyer belt and run through a scanner that predetermines its cross section in advance, moving the product along to the mechanical slicer producing slices of the same weight, by varying the thickness.

Lock out before disassembly and or cleaning.

THE MEAT SLICER

While the construction of meat slicers may differ, they are basically identical in function. Some models are fully automatic for volume cutting and can be easily converted to manual operation. They can be adjusted to regulate the thickness of the slice and the length of the stroke.

Most models can be broken down to four main parts for easy cleaning: a meat table, a slice deflector guard, a knife guard and a built-in sharpener. All parts in contact with food are usually stainless steel.

A spiked plate holds the product firmly and protects the fingers when cutting and slicing small pieces.

The sharpener is fitted with two stones for double action. When out of use, the sharpener disappears from sight, and its cover becomes an integral part of the knife housing. At the same time, the complete unit can be removed for cleaning purposes.

The sharpener, an integral part of the slicer, should be carefully handled. The angle of the two grinding wheels is pre-set to give the precise grinding bevel to the knife.

Simply lift, turn and lower over the edge of the knife. One finger controls the pressure of the stones against the knife. The machine is then run. After use blade should be cleaned of any grinding dust to prevent contamination of the food.

Meat Slicers Safety Checklist

- ✓ **Lock out** before checking, disassembling and/or cleaning.
- ✓ Keep all guards in place when in use.
- ✓ **Adjust blade thickness setting to zero after use.**
- ✓ Keep the sharpening stones in good condition and functioning properly.

Lock out sign
Credit: Master Lock Canada

✓ Only one person operating the machine at one time.
✓ When using fully automatic slicing machines, keep hands well clear during cutting at all times. To clear meat blockages or inaccurate cuts **push** the **cancel** button on the computer console. Then **lock out** machine before rectifying the problem.

BIRO Slicer
Credit: Biro Model B300M
Gravity Feed Manual Slicer

Hobart manual & automatic slicer
Credit: TRU Retail Meat Processing Program

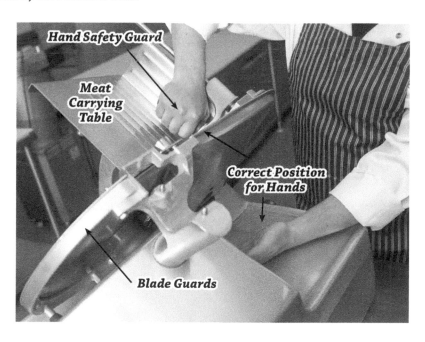

Correct hand position for use of a manual operated slicer
Credit: TRU Retail Meat Processing Program

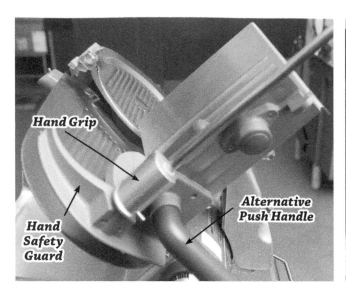

Hand Grip

Hand
Safety
Guard

Alternative
Push Handle

Slicer with blade wide open – Use all safety guards with blade open.
Do not leave machine running and un-attended.
Credit: TRU Retail Meat Processing Program

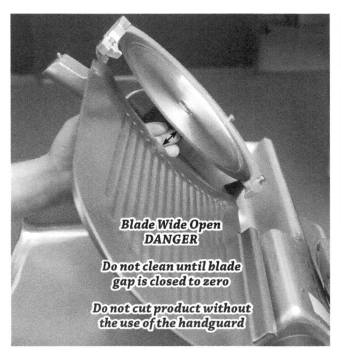

Blade Wide Open
DANGER

Do not clean until blade
gap is closed to zero

Do not cut product without
the use of the handguard

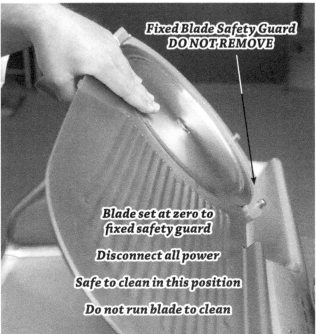

Fixed Blade Safety Guard
DO NOT REMOVE

Blade set at zero to
fixed safety guard

Disconnect all power

Safe to clean in this position

Do not run blade to clean

Slicer blade open to maximum, fully closed to 'ZERO' depth
Credit: TRU Retail Meat Processing Program

SAUSAGE MIXERS

The mixer mixes the many ingredients of which a batch of sausage is composed of into one homogenous mass (batch) so that the product can be filled by means of the stuffer into casings.

It consists of a trough-like shaped stainless steel container, which can be tilted for speedy discharging. Through its centerline, parallel to the angle of tilt, runs a shaft onto which several oval paddles are attached. The turning shaft moves the paddles, which then mix the contents of the container. Some types work on the principle of two sets of paddles, which shortens the mixing time, which means less chance of warming and smearing the product.

The machine is used for the following:

1. To combine fine dough prepared in the cutter and coarse material which has gone through grinder to the finished stage.
2. To blend material that has been ground to different coarseness and finish processing in mixer or transfer for further cutting and blending to cutter.
3. To pre-salt material for storage or blending of seasoning into mix, etc. Stress importance of timing in order to avoid warming up and smearing.
4. It is important to mix batches of formula within specific time limits, avoiding overhead, smearing or improper and insufficient blending.

Lock out sign
Credit: Master Lock Canada

Sausage Mixer - Lock Out & Safety Procedure

1. **Lock out** machine before checking, disassembling or cleaning.
2. Turn the control dial or switch on the sausage mixer to the "O" (off) position.
3. Unplug machine.
4. Have the plug in in front of your body to ensure that no one else plugs the machine in.
5. When work on the sausage mixer is complete, the machine can be plugged back in. Ensure that no hands or other body parts are near the operating unit.
6. Only one person at a time should operate the machine to avoid distractions.

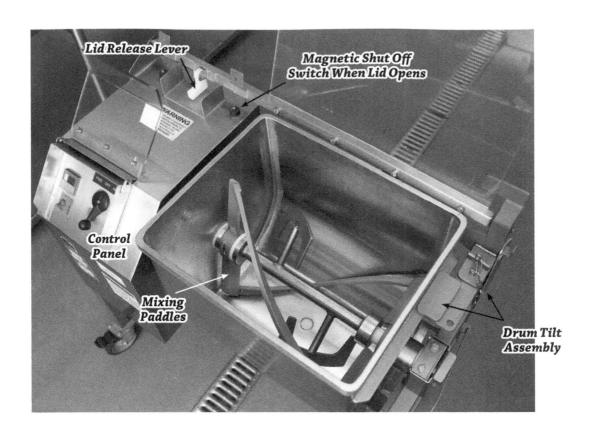

Meat mixer
Credit: TRU Retail Meat Processing Program

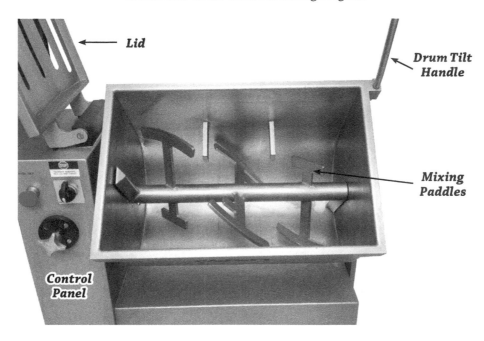

Koch Meat mixer
Credit: NAIT Professional Meat Cutting & Merchandising Program

SILENT CUTTER

The name of this piece of equipment is somewhat ironic as it is one of the noisiest machines used in processing. This machine speeds up the chopping process and compared to the grinder gives a more evenly pictured meat that doesn't smear.

The operation consists of sharp knives rotating vertically and rapidly above a turning bowl. The number of knives can vary depending upon the type of machine and the operator's preference. Temperature control is a major concern because the fast-turning knives create friction and therefore warmth.

The silent cutter can do the work of a meat grinder, mincer and mixer. Since the cutter is a machine capable of working at extremely high speeds, its multi-knife head can rotate up to 3,000 – 4,000 revolutions and more per minute. All safety factors involved are of paramount importance. Cutter knives should always be very sharp and steeled after every use to assure a consistent product stability and quality. The transmission and drive train of the silent cutter is running in an oil bath with a filter, which should be changed after every two hundred hours of operation. Cleaning procedures should start with a rinse of cold water then soap, brushing, rinsing and sanitizing. The last item can be eliminated if the machine is made of stainless steel only (bacteria doesn't grow on stainless steel). Operating the silent cutter is one of the most responsible jobs in the meat sausage industry.

Silent Cutter Safety Checklist

Lock out sign
Credit: Master Lock Canada

✓ **Lock out** before disassembling or cleaning.

✓ Do not attempt to talk to anyone else while operating this machine.

✓ Only one operator at a time using the machine.

✓ Observe the temperature of product carefully while machine is operational.

✓ While machine bowl is rotating and the operator must manipulate emulsion from the edge of the bowl to the centre, keep hands only near the centre of the open portion of the bowl.

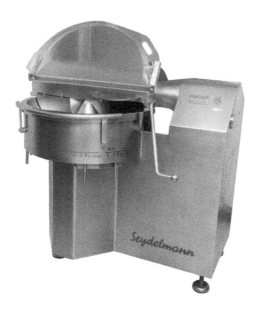

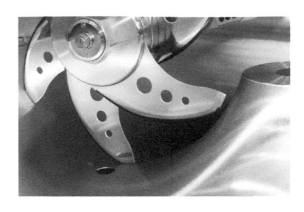

Silent or Bowl Cutter
Credit: NAIT Professional Meat Cutting &
Merchandising Program

Silent cutter blades
©istock.com / credit to rqsinboxru

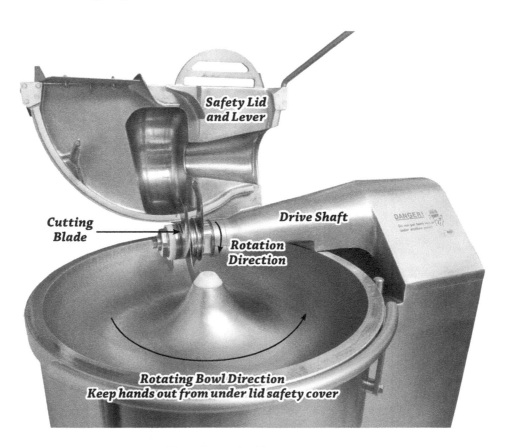

Safety Lid and Lever

Cutting Blade

Drive Shaft

Rotation Direction

Rotating Bowl Direction
Keep hands out from under lid safety cover

Silent Cutter inside view
Credit: NAIT Professional Meat Cutting & Merchandising Program

VACUUM PACKAGING MACHINE

Today's modern meat-processing plant and retail outlet cannot be without the application of vacuum packaging techniques. The advantages are obvious. Fresh meat (for aging, maturing) or processed meat products of any kind (sausage, bacon, ham, etc.) can easily be packaged and will retain freshness, colour, flavour resulting in an improved appearance, longer shelf life and less weight loss.

The basic vacuum machine consists of a vacuum chamber into which the vacuum bag with product is placed with the open end of the bag laid over the heat seal bars. After the lid has been closed, a vacuum pump located in a closed housing underneath the chamber extracts the air contained in the pouches or bags and the chamber. After the air is extracted, the sealing bars heat and seal along the open edge of the pouch containing the product. The lid then opens automatically.

Vacuum packaging machines allow for decorative coloured packages as well as shrink packaging in which the packaged contents being vacuum sealed are either run through a steam tunnel or dipped into a boiling water bath thus shrinking the package down to the size of the product and creating a tight outer skin. These machines also have the capacity to package meats in cooking pouches of plastic or metal foil after which the product can be cooked and kept refrigerated, increasing the products shelf life. Vacuum packaging reduces the chances of freezer burn in frozen products (dependent upon handling procedures).

There are of course some disadvantages. Packaging of fresh pork for prolonged storage is not recommended because the vacuum speeds up the process by which pork fat becomes rancid. Although slowed down, discolouration still occurs, especially when exposed to intensive light sources. Even vacuum packaged products need to be refrigerated at low temperatures. Some bacteria do not need air to multiply and under certain conditions will start multiplying again. Therefore if product is to be stored for a longer period, it should be frozen before bacteria develop.

Leakers (bags with either a hole or an improper seal) should either be used immediately or repackaged. The reason for leakers could be:

- Wrinkles in the seal
- Meat particles and/or fluid in the seal area
- A hole due to either a sharp object on the product inside the package
- Inappropriate handling

Some Technical Data

The Vacuum packaging machine has a vacuum chamber with an airtight lid. When product is laid in properly, (open end of the package over the vacuum bar, straight with no wrinkles and not sticking over vacuum bar more than 3 cm) the lid will be closed, and the pump will begin to evacuate the chamber.

After all the air is evacuated, the heat seal bar comes down and welds the open end together. The desired amount of vacuum is controlled by the operator as well as the welding time, which will vary depending on the thickness of the bag.

Cleaning and Maintenance

The chamber and seal bar(s) should always be kept free of meat particles or fluid of any sort since such items could easy end up in the compressor creating a damaging effect or hamper the operation of the seal bar thus creating leakers.

Special attention should be given to the seal in the lid and the Teflon band covering the seal bar. Both should always be intact to avoid insufficient evacuation of the chamber and burning seals. The compressor has an oil bath and oil filter that should be changed after every 2000 hours of operation. The oil level must always be kept up to the full mark. Vacuum hoses and joints must be checked regularly for leakage. All maintenance of this machine is to be done by trained personnel only.

Following all the above mentioned points will make the vacuum packaging machine one of the most profitable equipment items.

Vacuum Packing Machine Safety Checklist

✓ **Lock out** before disassembling, cleaning or general maintenance.
✓ Do not overload or force product that is too large into the machine.
✓ On all vacuum machines and especially dual chambered units, make sure the hands of co-workers are clear of the machine before depressing the chamber lid down.

Lock out sign
Credit: Master Lock Canada

Dual chamber vacuum machine
Credit: NAIT Professional Meat Cutting & Merchandising Program

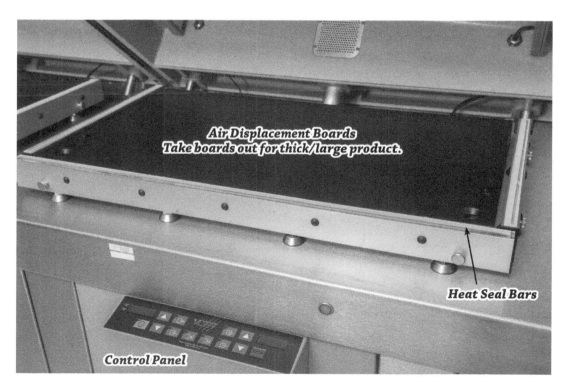

Vacuum machine heat seal bars & air displacement boards
Credit: NAIT Professional Meat Cutting & Merchandising Program

Vacuum machine in action
Credit: Two Rivers Specialty meats

Steak & Sausage vacuumed
Credit: Bunzl Processor Division/
Koch Supplies

Sandwich meats & cheese vacuumed
Credit: Bunzl Processor Division/
Koch Supplies

Salmon fillet in Gold foil vacuum pouch
Credit: Bunzl Processor Division/
Koch Supplies

THE TUMBLER

The tumbler was invented to maximize protein extraction and cooking yields without the addition of phosphates and non-meat proteins to the cure. It looks like a commercial dryer with a rotating drum. Inside the drum are two rods which transport the piece of meat almost up to the top of the drum, and due to gravity it falls back down to the bottom of the drum, from where it starts going up to fall down again. The impact of the fall has a massaging effect and will therefore help to solubilize the water and salt soluble proteins. The newer tumbler systems have air pressure control, which regulate the atmosphere pressure up to 95% vacuum.

Tumbler Safety Checklist

- ✓ **Lock out** before checking, disassembling, cleaning or general maintenance.
- ✓ Operate to manufacturer's specifications. Do not overload machine.
- ✓ Keep hands away from all moving parts.

Lock out sign
Credit: Master Lock Canada

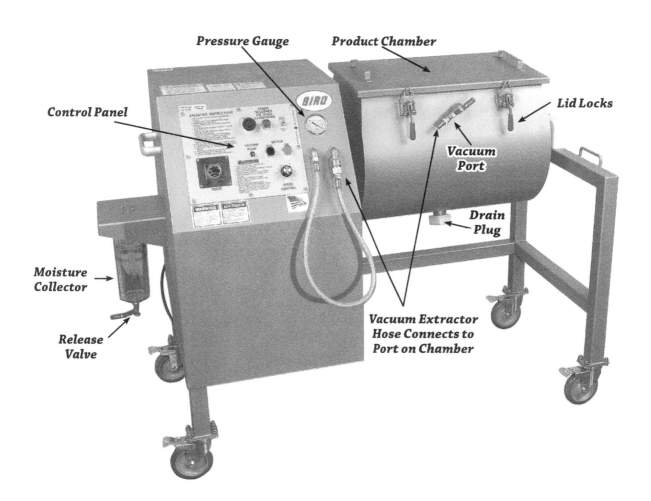

Free-standing vacuum tumbler
Credit: BIRO - Model VTS-100 Vacuum Tumbler

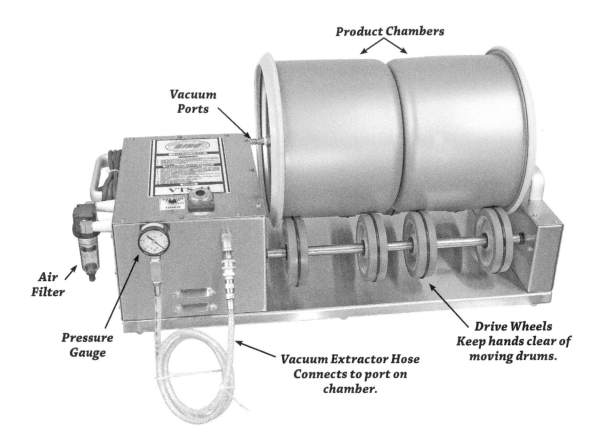

Product Chambers

Vacuum Ports

Air Filter

Pressure Gauge

Vacuum Extractor Hose Connects to port on chamber.

Drive Wheels Keep hands clear of moving drums.

Tabletop dual chambered vacuum tumbler
Credit: BIRO - Model VTS-44 Vacuum Marinating Tumbler

THE SAUSAGE STUFFER

To stuff sausage meat into its designated casing requires some sort of a stuffing machine. Many years ago, sausage makers would slide a casing onto the narrow tube of a horn attached to a cylinder. The cylinder was then filled with sausage meat and a plunger pushed the meat down the cylinder through the horn and out into the casing. As times changed hand-driven machines were better developed. These consisted of a cylinder with a piston (plunger) inside, which could with the aid of a transmission be driven up or down. On the bottom end

of the cylinder was a spout (horn) that the sausage meat was pressed through and into a casing. Further development changed the hand drive into an electric floor model that moved the cylinder up and down with water pressure. Further development of the hand style crank model saw the transmission with its gears replaced with hydraulics. That was the stuffing machine for decades. In the mid-nineteen seventies, a German engineer developed a revolutionary new system, where the stuffer has a hopper located above a system of small rotating augers in the neck chamber of the machine. The spout was attached at the exit point of the augers. The meat was sucked into these rotating augers with the help of a vacuum pump, removing all the air contained in chamber and the sausage meat, and then pushed the meat into the spout, and from there into the casing. This process sounds complex, but it really is not.

Lock out sign
Credit: Master Lock Canada

Sausage Stuffer Safety Checklist

- ✓ **Lock out** before checking, disassembling, cleaning or general maintenance.
- ✓ When closing the pressure lid, keep fingers clear of opening.
- ✓ Handle heavy parts such as removable lids with care so as not to drop them on your or anyone else's feet.
- ✓ Do not over pressurize the stuffer when evacuating air from the cylinder prior to beginning stuffing.

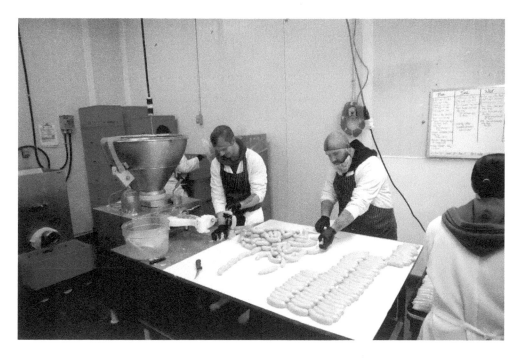

Sausage stuffer in action
Credit: Two Rivers Specialty Meats

*Manual operated tabletop
sausage stuffer
Credit: Friedr. Dick*

*Small hydraulic sausage stuffer
Credit: TRU Retail Meat
Processing Program*

*Hydraulic vacuum sausage stuffer
with hopper & auto linker
Credit: NAIT Professional Meat
Cutting & Merchandising Program*

SMOKEHOUSE

Technical advances made during the last decade in the development of machinery and equipment for the food processing industry have certainly made their impact on the modern smokehouse. The smokehouse is one of the oldest inventions in use to preserve meat and meat products from being spoiled by exposing them to smoke created by slowly smouldering, tar-free wood chips or shavings.

The modern smoker is a totally sealed and enclosed unit, independent of the climate outside. The whole ductwork inside, including ventilation, rotating, recycling, intake and release, humidification and de-humidification systems and heating and cooling units, has been created to ensure a totally equal climate and humidity level in every area inside the smoker. The system allows the operator to be in full control of the environment inside. That means that temperature, humidity, air circulation, airflow, smoke and air intake and release can be fully adjusted to any desired level for any particular product. These features enable the production of a consistent product all year independent of the outside environment.

Contrary to the above described automated smoker, older models and small fashioned home smokers depend on the outside environment or weather (humidity, etc.), and therefore products produced using them will always vary in quality and finish.

A smokehouse today, however, has become a very complicated apparatus, though still working by the same principle. Its many functions can be programmed according to the requirements of the material to be processed and will then automatically proceed through the different modes.

The basic working cycles of the smokehouse are as follows:

1. Reddening
2. Drying
3. Hot & Cold Smoking
4. Baking
5. Cooking
6. Evacuation
7. Shower

Optional additional features may include but are not limited to the following:

1. Multiple smoke applications (smouldering, friction or liquid)
2. Cooling and holding
3. Internal cleaning

Evacuating is a very important cycle because smoke after being kept in a sealed unit for more than half an hour starts to develop an explosive gas, which if not released could blow up the smokehouse. Therefore the maximum smoke time without evacuation

is 30 minutes. Modern smokehouses can be preprogrammed to cycle the evacuation of smoke. If properly programmed automatic evacuation will be activated at the end of each smoking cycle. If the smokehouse is semi-programmable, meaning it has a timer and is operated manually, then after every half an hour of smoking an alarm will sound reminding the operator to evacuate manually; but remember, the timer is set manually, and if not attended to, the smoke generator will continue to push smoke into the chamber. Don't forget because neglect could be disastrous.

The smoker should be cleaned of tar and purge build-up once a day when heavily used, and once a week when lightly used. Thorough cleaning should be done weekly and is accomplished with the use of a non-toxic chemical designed for this purpose. The use of toxic or homemade cleaning cocktails (the mixing of chemicals such as ammonia and bleach, etc.), will be hazardous to you and your health. Cleaning agents must be used carefully, paying strict attention to the manufacturer's directions on the label.

There are many types of smokehouses available today, from the homemade brick or block smokehouse with a fire pit in the corner to the fully programmed computer operated systems that can cost well over $100,000. The average smokehouse with the normal working cycles as listed above would require the following safety checklist.

Note: Smokehouses vary in size, model and capacity. Each, however, has similar features, and below we try to capture most.

✓ **Lockout** and keep the smokehouse door open before checking, disassembling, cleaning or general maintenance.

✓ Sawdust **Water tray,** Extinguisher
Check water level in the sawdust hopper and if a manual function, top-up daily (fill 2/3 capacity).

✓ **Smoke pipes**
Clean or change out removable pipes daily to avoid tar build-up and fire.

✓ **Sawdust Feeder or Hopper**
Depending on type of smokehouse some have augers that look like a wood auger bit that dispense the sawdust from the hopper to the hot plate. This auger requires cleaning or brushing off daily to avoid fine particle and tar build-up, which could start a fire. Other more modern units have the smoke generator built into the door. The heat element, ash dispenser and smoke distribution pipe must be cleaned daily prior to use.

✓ Use **insulated gloves** when removing hot meat racks or product from the smokehouse.

✓ Make sure that all products hanging in the smokehouse are hung carefully to avoid dropping to the floor of the smokehouse.

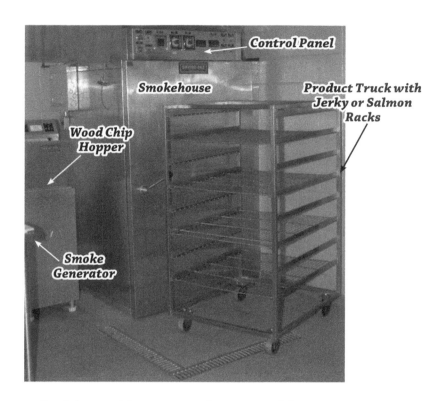

Smokehouse with separate smoke generator & hopper
Credit: Jakes & Associates

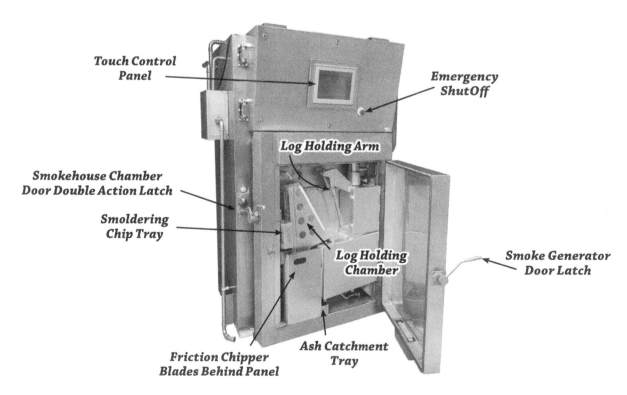

Automatic Smokehouse showing built-in wood chipper & smoke generator
Credit: NAIT Professional Meat Cutting & Merchandising Program

There are different types of brine injectors available, all doing basically the same job. The difference is that some are slower and less accurate, like hand-driven injectors, which of course represent the smallest investment. The next step is a motorized pump-driven manual injector, which is somewhat faster and a little more accurate, but is much more expensive. These machines will do the job for a small to medium meat processor.

The automatic brine pump has a system of ten or more vertically arranged needles, with small openings on the lower end of the needle toward the tip, which move up and down. At the lower part of its down-stroke into the product, the brine, which is taken up by means of a pump from a tank below the unit, travels through a filter via the intake hose into the needles and is discharged (injected) into the product to be cured.

The amount of brine injected into the product is regulated by means of a pressure-control valve with indicator and varies for different products. At the same time while the needles are in the up position, a conveyor belt carries the product moving it a certain distance ahead (variable) and thereby transports the material through the process of injection. The correct pressure combined with the selected forward movement and the formula of the brine guarantee a consistent product. The needles are spring-mounted, and the mechanical down movement will not force them beyond a certain point of penetration and cause them to break if the needle hits a solid object such as a bone in a

Automatic brine injector
Credit: ©istock.com-credit to IP Galanternik D.U.

ham, thereby making it possible to process material that contains bones, for example: bone-in hams, pork loins, pork-hocks, etc.

Although all metal parts of the injector that have contact with the brine are made of stainless steel, due to the high corrosion factor of the brine, great care must be taken that the machine is cleaned thoroughly after every use. The element in the intake filter must be taken out and cleaned after every use; after reassembly, lukewarm water should be run through the injector for 1 - 2 minutes in order to remove all brine residues. The perforation of the needles must be checked for blockage; all remaining meat particles must be removed. The conveyor can be taken off for easier cleaning and the removal of meat and fat particles.

The most common method of pickling meats today for smaller businesses is with the electric brine pump, which consists of a small electric motor, pump, pressure gauge and hoses and an assortment of pumping needles either single or triple headed that are interchangeable. Small hand operated pumps are also available.

The operator usually uses the multiple needle heads for boneless products and the single needle head for bone-in products. The operator then manually inserts the needles into the product in a prearranged pattern injecting the product by releasing the brine through a handheld pressure nozzle, which has the needles screwed into it.

Electric brine pump
Credit: Bunzl Processor Division/
Koch Supplies

Electric brine pump with table & brine barrel
Credit: Bunzl Processor Division/
Koch Supplies

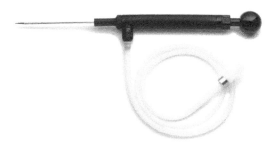

Manual hand pump
Credit: Friedr. Dick

✓ **Lockout** power before checking, disassembly, cleaning or maintenance.

✓ Flush out pump hoses and needles with 10 to 40 litres of lukewarm water after use. Amount of water used depends on the size and type of pump.

✓ Avoid random spray of brine. Keep hand over injection area or use a plastic spray guard, so spray does not get into eyes or on clothes or walls. Although salt is not dangerous in diluted form, if splashed in the eyes, it can be very painful (Flush eyes with cold water until irritation ceases).

✓ Insert pickle needles into flesh carefully. They are sharp. Keep opposite hand behind the needle until it is fully inserted to avoid stab wounds and possible injection of brine into your own body.

✓ Wear safety or splash goggles.

THE CLIPPING MACHINE

This machine fixes a clip on the end of the casing to prevent the sausage meat from squeezing out. It is available in three forms: manual, air pressure driven or electrical. A potential danger is that the metal clip used to hold the product together could easily rip a weaker casing. Sausage making students or apprentices should learn how to tie casing manually with string before using a clipper or automatic string tying machine.

Lock out sign
Credit: Master Lock Canada

Sausage clipper
Credit: NAIT Professional Meat Cutting &
Merchandising Program

Sausage hand clipper & off set clips
Credit: Stuffer's Supply

THE COOKING KETTLE

Cooking Kettles haven't been totally replaced as many sausage makers still use them in the production of liver sausage, head cheese and other cooked sausages such as lyoner, jagerwurst and blood sausage, etc., all needing either steam or a hot water bath for cooking. After cooking these products are then placed in an ice bath for quick cooling. The use of cooking kettles is an older method used to cook meat or sausages in water instead of steam and requires somewhat different cooking techniques and times.

Cooking kettles are available in either stainless steel, which is preferable or aluminum. Today they are still very popular with restaurants and culinary schools in the production of stocks and sauces. Kettles can be heated with wood and coal, steam, electricity, propane, natural gas or oil. Modern kettles are thermostatically controlled to maintain a desired temperature and most are gas or electric.

The kettle should be washed with an antibacterial cleaner and rinsed thoroughly after each use. A residue of rinsing water inside should be prevented.

Sausage Cooking kettle
Credit: NAIT Professional Meat Cutting & Merchandising Program

STUFFING HORNS OR TUBE HORNS

The stuffing horn is used to stuff cured and/or tumbled meats or fresh items into a netting or casing, which can be fiber, cloth or cellophane to hold products together and give them a unique shape and appearance after smoking and/or cooking. These casings are not edible, although some edible products are in development.

There are two types of stuffing horns: manual and electric, which is compressor driven. It consists (in either form) of different sizes of plastic pipe or an expandable stainless steel pipe that basically fits all diameters of product. The netting slides onto the pipe, is clipped or tied on the front end and then the product is pressed through the pipe (either manually or by the compressor) and is pushed firmly into the netting or casing. Then the rear end of the netting or casing is clipped or tied to prevent the product from squeezing out. After this, the product is ready to be smoked and/or cooked or finished otherwise.

Stuffing horn (expandable steel)
Credit: Bunzl Processor Division/Koch Supplies

Bullet stuffing Horn in action
Credit: Canada Beef

GRAVITY CONVEYORS

Gravity conveyors are used in higher production areas such as supermarkets. They are less common to the independent outlet. Most gravity conveyors are sloped toward a slicing, packaging and/or pricing machine. Product is placed at the top of the conveyor, which by way of gravity feeds another step in the production phase of the product.

1. Be sure they roll freely and are safely supported.
2. Protect any sharp corners on the side rails.

ROTISSERIE MACHINES

This piece of equipment is somewhat self-explanatory and really shouldn't need much explanation. In short, the rotisserie is used for cooking product evenly while rotating it on a spit within a contained environment. Rotisseries vary in size, features and capacity. Rotisseries are popular on barbeques, in restaurants, in delicatessens and even in homes as small appliances.

Chicken on a BBQ rotisserie
©istock.com / credit to KaraGrubis

Chickens on a commercial rotisserie
©istock.com / credit to Jimmy Truno

1. **Lockout** before disassembling and/or cleaning.
2. Use suitable gloves and tongs for removing hot spits.
3. Keep all drive rods, gears or worm drives suitably covered by guards.

DANGER

LOCK OUT TAG OUT POWER BEFORE SERVICING, REPAIRING, CLEANING, OR RETOOLING EQUIPMENT

Lock out sign
Credit: Master Lock Canada

WORKTABLES

Worktables can be any table used in a food establishment in the production of food. It can be used for storing boxes, product, supplies or any materials needed by the employees. Most commonly, worktables were designed for working on or at. For us they are used to cut meat, make sausage or to wrap product on.

1. Check that legs are sturdy and secure and that knife racks are solidly attached.
2. Ensure the tops of wooden blocks are fairly level and safe for working on.
3. Locate wooden blocks out of the path of traffic and swinging doors.
4. Ensure all worktables are free of sharp edges and corners.
5. Ensure that worktables with plastic cutting surfaces have secure slots for vertical storage of cutting surfaces after cleaning and sanitizing.

Open base cutting table
Credit: Columbia Products, USA.

Wooden top cutting tables
Credit: NAIT Professional Meat Cutting &
Merchandising Program

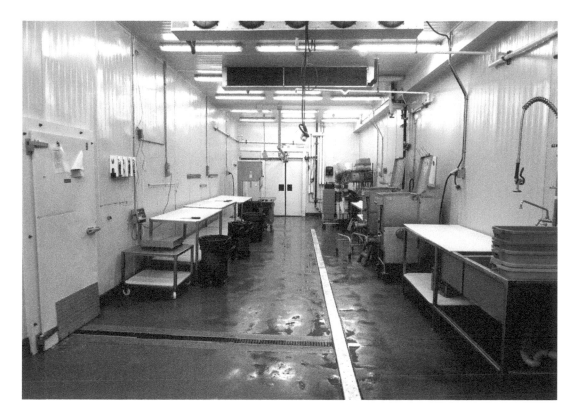

Cutting tables in a commercial processing operation
Credit: Two Rivers Specialty Meats

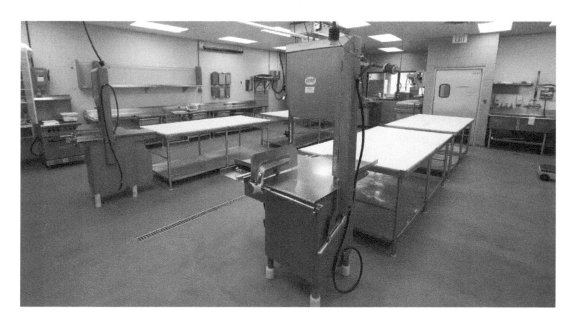

Cutting tables in a training operation
Credit: TRU Retail Meat Processing Program

MSD sheet
Credit: Diversey, USA

Protective equipment
Credit: Bunzl Processor Division/Koch
Supplies

1. Use only approved chemical cleaners and sanitizers when cleaning (Read all S.D.S. [Safety Data Sheets] material before using chemicals).

2. **Lockout** all power equipment before disassembling or cleaning.

3. Always use approved eye protection when using chemical sprays or foams and know the location of your eye wash station.

4. Never spray toward other workers.

5. Never use chemical cleaners or sanitizers while food production is in process.

6. Use safety gloves where indicated to do so.

7. Use waterproof aprons and boots during cleanup process to avoid hot water and chemical spillage on your feet, legs or body.

8. Use only approved amounts of chemical cleaners and sanitizers (if in doubt, don't use them until instructed otherwise). (Keep all containers clearly marked as to contents in a safe storage area.)

9. Handle equipment and tools carefully when disassembling. Some equipment pieces are heavy and can easily crush feet or legs if dropped or pushed over.

10. Never leave knives or sharp parts of equipment immersed in water before cleaning.

11. Don't throw pieces of equipment to other workers in an attempt to save time.

Eyewash station in action
Credit: Guardian eyewash equipment

Tap mounted eyewash system
Credit: Guardian eyewash equipment

Refrigeration

HOW REFRIGERATION WORKS

Refrigerators work on the same principle as the heat pumps that some people use to heat and cool their homes. The refrigerator uses a refrigeration gas to draw heat out of the inside of the refrigerator and release it to the outside air.

Nevertheless, to draw heat from inside the refrigerator, the gas must be colder than the refrigerator's temperature. To release heat to the outside, it must be warmer than the outside air.

So the trick is getting the gas to go through temperature change done mostly through pressure changes.

The refrigerator's motor drives a compressor. The compressor puts pressure on the gas, causing it to heat up. The hot, dense gas leaves the compressor and enters the condenser, a system of tubes with lots of room for outside air to circulate around them. In the condenser the gas gives up heat to the outside air and condenses into liquid as a result.

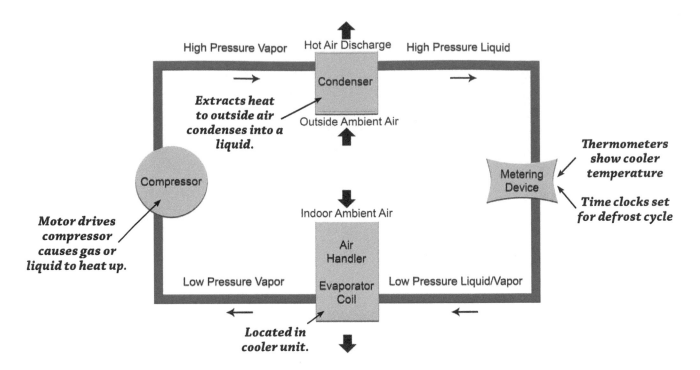

High Pressure Vapor   Hot Air Discharge   High Pressure Liquid

Condenser

Extracts heat to outside air condenses into a liquid.

Outside Ambient Air

Compressor

Thermometers show cooler temperature

Metering Device

Time clocks set for defrost cycle

Motor drives compressor causes gas or liquid to heat up.

Indoor Ambient Air

Air Handler

Evaporator Coil

Low Pressure Vapor   Low Pressure Liquid/Vapor

Located in cooler unit.

Cooler coil system layout diagram
©David Spates / Dreamstime

THE COMPRESSOR UNIT

This is the unit that is hooked up to and works in conjunction with the cooling system in the cooler or freezer. Compressor units are usually located well away from the merchandising and processing areas. Most large-volume outlets have a mechanical room, which has been designed to house all the compressor units in that store. Most companies find it more economical and practical to have regular service maintenance in the case of multiple units, and under these circumstances, all departments experience minimum inconvenience.

Next, the refrigeration gas, now under high pressure, passes liquid through a valve into a low-pressure zone.

The drop in pressure causes some of the refrigeration gas to vaporize in the cooler unit. This act of vaporizing chills the refrigeration gas.

Finally the chilled, low-pressure gas liquid mixture makes its way into the part of the piping circuit and through an expansion valve into the evaporator (the cooler unit inside the cooler). There the cold gas draws heat from the air. The heat causes the gas to vaporize completely. The gas then heads back to the compressor to begin the cycle again.

Refrigeration compressor units in a large Supermarket
Credit: Save on Foods

Refrigeration evaporator unit
Credit: TRU Retail Meat Processing Program

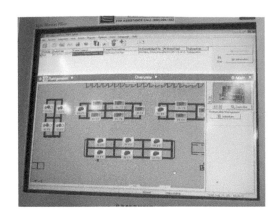

Computer system for monitoring a large supermarket refrigeration units
Credit: Save on Foods

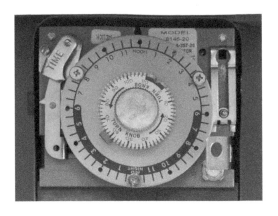

Defrost cycle timing clock in a smaller meat store
Credit: Summit Gourmet Meats

BASIC REFRIGERATION

The walk-in cooler is the means of safeguarding fresh meats against spoilage. It's a place to hold the meat until it can be processed and moved to the display cases. Remember that the faster you move and sell meats, the less shrinkage and loss occurs. Also remember the abbreviation "FIFO" - first in, first out. In other words, sell the oldest meat first. Move the product on hand forward near the door to your cooler as new orders are received, so the physical arrangement of meats in the cooler indicates what products should go first. Place related items together, such as all pork, lamb, veal, etc., to simplify inventory control.

In planning "a place for everything and everything in its place" for your walk-in cooler, put fresh meats away from the cooler door to reduce drying out to the temperature at which water freezes. The temperature at which most meat freezes is about -2°C. For this reason the temperature should not be allowed to go any lower than -2°C since the slow freezing action will cause the surfaces of beef, veal and lamb to darken.

It used to be that a good thermometer would be kept in the cooler about 1.5 m above the flood (eye-level) and away from coils and cold airstreams of metal surfaces. These days almost all thermometers are digital and embedded in the outside wall of the refrigeration unit. Temperatures can be monitored daily with a handheld device or by the old-fashioned method of placing a thermometer inside the unit. Thermometers should be checked and temperatures recorded in the refrigeration data log daily to monitor any fluctuations caused by interruptions such as deliveries, defrost cycles and down time.

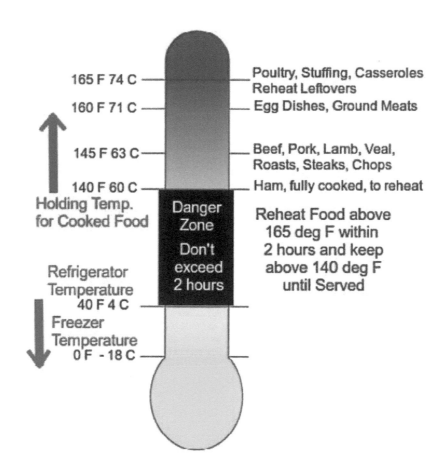

165 F 74 C — Poultry, Stuffing, Casseroles
Reheat Leftovers

160 F 71 C — Egg Dishes, Ground Meats

145 F 63 C — Beef, Pork, Lamb, Veal,
Roasts, Steaks, Chops

140 F 60 C — Ham, fully cooked, to reheat

Holding Temp.
for Cooked Food

Danger
Zone

Don't
exceed
2 hours

Refrigerator
Temperature
40 F 4 C

Freezer
Temperature
0 F - 18 C

Reheat Food above
165 deg F within
2 hours and keep
above 140 deg F
until Served

Food safe temperature chart
Credit: Dr. John Anderson

Note: For further details on Bacterial growth & Safe Meat Handling see the thermometer guides, appendix pages 746-747.

CIRCULATION IN WALK-IN COOLERS

The most common type of cooling unit today is the blower coil system in which air is drawn from the floor area up through the cold coils and then driven back into the cooler area. Rapid circulation of the air is assured by the type of cooling unit, the power of the fans to distribute cool air, the location within the walk-in cooler of the cooling units and the number of fans circulating the air. It is interesting to note that with some older model walk-in coolers, you may run across warm spots created by the passage of the air stream caused by the maturing cooling unit. These units have adjustable deflectors that direct the airflow, and they might need monitoring to avoid warm spots. If need be, these warm spots can be pinpointed by arranging a series of thermometers at strategic places. The deflectors on the front of the blower can be adjusted to rectify most of these warmer sections until a fairly constant temperature prevails. However, if any warm spots cannot be eliminated, avoid placing items which need cold air in those sections.

The floor areas should be kept free of cartons stacked directly in the path of air streams. If cartons of products have to be placed in the cooler, store them on mobile stacker trolleys or permanent and secure storage racks; otherwise, put them on pallets on the floor staggered to allow air to circulate around them. It may be more practical to place them against the wall directly underneath the blower unit, but not stacked too high. In this way they will not interfere with the air stream.

Since the air stream is the only medium of cooling free flow of air through the blower itself, it must be considered as important as the physical layout of the cooler. The coil system is designed similar to a car radiator, and if the delicate cooling vent fins are damaged, they may prevent the flow of air through the blower. Practices such as chipping away ice build-up with a cleaver, boning knife or any other sharp object can bend the fins or possibly puncture the refrigeration lines, resulting in loss of refrigerant. For these reasons, such practices should be shunned. When ice build-up is observed, it is usually a symptom of mechanical failure or poor operational usage. Both cases warrant professional attention.

THE HUMIDITY FACTOR

Lean beef is usually made up of about 70% moisture. This moisture represents flavour, sales appeal and value in the product. If any of this moisture is lost, shrinkage occurs. Shrinkage is continuous if the product is exposed in the wrong environment. Even under ideal conditions a minimal amount of shrinkage will occur. A hindquarter of beef can shrink approximately 1.5% during a weekend of holding in the cooler; this means $1.50 loss in every $100 worth of product, which represents a loss of net profit in sales. The humidity factor is of less importance in meat markets that deal strictly in block-ready vacuum packed meat products.

The moisture content of the air is expressed as the relative humidity and is measured in percentage. When the air is saturated with moisture, the relative humidity is 100%, which means the air is holding all the moisture possible at that temperature. It is at this saturation point that rain or other forms of precipitation occur. When we say the humidity is 75%, we are saying that the air contains three-quarters of the moisture necessary to cause saturation of that air.

If the air in the walk-in cooler drops below 70% relative humidity, undue shrinkage will result. If the relative humidity is too high, moisture will condense on the meat, providing an excellent medium for bacteria growth, which can result in the meat spoiling much sooner than otherwise. When this starts, trimming losses are heavy. Therefore the humidity in the walk-in cooler should be maintained at approximately 75% to 80%.

Coolers that are made and installed by reputable manufacturers are designed to maintain the proper humidity level automatically. Keeping the proper difference in the temperature between the coils, which cool the air and the air itself, does this. For example, in a correct cooler system, coils will maintain a temperature of -6 to -5 °C while the air in the cooler area is approximately 0 - 2°C. This temperature differential results in the right humidity in the cooler. However, if that same cooler had a cooling mechanism, which was too small for the size of cooler, the mechanism would have to work overtime to cool the air. This would mean that the coils proper temperature would be substantially colder than the air. Or while the air was at 2°C the coils might be registering -10°C. This degree differential would result in moisture from the air condensing on the coils, lowering the humidity and beginning to dry out the meat.

If too much moisture is allowed to reach the coils, ice may form, which will block up the delicate fins of the unit thus slowing down the flow of cold air and lowering the temperature. A normal cooling mechanism will automatically relieve the coil area of any frost deposit before ice build-up occurs by going into a defrost cycle. During this cycle, the refrigeration action is stopped, and heating elements in the coil system are allowed to melt away any frost deposit. This action is balanced with a cooler air temperature, and as the air temperature rises, the heaters are stopped and normal refrigeration takes over. The normal defrost cycles usually last for 20 to 60 minutes (according to the circumstances) with duration and frequency being set for those times when the cooler is at minimum usage and the air temperature is at its norm. This is usually late evening or early morning.

The humidity of the cooler can be upset by introducing extra moisture, such as by leaving water on the floor or taking in a bucket of hot water for cleaning purposes. Moisture from these sources will be drawn off and deposited as frost on the coils. Special effort must be made to keep the cooler area as dry as possible, particularly the floor on which meat purge may drain. If a build-up of ice on the coils occurs despite all good practices, a refrigeration mechanic should be called in to rectify the situation.

1. Keep the area around the unit free from unnecessary material. Make sure the area is well ventilated.
2. Post information such as running temperatures on doors of coolers and freezers, times of defrost cycles, and temperature of cooler during defrost cycles.
3. Do not interfere with the control settings if you have no knowledge of the system.
4. Keep the cooler area dry.
5. Keep cooler doors closed when not being used.
6. Have a cooler layout, which does not seriously impede the airflow of the blower unit.
7. If thorough cleaning of cooler area is called for, make sure all meat has been removed and the compressor unit switched off at the main source.
8. Keep a lid on any container that holds fluid, e.g., brine tank.
9. If condensation (beads of water) is seen on walls or ceilings of cooler, seek the advice of a serviceman.
10. Make sure that good-quality thermometers are present in cooler areas.
11. Measure the differential of coil and air temperature periodically with two thermometers. Or measure the humidity with a psychrometer, an inexpensive device available from a good hardware store.

MEAT FREEZER

Meat freezers operate under the same principles but at obviously lower temperatures. It is extremely important that frozen product is placed in the freezer as soon as it is received. It should never be stored in the cooler. Only when product **needs to be thawed** is frozen product placed in the cooler.

Meat Cooler & Freezer Safety Practices

1. Keep racks securely fixed to the walls.
2. Keep floors clean and dry to provide good traction.
3. Use vapour-proof light globe protectors.
4. Be sure doors can be easily opened from the inside.
5. Allow adequate space for lifting heavy cartons of products onto a mobile dolly.
6. Keep a hard hat available for use in the cooler and freezer.

7. Provide a "step leveller" or ramp to allow easy movement of mobile dollies into the cooler or freezer units.
8. Provide warm coats, gloves and hats for working in freezer.

SELF SERVICE & FULL SERVICE DISPLAY CASES

As coolers affect profit during the holding and processing of bulk meats and cuts of meat, the display cases are critical to the saleability of the finished packages. The merchandising period is one of the most crucial times, as each package of meat must maintain the "buy me" appeal. When packages of meat are returned to the back room because of loss of appeal, a loss of money results. Consequently, it is of equal importance that the self-service display case be kept in good operating order.

Self closing freezer door
Credit: TRU Retail Meat Processing Program

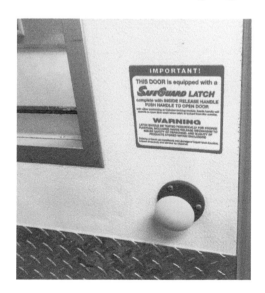

Freezer door with inside safety release push handle and safety warning
Credit: Jakes & Associates

Self service meat case
Credit: Canada Beef

Full service meat case
Credit: Canada Beef

Full service case layout
©istock.com / credit to wirOman

Self service meat case
Credit: NAIT Professional Meat Cutting & Merchandising Program

SUMMARY

TERMS FOR REVIEW

Bandsaw	Meat mixer	Steel
Bowl cutter	Meat slicer	Twine
Brine pumps	Mixer grinder	Vacuum machine
Cry-o-vac	OHS	Vacuum tumblers
Discolouration	Sausage stuffing machine	Whole muscle needle tenderizer
Grinder	Scabbard	Whole muscle steak slicer
Hand tools	Steak tenderizer	

DISCUSSION QUESTIONS

1. Define Hand & Power Tools.

2. Explain in your own words how accidents are usually caused.

3. Discuss the cause and effects of a dull knife.

4. Explain what OHS has to say about impairment on the jobsite.

5. Why should a person never catch a falling knife?

6. Explain the usefulness of scabbards.

7. What function does the tool known as a "Steel" have?

8. Why should we "lock out" equipment before making adjustments to it?

Chapter 4

Meat Science

Meat Science is the study of the composition, nutritional value, wholesomeness and consumer acceptability, largely determined from the initial conception, growth and development of the domestic animal to the time of harvest and to the ultimate processing, preparation, distribution, cooking and consumption of its meat.

The chapter takes a look at what makes some cuts more tender than others, the difference between locomotion and support muscles of a carcass, their fibre and colour, the effect of age and the aging of meat. It also looks at a few abnormalities in meat, the use of hormones and antibiotics and what it means to be naturally raised.

The science of meat includes the effects of heat on meat, cooking methods used to cook meats, and how seasoning, marinating and coating meat alters or enhances its flavour.

Meat Science

In this chapter we're going to have a look at the composition of meat, its structure, harvesting (slaughter), aging, colour and some tenderness factors. We'll also look at a few imperfections and their causes as well as the nutritional value of meats, which includes meat cookery, as both nutrition and cookery have science at their root. This chapter does have some science to it, but we do our best to keep it simple and practical. For the most part the information is well circulated in other books, magazines, periodicals, documentaries and the Internet, etc. We have no new discoveries and nothing new on the make-up of meats that we haven't used in the past. What we do have is a new approach to organizing the information available utilizing our educational backgrounds, classroom experience and the materials we've developed over the last four or five decades.

Composition

Meat is the muscle tissue of an animal and consists of three major components: water, protein, and fat.

Water is about 75% of muscle. It is this high percentage that concerns us when it comes to aging of meat as aging brings about shrinkage. Shrinkage brings about moisture loss, and moisture loss brings about an increase in costs. It should also be noted that all things living in water or out of water need water to survive. The healthiness of the foods we eat for our nourishment relies on water as a staple for their microbiological and biochemical systems and functions.

Protein is an important nutrient and the most abundant solid material in meat. It is responsible for meat colour, muscle function and approximately 20% of muscle tissue is protein. The main proteins in meat that concern the industry are contractile proteins, sarcoplasmic proteins, plasma proteins, and connective tissue proteins. (See Structure of Meat)

Fat dispersed intramuscularly makes up about 5% of muscle tissue. However, a carcass can have as much as 30% fat between and around muscle groups, something we refer to as "fat cover" when found to be on the exterior of a carcass and "fatty" when found between muscle groups. From an industry standpoint, fat is our friend. Fat contributes to flavour, colour and texture.

Structure of Meat

Water is an important component of muscle and cellular life. The amount of water in meats varies between species. Water is the medium the body uses to move nutrients, metabolites (small molecules having various functions such as providing fuel, structure, signalling, stimulating and inhibitory effects on enzymes, defense and interactions with other organisms) and hormones. Water is also used to transport waste materials from cells to excretion sites as with urine and feces. Without water these metabolic and other biochemical reactions would cease to function; thus, the importance of keeping hydrated.

MUSCLE COMPONENTS

Moisture	60 – 75%
Protein	10 – 20%
Fat	4 – 22%
Ash & Other	1%

The muscles of meat are made of fibres bound together with connective tissue known as **collagen**. Carcass muscles are linked together or attached directly to the bone structure. These muscles land in one of two groups: Locomotion or Support muscles. Locomotion muscles are those muscles attached to the skeletal structure of the shoulders, neck, arm and shank areas; they are the more exercised muscles of the carcass. Support muscles run along the back of an animal or those that support the spine; these are less exercised and therefore have more utility with respect to cut-ability. They include but are not limited to the rib section, loin, tenderloin, parts of the hip and even the kidneys.

On larger bones such as shanks it is easy to see the muscle groups in bundles bound together surrounded by collagen fibres. On the hind shank we see these bundles with their endpoints attached to the tarsal bones (hock end) and Achilles by tough tendons known as elastin. Looking at a cross section of a cut shank, we also see stronger more pronounced collagen strands (called silver skin) surrounding bundles of muscle groups.

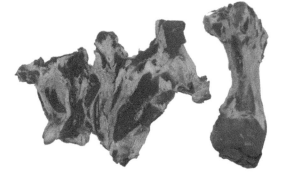

Hind shank cross sections with collagen around muscle groups
Credit: Jakes & Associates

Fore shank boneless showing collagen covering on muscle groups
Credit: Jakes & Associates

The muscle fibres are known as myofibrils. **Myofibrils** are composed of thick and thin filaments arranged in a repeating pattern alongside other myofibrils. One unit of a bundle is called **sarcomere** or little muscle. The thick filaments are the contractile protein **myosin**. The thin filaments known as **actin** contain two other proteins called **troponin** and **tropomyosin** that help regulate muscle contraction.

Outside round showing (silver skin) collagen connective tissue on a flat muscle.
Credit: Jakes & Associates

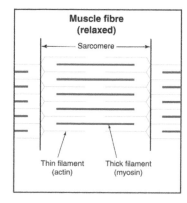

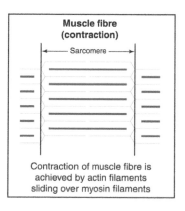

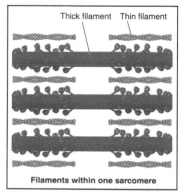

Muscle fibre (relaxed)

Sarcomere

Thin filament (actin)   Thick filament (myosin)

Muscle fibre (contraction)

Sarcomere

Contraction of muscle fibre is achieved by actin filaments sliding over myosin filaments

Thick filament   Thin filament

Filaments within one sarcomere

Muscle fiber contraction showing sarcomere, actin & myosin filaments
©Legger / Dreamstime

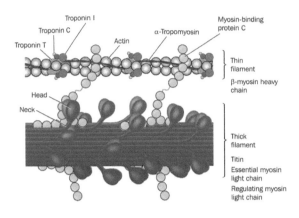

Actin & Myosin with troponin & tropomyosin
proteins in action
©Legger / Dreamstime

Proteins constitute an important class of chemical compounds in the body. Some proteins are necessary for the body's structure, and other proteins function in vital metabolic reactions. In carcass meats most of the protein present is in muscle and connective tissues. These are the fibrous proteins that form structural units and the **globular** proteins, which include the numerous enzymes that cause or accelerate metabolic reactions.

Fat (or adipose tissue) is the main form of lipid storage in all higher animals. It is deposited in specialized cells of adipose tissue (such as energy storage fat that also cushions and insulates the body) and is composed mainly of large molecular weight compounds of neutral lipids (known as triglycerides - the main components of natural fats and oils) and phospholipids that help form membranes in cells. Between fat cells are a number of other cells together

with collagen fibres and elastin networks. Sufficient lipids are stored as **triglycerides** (see Nutrition) in the cytoplasm of the fat cells as an energy source used for periods of starvation or fasting; it also helps regulate temperature. The majority of lipids are stored as adipose tissue between the loose connective tissue of the muscle bundle sheath fibres, creating what is commonly referred to as **marbling** (intramuscular fat).

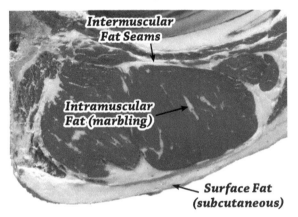

A well marbled rib eye section
Credit: Canada Beef

Chemically fats and oils are very similar compounds, but fats are solid at room temperature where oils are liquid. Fat deposits are not stationary; lipids are continuously being mobilized and re-deposited. When stress conditions develop in the animal such as starvation, prolonged exercise or rapid fear responses in terms of violent exercise or as can occur during harvesting, adrenaline from the bloodstream binds with specific receptors in the fat cell surface and triggers a response. A hormone sensitive lipase (a digestive enzyme) is activated, rapidly converting triglycerides to diacylglycerols and Free Fatty Acids (FFA) as a source of fuel for the body.

Fat in meat is not altogether undesirable and wasteful. In moderation fat gives a "finished" look. Without some fat cover, a carcass is judged to be deficient. Fat as marbling contributes to the juiciness of cooked meats because it melts between the bundles of muscle fibres (See Meat Cookery). Fat also protects the kidneys, a delicate internal organ and acts as insulation against cold as well as being a source of energy in times of food shortage.

Well finished beef front quarter
Credit: Jakes & Associates

Well finished beef hind quarter
Credit: Jakes & Associates

Well marbled wing grilling steak
Credit: Jakes & Associates

Beef kidney in its natural fat covering
Credit: CPMCA image collection

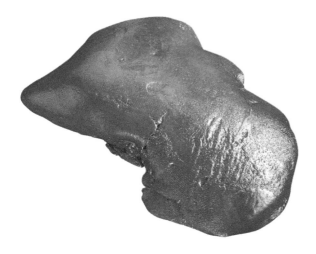

Carbohydrates are stored in the liver and skeletal muscles as polysaccharide glycogen (starch and sugar molecules). The glycogen is a high-energy compound that is converted into glucose (sugar) as a source of instant energy for muscle tissue. Carbohydrates have an important role in energy metabolism and in the growth and repair of structural tissue.

Beef liver
Credit: Canada Beef

Skeletal Structure

Cartilage is composed of cells and extra-cellular fibres that are embedded in a gel-like matrix. Cartilage and bone constitute the supportive elements of the skeletal structure. During embryonic development, most of the skeleton is formed as cartilage that is later converted to bone. Most bone growth occurs through the cartilage intermediary. Some cartilage remains such as the articular disks of bone joints that persist throughout the life of the animal. Cartilage is categorized as hyaline (glassy or clear), elastic and/or fibro cartilage. Hyaline cartilage is the most abundant type in the body and is found on the surfaces of bones at joints, the ventral ends of the ribs (costal cartilage), the dorsal tips of the thoracic vertebrae (button bones), and as the cartilaginous tissue associated with the lumbar and sacral vertebrae. As an animal matures, the cartilage ossifies, giving evidence of age and is used by graders to determine age of carcass.

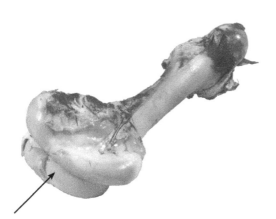

Round bone showing hyaline cartilage
around the knee joint
Credit: Jakes & Associates

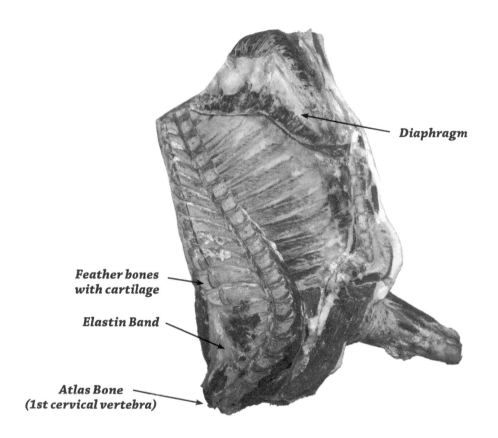

Feather bones with cartilage

Elastin Band

Atlas Bone (1st cervical vertebra)

Diaphragm

Beef front quarter showing locations of white cartilage, elastin, 1st vertabrae, diaphram and split feather bones.
Credit: Jakes & Associates

Bone held together by fibrous connective tissue, supports a meat animal's body, produces red and white blood cells, stores minerals, protects organs (heart, lung, etc.) and enables mobility. Three types of tissue (bone, fibrous connective and adipose tissues), though they differ radically in appearance and properties, are all classified as types of connective tissue. All three types contain cells located in a matrix with fibres. In bones both the matrix and the fibres make an important contribution to mechanical strength. The hardness of bone originates from a calcified matrix, made up of calcium, magnesium, phosphorus, sodium and other trace minerals. Strength comes from embedded collagen fibres and the tubular shape of bones such as the shank and hip bones. The cells of bone known as osteocytes are trapped in small cavities called lacunae.

Beef marrow bone cross section
©istock.com / credit to yommy 8008

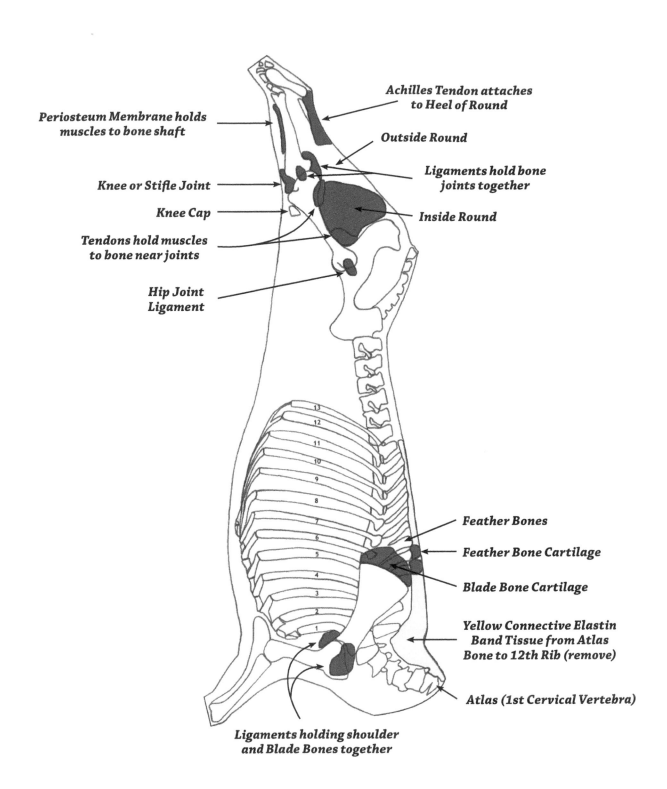

Periosteum Membrane holds
muscles to bone shaft

Achilles Tendon attaches
to Heel of Round

Outside Round

Knee or Stifle Joint

Ligaments hold bone
joints together

Knee Cap

Inside Round

Tendons hold muscles
to bone near joints

Hip Joint
Ligament

13
12
11
10
9
8
7
6
5
4
3
2
1

Feather Bones

Feather Bone Cartilage

Blade Bone Cartilage

Yellow Connective Elastin
Band Tissue from Atlas
Bone to 12th Rib (remove)

Atlas (1st Cervical Vertebra)

Ligaments holding shoulder
and Blade Bones together

*Carcass bone structure highlighting, bone joints,
ligaments, tendons, cartilage, elastin & periosteum
Credit: Jakes & Associates*

Gristle in a carcass is formed from tendons that muscles pull on bone for movement, from ligaments that hold bones together at the joints of the skeleton and from aponeurosis known as sheets of pearly white fibrous tissue that takes the place of tendon. Aponeurosis also covers some muscles and forms a thin sheet of fibrous tissue called fascia (fasciae or fascicles), enclosing a muscle or organ by forming strong sheets between muscles. The dominant protein in gristle is collagen. Since connective tissue is found in nearly all parts of the body at the microscopic level, collagen is the most abundant protein in the animal body.

Skeletal Muscle

Skeletal or striated muscles are the principal source of muscle tissue in meat, although a small amount of smooth muscle also exists as blood vessels. Smooth muscle contains a significant amount of elastin and collagen, with no particular fibre grain. Skeletal muscle is composed of strings of myofibrils that are tubule shaped. The muscle and connective tissues are the dominant components of the meat animal's carcass. It is important to distinguish between muscle and connective tissue or collagen such as silverskin in meat and to understand the respective structure and composition. Most meat items are cut across the tubule muscles or across the "grain" to maximize tenderness and what is called palatability.

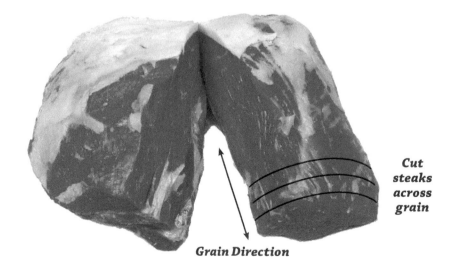

Cut steaks across grain

Grain Direction

Top sirloin (cap removed) split, showing myrofibril grain direction
Credit: Jakes & Associates

Contractile proteins generate force for muscle contraction and organ muscle function as with the heart. Chemically, skeletal muscles are composed of a number of amino acid sequences that form the contractile proteins actin and myosin, both salt-soluble. **Myosin** is a motor protein involved in muscle contraction, and **Actin** helps form filaments that are also involved in muscle contraction. **Troponin** is attached to the protein tropomyosin and lies within the groove between actin filaments in muscle tissue. In a relaxed muscle, **tropomyosin** blocks the attachment site for the myosin cross- bridge and prevents contraction. Tropomyosin and troponin are considered regulatory proteins and function like a switch that starts and stops shortening of the muscles .Muscle contraction takes energy supplied biochemically by *Adenosine Triphosphate* (**ATP**). ATP is the source of energy used in the contraction of working muscles. ATP comes from three different biochemical systems in muscle: phosphagen, glycogen-lactic acid, and aerobic respiration. The source of energy required (system) depends on muscle demand for that energy.

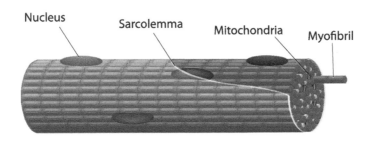

Muscle fiber showing Sarcolemma and a Myofibril
©Designua / Dreamstime

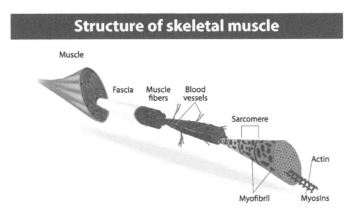

Actin & myosin, troponin & Tropomyosin on thick and thin filaments of muscle tissue
©Legger / Dreamstime

Sarcoplasmic reticulum is a mesh-like or sleeve-like structure found around each myofibril. At the end of the reticulum there are lateral sacs connected by a series of small tubular elements. These lateral sacs store calcium that is released following membrane excitation (movement). It is the release of this calcium during electrical stimulation of the muscle tissue and the breakdown of myosin that causes moisture loss and shrink.

Sacolemma Band surrounding muscle fibers

Myofibrils

Sarcoplasmic Reticulum

Sacoplasmic reticulum
Credit: Mairi Budreau, Artist

Plasma is the liquid portion of the blood and consists of a large number of inorganic substances such as salt and minerals dissolved in water. These proteins are water-soluble and help make-up purge or drip that occurs when meat is stimulated or hung to age. Most plasma proteins can be classified according to certain physical and chemical reactions into three broad groups: albumins that keep blood from leaking out of blood vessels, globulins that bind with hemoglobin blood colour and fibrinogen, a soluble

protein found in blood plasma that functions in blood clotting. The albumins are by far the most abundant of these groups and are synthesized by the liver. Plasma drip is due to the rupturing and severing of the blood vessels found within the muscle tissue.

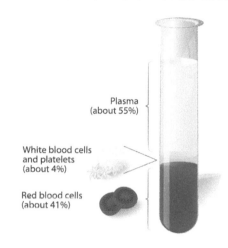

Plasma
(about 55%)

White blood cells
and platelets
(about 4%)

Red blood cells
(about 41%)

Composition of blood
showing Plasma percent
©Designua / Dreamstime

Connective Tissue proteins have as their major function connecting, anchoring, and supporting the structures of the body. These cells typically have a large amount of extra-cellular material between them. The cells themselves include those in the loose mesh work of cells and fibres underlying most epithelial layers that line the cavities and surfaces or blood vessels and organs plus other types as diverse as fat-storing cells, bone cells and red and white cells. These extracellular fibres include rope-like collagen fibres, which have a high tensile strength and resist stretching, rubber-band-like elastin fibres and fine, highly branched reticular fibres that crosslink to form a fine meshwork.

Harvesting

Here with harvesting we're looking at the science component, what happens to the meat at harvest time. The topic of harvesting domestic animals is covered in more detail in Chapter 12.

Prior to harvesting (slaughter), animals are vulnerable to stress that can and do alter their **pH (potential hydrogen)**. pH is measured on a scale of 0 to 14 with 7 being neutral.

- pH above 7 = alkaline
- pH below 7 = acid

Changes in pH brought about by stress are most likely to occur with domestic cattle and pigs processed for food. A change of pH in stressed animals can cause discolouration that is visible in the finished product. Therefore, it is important to understand how these changes occur and how they may affect product presentation, colour and flavour.

The key to minimizing stress is to handle the animals as quickly and gently as possible assuring their pH remains stable prior to death—around 6.5 (neutral) and dropping to about 5.6 to 5.2 **post mortem** (after death) during the first 24 hours of cooling when the carcass temperature is forced down to 4°C.

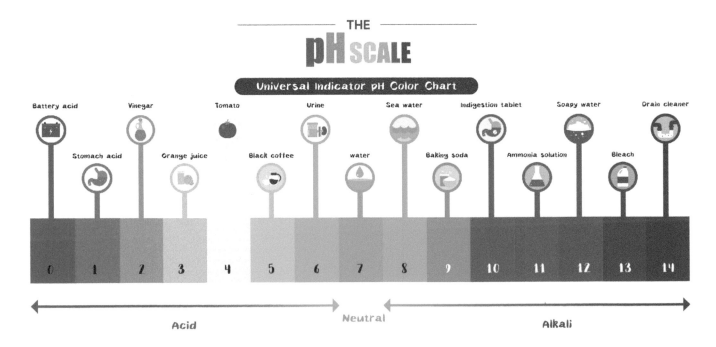

Universal pH scale showing colours & different pH examples
©Tuksaporn Rattanamuk / Dreamstime

All the factors outlined above have some effect on the animal's pH. As the animal ceases to breathe and as blood leaves the animal with the heart still pumping, about 50% of the blood is removed. It takes about four to six minutes before the heart ceases to beat. As the pH begins to drop below 6.5, **lactic acid** is produced, increasing the **acidity.** Lactic acid serves as a preservative, lessening deterioration of the carcass until the temperature of the muscles reaches 4°C.

At this point, **rigor mortis** (the stiffening of the muscles in death) begins to set in. This usually takes between 12 and 24 hours depending on the size of the carcass and amount of exterior fat covering.

There are three stages to rigor mortis:

- Pre-rigor
- Rigor maximum
- Rigor resolution

Pre-rigor: The muscle fibres begin to shorten due to the depletion of adenosine triphosphate (ATP), causing the muscles to become less extendable while hanging under load. With less oxygen available, the myosin and actin proteins form **actomyosin** after death occurs. The actomyosin produces a **cross bridge** between the actin and myosin filaments. In the living animal, these cross bridges are broken during the relaxation phase of a normal contraction cycle (e.g., movement such as walking). However, after death (post mortem) cross bridges are formed permanently as the muscles shorten.

Rigor maximum: The muscle fibres reach maximum shortening, resulting in stiff muscles. The cross bridges are now firmly in place.

Rigor resolution: The now stiff muscle fibres begin to extend again and stretch out to almost their original length. As this extension occurs, the cross bridges create a tearing effect. This phase results in **tenderization** during **dry aging** (hanging) or **wet aging** (storing in **vacuum packaging**) of carcass meat and is most noticeable in prime meat cuts from the short loin, sirloin, and 7-bone rib of beef. Another chemical process develops during this phase in which the still living cells begin to produce lactic acid. Lactic acid is normally removed by the circulatory system of living animals; however, in rigor resolution it remains in the muscles, causing the pH to drop until the core temperature of the carcass reaches 4°C.

Rigor mortis takes different times to activate depending on the size of the animal and, in some cases, the species. (Table 1, page 168)

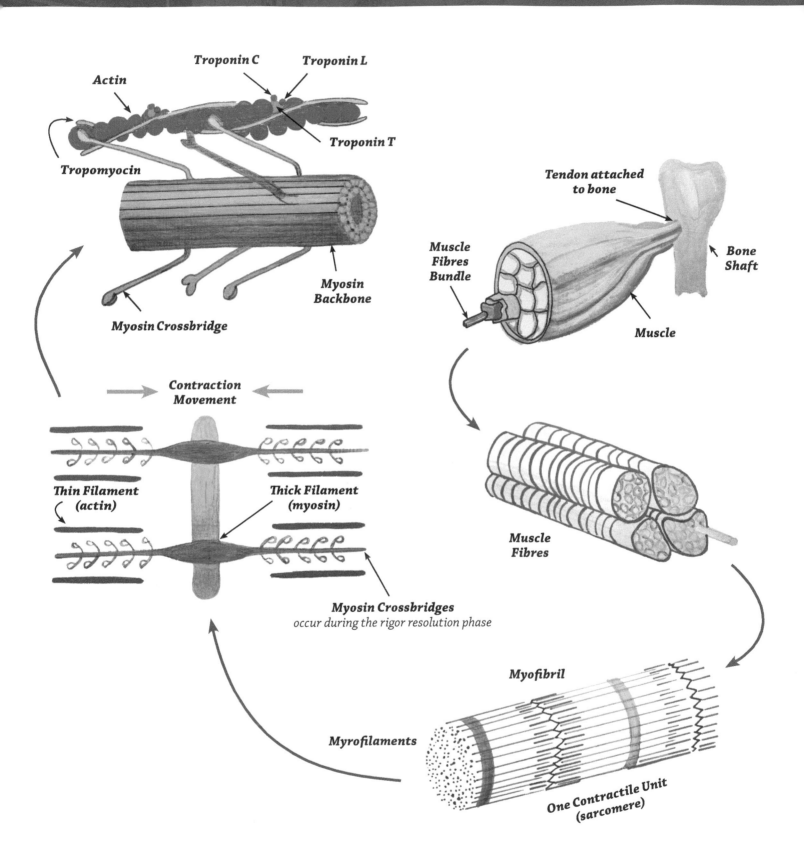

Actin

Troponin C **Troponin L**

Troponin T

Tropomyocin

Myosin Backbone

Myosin Crossbridge

Tendon attached to bone

Bone Shaft

Muscle Fibres Bundle

Muscle

Contraction Movement

Thin Filament (actin)

Thick Filament (myosin)

Muscle Fibres

Myosin Crossbridges
occur during the rigor resolution phase

Myofibril

Myrofilaments

One Contractile Unit (sarcomere)

Diagram of cross bridges in post mortem carcass
Credit: Mairi Budreau - Artist

Beef carcass hanging
Credit: Canada Beef

Lamb carcass
Credit: Sungold Specialty meats Ltd

Pork carcass
Credit: CPMCA image collection

Species	Time for Rigor Mortis to Activate
Beef	6 to 12 hours
Lamb	6 to 12 hours
Pork	15 minutes to 3 hours
Turkey	Less than 1 hour
Chicken	Less than half an hour
Fish	Less than 1 hour

Table 1: Length of time required for rigor mortis to activate.

To further understand the three stages of rigor mortis in relation to meat tenderness, consider the following example: A beef animal has endured a stressful separation from its home farm and a prolonged road trip to the harvesting plant. During the trip, the animal became very dehydrated, thus arriving at the plant in a weakened and agitated state and could not be settled down prior to slaughter.

In this example, the animal's pH could be above 7 (neutral) into the alkaline part of the pH scale (8-14) before harvest. This could cause the carcass (post mortem) to never reach rigor resolution, remaining in the rigor maximum stage, where the muscle fibres are at maximum stiffness. Therefore the carcass would remain tough even after the normal aging process.

Electrical stimulation (ES) is a method of accelerating the normal decline of pH onset post mortem. In Canada, it is used mainly on lamb carcasses to enhance the tenderization process and protect from **cold shortening**. Cold shortening can occur with smaller carcasses and refers to cooling too rapidly, preventing the rigor resolution stage from being reached. ES is used to kick-start the rigor maximum stage to reach the rigor resolution stage, which improves meat tenderness and maintains the bright red colour and muscle firmness.

The standard voltage for ES is 504 volts at 3 amps. If used immediately after stunning, ES can be applied at lower voltage. However, higher voltage is more effective. If ES is delayed for one hour after stunning, a massive 1,600 volts is required to kick-start the process.

Aging

The aging of meats has been a topic of discussion for several decades and dates back hundreds of years. All fresh meat is aged for at least a few days and most red meats (beef) for several days and even weeks to allow enzymes naturally present in the meat to break down the muscle tissue, resulting in improved texture and flavour. These days most beef is aged in vacuum-sealed bags, a process known as wet aging. The two methods of aging are wet aging and dry aging.

Inside round vacuum sealed

Prime rib boneless vacuum sealed

Credit: CPMCA image collection

Wet aging refers to aging of meats packaged in plastic vacuum bags. The advantage to wet aging is that the packaging protects the product from bacteria, mold, and prevents weight loss due to drying. The enzymes naturally found in meat continue to break down the muscle tissue vacuumed in the bag but at a slower rate. Products set aside for wet aging have to be refrigerated. The quality of wet aged products depends on the quality of the meat, the amount of aging time before packaging, the vacuum seal of the package and the consistent temperature of refrigeration. It also depends on the amount of purge or moisture inside the package (as the longer the product rests in its own juices, the more it takes on the flavour of those juices), and the amount of time the product is allowed to rest outside of its packaging. All wet aged products should rest a minimum amount of time to air, allowing any gases built up during the vacuum stage to dissipate before using. There are time limits to the practice of wet aging of meats, and it's best to investigate what they are before engaging in the activity. Most beef items can be wet aged up to thirty days.

Carcass beef dry aging in a Federal plant
Credit: Canada Beef

Dry aging is a process of either hanging carcasses on the rail or placing block ready cuts on racks under refrigeration, where air circulation is guaranteed and temperature and humidity are controlled to prevent spoilage. Compared to wet aging, dry aging involves considerable expense as the practice is done with higher quality meats having sufficient fat cover and marbling and results in moisture loss.

Dry aged meats are exposed to dehydration or moisture loss that intensifies the flavour of the meat. The duration or length of time for dry aging depends on the desired outcome with respect to texture, flavour and tenderness. Dry aging can be as short as 9-14 days or as long as 21-60 days depending on the cut of meat. Most dry aging takes place in smaller butcher shops (and some restaurants), where the focus is on natural flavour and tenderness, both attributes consumers who frequent them appreciate.

Carcass beef dry aging in a Provincial plant
Credit: CPMCA image collection

Meat Colour and Tenderness

Under cross-sectional inspection, muscles from different parts of the animal's body display bundles of fibres that appear as irregularly shaped polygons. The bundle size and thickness of the **connective tissue septa** (dividing wall) determine the texture of the muscles. Those with small bundles and thin septa have a fine texture, and those muscles with larger bundles and more connective tissue with thick septa have a coarser texture.

The finer the meat texture, the more precision of movement from the muscle such as with tenderloin. The coarse-textured muscles such as shanks and shoulders are the heavy locomotion muscles of the body that support the full weight of the animal and therefore require less precision of movement.

Science can help explain why some muscles on a beef animal are more tender than others. There are actually three types of skeletal muscle known as **twitch fibres**, with differing speeds of movement and with different colours: fast glycolytic (white), fast oxidative (red) and slow oxidative (red/white intermediate).

Fast glycolytic (white) are fast twitch fibres; they are found in skeletal muscle such as shanks, shoulders and hips and are known as "voluntary muscles." They require no oxygen, and they move faster.

*Hip of beef showing hind shank
Credit: Jakes & Associates*

*Beef shank muscle a 'voluntary muscle'
©istock.com / credit to Chengyuzheng*

Beef diaphragm has slow twitch fibers
Credit: CPMCA image collection

Beef tenderloin has fine textured muscles
and slow/fast twitch fibers
Credit: Jakes & Associates

Slow oxidative (red/white intermediate) are slow/fast twitch fibres; they are found in precision muscles such as the tenderloin and strip loin that don't need to move as fast as skeletal muscles.

Fast oxidative (red) are slow twitch fibres; they are found in the diaphragm, heart, arteries, veins, stomach and intestines and are known as " Involuntary muscles." They require oxygen to operate, and they move slowly.

Beef striploin has fine textured muscles
and slow/fast twitch fibers
Credit: Jakes & Associates

Beef heart
©istock.com / credit to VladyslavDaniln

Twitch Fibres	
Colour	**Action**
White	Are fast twitch fibres
Red	Are slow twitch fibres
Red/White Intermediate	Are slow/fast twitch fibres

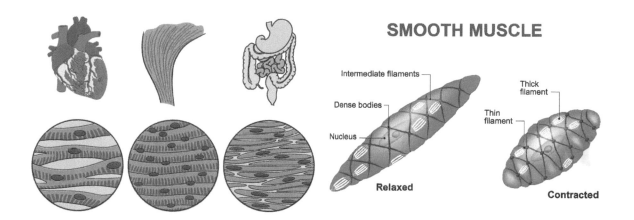

SMOOTH MUSCLE

Muscle types from left to right:
Cardiac, Skeletal and Smooth
©Udaix4 / Dreamstime

Muscle tissue diagram showing Skeletal,
smooth & cardiac muscle.
©Designua / Dreamstime

The post mortem colour development of meat varies greatly from one species to another, with variations in fresh beef being very prominent. Beef shows a range of colour from first being cut to the end of its shelf life (about three days).

Typical meat colour for different species is shown in Table 2.

Species	Colour
Beef	Bright cherry red
Fish	Pure white to grey-white or pink to dark red
Horse	Dark red
Lamb and mutton	Light red to brick red
Pork	Greyish pink
Poultry	Varies from bluish white, greyish pink to dull red
Veal	Brownish pink

Table 2: Typical colour of meat from different species.

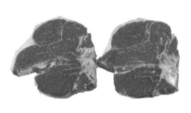

Beef meat colour - Porterhouse grilling steaks
Credit: Jakes & Associates

Fish colour – Salmon steaks
Credit: Fisherman's Market

Fish colour – Halibut fillet
Credit: Fisherman's Market

Horse meat colour
©istock.com / credit to
EddWestmacott

Lamb meat colour - Lamb loin chops
Credit: Jakes & Associates

Pork meat colour -
Pork loin center portion
Credit: Jakes & Associates

Chicken meat colour – Chicken breast boneless / skinless
Credit: Jakes & Associates

Veal meat colour
©istock.com / credit to yvdavyd

Meat colour is significant to consumer acceptance of products. The bright red colour of good quality beef, sockeye salmon and young lamb are naturally appealing, whereas the paler colours of veal and other fish species are less appealing to many, although more sought after by some ethnic groups. Dark meats such as horse are more popular in Quebec and European countries. Mutton (sheep over 12 months of age with darker flesh) appeals to an even smaller range of customers.

FACTORS AFFECTING COLOUR

Poultry provides a good opportunity to see and learn about the differences in meat colour. Meat cutters and cooks may often be asked why different parts of a chicken have **white meat** and other parts have **dark meat**, or why duck or game birds have mostly dark meat.

Poultry white meat –
Chicken breast boneless - skin on
Credit; Jakes & Associates

Poultry dark meat –
Chicken thigh boneless skinless
Credit: Jakes & Associates

Duck meat
Duck boneless breast
©istock.com / credit to bonchan

The colour of the meat is determined by how the muscle is used. Upland game birds such as **partridge** and grouse that fly only for short bursts have white breast meat. In contrast ducks and geese and most other game birds that fly long distances have exclusively dark meat. In domestic poultry (chickens and turkeys), there is a difference between breasts (white meat) and thighs and drumsticks (dark meat).

Meat colour is associated with two proteins: **myoglobin** (iron and oxygen binding protein in muscle tissue) and **hemoglobin** (a red protein transporting oxygen in the blood). When animals are no longer alive and air comes in contact with the meat, myoglobin reacts with oxygen in an attempt to reach a state of equilibrium, at which point no further changes occur. As this process happens, the meat colour goes through three stages and three colours that are easy to see, especially on fresh cuts of beef.

1. Purplish red (myoglobin) occurs immediately after a **steak** is sliced.
2. Cherry red (**oxymyoglobin**) occurs several minutes after cutting and after exposure to oxygen (referred to as **bloom**).
3. Brown (**metmyoglobin**) occurs when the iron in the myoglobin is oxidized, which usually takes about three days after cutting.

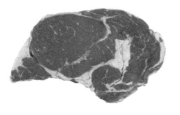 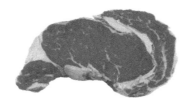 

Purplish Red when first cut –
(myoglobin colour)

Bright cherry red, the blooming
of the steak at its best –
(oxymyoglobin colour)

The browning phase of the steak
near the end of its visual shelf
life – (metmyoglobin colour)

Credit: Summit Gourmet Meats

Oxygen plays two important roles, which affect the colour in opposite ways. As soon as meat is cut, oxygen reacts with the myoglobin and creates the bright red colour associated with oxymyoglobin. This will continue to develop until the iron in the myoglobin oxidizes to the point of the metmyoglobin stage.

Oxidation can also occur when iron in the meat binds with oxygen in the muscle. This can often occur during the processing of round steak from the hip primal and can be identified by the rainbow-like colours that appear from the reflection of light off the meat surface. The condition will remain after the product is cooked and can often be seen on sliced roast beef used in sandwich making. This condition does not alter the quality of the meat; however, it is generally less attractive to consumers.

Rainbow colour shown on Outside round muscle (cooked & sliced corned beef)
Credit: Jakes & Associates

Maintaining the temperature of fresh meat near the freezing point (0°C/32°F) helps maintain the bright red colour of beef meats for much longer and prevents discolouration.

Meat should be allowed to bloom completely (the bloom usually reaches its peak about three or four days after cutting) or be wrapped on a meat tray with a **permeable** wrapping film as in supermarket meat displays. If portioned steaks are to be vacuum packed, doing so immediately after cutting (but before the bloom has started) will allow the steaks to bloom naturally when removed from the vacuum packaging.

A comparison between a well aged brown T-Bone steak & a Prime rib steak that has just bloomed
Credit: Summit Gourmet Meats

Certain phases of meat processing can also trigger discolouration. Oxidation browning (metmyoglobin) can develop more rapidly than normal if something occurs to restrict the flow of oxygen once the bloom has started but has not been allowed to run its full course. The two most common examples are:

- Cut meat surfaces stay in contact too long with flat surfaces such as cutting tables, cutting boards or trays.
- Meat is wrapped in paper (which means there is no further exposure to air and therefore no oxygen, which speeds up the browning effect).
- The browning effect will occur naturally once the meat is exposed to oxygen.

There are two other types of discolouration that commonly occur with beef and pig meat. Although the cause of both types occurs before death (**ante mortem**), the actual change does not show up until after death (post mortem). The discolouration is a result of chemical reactions in the animal's body due to stresses known as **pre-slaughter stress syndrome (PSS)**. (See Imperfections)

Both the age of the animal, the handling at the time of processing and the post mortem aging affect tenderness (or toughness). The amount of connective tissue in meats and its solubility (the degree it dissolves during cooking) can directly influence the tenderness of meat. There are two main forms of connective tissue: collagen and elastin. Cross-links are found in older animals, making meats from those animals less palatable. **Cross-linking** refers to elastin and collagen rings that hold muscle fibres in place. As the animals age more elastin and collagens rings form. More cross-links are a direct result of age, and therefore meat toughness increases with age.

The older the animal is, the tougher the meat will be. The younger the animal, the more tender it will likely be (for the most part). As well, regardless of age, the more exercised parts of an animal contain more elastin rings than less exercised parts.

Tenderness is also a factor of biochemical reactions within the meat. Meat can be tough when **actomyosin** (a complex of actin and myosin of which the contractile protein filaments of muscle tissue are composed) or myofibrils (elongated contractile threads found in striated muscle cells) have overlapped. Post mortem aging at the resolution stage of rigor mortis helps eliminate actomyosin toughness. Table 3 shows the ideal age of animals for processing different domestic species harvested for their meat. Animals processed under stress or older than the age indicated will have increased levels of toughness.

Meat type	Approximate age of animal at processing
Beef	18 to 30 months
Veal	Less than 12 months
Baby veal	3 to 6 months
Pork	6 to 8 months
Lamb	3 to 12 months
Poultry	3 to 8 weeks (Game hens & Chickens)

Table 3: Approximate processing ages of different animals.

The pale muscles of veal carcasses indicate an immature animal, which has a lower myoglobin count than those of more mature animals. Young cattle are fed primarily milk products to keep their flesh light in colour. However, once a calf is weaned and begins to eat grass, its flesh begins to darken. Intact males such as breeding bulls have muscle that contains more myoglobin than females (heifers) or steers (castrated males) at a comparable age.

Generally, beef and lamb have more myoglobin in their muscles than pork, veal, fish and poultry. Game animals have muscles that are darker than those of domestic animals, in part due to the higher level of physical activity, and therefore they also have higher myoglobin.

Imperfections

The discolouration is a result of chemical reactions in the animal's body due to stresses known as PSS.

PSS can result in two different types of discolouration: PSE and DFD.

PSE (pale, soft and exudative) occurs mainly in pigs (and in some cases has been found to be genetic). PSE is brought about by a sudden increase of lactic acid due to the depletion of glycogen before slaughter, which in turn causes a rapid decline in the pH post slaughter. The trained eye can detect the visible signs of PSE by inspecting the pork loin primal, where the flesh appears much paler than normal. The muscle meat is softer and may be very sloppy and wet to the touch and might be leaking meat juices, a result of a high proportion of free water in the tissues.

Although product with PSE is safe to eat, its shelf life is limited, and it may become tougher sooner if overcooked.

Normal pork colour (Comparison)
Credit: Jakes & Associates

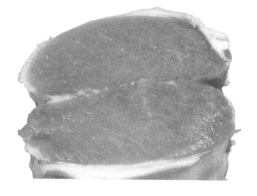

PSE pork colour
Credit: Jakes & Associates

Products with PSE have limited use as fresh products but are used to manufacture cooked products such as formed ham and certain sausage varieties with a recommended limit of 10% (i.e., one part PSE to nine parts of regular meat), due to the high water content.

DFD (dark, firm and dry) occurs mainly in beef carcasses but sometimes in lamb and turkey. In the meat industry these carcasses are referred to as **dark cutters**. Unlike PSE meat, DFD meat shows little or no drop in the pH after slaughter. Instead, there may be an increase of stress hormones such as **adrenaline** released into the bloodstream. Consequently, **glycogen** (muscle sugar) is depleted before slaughter due to stresses.

This decreases the lactic acid, which in turn affects the pH, causing it to not drop fast enough after slaughter. Therefore the muscle meat, typically in the hip area of the carcass, may become very dry and dark.

Even after the carcass is aged and the meat has been processed and displayed, the dark appearance remains, and bloom will not occur. In addition, the meat may also feel sticky to the touch, which limits shelf life. DFD meat is generally considered unattractive to the consumer; however, the meat remains edible and is still suitable for use in cooked products and sausage emulsions but should be limited to 10% (one part DFD to nine parts of regular meat).

Listed below are some causes of DFD that should be avoided:

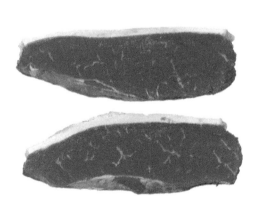

Normal Meat Colour
Credit: Jakes & Associates

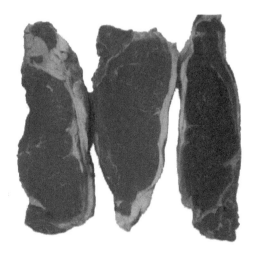

Striploin steaks: (L to R) Fresh Cut Colour,
Bloomed Steak Colour, DFD Colour
Credit: Dr. B. Bohrer - University of Guelph,
Food Sciences.

- Transferring animals to strange surroundings (kill plant) and holding them for too long
- Treating animals roughly prior to and during transport (e.g., using cattle prods)
- Overcrowding cattle during shipping
- Mixing cattle with other animals they are not used to
- Preventing animals from having sufficient rest at the slaughterhouse prior to harvesting
- Dehydrating animals (not giving them enough water) prior to slaughter
- Causing over-excitement, pain, hunger, excessive noise, smell of blood
- Exposing animals to temperature extremes during transportation
- Shipping stress-susceptible animals such as intact males (bulls), during severe weather

Note: DFD can occur anywhere between 12 and 48 hours prior to an animal's slaughter.

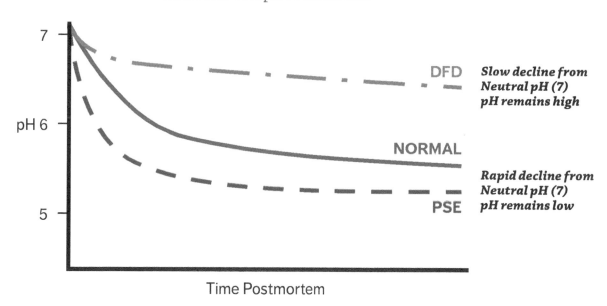

DFD AND PSE pH REACTIONS

Credit: Dr. B Bohrer - University of Guelph, Food Sciences

Large Liver abscess
Credit: Jakes & Associates

Even though meats arriving at their final destination (point of sale) have usually been approved and inspected, the product still requires further checks prior to sale and eating in case **abnormal** meat inconsistencies were missed in the inspection process. Some of these are caused by injuries or disease that occurred while the animal was alive while others are naturally occurring parts of the animal's body (glands in particular) that are removed prior to or during the cutting process.

Some examples of **abnormalities** are given here:

- **Abscesses and cysts:** infected or non-infected tumours from old injuries that are imbedded in muscles and sometimes close to bones.
- **Blood spots and clots:** usually from more recent injuries and also found imbedded in muscles or between muscle seams or on or near bone joints.
- **Fibrous tissue:** scar tissue, usually from very old injuries, with the appearance of white fatty seams or thin strands tightly bound together, making the muscle tough and unsightly.
- **Lymph nodes and glands:** lymph nodes are glands in the throat and back of the tongue that give a good indication of the general health of the animal. These are inspected on the animal carcass at the harvesting plant prior to being sold, but internal or inter-muscular glands are not examined unless further inspection by a veterinarian is recommended. Consequently, three major glands are removed from beef, pork and lamb during processing to ensure the public does not see them. They are the **prescapular gland**, located in the neck and blade sub-primal cuts, below the junction of the fifth cervical vertebra, the **prefemoral gland**, located at 90 degrees to the round bone on the hip, on the exterior of the sirloin tip imbedded in the cod fat pocket and the **popliteal gland**, located in the outside round sub-primal in the hip primal between the eye of the round and the outside round flat under the heel of round, imbedded in a fat pocket.

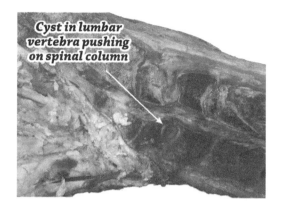

Lumbar spine cyst

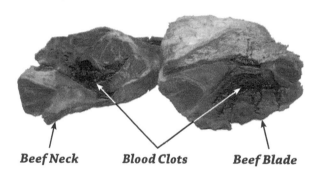

Blood clots from horn gore wound

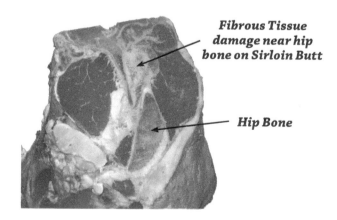

*Fibrous tissue damage near
hip bone on sirloin butt
Credit: Jakes & Associates*

Lymph nodes and glands are the control or police units in the body, and their function is to discard bad and damaged cells. Also this glandular system neutralizes any foreign antibodies that enter into the system either through genetic cell alternations or through environmental elements. Figure 1 outlines the lymphatic gland systems as seen on a side of beef, which can be applied to all meat species.

As illustrated in Figure 1, there is an extensive glandular system that helps the body to function normally. Not shown in this figure is a chain of lymph glands situated at the base of the tongue, directly in front of the atlas joint. During the slaughter process, inspectors examine the glandular lymph nodes for any signs of irregularity such as colour, sandy-gritty texture, cysts, blood spots, etc. Glands in healthy animals are whitish in colour with light shades of brown and a soft sponge-like texture.

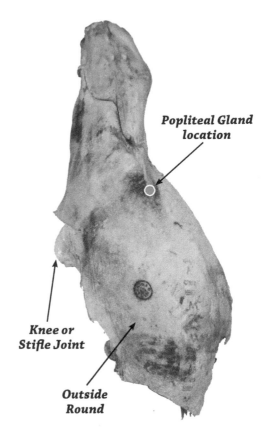

Popliteal Gland location

Knee or Stifle Joint

Outside Round

Beef hip
Credit: Jakes & Associates

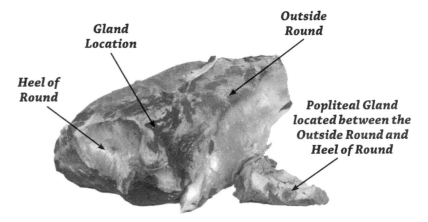

Gland Location

Heel of Round

Outside Round

Popliteal Gland located between the Outside Round and Heel of Round

Outside round showing popliteal gland location
Credit: Jakes & Associates

Bovine Spongiform Encephalopathy (**BSE**) is a chronic, degenerative disorder affecting the central nervous system of cattle first recognized in Britain in 1986. Research conducted by food science and technology institutions have demonstrated that BSE may have originated from feeding infected *Meat and Bone Meal* (**MBM**) to cattle, especially MBM that may have originated from sheep or goats that were infected with *Transmissible Spongiform Encephalopathy* (**TSE**) or scrapie. Because of this, Scientists in the UK started doing research on scrapie, TSE in sheep, and have shown that the only rendering system found to reduce the amount of scrapie agent to an undetectable level was heating it to a temperature of 133°C at 3 bar pressure for a minimum of 20 minutes. However, this has not as yet been shown to be an effective sterilization process of MBM in the eradication and spread of BSE. In Canada it is illegal to feed any form of MBM to ruminants. It is, however, allowed for pigs and poultry providing all *Specified Risk Materials* (**SRM**) have been removed and the product has been heat-treated (more on SRM in Chapter 12 on Harvesting).

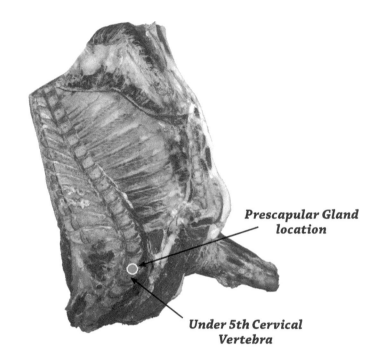

Prescapular Gland location

Under 5th Cervical Vertebra

*Beef front – prescapular gland
Credit: Jakes & Associates*

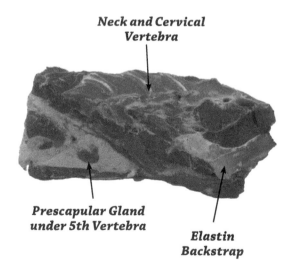

Neck and Cervical Vertebra

Prescapular Gland under 5th Vertebra

Elastin Backstrap

*Beef neck – showing prescapular gland location
Credit: Jakes & Associates*

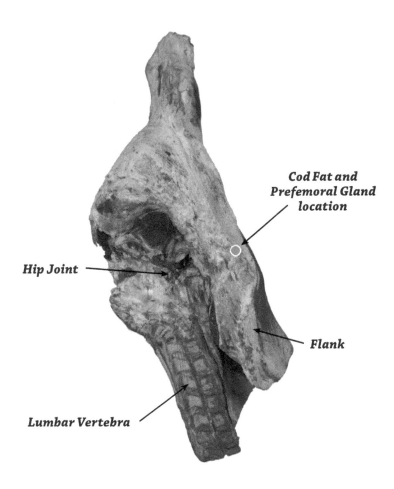

Cod Fat and Prefemoral Gland location

Hip Joint

Flank

Lumbar Vertebra

Beef hindquarter – showing prefemoral gland location
Credit: Jakes & Associates

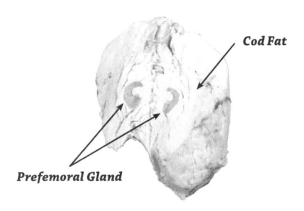

Cod Fat

Prefemoral Gland

Cod fat – showing prefemoral gland inside fat
Credit: Jakes & Associates

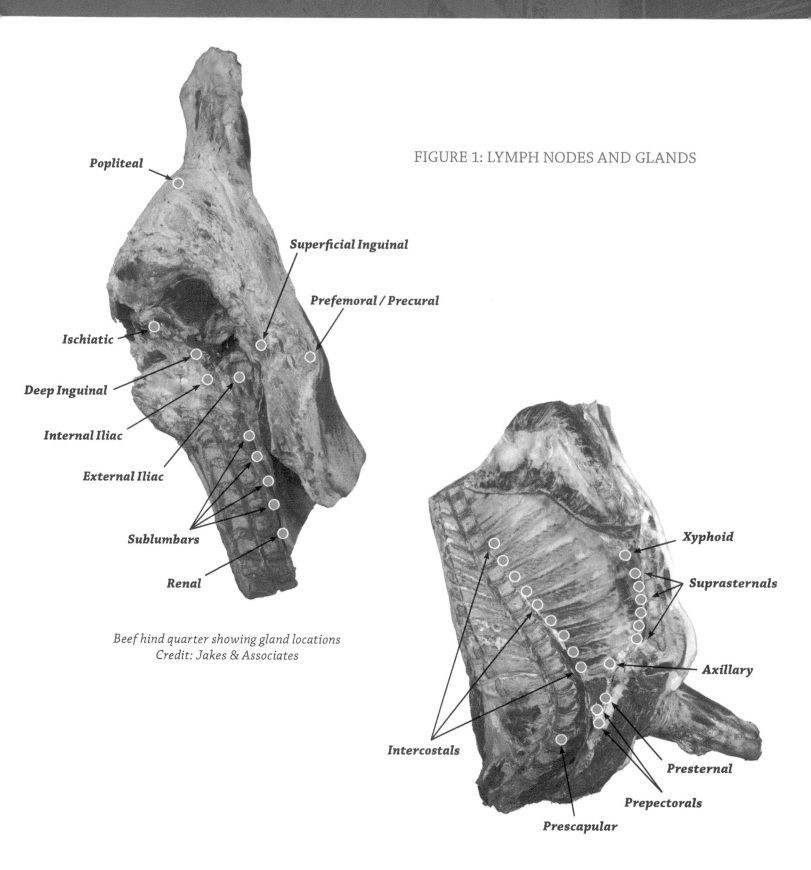

FIGURE 1: LYMPH NODES AND GLANDS

Popliteal

Superficial Inguinal

Prefemoral / Precural

Ischiatic

Deep Inguinal

Internal Iliac

External Iliac

Sublumbars

Renal

Beef hind quarter showing gland locations
Credit: Jakes & Associates

Xyphoid

Suprasternals

Axillary

Intercostals

Presternal

Prepectorals

Prescapular

Beef front quarter showing gland locations
Credit: Jakes & Associates

Note: Most of the smaller glands are visible on the carcass prior to processing however, the deeper set glands are not visible until that portion of the carcass where the gland is located is cut into retail cuts. It is the responsibility of the Meat Cutter to remove the glands to improve the appearance of the product.

Residues in Meat

The two major residues that are or have been used by the meat industry are both well documented and controversial because they are used to manipulate growth and development in animals. These residues are 1) **sub-therapeutic hormones** that produce more lean muscle and less fat, and 2) **antibiotics** used to maintain the health of the animals in mass-production operations.

Today the addition of these residues is strictly controlled and monitored by the government. Health Canada sets the standards for levels of hormones and antibiotics that can be left in food and regulates the use of hormones and antibiotics in Canada so that they do not pose a risk to the public. The Canadian Food Inspection Agency (CFIA) is responsible for the monitoring and testing of food products to ensure that they meet the regulatory requirements.

Hormones are a product of living cells that circulate in body fluids (such as blood) or sap. They produce a specific stimulatory effect on the activity of cells. Hormones are naturally occurring in all animals and plants, so when people discuss the use of hormones in food, they are usually referring to the addition of sub-therapeutic or **growth hormones** such as zeranol (synthetic estrogen), melengestrol acetate (synthetic progesterone) and trenbolone acetate (synthetic testosterone). The use of growth hormones has been illegal since the 1960s for poultry and pork produced in Canada as well as for dairy cattle. Growth hormones are still in use by some beef cattle producers, but the residue levels are carefully regulated and monitored.

Antibiotics are used to treat animals that are sick, manage and prevent disease in animals and fruit crops and promote the healthy growth of certain animals. In Canada antibiotics are approved for regulated use in beef, dairy cattle, chicken, laying hens, turkey, pork and fish.

Should a dairy cow be treated with antibiotics, its milk can be tested for antibiotic residues. Any milk testing positive for antibiotic residue is not sold for human consumption but is discarded. When poultry are treated with antibiotics, the eggs they lay are discarded.

As with hormones, the use of antibiotics is closely regulated, and food products are regularly tested to ensure compliance. In addition, there is a move to reduce the overall use of antibiotics in Canada, both in agriculture and for treating human disease due to the increase of antibiotic-resistant bacteria.

Naturally raised products in the last 25 years have seen a significant increase in consumer demand. Animals designated for the plates on our tables, meat and poultry products, are being scrutinized by consumers wanting an organic product; one that has been raised in a humane manner with no added growth hormones or antibiotics, and in the case of poultry, with access to the outdoors. From a health standpoint, consumers want to know more about the meat they purchase, and many smaller producers and processors now cater to a rapidly growing number of clients who desire meat and poultry that they are confident has come from a **"clean"** source. Of course there is no guarantee that naturally raised products are any safer or healthier than products deemed unnatural by consumers.

Beef cattle in a free-range location
Credit: Canada Beef

Lambs in a free-range location
Credit: Jay Springs Range

Pigs in a free-range location
Credit: Raven Ridge Farms

Products may be labelled as natural, free-range and/or organic, providing they meet the criteria set out by CFIA and their standards for organic production systems. When promoting products that are naturally raised in accordance with regulations as free of hormones and antibiotics, the following statement must be used: "No additional hormones or antibiotics." The word "additional" is required because all animals have natural hormones. Certified organic meats must meet strict requirements of the certifying bodies such as the Certified Organics Association of British Columbia, Alberta Organic Producers Association, Sask Organics, Organic Producers Association of Manitoba, Organic products Certification of Quebec and the Atlantic Canadian Organic Regional Network, which set standards for feed, pasture and humane treatment of animals that are certified organic in correlation to the Canadian Organic Standards.

The following is in accordance with CFIA definitions and regulations:

Free-range claims refer to chickens having access to regularly roam and graze outdoors. There are no specific requirements such as the length of time spent outdoors or the type of environment in order to use these claims.

Natural claims mean the food product or ingredient of the food product does not contain added vitamins, nutrients, artificial flavours or food additives. In addition, the product cannot have something removed from it (except for water) or have been significantly changed.

Organic claims and the organic logo are only permitted on products that have 95% or more organic content and have been certified according to Canadian requirements for organic products. An organic claim does not mean the food product has superior nutritional content or is safer than other

Chickens in a free-range location
Credit: Raven Ridge Farms

Turkeys in a free-range location
Credit: Raven Ridge Farms

food products. Organic products that are imported or sold between provinces or that bear the Canada Organic logo, must meet the Organic Standards, which state how animals can be housed, fed, transported and slaughtered and how crops can be grown, processed and stored. In addition, it dictates which substances such as pesticides, antibiotics and hormones can be used to prevent pests and diseases.

Nutrition

The basis for health is good quality food - a source of raw materials needed for the repair and functioning of the body. The idea of nourishing the body with nutrients is becoming more the norm as more and more people are becoming health conscious. There is, however, a big difference between being well-fed and being well-nourished. Sufficient calories will maintain weight, but in the absence of the fifty-odd nutrients needed, the human machine doesn't function at top-notch efficiency.

The human body is a dynamic organism. It is composed of cells, which are in turn, made of chemical compounds. These cells live and die and are constantly being replaced. In order for the body to replace its dying cells, the chemical compounds of which they are made must be present. Fortunately, the body can manufacture most of these compounds; those that cannot should be obtained in the diet. These compounds are called nutrients. Protein, carbohydrate, fat, vitamins and minerals are all nutrients required for the body to function. Some foods are better suppliers of nutrients than others.

Food is stored energy and is the fuel for the body. The amount of energy stored in food has traditionally been measured as Calories (with a capital "C") or kilocalories. These two terms are synonymous. With metric conversion, food energy is to be measured as kilojoules. There are 4.2 kilojoules in one Calorie (kilocalorie). For a rough estimate, divide kilojoules by four to give Calories (kilocalories). For example, in 4,000 kilojoules there are 1,000 Calories (kilocalories).

Food has three main sources of Calories: 1) Protein derived from meats, including seafood, dairy and plants (nuts, soy, etc.), 2) Carbohydrates, derived from starches and sugars. Carbs have two categories, simple (refined foods) and complex (unrefined foods), and, 3) Fat, supplying the essential fatty acid called linoleic acid found abundantly in oils. Fat is also a carrier of fat-soluble vitamins A, D, E and K. Fats are derived from fats and oils, meats, poultry, fish and dairy products.

CALORIES GUIDE: for each group of foods

Food list	Calories	Carbohydrate	Fat	Serving example	Volume
Vegetables	25	5 g		Raw vegetables Cooked vegetables	1 cup = 250 g ½ cup = 115 g
Fat-free & very low-fat milk	90			1% or fat free milk Low fat yoghurt	1 cup = 250 ml ¾ cup = 188 g
Very lean protein	35		1 g	Fish fillet, lean Cooked beans	1 oz = 28 g ½ cup = 125 g
Fruits	60	15 g		Fresh berries small apple or banana	1 cup = 100 g
Lean protein	55		2-3 g	Salmon or herring Chicken dark meat-skin off	1 oz = 28 g 1 oz = 28 g
Medium fat proteins	75		5 g	Beef Tofu	1 oz = 28 g 4 oz = 112 g
Starches	80	15 g		Cold cereal Cooked pasta	¾ cup = 188 g ½ cup = 125 g
Fats	45		5 g	Bacon Mayonnaise	1 slice 1 tsp = 15 g

Not all nutrients provide energy. While vitamins and minerals do not provide energy, protein, fat and carbohydrates do. The carbon and hydrogen in protein, fat and carbohydrates combine with oxygen from the air we breathe and produce energy and carbon dioxide. The amount of protein, carbohydrates and fat in food determines how much energy is available.

Meat plays a significant role in the Western diet. Meat is almost completely digestible and rates high on the nutritional scale as it contains high levels of **proteins**, consisting of amino acids. **Amino acids** fall under one of three groups: Essential (indispensable), Non-essential (dispensable), and Conditional (Table 4). Amino acids are organic compounds that combine to form proteins, and the two (amino acids and proteins) are the building blocks of life.

When proteins supplied in food are digested or broken down by the body, amino acids are left. The body then uses these amino acids to make proteins for the body to break down food, to grow, to make repair and to perform other body functions. In other words, amino acids are used as a source of energy by the body for the body.

The body cannot make essential amino acids; they need to be supplied on a daily basis by diet. However, the human body is capable of producing non-essential amino acids on its own. Meat and other animal proteins supplies all the essential amino acids required for the human body.

Essential	Non-essential	Conditional
Histidine	Alanine	Arginine
Isoleucine	Asparagine	Cysteine
Leucine	Aspartic acid	Glutamine
Lysine	Glutamic acid	Glycine
Methionine		Ornithine
Phenylalanine		Proline
Threonine		Tyrosine
Tryptophan		Serine
Valine		

Table 4: Amino Acids

Vitamins and minerals are dietary essentials, which are lumped together because they all contain carbon, do not provide energy and are needed in small amounts in the diet to regulate biological reactions. Aside from these characteristics, vitamins and minerals are totally unrelated. A substance can be a vitamin for one species yet not for another, depending on whether the animal's body can make the vitamin.

Meat is also rich in B complex **vitamins** such as thiamine, riboflavin and niacin, but the fat-soluble vitamins are not all found in meat. Minerals essential for the diet, with the exception of calcium, are found in meat, including phosphorus, iron, copper and trace minerals. (Tables 5, 6, & 7)

Vitamins are often grouped according to solubility, those dissolving in water and those dissolving in fat. There are 13 recognized vitamins: 4 fat-soluble and 9 water-soluble (Table 6).

The term minerals refer to elements such as iron that cannot be broken down into simpler compounds. They are inorganic (contain no carbon) substances, which are present in rock or soil and make-up about 4% of the body's weight. Of the sixty known minerals, about sixteen are known to be essential to humans (Table 7).

Meat, fish and poultry provide a variety of vitamins and minerals. The Health Canada website (www.hc-sc.gc.ca) and their food guide provide an overview of the most prominent nutrients supplied by meats.

Vitamins found in Meats and Meat Products	
Vitamins	**Source**
A	Certain oils, egg yolk, mammalian liver
D	Fresh liver oils (including that of fish) and fatty tissues
E	Green leafy veggies, animal organs (pituitary gland, adrenals, pancreas, spleen), milk, butter and abdominal fat
K	Green veggies, potatoes, fruits, live oils
Thiamine (B1)	Meat, liver and kidney
Riboflavin (B2)	Milk and meat
B6	Red meat, liver, kidney, brain, cod liver, egg yolk and milk
B12	Liver, kidney and egg yolk
Niacin	Liver and red meats
Pantothenic Acid	Liver, kidney, muscle, brain and egg yolk
Biotin	Liver, kidney, meat, egg yolk and milk
Folic Acid	Liver, kidney, muscle, milk and cheese

Table 5: Vitamins found in meats

Fat-soluble and Water-soluble Vitamins	
Fat-soluble	A, D, E and K.
Water-soluble	Thiamine, riboflavin, niacin, vitamin B6, folacin, vitamin B12, pantothenic acid, vitamin C, and biotin.

Table 6: Fat- and Water-soluble Vitamins

Minerals Present in the Human Body	
Relatively Large amounts	Calcium, phosphorus, potassium, sulphur, sodium, chlorine, magnesium.
Trace amounts	Iron, zinc, selenium, manganese, copper, iodine, molybdenum, chromium, fluorine.

Table 7: Minerals

CHOLESTEROL CONTENT OF MEAT

Molecules called lipoproteins carry cholesterol in the blood. Two important kinds of lipoproteins are low-density lipoprotein (LDL) and high-density lipoprotein (HDL). When checking your blood for the level of cholesterol, doctors include another type of fat called triglycerides. Total cholesterol count includes HDL, LDL and triglycerides.

- **LDL** makes up the majority of the body's cholesterol and is known as the "bad guy" as they lead to hardening of the arteries resulting in heart problems and stroke.
- **HDL** cholesterol absorbs other cholesterol and carries it back to the liver, which flushes it from the body. HDL is known as the "good guy" cholesterol. Having higher levels of HDL can reduce the risks of heart disease and stroke.
- **Triglycerides** are a type of fat found in the blood that the body uses for energy. The combination of high levels of triglycerides with low levels of HDL or high LDL can increase your risk of heart attack and stroke.

There is a perception that red meats are high in cholesterol, whereas other sources of protein (poultry/seafood) contain much lower quantities of cholesterol per serving. Charts (Table 8) which list the cholesterol content of meat and seafood indicate that red and white meats have very similar cholesterol contents, although some fish (e.g. cod, salmon) do have significantly less cholesterol content than meat (red and white). Check with the Canadian Food Guide to make sure you're getting the correct type and amount of recommended daily intake of foods containing cholesterol.

Meat Cookery

Meat Cookery refers to the cooking of meats to obtain a particular desired result using various heat applications. Any cookbook supplies a number of methods toward that end. However, skillful cooks know exactly how to employ the methods needed to produce the desired change in meat. We are not saying that after reading this portion of the chapter you'll be a skillful cook. That comes with experience, but we are advocating that after reading this content you should know what cooking does to meat.

As we know, meats are composed of water, protein and fat as well as small amounts of carbohydrates, vitamins, minerals and pigment and flavour elements. When meat is placed under a particular heat application (frying, broiling, braising or roasting, etc.), it changes colour, texture (structure) and appearance, not to mention flavour.

Food	Amount	Cholesterol (mg)
Oysters, Salmon	87 grams	40
Clams, Halibut, Tuna	87 grams	55
Poultry, Light Meat	87 grams	67
Beef & Pork	87 grams	75
Lamb, Veal & Crab	87 grams	85
Shrimp	87 grams	130
Lobster	87 grams	170
Kidney	87 grams	680
Liver	87 grams	370
Heart	87 grams	230
Egg	Each one	250

Table 8: Cholesterol in Meat

The protein molecules are in bonded cells, and as heat is applied, the bonds break and the coils start to unwind (the collagen, connective tissue and sarcoplasmic reticulum of myofibrils, etc.). As this takes place, the water content in the muscle fibres start to purge (evaporate), shrinking the product. If it's red meat, it starts to turn brown as the myoglobin reacts to the heat. The iron atoms in the protein lose an electron, gradually changing the colour from red to brown. White meat has far less myoglobin, and when cooked, the pale bluish/pinkish colour of the raw product turns white.

The following are useful points to remember about what happens to meats when heat is applied to it.

Water when boiled gets hot, produces steam and evaporates. Under heat, water not bonded in meat rises to the surface and evaporates, leaving the product less moist or dry.

Protein in meat coagulates (changes from raw to solid) when heated. The amount of coagulation depends on the amount of heat and cooking time. The firmer the coagulation, the more shrink the product experiences; more shrink means a tougher product. The addition of acidic additives such as lemon, tomato, etc., help breakdown and tenderize connective tissue protein under moist heat conditions.

Carbohydrates are found in small amounts in meats. They contain starches and sugars needed for caramelizing of meats. It's the carbs in meats that produce the grill marks on BBQ steaks known as the Maillard reaction.

Fats are an important cooking medium. Different types of fat have different melting points. Fat provides flavour, moisture and tenderness (marbling).

Collagen is converted from strong fibres to jelly (gelatin) by the action of moist heat application during cooking such as in the locomotion muscle of the animal (shanks and shoulder areas).

Cooking Methods

There are two primary methods of cooking meat. One is the "**dry**" heat application, and the other is "**moist**" heat application. The meaning of the term "**doneness**" depends on whether the cooking method uses dry or moist heat application. With the application of dry heat, meat is "done" when the proteins have reached the desired degree of coagulation as indicated by internal temperature (Table 9). The idea of dry heat application is to achieve a desired doneness while preserving natural juices and tenderness, whereas with the application of moist heat, meat is "done" when connective tissues have broken down enough for the meat to be palatable. And meat cooked using moist heat applications is always well done. Low temperature is key to avoiding toughness with moist heat application as doneness is determined by tenderness, not temperature.

Using the Meat Thermometer	
Meat Temperature	Degree of Roasting
50°C	Rare
55°C	Medium Rare
60°C	Medium
70°C	Well Done (Red Meat)
75°C	Well Done (Veal & Lamb)
85°C	Well Done (Pork)

Meat thermometer
Credit: Canada Beef

Table 9: Cooking Temperatures.

Dry Heat Applications are those in which heat is applied without moisture by hot air, hot metal, induction, radiation or hot fat. Dry heat applications are divided into two categories: without fat and with fat. Examples of dry heat application without fat are roasting, baking, broiling, grilling, griddling and pan-broiling. Examples of dry heat application with fat are pan-frying, sautéing, deep-frying and pressure frying.

Roasting & Baking. To "roast" and to "bake" means to cook using hot dry air as in an oven or a barbecue. Roasting usually applies primarily to meats and poultry while baking usually applies to fish. Roasted or baked meats are commonly cooked at

temperatures between 163°–177° C, in a preheated environment (oven or barbecue).

Prime rib roast
Credit: Canada Beef

Broiling. Broiling means to cook with radiant heat from above. Broiling uses radiant heat from an overhead source to cook. The best results for broiling are obtained if the temperature is 177° C.

Broiled steak
Credit: Canada Beef

Grilling, Griddling, and Pan-broiling are all dry heat cooking methods opposite to broiling in that they use heat from below.

Grilling is done on an open grid (rack) over a heat source that can be either charcoal, electric or gas.

Steak on a grill
Credit: Canada Beef

Griddle. Griddling is done on a solid surface, opposite to grilling.

Steak on a griddle
©istock.com / credit to Image Sourc

Pan-broiling. Pan-broiling is like griddling, cooking meat on a flat surface in a heated frying pan with no oil or lid.

Pan broiling a steak
Credit: Canada Beef

Sautéing is cooking small pieces of food by using high heat and a small amount of fat.

Tenderloin steaks sautéing in a Pan
©Darryl Brooks / Dreamstime

Pan-frying. Pan-frying means to cook in a moderate amount of fat over a moderate rate of heat.

Beef steaks frying in a pan
©Misha Belly / Dreamstime

Deep Fat Frying involves submerging meat into hot oil. Many foods (especially fish) are dipped in a breading or batter before frying. The best temperature for the oil is 177°C.

Fish cooking in a deep fat fryer
©istock.com / credit to kondor83

Moist Heat Applications are those in which heat is applied with moisture by poaching, simmering, boiling, steaming, blanching and braising. The temperature of the liquid determines the method. Sous vide and canning are also moist heat applications.

Poaching means to cook in liquid that is hot but not boiling. Poaching temperatures range in the area of 71 - 82°C.

Poached egg
© Seggey Milyanchikov / Dreamstime

Simmering. To simmer means to cook in a liquid that is gently bubbling. Simmering temperatures vary from 85 - 96°C.

Stew in a pot
©istock.com / credit to Lisovskaya

Boiling means to cook in liquid that is boiling or bubbling rapidly. Water boils at 100°C at sea level

Blanching means to very briefly and partially cook food in boiling water (or hot fat).

Steaming means to cook foods by exposing them directly to steam. Steaming can also mean cooking an item tightly wrapped or in a covered pan so that it cooks in the steam formed by its own moisture.

Braising means to cook covered in a small amount of liquid, usually after browning the product in a frying pan. In almost all cases, the liquid used in braising is served as part of the recipe, as with stews.

Sous vide means to cook food sealed in a container (plastic or foil bag or glass) in a temperature controlled water bath well below boiling point. This method doesn't expose meats to high levels of heat and prevents overcooking, as the product cannot get hotter than the preset water bath temperature (temp range is 55 – 60°C). Depending on the product and the desired outcome, cooking times can be as short as one hour or as long as 48 hours.

Sous vide machine
©Fedor Kondratenko

Canning means to preserve food by cooking it in an airtight sealed container (either tin, foil bag or glass), usually a pressure canner, though some still use the hot water bath. Temperature for canning is 100°C and must be maintained to control the growth of unwanted spoilage organisms inside the container. The canning of meats is popular with cuts of corned beef, ham, spam, meat spreads and seafood (tuna, salmon, crab, etc.).

Home canning cooker
©istock.com / credit to sarasang

Pressure cooker
©istock.com / credit to jgroup

Seasoning enhances the natural flavours of food without dramatically changing its taste; salt and pepper are the most common seasonings. The trick to seasoning foods is to season them at the beginning and during the cooking process, sampling and adjusting as you go along. Adding seasoning at the end (finished product) doesn't allow for the seasoning to blend in or be absorbed.

Flavouring adds new taste to a food and alters its natural flavours; flavourings include herbs, spices, vinegars and condiments. Flavouring ingredients can also be added at the beginning, middle or end of the cooking process. Most flavourings need heat to release their flavours and time for the flavours to blend, so it would be a good idea to know in advance what flavourings your recipe calls for and when to add them. An important factor to flavouring is time, the time of cooking.

Though there is a distinct difference between seasoning and flavouring, rightly or not, the two are most often used interchangeably. The thing to remember is that your main ingredient (meat, poultry or fish) is your main source of flavour, and any seasoning or flavouring you add enhances the interest of the natural flavour already there and does not mask it. Poorly prepared food cannot be rescued with last minute seasoning or flavouring.

MARINATING MEATS

Marinating means to soak meats in a seasoned liquid in order to, 1) flavour the meat, and 2) tenderize the meat. Marinades have three categories of ingredients: **oil, acid** and **flavour**. Oils help preserve the meat's moisture, acid (mostly from vinegars, lemons, tomatoes or wines) helps tenderize the meat and flavour (from herbs and spices) adds to the eating experience.

There are three types of marinades: cooked, raw and instant.

1. **Cooked marinades** have a longer shelf life (bottled), are tastier (tangy) and easier to use. The advantage of cooked marinades is that the spices release more flavour into the marinade when it's cooked. Most cooked marinades are used as rubs as with the barbecuing of ribs.
2. **Raw marinades** are used under refrigeration where the meats are soaked in the marinade and refrigerated for a period of time before cooking.
3. **Instant marinades** (prepackaged/premixed products) can be used instantly (no pun intended) or to marinate for several hours.

The basic guidelines to marinating are:

- marinate under refrigeration
- thicker portions require more time to marinate
- use acidic-resistant containers (not all plastics are)
- bagged (sacked) spices should be tied shut for easy removal
- cover meats completely with marinade

DRY METHODS OF COOKING

Grilling
Sauteing
Baking
Pan Frying
Pan Broiling
Deep Fat Frying
Oven Roasting
Broiling

MOIST METHODS OF COOKING

Pot Roasting
Stewing
Poaching
Braizing
Steaming
Boiling

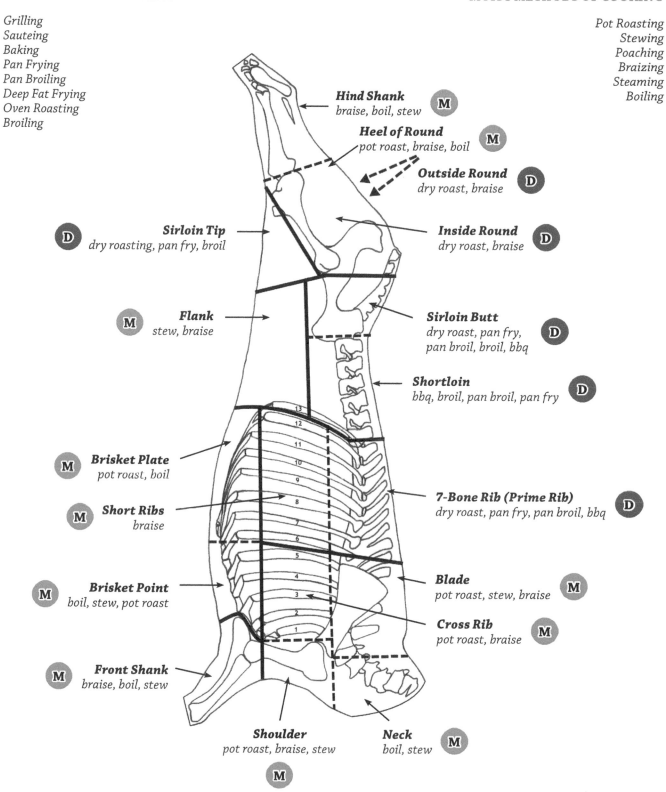

Hind Shank (M)
braise, boil, stew

Heel of Round (M)
pot roast, braise, boil

Outside Round (D)
dry roast, braise

Sirloin Tip (D)
dry roasting, pan fry, broil

Inside Round (D)
dry roast, braise

Flank (M)
stew, braise

Sirloin Butt (D)
dry roast, pan fry,
pan broil, broil, bbq

Shortloin (D)
bbq, broil, pan broil, pan fry

Brisket Plate (M)
pot roast, boil

Short Ribs (M)
braise

7-Bone Rib (Prime Rib) (D)
dry roast, pan fry, pan broil, bbq

Brisket Point (M)
boil, stew, pot roast

Blade (M)
pot roast, stew, braise

Cross Rib (M)
pot roast, braise

Front Shank (M)
braise, boil, stew

Shoulder (M)
pot roast, braise, stew

Neck (M)
boil, stew

Cooking methods guide for beef cuts
Credit: Jakes & Associates

COATINGS

Breading means to coat with breadcrumbs before deep-frying, pan-frying or sautéing. There is a set standard that has three stages to breading: flour, egg wash and crumbs.

- Flour helps the breading stick to the meat
- Egg washes give greater binding properties, and
- Crumbs create a crisp golden appearance

Coating meat with flour is known as "**dredging**." The purpose of dredging is to give an even thin coating of flour to the meat.

Batters are used in deep-frying to give a crisp and flavoured coating (crust). There are many types of batters and batter formulas. Many different liquids are used in batters, including milk, water or beer. Eggs may or may not be used.

SAUCES

A sauce is a seasoned and flavoured liquid, thickened and used to flavour foods. A sauce adds two qualities to food: moisture and flavour. Flavoured butters, salsa, relishes and pan gravies are examples of modern sauces. Classic hot sauces (not hot as in spicy) are divided into two groups: **basic** (known as mother sauces) and **derivative** (small compound sauces).

The structure of **basic** sauces are made of **three** kinds of **ingredients**:

- A liquid (the body of a sauce)
- A thickening agent (a starch)
- Seasoning and flavouring ingredients (salt, pepper, herbs and spices)

Basic sauces are made from one of **five liquid bases**:

- White stock (mainly chicken)
- Brown stock (mainly from beef stock)
- Milk
- Tomato (plus a stock)
- Clarified butter

Degree of Doneness

As meat cooks, the pigments change colour, and this change indicates the degree of doneness. During heat application the outer texture of red meats (like beef, bison or lamb) changes from its red colour to pink to grey while white meats (veal, pork and poultry) change from pink or grey-pink to white or off-white (Table 10).

Internal Colour Indicating Degree of Doneness			
Species	**Rare**	**Medium**	**Well Done**
Beef	Red	Pink	Grey
Bison	Red	Pink	Grey
Lamb	Red	Pink	Grey
Veal	Pink	Grey-Pink	Grey
Pork	Pink	Grey-Pink	Grey
Poultry	Pink	Grey-Pink	Grey

Table 10: Degree of Doneness

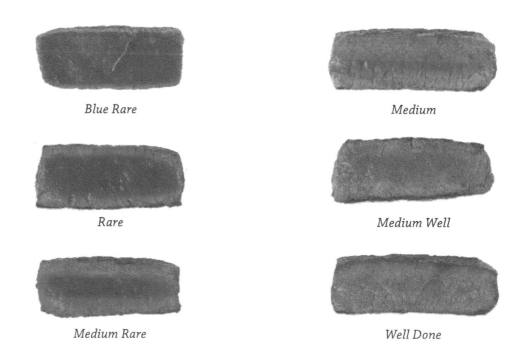

Blue Rare   *Medium*

Rare   *Medium Well*

Medium Rare   *Well Done*

Steak Doneness Chart
Credit: Canada Beef

SUMMARY

Aging	Collagen	Marinade
Amino Acids	Connective Tissue	Meat Colour
Antibiotics	Cross Bridges	Moist Heat
ATP	Doneness	Natural
Bloom	Dry Heat	Organic
Bone	Free-Range	Oxidization
Carbohydrates	Gristle	Protein
Cartilage	Hormones	Rigor Mortis
Cholesterol	Marbling	SRM

DISCUSSION QUESTIONS

1. Which two proteins regulate muscle contraction?

2. Acknowledging that too much fat or fatty meats are undesirable, why do we still say, "Fat is our friend"?

3. Skeletal structure is made of three components. What are they?

4. Explain the three stages of rigor mortis.

5. What does pH mean, and how is it measured?

6. What are the two methods used to age meats? Explain each.

7. Explain the difference between white meat and dark meat in poultry.

8. Which two proteins are associated with meat colour?

9. What is PSE and DFD, and how can they be avoided?

10. What function do lymph nodes and glands have?

11. What difference, if any, are there between natural, organic or free-range?

12. What are amino acids? Are they categorized? If so, list the categories and explain them.

13. Are there different types of cholesterol, and is cholesterol good for you?

14. Explain the differences between dry heat and moist heat applications.

15. What does the term "doneness" refer to?

Chapter 5

Bovine Meats

With the onslaught of technology, carcass animals are becoming increasingly difficult to obtain from the larger Meat Packing Plants. Most bovine carcass meats are now cry-o-vac'd in atmosphere controlled packaging and sold as: Block Ready, Knife Ready, or Counter Ready Meats. The main reason for this is marketing. Other benefits are an extended shelf life, handling, storage and shipment.

Major topics of this chapter cover the production and processing of bovine carcasses, the identification and characterisitics of primal and sub-primal cuts and the processing of sub-primal cuts into retail cuts of meat. Included are offals, grading and labelling requirements of each species. The chapter is a guide to the development of hands-on skills in the processing of bovine carcasses. Included is a collection of retail images charted in cutting sequence from primal to retail cuts.

Bovine Meats

History

While Bison are indigenous to our prairie provinces, cattle are not. Cattle were introduced to our landscape when the explorers and settlers first started arriving back as early as 1518. Jacques Cartier brought the first cattle to Quebec in 1541 when he equipped his settlement at Cap Rouge, just upstream of present day Quebec City. During those early years when explorers and settlers came to the new land, they brought with them cows and bulls in hope, that once settled, they could extend their herds; but the land was a little more hostile than first anticipated and both settlers and cattle didn't fare well. For the most part, during those early years of exploration, cattle were consumed for their meat. History shows initial attempts to breed and herd cattle in the new land failed, as the climate and terrain of our northern trading posts were not kind to them.

Perseverance finally paid off and early Canadian settlements raised cattle for food (dairy and meat) and hides. Cattle were one of the mainstays of mixed farming (as were other farm animals) that spread across the country with rural settlement, and ranching became particularly important in the rangelands of Western Canada where cattle began to flourish.

Some of the breeds introduced to Canada are the Angus and the Galloway from Scotland (1850's), the British Hereford (1860's), the Longhorn from southern United States (1860's) and the Shorthorn from Scotland (1825). During the late 1960s and throughout 1970s, a number of European breeds gained entry into Canada. From France came the Limousin, Blonde d' Aquitaine, Maine-Anjou and the Saler. From Germany we purchased the Gelbvieh. From Switzerland came the Simmental, and from the United States came the French breed, Charolais. Once acclimatized, these exotic breeds were bred and cross-bred for commercial purposes, beef.

According to the Canadian Beef Breeds Council, the following is a list of registered cattle breeds raised for their beef in Canada: Angus, Blonde d'Aquitaine, Braunvieh, Charolais, Dexter, Galloway, Gelbvieh, Hays Converter, Hereford, Limousin, Lowline, Maine-Anjou, Salers, Simmental and Speckle Park. The more common breeds in alphabetic order are as follows:

Angus steer
©Kiwimate / Dreamstime

Blonde d'Aquitaine steer
Credit: Canadian Blonde d'Aquitaine Association

Charolais steer
Credit: Canadian Charolais Association

- **Angus** is Canada's leading beef breed imported from Scotland in 1859. They can be black or red, extremely fertile, naturally polled (no horns), easy to keep, stay healthy for fourteen plus years and as a product it has proven tenderness and consumer's acceptance with over 150 years in beef production. Angus bulls average out to just over 1,000 kilograms while the cows average out to just less than 600 kilograms.

- **Blonde d'Aquitaine** arrived in Canada in the early 1970s from France. They are known to be thin-boned, well muscled and have high yielding carcasses. Mature bulls average out to be 1,100 kilograms with females averaging out to between 700 - 800 kilograms.

- **Charolais** is originally from France and one of their oldest breeds. They were imported form the United States in 1956. This breed has been proven to be highly adaptable to the Canadian climate and terrain, has a polled strain, grow rapidly and produces lean, high yielding carcasses. Mature bulls average out to 1,100 kilograms while cows average to just over 700 kilograms.

- **Gelbvieh,** imported from Germany in 1972, are of moderate size, docile, fertile and used for cross-breeding programs. They have lean/muscular carcasses and impressive feed efficiency (conversion of beef to muscle).

Gelbvieh steer
Credit: Gelbvieh, Tasmania

- **Hereford,** were brought over from England in 1860. They are one of the oldest and numerous beef cattle breeds in Canada. They are hardy animals with a high growth rate and well-defined beef characteristics. Herefords are leaders in docility, resulting in lower production costs and better meat quality. Mature bulls average out to be approximately 1,000 kilograms with cows averaging 700 kilograms.

Hereford steer
©Phillip Minnis / Dreamstime

- **Limousin,** imported into Canada in 1969 from France, have proven to be the top breed for feed conversion. They have superior muscle and are uniform in size and colour.

Limousin steer
Credit: Canadian Limousin Association

- **Simmental** was imported from Switzerland in 1969. It has become one of the nation's most influential breeds, has outstanding growth and performance records, is docile, profitable and has superior carcass characteristics. This breed is large-framed and muscular with excellent maternal and beef characteristics. The mature bull averages out to be 1,200 -1,300 kilograms in weight, with females averaging just over 700 kilograms. Simmentals are the breed of choice for cross-breeding programs.

Simmental heifer
©istock.com / credit to Frizi

The Red Meat Industry

The Department of Agriculture and Agri-Food Canada reports regularly on the red meat industry, which includes beef and veal, pork, lamb and mutton, goat, rabbit, horse as well as venison and bison. According to Agriculture and Agri-Food Canada statistics, the red meat industry had annual shipments worth 19.4 billion dollars in 2015. In this chapter we concentrate on the red meat of bovine: beef, veal and bison.

BEEF

The Canadian Cattlemen's Association boasts that Canada is one of the largest exporters of red meat and livestock in the world, exporting around 45% of Canadian beef and cattle production each year. According to the Canadian government, in 2015 there were 11.92 million cattle and calves on approximately 82,240 Canadian farms and ranches. Alberta accounts for approximately 41% of this inventory. Farm cash receipts from the sale of cattle and calves in 2014 totalled 9.8 billion dollars. The Canadian beef industry ships to fifty-six countries but is reliant on the United States for 75% of all beef exports. The next largest export markets are mainland China and Hong Kong (8%), Japan (6%), Mexico (4%) and South Korea (2%) accounting for 96% of total export volumes with all other markets taking up the remaining 4%.

VEAL

For the most part veal farming is a by-product of the dairy industry. Dairy cows must be impregnated annually to continue producing milk. About half of their calves are males designated for either beef or veal production. It should be noted that not all female dairy calves are raised as future milk producers; most of these are also designated for beef or veal production. The provinces that produce the most veal for market are Ontario and Quebec. The provinces with the highest calf populations are Alberta and Saskatchewan with 61% of the Canadian calf inventory, which is approximately 4 million head.

BISON

There are two breeds of bison, Wood Bison and Plains Bison. The Wood Bison dominated Northern Canada and the Plains Bison the prairie provinces of Alberta, Saskatchewan and Manitoba as well as parts of the Yukon. Back in the day, it is estimated there were as many as thirty million bison roaming the Great Plains of North America. Hunting, industrialization and westward migration of people and their animals brought about the demise of the bison. By the nineteenth century bison were nearly extinct, making their rangelands available to settlers and cattle ranchers alike. Only in the last thirty years has there been a concerted effort to bring back bison populations to a sustainable level and to the point where some ranchers now raise them as food animals.

Agriculture and Agri-food Canada's report in 2014 states that there were 125,142 head of bison on about 1,211 farms in Canada. The majority of bison are concentrated in the west with 77% of the herd concentration in Alberta and Saskatchewan. Exports of bison meat are primarily to the United States, but boneless product is also shipped to countries in Europe, most notably France, Germany and Switzerland. Bison raised for their meat are ready for harvesting between twenty and thirty months of age. Domestically, bison are sold at premium due to the demand from other global markets. Anatomically, bison is comparable in quality to beef and is handled from a retailing perspective in similar fashion. The main differences between bison and beef are feed, size and flavour, with bison having a milder, juicier and sweeter taste. Though bison are now herded and farmed on the lands that were once native to them, they are still considered to be wild and not yet domesticated.

Bovine health and wellness falls into the arm of the Canadian Food Inspection Agency (CFIA), which is responsible for all federal inspection programs related to the feed production for cattle, animal health and processing of cattle, bison, veal as well as plant safeguards such as HACCP.

All federal Canadian meat plant harvesting facilities are strictly monitored by CFIA, and all provincial meat plant harvesting facilities are strictly monitored by provincial inspection, including animal handling protocols and HACCP plans for all aspects of animal care and humane slaughter.

TRACEABILITY

Federal, provincial and territorial governments in partnership with industry are working together through the Industry Government Advisory Committee (IGAC) in establishing an effective and sustainable livestock traceability system in Canada.

Livestock traceability systems in Canada are built on three basic elements: 1) animal identification, 2) premise identification, and 3) movement reporting. Animal identification for cattle (including calves) and bison is mandatory in Canada. These programs are regulated and enforced by the CFIA.

Leading the charge for the traceability of cattle is the Canadian Cattle Identification Agency (CCIA), a non-profit group. CCIA is an industry led organization established to promote and protect animal health and food safety concerns in the Canadian cattle herd. As of July 1, 2010, in addition to premises location allocator identification number (PID), all cattle are

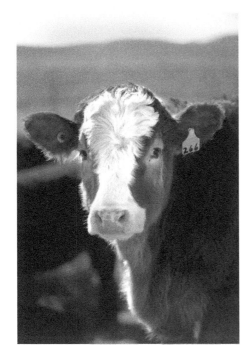

PID & RFID tags on a beef animal
Credit: Canada beef

tagged with an approved Radio Frequency Identification (RFID). The combined PID and RFID tags hold valuable information about the animal: its age, health, origin, breed and movement.

The bison identification program is a Canadian Bison Association initiated industry program. The bison traceability system is operated in conjunction with the CCIA system. All bison leaving their herd of origin are tagged with an approved RFID. Bison RFID tags are part of a number sequence allocated to bison and are white in colour. These white coloured tags can only be purchased from the Canadian Bison Association.

Beef Production

Beef cattle production has three stages: 1) cow-calf operations that produce weaned calves, 2) stocker operations that feed calves to maturity, and 3) finishing operations that feed cattle intensively for the purpose of reaching animal harvest weight. These three stages can operate separately or can be combined on a single farm. Most large-scale farms specialize in just one of the three stages as with feedlots.

Cow-Calf operations maintain a breeding herd of beef cows and oversee their reproduction. According to Canfax, Canada's beef-cow herd is estimated to be approximately five million head. Herds range in size from five to ten cows on small farms to several hundred, even thousands, on large ranches. Herds can consist of a specific breed or cross-breeds suited to specific demographics, needs or demand. In each case quality traits are assessed and evaluated regarding mothering, calving (birthing), milk production, temperament, etc.

Breeding takes place in summer when cows in pasture are exposed to bulls for a period of one to two months. Unlike dairy production, which relies on artificial insemination, most cow-calf operations use live bulls to detect cows that are in heat and ready to mate. Calving takes place from February to March and each calf is marked with a PID and RFID tag. In late spring, the cow-calf pairs are rounded up and separated (weaned). If need be, calves are polled (dehorned), the males castrated, vaccinated and depending on the size and type of cow-calf operation, an artificial hormone pellet is implanted in the ear to stimulate growth. Larger operations will separate pregnant yearlings and heifer calves for breeding the next spring. Both steers and heifers calves may be sold to stocker operations.

Stocker operations specialize in getting calves ready for finishing. Their focus is on maximizing skeletal structure and muscle growth before moving the animals to the feedlot stage. Stocker operations require large sustainable pastures for summertime grazing and wintertime feeding.

Finishing operations is the final step in the maturity of calf-to-cow life cycle. Finishing operations live up to their name. They finish cattle with a nutritious mix of feed designed to put on weight by building bone and muscle for marketing purposes. This stage is known as the end of the road for cattle. After finishing operations are complete, meaning the cattle have reached the desired weight and muscle gain, the cattle are sent to the harvesting facility; from there they become known as and are processed as beef.

Beef Processing

In 1991, CFIA developed the Food Safety Enhancement Program (FSEP) in order to promote and support development, implementation and maintenance of HACCP systems in all food processing plants. FSEP started as a voluntary program, but in November 2005 it became mandatory for all federally registered meat and poultry abattoirs, processing plants and storage facilities in Canada.

Working Conditions: To maintain product quality and shelf life, meat cutting and packing is performed at temperatures at or below 4° Celsius. The work requires skill and knowledge in proper cutting techniques and the use of equipment designed to make working easier, safer and more efficient. It also requires physical strength and endurance to maintain demanded productivity levels.

Continuous improvement of plant production processes and vigilant enforcement of safety regulations contribute to ever-increasing levels of employee safety and the elimination of any repetitive motion injuries. On-site health care, ergonomic training sessions and job task rotation assist employees and managers remain up to date on the latest techniques and tools available to minimize work-related injuries.

Inspection & Grading

Federal meat inspection is carried out by the CFIA. Meat shipped from province to province or exported out of country must be federally inspected. The remainder is subject to provincial inspection, which is similar to the federal system of inspection. Inspection is a guarantee of wholesomeness, not quality or tenderness. Inspected meats assures us the product(s) are fit for human consumption, are clean and free of disease causing organisms as indicated by an inspection stamp.

The Canadian Beef Grading Agency (CBGA), a private non-profit corporation, carries out the grading of beef in Canada. The CBGA is accredited by the CFIA to deliver grading services for beef in Canada. The grade standards are set by the Federal Government based on recommendations from the Industry/Government Consultative Committee on Beef Grading. Unlike inspection, the grading of beef is voluntary and not required by law.

Grading is intended to place carcasses into uniform categories of similar quality, yield and value in order to facilitate marketing and production decisions. Grading may be used as a basis for producer settlement, but its main focus is marketing. Grading is intended to ensure that consumers have consistency and predictability in the eating quality.

Federal Inspection stamp

Example of a Provincial Inspection stamp
Credit: CPMCA image collection

BEEF GRADES

There are thirteen beef grades in Canada. The four top grades start with Canada Prime, then Canada AAA, Canada AA and Canada A, all from young animals and indicated by a red stamp. About 90% of all graded beef carcasses fall within the top four grades, and all major retailers carry one or more of them. The top four grades are also stamped with a yield stamp indicating the ratio of lean useable meat to fat and bone (Table 1: Yields).

Prime and A grade Yields	
Canada 1	59% or more lean useable meat
Canada 2	54-58% lean useable meat
Canada 3	53% or less lean useable meat

Table 1

Canada AAA stamp & yield 1 stamp
Credit: Canada Beef

Note: For more on beef harvesting, inspection and grading refer to Chapter 12.

Canadian Beef Primal Cuts

Beef is derived from dressed carcasses of bovine animals having a warm weight of 160 kg or more. Beef may be derived from male or female animals or from steers (a castrated male). Dressed beef carcasses are beef carcasses from which the skin, head, developed mammary glands and feet at the carpal and tarsal joints have been removed and the carcass has been eviscerated and split into two equal sides. Sides of beef refer to one of the two approximately equal portions of the dressed beef carcass obtained by cutting (splitting) from the tail to the neck along the median line (centre of the spine). For transport purposes and ease of handling, sides of beef are further portioned into front and hind quarters. The Front Quarter refers to the anterior portion of the beef side, which is separated from the hind quarter by a cut passing between the twelfth and thirteenth rib, and the Hind Quarter refers to the posterior portion of the side of beef, which is separated from the front quarter as described, between the twelfth and thirteenth rib.

According to the CFIA Meat Cuts Manual for beef, there are seven or alternatively eight primal cuts: Chuck (or Square Cut Chuck), Rib (or Rib Section), Full Brisket (or alternatively split into Plate and Brisket), Shank, Flank, Loin, and Hip.

Note: As with all Primal and Sub Primal Cuts, where there is more than one identifier used (i.e. name in brackets) either use is acceptable as they mean and refer to one and the same cut of meat. For example, the Primal cut "Chuck" can also be called a "Square Cut Chuck" or as with the term "Loin" is also synonymous with the term "Long Loin."

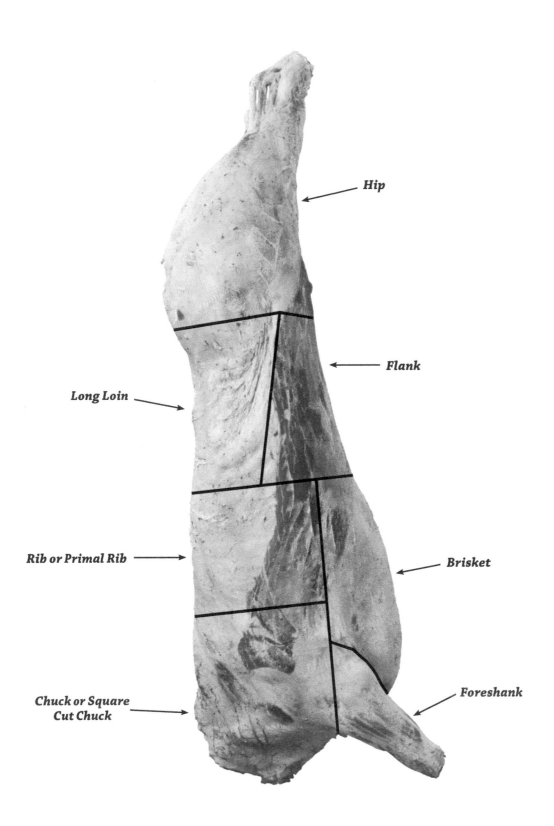

Hip

Flank

Long Loin

Rib or Primal Rib

Brisket

Chuck or Square
Cut Chuck

Foreshank

Beef side primal cuts
Credit: Canada Beef

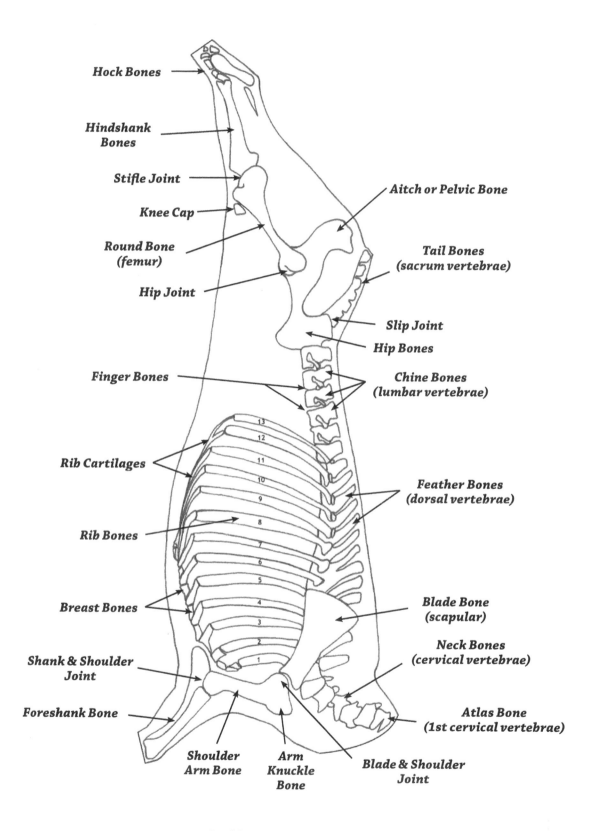

Hock Bones

Hindshank Bones

Stifle Joint

Knee Cap

Round Bone (femur)

Hip Joint

Aitch or Pelvic Bone

Tail Bones (sacrum vertebrae)

Slip Joint

Hip Bones

Finger Bones

Chine Bones (lumbar vertebrae)

Rib Cartilages

Feather Bones (dorsal vertebrae)

Rib Bones

Breast Bones

Blade Bone (scapular)

Neck Bones (cervical vertebrae)

Shank & Shoulder Joint

Foreshank Bone

Atlas Bone (1st cervical vertebrae)

Shoulder Arm Bone

Arm Knuckle Bone

Blade & Shoulder Joint

13
12
11
10
9
8
7
6
5
4
3
2
1

Beef Carcass Bone Structure
Credit: Jakes & Associates

- **Chuck (or Square Cut Chuck)** means that portion of the **Front Quarter**, which is separated, from the **Rib**, **Plate**, **Brisket** and **Shank** by two (2) straight cuts at right angle to each other. The first cut passes between the 5th and 6th rib and separates the **Chuck**, **Brisket** and **Shank** from the **Rib** and **Plate**. The second cut passes at a point slightly above (dorsal to) the elbow joint (distal extremity of the humerus) and through the cartilaginous juncture of the first (1st) rib and sternum, and separates the **Chuck** from the **Brisket** and **Shank**.

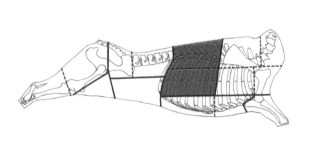 

- **Rib (or Primal Rib):** means that portion of the **Front Quarter** which is separated from the **Chuck** and **Brisket** by a straight cut passing between the 5th and 6th rib and from the **Plate** by a straight cut passing across the ribs at right angles to the first cut, at a point slightly below (ventral to) the centre of the rib cage.

Note: This cut includes seven (7) ribs (6th to 12th inclusive) and may contain a small portion of the blade bone (scapula) and cartilage. It should not be confused with **Prime Rib**, which includes 6 ribs (7th to12th).

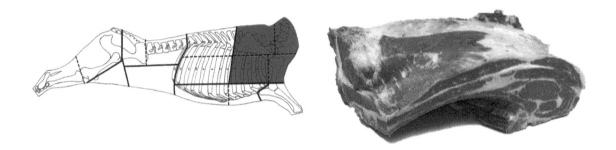

- **Plate (or Brisket Plate alternative):** means that portion of the **Front Quarter** which is separated from the **Chuck** and **Brisket** by a straight cut passing between the 5th and 6th rib and from the **Rib** by a straight cut passing across the ribs at right angles to the first cut at a point slightly below (ventral to) the centre of the rib cage.

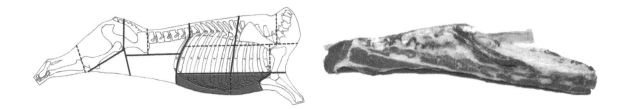

- **Brisket (or Brisket Point alternative):** means that portion of the **Front Quarter** which is separated from the **Plate** by a straight cut passing between the 5th and 6th rib, from the **Chuck** by a cut at a right angle to the first cut, passing at a point slightly above (dorsal to) the elbow joint (distal extremity of the humerus) and from the **Shank** by a cut which follows the natural contour of the elbow bone (olecranon process of the ulna).
- **Full Brisket:** refers to the portion containing both the **Brisket** and **Plate**.
- **Shank (or Foreshank):** means that portion of the **Front Quarter** which is separated from the **Chuck** by a cut passing at a point slightly above (dorsal to) the elbow joint (distal extremity of the humerus) and from the **Brisket** by a cut which follows the natural seam of the elbow bone (olecranon process of the ulna).

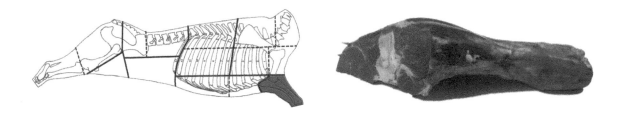

- **Flank:** means that portion of the **Hind Quarter** which is separated from the **Loin** by a straight cut passing approximately parallel to the lumbar back bones (lumbar vertebrae), beginning in close proximity to or through the flank lymph node (prefemoral) and from the **Plate** by a cut passing between the 12th and 13th rib and cartilage.

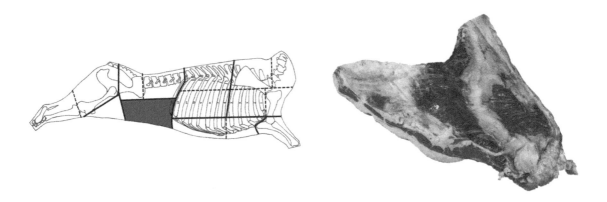

- **Loin (or Long Loin):** means that portion of the **Hind Quarter** which is separated from the **Flank** as described in item 5.1, from the **Sirloin Tip** (see 5.3.5) and from the **Hip** by a cut which passes in front of (anterior to) the rump knuckle bone (head of the femur/acetabulum), thereby cutting the pelvic bone (os coxae) into approximately two equal parts.

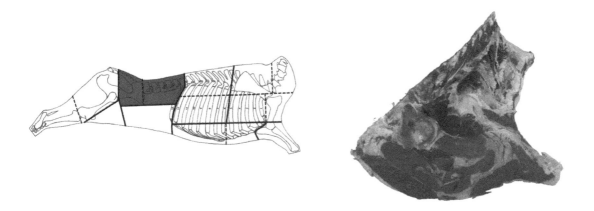

- **Hip:** means that portion of the **Hind Quarter** which is separated from the **Loin** by a straight cut which passes in front of (anterior to) the rump knuckle bone (head of the femur/acetabulum), thereby cutting the pelvic bone (os coxae) into approximately two (2) equal parts known as the Pin Bone in the Loin primal cut and Aitch Bone in the Hip.

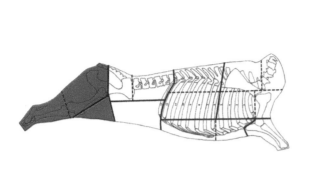

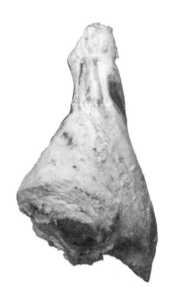

Sub-Primal & Retail Cuts

Sub-primal cuts are derived from primal cuts. The primal cuts of beef can and are usually further processed into sub-primal cuts for ease of handling and storage. This further processing can be done either at plant level or store level depending on the nature of the operation. Some retail outlets still prefer to break quarters of beef to better suit the needs of their operation and the consumer demand for in-house fabricated cuts. Primal cuts are broken into sub-primal cuts for later use. The sub-primal cuts are then further processed or fabricated into retail cuts. The CFIA Meat Manual identifies several sub-primal possibilities for each of the primal cuts of beef.

The sub-primal cuts of the **Square Cut Chuck (or Chuck)** are: Shoulder Clod, Top Blade, Top Blade Portion, Blade, Bottom blade, Neck, Cross Rib, Shoulder (or Shoulder Arm), and Chuck Short Ribs.

- **Shoulder Clod:** means that large muscle mass of the **Chuck** which lies outside (lateral side) of the blade bone and ventral to the ridge of the blade bone, extending from the shoulder joint to the tip of the blade bone cartilage. It is obtained by two (2) main straight cuts approximately parallel to each other. The first cut passes along the ventral side of the ridge of the blade bone and the other over the ribs. The **Shoulder Clod** is the largest, leanest muscle of the Square Cut Chuck. It is also the main muscle found in the **Cross Rib**. Classic cuts are boneless cross rib roast and boneless cross rib simmering steaks.

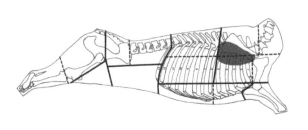

- **Top Blade:** means the portion of the **Shoulder Clod,** including the muscles infraspinatus (known as the **Flat Iron**), triceps brachii and deltoideus found outside (lateral side) of the blade bone (scapula). In recent years, the flat iron portion of the chuck is tender enough to be retailed as a grilling steak. There is a layer of collagen running in the middle of this muscle that a retailer needs to be aware of.

- **Top Blade Portion:** means that large round cylindrical V- shaped muscle (supra-spinatus, also known as the **Mock Tender**) of the **Blade** which lies outside (lateral of side) of the blade bone (scapula) and dorsal to the ridge of the blade bone or the infraspinatus muscle which lies outside of the blade bone and ventral to the ridge of the blade bone. They are separated from the blade bone and adjacent muscles through natural seams. This muscle is retailed as stewing beef, and pot roast, and is tender enough as top blade cutlets, top blade stir-fry, and marinated or tenderized top blade kabobs.

- **Blade:** means that portion of the **Chuck** which is separated from the **Neck, Cross Rib** and **Shoulder** by two (2) straight cuts at right angles to each other. The first cut passes at a point slightly in front of (anterior to) the shoulder joint and the anterior tip of the blade bone (scapula), thereby separating the **Neck** and **Shoulder** from the **Blade** and **Cross Rib**. The second cut passes through the interior edge of the seventh (7th) neck bone (cervical vertebra) and through the blade bone (scapula) separating the **Neck** from the **Shoulder** and the **Blade** from the **Cross- Rib**. At one time this cut was fabricated into chuck steaks but today is muscle seamed, deboned, and further retailed as chuck blade boneless items such as braising steaks and slow roasting or pot roasts.

Note: The blade may contain small portions of the 5th and 6th neck bones (cervical vertebrae).

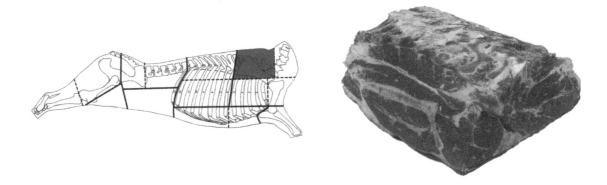

- **Bottom Blade (Inside Blade):** means the portion of the **Blade** located inside (medial side) of the blade bone (scapula), including the muscles teres major, subscapularis and serratus ventralis. The bottom blade can be retailed as a bottom blade roast (slow roasting or pot), bottom blade braising steak, or further cut for stewing beef and lean ground beef.
- **Neck:** means that portion of the **Chuck** that is separated from the **Blade, Cross Rib** and **Shoulder** as described above. The neck is very tough and is used for trimmings; for either stewing meat or ground meats.

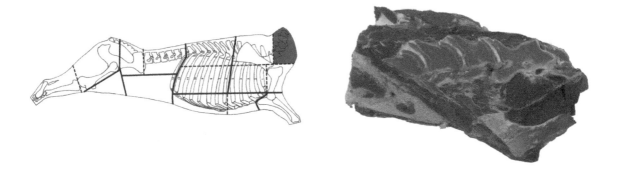

- **Cross Rib:** means that portion of the **Chuck** separated, from the **Blade, Neck** and **Shoulder** as described above. The cross rib can be versatile as it contains most of the shoulder clod. Traditionally the cross rib was retailed as a bone-in item, and now outside of custom cutting operations there is little demand for it. Today the cross rib is commonly fabricated boneless, offering the retailer more merchandising options.

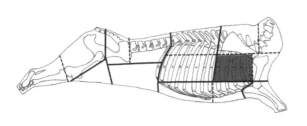

- **Shoulder (or Shoulder Arm):** means that portion of the **Chuck** separated from the **Cross Rib**, **Blade** and **Neck.** It used to be that the shoulder arm was cut and trimmed as a braising roast, but now it is rarely used for anything other than stewing beef or ground beef.

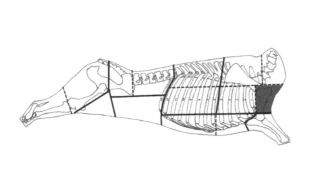

- **Chuck Short Rib:** is an alternative portion of the **Chuck**. It is separated from the **Neck** and **Shoulder** and from the **Blade** by a straight cut passing on the superior edge of the body of the 7th neck bone (cervical vertebra) and through the middle of the blade bone (scapula) and from the **Cross Rib** by a straight cut passing below (ventral to) the anterior tip of the blade bone (scapula) and in proximity to the shoulder joint. In simple language, retailers know this cut as the cross rib cap (beef ribs). It can be retailed as a marinated item, braising item, or as short ribs. The chuck short rib falls under the category of comfort food (slow cookery).

  Note: The **Blade** and **Cross Rib** portions resulting from the removal of the **Chuck Short Rib** are alternative portions of the **Chuck**. The sub-primal cuts of the **Rib (Primal Rib)** are: Rib Eye, Boneless Rib, Short Ribs, and Prime Rib.

- **Rib Eye:** means that boneless portion of the **Rib** containing the large round-shaped muscle (longissimus dorsi) located at the vertebral end of the ribs. It may contain the closely adjacent muscle, spinalis dorsi (and most always does). The rib eye can be cut into grilling steaks. Rib eye steak is a popular BBQ steak. At times you might see this item sold whole or in large chunks as a roast, but its main resolve is steaks. We have seen the rib eye steak sold as rib eye lip-on because the complexus muscle (commonly referred to as the lip) is still attached.

Note: The term **Boneless Rib** should be used if any other muscles are present.

- **Short Ribs (Short Braising Ribs):** is the rib end portion of the **Rib** and **Plate** obtained by making a straight cut parallel and adjacent to the cut which separates the **Rib** from the **Plate**. Short ribs fall in the category of comfort food. When they are sliced thinly (1/2 inch width), they can be marinated and seasoned for BBQ use. They can also be sold boneless. In short (no pun intended), this is a braising item.

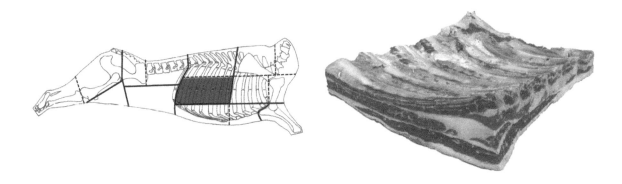

Note: **Short Ribs** contain no rib cartilage (costal cartilage).

- **Prime Rib:** is an alternative portion of the **Rib** and refers to the portion containing the posterior six (6) ribs of the 7 bone **Standing Rib** (7th to 12th inclusive). Prime rib has excellent utility and a strong following among cooks, BBQ enthusiasts, and consumers. This cut can be well marbled, has good fat cover, and is tender as a prime rib roast or prime rib grilling steaks. Classic cuts are: prime rib roast, oven ready prime rib (bones removed), prime rib roast cap off, rib eye roll, prime rib steak, rib grilling steak cap removed and beef grilling ribs (also referred to as beef grilling back ribs).

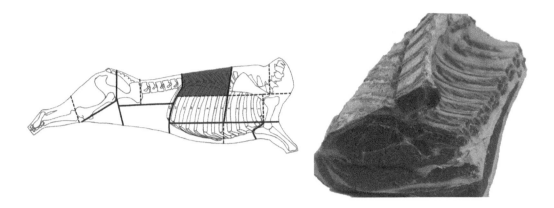

There are no further sub-primal cuts for the **Brisket Plate, Brisket Point, Full Brisket, Shank or Foreshank**, and **Flank**; however, these primal cuts are fabricated into retail meat cuts as follows:

- **Brisket Plate** is almost always used for trim, and trimmings of beef can be utilized for various other items from meatballs to ground beef. It used to be the boneless plate was wrapped around the boneless brisket point and sold as a boned and rolled brisket. Some independent retailers even made that item into corned beef. Today most corned Beef is made strictly from boneless brisket points.

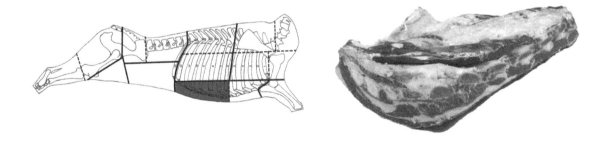

- **Brisket Point** is deboned, trimmed, and sold whole or cut into manageable portions. With today's craze around BBQ meats, brisket points have become somewhat of a celebrity of preferred BBQ cuts. The brisket point can also be used for other braising items like boneless brisket pot roasts.

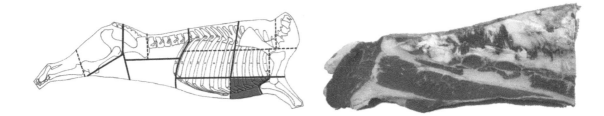

- **Shank** is an item strictly for braising unless deboned for lean trim. The amount of collagen in this primal is attractive to customers who enjoy comfort foods (slow cooked or braised meats).

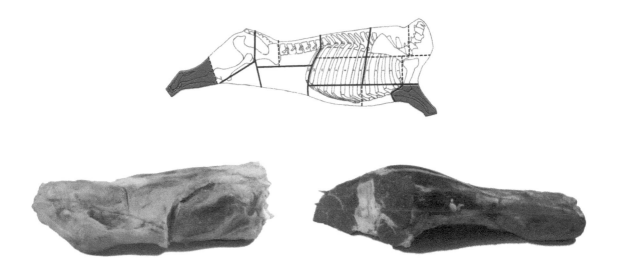

- **Flank** has the flank steak located on the inside of the primal on top of the cod fat containing the flank lymph node (prefemoral). The flank steak is retailed whole or fabricated into a flank steak, London broil, by sending it once through the tenderizer and layering thin slices of the cod fat on one side then rolling it into a cylinder shape, producing a pin wheel appearance when cut. The main marbled muscle running parallel to the flank steak is also retailed as either stewing meat or as steak tails (known in the restaurant industry as flank skirt).

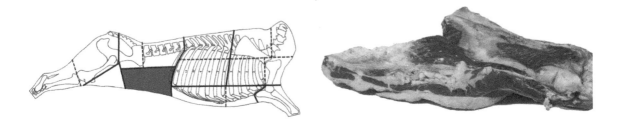

The sub-primal cuts of the **Loin** are: Short Loin, Porterhouse, T-bone, Wing, Tenderloin, Strip Loin, Sirloin, Sirloin Tenderloin Removed, Top Sirloin, Bottom Sirloin, and Sirloin Cap.

- **Short Loin:** means the anterior portion of the **Loin** which is separated from the **Sirloin** by a straight cut which passes at a point immediately in front of (anterior to) the pin bone (ilium or tuber coxae). This cut is most common to Block Ready Beef, where for ease of handling and storage it is vacuum packaged, labelled, and crated for shipment. From this sub-primal we get the grilling steaks porterhouse, T-bone, and wing.

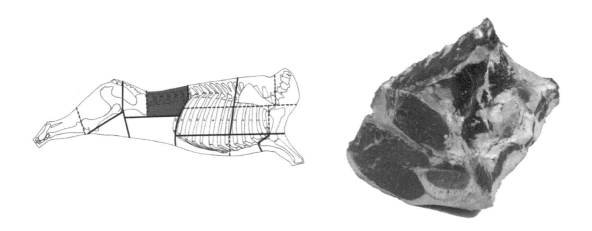

- **Porterhouse:** means that portion of the **Short Loin** which is separated from the **T-bone** by a straight cut passing immediately in front of (anterior to) the tip of the gluteus medius muscle and approximately through the centre of the body of the 4th lumbar vertebra. Porterhouse steaks are large in size and have as a characteristic the gluteus medius muscle. If there is no evidence of the gluteus medius muscle on a Porterhouse steak, then it is to be referred to as a T-bone.

Note: **Porterhouse** may also be referred to as **T-bone**, yet **T-bone**, as described, may not be referred to as porterhouse.

- **T-bone:** means that portion of the **Short Loin** which is separated from the **Porterhouse** and from the **Wing** by a cut passing approximately through the centre of the body of the 1st lumbar vertebra and along the back (posterior) side of the last rib (13th rib). T-bone steaks have been a main stay of the loin cuts for many years. T-bones are becoming harder to find (as with porterhouse steaks) due to their size. Consumers of today are looking for smaller portions with similar characteristics involving tenderness and marbling.
- **Wing:** means that portion of the **Short Loin** separated from the **T-bone**. It includes the 13th rib or part thereof. Wing steaks are a rarity and most commonly fabricated into strip loin steaks.
- **Tenderloin:** means the cylindrically shaped main muscle (psoas major and minor) located on the inside (ventral side) of the **Loin**. Tenderloin is cleaned of fat and silverskin and cut into portions or sold whole. The tapered ends can be butterflied to present a larger surface for presentation purposes.
- **Strip Loin, Bone-in (Shell Loin):** means that portion of the **Short Loin** from which the tenderloin has been removed. It contains portions of the abdominal muscles: obliquus abdominis externus,; obliquus abdominis internus;, transversus abdominis and loin muscles,; gluteus medius;, longissimus dorsi; and multifidus dorsi, or portions thereof. This item is rare and not normally retailed, but if it is, the classic cut will be called bone- in strip loin grilling steaks.

Note: This primal can be called strip loin, bone- in or shell loin as each is synonymous with the other.

- **Strip Loin:** means that portion of the **Short Loin** from which the **Tenderloin** and bones have been removed. It contains three (3) muscles: gluteus medius; longissimus dorsi; and multifidus dorsi, or portions thereof. The strip loin is often fabricated or processed into steaks or medallions for grilling. The medallions present an even, smaller, and thicker cut for grilling than the regular full size steak.
- **Sirloin:** means the posterior portion of the **Loin** which is separated from the **Short Loin** by a straight cut which passes at a point immediately in front of (anterior to) the pin bone (ilium or tuber coxae). Classic retail cuts are referred to below (top sirloin).

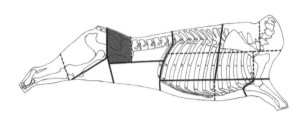

- **Sirloin, Tenderloin Removed:** means the **Sirloin** from which the **Tenderloin** is removed. This tenderloin portion is commonly referred to as the butt tender. The butt tenderloin is retailed as tenderloin or butt tenderloin, whole or cut into steak size portions.

- **Top Sirloin:** means the dorsal portion of the **Sirloin** that includes the gluteus medius and may include the biceps femoris (cap) but doesn't include the butt tender. Classic cuts are top sirloin roast, top sirloin steaks (regular and& fast- fry) and stir-fry, ground sirloin, sirloin kabobs cut from the biceps femoris (cap).

- **Top Sirloin, Cap Removed (Top Sirloin Portion):** means the **Top Sirloin** from which the biceps femoris is removed.

- **Bottom Sirloin:** means the ventral portion of the **Sirloin** that includes the muscle tensor fasciae latae. Classic cuts of the bottom sirloin are tri-tip sirloin roasts, ground sirloin, sirloin kabobs, bottom sirloin steaks, and sirloin stir-fry.

The sub-primal cuts of the Hip are: Rump, Round, Inside Round, Outside Round, Eye of Round, Heel of Round, Shank, and Sirloin Tip.

- **Rump:** means that portion of the **Hip** which is separated from the **Round** by a straight cut passing approximately parallel and in proximity to the aitch-bone (ischium), leaving no portion of the aitch-bone (ischium) in the **Round**. Custom operations still produce this cut for their clientele, but it's not a popular item in most metropolitan areas. It still might be a cut fabricated in some rural settings, but for the most part it's obsolete. Think about it, the rump has the aitch-bone in it. For it to be attractive, the bone would need to be removed and the muscles held together to make a good presentation. The rump has as part of its makeup the outside round, including the eye or round and the inside round.

- **Round (Full Round):** means that portion of the **Hip** which is separated from the **Rump**, and from the **Sirloin Tip** by a straight cut which passes at a point in front of (anterior to) the shaft of the leg bone (femur) and from the **Heel** of **Round** by a straight cut which passes through the base of the shaft of the leg bone (distal extremity of the femur). The cut may extend into the **Rump.** Not many retailers sell the full round as described. Those companies that cater for large functions might want it, but the full round in retail is separated as described further below.

Note: The **Round** contains no part of the gastrocnemius muscle (inner shank muscle).

- **Inside Round:** means that boneless portion of the **Round** located inside (medial side) of the leg, which is separated from the **Outside Round** by cutting lengthwise along the natural seam. The cut may extend into the **Rump**. It contains four (4) muscles, namely: pectineus, adductor, gracilis and semimembranosus. The adductor muscle is the most tenderest part of the inside round and can be used for kabobs and stir-fry. In some European countries the adductor muscle is utilized as a grilling item. By Canadian standards the inside round is not a grilling item unless it has been thin sliced and tenderized. Classic cuts of inside round are: roasts, marinating steak, minute steak, marinating strips, rouladen, and diced beef. The inside round does have excellent utility and can be fabricated into several value-added items such as stuffed and seasoned rouladen, marinated kabobs, stir-fry, and beef jerky, etc..

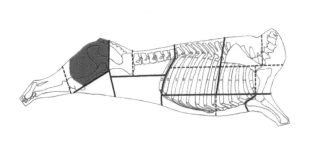 

- **Outside Round:** means that boneless portion of the **Round** located outside (lateral side) of the leg, which is separated from the **Inside Round** as described. The cut may extend into the **Rump**. It contains three (3) main muscles, namely: vastus lateralis, biceps femoris and semitendinosus (eye of round). It may exclude the **Eye of Round**. If the retailer is purchasing block ready outside rounds to further fabricate into retail cuts, more than likely it will not include the eye of round. The eye of round is processed separately at plant level for cost effective measures (called packinghouse merchandising). As far as the outside round goes, the retailing of this cut is limited as it's a very dry and tough cut especially if the consumer over cooks it. Classic cuts of the outside round are roasts, braising steaks (also known as Swiss steak). The tenderer portion located at the rump end can be utilized as kabobs, stir-fry, or minute tenderized steaks. Often the outside trimmings are used for extra lean ground beef or even beef jerky (providing the facility has the capability to do so).

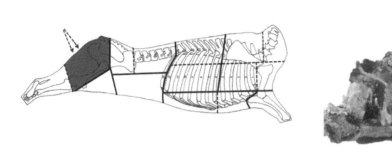

- **Eye of Round:** means the round- shaped muscle (semitendinosus) found at the outer (posterior) extremity of the **Outside Round** and extends into the **Rump**. Eye of the round is utilized for stir-fry, eye of round roasts and steaks (seasoned and regular), beef kabobs (if marinated), and cutlets.
- **Heel of Round:** means that portion of the **Hip** which is separated from the **Round** by a straight cut which passes through the base of the shaft of the leg bone (distal extremity of the femur) and from the **Shank** by a straight cut passing through the stifle joint (knee joint), the tibio-femoral articulation). The heel is utilized by cutting into stewing beef and or lean ground beef.
- **Shank (Hind Shank):** means that portion of the **Hip,** which is separated from the **Heel of Round** by a straight cut passing through the stifle joint (tibio-femoral articulation). Classic cuts from the shank are centre cut shank, marrow soup bones, knuckle soup bones, lean ground beef, and stewing beef.
- **Sirloin Tip:** means that portion of the **Hip** obtained by a "V-shaped" cut beginning approximately at the knee cap (patella) following the full length of the leg bone (femur) up to the vicinity of the rump knuckle bone (head of femur/acetabulum) then towards the flank lymph node (prefemoral). It contains three (3) main muscles, namely: vastus lateralis, rectus femoris and vastus medialis. Classic cuts of the sirloin tip are: sirloin tip roast, sirloin tip eye removed, sirloin tip steaks, and sirloin tip medallions.

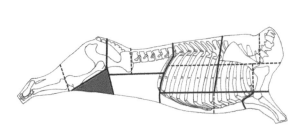 

- **Eye of Sirloin Tip:** means the triangular-shaped muscle (vastus lateralis) located outside (lateral side) of the **Sirloin Tip**. Classic cuts are stir-fry, sirloin tip sandwich steak, minute steaks, and kabobs.
- **Sirloin Tip, Eye Removed:** means the **Sirloin Tip** excluding the **Eye of Sirloin Tip**. Classic cuts are as per above.

VARIETY MEATS

Variety meats are edible parts of an animal other than skeletal muscle. Listed below are those of beef.

- Heart
- Liver
- Kidney
- Tripe
- Sweetbreads
- Suet
- Tongue
- Oxtail

Beef heart
Credit: © istock.com
VladyslavDanilin

Beef liver
Credit: Canada Beef

Beef kidney
Credit: Canada Beef

Beef Tripe
Credit: Canada Beef

Beef sweet breads
(thymus glands)
Credit: CPMCA image
collection

Beef suet (kidney fat)
Credit: CPMCA image
collection

Beef tongue
Credit: Canada Beef

Beef tail or ox tail
Credit: Canada Beef

CFIA Nomenclature Requirements for Beef

CFIA developed a meat manual for uniformity and consistency within the industry regarding various cuts of meat and their nomenclature. By no means was the intent to stymie creativity among competitors but simply to develop a standard that all Canadians could identify with in the naming of meat items. Different outlets and plants design processing methods according to their needs and customer demand; however, this doesn't give them license to arbitrarily change parameters set forth by the regulations regarding standards. Meat cuts are based on two factors: a) the muscle and bone structure, and b) appropriate use. Both are clearly identified in CFIA's Meat Manual by the cutting and breaking markers, explanations and the nomenclature assigned to each item.

Retailers are responsible for ensuring that the names used to describe meat cuts on labels and in advertisements include the appropriate specific terms. The name used to describe all meat cuts must include an indication of the species with the exception of beef.

The name used to describe all **variety meats** (listed further on under Variety Meats) must include an indication of the species with no exceptions.

RETAIL MEAT CUTS LABELLING REQUIREMENTS FOR BEEF

Prepackaged beef meat cuts offered for sale at retail do not require identification of the species but must be marked with the following:

- the name of the cut,
- the name of the retailer,
- the net quantity,
- the packaging date,
- the durable life of the meat cut unless the durable life is indicated on a poster next to the product, and
- the words "previously frozen" if a meat cut that has been frozen is thawed prior to sale, unless the words "previously frozen" appear on a poster next to the product.

LIST OF BEEF MEAT CUT MODIFIERS

Modifiers are descriptions used to explain in more detail what the cut of meat is or what alterations have been done to the primal/sub-primal cut to obtain the outcome you have before you.

- Bone-in
- Boneless
- Butterfly
- Cap removed
- Delicatize(d)
- Diced Beef
- Kabob
- Medallion
- Minute Steak
- Pot Roast
- Roast Beef
- Rolled
- Semi-Boneless
- Steak
- Stewing Beef
- Tenderize(d)
- Tied
- Tournedos
- Trimmed

Note: While not required, these modifiers may be used to describe beef cuts provided they are informative and not misleading.

Primal, Sub-Primal/ Retail Cut /Modifier

- **Sample:** Chuck Bottom Blade (Primal, Sub-Primal) Steak (Retail Cut) Boneless (Modifier)

Credit: Canada Beef

Hip:

- Inside Round - Inside Round Steak/ Roast.
- Rouladen, if cut from the inside or outside, must be labelled accordingly - Inside Round Rouladen; Outside Round Rouladen.
- Tenderized hip can come from any portion of the hip except the heel. Tenderized heel must be labelled - Heel of Round Tenderized Steaks, or simply Heel of Round.
- Outside Round Roast with the Heel attached must be labelled - Outside Round Roast, Heel Attached.

Sirloin Tip:

- Sirloin Tip Steaks / Roast.
- If the Sirloin Tip Eye is removed from the Sirloin Tip, the label must indicate - Sirloin Tip, Eye Removed.
- If steaks are cut from the "Eye", the label must indicate - Eye of Sirloin Tip Steaks.

Loin (Long Loin):

- Porterhouse may be referred to as T-Bone.
- Porterhouse Steaks have the gluteus medius muscle present.
- Sirloin Steak has the tenderloin, bottom & top sirloin and the bone.
- Sirloin Boneless has all the above except is boneless.
- Sirloin Boneless Tenderloin Removed is the same as above except the tenderloin has been removed.
- Top Sirloin implies boneless with no Bottom Sirloin or Tenderloin attached.
- Bottom Sirloin implies "Boneless" with no Top Sirloin or Tenderloin attached.

- The terms Top Sirloin Portion or Top Sirloin, Cap Removed may be used to describe a Top Sirloin from which the cap is removed. The Cap muscle (biceps femoris) may be described as Sirloin Cap or as Top Sirloin Portion.

Flank:

- If the flank steak is stuffed and rolled for London Broil, the label must indicate - Flank London Broil Stuffed.

Chuck (Square cut Chuck):

- Blade steaks can be cut up to the prescapular gland in the neck.
- Blade Steaks cannot be called Chuck Steaks, but may be called Chuck Blade Steaks.
- If the blade is seamed, the options are Top or Bottom Blade - to be used for both steaks and roast.
- If the Cross Rib is split lengthwise, both sides must carry the word "portion" on the label.

Shoulder:

- Shoulder Arm bone is that portion of the shoulder only containing the shaft of the humerus (arm bone). The whole shoulder portion may be deboned for further processing.

Neck:

- Neck is that portion of the chuck which is separated from the blade, cross-rib and shoulder. The neck contains the prescapular lymph gland.

Rib:

- Prime rib is 6 ribs - when sides are separated between the 12th and 13th ribs.
- Standing Rib or Rib can be used on the label for all portions of the rib.
- If you remove the Rib Cap, it must be indicated on the label.
- The rib cap cut into strips must have Rib Cap on the label but not the word Short Rib.
- The ribs from Rib can be labeled Beef Ribs - you need the word "Beef".
- The Rib Eye has only two muscles and no tail attached
- The term Short Ribs can only be used for items coming from the actual short rib portion.

Shank (Foreshank):

- Shin Beef must be referred to as Shank Meat.

Brisket (Brisket Point):

- You cannot call the Brisket Point Boneless Short Ribs.

Additional points:

- Stew Beef is correct - not "Beef Stew".
- Fat Added - this term must be declared when fat is added other than the normal fat layer attached to the specific cut. For example:

  Outside Round Roast Fat Added for the rotisserie.

  Flank Steak, Fat Added.
- Tenderized steaks - the primal cut may be used to describe the common name of the product. For example:

  Inside Round Steak, options are - Hip Minute Steak, Tenderized Inside Round, or Tenderized Round.
- Meat from any portion of the carcass which is broken down into small pieces or prepared as stewing meat or shish kabob, etc., need not be referred to by the name(s) of the cut(s) from which it originates, e.g. Beef Shish kabob.

GROUND MEATS

The following items are exceptions and do not need to be labelled as to carcass origin (Primal-Sub-primal).

- Regular Ground Beef
- Medium Ground Beef
- Lean Ground Beef
- Extra Lean Ground Beef
- Mechanically Separated Beef

The name(s) of the cut(s) from which ground beef is prepared must not be used to describe this product. Section B.14.015 of the Food and Drug Regulations requires that ground beef be labelled exclusively as Regular Ground Beef, Medium Ground Beef, Lean Ground Beef, Extra Lean Ground Beef, or Mechanically Separated Beef. Fat Content of Ground Meat and Correct Labelling:

- **Regular Ground** (naming the species) when meat from the named species is processed by grinding and does not contain more than 30% fat;
- **Medium Ground** (naming the species) when meat from the named species is processed by grinding and does not contain more than 23% fat;
- **Lean Ground** (naming the species) when meat from the named species is processed by grinding and does not contain more than 17% fat;
- **Extra Lean Ground** (naming the species) when meat from the named species is processed by grinding and does not contain more than 10% fat.

Credit: Canada Beef

Note: The name(s) of the cut(s) from which ground meat is prepared need not be used to describe this product.

Hobart fat testing machine
Credit: TRU Retail Meat Processing Program

HFT 2000 fat analyser machine
Credit: Costco

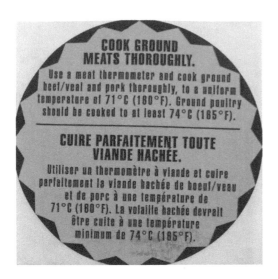

Ground beef safe cooking guide label
Credit: Credit: Costco

The Hobart fat analyser requires 2 ozs of ground meat which is then spread over a donut shaped aluminum disk and placed on top of the funnel under the cooking unit. The process takes 15 minutes to cook the patty with the juices and fats dripping into a test tube below the funnel. The hot fat floats to the top of the test tube where a sliding scale is adjusted to the edge of the test tube at the bottom & top of the fat layer. Once the slide is adjusted accurately the fat content can be read off the scale.

The DSC – HFT 2000 fat analyser requires 5 grams of ground meat which is then spread between 2 thin fibre glass disposable disks and placed in the machine. The lid is closed, and the cooking process takes 20 minutes. A digital read out shows the results on the machine screen.

"Fresh" Ground Beef - the unmodified use of the term "fresh" when used to describe food, means "offered for sale at the earliest possible time." According to industry practice, the "earliest possible time" after grinding is on the same day that it is first ground. The term "fresh" should therefore **not be used** to describe ground beef that is first offered for sale a few days after grinding.

Block & Knife Ready Beef Products

With ever-growing costs concerning the operation of a business, one-thing entrepreneurs look to is ways in which they can save overhead expenses without compromising quality or value. Block and knife ready meats come vacuum packaged in boxes, separated according to primal and sub-primal cuts and are easier to stock, stack and store. This product does not need the overhead rails and fridge space that swinging carcasses need. Block and knife ready meat has been portioned at plant level into large manageable primal and sub-primal sections that take up less room and can be used as demand dictates much quicker than that of swinging quarters of beef.

Some of the more common block and knife ready meats of beef include but are not limited to the following:

- Boneless Trim
- Chuck Blade (regular and boneless)
- Chuck Cross Ribs (regular and boneless)
- Short Ribs
- Standing Ribs

- Rib Eyes (regular and lip on)
- Brisket Points (boneless)
- Flank Steaks
- Sirloin Tips (regular and peeled)
- Inside Rounds (regular or denuded)
- Eye of Rounds
- Outside Rounds
- Sirloin Butts or Top Sirloins
- Short Loins or Strip Loins
- Tenderloin or Butt Tenders

Counter Ready Beef Products

Counter ready meats refer to those beef items that have been processed and fabricated at plant level, are packaged for displays, boxed and shipped to store level. With these there is no need of a meat cutter. The product is finished and ready for in-store labelling and displaying. Counter ready meats come in one of two forms: fresh or processed (meaning fermented, cooked, brined, frozen and fresh sausages, etc.). There is a movement within the industry to return to full service counters as customer demand dictates. However, there do exist large box store operations that offer counter ready meats as a cost alternative to full service outlets. Consumers determine which one they prefer. In recent years it has been our observation that most clientele are now looking for information about their purchase not normally found on a package label. They wish to speak to knowledgeable staff and qualified meat experts to assist them. People in general want more information about where the meat comes from, how to handle it, store it, prepare it, portion it and decide the size per serving, too much information to put on a label.

Value-Added Retail Meat Cuts

Value-added means adding value to meat. It's an age-old concept where in times gone by meat cutters and operators of meat shops and supermarket departments formulated value-added items to utilize as much of their product inventory as possible.

Items such as trimmings and offal weren't all that popular and didn't command a high return on investment. Due to low demand, these items were offered cheap to consumers. Operators looked for and formulated recipes that enhanced these items and advertised them as value-added. For example, ground meats became fresh sausages, seasoned meatballs and hamburger patties. The collection of fat from trimmings was ground, shaped into baseball size and rolled in seeds to be sold as bird-balls. Beef tongues were pickled, cooked and sliced as luncheon meat. Kidney and hearts were added to meat pies, and scraps of trimmings were ground for pet food.

As lifestyle patterns change, so does the industry. More and more consumers are looking to convenience foods, and both shops and meat plants are responding with new products and strategies that might entice consumers to purchase their products. Product diversity has grown from fresh/frozen to seasoned/cooked/heat and serve. For the most part value-added meats are boneless for consumer convenience and versatility. All value-added meats are designed to help consumers make dinner and enjoy food. Shoppers look for ideas and products that match their skill and taste.

In consideration are home appliances used in the preparation of items that might attract consumers. Products have as part of their design cooking instructions, nutritional value, ingredients and are trendy, taking advantage of the latest craze with respect to flavour (seasoning/spices). The Food Network has greatly contributed to the interest in food: its preparation, presentation, taste and competition.

Veal Processing

The processing of veal falls under the guise of the CFIA and all applicable regulations administered by them on a federal level. In addition, on a provincial level the standards are the same as they mirror those of the federal level. As with all meats, veal as meat cannot be sold or retailed unless it has undergone either federal or provincial inspection (see section above on beef processing). Again, federally inspected meats may be sold across provincial and international boarders but provincially inspected meats may not. Provincially inspected meats can only be sold within the boundaries of the province and its jurisdiction.

Working Conditions: At plant level the working conditions aren't any different than those who harvest beef. In most cases they may be the same plant. Just know that it is very likely to be a cool or cold environment considering the nature of the industry.

Larger federal plants operate on a larger scale and therefore their processing lines are more rigorous with respect to production and repetition. Smaller plants such as local abattoirs have more leeway when it comes to production schedules and flexibility of employee assignments. Employees of smaller facilities tend to be more versatile due to the size and scope of an independent operation.

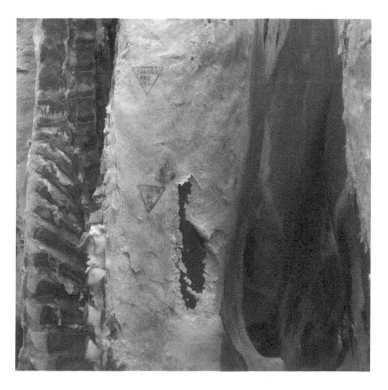

Veal carcasses, graded
Credit: Canadian Beef Grading Agency

Categories of Veal

Almost all packers in their processing of veal and veal carcasses have generalized the terms used to describe the variance in veal carcass size and weight to suit the local market, falling under one of the two categories either "**ligh**t" (9 -68 kilograms) or "**heavy**" (68 – 180 kilograms). Industry terms common to these two categories are: Baby Veal, Bob Veal, Vealers, Calves, and Nature (White Veal).

Light Veal: Baby Veal, Bob Veal or Vealers are terms used by industry in their attempts to describe the age, weight and colour of the veal. For example, baby or bob veal can be anywhere from two days to one month old (thus the name "baby"). Milk fed calves known as vealers are anywhere from one to three months old. Vealers are raised for colour, tenderness and flavour.

Heavy Veal: Calves and Nature (White Veal) are terms used by industry to describe the heavier carcasses of veal. Calves can be up to twenty weeks old. At that age, the calf's anatomical makeup is in the process of change from veal to more of that like beef. These carcasses weigh in the neighbourhood of 68 -140 kilograms. Their diet consists of mainly milk, grains and hay combinations. Nature veal also known as white veal could range to a maximum age of twenty weeks attaining carcass weight between 80 and 110 kilograms. These animals are raised on a controlled diet, kept in separate pens and limited in both movement and exercise to prevent excessive muscular development. This is to produce a white or pinkish colour of lean meat and is the most expensive type of veal on the market.

It should be noted that any such classification(s) (defined by industry) do not supersede or override the regulations governing veal. It should also be noted that veal being what it is (young carcasses of the bovine species) comes in various weight ranges. In recognition of this problem, the CFIA has established specific breaking guidelines in the identification of veal primal cuts and sub-primal cuts (herein provided) for both "light" and "heavy" veal carcasses.

Inspection & Grading of Veal

Inspection on a federal level is the responsibility of the CFIA, as is the grading, which is facilitated in coordination with the CBGA. If inspection is done at the provincial level and grading is desired, then the CBGA takes that role.

VEAL GRADES

There are ten grades of veal carcasses with the grade names Canada A1, Canada A2, Canada A3, or Canada A4,; Canada B1, Canada B2, Canada B3, Canada B4, Canada C1 and Canada C2. For a Dressed Veal Carcass to be graded it must fall into the weight range of 80 -180 kilograms.

Note: For more on veal harvesting, inspection and grading refer to Chapter 12.

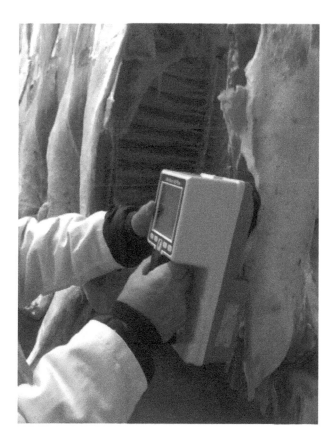

Veal colour meter is placed on the fresh cut
brisket to assess brilliance
Credit: Canadian Beef Grading Agency

Canadian Veal Primal Cuts

Veal is meat derived from dressed carcasses of bovine animals that have the maturity characteristics set out in Schedule I, Part IV of the Livestock Carcass Grading Regulations and a warm carcass weight of less than 205 kilograms with the hide on or less than 180 kilograms with the hide removed.

Maturity Characteristics are as follows:

- Bones that are soft and reddish in colour
- Ribs that are narrow and slightly rounded
- A sternum that shows distinct divisions
- An aitchbone that is covered by cartilage.

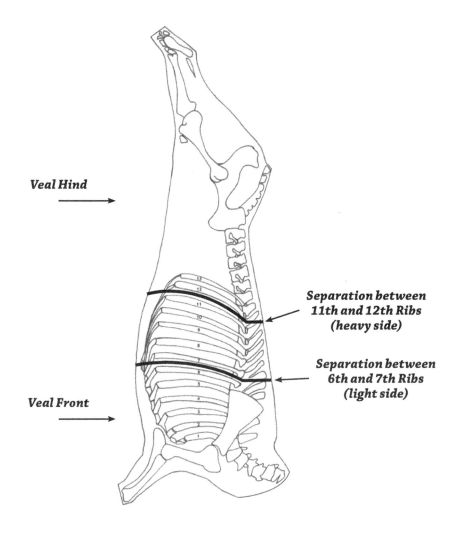

Veal side - front & hind separation point
Credit: Jakes & Associates

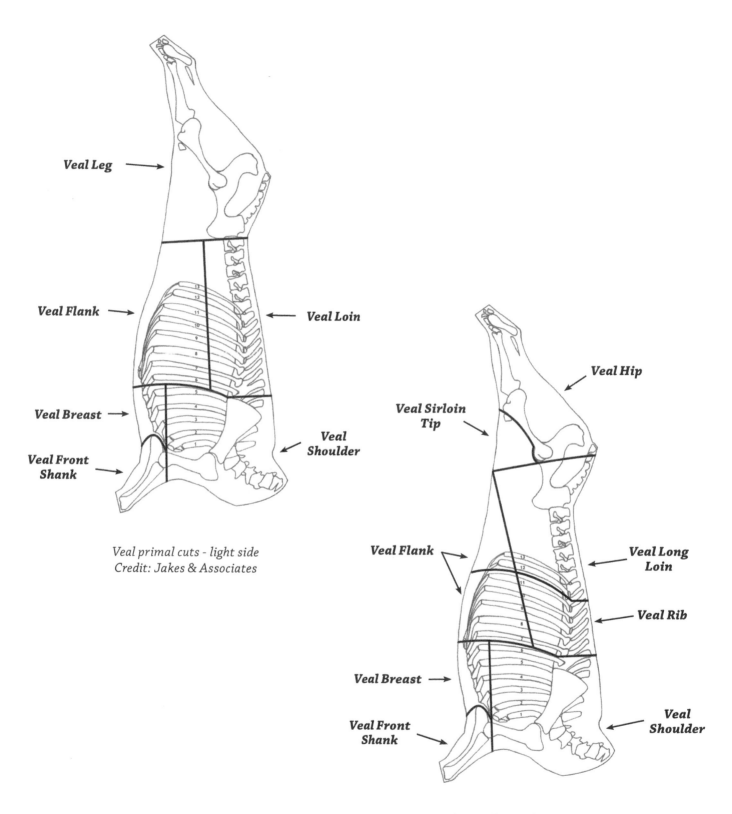

Veal Leg

Veal Flank

Veal Loin

Veal Breast

Veal Shoulder

Veal Front
Shank

Veal primal cuts - light side
Credit: Jakes & Associates

Veal Hip

Veal Sirloin
Tip

Veal Flank

Veal Long
Loin

Veal Rib

Veal Breast

Veal Shoulder

Veal Front
Shank

Veal primal cuts - heavy side
Credit: Jakes & Associates

A **Dressed Veal Carcass** means a veal carcass from which the skin, head and feet at the carpal and tarsal joints have been removed and the carcass has been eviscerated. Sides of veal refer to one of the two approximately equal portions of the dressed veal carcass obtained by cutting (splitting) from the tail to the neck along the median line (centre of the spine). For transport purposes and ease of handling, sides of veal are further portioned into front and hind quarters. The Front Quarter refers to the anterior portion of the veal side, which is separated from the hind quarter by a cut passing between the 11th and 12th rib, and the Hind Quarter refers to the posterior portion of the side of veal which is separated from the front quarter as described, between the 11th and 12th rib.

The CFIA regulations don't discriminate in their meat cuts manual the difference between what they call the **Front Half** from the **Front Quarter**. It's the same for the **Hind Half** and the **Hind Quarter**. The breaking markers are identical as are the explanations describing each quarter. The terms are used to distinguish an alternative to heavier or lighter veal carcasses. Therefore it is determined that either descriptor, i.e., Front Half is interchangeable with Front Quarter (referring to the same thing) as it is also with Hind Half and Hind Quarter.

There is a difference between what CFIA calls a **Front** and a **Front Half** (or **Front Quarter)**; these are not synonymous with each other or interchangeable. Here the regulations speak specifically to the category of Veal.: Light or Heavy – referring to the alternative methods suited to various weight and size ranges of Dressed Veal Carcasses. For example, below is a description of the **Front** and **Front Double** primal cuts. Note that they have the same number of ribs and that they are separated between the same ribs (6th and 7th). When CFIA indicates the term "**Double**" they are referring to a "light" Dressed Veal Carcass that has been left whole. When indicating the terms Side, Front Quarter, Front, Hind Quarter, Leg, Whole Loin, Flank, and Rib and Flank, they are referring to a "heavier" Dressed Veal Carcass that has been split from the tail to the neck along the median line (centre of the spine). The following descriptions for Primal and Sub Primal Cuts derived from the **Front Half**, **Front Quarter**, **Hind Half** and **Hind Quarter** of **Dressed Veal Carcasses** are designed around meeting that purpose, the variation and size differentiation of veal carcasses.

According to the CFIA governing regulations regarding the breaking and naming of veal cuts, the primal cuts are: **Front – Front Double, Leg – Leg Double, Whole Loin, Whole Loin Double, Flank, and Rib (Rack) and Flank, Double.**

- **Front:** means that portion of the side, which is separated from the Whole Loin and Flank by cutting (ribbing) between the 6th and 7th rib.
- **Front Double:** means the anterior portion of the Front Half which is separated from the Rib and Flank, Double by a straight cut passing between the 6th and 7th rib.
- **Leg:** means the posterior of the Side, which is separated from the Whole Loin and Flank by a straight cut which passes in front of (anterior to) the pin bone (ilium or tuber coxae).
- **Leg, Double:** means the posterior portion of the Hind Half, which is separated from the Loin, Double and Flank by a straight cut passing immediately in front of (anterior to) the pin bone (ilium or tuber coxae).
- **Whole Loin:** means that portion of the Side which is separated from the Front and Leg as described above, respectively, and from the Flank by a straight cut, approximately parallel to the back bones (vertebra column) passing at a point slightly above (dorsal to) the costal cartilage of the 12th rib.
- **Whole Loin Double:** means that portion of the Dressed Veal Carcass which is separated from the Front, Double and Leg, Double as described and from the Flanks, by a straight cut approximately parallel to the back bones (vertebra column) passing through the 13th rib, approximately at the beginning of the costal cartilage. It consists of the Loin, Double and Rib (Rack), Double, attached.
- **Flank:** means that portion of the Side, which is separated from the Front, Leg and Whole Loin as described above.
- **Rib (Rack) and Flank, Double:** means the posterior portion of the Front Half, which is separated from the Front, Double, as described. It consists of the Rib (Rack) and the rib portion of the Flank attached.

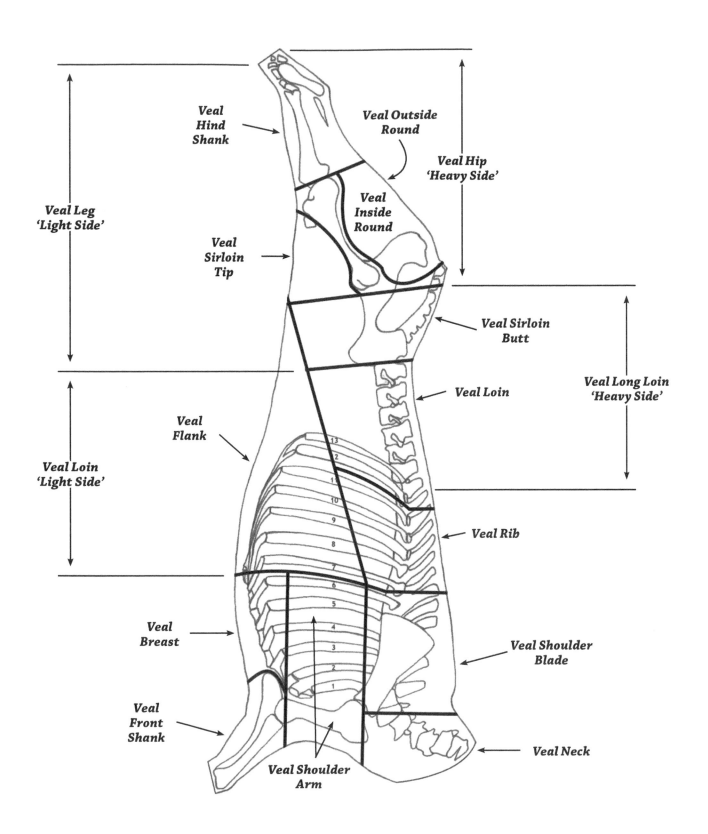

Veal Hind Shank

Veal Outside Round

Veal Hip 'Heavy Side'

Veal Leg 'Light Side'

Veal Inside Round

Veal Sirloin Tip

Veal Sirloin Butt

Veal Loin

Veal Long Loin 'Heavy Side'

Veal Flank

Veal Loin 'Light Side'

13
12
11
10
9
8
7
6
5
4
3
2
1

Veal Rib

Veal Breast

Veal Shoulder Blade

Veal Front Shank

Veal Neck

Veal Shoulder Arm

Veal light & heavy sub-primals
Credit: Jakes & Associates

Sub-primal & Retail Cuts of Veal

According to the CFIA's governing regulations regarding the breaking and naming of veal cuts, the sub-primal cuts are: **Neck, Shoulder - Shoulder Double, Breast, Shank, Leg Shank Portion, Leg Butt Portion, Heel of Round, Sirloin Tip, Sirloin -Sirloin Double, Leg Short Cut, Rump, Round, Inside Round, Outside Round, Eye of Round, Loin - Loin Double and Rib – Rib Double**.

As you will see and experience, classic retail cuts of veal are not much different from those of beef as they are presented, marketed, and merchandised in similar fashion.

- **Neck:** means that portion of the Front that is separated from the Shoulder by a straight cut passing through the 5th neck bone (cervical vertebra). Classic cuts are: veal stewing meat, lean ground veal and veal soup bones.
- **Shoulder:** means that portion of the Front, which is separated from the Neck as described above and from the Breast and Shank by a straight cut that passes through the base of the shaft of the arm bone (distal extremity of the humerus). In beef terms this would be the chuck. Classic cuts are veal shoulder roasts (regular and boneless), veal shoulder steaks (regular and boneless), veal stewing meat, veal shoulder short ribs, veal shoulder cutlets, and veal shoulder stir-fry.
- **Shoulder, Double:** means that portion of the Front, Double which is separated from the Neck, Breast and Shank as described. Classic cuts are the same as above with the word "Chop" replacing the word "Steak."
- **Breast:** means that portion of the Front, which is separated from the shoulder as described above, and from the Shank by a cut which follows the natural (dividing) seam. This cut is parallel to that of the Brisket Point in beef. Classic cuts are boneless veal breast, boned and rolled veal breast, veal stewing meat, and veal boneless short ribs.
- **Shank (Foreshank):** means that portion of the Front, which is separated from the shoulder and Breast as per above.
- **Shank (Hind Shank):** Means that portion of the Leg, which is separated from the Leg, Shank Portion or Heel of Round by a straight cut passing through the stifle joint (tibio-femoral joint). Classic cuts from the veal shank are centre cut veal shank, veal stewing meat, ground veal and veal soup bones.
- **Leg, Shank Portion (Leg, Shank End):** means that portion of the Leg, which is separated from the Shank and from the Leg, Butt Portion by a straight cut, which passes approximately through the centre of the shaft of the leg bone (femur)

approximately at right angles to it. Classic cuts from this sub-primal depend on size. This cut produces veal cutlets, veal stewing meat, veal stir-fry, veal scallopini, and veal leg roasts (regular and boneless).

- **Leg, Butt Portion (Leg, Butt End):** means that portion of the Leg, which is separated from the Leg, Shank Portion. Classic cuts are same as those from the leg, shank portion.
- **Heel of Round:** is an alternative portion of the Leg, which is separated from the Shank and from the Round by a straight cut passing through the base of the shaft of the leg bone (distal extremity of the femur). This cut is not a popular cut as for the most part carcass veal is deboned and muscle seamed for greater utility and value.
- **Sirloin Tip:** is and alternative portion of the Leg obtained by a "V-shaped" cut beginning at the knee cap (patella) and following the full length of the leg bone (femur) up to the rump knuckle bone (head of femur/acetabulum) then toward the flank lymph node (prefemoral). Classic cuts are veal sirloin tip, veal stir-fry, veal cutlets, and if seamed, veal scallopini.
- **Sirloin:** is an alternative portion of the Leg, which is separated from the Sirloin Tip and from the Rump by a straight cut which passes in front of (anterior to) the rump knucklebone (head of femur/acetabulum). Classic cuts are boneless veal top sirloin chops or steaks, boneless veal top sirloin roasts, and veal trimmings.
- **Sirloin, Double:** means the anterior portion of the Leg, Double which is separated from the Leg, Short Cut.
- **Leg, Short Cut:** means the Leg from which the Sirloin has been removed. Classic cuts are the cuts you would get from the sirloin tip, heel of round, leg, butt and shank portions.
- **Rump:** is an alternative portion of the Leg, which is separated from the Sirloin and from the Round by a straight cut approximately parallel and behind (posterior to) the aitch bone (ischium).
- **Round:** is an alternative portion of the Leg, which is separated from the Sirloin Tip and Rump respectively, and from the Heel of Round by a straight cut which passes through the base of the shaft of the leg bone (distal extremity of the femur). The cut may extend into the Rump.

  Note: The round contains no part of the gastrocnemius muscle (aka inner and outer shank).

- **Inside Round:** Same as that of beef.
- **Outside Round:** Same as that of beef.

- **Eye of Round:** Same as that of beef.
- **Loin:** means the posterior portion of the Whole Loin, which is separated from the Rib by a straight cut which passes behind (posterior to) the last rib. Classic cuts of the loin are referred to as "Chops."

   Note: The Loin contains no part of the rib.

- **Loin, Double:** means the posterior portion of the Whole Loin, Double which is separated from the Rib, (Rack) Double by a straight cut passing behind (posterior to) the last rib (13th rib).

   Note: For Both the Strip Loin and Tenderloin refer to Beef.

- **Rib:** means the anterior portion of the Whole Loin, which is separated from the Loin.

   Note: The complete Rib or part thereof prepared as a roast, may be referred to as **Rack.**

- **Rib, Double:** means that anterior portion of the Whole Loin, Double which is separated from the Loin, Double.

   Note: For Rib eye refers to Beef.

VEAL VARIETY MEATS

- Brain
- Heart
- Kidney
- Liver
- Sweetbread
- Tongue

Calf liver is similar to beef liver. It is light reddish brown in colour, very tender and the mildest of all livers. It weighs approximately 900 g to 1500 g and is the most expensive to buy. It does not need skinning prior to cooking.

Veal kidney is much like beef kidney, but milder in flavour and so tender that it can be fried. Average weight is approximately 175 g.

Veal tongues are usually processed commercially into processed meat or bottled products but can be ordered from the packers for specific orders.

Veal Heart weighs from 500 g to 1.5 kg. Its colour ranges from light reddish brown to a pale pinkish brown. It is conical in shape with a border of soft, creamy fat at the base. It can be retailed whole, halved, or cut into thick slices.

Veal or Calf Sweetbreads are considered a great delicacy. They are largest in size, reaching 500 g to 700 g when the calf is five to six weeks old and decreasing in size as it becomes older. Sweetbreads are the thymus glands.

CFIA Nomenclature Requirements for Veal

Nomenclature of veal retail cuts is no different than that of beef. Veal primal and sub-primal cuts are based on two factors, a) the muscle and bone structure of the carcass, and b) appropriate use. Both are clearly identified in CFIA's Meat Manual by the cutting and breaking marker explanations and the nomenclature assigned to each item.

As far as labelling requirements go, the name of the species "veal" shall accompany the name of all cuts of veal. In other words, the name used to describe all meat cuts must include an indication of the species. For additional information to be included on labels identifying cuts of veal, see the Retail Meat Cut Labelling Requirements of Beef section in this chapter.

LIST OF MEAT CUT MODIFIERS FOR VEAL

- Bone-in
- Boneless
- Cap Removed
- Chop
- Cutlet
- Delicatize(d) or Delicated
- Diced Veal
- Frenched Rib Chop
- Medallion
- Portion
- Rack

- Roast
- Rolled
- Scallopini
- Semi-Boneless
- Steak
- Stewing Veal
- Stuffed
- Tenderize(d)
- Tied
- Trimmed

Veal (species), Retail Cut (primal-sub-primal), Modifier (What was done to it). **Note**: Sample Modifier:

Veal/ Breast/ "stuffed"

The following items are exceptions (do not require the Specie name "Veal" preceding the retail name):

X-Lean, Lean, Medium, or Regular Ground Veal; and Stewing Veal.

The term "**baby beef**' is not to be used to describe veal. With such items as Veal liver, heart, sweetbreads, tongue and brains are, however, prefaced with the term calf, e.g. "**Calf Liver**".

Veal Cutlet: A boneless slice of meat obtained from any portion of the leg from which the shank and heel of the Round are removed. **Veal cutlets** processed from other than the leg portion (as stated above) _must be identified_ with the primal or sub-primal from which they came, e.g. Veal Cutlets made from the shoulder area shall be labelled as "Veal Shoulder Cutlets".

Bison Processing

There isn't much to record regarding the processing of bison. These food animals are treated in similar fashion to that of beef. The handling of a Dressed Bison Carcass is subject to the same CFIA and FSEP regulations as beef. Due to their compatibility, bison primal, sub-primal and retail cuts have the same guidelines and parameters as beef. Bison as a species have anatomical structure and conformation parallel to that of beef with the exception of the front quarter. Bison front quarters are larger in the shoulder (thoracic vertebrae) and ribs, making them a little more awkward to handle.

Inspection & Grading of Bison

Here as with the CFIA cutting guidelines for beef, Bison follows the same rules and regulations during inspection and grading. Bison are evaluated both pre and post mortem, making sure they are fit for human consumption.

Bison Grades

There are ten grades for bison with the grade names Canada A1, Canada A2, Canada A3 and Canada A4 at the top. Again, as with beef grading is not mandatory but recommended if retailing to product conscious consumers.

Bison
Credit: © Isselec / Dreamstime

Farmed bison grazing
Credit: ©Accountrwc / Dreamstime

Canadian Bison Primal, Sub-primal & Retail Cuts

Bison is derived from dressed carcasses of bovine animals having a warm weight of 160 kg or more. Bison may be derived from male or female animals. Dressed bison carcasses are bison carcasses from which the skin, head, developed mammary glands and feet at the carpal and tarsal joints have been removed, and the carcass has been eviscerated and split into two equal sides. Sides of bison refer to one of the two approximately equal portions of the dressed bison carcass obtained by cutting (splitting) from the tail to the neck along the median line (centre of the spine). For transport purposes and ease of handling, sides of bison are further portioned into front and hind quarters. The **Front Quarter** refers to the anterior portion of the bison side, which is separated from the hind quarter by a cut passing between the twelfth and thirteenth rib and the **Hind Quarter** refers to the posterior portion of the side of bison which is separated from the front quarter as described, between the twelfth and thirteenth rib.

For further breaking and processing guidelines for bison primal, sub-primal and retail cuts refer to the section on beef (above).

Bison Variety Meats

Variety meats are edible parts of an animal other than skeletal muscle. Listed below are those of bison:

- Heart
- Liver
- Kidney
- Tripe
- Sweetbreads
- Suet
- Tongue
- Bison Tail

Retail Meat Cuts Labelling Requirements for Bison

As far as labelling requirements the name of the species "Bison" shall accompany the name of all cuts of bison. In other words, the name used to describe all bison meat cuts must include an indication of the species. For additional information to be included on labels identifying cuts of bison see *Retail Meat Cut Labelling Requirements* of the beef section in this chapter as the regulations governing Bison mirror that of those regulating Beef.

Wholesale Meat Specifications

Suppliers of food service cuts follow a set of specifications called Institutional Meat Purchase Specifications (IMPS). The specifications are a result of a 1992 decision by the Canadian Meat Council (CMC) and the American Institutional Meat Purchasing Specifications Council to synchronize their naming systems in order to reduce cross-border and domestic confusion. Based on feedback from stakeholders, the IMPS were revised in November of 2014 to adopt common trade language with respect to terminology used for meat cuts traded between our two countries.

In February of 2015, the CFIA's Wholesale Meat Specifications Document (WMSD) was released. The WMSD is the result of a thorough review of the current wholesale meat-cut nomenclature. The CFIA administers the Meat Inspection Act and Meat Inspection Regulations, the Food and Drugs Act and the Food and Drug Regulations and the Consumer Packaging and Labelling Act and Consumer Packaging and Labelling Regulations, which require that meat cuts, organs and other carcass parts be identified on labels with proper common names. The information about meat cut names and their specifications and item numbers contained in the WMSD are identical to that found in the IMPS documents (Table 1).

The WMSD document provides industry and consumers with a simple and informative system of nomenclature (naming convention) that will ensure the use of standardized terms in the naming of meat cuts, discourage any misuse of these terms and provide consumers with information to compare prices and select cooking methods.

IMPS/WMSD Meat Categories	
Series Number	Series Name
100	Beef
200	Lamb
300	Veal
400	Pork
500	Cured, Cured & Smoked and Cooked Products
600	Cured, Dried, and Smoked Beef Products
700	Variety Meats & Edible By-products
800	Sausage Products
11	Goat

Table 1: IMPS/WMSD Categories

Note: Bison is not listed.

SUMMARY

Baby Veal	Label Modifiers	Traceability
Block Ready	Nomenclature	Value-Added
Bob Veal	PID	Veal
CBGA	Primal Cuts	Vealers
Counter Ready	Red Meat Industry	WMSD Categories
Dressed Carcass	RFID	Yield
Knife Ready	Sub-Primal Cuts	

DISCUSSION QUESTIONS

1. Canada has many breeds of cattle used in the production of beef, but we have only identified seven. Discuss the differences between these breeds and why perhaps these seven were chosen over other breeds of cattle.

2. The Red Meat Industry isn't just beef. What other species of meat make up this industry?

3. What percentage of our beef and cattle production is exported each year?

4. Which provinces have the highest calf populations?

5. Which red meat species is most comparable to bison?

6. Is traceability important to Canada? Why? And how is it implemented?

7. What are the three stages of beef production?

8. Which government agency is responsible for the inspection and grading of bovine animals?

9. What does a "Yield Stamp" indicate?

10. With respect to the labelling of red meat, is it mandatory that all red meats be identified by species?

11. How many primal cuts does beef have? How many do bison have?

12. Referring to beef, is "Loin" and "Long Loin" the same thing? Why or why not?

13. Why has the Red Meat Industry introduced "Block Ready" beef?

14. What do we mean when we say a product is Value-Added?

15. How many categories of veal are there, and what are they?

Beef Retail Meat processing options:

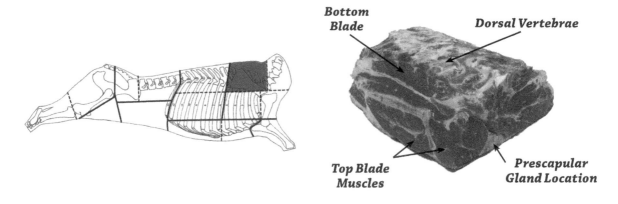

Blade sub-primal – top blade (L) under blade bone bottom blade (R) top

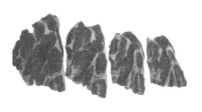

Blade simmering steaks bone in

Chuck blade short rib roast (L)
Blade roast bone in (R)

Chuck short rib or Blade roasts
bone in

Bottom (L) & top blade
muscles (R)

Bottom blade whole

Bottom blade marinating steaks

Top blade marinating steaks
(from flat iron)

Bottom blade pot roast

Top blade portion marinating
steaks from
(blade mock tender)

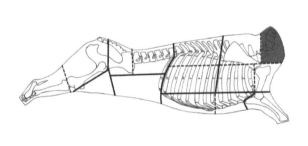

Neck whole showing prescapular gland

Neck with cervical vertebrae removed

Neck vertebrae 1-6 L to R

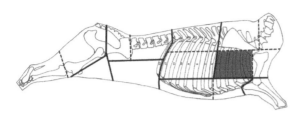

Cross rib whole shank end view

Cross rib blade end view

*Cross rib muscle groups
seamed out*

Cross rib main muscle (L) & Rib cap

*Cross rib split with 2 ribs each
reversed on roast*

*Cross rib cut into 4 pot roasts
bone in*

*Cross rib cap (Beef ribs 4-bone)
ready to cut.*

Grain Direction →

Cut Line Direction

Remove this muscle first before cutting

Beef ribs for braising or marinating (Maui style)

Cross rib ready to slice into steaks

Cross rib marinating steaks

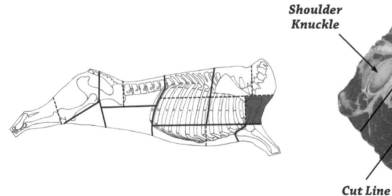

Shoulder Knuckle

Common part of shoulder used for steak and roasts (mainly custom cut operations)

Cut Line Direction

Figure 8 on shoulder arm bone where foreshank is removed from the beef front quarter

Shoulder arm whole

Shoulder arm boned showing shoulder arm bone

Shoulder arm pot roasts bone in

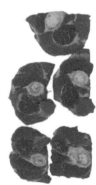

Shoulder arm simmering steaks bone in

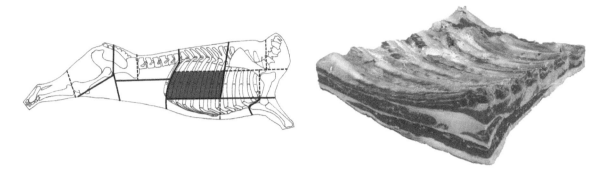

Short ribs sub-primal

Short ribs cut at 1.5 in

*Short ribs simmering
(variety of cut styles)*

Short ribs cut thinner for braising

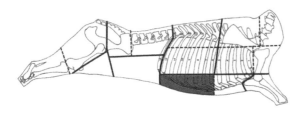

Brisket plate

Brisket plate trimmed & ready to roll

Brisket plate pot roast (whole)

Brisket plate pot roasts

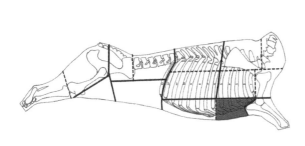

Brisket point sub-primal

Brisket point boneless
outside view

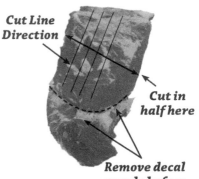

**Cut Line
Direction**

**Cut in
half here**

**Remove decal
muscle before
cutting braizing
pieces**

Brisket point boneless inside view

Brisket point brazing pieces

Brisket point pot roasts

Alternative retail option,
boneless point & plate
tied together

Brisket Point & Plate pot roasts

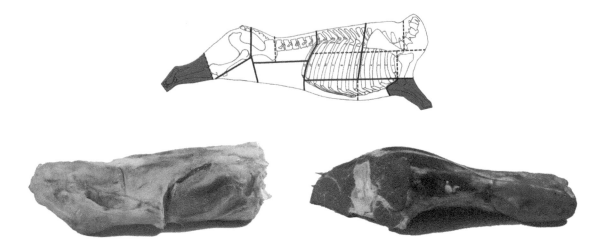

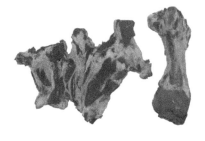

Hind shank whole tendon side view

Fore shank whole outside view

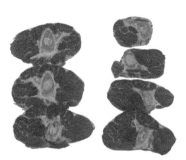

Hind shank boned out

Fore shank boned out

Hind shank cross cut

Fore shank cross cut

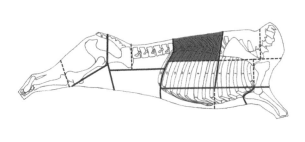

7-Bone rib whole (chine bone on)

7-Bone rib chine & feather bones off

7-Bone rib end view with beef back ribs off

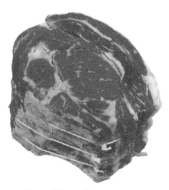

Standing rib oven roast

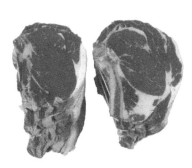

Prime rib oven roasts

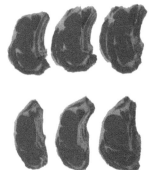

Prime rib grilling steaks

Rhomboidious Muscle

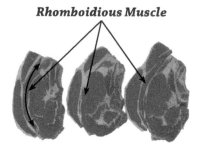

Rib grilling steaks showing Rhomboidious muscle location

Note: If the rhomboidious muscle is present the steaks must be sold as rib grilling steaks not Prime Rib grilling steak. Rib steaks are cut from the standing rib of the 7-Bone rib.

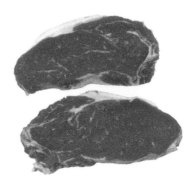

Rib eye with blade cartilage, side seam &
rhomboidious muscles off

Rib eye grilling steaks

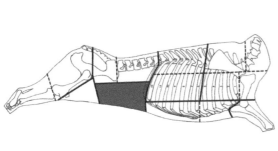

Flank whole inside view

Flank marinating steak
inside view

Flank marinating steak (scored)
outside view

Flank marinating steak sliced thin
(cut across grain)

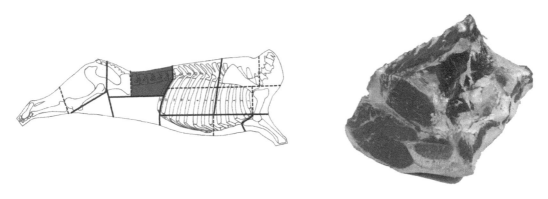

Short loin porterhouse end view

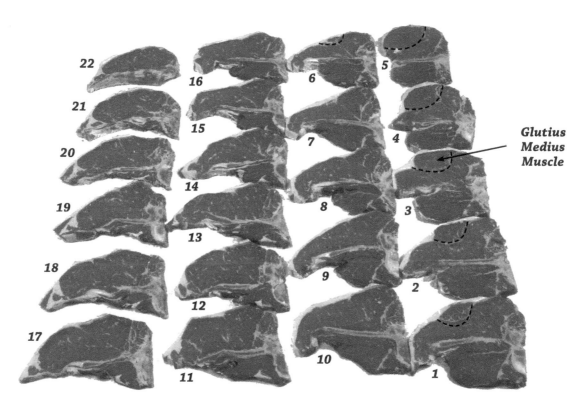

Glutius Medius Muscle

Short loin all bone in steaks

Note: The glutius medius muscle on the steaks numbered 1–6 and indicated with the dotted lines are all Porterhouse Steaks.

Steaks numbered 7–20 are all T-Bone steaks.

Steaks numbered 21–22 are Wing Steaks.

A Porterhouse grilling steak can be sold as a T-Bone grilled steak, however a T-Bone grilling steak cannot be sold as a Porterhouse grilling steak.

*** Number of steaks per shortloin depends on steak thickness!

Striploin whole Porterhouse end view

Striploin deboned showing lumbar vertebrae

Striploin grilling steaks

Tenderloin trimmed side muscle off

Tenderloin grilling steaks

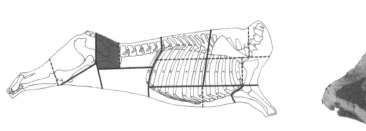

Sirloin butt short loin end view

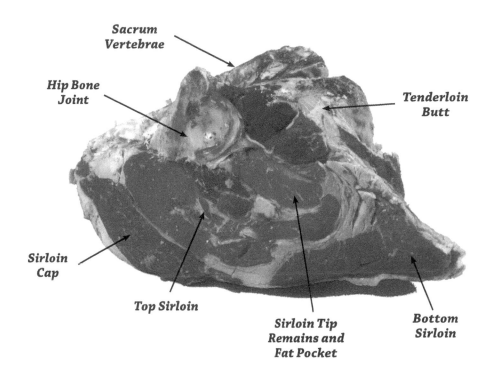

Sacrum Vertebrae

Hip Bone Joint

Tenderloin Butt

Sirloin Cap

Top Sirloin

Sirloin Tip Remains and Fat Pocket

Bottom Sirloin

Sirloin butt – hip end view

Sirloin butt - tenderloin butt off

Sirloin butt – tenderloin & lumbar vertebrae off

Sirloin butt fully boned out

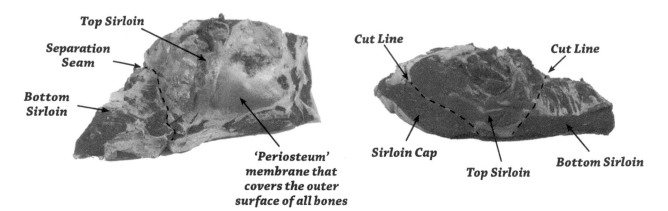

Top & bottom sirloins

Top & bottom sirloin

Top & bottom sirloins separated

Top sirloin outside view with inspection stamp

Top sirloin and cap inside view

Sirloin cap trimmed & Sirloin cap grilling steaks

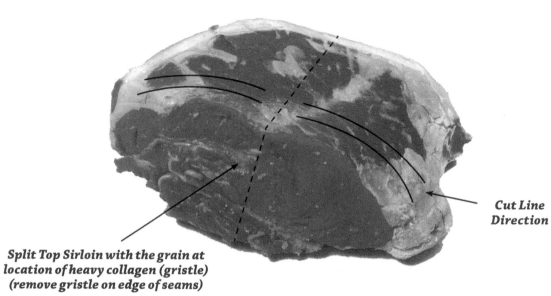

Split Top Sirloin with the grain at location of heavy collagen (gristle) (remove gristle on edge of seams)

Cut Line Direction

Top sirloin cap removed

Top sirloin split at the gristle

Top sirloin grilling steaks

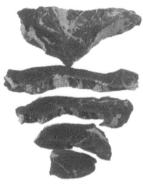

Bottom sirloin grilling steaks (Tri-tip)

Tenderloin butt un-trimmed

Tenderloin butt grilling steaks

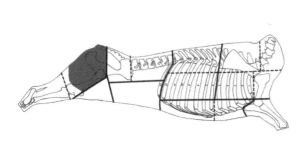

Beef hip – Inside round view

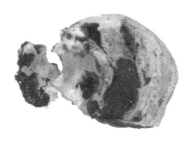

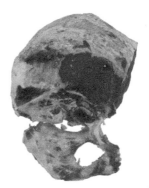

Inside round whole pelvic bone on

Inside round pelvis oyster meat off

Inside round pelvis removed

Inside round out side view

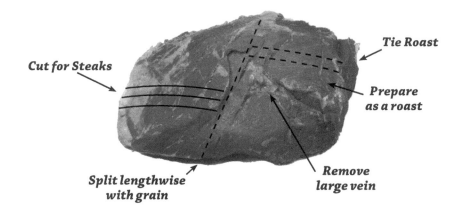

Cut for Steaks

Tie Roast

**Prepare
as a roast**

**Split lengthwise
with grain**

**Remove
large vein**

Inside round inside view

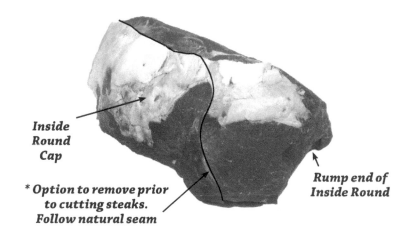

**Inside
Round
Cap**

*** Option to remove prior
to cutting steaks.
Follow natural seam**

**Rump end of
Inside Round**

Inside round split rump or pelvis end view

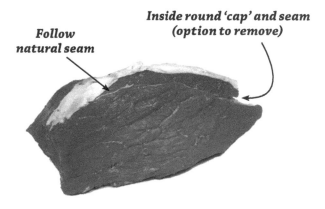

**Follow
natural seam**

**Inside round 'cap' and seam
(option to remove)**

Inside round split, inside view with cap showing

Inside round oven roast

Inside round oven roasts, Inside view

Inside round marinating steaks rump or pelvis end

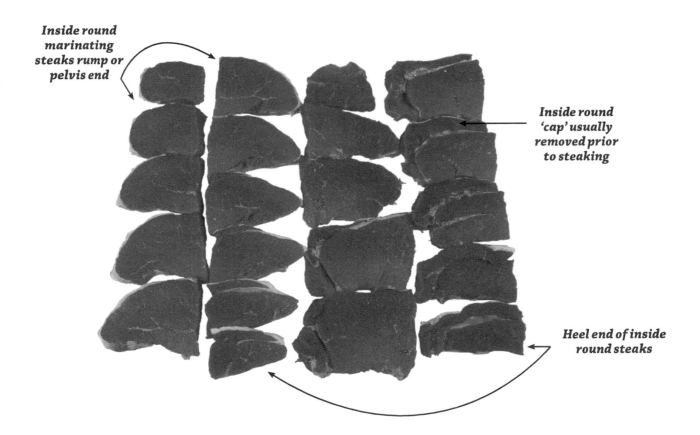

Inside round 'cap' usually removed prior to steaking

Heel end of inside round steaks

Inside round marinating steaks from the whole inside

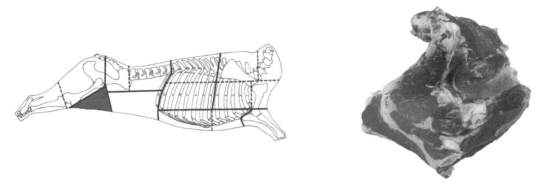

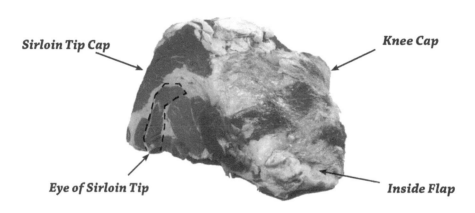

Sirloin tip-inside view

Sirloin Tip Cap

Knee Cap

Eye of Sirloin Tip

Inside Flap

Sirloin tip – hip end view

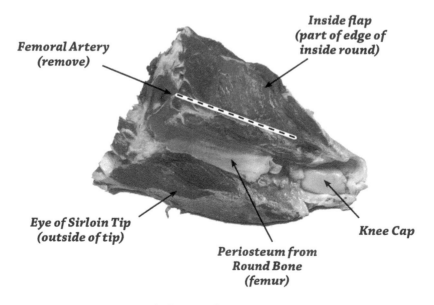

Femoral Artery (remove)

Inside flap (part of edge of inside round)

Eye of Sirloin Tip (outside of tip)

Periosteum from Round Bone (femur)

Knee Cap

Sirloin tip- knee cap side view

Sirloin tip eye & cap muscles removed

Sirloin tip eye removed oven roast- hip end view

Sirloin tip eye removed oven roast- hip end inside view

Sirloin tip eye removed oven roasts

Sirloin tip cap-inside view

Sirloin tip cap-outside view

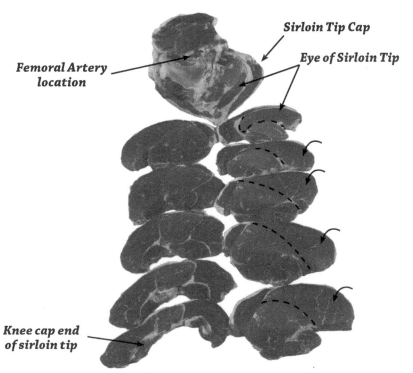

Femoral Artery location

Sirloin Tip Cap

Eye of Sirloin Tip

Knee cap end of sirloin tip

Sirloin tip marinating steaks (all)

Eye of sirloin tip-outside view

Eye of sirloin tip-inside view

Eye of sirloin tip marinating steaks

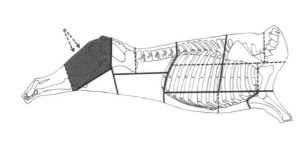

Beef hip – outside round view

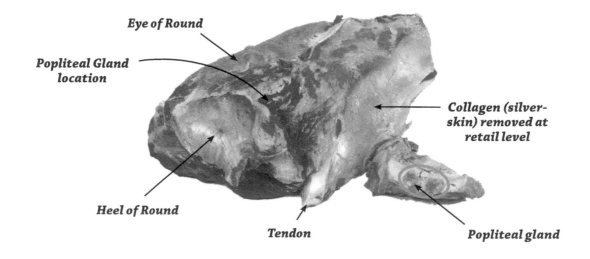

Eye of Round

Popliteal Gland location

Collagen (silver-skin) removed at retail level

Heel of Round

Tendon

Popliteal gland

Outside round – Popliteal gland & fat removed

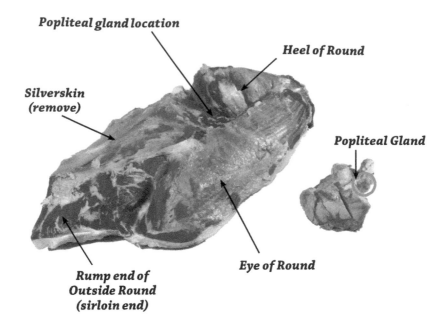

Popliteal gland location

Heel of Round

Silverskin
(remove)

Popliteal Gland

Rump end of
Outside Round
(sirloin end)

Eye of Round

Outside round – Eye of round & rump end view

Outside round flat with heel of round attached

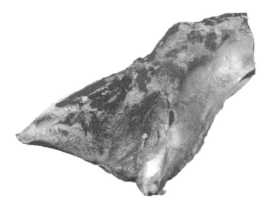

*Outside round flat heel end view
heel of round removed*

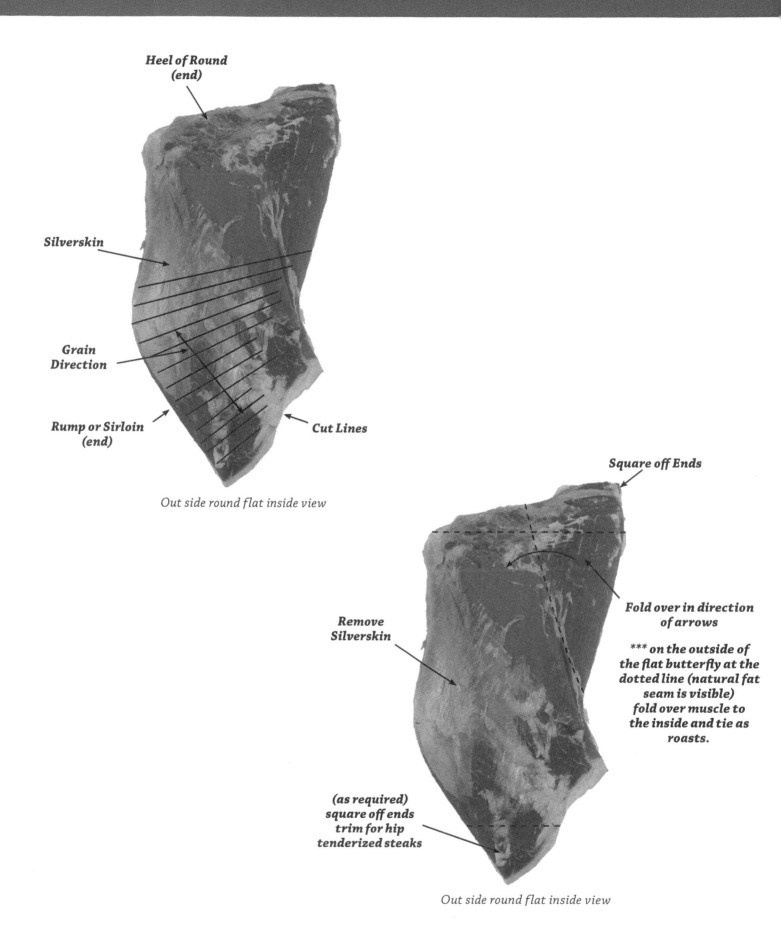

Heel of Round (end)

Silverskin

Grain Direction

Rump or Sirloin (end)

Cut Lines

Out side round flat inside view

Square off Ends

Remove Silverskin

Fold over in direction of arrows

*** on the outside of the flat butterfly at the dotted line (natural fat seam is visible) fold over muscle to the inside and tie as roasts.**

(as required) square off ends trim for hip tenderized steaks

Out side round flat inside view

Rump or Sirloin end

Heel of Round end

Outside round marinating steaks

Outside round flat showing flap folded from the outside to the inside

Outside round oven roast-showing flap fold over

Outside round oven roast-Sirloin or Rump end view

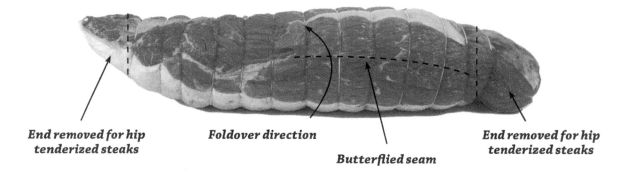

End removed for hip tenderized steaks

Foldover direction

Butterflied seam

End removed for hip tenderized steaks

Outside round flat showing butterflied cut & flap folded over

Heel of round with Superfiscal digital flexor, SDF (lifted)

Heel of round with SDFmuscle off (inside view)

Heel of round with SDF muscle off (outside view)

Eye of round whole (trimmed)

Eye of round (butterflied)

Eye of round oven roast-sirloin & heel end view (butterflied)

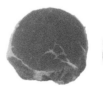

Eye of round oven roast-inside view (butterflied)

Eye of round marinating steaks

Pork

Pork is not only very popular in North America but around most of the world, and has been for many years. It can be retailed fresh, cured or smoked, and can bring considerable profit if it is merchandised in a variety of ways.

Unlike the bovine specie of beef, pork is not aged and should be processed and retailed as soon as possible after receiving to maintain freshness and flavor. The topic of this chapter differs little to that of bovine meats with respect to volunteering information on the production, processing and fabrication of pork and pork retail cuts.

Major topics are hog production, hog processing, grading of hogs, Canadian primal and sub-primal cuts of pork, pork offals and labelling requirements for pork.

Most descriptions of primal and sub-primal cuts of pork are enhanced with graphics and images assisting identification of pork cuts as a guide to the development of hands-on skills in the processing of pork and pork cuts. Included is a collection of retail images charted in cutting sequence from primal to retail cuts.

Pork

History

French settlers first brought pigs to Canada in the late 1500s and early 1600s. Apart from wild game, pork was the most popular meat of the early settlers. Most settlers and landowners of times gone by raised pigs as a food source and as a means for controlling waste materials produced by the land and by humans. Pigs had unrestricted access to the outdoors, were confined to a reasonably large portion of the landscape, and were free to breed and give birth whenever and wherever they wanted. Litters could be as small as three or four piglets and as many as twelve. Of course, large litters brought about some problems as sows would accidently kill their piglets when they rolled over, suffocating the little critters, and boars at times would eat the wandering young. Piglets were also subject to other hazards outside the farmyard. Wolves, badgers, coyotes and foxes all took their turn at helping themselves to a little pork.

It didn't take long to raise pork and as the decades passed pigs became hogs and were confined to barns designed to keep predators out and piglets in. Grazing was restricted to well-fence farmyards. Feed still included human scraps as well as harvest leftovers. The size of the herd increased as the need for protein within the community grew. Byproducts of the animal were utilized for other necessities such as hide hair (used for brushes), the skin (used for leather), the fat (rendered as lard and used as cooking oil, soap and as a sealer for canned meats), the bones (for small hand tools) and of course gelatin extracted from stocks made from pork bones. The meat of pigs could be preserved in brine or salt making it available as a source of protein during the winter months, all before refrigeration became commonplace.

Hog history hasn't been well documented from the time they were first introduced to Canada, at least not until the early part of the nineteenth century when the Canadian government started taking census and recording statistics based on population, agriculture and natural resources, etc. Up to that point, almost all-rural landowners had pigs for the reasons already mentioned.

Statistics Canada's census of population and agriculture for 1921 show the Canadian population to be just under nine million people and about seven hundred thousand farms of which four hundred and fifty thousand reported having pigs with a combined total count of just over three million. Compare those numbers to the 2011 census where our population was reported to be over thirty-three million people and two hundred thousand farms of which only seven thousand reported having pigs with a combined total count being a little under thirteen million pigs. This demonstrates how over time our hog operations have changed. Canada has moved from small family farm operations to large-scale corporate farm operations.

Today hogs are fed a carefully programmed diet. The diet consists of a balance of proteins, carbohydrates, fats and minerals. They derive these from a variety of sources such as corn, rye, barley, vegetable oils, alfalfa, skim milk, fishmeal, feed grains and protein supplements. Pigs are now raised in computer-controlled barns that regulate heat, air circulation, and water supply. Sows, in groups as large as sixteen are kept separate from boars except during times of breeding. Pregnant sows are moved to individual quarters during gestation for health and safety reasons. A pregnant sow delivers her piglets in a farrowing room, which has supplemental heat and an appropriate floor surface for both sow and piglets. Weaned piglets are moved to a nursery barn until they reach an average weight of 27 kilograms after which they are again moved to a feeder barn where they stay until they are six months old or weigh between 100 - 110 kilograms.

The flesh of youthful hogs is very tender because of an absence of heavy connective tissue. Unlike beef, pork doesn't have to be aged and should be processed and retailed as soon as possible after receiving to maintain freshness and flavour. The flesh has a pinkish colour, a fine texture and very greasy white fat. The fat enhances the flavour of the pork and therefore some fat should be left on each cut. Leaner cuts are divided from the loin and the leg.

Choice butcher hogs are approximately six months old at the time of slaughter. Packinghouses can more readily utilize the less marketable products of pork as by-products: pork fat can be processed into pure lard and other profitable items; intestines are used for casings and the head, feet and skin have other uses. Whole carcasses are seldom sold to retailers, though they are still available.

Pork is very popular in Canada and has been for many years. It can be retailed fresh, cooked, cured or smoked, and it will bring considerable profit if it is merchandised in a variety of ways. The bulk of pork is processed for export markets.

Hog Production

Canada produces approximately thirty million pigs annually. The majority of this production occurs in five provinces: Alberta, Saskatchewan, Manitoba, Ontario and Quebec. Major breeds include the Yorkshire (42% of the national herd), Landrace (32%) and Duroc (25%). Each breed is characterized by unique qualities related to litter size, growth rate, feed conversion, carcass structure and composition.

The Yorkshire female, commonly known as the Large White, is used successfully in many crossbreeding programs and has come to represent the ultimate in sow productivity. With its high carcass quality, the Canadian Yorkshire plays an increasing role in maintaining consumer demand for high-quality pork in Canada and its export markets.

Yorkshire female
Credit: Canadian Swine Breeders Association

The Landrace female, also used in pure-bred and crossbreeding programs, is well known for its excellent mothering ability, temperament, longevity and prolific reproduction. This breed is highly desired for its average daily gain, feed conversion and leanness. The Landrace is a well-muscled white animal noted for overall high-quality carcass traits and particularly high yield percentages of belly (bacon) and leg (ham) conformation and quality.

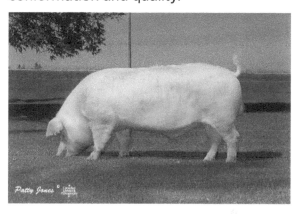

Landrace male
Credit: Canadian Swine Breeders Association

The Duroc breed dominates the male lines in Canada. The Duroc is a solid, pinkish-red meat animal noted for its feed-efficiency and for excellent carcass qualities of intramuscular fat, tenderness and juiciness. Strong feet and legs make the Duroc an excellent choice for rugged commercial feeding conditions. This breed is also noted for large litters, a characteristic retained even when used in crossbreeding programs.

Duroc female pigs
Credit: Canadian Swine Breeders Association

Canadian success in producing consistency with its hog production is a significant advantage to the meat processing industry. The fact that Canadian pork producers use primarily three breeds of hog, animals that grow and finish with excellent carcass conformation, is something breeders and meat processors appreciate in meeting consumer demand.

Hog Health and Wellness falls into the arm of the Canadian Food Inspection Agency (CFIA), which is responsible for all federal inspection programs, related to the feed production of hogs, animal health and processing of hogs as well as plant safeguards such as hazard analysis and critical control points (HACCP). To enhance on-farm food safety programs, CFIA also provides a system for formally recognizing HACCP programs based on technical dependability and delivery. All federal Canadian meat plant harvesting facilities are strictly monitored by CFIA and all provincial meat plant harvesting facilities are strictly monitored by provincial inspection including animal handling protocols and HACCP plans for all aspects of animal care and humane slaughter.

Traceability is a national initiative led by the Canadian Pork Council (CPC) in cooperation with its provincial members and the CFIA. To date, traceability is related to live animals and consists of monitoring swine movement so that any disease outbreak can be contained and controlled. This initiative is structured around a national identification and traceability standard that require all pig farmers and pig custodians (auction markets, transporters, breeders, etc.) to properly identify, keep records and report the movement of pigs under their care or control from birth or import to slaughter or export. This includes the wild boar industry. For more on this visit www.pigtrace.ca.

Hog Processing

In 1991 CFIA developed the Food Safety Enhancement Program (FSEP) in order to promote and support development, implementation and maintenance of HACCP systems in all food processing plants. FSEP started as a voluntary program, but in November 2005 it became mandatory for all federally registered meat and poultry abattoirs, processing plants and storage facilities in Canada.

Working Conditions: To maintain product quality and shelf life, meat cutting and packing is performed at temperatures at or below 4° Celsius. The work requires skill and knowledge in proper cutting techniques and the use of equipment designed to make working easier, safer and more efficient. It also requires physical strength and endurance to maintain demanded productivity levels.

Continuous improvement of plant production processes and vigilant enforcement of safety regulations contribute to ever-increasing levels of employee safety and the elimination of any repetitive motion injuries. On-site health care, ergonomic training sessions and job task rotation assist employees and managers with remaining up to date on the latest techniques and tools available to minimize work related injuries.

Grading

The Canadian pork grading system was developed to facilitate the trade of carcasses by describing the commercially important attributes of pork carcass conformation. Quality evaluation of the composition, amount of lean, and the weight of a carcass are three important criteria used to determine the value of a pork carcass to the packer as demanded by their consumers. Objective instrumentation based on **light reflectance** (probe), **ultrasound**, or **electromagnetic conductivity** can be used to measure composition and carcass value (See more on Grading of Pork in Chapter 12).

Canadian Pork Primal Cuts

Pork is derived from dressed carcasses of porcine animals. It may be derived from male or female, ridgling (a male pig with one or both testicles undescended) or castrated animals. A **Dressed Pork Carcass** is a carcass from which the hair, toenails, developed mammary glands or skin and head have been removed and the carcass has been eviscerated and split into two equal sides. **Sides of Pork** refers to one of the two approximately equal portions of the dressed carcass obtained by a straight cut from the tail to the neck along the median line (centre of the spine). When referring to the **Head**, we mean that portion of the dressed carcass severed at the atlas joint (first cervical vertebra) and it may exclude the jowl.

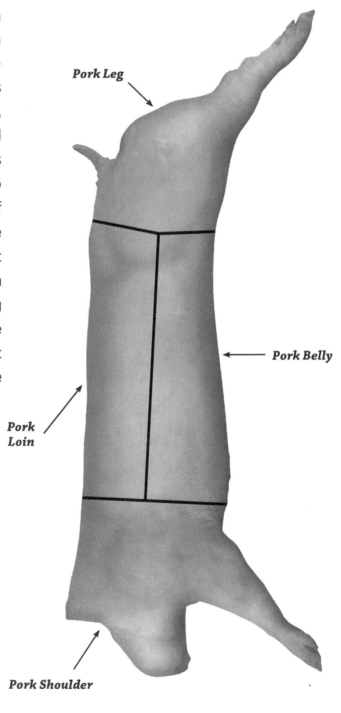

Side of pork
Credit: Canada Pork International

Pork carcass (2 sides)
Credit: CPMCA image collection

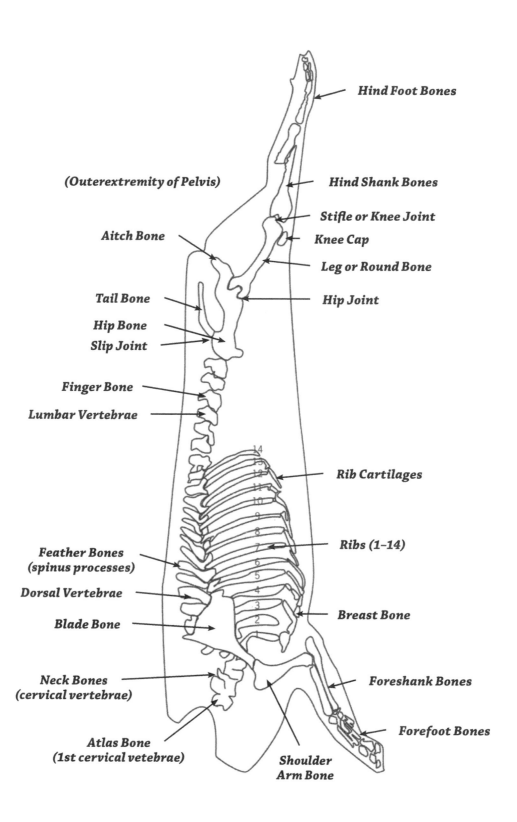

Hind Foot Bones

(Outerextremity of Pelvis)

Hind Shank Bones

Aitch Bone

Stifle or Knee Joint

Knee Cap

Leg or Round Bone

Tail Bone

Hip Joint

Hip Bone

Slip Joint

Finger Bone

Lumbar Vertebrae

14
13
12
11
10
9
8

Rib Cartilages

7

Ribs (1–14)

**Feather Bones
(spinus processes)**

6
5
4

Dorsal Vertebrae

3
2

Breast Bone

Blade Bone

**Neck Bones
(cervical vertebrae)**

Foreshank Bones

Forefoot Bones

**Atlas Bone
(1st cervical vetebrae)**

**Shoulder
Arm Bone**

Skeletal bone structure of Pork
Credit: Jakes & Associates

According to the CFIA Meat Cuts Manual for pork, there are four primal cuts: Shoulder, Leg, Loin and Belly.

- **Shoulder:** means that portion of the carcass, which is separated from the Loin and the Belly by a straight cut passing posterior to the second thoracic vertebra and between the second and third rib.

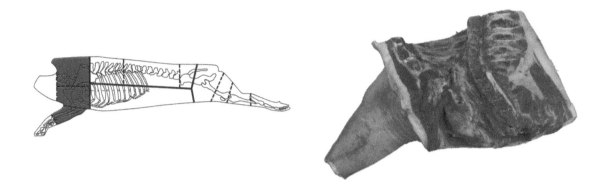

- **Leg:** means that portion of the carcass, which is separated, from the loin and belly by a straight cut passing through the narrow part of the hip bone (shaft of the ilium or pelvic bone).

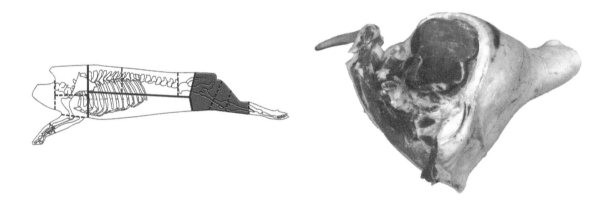

- **Loin:** means that portion of the carcass, which is separated from the leg and shoulder as described above, and from the belly by a straight cut, which passes slightly below (ventral to) the fourth chine bone (thoracic vertebra or rib end) and tenderloin muscles (psoas major and minor or sirloin end).

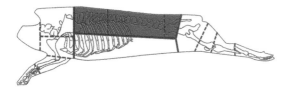 

- **Belly:** means that portion of the carcass, which is separated from the shoulder, leg, and loin as described above. In other words, if you break the carcass as prescribed, you're left with the belly

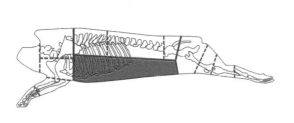 

Sub-primal & Retail Cuts

Sub-primal cuts are derived from primal cuts. The four primal cuts of pork can and usually are further processed into sub-primal cuts for ease of handling and storage. This further processing can be done either at plant level or store level depending on the nature of the operation. Some retail outlets still prefer to break sides of pork to better suit the needs of their operation and consumer demand for in-house fabricated cuts of pork. Primal cuts are broken into sub-primal cuts for later use. The CFIA Meat Manual identifies several sub-primal possibilities for each of the primal cuts of pork.

The sub-primal cuts of the **Pork Shoulder** are: Foot, Hock, Lacone, Jowl, Neck Bones, Riblets, Shoulder Picnic and Shoulder Blade.

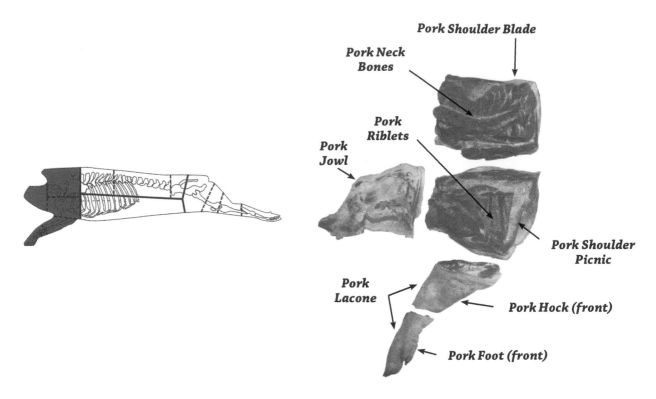

Pork Shoulder Blade

Pork Neck Bones

Pork Riblets

Pork Jowl

Pork Shoulder Picnic

Pork Lacone

Pork Hock (front)

Pork Foot (front)

Credit:Canada Pork International

- **Foot:** means that portion of the shoulder, which is separated from the hock by a straight cut at the wrist (carpal) joint. Splitting it down the centre lengthwise starting between the toes is how the **Pork Foot** (pigs feet) is usually retailed.

- **Hock:** means that portion of the shoulder, which is separated from the foot as described above, and the shoulder picnic by a straight cut which passes through the base of the shaft of the arm bone (distal extremity of the humerus). The **Pork Hock** is either retailed whole or split to reveal the shank meat and is sometimes even cured and smoked.

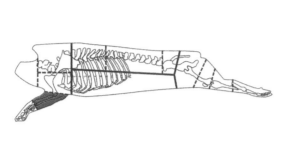

- **Lacone:** is a term used to describe the entire front leg, namely the foot and hock. This cut is not common to the retail market and is sold whole.

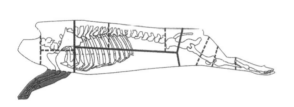

Credit: Canada Pork International

- **Jowl:** means that portion of the shoulder, which is separated from the shoulder picnic by a straight cut, which passes near the inside of the ear dip. The **Pork Jowl** is also retailed whole. It is important you remove all visible glands and score the rind in a criss-cross pattern for decorative looks as well as for cooking and carving purposes.

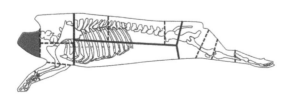

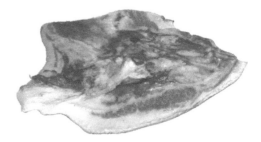

- **Neck bones:** refers to most of the neck bones (cervical vertebrae) and up to the first three backbones (thoracic vertebrae) with adjoining ribs along with the adhering meat. **Pork Neck Bones** are mainly used for soup stocks and soups. To retail these we normally cut them into same cube size on the bandsaw.

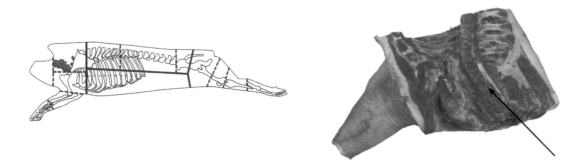

- **Riblets:** means the rib portion of the neck bones. **Pork Riblets** can be retailed whole, sternum removed or split (cut) through the ribs similar to pork side ribs.

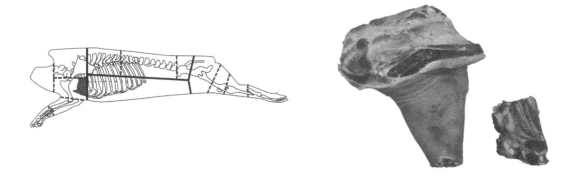

- **Shoulder Picnic:** means that portion of the shoulder which is separated from the Lacone, Neck bones, and Jowl as described above, and from the shoulder Blade by a straight cut passing through the neck of the blade bone (scapula) and a right angle to the jowl cut. Pork Shoulder Picnics can be retailed whole, boneless (as roasts) or cured and smoked. Because of the large knuckle on the arm bone very rarely is this cut sliced into Pork Shoulder Picnic Steaks.

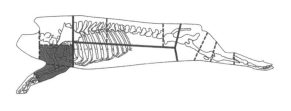 

- **Shoulder blade:** means that portion of the shoulder, which has been separated from the neck bones, jowl, and shoulder picnic as described above. In other words, it's what you're left with when you've followed the above order of processing the shoulder. For the most part, the pork shoulder blade is retailed boneless both as **Pork Shoulder Blade Roast Boneless** and as **Pork Shoulder Blade bone in and Boneless Steaks**. More often than not the pork shoulder blade is separated into top and bottom blades with the bottom serving as already mentioned roasts and steaks and the top for **Fresh Pork Cubes**, **Pork Stewing Meat** or **Lean Ground Pork**.

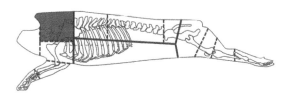 

The sub-primal cuts of the **Pork Leg** are Foot, Shank, Leg Shank Portion, Leg Centre, Leg butt Portion, Leg Shank Half, Leg Butt Half, Leg Inside, Leg outside, Leg Eye and Leg Tip. Less common today are the cuts of Leg shank Portion, Leg Centre, Leg Butt, Leg Shank Half and Leg Butt Half; all of which are more common to smoked cooked hams than fresh hams.

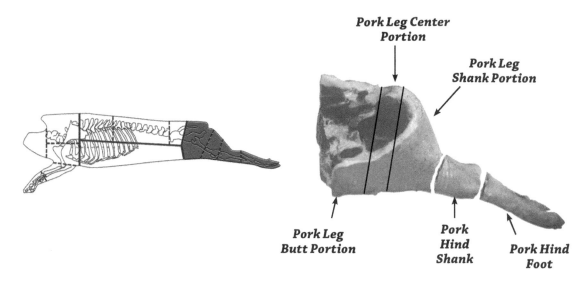

Pork Leg Center Portion

Pork Leg Shank Portion

Pork Leg Butt Portion

Pork Hind Shank

Pork Hind Foot

Credit: Canada Pork International

- **Foot (Hind Foot):** means that portion of the leg, which is separated from the shank by a straight cut passing through the hock (tarsal) joint.

- **Shank:** means that portion of the leg, which is separated from the Foot as described above and from the **Leg, Shank Portion** by a straight cut passing through approximately the mid-point of the shank bones (tibia and fibula). The **Pork Shank** can be retailed similar to the **Pork Hock**.

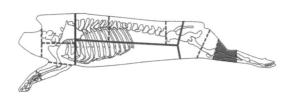 

- **Leg Shank Portion:** means that portion of the leg, which is separated from the Shank as described above, and from the leg centre by a straight cut passing approximately at a right angle to the base of the shaft of the leg bone (distal extremity of the femur). The **Pork Leg Shank Portion** is rarely retailed as such. When on sale or sold as a loss leader stores might have them in stock. You see this cut more as a ready-to-eat (**RTE**) or ready-to-serve (**RTS**) **Ham** than a fresh item. We should also mention that these bone-in fresh leg cuts are more popular among custom cutting operations than retail ones.

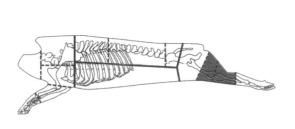 

- **Leg Centre:** means that portion of the leg which is separated from the leg, shank portion as described above, and from the **Leg, Butt Portion** by a straight cut passing at right angle to the proximal end of the shaft of the leg bone (femur), at a point behind (posterior to) the ischium (pelvic bone) and does not include the knuckle portion of the femur pelvic joint. Again, the **Pork Leg Centre** appears when **Pork Legs** are on sale because the retailer made a special buy on fresh legs. The centre cut is a means of merchandising a part of the leg for a better return. This cut isn't something you'll see that often as a fresh item, as it is more common to the cured, cooked and smoked ham.

Custom cutting facilities process the fresh ham to produce this item for their customers as it takes far less time to do so than it does to debone and merchandise it as described in this text further below.

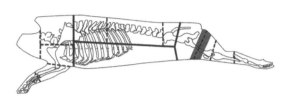 

- **Leg Butt Portion:** means that portion of the Leg separated from the leg centre as described above. This cut too is not often seen in fresh counters these days as retailers can command a better dollar when the fresh ham is deboned, muscle seamed and processed as individual parts (see below- inside, outside and tip). Once again, this cut is more common to the cured, cooked and smoked ham and custom cutting operations.

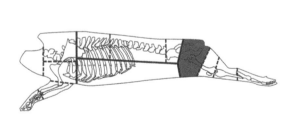 

- **Leg Shank Half:** refers to an alternative portion of the leg, which may include the shank and is separated from the leg butt half by a straight cut passing at a right angle to the middle of the shaft of the leg bone (femur). As for the above cuts from the pork leg, it is mostly sold as a ready to eat (RTE) item.

- **Leg Butt Half:** refers to an alternative portion of the leg separated from the leg shank half as described above and retailed in similar fashion.

The Pork leg can be further merchandised in to the following sub primals

Note: Retail cut Image sequences from these subprimals are found at the end of the chapter.

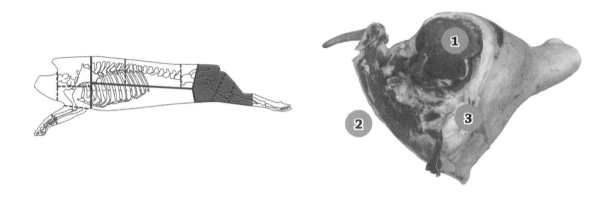

Pork Leg inside 1 Pork leg outside 2 (underneath) Pork leg tip 3

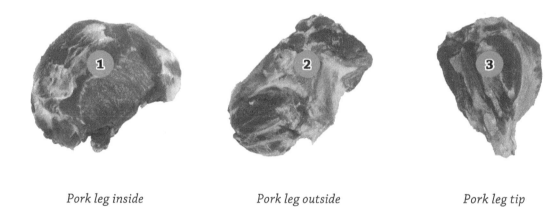

Pork leg inside *Pork leg outside* *Pork leg tip*

- **Leg Inside:** means that portion of the leg located inside (medial side) of the leg, which is separated from the **Leg Outside** by cutting lengthwise along the natural seam. It contains two main muscles, namely: semimembranosus and adductor. We refer to these as **Denuded Pork Inside Rounds** as the description doesn't include the cap, which covers these muscles. When retailing this cut the cap is removed and the **Pork Inside Round** can then be merchandised as either a **Pork Leg Inside Round Roast** or **Pork Leg Inside Round Steaks**. As with all the leaner boneless pork leg cuts it can also be used to make **Pork Inside Round Schnitzel, Pork Leg Cutlets, Pork Leg Cubes, Pork Leg Kabobs** and **Pork Stir Fry** or **Pork Stewing Meat**.

- **Leg Outside:** means that portion of the Leg located outside (lateral side) of the leg, which is separated from the Leg Inside as described above. It contains two muscles, namely: semitendinosus and biceps femoris. It may exclude the Leg Eye (semitendinosus). The meat industry retails this cut as a **Pork Leg Outside Round Roast**. It can also be used for **Pork Stewing Meat**, **Pork Leg Cubes**, **Pork Leg Cutlets**, **Pork Stir Fry**, and worst-case scenario for **Fresh Lean Ground Pork**.

- **Leg Eye:** means the round-shaped muscle (semitendinosus) found at the outer (posterior) extremity of the leg outside. This cut use to be left on the outside. Nowadays it's separated and merchandised as a lean cut used for **Pork Leg Eye Roast**, steaks, or cubes. It's also used to make cutlets, kabobs, and stir-fry (as per all of the above, proper nomenclature applies).

- **Leg Tip:** means that portion of the **Leg** located in front of (anterior to) the leg bone (femur), obtained by two (2) straight cuts at right angles to each other. The first cut begins approximately at the knee cap (patella) and follows the full length of the leg bone (femur) up to the vicinity of the knuckle-bone articulation (head of femur/acetabulum). The second cut is at right angle to the first and intersects the first cut at the articulation. It contains three (3) main muscles, namely: vastus medialis, rectus femoris and vastus lateralis. Pork leg Tip is retailed as either a **Pork Leg Tip Roast** or **Pork Leg Tip Steaks**. As with the pork inside and outside, the **Pork Tip** has the same utility.

The sub-primal cuts of the **Pork Loin** are: Rib Chop or Rib Roast (also used for Country Style Ribs), Loin Centre, Sirloin, Loin Rib Half, Loin Sirloin Half, Back Ribs, Tenderloin, and Button Bones. It should be noted that Button Bones are a commodity not often seen in retail outlets but still available upon request; for the most part, they are sold as a seasoned, coated, and precooked item in the larger supermarkets.

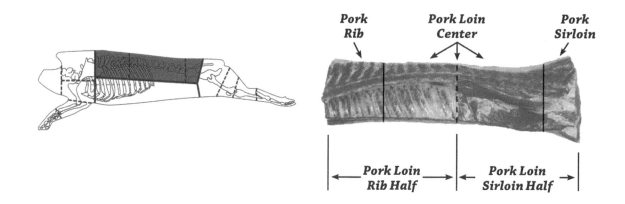

- **Rib Chop or Rib Roast:** means that anterior portion of the **Loin**, which is separated from the loin centre by a straight cut passing behind (posterior to) the seventh chine bone (thoracic vertebra). **Pork Rib Chops** and **Pork Rib Chops Boneless** are the more common cuts processed or fabricated from this part of the pork loin. You can also be creative and make **Pork Loin Rib Country Style Ribs, Seasoned** or **Pork Rib Chops Stuffed Boneless** or **Roasts**, **Pork Loin Cutlets**, **Pork Loin Kabobs**, **Pork Stir Fry**, etc.

The Pork Loin can be merchandised in to the following subprimals

Note: Additional retail cut Image sequences for this primal are found at the end of the chapter.

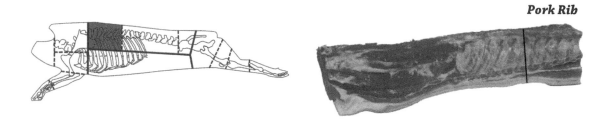

Pork Rib

- **Loin Centre:** means that central portion of the loin containing no cap muscle (trapezius), which is separated from the **Rib Chop** or **Rib Roast** as described above, and from the **Sirloin** by a straight cut which passes through a point in front (anterior) of the pin bone (ilium or tuber coxae). As with the **Pork Loin Rib** (above) the **Pork Loin Centre** can be merchandised into regular and boneless chops. The funny thing here is **Pork Loin Centre Cut Chops** (meaning regular) may or may not have some tenderloin attached to them depending from which end they are cut, close to the rib or closer to the sirloin.

  Note: the Pork Loin, Centre contains no pin bone (ilium) and no cap muscle (trapezius).

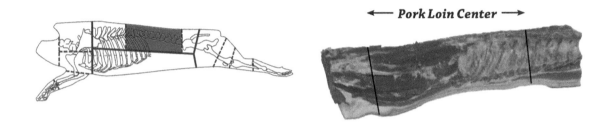

← *Pork Loin Center* →

- **Sirloin:** means that posterior portion of the loin, which is separated from the loin centre as described above. **Pork Sirloin Chops** are sold with bone or without bone. With bone intact the **Pork Sirloin Chop** will have a portion of tenderloin attached and the boneless version will not. The **Pork Sirloin Boneless Portion** of the loin is sometimes referred to as the buckeye. **Buckeye** is a packinghouse term and is not accepted as a product term on labels.

  Note: the Sirloin contains the anterior half of the pin bone (ilium).

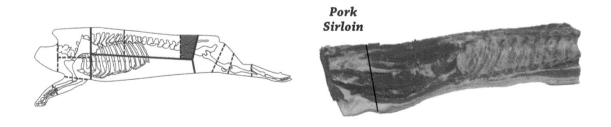

Pork Sirloin

- **Loin Rib Half:** means that anterior portion of the loin, which is separated from the **Loin, Tenderloin Half** by a straight cut which passes behind (posterior to) the last rib (alternative cut). If you're reading these descriptions in the order they have been written then you'll know the potential retail cuts this sub-primal produces.

  Note: the Loin, Tenderloin Half contains no rib or parts thereof.

- **Loin Sirloin Half:** means that posterior portion of the loin, which is separated from the **Loin, Rib Half** as described above (alternative cut). With respect to retail cuts processed from this sub-primal you'll find them in the above literature.

Pork Loin Sirloin Half   Pork Loin Rib Half

Pork loin sirloin & rib halves

- **Back Ribs:** refers to the ribs with adhering meat obtained from the **Rib Half** or **Rib End** of the loin. **Pork Back Ribs** are retailed as is. They can be portioned into smaller sections but doing so doesn't alter the nomenclature assigned to this cut.

Pork Back Ribs

Pork loin with back ribs (right half)

- **Tenderloin:** means the cylindrically shaped muscle (psoas major and minor) located on the inside (ventral side) of the **Loin Sirloin Half**. **Pork Tenderloin** can be sold whole, stuffed, marinated, seasoned, or portioned into **Pork Tenderloin Medallions**.

Pork Tenderloin

- **Button Bones:** that portion of the backbones (transverse process of the lumbar vertebrae) with adherent connecting meat tissues removed from the Loin (not a common cut but still available). This cut was more popular in times gone by and may yet make a comeback. Most are retailed and sold as a seasoned, coated, and deep-fried product that needs reheating. There are retailers who process their own pork loins that do from time to time have this item fresh on hand.

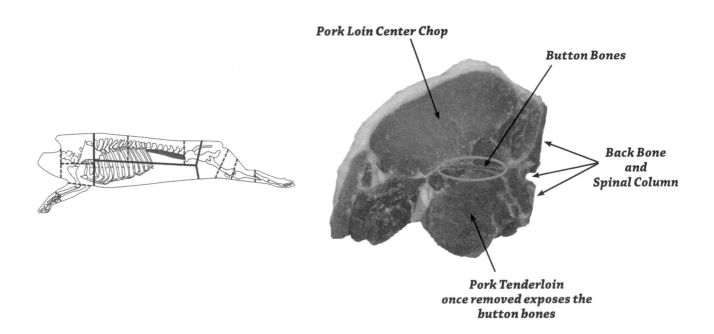

Pork Loin Center Chop

Button Bones

Back Bone and Spinal Column

Pork Tenderloin once removed exposes the button bones

The sub-primal cuts of the **Pork Belly** are: Side Ribs, Side Rib Centre Cut, Side Rib Centre Off, Breast Bone/Pork Bones, Side Ribs Breast Bone Off, Side (Boneless Belly) and Skirt. Traditionally the skirt of the Side Ribs is left on.

The Pork Side Ribs can be further merchandised into more retail cuts.

Note: Retail cut Image sequences from these primal are found at the end of the chapter.

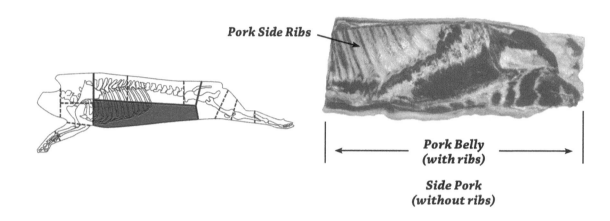

Pork Side Ribs

*Pork Belly
(with ribs)*

*Side Pork
(without ribs)*

Side Ribs: means that portion of the belly containing the ribs and adhering meat, which is separated from the **Side (Boneless Belly)** by a cut following the contour of the breastbone (sternum) and rib cartilage (costal cartilage). **Pork Side Ribs** are retailed in various ways, as you'll see below. This item is sold with sternum bone removed, cut down the middle of the ribs, wrapped in size appropriate packaging.

- **Side Rib, Centre Cut:** that portion of the **Side Rib** from which the breastbone and the rib cartilage have been removed.

- **Side Rib, Centre Off:** that portion of the **Side Rib** from which a portion of the centre cut has been removed; it is comprised of a portion of the centre cut, the breastbone and rib cartilage.

- **Breast Bone/Pork Bones:** that portion of the **Side Ribs** from which the Pork Side Ribs Centre Cut has been removed and only the breastbone and/or cartilage remains.

- **Side Rib, Breast Bone Off:** refers to that portion of the **Side Rib** from which the Breastbone has been removed.

- **Side (Boneless Belly):** means that portion of the belly from which the side ribs have been removed as described above (see Side Ribs). The **Pork Side Belly** is retailed as **Pork Fresh Sliced Side**, **Pork Fresh Side**, or cubed, marinated, and seasoned **Salt Pork**. **Side Pork Bellies** are common to the processing of **Side Bacon**.

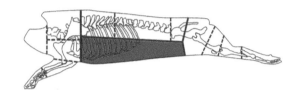

Pork side ribs whole (Outside view)   *Side pork whole*

- **Skirt:** means the muscular costal part of the diaphragm. In retail counters skirt is more common to beef than it is to pork.

Pork Skirt (diaphragm)

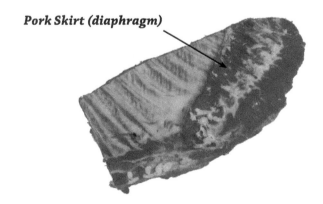

Pork side ribs with skirt

Pork Variety Meats

Variety meats are edible parts of an animal other than skeletal muscle. Listed below are those of pork.

Variety meats also referred to as "offal" have gained some notoriety as comfort food. Some dishes containing offal remain part of a region's cuisine and may be consumed especially in connection with holidays such as the Scottish tradition of eating haggis on Robbie Burns Day.

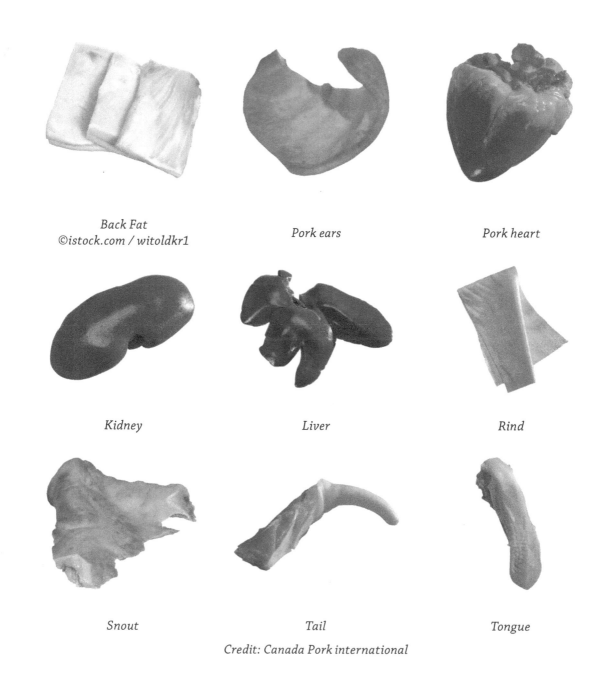

Back Fat
©istock.com / witoldkr1

Pork ears

Pork heart

Kidney

Liver

Rind

Snout

Tail

Tongue

Credit: Canada Pork international

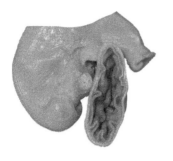

Tripe
©istock.com / poongpeed

Feet
Credit: Canada Pork International

Brain
Credit: Canada Pork International

Pork Liver is most often dark reddish brown (sometimes almost black) in colour, and is less tender than other livers. It usually has a pronounced strong flavour and does not enjoy the same popularity as beef or veal liver. The strong flavour can be tempered by soaking the liver slices in milk. Pork liver is not skinned prior to cooking and can be identified from other livers by its course spotty marked skin.

Pork Kidney is dark reddish brown in colour and very strong flavoured. It is not suitable for use in conjunction with stewing beef. It is smooth, elongated and bean-shaped and can be purchased in bulk, either fresh or frozen. A very small volume seller, pork kidneys weigh from 175 g to 225 g. They are purplish grey in colour and have a characteristic flavour.

Pork Hearts & Tongues, though some ethnic groups enjoy them, they are usually processed commercially into processed meat or bottled products but can be ordered from the packers for specific orders.

Pork Tripe is another offal item whose retail demand is dependent upon market locale. This is processed from the muscular inner lining of the stomach. It can be smooth tripe (plain) or honeycombed and with pork it is very slimy. Where in demand, it is sold fresh. Tripe is usually partially cooked during processing. Most pork tripe from the packers is used in commercially prepared sausage and luncheon meats.

Pork Skin (Rind): means skin obtained from a **Dressed Pork Carcass** or portions thereof and excludes the snout, lips, scalp and ears.

CFIA Nomenclature Requirements for Pork

Retailers are responsible for ensuring that the names used to describe meat cuts on labels and in advertisements include the appropriate specific terms. The name used to describe all pork meat cuts must include an indication of the species. For example, the term "pork" must appear in conjunction with the term "shoulder" when a pork shoulder roast is offered for sale. The name used to describe all variety meats (listed further on under Variety Meats), must include an indication of the species.

RETAIL MEAT CUT LABELLING REQUIREMENTS FOR PORK.

Prepackaged pork meat cuts offered for sale at retail must be marked with:

- the name of the species and cut,
- the name and address of the retailer,
- the net quantity,
- the packaging date,
- the durable life of the meat cut unless the durable life is indicated on a poster next to the product, and
- the words "previously frozen" if a meat cut that has been frozen is thawed prior to sale unless the words "previously frozen" appear on a poster next to the product.

LIST OF PORK MEAT CUT MODIFIERS

Modifiers are descriptions used to explain in more detail what the cut of meat is or what alterations have been done to the primal/sub-primal cut to obtain the outcome you have before you. As with the fabrication of a Boneless Pork Shoulder Bade Roast or a Butterfly Loin Pork Chop, there are steps taken to obtain them. First off with boneless items you have to remove the bones. With items identified as roasts, you either net them or tie them into a shape common to their purpose, as with roasting, thus the modifiers "Boneless" and "Roast". With the term "Butterfly" it is understood the cut (chop) is boneless, therefore chops that are butterflied have to be boneless or they can't be labeled as "Butterfly."

- Bone in
- Boneless
- Breaded
- Butterfly Chop
- Cap removed
- Chop
- Chop with pocket
- Cutlet
- Crown
- Crown roast
- Delicatize(d)
- Diced Pork
- Frenched Chop

- Kabob
- Medallion
- Portion
- Roast
- Rolled
- Seasoned
- Semi-Boneless
- Skinless, Skinned
- Steak
- Stuffed
- Tenderize(d)
- Tied
- Trimmed

Note: While not required, these modifiers may be used to describe pork cuts provided they are informative and not misleading

PORK LEG TIP
STEAK (BL)

PORK TENDERLOIN
(Medallions)

PORK SIDE RIBS
(Breast Bone Removed)

Packed On	Best Before	Sell By
Net Wt/Ct	Unit Price	Total Price

Packed On	Best Before	Sell By
Net Wt/Ct	Unit Price	Total Price

Packed On	Best Before	Sell By
Net Wt/Ct	Unit Price	Total Price

Pork leg tip steaks boneless

Pork tenderloin medallions

*Pork Side Ribs breast bone
removed or off*

Credit: TRU Retail Meat Processing Program

BASIC LABELLING REQUIREMENTS FOR PORK

Label: Pork (Species), Retail cut (Primal/Sub-primal), Modifier (if altered).

Sample: Pork (Species), Loin Centre Cut Chops (Primal/Retail cut), Boneless (Modifier).

The following items are exceptions that do not require the primal name preceding the retail name: Pork Feet, Pork Jowl, Pork Hock, Diced Pork, Pork Stir Fry, and any variety of Ground Pork.

The term "**Pork Neck Bones**" may be used to describe the neck bones and adhering meat, including the cervical vertebrae part of the occipital bone and up to three thoracic vertebrae with adjoining ribs (see Sub-primal Cuts: Pork Shoulder).

The term "**Pork Riblets**" may be used to describe the rib portion of the neck bones (see Sub-primal Cuts: Pork Shoulder).

The term "**Pork Back Ribs**" may be used to describe the strip or individual pieces of rib bones, including the adherent connecting meat tissue obtained from the rib half of the loin (see Sub-primal Cuts: Pork Loin).

The term "**Pork Tenderloin**" may be used to describe the main muscle (psoas major and minor) removed from the inside (ventral) portion of the loin (see Sub-primal Cuts: Pork Loin).

The term "**Button Bones**" may be used to describe that portion of the backbones (transverse process of the lumbar vertebrae) with the adherent connecting meat tissues removed from the loin (see Sub-primal Cuts: Pork Loin).

Pork Leg:

Boneless Pork Leg Roast must contain all three main sub-primal parts –Tip, Inside, Outside and Eye.

Cutlets from the Leg must indicate the primal on the label, e.g. Pork Leg Cutlets.

Roasts or Steaks cut from any of the four main leg sub-primal muscles must be indicated on the label, e.g. Pork Leg Inside Roast or Steak, Pork Leg Tip, Pork Leg Outside or Pork Leg Eye.

Small pieces of unidentifiable muscles of meat do not need the primal on the label, e.g. Pork Stir Fry.

Pork Loin:

All cuts from the pork loin must state the section of loin: Pork Rib, Pork Loin Centre, Pork Sirloin, Pork Loin Rib Half, and Pork Loin Sirloin Half.

Belly:

Pork Belly can be referred to as Side Pork if side ribs have been removed.

The breastbone from the side ribs must be labelled Pork Breast Bone.

To be labelled Pork Side Ribs, the entire side ribs must be present; if not, the modification should be indicated on the label, i.e. Pork Side Ribs Centre, Pork Side Ribs Centre Cut, or Pork Side Ribs Centre Cut Off, as the case may be.

Shoulder:

Retail cuts from the Shoulder blade and the Shoulder Picnic must indicate "Shoulder" on the label, e.g. Pork Shoulder Blade or Pork Shoulder Picnic.

Pork Shoulder Picnic must not be labelled as Picnic "Ham", as Ham is reserved for the Pork Leg

GROUND MEATS:

Ground Pork must be labelled as Extra Lean, Lean, Medium, or Regular and must comply with regulated fat content.

- **Regular Ground** (naming the species) when meat from the named species is processed by grinding and does not contain more than 30% fat;
- **Medium Ground** (naming the species) when meat from the named species is processed by grinding and does not contain more than 23% fat;
- **Lean Ground** (naming the species) when meat from the named species is processed by grinding and does not contain more than 17% fat;
- **Extra Lean Ground** (naming the species) when meat from the named species is processed by grinding and does not contain more than 10% fat.

Block & Knife Ready Pork Products

With ever-growing costs concerning the operation of a business one-thing entrepreneurs look for is ways in which they can save overhead expenses without compromising quality or value. Block and knife ready meats come vacuum packaged in boxes, separated according to primal and sub-primal cuts, and are easier to stock, stack, and store. This product does not need the overhead rails that swinging carcasses need. Block and knife ready meats have been portioned at plant level into large manageable primal and sub-primal sections that take up less room and can be used as demand dictates much quicker than that of swinging sides of pork.

Some of the more common Block and Knife Ready meats of pork include the following:

- Pork Shoulders (Montreal style)
- Pork Picnics (Regular and Boneless)
- Pork Blades (Regular and Boneless)
- Legs of Pork (Regular, Boneless, and segmented muscles) (Insides etc.))
- Pork Loins (Regular and Boneless)

- Pork Sirloin (Boneless)
- Pork Back Ribs
- Pork Tenderloins
- Boneless Pork Bellies
- Pork Side Ribs
- Jowls
- Trim (50/50; 60/40; 70/30 lean to fat)

Counter Ready Pork Products

Counter ready meats refer to those pork items that have been processed and fabricated at plant level. They are packaged for displays, boxed and shipped to store level. With these products, there is no need of a meat cutter. The product is finished and ready for in-store labelling and displaying. Counter ready meats come in one of two forms: fresh (as listed below) or processed (meaning fermented, cooked, brined, frozen and fresh sausages etc.).

Some larger supermarket chains carry fresh pork counter ready meats due to a shortage of skilled labour in their area for people who know how to cut, wrap, price, and display products. There is also the argument that counter ready meat costs less when taking into consideration the costs associated with labour and space allocation. It is suspected that where counter ready meats are sold, it is due to one or the other aforementioned reasons.

Some of the more common Fresh Pork Counter Ready Products are:

- Netted Boneless Pork Shoulder Picnic Roasts
- Netted boneless Pork Shoulder Blade Roasts
- Boneless Pork Shoulder Blade Steaks
- Netted Boneless Pork Leg Roasts
- Pork Leg Cutlets (Regular, Seasoned or Breaded
- Pork Loin Chops (Rib, Centre, and Sirloin)
- Boneless Pork Loin Chops (Rib and Centre)
- Pork Tenderloins
- Pork Side Ribs Breastbone Removed

- Pork Back Ribs
- Side Pork (sliced and pieces)
- Ground Pork

Some of the more common Processed Pork Counter Ready Products include but are not limited to the following:

- Smoked Pork Picnics
- Capocollo/ Capicola/ Cappa etc.
- Fresh and Frozen Pork Sausages (various flavours)
- Fresh and Frozen Pork Sausage Meat (seasonal fluctuations)

- Sausage Patties
- Cooked Boneless Pork Leg Roasts
- RTE and RTS Hams (Whole, Half, Centre Cut Steaks, or Boneless)
- Kaiser Pork Loin/Chops (AKA Kassler)
- Back Bacon (Regular or Peameal)
- Cooked Back Ribs
- Salt Pork
- Bacon (Side, Sliced or Pieces)
- Cooked Side Ribs

Value-Added Pork Cuts

Value-added cuts of pork are innovative cuts designed to attract consumer attention and interest. These cuts give consumers more options for their favourite meats and cooking methods. Retailers formulate value-added items for one of two reasons, to brand a product item available only through them and/or to take advantage of a popular trend or demand.

Value-added pork items have gone from a simple seasoning to cooked ready to reheat items. These items include ribs, roasts, chops, sausages, and deli meats such as pies and stuffed pastries (sausage rolls) and salads. Most supermarkets and some independents now carry takeout foods where prepared meats like sweet and sour ribs, meat sauce for spaghetti and fish and chips are readily available.

As lifestyle patterns change so does the industry. More and more consumers are looking to convenience foods, and both shops and meat plants are responding with new products and strategies for enticing consumers to purchase their products. (More on value-added in Chapter 5: Bovine Animals)

Food service products are a direct response by the industry to fill a demand made by retailers for the need for variety and versatility. Food service cuts cater to food service outlets but that doesn't mean all products designed for food service end up in food service facilities such as restaurants. For more on food service cuts see chapter 5.

SUMMARY

Block Ready Meats	Labelling Modifiers	Swine
Butcher Hogs	Nomenclature	Traceability
CFIA	Pork Grading System	Ultrasound
Duroc	Primal Cuts	Wild Boar
HACCP	Probe	Variety Meats
Landrace	Sub-primal Cuts	Yorkshire

DISCUSSION QUESTIONS

1. From 1921 to 2011 the Canadian hog population increased by 10 million. Explain why.
2. Why do we not have to age pork?
3. To what weight do we finish butcher hogs?
4. There are three main breeds of hogs used in Canada in the production of pork. Discuss their differences.
5. Why does Canada have a "traceability" program for swine? Does this program include wild boar?
6. How is pork graded and why?
7. CFIA has labelling requirements for all species. What are they for Pork?
8. How many primal cuts does a side of pork have, and what are they?
9. Pork can be purchased in carcass form (sides of pork), besides retail, in what other bulk forms can pork be purchased?
10. What is the meaning of "value-added" as it relates to pork?

Pork Retail Meat Processing options

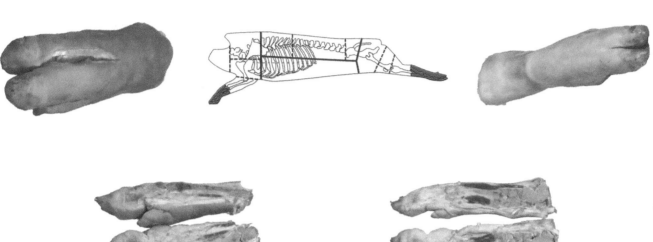

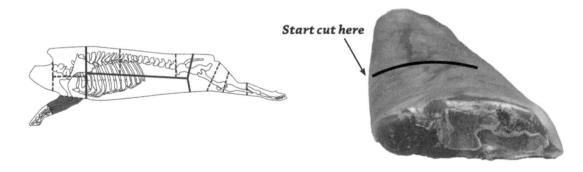

Pork feet split　　　　　　　　　　*Pork feet split*

Start cut here

Pork hock (start cut at narrow side of hock cutting through bone & muscle to one half inch from skin on opposite side & fold open.

Pork front hock cross cut side view　　　　　*Pork front hock cross cut retail view*

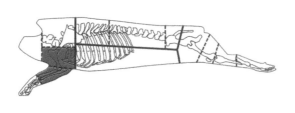
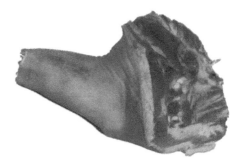

Pork shoulder picnic shank end view

*Pork shoulder picnic blade
end view*

*Pork shoulder picnic shank &
blade portions*

*Pork shoulder picnic
shank portion*

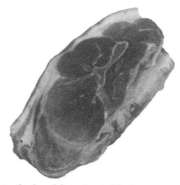

Pork shoulder picnic blade portion

*Pork shoulder picnic roast
boneless skin on*

*Pork should picnic roast boneless
skin on blade end view*

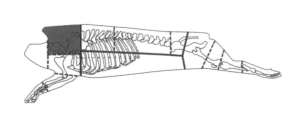

Pork shoulder blade loin rib end view

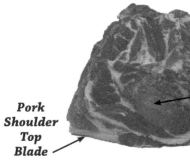

Pork Shoulder Top Blade

Pork Shoulder Bottom Blade

Pork shoulder blade neck bones off, blade bone in

Pork shoulder blade steaks bone in

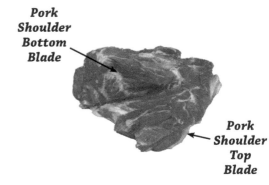

Pork Shoulder Bottom Blade

Pork Shoulder Top Blade

Pork shoulder blade boneless

Pork shoulder blade roasts boneless

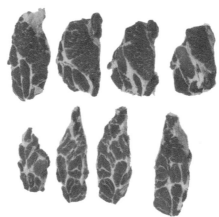

Pork shoulder bottom blade steaks

Pork stew (often from the top blade)

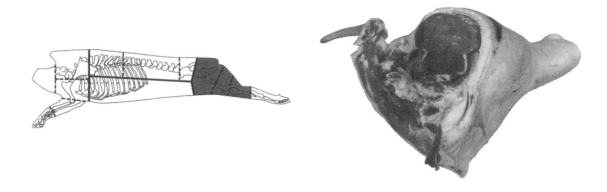

Pork leg whole

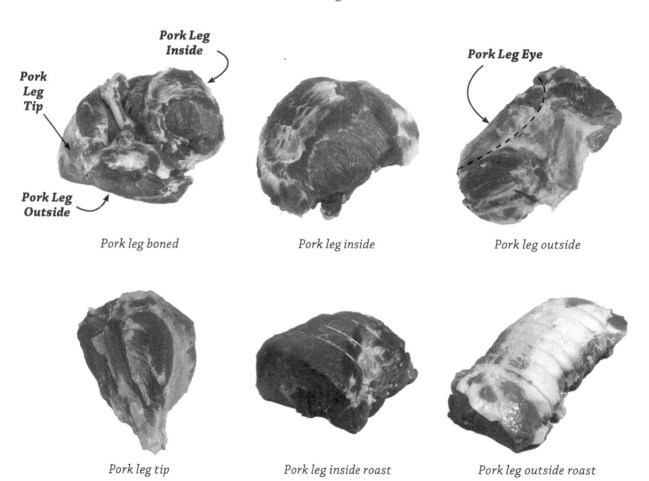

Pork Leg Inside

Pork Leg Tip

Pork Leg Outside

Pork Leg Eye

Pork leg boned

Pork leg inside

Pork leg outside

Pork leg tip

Pork leg inside roast

Pork leg outside roast

Pork leg tip roast & steaks   Pork leg inside steaks   Pork leg outside steaks

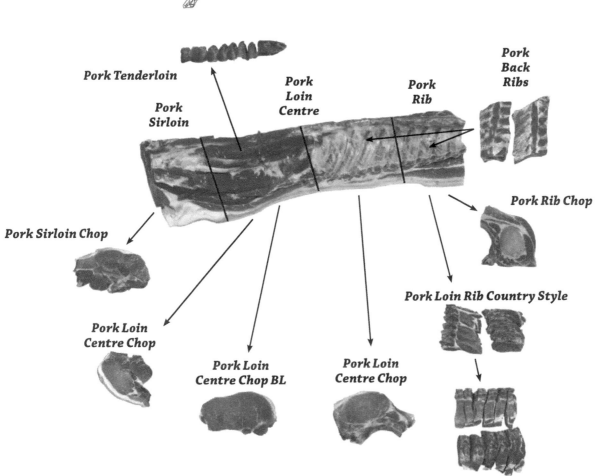

Pork Tenderloin

Pork Sirloin

Pork Loin Centre

Pork Rib

Pork Back Ribs

Pork Sirloin Chop

Pork Loin Centre Chop

Pork Loin Centre Chop BL

Pork Loin Centre Chop

Pork Rib Chop

Pork Loin Rib Country Style

Pork loin retail images with names

Pork rib bone-in & boneless

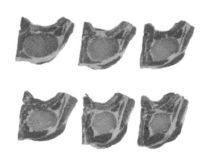

Pork rib chops

Pork loin center boneless

Pork loin center

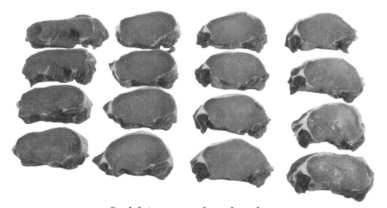

Pork loin center chops boneless

Pork loin center roast boneless

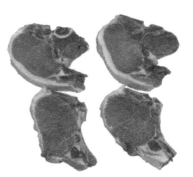

(Top)Pork loin center chops
(cut from sirloin end of loin)
(Bottom) Pork loin center chops
(Cut from rib end of loin)

Pork sirloin bone in

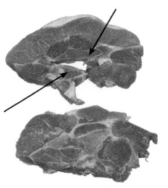

*Pork sirloin chops
(slip joint exposed)
Hip bone (Top)
Sacrum vertebra (Bottom)
is removed to create a more
appealing chop*

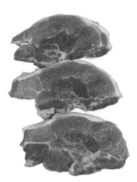

Pork sirloin chops

Pork sirloin boneless

Pork sirloin chops boneless

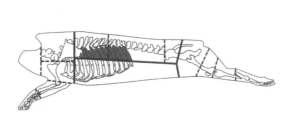

Pork back ribs

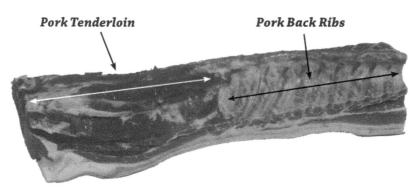

Pork Tenderloin **Pork Back Ribs**

Pork loin with back ribs (right half)

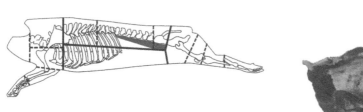

Pork tenderloin whole

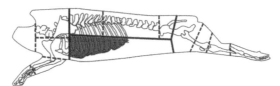

Pork side ribs (inside view)

Pork side ribs (outside view)

Pork side ribs center cut (bottom)
Pork side ribs center cut off (top)

Pork breast bone (top)
Pork side ribs center cut breast bone off (bottom)

Pork breast bone (top)
Pork breast bone cross cut (bottom)

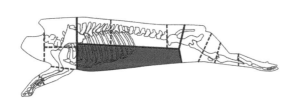

Side pork whole

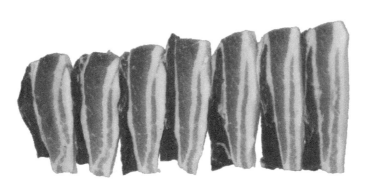

Side pork sliced thin

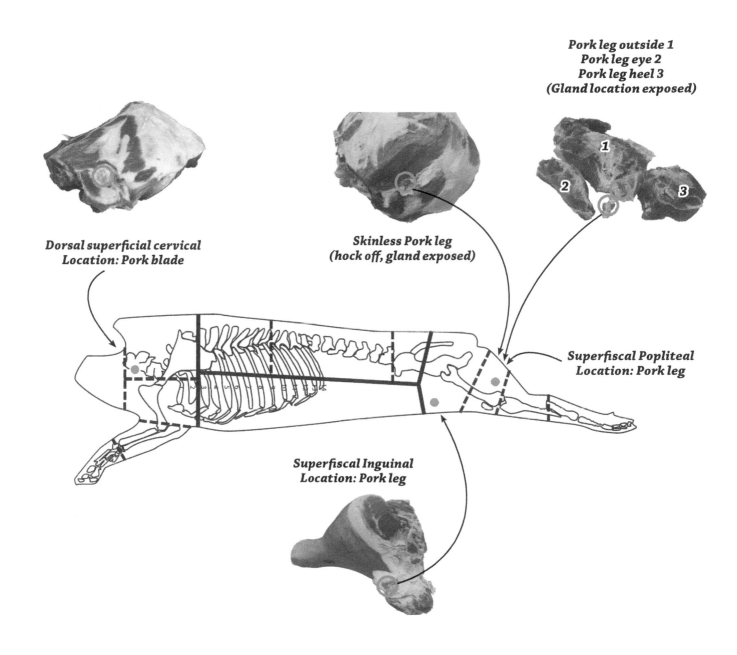

Pork leg outside 1
Pork leg eye 2
Pork leg heel 3
(Gland location exposed)

Dorsal superficial cervical
Location: Pork blade

Skinless Pork leg
(hock off, gland exposed)

Superfiscal Popliteal
Location: Pork leg

Superfiscal Inguinal
Location: Pork leg

The 3 major glands of the side of pork showing locations
(These are usually removed during Retail Processing)

Note: For further details on Bacterial growth & Safe Meat Handling see the thermometer
guides, appendix pages 746-747.

Chapter 7

Lamb

This chapter covers topics on various breeds of sheep and provides information on the processing, grading and labelling of lamb and lamb cuts.

Lamb is an Ovine animal having the same bone structure as Goat and Mutton. With ovine animals becoming more popular it's imparative Canadian meat cutters have knowledge of processing carcasses into primal, sub-primal and retail cuts.

In the processing of smaller carcass animals like those of ovine carcasses more care and skill is needed to avoid unnessecary waste. To assist with skill development and knowledge of lamb cuts the chapter provides descriptions of primal and sub-primal cuts of lamb highlighted with graphics and images. These graphics and images are arranged in sequence of fabrication assisting the reader with linking retail lamb cuts to their primal and sub-primal origin.

Lamb

History

Sheep are ruminant herbivores (ovine animals), meaning they eat only plants (true vegans) and digest their food in four stomachs, just like cattle, goats and deer. Female sheep are called Ewes and males are called Rams.

Sheep in Canada can be traced back to pioneer days when settlers from France, England and other parts of Europe took the long trek to the new land of Eastern Canada looking for a better life. The sheep they brought with them across the Atlantic Ocean were used for their wool as well as for their meat. Sheep wool was used in the production of clothing and sheep offspring (lamb) for meat, providing both attire and protein for the settlers. At the time, mid to late 1600s, there were reported to be approximately 500 sheep in eastern Canadian settlements. Like all small farm animals of that time, lamb was subject to predators and needed human intervention for protection.

With the migration of settlers heading west, the sheep population grew, and according to Statistics Canada by the early 1900s reached numbers of approximately 3.5 million. Of course back then and before the introduction of manufactured fabrics and synthetic materials, sheep were an important commodity as their wool was used in the manufacturing of clothing in both Canada and abroad. However, after the Second World War things changed for sheepherders as the wool of their sheep didn't carry the same demand. Sheep farmers had to change their operations from mainly wool to mainly meat. The sheep population of 3.5 million started to dwindle and by the mid-1970s reached the number of approximately half a million (500,000). With the resurgence of lamb as a red meat alternative, Canada now boasts a sheep population of over one and a half million (1,500,000) with the majority being raised in Quebec, Ontario and Alberta (Statistics Canada 2016).

Lambs are young sheep aging no more than fifteen months with the vast majority in the twelve-month category. Lamb production is part of the Red Meat Industry talked about in the chapter on beef. The meat of lamb is tender, due to its age, and has a distinct flavour profile from other red meats attributed to diet and the content of fatty acids. Lamb popularity is on the rise as is the cost of lamb. Canadian lamb continues to claim a significant price point due to demand and cost of production. Canadian lamb production makes up less than half of the overall consumption of lamb in Canada (about 40%), with the majority bowing to imported Australian and New Zealand lamb.

Lamb Production

There are more than two hundred breeds of sheep in the world. Most are selected for traits such as flocking instinct and meat quality as well as wool; wool is still viable today though not experiencing the same demand as that of the 16, 17, 18 and early 1900s. The entire sheep population of Canada lives on about eleven thousand farms. Typically sheep live outdoors on lands not used or fit for agricultural purposes paying tribute to the resilience of the animal. On average ewes give birth to anywhere from two to four lambs at one time once a year. Lambs are nursed for six to ten weeks depending on rate of growth and herd management.

The more popular breeds of sheep in Canada are Suffolk, Dorset and Arcott.

Suffolk: This is a large breed of sheep with a mature weight range of one hundred and ten kilograms (110 kg) for ewes and one hundred and sixty kilograms (160 kg) for rams. They are large framed, muscular and characteristically have a black head and black legs. They are raised for their meat as Suffolk lambs exceed all other breeds in rate of gain, with excellent growth and desired carcass traits.

Suffolk sheep
Credit: Canadian Sheep Breeders' Association

Dorset: This breed has two lineages, the Horned Dorset and the Polled Dorset. Of the two, the Polled Dorset is more popular. The Dorset is known for prolific lambing, with the ewes producing two lambing seasons per year. Mature ewes can reach a weight of ninety kilograms (90 kg) and rams one hundred and twenty five kilograms (125 kg). The Dorset is a stout breed, shorter in length and height than the Suffolk.

Dorset sheep
Credit: Canadian Sheep Breeders' Association

Arcott sheep
Credit: Canadian Sheep Breeders' Association

Arcott: This breed is native to Canada, a result of a cross breeding program at the Agriculture Canada research station near Ottawa. It is a medium size, short and thick sheep with strong meat characteristics. The Arcott has been selectively bred for higher fertility, multiple births and growth rate. Ewes are easy to breed, requiring minimal maintenance. The ewes finish out at a mature weight of about one hundred and fifteen kilograms (115 kg) and the rams at a weight of one hundred and fifty kilograms (150 kg).

Ovine Health and Wellness falls into the arm of the Canadian Food Inspection Agency (CFIA), which is responsible for all federal inspection programs related to the feed production of ovine animals, animal health and processing of lamb as well as plant safeguards such as HACCP.

Traceability for lamb is the same as for beef, veal and bison. The tagging of lambs is a national program initiative governed by the CFIA and is mandatory.

Lamb Processing

Lamb processing takes place in provincially inspected local abattoirs or federally inspected meat plants. Provincial abattoirs handle both custom work as well as wholesale carcass lamb for retailers. Custom work involves harvesting lamb for individuals who raise lamb for their own use. Wholesaling lamb involves harvesting lamb bought at auctions or from feedlots/farming operations and selling them to retailers who want carcass lamb for their clientele. Federal lamb processing plants procure lamb for the sole purpose of wholesaling carcass lamb and block, knife or counter ready lamb cuts to retailers.

Grading of Lamb

There is a grading system for lamb and other ovine animals such as goat; however, from a local standpoint this system is rarely used. There are five grades of ovine carcasses with the grade names of Canada AAA, Canada C1, Canada C2, Canada D1 and Canada D4. (See more on Grading of Lamb in Chapter 12).

Canadian Lamb Primal Cuts

Lamb is derived from dressed carcasses of ovine animals that meet the maturity characteristics prescribed in the Livestock Carcass Grading Regulations. These maturity characteristics are as follows:

1. Fewer than two permanent incisors.
2. Two break joints or, in the case of a carcass with one break joint and one spool joint, the break joint has four intact and well-defined ridges with at least a slightly red and slightly damp surface.
3. Ribs that are no more than slightly wide tend to be rounded rather than flat and are reddish in colour.

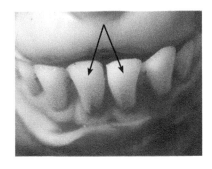

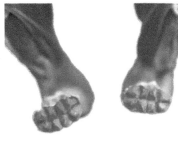

Lamb incisor teeth
Credit: CPMCA image collection

Lamb break joint
Credit: Summit Gourmet Meats

Lamb break joints - front shanks
in the back ground
Credit: Summit Gourmet Meats

Meat derived from a dressed carcass of an ovine animal that does not meet the specifications prescribed for **Lamb** shall be referred to as **Mutton**.

A **Dressed Lamb Carcass** is a carcass of lamb from which the skin, head and feet at the carpal and tarsal joints have been removed and the carcass has been eviscerated.

Lamb carcasses can be sold **Whole**, by the **Front Half** (meaning the anterior portion of the carcass), **Hind Half** (meaning posterior portion of the carcass separated between the 11th and 12th rib), and by the **Side** (meaning one of two approximately equal portions of the carcass split from tail to neck along the median line). Carcass Lamb is more commonly sold to retailers as **Whole** or as Block Ready (explained further on).

According to the CFIA Meat Cuts Manual for lamb, there are four primal cuts: **Front, Leg, Whole Loin**, and **Flank**. It also refers to these primal cuts as "Double," where the carcass has not been split into a Side. Whether a Side or a "Double" primal cut, the breaking points and parameters are the same.

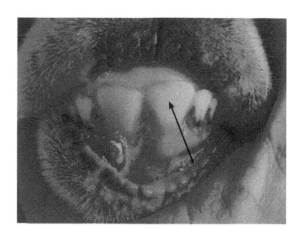

*Older sheep teeth at
1-2 years indicates - Mutton.
Credit: CPMCA image collection.*

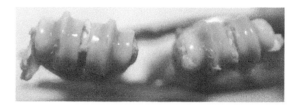

*Older sheep develop spool joints
instead of break joints
Credit: CPMCA image collection*

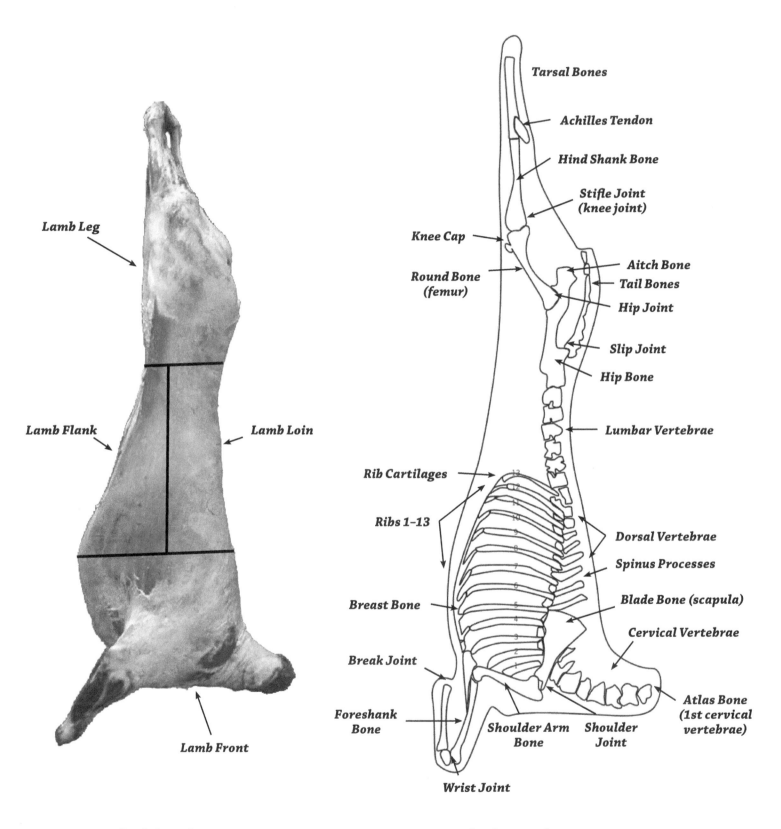

Lamb Leg

Lamb Flank

Lamb Loin

Lamb Front

Tarsal Bones

Achilles Tendon

Hind Shank Bone

Stifle Joint
(knee joint)

Knee Cap

Round Bone
(femur)

Aitch Bone

Tail Bones

Hip Joint

Slip Joint

Hip Bone

Lumbar Vertebrae

Rib Cartilages

Ribs 1–13

Dorsal Vertebrae

Spinus Processes

Blade Bone (scapula)

Cervical Vertebrae

Breast Bone

Break Joint

Foreshank
Bone

Shoulder Arm
Bone

Shoulder
Joint

Atlas Bone
(1st cervical
vertebrae)

Wrist Joint

Lamb dressed carcass

Lamb carcass bone structure

Credit: Jakes & Associates

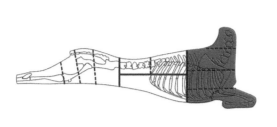

Lamb front double

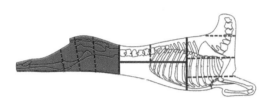

Lamb leg double

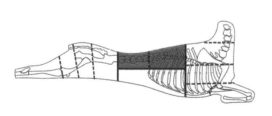

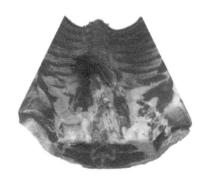

Lamb loin double

- **Front:** means that portion of the carcass which is separated from the **Whole Loin** and the **Flank**, by a straight cut passing between the sixth (6th) and seventh (7th) rib.

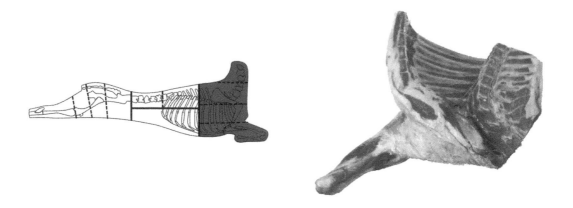

- **Leg:** means the posterior portion of the carcass, which is separated from the **Whole Loin** and **Flank** by a straight cut passing immediately in front of (anterior to) the pin bone (ilium or tuber coxae).

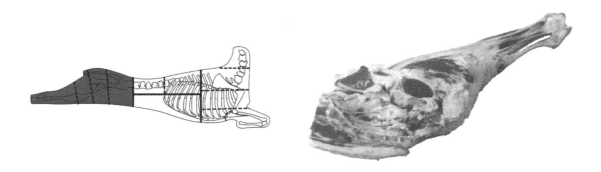

- **Whole Loin:** means that portion of the carcass which is separated from the **Front** and **Leg** as described above, respectively, and from the **Flank** by a straight cut approximately parallel to the backbone (vertebral column) passing through the thirteenth (13th) rib, approximately at the beginning of the costal cartilage.

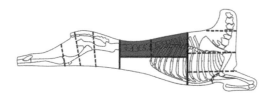 

- **Flank:** means that portion of the carcass, which is separated from the **Front**, **Leg**, and **Whole Loin** as described above.

Note: this primal has no sub-primal cuts and has been traditionally retailed as Lamb Flank Ribs. It can be merchandised into Ground Lamb, Lamb Stewing Meat, or deboned, stuffed and rolled as a Stuffed Lamb Flank. Innovation and creativity has seen this item deboned, trimmed and cured as Lamb Bacon.

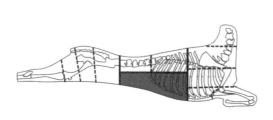 

Sub-primal & Retail Cuts of Lamb

Sub-primal cuts are derived from primal cuts. The four primal cuts of lamb can and usually are further processed into sub-primal cuts for ease of handling and storage. This further processing can be done at either plant level or store level, depending on the nature of the operation. Some retail outlets still prefer to break carcasses of lamb to better suit the needs of their operation and consumer demand for in-house freshly fabricated cuts of lamb.

The CFIA Meat Manual identifies several sub primal possibilities for each of the primal cuts of lamb.

The sub primal cuts of the **Lamb Front** are: Shank, Breast, Neck and Shoulder

- **Shank:** means that portion of the **Front**, which is separated from the **Breast** by a straight cut passing through the base of the arm (distal extremity of the humerus) and follows the natural seam of the elbow. Classic cuts of **Lamb Shank** are whole, split or notched several times just through the radius leaving the muscle intact.

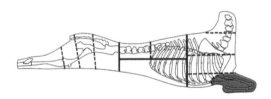 

- **Breast:** means that portion of the **Front** which is separated from the **Shank** as described above, and from the **Shoulder** by a straight cut which passes through the base of the shaft of the arm bone (distal end of the humerus) approximately at right angles to the cut edge of the **Front**. Classic cut of the **Breast** is whole, cubed (bone-in) or boneless and trimmed.

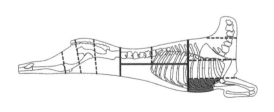 

- **Neck:** means that portion of the **Front**, which is separated from the **Shoulder** by a straight cut passing through the fifth (5th) neck bone (cervical vertebra). The **Neck** is usually deboned and used for trim or cut whole into chunks for lamb stew.

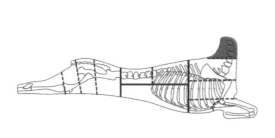

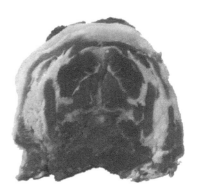

- **Shoulder:** means that portion of the **Front**, which is separated from the Breast and Neck (it's what you're left with when you follow the above steps). Traditionally the shoulder is used for **Lamb Shoulder Chops** but can also be boned and rolled for **Lamb Shoulder Roast** boneless.

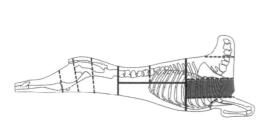

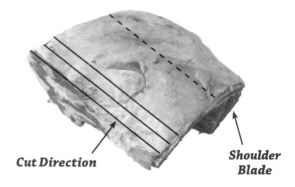

Cut Direction *Shoulder Blade*

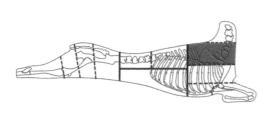

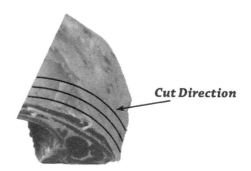

Cut Direction

The sub primal cuts of the **Lamb Leg** are:

Shank, Leg Shank Portion, Leg Butt Portion, Sirloin, and Leg Short Cut.

- **Shank:** means that portion of the leg, which is separated from the **Leg Shank Portion** by cutting through the stifle joint (tibio-femoral joint). As mentioned above, **Lamb Shanks** can be sold whole, split or notched. They can be braised or used as a stewing item.

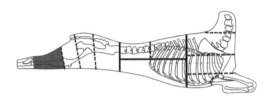 

- **Leg Shank Portion:** has two alternatives 1) means that portion of the **Leg** which is separated from the **Shank** as described above, and from the **Leg Centre** by a straight cut passing through the middle of the shaft of the leg bone (femur) approximately at right angles or 2) that portion of the leg which is separated from the **Shank** as described, and from the Sirloin by a straight cut passing in front of (anterior to) the rump knuckle (acetabulum/head of femur). This particular cut is found mostly in custom operations where lamb owners have their carcass cut, wrapped, and frozen for their own consumption. **Retail classic cuts** from the lamb leg are Lamb Leg Whole Boneless, as well as muscle seamed cuts producing the **Lamb Leg Inside, Lamb Leg Outside, Lamb Leg Tip** and **Lamb Leg Sirloin**; which are then further fabricated into either roasts or chops with trimmings used for **Lamb Stewing Meat, Ground Lamb** or **Fresh Lamb Sausage**. The seamed leg muscles can also be used for **Lamb Stir Fry, Lamb Kabobs,** or **Lamb Marinated Cubes**.

- **Leg Butt Portion:** means that portion of the **Leg**, which is separated from the **Leg, Shank Portion** by a straight cut passing through the middle of the shaft of the leg bone (femur) approximately at right angles. For classic cuts from the leg see **Leg Shank Portion** above.

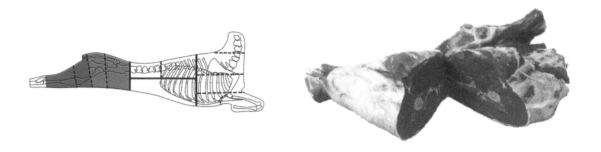

Lamb leg shank portion (L) & butt portion (R)

- **Sirloin:** is an alternative portion of the Leg which is separated from the **Leg, Shank Portion** or **Leg Short Cut** (below) by a straight cut passing immediately in front of (anterior to) the rump knuckle bone (acetabulum/head of femur).

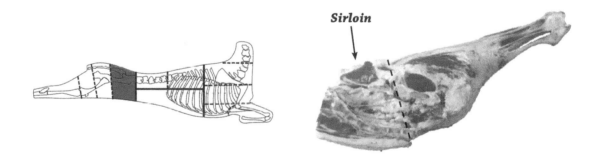

- **Leg Short Cut:** means the Leg from which the Sirloin has been removed. Short Cut Legs of Lamb are more common to imported frozen product usually retailed and sold whole.

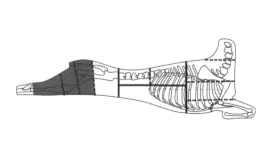

The sub-primal cuts of the **Lamb Whole Loin** are Loin and Rib.

- **Loin:** means that posterior portion of the **Whole Loin**, which is separated from the **Rib** by a straight cut passing behind (posterior to) the last rib (13th rib).

  Note: the **Loin** shall contain no part of the rib.

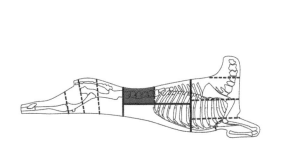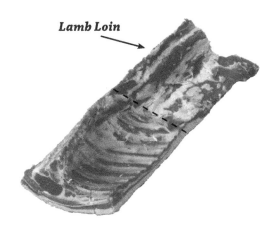

Lamb Loin

Lamb loin whole & Lamb loin portion

- **Rib:** means that anterior portion of the **Whole Loin**, which is separated from the **Loin** as described above.

Note: the **Rib** or part thereof prepared as a roast may be referred to as **Rack**.

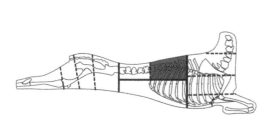

Lamb rib

Lamb Variety Meats

Variety meats are edible parts of an animal other than skeletal muscle. Listed below are those of lamb.

Variety meats, also referred to as "offal," have gained some notoriety as comfort food. Some dishes containing offal remain part of a region's cuisine and may be consumed especially in connection with holidays, such as the Scottish tradition of eating haggis on Robbie Burns Day.

- Liver
- Kidney
- Heart
- Tongue
- Sweetbread

Lamb liver is highly accepted by Europeans as a delicacy. It does not enjoy the same popularity as beef liver, but it is very tender and mild. It is not skinned prior to cooking and does not need soaking.

Lamb liver
Credit: Jakes & Associates

Lamb kidneys are very small, bean-shaped and dark brown in colour and each lamb yields approximately 60 - 90 grams of kidney. Only limited amounts are available from the packers, however, they are available in bulk frozen form from New Zealand.

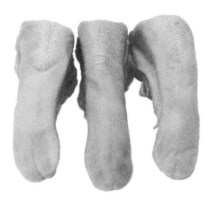

Lamb tongues
Credit: Sungold specialty meats

Lamb kidneys with fat
Credit: Jakes & Associates

Lamb hearts are dark reddish brown in colour. They are limited in supply, and weigh from 125 g to 175 g each. They are a very small volume seller, usually more popular with Europeans.

Lamb sweetbreads are the thymus glands from the neck or the pancreas near the heart. The gland is sweet to the taste hence the name Sweetbread. They are more popular in Eastern Canada with different ethnic groups and are mainly imported from New Zealand or Australia.

Lamb heart
Credit: Jakes & Associates

Lamb tongues are usually processed commercially into processed meat or bottled products but can be ordered from the packers for specific orders.

Lamb sweetbreads
Credit: Sungold specialty meats

It should be noted here that **Goat** is too becoming popular as an alternative red meat and is handled in similar fashion to that of lamb. As the Canadian population continues to grow in ethnicity, so will the demand for other meat alternatives.

CFIA Nomenclature Requirements for Lamb

Retailers are responsible for ensuring that the names used to describe meat cuts on labels and in advertisements include the appropriate specific terms. The name used to describe all lamb meat cuts must include an indication of the species. For example, the term "lamb" must appear in conjunction with the term "shoulder" when a lamb shoulder roast is offered for sale. The name used to describe all variety meats (listed further on under Variety Meats) must include an indication of the species.

LAMB RACK

Packed On	Best Before	Sell By
Net Wt/Ct	Unit Price	Total Price

Credit: TRU Retail Meat processing Program

RETAIL MEAT CUT LABELLING REQUIREMENTS FOR LAMB

Prepackaged lamb meat cuts offered for sale at retail must be marked with the following:

- the name of the species and cut,
- the name and address of the retailer,
- the net quantity,
- the packaging date,
- the durable life of the meat cut unless the durable life is indicated on a poster next to the product, and
- the words "previously frozen" if a meat cut that has been frozen is thawed prior to sale unless the words "previously frozen" appear on a poster next to the product.

LIST OF LAMB MEAT CUT MODIFIERS

Modifiers are descriptions used to explain in more detail what the cut of meat is or what alterations have been done to the primal/sub-primal cut to obtain the outcome you have before you.

- Boneless
- Chop
- Crown
- Diced Lamb
- Frenched (Rib Chop)
- In basket
- Medallion
- Partially Boneless
- Rack

- Roast
- Rolled
- Semi-Boneless
- Steak
- Stewing
- Stuffed
- Tied
- Trimmed

Note: While not required, these modifiers may be used to describe lamb cuts, provided they are informative and not misleading

BASIC LABELLING REQUIREMENTS FOR LAMB:

Label: Lamb (Species), Retail cut (Primal, Sub-Primal), Modifier (if modified).

Sample: Lamb (Species) Flank (Primal) Stuffed (Modifier)

Credit: TRU Retail Meat processing Program   *Credit: TRU Retail Meat processing Program*

Lamb:

The edible flesh, with adhering bones and fat, from a young animal of ovine (ovinus) (sheep) species. It includes hoggets (yearling sheep), and wethers (male sheep castrated before sexual maturity).

> **Note:** The edible flesh, with adhering bones and fat, from older animals of that species, such as ewes, muttons, and rams, shall be referred to as **Mutton**.

Leg:

All cuts from the leg must have the primal "Leg" on the label.
Sirloin Chops cut from the leg must have "Leg" on the label, e.g. Lamb Leg Sirloin Chops.

GROUND MEATS

- **Regular Ground** (naming the species) when meat from the named species is processed by grinding and does not contain more than 30% fat;
- **Medium Ground** (naming the species) when meat from the named species is processed by grinding and does not contain more than 23% fat;
- **Lean Ground** (naming the species) when meat from the named species is processed by grinding and does not contain more than 17% fat;
- **Extra Lean Ground** (naming the species) when meat from the named species is processed by grinding and does not contain more than 10% fat

Block & Knife Ready Lamb Products

We have written about the growing concern of costs associated with running a business, and entrepreneurs/retailers look to ways in which they can save overhead expenses. Purchasing lamb as Block or Knife Ready is one of those considerations. Though fresh lamb is commonly sold in carcass form, Canada does produce a block ready lamb product as an alternative.

Some of the more common Block and Knife Ready meats of lamb include the following:

- Lamb Shoulders
- Lamb Shoulders Boneless
- Lamb Racks
- Lamb Racks Frenched
- Lamb Loins
- Lamb Loins Boneless
- Lamb Shanks
- Lamb Legs
- Lamb Legs Boneless
- Lamb Shanks
- Lamb Trim (50/50; 60/40; 70/30 lean to fat)

Counter Ready Lamb Products

Counter ready meats refer to those lamb items that have been processed and fabricated at plant level, are packaged for displays, boxed and shipped to store level. With these there is no need of a meat cutter. The product is finished and ready for in-store labelling and displaying. Counter ready meats come in one of two forms: fresh (as listed below) or processed (meaning fermented, cooked, brined, frozen and fresh sausages, etc.).

Some larger supermarket chains carry fresh lamb counter ready meats due to a shortage of skilled labour in their area of people who know how to cut, wrap, price and display products. There is also the argument that counter ready meat costs less when the costs associated with labour and space allocation are taken into consideration. It is suspected that where counter ready meats are sold, it is due to one or the other aforementioned reasons.

Some of the more common Fresh Lamb Counter Ready Products are as follows:

- Netted Boneless Legs of Lamb
- Netted Boneless Shoulder of Lamb Blade
- Lamb Shoulder Chops
- Loin Lamb Chops
- Boneless Lamb Loins
- Ground Lamb

Value-Added Lamb Cuts

Value-added cuts of lamb are innovative cuts designed to attract consumer attention and interest. These cuts and merchandising them are often two of the most important aspects of retailing meats. Value-added meats give consumers more options for their favourite meats and cooking methods. Retailers formulate value-added items for one of two reasons: to brand a product item available only through them and/or to take advantage of a popular trend or demand.

Examples of value-added lamb cuts are as follows:

- Lamb Rack, Crown Roast
- Lamb Rack
- Lamb Chops Frenched
- Lamb Stuffing
- Lamb Leg Boneless and Stuffed
- Lamb Shoulder Marinated

Wholesale Meat Specifications for Lamb

Food service products are a direct response by industry to fill a demand made by retailers for the need for variety and versatility. Food service cuts cater to food service outlets, but that doesn't mean all products designed for food service end up in food service facilities such as restaurants. For more see Chapter 5.

SUMMARY

TERMS FOR REVIEW

Arcott	Lamb Breast	Lamb Shank
Break Joint	Lamb Flank	Lamb Shoulder
Dorset	Lamb Front	Mutton
Dressed Lamb	Lamb Grades	Ovine
Ewes	Lamb Leg	Rams
Goat	Lamb Loin	Spool Joint
Herbivores	Lamb Rack or Rib	Suffolk
Lamb	Lamb Rib Crown Roast	Sweet Breads

DISCUSSION QUESTIONS

1. Explain why Canada's sheep population numbers reached an all-time low of approximately half a million sheep in the 1970s. What brought that population back to one and a half million?

2. List and describe the three main breeds of Canadian sheep.

3. What is an abattoir?

4. How many grades are assigned to Lamb? Do these grades apply to other ovine animals? Which ovine animals do the grades apply to?

5. List the primal cuts of Lamb.

6. What considerations are there in determining what constitutes a "Rack of Lamb?"

Lamb Retail Meat Processing options

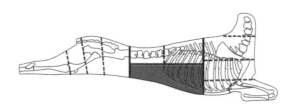

Lamb flank

Lamb flank partially boned

Lamb flank ribs

Lamb hind shank

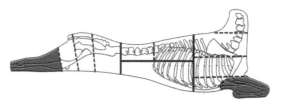

Lamb front shank

Lamb hind shank cross cut

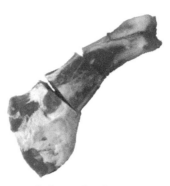

Lamb front shank cross cut

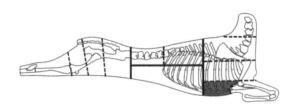

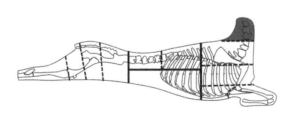

Lamb breast mainly used for trim

Lamb neck cut as chops or for stew

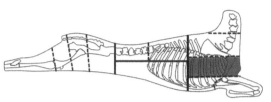

**Lamb shoulder arm**   **Lamb shoulder blade**

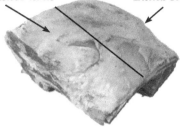

*Lamb shoulder with cut line
direction for shoulder arm chops*

Lamb shoulder arm, shank & breast off

Lamb shoulder arm chops

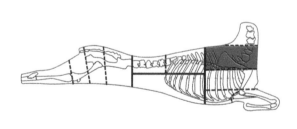

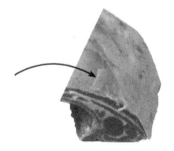

Lamb shoulder blade with cut line direction

lamb shoulder blade chops

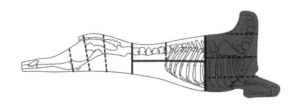

Lamb front

Lamb front boning out sequence

Step 1: Lamb front with breast bone part removed

Step 2: Lamb front breast, ribs and dorsal back bone off

Step 3: Lamb front blade bone exposed

Step 4: Lamb blade bone separated from shoulder arm bone joint

Step 5: Place finger under blade bone cup & pull firmly toward you while pushing against the arm bone knuckle to peel out blade bone

Step 6: Shoulder knuckle bone exposed by careful tunnel boning to release tendons while rotating the shank as you cut tendons & ligaments

Step 7: Rotate shank 360 degrees several times while pulling slowly to release arm bone.

Step 8: Arm bone & shank after removal

Step 9: Remove prescapular gland and fat pocket

Step 10: level the boneless shoulder by butterflying (fold over)part of the cross rib muscle (where the knife is) to fill in the shallow side to the left

Step 11: Roll roast from the blade end (top) to the breast (bottom) & tie up.

Step 12: Cut whole rolled shoulder in half for Lamb shoulder roast portions boneless.

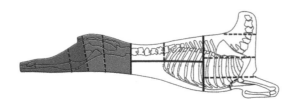

Lamb Leg shank (L) & butt portions (R)

Lamb leg shank portion

Lamb leg butt portion

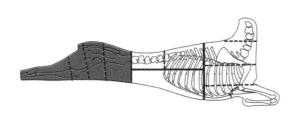

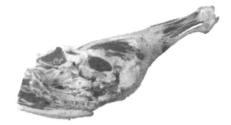

Lamb leg

Lamb leg boneless whole

Lamb leg roast portion boneless

Lamb leg roast portion boneless

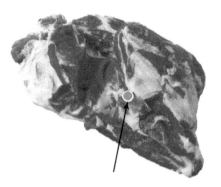

Lamb leg whole part boned

Lamb leg whole fully boned
Popliteal gland location

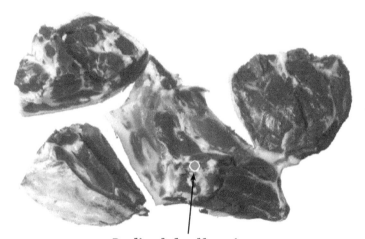

Popliteal gland location

Lamb leg muscle groups
Lamb leg tip (left)
Lamb leg sirloin (top)
Lamb leg outside (centre)
Lamb leg inside (right)

Lamb leg tip

Lamb leg tip steaks

Lamb leg Sirloin

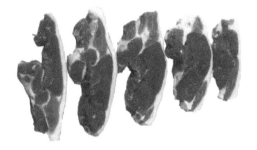

Lamb leg sirloin steaks

Lamb leg inside

lamb leg inside steaks

Lamb leg outside

Lamb leg outside steaks

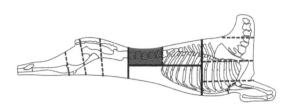

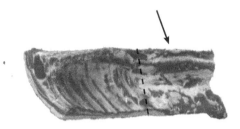

Lamb loin section

Lamb loin chops pre-cut, saw ready

Lamb loin chops

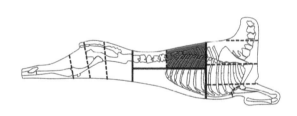

Lamb loin rib section

Lamb rib

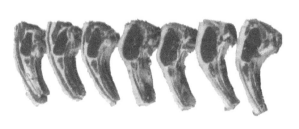

Lamb rib chops

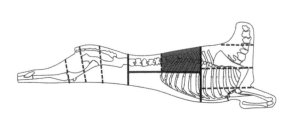

Lamb rib or rack

Preparing a Lamb rack

Step 1: start your first cut close to the loin eye

Step 2: peel off rib meat to edge of rib loin muscle

Step 3: cut out muscle meat between ribs with a straight cut at the fat line

Step 4: ribs must be nice and clean

Step 5: cut off chine bone carefully to separate feather bones & shorten ribs bones if needed

Step 6: remove outside fat if required

Step 7: Lamb rack underside view

Step 8: Lamb rack outside & best view

Step 9: or 2 Lamb racks from the same carcass can be tied together as a Lamb rib Crown roast

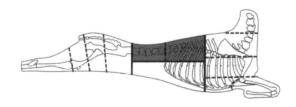

Lamb loin

Step 1: Lamb loin roast boneless - Lamb loin with tenderloin partly removed

Step 2: Lamb tenderloin

Step 3: lamb loin rib & backbone removed

Step 4: Lamb loin sections ready to roll together

Step 5: Lamb loin section rolled together as a roast

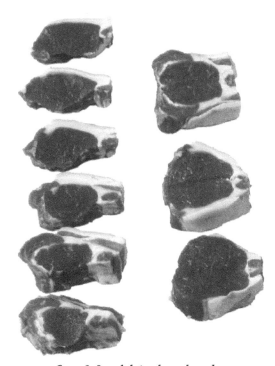

Step 6: Lamb loin chops boneless

Chapter 8

Poultry

Poultry has become the alternative red meat. Poultry is high in protein and low in cholesterol and comes in many varieties, size and shape. Poultry includes but is not limited to the common species of chickens, ducks, geese and turkeys. Each species of poultry is handled and processed differently.

This chapter provides descriptions of the more common species of poultry the meat industry promotes. It covers the topics of poultry production, processing and grading. The main concern of the chapter is the Canadian standards regarding proper handling of poultry, cuts of poultry and the labelling thereof.

All poultry descriptions and their cuts are enhanced with images to assist with identification and knowledge of poultry cuts. These graphics and images are intended to guide the development of hands-on skills in the processing of poultry retail cuts.

Poultry

History

Before the Canadian population became interested in domestic poultry, game birds-both migratory and non-migratory-were a source of food and protein for indigenous peoples, explorers and early settlers. Geese, ducks and wild turkey were more popular ones, but they also hunted seabirds, crane, rail, pigeon and game birds like the grouse and pheasant. The eating quality of wild birds rested with their age. Younger birds are more tender and flavourful than older birds, a fact held true today. Though most birds didn't offer a lot of meat per carcass, they did provide an alternative source of protein between large wild game catches such as caribou, moose, or deer.

Early settlers that made the voyage across the Atlantic to the new land brought with them domestic poultry, chickens, ducks, and geese. These birds were housed in coups and fenced in to protect them from natural predators. At the time poultry was kept for reproduction (breeding), for their

eggs and their meat. With respect to chickens, these were kept solely for their eggs and eating chicken was a by-product of egg production. Chickens that were too old to lay eggs or those chickens that didn't lay eggs were killed and eaten. Even today homesteaders rely on poultry (chickens) as their year-round source of protein.

When one thinks of poultry they're most often referring to chicken, but chicken doesn't make up the whole gamut of poultry. Granted chicken currently has the largest share of the Canadian poultry market, but that doesn't mean there isn't a demand for other types of poultry that we raise. Thanks to the global market, research and development, and crossbreeding practices by producers, we now have a stable variety of stable poultry species in Canada available to the consuming public. The more common types of poultry Canadians prefer are: Chicken, Duck, Goose and Turkey.

Chicken: (*Gallus gallus domesticus*) is a type of domestic fowl, a subspecies of the red junglefowl. There are only two breeds of chicken developed in Canada, the Chantecler and the Red Shaver, both more suited to home or small farm operations. The more common species found in Canada are bred for large-scale operations, and include the White Leghorn for white egg production, and the Rhode Island Red, Barred Plymouth Rock and New Hampshire for brown egg production. Birds used and crossbred for meat (known as broilers) are the White Plymouth Rock, the New Hampshire and Cornish breeds. Chicken broilers are harvested between 35 and 42 days of age.

Chicken White Leghorn
©istock.com / credit toX2Photo

Chicken White Plymouth Rock
©Holly Kuchera / Dreamstime

Duck: (*Anas platyrhynchos, Cairina moschata*) is a domesticated bird primarily kept for meat because of their rapid growth, hardiness and ease of handling. Rapid growth combined with good egg production make the White Pekin the most popular breed of duck raised for meat. Ducks are harvested for their meat at about seven or eight weeks of age.

Pekin Duck
©istock.com / credit to sebastianosecondi

Goose: (*Anser anser domesticus or Anser cygnoides domesticus*) is a domesticated bird with the three most popular breeds in Canada being the Emden, Chinese, and Toulouse goose. Traditionally geese were kept for their meat, eggs, and down feathers. The harvesting age of geese for meat depends on the desired weight range of the finished product: the average is under 24 weeks of age.

Domestic Goose
©istock.com / credit to chas53

Turkey: (*Meleagris gallopavo*) is a domesticated bird raised for their meat. It's especially popular during the holiday seasons as a part of Thanksgiving and Christmas dinners. The Broad Breasted White is the commercial turkey of choice for large-scale industrial turkey farms and consequently is the most consumed variety of turkey in Canada. The harvesting age of turkey depends on the desired weight range. On average turkeys are harvested between five and six months of age.

Turkey-tom.
©istock.com / credit to nbiebach

Poultry Production

The poultry cycle from producer to consumer starts at the farm where the age-old question is, "Which came first, the chicken or the egg?" Though we aren't here to answer that, we can tell you it starts at the pullet barn where young hens (baby chicks) are brought to breeding age. From the pullet barn the hens move to the breeding barn. There, fertile hens are bred or artificially inseminated. Eggs are laid, incubated and hatched, or they are graded and end up in someone's omelet. From the hatchery, chicks are moved to open growing barns with access to food and fresh water until they reach the age of harvest. From growing barns the poultry is shipped to a processing facility where, if suspect, a veterinarian inspects them and they are slaughtered. Then the carcasses are inspected and further processed for market consumption.

Canadian Breeders have developed hybrid strains of chickens for commercial egg and meat production; the same can be said of turkeys but to a lesser degree. As the Canadian ethnic population grows so does the demand for other types of poultry. Duck is becoming more popular and some duck farmers in Canada are now processing their own crop from start to finish. Other poultry farmers have formed cooperatives and begun pooling their resources as a means of marketing their product(s) from farm gate to the consumer's plate.

The production of poultry raised and used for meat is regulated federally by the Agricultural Products Marketing Act and provincially by Agricultural Marketing

Boards. Federal agencies allocate production quotas to the provinces and remove market surpluses. They also regulate the import and export of poultry products. Provincial boards allocate production quotas to their respective producers, set prices, advertise the product and deduct predetermined levies from producers for their operating costs.

Health and Wellness of poultry starts at the farm with an On-Farm Food Safety Program. On-Farm Food Safety Programs are developed for various commodities to enhance food safety, maintain consumer confidence and facilitate market access. They use management approaches such as Hazard Analysis and Critical Control Points (HACCP) to reduce potential risks and hazards within production to a safe level. On-Farm Food Safety Programs comply with federal, provincial and territorial legislation and are delivered by a provincial delivery agent or by the national industry organization that owns the program. They have all gone through a thorough technical review process led by the Canadian Food Inspection Agency (CFIA) as part of the federal Food Safety Recognition Program. The complete process from the farm to the fork therefore falls into the arm of the CFIA, which is responsible for all federal inspection programs related to the feed production of poultry, the health and processing of poultry, as well as plant safeguards such as HACCP.

Traceability is a crucial and a mandatory component of animal health and food safety systems in Canada. The program design is to protect public health and strengthen food safety as well as provide rapid response to disease outbreaks (such as Avian Flu) and natural disasters (such as floods etc.) that affect our Canadian animal resource base. Determining where livestock are and where they have been allows, when needed, efficient emergency planning and response. As we learned in chapter 5, all traceability programs have three fundamental pillars: identification of premises, animal identification and animal movement.

Each poultry farm must possess or have a Premises Identification number (PID) associated to where the poultry are located (raised and cared for). In addition, whenever the poultry is moved or shipped a Radio Frequency Identification chip (RFID) was used to track such movement or shipment from its place of origin to its destination. The RFID chip would be placed on the transport or shipment of poultry leaving the farm for tracking purposes complete with PID info. The RFID chip information was then entered into a national database and at each designated stop the shipment's RFID chip is updated tracking the movement of the shipment to its final destination or stop The RFID is now no longer in use and was replaced by a Flock Information Reporting Form which functions in similar manner as the RFID chip.

FLOCK INFORMATION REPORTING FORM
VERSION 8.0

Producer/Enterprise Name	Producer Code/Quota/Premises ID	Placement Date of Chicks/Poults

Barn #	Species	Category/Sex	Age of Birds	# Birds Placed	Birds Shipped	Mortality Rate (%)**	Kg/Bird

CFC OFFSAP/TFC OFFSP Certification: ☐ Yes ☐ No   Grow-out Density: ___   ☐ kg/m² ☐ lb/ft² ☐ kg/ft² ☐ space/bird

SECTION A - MEDICATION AND VACCINE INFORMATION

		If Yes:
1.	Were medications or vaccines administered at the hatchery?**	☐ Yes ☐ No	A through F*
2.	Were vaccines administered on-farm?**	☐ Yes ☐ No	A through G*
3.	Were any medications administered for treatment during the flock?**	☐ Yes ☐ No	A through H*
4.	Were any non-treated diseases or syndromes diagnosed during the flock?**	☐ Yes ☐ No	H
5.	Were any medications with a withdrawal time used in the last 14 days prior to shipment?	☐ Yes ☐ No	A through G*
6.	Were any extra-label medications used?**	☐ Yes ☐ No	A through F*
7.	Were any Category I medications (e.g., ceftiofur - Excenel™, enrofloxacin – Baytril™) used on-farm in a preventive manner?	☐ Yes ☐ No	A through G*

**For mature turkeys, this information must be provided for the last 120 days of life.

*Attach prescriptions for all extra-label medication use

RECORD ANY "YES" ANSWERS IN THE TABLE BELOW (USE THE GUIDE ABOVE TO FILL IN THE COLUMNS):

Question # (i.e. 1-7 above)	(A) Medication or Vaccine Name	(B) Route (i.e. feed, water, injection etc.)	(C) First treatment date	(D) Last treatment date	(E) Withdrawal Period (days)	(F) Safe Marketing Date (if any)	(G) Dose	(H) Disease or Syndrome & Flock Recovery Date

SECTION B - FEED WITHDRAWAL AND LOADING INFORMATION

Planned catching time:	M D Time ☐AM ☐PM	Actual start of catching:	Time ☐AM ☐PM
Planned processing time:	M D Time ☐AM ☐PM	Time of last access to water:	Time ☐AM ☐PM
Was the feed supply disrupted in the last 48 hours? ☐ Yes ☐ No		Feed withdrawal time provided by processor:	Time ☐AM ☐PM
Time feed was no longer accessible: M D	Floor#1 Time ☐AM ☐PM	Floor#2 Time ☐AM ☐PM	Floor#3 Time ☐AM ☐PM

Additional Comments: _____

Provide any additional comments on flock condition during the brooding/grow-out period and/or the catching process on a separate sheet of paper if desired.

I confirm that, to the best of my knowledge, the information contained on this flock information reporting form is accurate and complete and that any diseases that were diagnosed in the flock as a result of laboratory tests and/or readily observable clinical signs have been identified and reported on this form, and that I have followed required withdrawal times as per the veterinary prescription, labeling indication and/or feed mill instructions.

Producer's Signature: _____

(EMAIL) (SAVE) (PRINT) (CLEAR FORM)

Note: This information is confidential between the producer and the processor.

Flock Information Reporting Form (FIRF)
Credit: Canadian Poultry and Egg Processors Council

Poultry Processing

Poultry processing takes place in provincially inspected local abattoirs or federally inspected poultry plants. On-site inspectors and veterinarians from the CFIA monitor processing facilities under federal jurisdiction, and provincial inspectors and veterinarians monitor those under provincial jurisdiction. Provincial abattoirs handle custom work for individuals who raise poultry for their own use, as well as wholesale poultry to retailers. Wholesaling poultry involves harvesting birds bought at auctions or from farming operations and selling them to retailers who want fresh local poultry for their clientele. Federal poultry processing plants procure birds like chickens, ducks, geese, turkeys, etc. for the sole purpose of wholesaling them to retailers. Most large plants build and carry inventories of poultry to accommodate the demands of seasonal fluctuations, such as those of Thanksgiving, Christmas and Easter—times that dictate larger orders for poultry and poultry products.

Note: for more on harvesting refer to chapter 12.

Poultry transportation crates
Credit: Canadian Poultry and
Egg Processors Council

Depending on the need or time of year, the retailer may purchase poultry either fresh or frozen. Due to its popularity, chicken is readily available as both fresh and frozen year-round. Other poultry, such as duck, goose and turkey, are subject to seasonal fluctuations. However, facilities like that of King Cole Ducks located in Ontario operate a vertically integrated agri-business meaning a farm-to-fork operation. King Cole Ducks Limited has and does everything from breeding, to growing, to processing, to wholesaling and retailing their ducks year round.

Modern poultry processing plant
Credit: ©istock.com/credit to roibu

Poultry processing line in action
Credit: ©istock.com/credit to roibu

Poultry is one of the more perishable meat products retailers carry, so proper handling is important to food safety and food quality. Upon receipt, all poultry should be put under refrigeration. If poultry is purchased fresh it should always be stored in the coldest section of the refrigerator, covered and packed with ice; if poultry is purchased frozen then it should be kept completely frozen until it is to be displayed frozen, defrosted or cooked.

To properly defrost frozen poultry, it should be kept in its original vacuum package and allowed to thaw out slowly in the refrigerator. If it must be defrosted quickly, the safest method is to place the bird breast down in cold water. Always remember to keep the water very cold by refreshing it regularly.

When preparing poultry for displays it's important to keep the cutting and handling of it separate from other meats so as to avoid any possibility of cross-contamination. Poultry is a common carrier of Salmonella and therefore the proper handling of poultry is vital to food safety. Most establishments have separate cutting rooms designated just for poultry, but if that is not the case then the meat cutter preparing cuts of poultry must take into consideration applicable food safety precautions.

When displaying poultry in the service case, keep it separate from other products (particularly fish) to avoid the absorption of lingering odours and possible cross-contamination. Though packaging materials have advanced greatly in strength and seal, poultry products release purge that might escape the package and weep into the display case, and for this reason retailers need to be diligent about keeping poultry displays fresh.

Frozen poultry that has been packaged for consumers at plant level is ideally suited for display in self-service freezer cases. These products must be kept frozen until served to the customer. Care should be taken in the handling of frozen poultry so as not to damage the packages (the cause of freezer burn) since eye appeal of the product is important to selling. Always protect the breast of any type of poultry, as poultry is displayed breast side up. Damaged packaging and dents in the breast lower the value and appeal of the bird. Should frozen poultry be displayed in a regular fresh meat counter, make sure that proper signage accompanies the display.

Note: Fresh bulk poultry now comes vacuum packaged in large sealed plastic bags, crated or boxed, with bags of ice packed on top of the sealed bags of poultry to help keep the product fresh and at temperatures well within the safe zone (below 4°C). Small processors may not have the technology to vacuum package poultry in large bags and in those cases the poultry will come in large bags with ice packed on top of the bags.

Frozen Poultry signage
Credit: CPMCA image collection

Note: For further details on Bacterial growth & Safe Meat Handling see the thermometer guides, appendix pages 746-747.

WHOLE POULTRY

Chickens are further classified as Cornish Game Hens, Frying Chickens, Broilers, Roasting Chickens, Capons, and Stewing Fowl (Hens). All classifications of chicken have both dark and light meat.

Cornish Game Hens (Rock Cornish Hens) are the smallest and youngest of the chicken classifications. Cornish chickens are harvested at 24 days of age with a weight range of approximately 800–1,000 grams.

Frying Chicken (Broilers) is the most common classification of the chicken family. Its youthfulness and versatility make it popular. Frying chicken may be purchased fresh, frozen, whole, cut up or segmented into parts.

Cornish Game hen
Credit: ©istock.com/credit to 4Kodiak

Broiler frying chicken
Credit: Jakes & Associates

WEIGHT BREAKDOWN OF CHICKEN

Segment	Approximate Percentage of Weight
Legs (drumstick and thigh}	30.5%
Breast (with small ribs)	28.9%
Back and neck	19.3%
Wings	12.5%
Gizzard, liver, heart	5.8%
Cutting loss	3.0%
Whole Chicken	100.0%

Roasting Chickens (includes Capon) are more mature birds. They are harvested between 50 and 70 days of age and can weigh between 2-3 ½ kilograms. Though they are classified as Roasting Chickens and not Fryers, these birds are still considered young and therefore tender. When Roasting Chickens are cooked, they don't produce the dark colour of bones that Frying Chickens do. This is because the bones of younger birds are more porous allowing the hemoglobin to penetrate through (escape from the marrow), producing a darker colour bone. Bones of younger birds are less developed and softer than those of more mature poultry such as Stewing Hens. The test is determining how flexible the keel bone (sternum) of the breast is: the younger the animal, the more flexible the cartilage of the keel bone will be; the older the animal, the more developed and hardened the keel bone will be.

Roasting chicken
Credit: Poultry Farmers of Canada

Capon is a bird that has been castrated surgically before it is six weeks of age. Capons do not develop in the normal way other chickens do. As a castrated animal they are calmer, grow more slowly and put on more fat than other chickens. Capons are rival to the Roasting Chicken for size, flavour and tenderness.

Capon
©Studiogi / Dreamstime

Stewing Hens are mature chickens. They are usually around 65 weeks of age at harvest time, depending on when they stop laying eggs. Stewing hens can weigh between 1 ½ – 3 ½ kilograms. These chickens are tough and the maturity of the bird dictates the cooking method: stewing.

Duck (dressed)
©istock.com / credit to Paul Cowan

Ducks contain all dark meat and weigh in the neighborhood of 2-3 kilograms. Their body shape is narrow and longer than that of chicken. Their keel bone is flatter than either the turkey or the chicken. They can be quite fatty as well as having a lower flesh-to-bone ratio than chicken or turkey.

Goose (dressed)
©istock.com / credit to Chengyuzheng

Geese have the same body shape as ducks. Geese have a larger cavity than ducks (are longer and wider). They usually weigh between 4-5 kilograms. Their flesh or meat is dark and, like ducks, geese are fatty.

Turkeys have a similar skeletal structure to that of chicken but are much larger. Their edible flesh to bone ratio is greater than that of chicken, duck or geese. Turkeys are classed as either hens (female) or toms (male). Toms are usually bigger in size than hens.

Turkey dressed (Hen)
©istock.com / credit to Paul Cowan

Grading of Poultry

There is a grading system for poultry. Canadian poultry grades are Canada Grade A, Canada Utility and Canada Grade C, with Canada Grade A being the best. (See more on Grading of Poultry in Chapter 12).

Canadian Cuts of Poultry

Poultry is meat derived from dressed carcasses of birds as defined by the Meat Inspection Act and regulations which states: "Bird means any species of bird that is slaughtered and processed as a meat product for human consumption and for which an inspection system has been established."

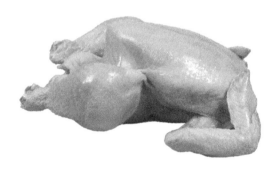

Poultry carcass whole

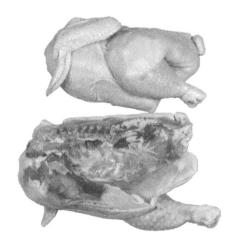

Chicken halves

A Dressed Poultry Carcass (Whole Poultry) means a poultry carcass from which the feathers, hair, head, the feet at the tarsal joints and uropygial gland (oil gland located at the base of the tail feathers) have been removed and the carcass has been eviscerated.

According to the CFIA Meat Cuts Manual for Poultry, the following is a description of poultry parts and their segments obtained from a Dressed Poultry Carcass.

- **Poultry Half (Half Poultry):** means one of two (2) approximately equal portions of a Dressed Poultry Carcass obtained by cutting through the backbones (thoracic vertebrae), pelvic bones (pelvis) and keel bone (sternum) along the median line and excluding the neck.

- **Front Quarter (Breast Quarter):** means is the front (anterior) portion of a Poultry Half obtained by cutting immediately behind (posterior to) and parallel to the rib cage (posterior to the seventh (7th) thoracic vertebra, seventh (7th) rib and sternum).

- **Hind Quarter (Leg Quarter) (Chicken Leg, Back Attached):** means the hind (posterior) portion of a Poultry Half, which is separated from the Front Quarter as described above.

  Note: the term "Leg, Back Attached" may also be used to identify this cut.

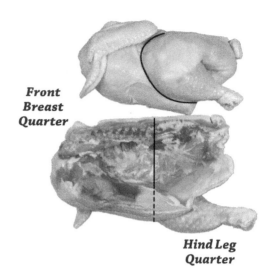

Front Breast Quarter

Hind Leg Quarter

Chicken front quarter & Chicken hind quarter

- **Wing:** Means the portion of the Whole Poultry obtained by cutting through the shoulder joint (articulation between the clavicle, coracoid and humerus). It includes Wing Drumette, the Winglet and may include the Wing Tip.

Chicken wings (outside view)

- **Wing Drumette:** means the proximal portion of the Wing, which is separated from the Whole Poultry by cutting through the shoulder joint as described, and from the Winglet by cutting through the elbow joint (articulation between the humerus and radius/ulna).

  Note: the Wing Drumette shall not be referred to as "Drumstick."

- **Winglet (V-Wings):** means the distal portion of the Wing obtained by cutting through the elbow joint (articulation between the humerus and radius/ulna). Part of the Wing Tip may be removed.

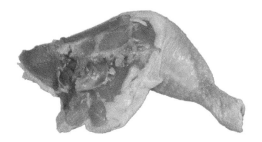

Chicken Leg (inside view)

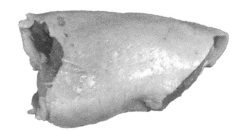

Chicken thigh

Chicken drumstick (outside view)

Chicken breast (full)

- **Leg:** means the portion of the Whole Poultry obtained by cutting at the natural seam through the hip joint (articulation between the femur and the pelvis). It includes the Thigh and Drumstick jointed or disjointed and may include pelvic meat. It excludes pelvic bones, back skin, abdominal skin and excessive fat.

- **Thigh:** means the proximal portion of the Leg which is separated from the Whole Poultry by cutting at the natural seam through the hip joint as described above, and from the Drumstick by a straight cut through the knee joint (femoro-tibial articulation). It may include pelvic meat but shall exclude pelvic bones, back skin, abdominal skin and excessive fat.

- **Drumstick:** means the distal portion of the Leg which is separated from the Thigh by a straight cut through the knee joint as described above.

- **Breast (Full Breast):** means that portion of the Whole Poultry which is separated from the Wing by cutting through the shoulder joint, from the neck by cutting approximately through the twelfth (12th) neck bone (cervical vertebra), from the Back by cutting through the ribs at the junction of the vertebral ribs and back and from the Hind Quarter by cutting immediately behind (posterior to) the rib cage (7th rib and sternum). The Breast includes the "Y" shaped ends of the ribs and excludes the neck skin.

- **Half Breast:** means one of the two (2) approximately equal portions of a Breast obtained by cutting through the breastbone (sternum) along the median line.

Note: the Breast may be portioned in two (2) approximately equal parts (Half Breast) as described or in three (3) parts by first removing the Wishbone portion then by cutting the breast bone (sternum) along the median line. For exact weight-making purposes, these parts may be substituted for lighter or heavier pieces and the package may contain two (2) or more of such parts without affecting the appropriateness of the product description as Breast.

- **Wishbone:** means the front (anterior) portion of the Breast obtained by a cut passing through the hypocledial ligament located between the tip of the wishbone (hypocledium) and the front point of the breast bone (carinal apex of the sternum), then between the wishbone (clavicle) and coracoid up to a point where the wishbone (clavicle) joins the shoulder. The neck skin shall be excluded.

- **Trimmed Breast:** means that portion of the Breast obtained by a cut passing along the junction of the vertebral and sternal ribs may be removed and the neck skin shall be excluded.

- **Half Trimmed Breast:** means one of two (2) approximately equal portions of a Trimmed Breast obtained by cutting through the breastbone (sternum) along the median line.

Note: the Trimmed Breast may be portioned in two (2) approximately equal parts (Half Trimmed Breast) as described, or in three (3) parts by first removing the Wishbone portion as described, then by cutting the breast bone (sternum) along the median line. For exact weight purposes these parts may be substituted for lighter or heavier pieces and the package may contain two (2) or more of such parts without affecting the appropriateness of the product description as Trimmed Breast.

- **Breast Fillet:** means the round, elongated fusiform muscle, (supracoracoid muscle or deep pectoral) found on each side of the keel bone (sternum).

Chicken back

- **Whole Back:** means the portion of the Whole Poultry, which is separated from the Breast as described above. It includes the neck, thoracic vertebrae, pelvic bones and tail. It may include parts of the vertebral ribs.

- **Back:** means the portion of the Whole Back which is separated from the Neck by cutting in the vicinity of the shoulder joint (approximately through the twelfth (12th) cervical vertebra). It includes the thoracic vertebrae, pelvic bones and tail, the skin and adhering meat. The vertebral ribs and/or scapula may be removed.

- **Stripped Back:** means the Back from which the meat adhering to the pelvic bones has been removed, commonly known as the oyster muscles that when removed remain on the thighs.

Chicken necks
Credit: ©Nicknicko / Dreamstime

- **Neck:** means the front (anterior) portion of the Whole Back or carcass obtained by cutting near the shoulder joint (approximately through the twelfth (12th) cervical vertebra). It may include the skin.

- **Poultry Giblets:** means is the liver, the heart or the gizzard or any combination thereof of the same species, obtained from a Dressed Poultry Carcass.

Poultry Variety Meats

Variety meats are edible parts of domestic birds harvested for human consumption. For poultry these are the following:

- Gizzard
- Heart
- Liver

Whole Cutup Fryers: is a Dressed Poultry Carcass of Chicken that has been cutup into segments and sold as Whole Cutup Frying Chicken. A whole cutup fryer must contain the wings, breasts and legs. The giblets, back and neck are optional. The breasts can be boneless or regular (bone-in). If the giblets, back and neck are to be included then the label must reflect that they are included.

Chicken livers and gizzard
Credit: Poultry Farmers of Canada

Chicken hearts
Credit: ©istock.com/credit to zhongyanjiang

CFIA Nomenclature Requirements for Poultry

Retailers are responsible for ensuring that the names used to describe poultry on labels and in advertisements include the appropriate specific terms. The name used to describe all poultry and poultry cuts must include an indication of the species of bird. For example, the term "Chicken," "Duck" or "Turkey" must appear in conjunction with the item whether that is a "whole" bird or a specific "segment" thereof. For example: "Chicken Breast," "Duck Breast" or "Turkey Drumsticks."

In addition to prepackaged foods, some non-prepackaged foods are required to carry a label. As the definition of label includes words belonging to or accompanying a food, the labels of non-prepackaged foods (meats sold from full service counters) may be on a tag or sign accompanying the food and not necessarily placed on the product itself. Since the majority of mandatory labelling requirements only apply to prepackaged foods, the labelling requirements for these foods (foods sold from full service counters) are limited.

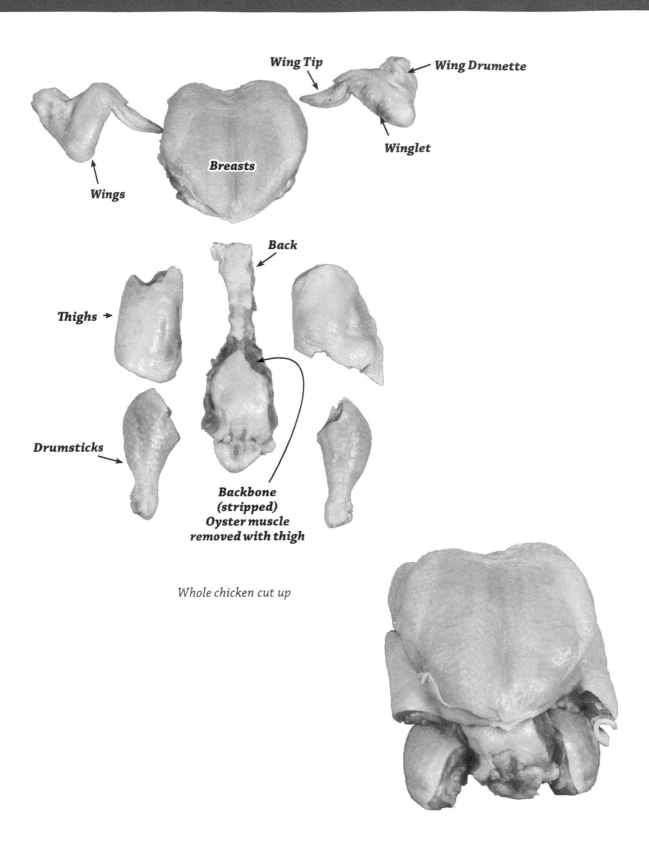

Wing Tip

Wing Drumette

Winglet

Breasts

Wings

Back

Thighs

Drumsticks

Backbone
(stripped)
Oyster muscle
removed with thigh

Whole chicken cut up

Chicken cut up (whole) on tray

Credit: Jakes & Associates

LABELLING REQUIREMENTS FOR POULTRY

Prepackaged poultry offered for sale at retail must be marked with:

- the name of the bird species and/or segment,
- the name and address of the retailer,
- the net quantity,
- the packaging date,
- the durable life of the poultry unless the durable life is indicated on a poster next to the product, and
- the words "previously frozen" if the poultry that has been frozen is thawed prior to sale unless the words "previously frozen" appear on a poster next to the product.

LIST OF POULTRY CUT MODIFIERS

Modifiers are descriptions used to explain in more detail what the bird (species) or segment is, or what alterations have been done to the poultry product in question. For example: a chicken breast that has the bones removed should be labelled "Chicken Breast Boneless."

Using the above example of "Chicken Breast Boneless" we note that the term "boneless" is optional; however, without it the description of the contents of the package is incomplete, keeping in mind the label identifying the content of a packaged item must be informative and not misleading. Here, as elsewhere noted, the phrase "while not required" refers to the option of removing the bone from the chicken breast or identifying the breast as "boneless" after all, we can label and sell a "Porterhouse" steak as a "T-bone" but we can't sell a T-bone as a Porterhouse even though they both come from the loin. The Porterhouse has the gluteus medius muscle whereas the T-bone does not. So too with chicken breasts, we can sell a boneless chicken breast as a regular chicken breast by just labelling it as "Chicken Breast" (implying the bones are still attached) but we can't sell or label regular chicken breasts as "Boneless".

Note: While not required, these modifiers may be used to describe cuts of poultry provided they are informative and not misleading.

**CHICKEN BREAST
(Stir-Fry)**

Packed On	Best Before	Sell By
Net Wt/Ct	Unit Price	Total Price

*Chicken breast stir-fry
Credit: TRU Retail Meat
Processing Program*

**CHICKEN LEGS
(back attached)**

Packed On	Best Before	Sell By
Net Wt/Ct	Unit Price	Total Price

*Chicken legs (back attached)
Credit: TRU Retail Meat
Processing Program*

**CHICKEN Thigh
(skinless)**

Packed On	Best Before	Sell By
Net Wt/Ct	Unit Price	Total Price

*Chicken thighs (skinless)
Credit: TRU Retail Meat
Processing Program*

POULTRY MODIFIERS:

- Basted
- Boneless
- Breaded
- Deep Basted
- Portion
- Pre-basted
- Rolled
- Self-Basting

- Semi-Boneless
- Skinless
- Stir Fry
- Stuffed
- Stuffed with
- Tied
- Trimmed

BASIC LABEL REQUIREMENTS FOR POULTRY

Label: Species name (when sold whole) ex: Turkey, Duck, Goose, or Species name, retail name, modifier

Sample: Chicken (Species) Breast (Retail Name), Boneless (Modifier).

Counter-Ready Poultry Products

Counter-ready poultry and poultry segments/cuts refer to poultry and poultry items that have been processed and fabricated at plant level, are packaged for displays, boxed, and shipped to store level. With these prepackaged and prepared products there is no need of a meat cutter. The poultry is finished and ready for in-store labelling and displaying. Counter-ready poultry comes in one of two forms: fresh or frozen.

Most larger supermarket chains carry fresh and frozen counter ready poultry for ease of handling and the convenience of storage and display. In all cases the poultry needs little attention outside stock rotation and refrigeration. When required or needed the poultry is simply removed from the containers or boxes it came in, labelled and priced, and displayed. There is also the argument counter-ready poultry provide better returns on investment with respect to costs associated with inventory, labour and sales. With counter-ready products knowledgeable staff can easily maintain displays during busy times avoiding customer disappointment looking to fill their appetite for poultry.

Some of the more common Counter Ready Poultry Products are:

- Whole Fresh Packed Frying Chicken
- Fresh Chicken Segments
  - Wings (Winglet & Drumette)
  - Legs (Thighs & Drums)
  - Breasts (Whole, Skinless, Halves, & Fillets)
  - Necks & Backs
- Whole Frozen Fryers
- Frozen Chicken Legs, Back attached
- Frozen Chicken Breasts
- Frozen Chicken Wings
- Ground Chicken
- Whole Fresh or Frozen Roasting Chickens
- Whole Fresh or Frozen Capons
- Whole Frozen Geese
- Whole Frozen Ducks
- Duck Breasts
- Whole Frozen Pheasant
- Whole Frozen Quail
- Whole Frozen Cornish Game Hens
- Whole Fresh or Frozen Turkeys
- Turkey Breast
- Turkey Rolls
- Turkey Drums
- Turkey Thighs
- Ground Turkey

Value-Added Poultry Cuts

Value-added cuts of poultry are no different than other value-added cuts of meat whether beef, veal, pork or lamb. Innovative cuts of poultry are designed to attract consumer attention and interest. Stocking and merchandising these cuts is one way to increase sales and profit margins. Value-added cuts of poultry give consumers more options for their craving, whether white or dark meat, chicken, duck or turkey. Value-added products take into consideration new product development, eating trends and flavours such as coated, seasoned, marinated, and oven-ready, precooked, or heat and serve. The versatility, popularity and relatively low cost of poultry make it attractive to all appetites.

Wholesale Meat Specifications for Poultry

Wholesale products are products that fill certain operational needs such as caselots of specific cuts of poultry, ex: Chicken Breast Tenders, Chicken Supremes, premade Cordon Bleu or Chicken Ballentines. They are ready-made products that the retailer might not be able to produce in large quantities due to operational restrictions and therefore are more economical to purchase in bulk from a food service provider. Such products are a direct response to industry demand made by retailers in order to meet a need for variety and versatility that keeps up with their clientele's keenness for adventure with food. With poultry, there appears to be more variety with choice of cut, texture and flavour.

SUMMARY

TERMS FOR REVIEW

Agro-business	Co-operative	Poultry Giblets
Broiler	Duck	Pullet
Capon	FIRF	RFID
Chicken	Freezer Burn	Roasting chicken
Chicken back	Frying chicken	Salmonella
Chicken breast	Gizzard	Seasonal Fluctuations
Chicken leg	Goose	Stewing fowl
Chicken necks	Hatchery	Turkey
Chicken thigh	Perishable	Winglet
Chicken wing	PID	

DISCUSSION QUESTIONS

1. How many breeds of chicken has Canada developed? Are they in commercial use? Explain.

2. List the four common types of poultry sold in Canada.

3. Which breeds of chicken are used in the production of white eggs?

4. Which breeds of chicken are used in the production of poultry in Canada?

5. Which breeds of chicken produce brown eggs?

6. Explain what On-Farm Food Safety Programs are.

7. Explain traceability as it applies to poultry.

8. Which bacteria is common to poultry products?

9. Which federally sponsored program monitors disease out breaks such as the Avian Flu?

Poultry Retail Meat Processing Options

Credits: Jakes & Associates

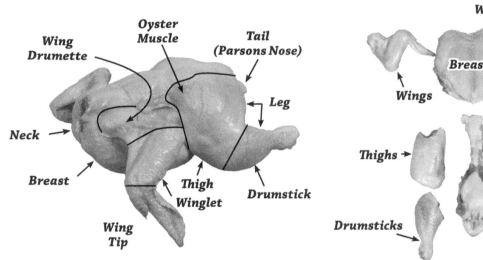

Poultry carcass whole

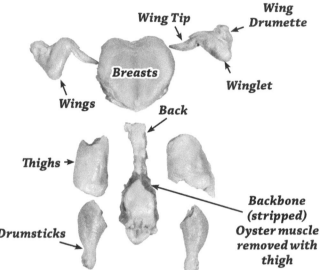

Chicken cut up whole with segment names

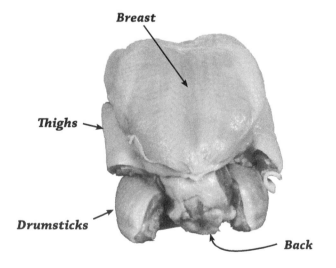

Chicken cut up whole

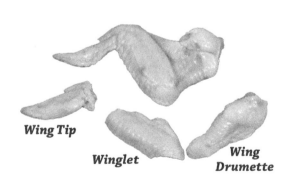

Chicken wing segments

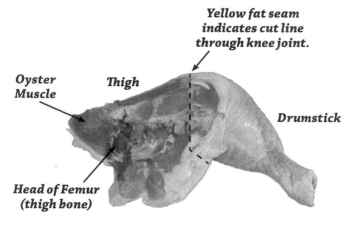

Yellow fat seam indicates cut line through knee joint.

Oyster Muscle

Thigh

Drumstick

Head of Femur (thigh bone)

Chicken leg (inside view)

Chicken leg (outside view)

Chicken leg back attached (inside view)

Chicken leg back attached (outside view)

Chicken thigh (outside view)

Chicken thigh (inside view)

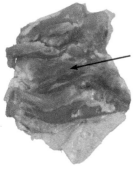

Chicken thigh boneless
(bone removed)

Chicken thighs skinless bone in

Chicken thigh boneless skinless

Chicken drumstick (outside view)

Chicken drumstick (inside view)

Chicken drumsticks skinless
(outside view)

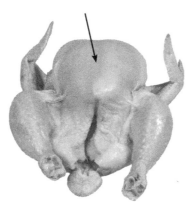

Whole chicken showing breast

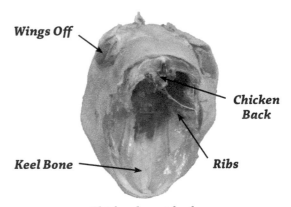

Wings Off

Chicken Back

Keel Bone

Ribs

Chicken breast back on

Chicken breast boneless (inside view)

Chicken breast boneless (outside view)

Chicken breast boneless / skinless

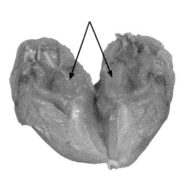

Chicken breasts boneless / skinless portions
Breast fillets arrowed

Chicken breasts boneless / skinless (with chicken breast fillets off)

Chicken breast fillets

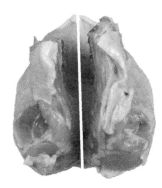

Whole chicken breast with center cut line for bone in breast portions

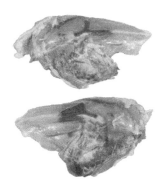

Chicken breast portion bone in (inside view)

Chicken breast portion bone in (outside view)

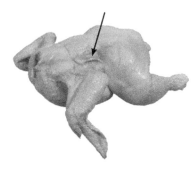

Chicken whole with back shown

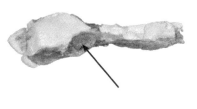

Chicken back stripped showing the exposed ilium depression where the oyster meat is removed with the chicken leg and therefore remains on the chicken thigh (outside view)

Meat case poultry display
Credit: Summit Gourmet Meats

Meat case Poultry display with value added marinated products
Credit: Save on Foods

Chickens necks
Credit: ©Nicknickko / Dreamstime

Processing sequence: Knife cutting a chicken.

Credits: CPMCA image collection

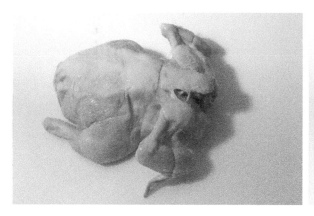

Step 1: Start position for knife cutting a chicken.

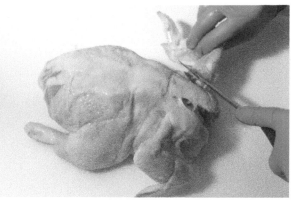

Step 2: Remove the wing at the shoulder bone joint

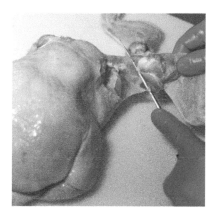

Step 3: Cut under the shoulder bone & leaving the breast meat on the carcass

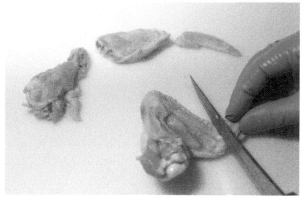

Step 4: Segmenting chicken wings - remove wing tip from outside of wing

Step 5: Chicken wing drumette, Chicken winglet & Chicken wing tip

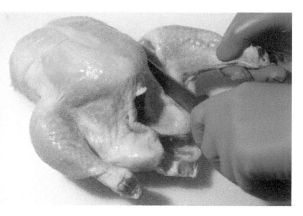

Step 6: Remove legs - cut through lose skin on inside of both legs

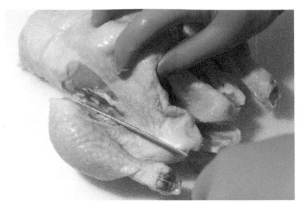

Step 7: Don't cut too deep into the leg seam & joint

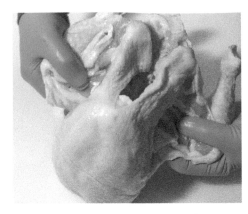

Step 8: Bend legs back at the hip to dislocate the hip joint on both legs

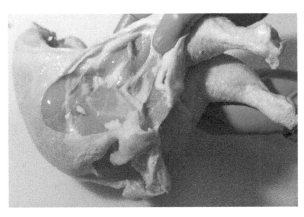

Step 9: The legs should now be in this position facing the cutter

Step 10: Hold the leg as shown & keeping the knife parallel to the backbone edge, cut towards the ilium cup & (oyster muscle)

Step 11: Score the edge of the Ilium cup with a forward slice and keep the knife pushing down

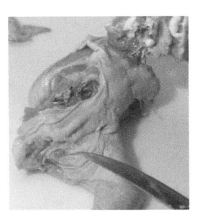

Step 12: This process pulls the 'oyster' muscle off the ilium keeping it on the chicken thigh

Step 13: Do the same on the opposite leg. Remember to adjust the chicken position to do this.

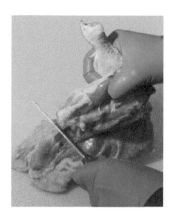

Step 14: See the hip joint and clean ilium cup with the knife hand applying downward pressure

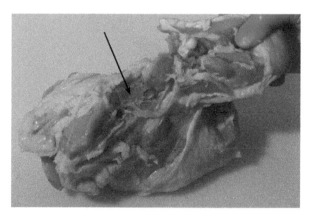

Step 15: The ilium cup is part of the back bone that holds the 'oyster' muscle

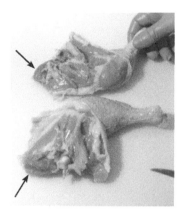

Step 16: Both chicken legs showing the 'oyster' muscle on the left outer edge of the legs

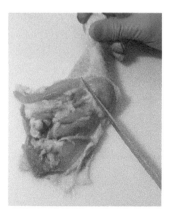

Step 17: Now separate the thigh & drumstick on the opposite leg at the yellow line and knee joint

Step 18: Chicken thigh & drumstick

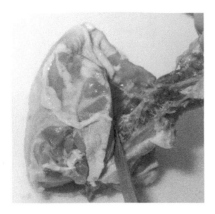

Step 19: Removing the back bone-while holding the back bone by the tail bone

*Step 20: Keep the knife edge as close to the back bone as possible with the knife tip up
Pull the knife down quickly with a vertical cut parallel to the edge of the back bone*

Step 21: Repeat on the opposite side & lift the back bone out - This skill will take time to learn

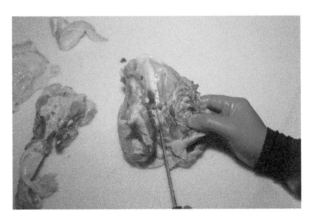

Step 22: Boning out the Chicken Breast-Scoring the white cartilage only to the edge of the keel bone

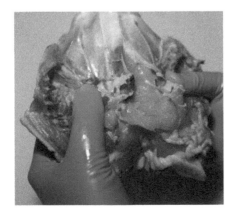

Step 23: Place thumb on one side of the keel bone and push down firmly with the opposite thumb to break away the bone edge of the keel bone-repeat on the opposite side

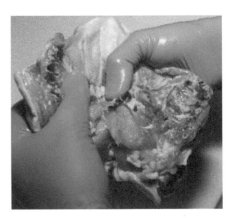

Step 24: Repeat on the opposite side of the keel bone

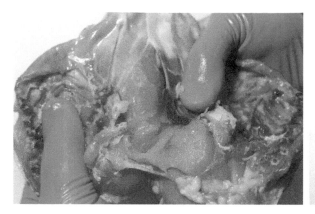

Step 25: Exposed edge of the keel bone after breaking the cartilage

Step 26: Slide your thumbs under the edges of the keel bone cartilage to release the flesh

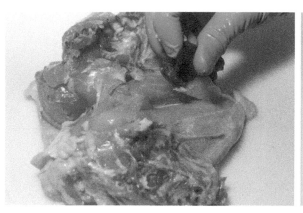

Step 27: Hold the bone end of the keel bone with thumb and first finger and pull up & out

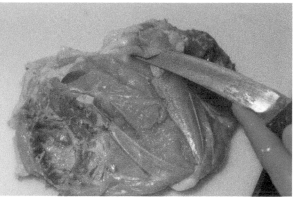

Step 28: Break the hidden wish bone in the upper centre of the breast if not already broken & slide knife edge under broken wish bone on the right of the breast

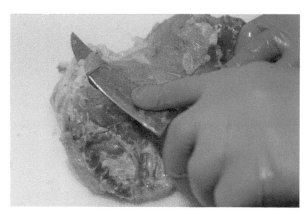

Step 29: Lifting the broken wish bone up on the left of the breast

Step 30: Full chicken breast with the keel bone removed

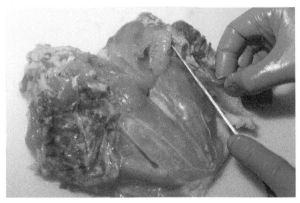

Step 31: Now cut under the rib bones to the coracoid bone on the right side of the breast

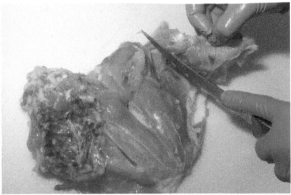

Step 32: Cutting over and under the coracoid bone

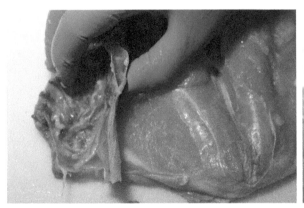

Step 33: Repeat on the left side of the breast

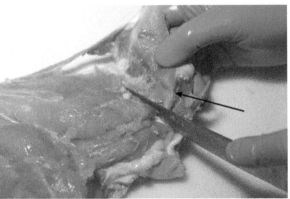

Step 34: The coracoid bone is between the knife & the thumb of the Cutter

Step 35: The fully boneless chicken breast

Step 36: Now peel off the skin from the thick end of the breast

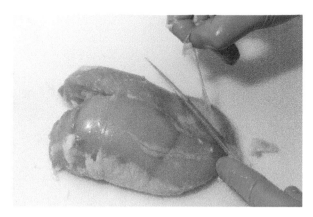

Step 37: Now trim off excess fat & membranes to present a clean chicken breast

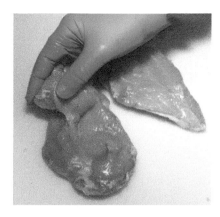

Step 38: After cutting the breast in half along the keel bone grove, remove the Chicken breast fillets

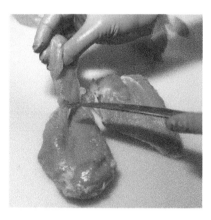

Step 39: Removing the chicken breast fillet from one half of the breast

Step 40: See left of center - Chicken breast fillet and Chicken breast fillet off

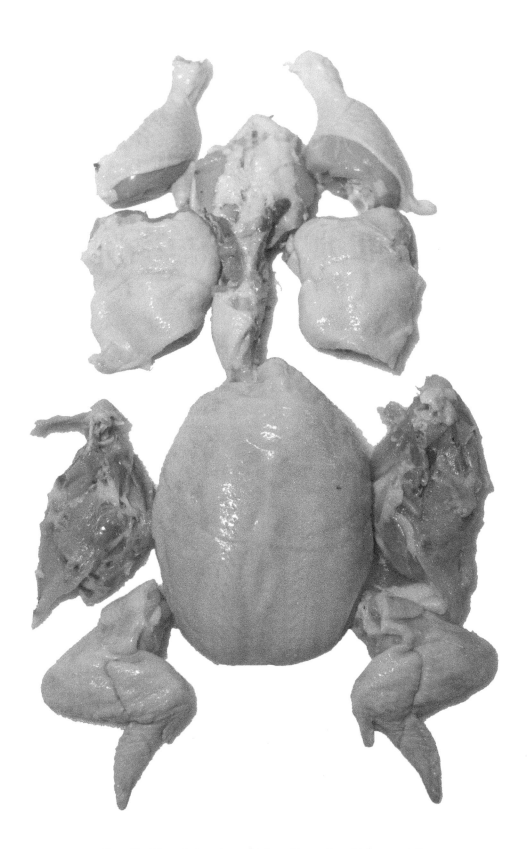

Step 41: The whole cut up chicken. Name the chicken parts?

Chapter 9

Seafood

Canada's fishing areas fall into four main divisions: Atlantic, Pacific, inland waters and aquaculture operations. Commercial fishing is important to the Canadian economy contributing billions of dollars annually to our gross domestic product.

This chapter talks about the different fishing methods used in commercial fishing in Canada, the types of fish caught in Canadian waters (saltwater, freshwater and shellfish), along with their common characteristics (flat fish, round fish, etc.). It also covers market forms of fish, fish processing and various species of fish and shellfish found in Canadian waters complete with a description of each and their distinguishing characteristics.

Again, the emphasis of the chapter is quality of product, presentation and quality controls. Other topics include microbiology as it affects seafood, bacteria that act as spoilage organisms and natural phenomena's that impact seafood. Included is the handling, storage, labelling and displaying of seafood along with information consumers of seafood should be aware of.

Seafood

History

When John Cabot arrived on the coast of Newfoundland in 1497 he found our Aboriginal peoples (Beothuk or Innu people of the region) catching fish for food and trade. He returned with some of the bounty to England and the news spread fast. The French and Portuguese consequently established a fishing industry in the Northwest Atlantic off the coast of Newfoundland in the early 1500s. At the time cod was plentiful. It was caught, salted, dried and sold as a valuable commodity during that period. Competing for the best spots, fishermen from England and Spain soon joined the French and Portuguese fishing vessels. Ships would arrive in early spring and stay through to September when they would leave Canadian shores with their catch headed toward their home of origin. As the land became established, the inhabitants began fishing from small open boats off the shores of Newfoundland and Nova Scotia.

As time passed the introduction of steel vessels replaced wood ships and canning technology of the time developed better methods of preserving fish leading to the canning of sardines and lobster by the late 19th century. The era also sees cod caught in larger netted traps replacing the hook and line method. The First Nations populations catch fish near spawning grounds of salmon on both our east and west coast rivers adding to the commerce of fur trading. By the 1880s the cod fishing and production peaked and began to decline and was replaced by halibut, lobster and salmon fisheries.

By the 1890s settlers move inland exploiting the inland lakes and rivers with seine methods of fishing. By the time of World War II the filleting and freezing of fish was well established in Newfoundland. Developments saw the introduction of radios, radar, sonar and otter trawling. Radios were used for communication between ships and shore and the sonar as a detection device. The use of otter trawling saw bigger catches. At the end of the war new fisheries were established for species such as red fish, flounder, scallops, shrimp and crabs. In 1947 the Fisheries Prices Support Board was founded, which helped stabilize returns to fishermen during downturns in the market.

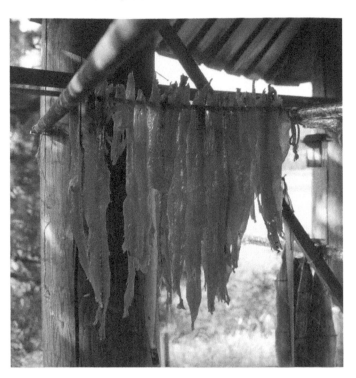

Fish drying in a camp
©Chris Boswell / Dreamstime

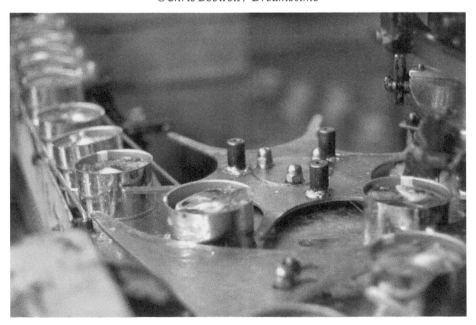

Canning operation
Credit: ©istock.com/credit to Anutik

With improved methods of preservation in the 1950s came greater demand for finished products. Groundfish gave way to frozen fish production, which increased as refrigeration and transportation methods advanced. By the 1960s foreign fishing off the Atlantic Coast saw Canadian fishing stocks starting to dwindle. In just 25 short years the industry went from underdevelopment to overcapacity. Canadians begin to experience regulatory controls to limit techniques, catch quotas and conflicts with outside groups for fishing rights. During this era the government began to determine who could fish, where they could fish, when they could fish, and how they could fish. By the 1980s Canada had the largest fishing zone, longest coastline, and was ranked in the top twenty fishing nations in the world.

Modern fishing boat
© Johann68 / Dreamstime

Seafood Production

Fishing is the oldest industry in Canada and fish and seafood is one of the largest food sectors exported by the country. Fisheries and Oceans Canada claim to be committed to the sustainability of this valuable natural resource. Extensive sea fisheries on both the Atlantic and Pacific coasts produce a wide variety of seafood in huge quantities, while the vast inland waters are also sources of many kinds of seafood, not to mention the ever-growing aquaculture operations (fish farms) inland and off shore. The term "seafood" and/or "fish" as used herein interchangeably refer to both finfish and shellfish (fresh & saltwater).

FISHING AREAS AROUND CANADA

Canada's fishing areas fall into four main divisions: Atlantic, Pacific, inland waters and aquaculture operations. Many commercially-important species are found in the Atlantic with lobsters currently ranked as the most valuable. Five species of salmon account for more than half of the Pacific catch value but many other varieties of ocean fish, including halibut and herring, are also part of the commercial industry. The principal freshwater fishing grounds are the Great Lakes, the lakes of the prairie provinces and the lakes of the Northwest Territories, notably Great Slave Lake, which yield a variety of fish; northern pike, whitefish, perch and walleye to name a few. There is also growing interest in the area of aquaculture, which now makes up a large portion of the salmon, trout, shrimp, clam and mussel production.

Worldwide aquaculture operations make up approximately 50% of the total world fish and seafood production for human consumption. Despite its extensive marine and freshwater resources, Canada is a relatively small producer, accounting for less that 0.3% of global aquaculture production and ranking 22nd in the world. However, Canada accounts for 8% of global farmed-salmon production, ranking 4th in the world behind Norway, the United Kingdom and Chile (Food and Agriculture Organization (FAO) 2009, The State of World Fisheries and Aquaculture 2008).

Canada has aquaculture operations in all provinces and in the Yukon. According to the department of Fisheries and Oceans Canada aquaculture operations now generates about two billion dollars in total economic activity, over one billion dollars in gross domestic product (GDP) and about half a billion in labour income. Aquaculture operations for several marine finfish and shellfish species are well established on the east and west coasts, while freshwater trout operations can be found in almost every province. In addition, Canadian finfish aquaculture also includes a small number of active tilapia, sturgeon, Atlantic halibut and other operations. The scope of aquaculture operations varies across the country depending upon the species being farmed, the environment (marine, freshwater) and the culture technologies used (hanging nets, socks, baskets or trays and bottom culture). The main types of growing operations include freshwater and saltwater net pens and land-based systems (tanks), bottom culture shellfish operations in intertidal and subtidal zones, long lines, and restocking operations in open water.

FISHERIES

Aquaculture is the aquatic equivalent of agriculture or farming on land. Defined broadly, agriculture includes farming both animals (animal husbandry) and plants (agronomy, horticulture and forestry in part). Similarly, aquaculture covers the farming of both animals (such as crustaceans, finfish and mollusks) and plants (like seaweed). While agriculture is predominantly based on use of freshwater, aquaculture occurs in both inland (freshwater) and coastal (brackish water and seawater) areas. Aquaculture is the cultivation of aquatic animals and plants, especially fish, shellfish and seaweed in natural or controlled marine or freshwater environments, known as underwater agriculture or fish farming. Aqua fish farms intervene in the rearing process to enhance production by providing regular stocking (hatching of fish), feeding (raising to mature state) and protection from predators (otherwise found in their natural habitat).

Aquaculture operation
©Megastocker / Dreamstime

Groundfish are fish that live on, in, or near the bottom of the body of water they inhabit. Some typical saltwater groundfish species are cod, flounder, halibut and sole. Related terms used in different contexts include **demersal fish** and **whitefish**, and more broadly, **bottom feeders**. Other examples of Groundfish are haddock, pollock and turbot.

Pelagic Fish can be categorized as coastal and oceanic fish, based on the depth of the water they inhabit. Coastal pelagic fish inhabit sunlit waters up to 650 feet deep, typically above the continental shelf. Examples of species include forage fish such as anchovies, sardines, shad and the predatory fish that feed on them. Oceanic pelagic fish typically inhabit waters below the continental shelf; they have agile bodies made for long distance migration and travel in schools while some are solitary that drift with ocean currents. Examples include

larger fish such as mackerel, swordfish, tuna and even sharks.

Shellfish is a fisheries term for exoskeleton-bearing aquatic invertebrates harvested as food including various species of **Molluscs** and **Crustaceans** such as clams, cockles, crabs, mussels, oysters, prawns, scallops, sea urchins and shrimp. Octopus, sea cucumbers and squid also fall into the category of shellfish.

FISHING METHODS

Gill Netting is a method of catching fish with a net suspended in the water. Fish are caught when they swim into the net and their gills become entangled in the webbing. This method is used extensively in British Columbia while harvesting herring and salmon. The nets are about 360 metres in length and 60 metres in width, but may vary depending on the species being targeted. Net size used in commercial fishing is regulated by the department of Fisheries and Oceans Canada.

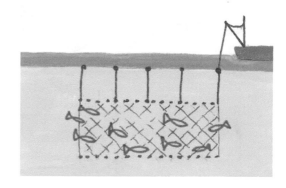

Gill net
Credit: CPMCA image collection

Longlining involves the use of a main fishing line to which are attached a series of shorter lines with baited hooks. Longlining is mainly used in catching black cod (sable fish), dogfish and halibut. The long line lies along the bottom of the ocean floor and, depending on conditions, up to 400 fish may be caught at one time.

Purse sein net
Credit: CPMCA image collection

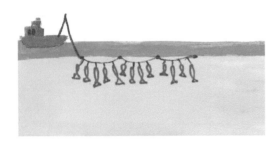

Long lining
Credit: CPMCA image collection

Purse Seining involves the use of a net, which can be "pursed up" to trap a school of fish. It is used extensively in the harvesting of migratory species such as herring and salmon. When a school of fish is located the seine net is set over the stern of the boat with a roller and/or hydraulically-controlled ramp. The boat then makes a large circle to surround the school of fish and the two ends of the net are then connected. This forms a giant floating fence encircling the fish. The purse line is then pulled tight to close the bottom of the net. The fish are trapped and the net is pulled up on board. A purse seine can capture as many as 1,000 tons of herring in one net.

Otter Trawling involves the use of a large bag-shaped net, which is dragged along the ocean floor. The net is a long wedged shape that narrows into a funnel called the "cod end." The mouth of the net is kept open during the trawl by metal or wood and metal doors that the water pushes against. As the net is towed along the ocean floor fish entering the net are forced into the cod end and cannot escape. In a single catch up to sixty tons of fish may be harvested. Otter trawling is used to catch flounder, lingcod, ocean perch and sole, not to mention whatever other species happens to be in the line of the trawl. A variation of the otter trawl is used for catching small shrimp.

Otter trawling net
Credit: CPMCA image collection

Trolling is a method whereby several fishing lines with numerous lures attached are dragged slowly through the water. This method is used to harvest albacore tuna, halibut and salmon. When a fish strikes the line it is hauled in, the fish is taken from the hook and the gear is reset. Trolling is regarded as the best method for ensuring quality and has the least stress on other renewable and sustainable resources.

Crab traps
© mlhead / Dreamstime

Trolling line
Credit: CPMCA image collection

Lobster boat & trap
©Jimphotos / Dreamstime

Trapping is a method used to catch both crabs and lobsters. Wooden or metal traps that look like large caged boxes with wired frames are baited and thrown overboard. Lobsters and crab walk along the ocean floor in depths of 7-30 metres. Traps rest on the bottom and are designed to let the crab or lobster walk right in and partake of the bait; once inside they become entrapped. The trap is pulled up after several hours and may contain more than one crab or lobster.

Types of Fish

Fish products from our four main divisions (Atlantic, Pacific, inland waters and aquaculture) are divided into two categories: finfish, or fish with fins and internal skeletons, and shellfish, fish with external shells but no internal bone structure.

Canadian Fish	
Saltwater Finfish	**Atlantic:** alewives, bass, catfish, cod, cusk, flounder, turbot, haddock*, hake, halibut, herring**, mackerel, plaice, pollock, rosefish, ocean perch, Atlantic salmon, shad, skate, smelt, sole, swordfish, tuna, witch and Boston blue fish.
	Pacific: Pacific cod, eulachon (or oolichan), flounder, halibut, herring, lingcod, rockfish, skate, sole, trout, steelhead, tuna, albacore, Alaska black cod (also called sable fish), anchovies (though anchovies for sale in Canada most likely come already prepared from Spain or Portugal) and salmon (chinook [both red and white], chum, coho, pink, sockeye, spring) all of which spawn in freshwater but live in saltwater.
Freshwater Finfish	**Inland Waters:** bass, white, buffalo fish, bullheads, cisco tullibee or lake herring, catfish, carp, chub, eel, gold-eye inconnu, lake trout, ling or burbot, perch, pickerel, blue, pike, sauger, sheepshead, smelt, sturgeon, sucker mullet, sunfish, tomcod, whitefish, bay pickerel and eel (which spawn in salt water and rear in fresh water).
Shellfish: Molluscs & Crustaceans	**Atlantic:** clams (bar, soft shell), quahaugs, crabs, lobsters, mussels, oysters, periwinkles, scallops and squid.
	Pacific: crabs, oysters, prawns, shrimps, clams (butter, geoducks and littlenecks), octopus and squid.
* Chicken haddie is usually a canned mixture of hake, cod and haddock: white flesh only. ** Small herring are known as sardines, pilchards, bristling and sprats.	

Characteristics of Finfish are lean or fat, come as round or flat and harvested from freshwater or saltwater. Lean fish may contain as little as 0.5 % fat, examples of which are Cod, Halibut and Sole. Fat fish can have up to 20% fat, examples of which are Mackerel, Salmon and Trout.

- **Round Fish** swim in a vertical position, have eyes on both sides of their head and their bodies may be truly round or oval in shape.

Round fish, Atlantic Salmon
©Alexander Raths /Dreamstim

- **Flat Fish** swim in a horizontal position, have both eyes on the top of their heads, have asymmetrical compressed bodies, and their skin is dark on top and white on the bottom.

Flat fish, Flounder
©Izuboky / Dreamstime

- **Freshwater Fish** come from lakes and rivers. Common freshwater fish include: catfish, perch, pickerel, pike and whitefish.

- **Saltwater Fish** come from saltwater oceans, seas and lakes. Bluefish, flounder, halibut and swordfish are commonly known saltwater fish.

- **Fresh Fish** is sold in varying forms from whole to steaks, fillets or ground. Fresh finfish comes in a variety of shapes and sizes but always from one of the three categories: lean or fat, round or flat, from fresh or saltwater.

MARKET FORMS OF FISH

Fish, including all forms of shellfish, is available on the market in many forms. It may be obtained whole, drawn, dressed, as steaks, fillets, butterflied fillets, sticks or tranches, and can be bought fresh, frozen, smoked, salted, pickled, dried, canned.

Whole Fish are marketed just as they are when taken from the water, complete with head, entrails, gills, fins and scales. Species such as smelts, herring, rainbow trout and sole are examples of whole fish caught and sold in markets.

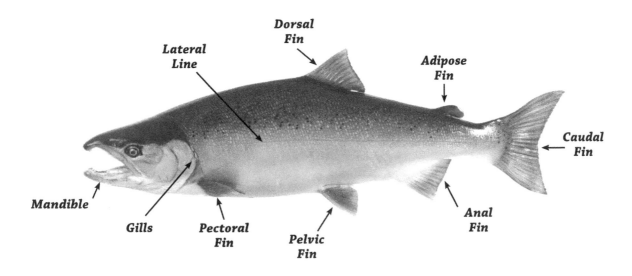

Identifying external parts of a whole round fish.
©Sneekerp / Dreamstime

Drawn Fish have their entrails (viscera) removed by making a slit along the belly, and are sold whole with head, fins and gills intact. Because the entrails have been removed, this market type of fish has a longer storage life. Food safety practices dictate drawn fish still need cleaning before preparation. Examples of drawn fish are pink salmon, Atlantic salmon, perch and trout.

Drawn fish - Steelhead trout
Credit: Fisherman's Market

Dressed Fish are whole with the entrails (viscera), head (includes the gills), tail, fins and scales removed. Perch, salmon, trout and herring can be marketed as dressed fish.

Dressed fish – Coho Salmon
Credit: Fishermans Market

Fish Steaks are cross section slices cut from medium to large size dressed fish. Fish steaks generally include the backbone. A few examples of fish cut for steak are halibut, Artic char and salmon.

Fish steaks – Coho salmon
Credit: Fishermans Market

Fish Fillets are the boneless sides of a fish cut lengthwise from the backbone. Fillets are practically boneless but can have some evidence of pin bones; very often the skin is also removed. Each side of a round fish provides a fillet whereas each side of a flat fish provides two fillets.

Fish fillets – Sockeye salmon
Credit: Fishermans Market

Fish Fillets Butterflied are produced from smaller fish where the backbone is removed and the fillets remain joined by the uncut skin.

Fish fillets butterflied
Credit: ©Ismael Tato Rodriguez - Dreamstime

Fish Sticks or Tranches are uniform cross section cuts from large fresh or frozen dressed fish.

Fish sticks or Tranches
Credit: ©istock.com / Credit to RusN

Shellfish have two categories: molluscs, like clams and oysters, and crustaceans, like crab and lobster. Shellfish can be marketed as whole fish. Both lobster and crab are also further processed by selling their meat as canned or by separating their parts (legs and claws). Octopus is a mollusc referred to as a cephalopod, which falls under the category of shellfish and can be sold whole or in portions.

- **Molluscs** are referred to as soft sea animals. There are three types of molluscs commonly caught and sold as seafood: univalves, bivalves and cephalopods.
  - **Univalves** have a single shell like that of a conch or snail.
  - **Bivalves** have a pair of hinged shells like those found on clams and mussels.
  - **Cephalopods** have a single thin internal shell called a cuttle-bone like that found in octopus and squid.

- **Crustaceans** are seafood animals with segmented shells and jointed legs like those of lobster, crab and shrimp.

HEALTH AND WELLNESS

The Government of Canada, via the Department of Fisheries and Oceans Canada, works to secure the future of Canada's wild fisheries by initiating conservative management practices that focus on sustainable development and responsible fishing. The Canadian Food Inspection Agency (CFIA) sets policies, requirements and inspection standards for fish products, federally-registered fish and seafood processing establishments, importers, fishing vessels and equipment used for handling, transporting and storing fish including aquaculture operations. All establishments that process fish and seafood for export or inter-provincial trade must be federally registered and must develop and implement a Hazard Analysis Critical Control Point (HACCP) system based on a Quality Management Program (QMP) plan.

Traceability is a crucial component of food safety systems in Canada; with seafood, traceability is accomplished through certification implemented by the United Nations' Food and Agricultural Organization (FAO). Buyers of fish and seafood are increasingly demanding independently verifiable evidence that these products come from legal and sustainable fisheries or aquaculture operations.

Traceability, defined as the ability to know where a product has been from "egg to plate," is commonly used in certification programs. Tracing wild or farmed fish and seafood as they travel through the supply chain demonstrates to consumers, retailers and export markets that the products being purchased come from operations that are managed in a safe and sustainable way. Traceability also contributes to seafood safety especially when, for example, food inspectors are able to locate products and inform recalls in case of health concern.

Through the International Organization for Standardization (ISO) TC234 Fisheries and Aquaculture Committee, Canada has been involved in the development of new international standards, helping to create a common global platform for documenting traceability. Until new international standards are in place, the onus remains with the Department of Fisheries and Oceans (DFO) guided by the Canadian Food Inspection Agency (CFIA) and corresponding governing bodies.

Seafood Processing

Canadian fisheries produce seafood in great variety. The product, however, is highly perishable and transporting it across the country is a major problem in keeping it fresh. The DFO and the fishing industry itself are continually working to improve methods of transportation. The most common methods of shipping involve packing fresh fish in ice and shipping across the country by rail (locally), or shipping by refrigerated road transport or airfreight. The result is that supplies of fresh fish can be obtained in the larger cities throughout the country, but further delay in distribution from these urban centres creates a problem of supply of fresh product in rural areas. The development of canning and quick freezing along with the wide use of frozen and canned storage throughout the country are helping to increase the supply of fish available to consumers.

Fresh seafood is shipped to all major metropolitan areas of Canada via airfreight or road transport. Finfish are processed as drawn or dressed and packed in containers and iced as are oysters, mussels and clams. Live fish, eel, lobster and crab are shipped in saltwater or freshwater tanks. These items are then further distributed by refrigerated transport truck packed in ice or, if live, in an appropriate insulated container.

Frozen seafood is also shipped across Canada having various destinations. Frozen finfish can be shipped whole, drawn or dressed and/or filleted. Shellfish can also be packaged, frozen and shipped in like manner. Frozen seafood is most commonly sold in cellophane or plastic packages, vacuum-sealed, labelled and/or boxed for ease of handling.

Canned seafood can be packed raw, smoked, cooked, dried or salted. Common canned seafood items are salmon, sardines and tuna. Canned seafood also includes crab, herring, mackerel, mussels, lobster, oysters and shrimp.

Species of Seafood

By no means do we expect to cover all fish found in Canadian waters, however, below we offer some of the more common species obtained by fisheries, caught in the wild and/or by farmed via aquaculture and marketed in Canada.

Bass: Largemouth bass is now one of the most widely distributed freshwater fishes in the world, mainly because of its popularity as a sports fish. In Canada this fish is found in lakes in Ontario and British Columbia (BC) as well as in some BC rivers. The smallmouth bass is a warm water fish found in southern Nova Scotia, southern and western New Brunswick and southern Quebec, through Ontario and at the south end of Lake Winnipeg in Manitoba, as well as central Saskatchewan and some parts of BC.

Distinguishing characteristics: Largemouth bass have large, long heads, a blunt snout and two joined dorsal fins with more separation than that of smallmouth bass. The top and back of the head are bright green to olive in colour. Smallmouth bass have large, long heads with dark bars that radiate back from the eyes. They have a blunt snout with a slightly lower jaw and two joined dorsal fins that appear as one. The head colour range is from brown to green with the sides of its body lighter in colour than that of the back.

Small Mouth Bass
©Tirrasa / Dreamstime

Largemouth Bass
©Jim Cottingham / Dreamstime

Clams: There are various species of clams. Wild clams live on the ocean floor bed but clams are also raised in aquaculture settings. BC is Canada's major clam producing province with their aquaculture industry farming butter clams, Manila clams, varnish clams, littleneck clams and the largest of clams, geoducks. Prince Edward Island (PEI) and Nova Scotia farm quahaug and soft-shell clams. All species of farmed clams are also harvested from the wild with butter clams dominating till the 1980s when native Manila and littleneck clams were caught and sold live as steamer clams.

Clams in shells
©Jiri Hera / Dreamstime

Distinguishing characteristics: Hinged shells. Manila and butter clams have horizontal lines that follow the contour of their shell and littleneck have vertical lines that flow from their hinge like a fan. The geoduck clam is native to the west coast and has a shell size that ranges from 15-20 centimetres in length with a neck (siphon) that is much longer, growing up to one metre in length. It is the largest burrowing clam in the world.

Geoduck Clams
©Vvoevale / Dreamstime

Cod: Atlantic cod is fished off the eastern shores of Canada, with the Pacific species off the western shores. Cod travel in schools and are found in deeper colder waters. Cod can grow to lengths of 2 metres averaging in weight between 4 – 10 kilograms. Historically, cod has been an important commodity both domestically and internationally. Cod is mild in flavour, has a low fat content with dense white flesh. This species of fish is also harvested for its oil (cod liver oil).

Distinguishing characteristics: Cod has three rounded dorsal and two anal fins. The pelvic fins are small and sit under the gill cover in front of the pectoral fins. Their upper jaw extends over the lower one. Cod have a distinct white lateral line running from the gill to the base of the caudal fin. Cod vary in colour depth from green/brownish to green/sandy colour with lighter sides and white bellies.

Cod
©Zhykharievavlada / Dreamstime

Crab: Canada is the world's largest producer of snow crab, producing two-thirds of the world supply. Off the shores of Nova Scotia the native blue crab is increasing in numbers and consumer interest. Dungeness and brown crabs are most common to Canadians.

Blue Crab has sapphire- tinted claws, molted, brownish shells, and are classified as both hard and soft-shelled. The abdomen is long and slender in males and wide and rounded in females. Mature females have red highlights on the tips of their pinchers. Blue crabs are harvested off shores of the Atlantic coastal provinces.

Blue Crab
©Pipa100 / Dreamstime

Brown Crab is found off the Atlantic coast of Canada. It is a robust crab of a reddish-brown colour having an oval hard-shell with a characteristic piecrust edge and black tips to the claws.

Brown crab
©Piotr Ryolzkowski / Dreamstime

Dungeness Crabs are the most important crab species harvested in Canada. Found mostly off the shores of BC, Dungeness crabs have found their way into more kitchens than the brown crab has. Dungeness crabs grow to be an average of 20 centimetres across the carapace (hard shell cover). At four to five years of age a Dungeness crab can exceed 25 centimetres and weigh approximately one to one and a half kilograms.

Dungeness crabs
©Vismax / Dreamstime

Snow Crab also known as Queen crab, are found in the north Atlantic and north Pacific oceans. In the Atlantic, snow crab are harvested off the coast of Labrador and Newfoundland. They prefer deep, cold-water conditions.

Snow crabs
©Rusty Elliot / Dreamstime

Distinguishing characteristics: Crabs have 10 legs (including claws) and are classified as decapods. Depending on the species they vary in size and hardness of shell called exoskeletons. Most crabs have two pairs of antennae and walk sideways.

Eels: The American eel resides in eastern Canadian fresh waters and is the most popular of the 35 species reported in Canada. Eels are typically elongated (snake like), round in cross section at the front and laterally compressed toward the back. They lack pelvic and dorsal fins and their anal fin is usually continuous with the tail fin. Most species lack scales. Eels are predaceous and tend to be nocturnal (hunt at night). Eels as food are sold fresh (live) or harvested and smoked.

Eels
©Dinoforlena / Dreamstime

Halibut: Pacific halibut are the largest flatfish in the world, weighing as much as 300 kilograms and reaching lengths of two and a half metres. Halibut are harvested from mid-March to mid-November by hook and line out of the waters off the BC coast. The average age of a commercially-fished halibut is 12 years. At birth halibut have an eye on each side of their head and swim like a round fish. They are classified as demersal fish and highly regarded as food.

Distinguishing characteristics: Halibut are dark brown on the top and off-white on the bottom. They have small invisible scales embedded in their tough skin with both eyes on top.

Halibut (top of fish)
©Pipa100 / Dreamstime

Lobster: Native to the Atlantic coast, lobsters are trapped and shipped live across Canada and to Europe. The American lobster is Canada's most valuable seafood export and the only species found in Canadian waters. Sometimes growing to lengths of 60 centimetres and weighing over 18 kilograms, lobsters can grow to be among the largest marine crustaceans. They are also the longest-living crustaceans, capable of reaching ages of up to 50 years.

Lobsters are active hunters feeding on a variety of seafood animals including crab, shellfish, marine worms, starfish, sea urchins and finfish. Canadian lobsters are found in the waters of the northwest Atlantic off the coast of Newfoundland, New Brunswick, PEI, Nova Scotia and the southern Gulf of St. Lawrence. At present lobsters are not being farmed in Canada.

Distinguishing characteristics: Lobsters have 5 pairs of legs, hard outer shells. The top two swimmerets (or feelers) on a female tail are soft, translucent and are crossed at the tips; they also have broader bodies than that of their male counterpart. A male's top two swimmerets are bony, opaque and point up toward his body.

Black Lobsters
©Cynoclub / Dreamstime

Red Lobsters
©Tusharkoley / Dreamstime

Mussels: The eastern blue mussel, western blue mussel and the Gallo/Mediterranean mussels are farmed in BC, Newfoundland, Nova Scotia, PEI and Quebec. Farmed mussels are grown to market size in mussel socks suspended from long-line systems (ropes) or rafts. Wild mussels grow all along the Atlantic coastline. These saltwater mussels are bivalves.

Distinguishing characteristics: Mussel shells are smooth, with a bluish black D-shaped shell. The meat of males is cream-coloured and females is coral-coloured. Live mussels have closed shells with dead ones displaying open shells.

Blue Mussels
©Mariuszks / Dreamstime

Octopus: Average size and age depends on the species of octopus (300 varieties) as some have a lifespan of six months while others five years. Their lifespan is limited by reproduction as males can live for only a few months after mating and females die shortly after their eggs are hatched. Octopus fisheries exist around the world, they live in every ocean and are eaten in many cultures, with the diversity of the Canadian population sharing in the cuisine delight of this marine animal.

Distinguishing characteristics: Has a soft body, eight arms with suckers for grip, is bilaterally symmetrical with two eyes and a beak and its mouth at the center point of the arms.

Octopus
©Michael Ansell / Dreamstime

Pacific Oysters
Credit: Fisherman's Market

Pacific shucked oyster
Credit: Fisherman's Market

Oysters: The American, or eastern oyster, and Pacific oysters are farmed in BC, New Brunswick, Nova Scotia, PEI and Quebec. They are placed on ocean floor beds or suspended in bags, cages, trays or rope lines. Wild oysters are harvested off both the Atlantic and Pacific coastlines and take on flavours natural to their environment. On the Atlantic shorelines oysters grow in vegetative waters, while the Pacific oysters grow in sandy waters.

Distinguishing characteristics: Generally Atlantic oysters have rough, thick shells with a tinge of green and Pacific oysters have white to black shells. It is said that wild Atlantic oysters have a salty, cucumber taste to them and the Pacific oysters have a sweet, creamy mineral flavour.

Perch: Perch are small to medium sized, carnivorous, bottom-dwelling, freshwater finfish usually with long, rounded, laterally compressed bodies and two dorsal fins. Canada records 16 species of perch with yellow perch as the most common. Perch inhabit warm to cool waters across Canada, from Nova Scotia to BC and into the Northwest Territories. The perch family also includes the Pacific ocean perch, a saltwater finfish known as Pacific rockfish, rose fish or red perch (named so after their body colour). It has a wide distribution in the North Pacific and is caught off the coast of BC. Ocean perch inhabit depths ranging from 40 to 600 metres. The saltwater variety is similar in shape and size to that of the freshwater variety.

Distinguishing characteristics: Yellow perch have sharp pointed spines on their dorsal, anal and pelvic fins. They have short, stubby, hunch-backed bodies, a large mouth and two dorsal fins. Their eyes are bright yellow to green. Yellow perch have a lateral pattern of seven green to brownish, tapered bars over a bright yellow to greenish under-coat. Ocean perch have a short, laterally compressed body that tapers toward their tail starting about midway down their length. They have a mouth with a protruding jaw, several sharp dorsal spines immediately followed by a flat dorsal fin and a tail with a slight indent. They are red in colour with blotches of olive.

Freshwater Perch
©Stevenrussellsmithphotos / Dreamstime

Ocean Perch
©Versh / Dreamstime

Pike: The northern pike is the fish most commonly thought of as pike. However, "pike" is the common name for a group of five species of predaceous freshwater fish belonging to the family *Esocidae*, order *Escoiformes*, class *Actinopterygii*. The northern pike can be found in freshwaters throughout Canada, except the Maritimes, most Arctic coastal areas and all but the northeast corner of BC. This species inhabits warm to cool lakes, rivers and large ponds usually in association with aquatic vegetation. Pike is a boney finfish and best caught during cooler months.

Distinguishing characteristics: Pike are large, soft-rayed fish with oval bodies. Their heads are flattened with duck-billed snouts and, as a predator finfish, are well armed with sharp teeth; the single dorsal fin and the anal and caudal fins are close together. Their bodies are patterned with horizontal rows of bean-shaped, yellow spots on a green to brown background. They have four to six pores on the underside of each lower jaw and the presence of scales over the whole of the cheeks and half of the gills.

Northern Pike
©Pipa100 / Dreamstime

Scallops: Sea scallops are bivalve mollusks and one of Canada's most important commercial shellfish. The scallop is possibly best known for its beautiful and distinctive circular shaped shell that can reach up to 20 centimetres in size. Sea scallops are found densely concentrated on sandy, gravel bottoms in waters at depths ranging from 10 to 380 metres along the coasts of PEI, Nova Scotia, New Brunswick, Newfoundland and Quebec. On average sea scallops need four to five years to reach commercial size. Bay scallops are native to the northwest Atlantic along the American coast from New Jersey to the Gulf of Mexico. The bay scallop used in aquaculture has been introduced from the US and is farmed in coastal waters off the shores of Canada in both the east and west. Bay scallops take anywhere from six months to three years to mature depending on the aquaculture operation and methods used to raise them—either on the bottom of the bay or the ocean floor or suspended in trays or netted bags. Bottom growing takes longer than that of suspended methods.

Distinguishing characteristics: Sea scallops are also known as Giant Scallops due to their size. Sea scallops are smooth, round and lean, and have a rich cream colour. Bay scallops are smaller, have the same shape, colour and texture.

Sea Scallops
©Ejwhite / Dreamstime

Bay Scallops
©Louella38 / Dreamstime

Shrimp: Shrimp are crustaceans with a hard outer shell that they must periodically shed in order to grow. They are found on soft, muddy bottoms, typically in waters between 150 to 600 metres in depth. Shrimp are found in both Canadian oceanic waters of the Atlantic and Pacific. Shrimp can grow to lengths of 15 centimetres, but the average size is about eight centimetres. Shrimp are the major prey of cod, haddock, halibut and ocean perch (all groundfish species). Shrimp are also farmed in Canada and abroad.

Distinguishing characteristics: Depending upon the species of shrimp their colour can vary from grey and green to pink. Regardless of the initial hue, all shrimp have the distinctive pink colour when cooked.

*Deveined shrimp
©Photoeuphoria / Dreamstime*

*Shrimp Black Tiger Prawns
©Thalang Itsaranggura Na Ayuddaya
/ Dreamstime*

Walleye: Also known as pickerel, walleye are members of the perch family and are a freshwater finfish native to Canada. Walleye can grow to lengths of 80 centimetres and weigh upwards of nine kilograms. They are large predators adapted to low light and are found in large, shallow, turbid lakes and the deeper waters of clear lakes.

Distinguishing characteristics: Long in body with a spiny dorsal fin followed by a soft dorsal fin. The caudal (tail) fin has a moderate indent. Walleye are olive green and gold in colour, fading to a white underside. They have dark spots on their backs and smaller dark spots on their fins. Their mouths are large with tiny razor sharp teeth.

*Walleye
©Vladyslav Danilin / Dreamstime*

Whitefish: Whitefish is a species of freshwater lake finfish found throughout much of Canada including the Great Lakes. They are deemed as a valuable commercial fish. The lake whitefish has a snout that overhangs its short lower jaw so that the mouth opens in a slightly inferior position, allowing it to feed on the bottom of lakebeds or grab food particulates out of the water or from the surface. Whitefish can grow to 75 centimetres in length and weigh upwards to 2.3 kilograms. The average size of a whitefish is approximately 50 centimetres in length, weighing approximately 1.8 kilograms.

Distinguishing characteristics: Their colour is typically silver to white with an olive to pale green or brown dorsal fin. The ventral fins are white and the tail is severely forked with a dark posterior edge.

Whitefish
©Viktor Nikitin / Dreamstime

Trout: Trout are both caught in the wild and farmed. Species of farmed trout are rainbow, steelhead, brown, lake char and brook with rainbow and brook being the most common. These are farmed in Alberta, BC, Manitoba, New Brunswick, Newfoundland, Nova Scotia, Ontario, PEI, Quebec and Saskatchewan. Farmed trout are raised in freshwater net pens, saltwater net pens (for steelheads) and land-based ponds or raceways. Ontario is the largest producer of farmed trout and is the third most valuable finfish species raised in Canada. In the wild trout is caught in the Pacific Ocean (steelhead), lakes and rivers. In their natural habitat, rainbow trout like cool freshwater, but some of them migrate into saltwater and become steelhead trout.

Distinguishing characteristics: Brook trout have a long, streamlined body with a large mouth that extends past the eyes. Colour variations include olive green, blue to grey or black above, and a silvery-white belly.

They have an adipose fin and a caudal fin that is slightly forked. The rainbow trout has seven fins, a pair of pectoral fins, a pair of pelvic fins, and anal fin, a dorsal fin and an adipose fin. Rainbow trout have sharp teeth on the roof of their mouths but have no lower teeth. Their colour is often times referred to as rainbow with colours on the back ranging from brown to olive to dark blue with a dominant pinkish band running the length of the body, thus their name rainbow trout.

Brook trout
©Daniel Thornberg / Dreamstime

Rainbow Trout
©Witold Krasowski / Dreamstime

Tuna: There are five varieties of tuna marketed globally: Albacore tuna, Bigeye tuna, Bluefin tuna, Skipjack tuna and Yellowfin tuna.

In Canada, Yellowfin, Bigeye and Albacore tuna catches in the Atlantic fisheries are referred to as "other tunas" and are managed through the DFO's Integrated

Fisheries Management Plan for Atlantic Swordfish and Other Tunas.

Albacore Tuna has a dark blue back with blue-grey flanks and belly. It is slow growing and can reach lengths of 140 centimetres long, weighing in at approximately 60 kilograms. The albacore fishery is a significant source of income for Canada's coastal communities, especially the Pacific coast. The Canadian fishery catches albacore primarily from the North Pacific and is valued at approximately 30 million dollars annually.

Albacore Tuna
©Zweizug / Dreamstime

Bigeye Tuna looks similar to Bluefin tuna, but the pectoral fin of the Bigeye is longer and its eyes are relatively larger compared to the size of its head. The estimated maximum length of this tuna is around 250 centimetres with a reported weight of up to 330 kilograms. It has a cigar-shaped body that is dark metallic brownish-blue to dark yellow on the back and whitish-grey along the belly, often with a bluish strip along the side. Bigeye tuna are found in Canadian waters of the Atlantic Ocean along the edge of the Gulf Stream and Georges Bank, the Scotian Shelf and the Grand Banks.

Adult Bigeye tuna swim at a greater depth than the Yellowfin tuna. Canadian vessels fishing in the Pacific Ocean do not catch Bigeye tuna.

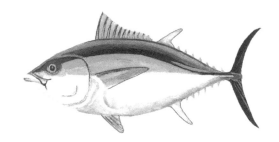

Big eye Tuna
Credit: CPMCA image collection

Bluefin Tuna is one of the largest tuna species. It is found distributed throughout the Atlantic and Pacific oceans. The popularity of this fish is reflected in highly lucrative global markets. Canada's western Atlantic Bluefin tuna fishery attracts more than 750 licensed harvesters who fish the western Atlantic Bluefin tuna stock in Canadian waters over the Scotian Shelf, in the Gulf of St. Lawrence, in the Bay of Fundy and off the coast of Newfoundland and Labrador.

Bluefin Tuna
©Lunamarina / Dreamstime

Skipjack Tuna grows up to a maximum size of 110 centimetres in length with a weight up to 34 kilograms. It is mostly found in tropical warm waters. It is a very important species for international fisheries. Skipjack is rarely found in Canadian waters; it is not caught by Canadian vessels or Canadian tuna harvesters.

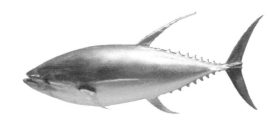

Species of Salmon are Atlantic, Chinook, Chum, Coho, Pink and Sockeye. Salmon live in saltwater but spawn in freshwater and therefore are classified as being anadromous; fish that do the opposite are known as catadromous.

Yellowfin Tuna is a mid-sized tuna, with commercially harvested fish ranging from 30 to 170 centimeters in length and weighing up to 90 kilograms. It has a dark blue-to-black coloured back, with silvery sides and bright yellow fins. Yellowfin tuna are normally found in the Pacific waters of Canada but are not harvested by the Canadian fleet, which typically targets northern Pacific albacore.

Distinguishing characteristics: The tuna has a sleek, streamlined body. It has two closely-spaced dorsal fins, seven to 10 finlets running from dorsal fins to a curved, crescent moon-shaped tail, which is tapered to pointy tips. The caudal is quite thin, with three stabilizing horizontal keels on each side. The tuna's dorsal side is usually metallic dark blue, while the belly is silvery or whitish in colour.

Pacific Salmon: The bounty of Canadian salmon helped shape many First Nations' cultures, and many Canadian communities on both the Atlantic and Pacific coasts still depend on salmon for their prosperity and livelihoods. Most Canadian salmon comes from the west coast of British Columbia and are referred to as Pacific salmon, with the sockeye being the most important commercial species. Wild Pacific salmon is available whole or dressed into a range of cuts such as steaks, fillets and sticks. A large percentage of sockeye and pink salmon is canned and a significant amount is exported.

Canadian wild salmon is available in many value-added products as well such as salmon caviar, hot and cold smoked salmon, marinated fillets, frozen salmon entrees, salmon jerky, salted salmon and salmon burgers and patties. Canadian seafood producers are always developing new value-added salmon products to bring to both the domestic and world markets.

Pacific Salmon
©Tab1962 / Dreamstime

Atlantic Salmon: Farmed Atlantic salmon makes up the bulk of Canada's salmon exports. On the Atlantic coast salmon farming began in New Brunswick's Bay of Fundy and is now widely practiced in Nova Scotia and, to a lesser extent, in Newfoundland. In British Columbia, salmon aquaculture is centered on Vancouver Island with the most common species being Atlantic salmon but also include Chinook and Coho.

Distinguishing characteristics: The anal fin on the Atlantic salmon has 12 or fewer rays.

Atlantic Salmon
©Alexander Raths / Dreamstime

Chinook Salmon: The number one sport fish on the west coast is Chinook salmon.

The flesh can be red, pink or white. This species has the widest colour range of all the salmon types. At full size, the Chinook can weigh between two and 14 kilograms and may reach a length of 150 centimetres. Chinook salmon over 14 kilograms are called Tyee (pronounced tie-ee) or King salmon.

Distinguishing characteristics: The Chinook salmon has a black tongue, black gums, black spots along the back and spots on both the top and bottom of the caudal fin.

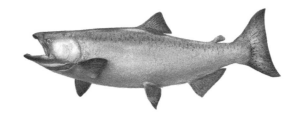

Chinook Salmon
©Daniel Thornberg / Dreamstime

Chum Salmon: This salmon has a very pale colour and is seldom used in retail markets for steaks of fillets, but is often sold drawn. At full growth chum salmon average 3.5 kilograms and have been found weighing 15 kilograms. They have been known to grow to lengths of 100 centimetres. Other names for this fish are dog salmon, Keta salmon or Silverbrite salmon.

Distinguishing characteristics: The chum salmon has a very silvery sheen, however, sexually mature chums will not have this distinguishing silver sheen. The chum salmon does not have spots along the back. The caudal, anal and pectoral fin has a solid black line on the end of each fin.

Chum Salmon
©Stanislav Komogorov / Dreamstime

Coho Salmon: The number two sport fish on the west coast is Coho salmon. The Coho has a nice dark pink colour. In the retail market Coho is sold in four market forms: drawn, dressed, steaks or fillets. At full growth a Coho can weigh up to five kilograms with lengths up to 98 centimetres.

Distinguishing characteristics: The Coho has a black tongue and white gums. It also has black spots, but only on the top half of the caudal fin.

Coho Salmon
©Sneekerp / Dreamstime

Pink Salmon: The most common type of salmon found on the west coast. Pink salmon has a light pink flesh tone and is often the cheapest salmon found in retail outlets. Fresh Pink salmon is sold as drawn, dressed, steaks or fillets. This salmon has a

soft delicate flesh texture, which is its most noteworthy characteristic. At full growth, Pink salmon can weigh up to 2.5 kilograms and reach a length of 76 centimetres.

Distinguishing characteristics: The Pink salmon has oval black spots along the back and on the tail. The Pink salmon also has very small and fine scales.

Pink Salmon
©Aleksey Sagitov / Dreamstime

Sockeye Salmon was the first salmon on the west coast to be commercially harvested. The Sockeye was also responsible for the start of the salmon canning industry. The dark red colour of their flesh makes the Sockeye the retail favourite. At full growth, Sockeye can average three kilograms in weight and reach 85 centimetres in length.

Distinguishing characteristics: Sockeye salmon have both white gums and a white tongue. Their skin has a silvery sheen and this salmon is almost toothless. The steaks have a very dark red colour.

Sockeye Salmon
Credit: ©istock.com / Credit to twildlife

Sockeye Salmon Fillets
Credit: Fishermans Market

Processed Seafood

CANNED SEAFOOD

Canadian seafood is widely distributed in canned form. The most important of the canned species from a standpoint of total annual production are: salmon, sardines, tuna and lobsters. Other familiar canned fishery products are: crab, clams, oysters, mackerel, chicken haddie*, shrimp and kippered snacks. There are also a variety of pickled and smoked fish and fish pastes (products of pounding, grinding, pressing, mincing, blending and/or sieving until it reaches the desired consistency) available.

Commercial Salmon Fishing Boat
Credit: ©istock.com / Credit to twildlife

Note: Chicken haddie is made up of several varieties of lean, white-fleshed Atlantic fish (cod, hake, haddock and cusk or moonfish). These are canned together as chicken haddie. The result is an inexpensive, mild-flavoured product suitable to any consumer's budget.

CURED, SALTED, SMOKED OR DRIED SEAFOOD

The most popular smoked fish include such varieties as: Atlantic cod, Alaska black cod, goldeye, cisco, haddock, salmon, sturgeon, herring, eels and whitefish.

Smoking produces a distinctive flavor, and although it helps to delay spoilage temporarily, it does not preserve the fish indefinitely. Smoked fish must be handled and stored with as much care as fresh fish. Kippered herring are both salt-cured and smoked. This is true for most smoked fish where some sort of curing or immersion in brine is done prior to the smoking operation.

Smoked Seafood Products
Credit: Save on Foods, Sahali

Dried salt fish may be purchased shredded or as boneless fillets. Boneless salted cod is usually packaged in 500 gram boxes. Salted herring comes in barrels, in glass jars or plastic containers and is readily available in bulk or various sized containers.

KAMABOKO (ALSO REFERRED TO AS SURIMI)

Originally formulated and made in Japan, Kamaboko is made from high-quality fish. It has protein content similar to that of eggs, is rich in calcium content, vitamins and minerals and low in fat. Kamaboko is processed from white-fleshed fish, flavoured, molded and surfaced with a red or pink food dye giving it a unique presentation. In our Canadian culture Kamaboko is processed and molded to shapes and artificially flavoured to resemble that of crab or lobster meat.

Kamaboko imitation Crab Meat
©dgstudio / Dreamstime

Surimi Imitation Crab leg meat
©Lepas / Dreamstime

Microbiology Affecting Seafood

In chapter 2, Professionalism, we discussed sanitation and basic microbiology as they pertain to our industry. Here we augment that to include seafood, considering the nature of this food source and its supply, as the subject is vitally important to food safety and public health.

The seafood handler has a responsibility to the customer to maintain the highest quality of seafood. To do so the handler must be aware of anything that will contaminate the product and know how to best handle all product sold. Any practice by fisherman, seafood processors, retailers or consumer that allows transfer of bacteria from raw seafood to ready-to-eat products poses a threat to food safety that may contribute to potential food poisoning.

Cross-contamination must be avoided when handling seafood. Cross-contamination occurs when clean, ready-to-eat products come in contact with a surface or food that is contaminated with bacteria. Examples of this can include: (1) storing and handling pre-cooked seafood in the same container previously used for raw seafood or other uncooked products; (2) handling ready-to-eat seafood with utensils, gloves or on work surfaces that have been previously used in handling raw seafood or other uncooked foods; and (3) wiping work surfaces and containers with soiled cloths.

BACTERIA

There are two groups of bacteria that are important to the seafood industry. The first group is considered food spoilage bacteria, and the second is food poisoning bacteria. Most types of bacteria can be controlled if proper handling, temperature controls and cleaning procedures are followed. Almost all cases of food-borne illness could have been prevented if proper procedures had been followed.

FOOD SPOILAGE BACTERIA

This bacterium is harmless to the consumer but destroys the quality of the product. Food spoilage bacteria grow well at cold temperatures, on damp surfaces and poorly-sanitized equipment and will cause a loss of sales (ability to sell) of the product. *Pseudomonades* are a type of food spoilage bacteria that survive in cold water and increase as a result of poor handling of the product; they usually discolour the product. Belly burn is a condition where the ribs no longer attach themselves to the gut cavity, which reduces the consumer appeal of the product. It is caused by enzymatic action but it is not bacterial. Luminescent bacterium, which is found in raw seafood, produces a glow on the product. It can also be found on cooked products such as shrimp meat, crabmeat and Kamaboko (imitation crab meat).

FOOD POISONING BACTERIA

These bacteria might be natural to the product or the product may be cross-contaminated with another bacteria not common to the product. Two of the most common type of bacteria found in fish is *Clostridium botulinum* and *Listeria monocytogens*. Both are of great concern to the seafood industry.

CLOSTRIDIUM BOTULINUM

Type E spores, which can be found in the intestines of fish and in shellfish, represent one of the many types of botulism. Botulism can produce spores, which produce a deadly toxin. Cooking and sanitizing (e.g. chlorination of water used in fish processing plants or chlorine dips and sprays for gloves, tools, equipment and use of heat) will kill these spores, however, at boiling water temperatures it takes a very long time to kill them. For this reason, processed fish in containers such as cans, jars, etc. is now sterilized by steam under pressure, to raise the temperature to well above 100°C. Botulism also grows in the absence of air. Because of this, fresh fish should never be kept in airtight packaging materials. Lox (brined salmon) and salmon products that are cold-smoked and vacuum-packed for sale can be sold in their packaging only if they are kept frozen. It is important to remind the customer to keep the product frozen prior to use. Botulism may also be found in canned products, but only if the product has been improperly sterilized or sealed. Proper handling can reduce the risk of botulism in all seafood products.

LISTERIA MONOCYTOGENS

Listeria is found in marine sediments, water and soil. This bacterium is fatal in 25% of reported cases. Listeria grows well in cold temperatures (as low as 3°C) and is very resistant to salt. Freezing will not kill the bacteria and it thrives in damp, moist conditions, the very conditions that are often associated with seafood handling. The best form of control is through proper cleaning procedures and through the use of an appropriate sanitizing agent in proper amounts. Cooking will also kill these bacteria.

RED TIDE (PARALYTIC SHELLFISH POISONING) AND OTHER BIO-TOXINS

Red tide is a natural occurrence, occurring annually as coastal waters warm up. It is a phenomenon whereby algae become so numerous that they discolour coastal waters, hence the name red tide. The algae deplete oxygen in the waters and/or release toxins that may cause illness in humans and other animals. Red tide affects shellfish that are filter feeders like clams, mussels and oysters. This toxin builds up in the mollusc and presents no hazard to the host, but is very dangerous and often fatal to humans. The muscle tissue of lobsters, crabs, shrimp and finfish are safe to eat during red tides since they do not accumulate the toxins. Scallops are a special case and, although they are bivalves, the toxin does not build up in the adductor muscle. Red tide can occur in isolated areas or over large areas. All shellfish that are commercially-harvested are required to have an identified harvest location. This is done to ensure that all shellfish harvested are safe to eat when they are sold at the retail level.

Red tide
©Michael De Hysschan / Dreamstime

It is recommended that shellfish be purchased only through a federally-inspected plant. Shellfish should not be purchased through back door traders.

While not wanting to alarm the consumer unnecessarily, there should be some additional comments made regarding marine bio-toxins. These have now been found in the viscera of crustaceans such as lobster and crabs, which have been feeding on bivalves with elevated levels of bio-toxins. Therefore the consumption of large amounts of the lobster's tomalley (liver) should be avoided.

Finfish are also potential carriers of bio-toxins. Ciguatera is caused by marine plankton (like red tide). It is mostly found in tropical countries and may be concentrated in predatory fish such as barracuda. Tetrodotoxin is found in Pufferfish that is served in sushi bars in Japan and some other countries. Scombrotoxin is caused by bacteria converting an amino acid prevalent in the flesh of some fish (e.g. tuna, mackerel, swordfish, mahi-mahi, anchovy, etc.) to a toxic derivative; this is also called histamine poisoning. The increase in shipments of fish from other parts of the world has increased the chances of contaminated fish being shipped to Canada and is why these shipments are monitored under the DFO's Import Inspection Program.

As filter feeders, bivalves may also accumulate pathogenic bacteria that pose a health risk to humans. The consumer is protected by the CFIA Canadian Shellfish Sanitation Program (CSSP), a federal food safety program jointly administered by the CFIA, Environment Canada (EC) and the DFO, which monitors shellfish growing waters and shellfish for the presence of bacterial contamination and for the presence of bio-toxins. Cooking destroys the pathogenic bacteria and largely eliminates this risk (bio-toxins are not destroyed by cooking).

Parasites in Fish

Because fish are in a free environment, there is little or no control over parasites in fish. Infected fish are not sick; parasites are a normal part of the life of the fish. The infection of fish by parasites does not pose a consumer safety issue if the fish has been frozen at -25°C for 24 hours, or cooked to a minimum temperature of 60°C. This temperature is reached during normal cooking procedures. Freezing the fish prior to salting, pickling or smoking will kill most parasites (however, parasites known as protozoans are not killed by freezing and are not harmful to humans). When salting fish, a concentration of 20% salt is required to destroy most species of unwanted bacteria and parasites. This means a fish that weighs 5 kilograms will be packed in 1 kilogram of salt.

There are four main varieties of parasites common to seafood: roundworms, protozoans, flatworms and parasitic crustacea.

Roundworms: Roundworms are also known as seal worms. They have two main groups: anisakine or nematodes. Roundworms can be reddish brown or translucent in colour and are mostly found in groundfish like cod. Processing plants are aware of the sensitivity of the issue from the consumer's perspective, so they candle the fish to remove as many worms as possible. Roundworms in fish fillets are usually harmless to the consumer but sometimes an allergic (hypersensitive) reaction may be triggered. This is called anisakiasis after the *Anisakis* worm.

Note: Candling means placing a bright light under the fillet to detect roundworms. It acts like an X-ray exposing the parasites. If too many are found, or the fillet is infested, then it is discarded.

Protozoans: Protozoans are one-celled animals that live on the flesh of the host animal. Also known as cysts, they are commonly found in all types of salmon. The cyst is usually white with a milky interior. Upon cooking the cyst will break down and have no form. Freezing will not kill the parasite but cooking will. This parasite is not harmful to humans and harms only the host species.

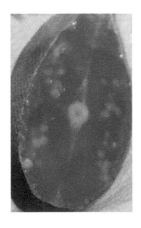

Protozoan cysts
Credit: Wikipedia

Flatworms: Flatworms, also known as tapeworms, are commonly found in most round fish fillets just under the skin or in the stomach cavity. They form a cyst in the flesh or stomach cavity and can be identified using the candling procedure. Cooking, freezing, salting or hot smoking will kill some of these parasites, but not all. The main hazard to consumers arises if raw fish is eaten. Humans who have contracted tapeworms can be medically treated to successfully eliminate the tapeworm.

Crustacea: Crustacea is a parasite found in most fish, but it is seldom observed. The copepod is the most common type of crustacea parasite. It is very large and looks like black round objects, which are often as big as marbles. Because of their size, copepods are easy to identify and remove from the fillets.

Flatworms
Credit: ©Drzaribu / Dreamstime

The Handling of Seafood

Seafood Handling is a normal part of any retail outlet that sells or handles seafood whether raw, cooked, or packaged. Below are some valuable, proven, practices most retailers employ managing seafood stocks.

- Newly arrived boxes of fresh fish and fish fillets must be placed under refrigeration without undue delay and, where necessary, should be re-packed with clean ice.
- All fresh and cooked fish products must be kept under refrigeration at all times and should not be frozen unless they are to be sold as frozen products.
- Fish products should never be stacked above the load line in self- and full-service display counters.
- Unfrozen smoked fish and salted fish products, which are not hard-dried, should be kept under refrigeration but should not be held in direct contact with ice.
- Marinated fish products, and all other prepared fish products that have not been frozen or heat treated/sterilized, should be kept under refrigeration.
- All fish and fish products in frozen storage should be protected from oxidation and dehydration.

- Only clean new and nontoxic packaging material should be used for wrapping fish.
- Cutting, filleting, and skinning boards of tables should be made of planed lumber or other material that is smooth and without cracks, and should be constructed in a manner approved by the local Department of Health.
- Containers for the disposal of fish waste should be provided and should be watertight, have well-fitted covers and constructed of metal or other material approved by the local Department of Health.
- Premises where fish is offered for sale should be maintained at all times in a clean and sanitary condition.
- When a vehicle is used for the purpose of retailing fish and fish products it should comply with applicable federal requirements.

HANDLING LOBSTERS

Lobsters should be kept alive in a saltwater environment, as fresh water is lethal to their system. When bought alive, lobsters should show movement of the legs. The tail of a live lobster curls under the body and does not hang down when the lobster is picked up. Lobsters taken out of salt water can remain alive for up to two weeks if they are kept in a cool, damp refrigerator. Once a lobster has died it must be cooked within a couple of hours. Failure to do so results in the meat becoming mushy and unpalatable. Lobsters are often transported to the retail store surrounded by damp material. They must be removed from the packing material immediately and placed into the saltwater tanks. Rubber bands are placed on the claws to prevent the lobsters from attacking one another or from pinching their handlers. This practice makes it easier to grip the lobsters so you should let the consumer know not to remove the bands until they're ready to cook them.

HANDLING CRABS

Crabs are usually retailed fresh and should be kept alive in saltwater tanks. Crabs should be active and show life when removed from the tank. Slow movement and claws that hang from the body are indications that the crab is not well. Any dead crabs should be removed from the tank immediately. Live crabs survive only a short time out of water and hence, when purchased, should be promptly cooked, cleaned and refrigerated.

HANDLING SHELLFISH

Top-quality shellfish have hard shells of varying sizes and shapes depending on the variety (clam, mussel or oyster). When alive, the shells are tightly closed or will close on handling. A gaping shell indicates a dead animal, which should not be used. Shellfish remain alive up to a week if kept at temperatures above freezing and below 5°C. Fresh shellfish will keep for seven to 10 days at these temperatures and if kept away from direct sunlight. Live shellfish should never be placed in an airtight container, as this will suffocate them. When displaying fresh shellfish, display them in a bed of ice but make sure they are displayed with the base down so they do not lose any internal moisture. Shucked shellfish should be plump and have clear liquid. Cartons containing shellfish should be refrigerated and placed on ice.

SCALLOPS

Scallops are shelled or shucked as soon as they are caught, as they do not survive out of water. The tender cube of white meat (abductor muscle) inside the shell makes up the scallop. Shucked scallops are marketed fresh or frozen. Fresh scallops have a slightly sweetish odour and should not be considered of poor quality if this odour is noticed. Scallops that are bad will smell like rotten turnips or cabbage. Frozen scallops should remain frozen until used and fresh scallops should be packed on ice. Scallops that have lost their fresh condition and developed a bad odour should be discarded. The shelf life of fresh scallops kept under proper refrigeration below 5°C is about three to five days.

SHRIMP

Shrimp comes in a variety of forms: raw whole, headless, peeled, peeled and deveined; and cooked, headless, peeled, peeled and deveined, etc. When marketed headless and peeled frozen, shrimp are sold by the count, which is expressed as a numerical range of shrimp per pound or 454 grams. A count of 30/40 means there are between 30 and 40 shrimp per pound (454 grams). Fresh shrimp should be handled and stored in similar fashion to that of other already mentioned shellfish (if fresh packed on ice and refrigerated, if frozen keep in the freezer or freezer display units).

FRESH FINFISH

Regardless of the species, whether drawn, dressed, or filleted, fresh finfish should be handled with the same care and attention as that of shellfish. Seafood is delicate and has to be kept cold (packed in or on ice) to maintain its freshness and natural appearance. Finfish stored and handled in this way remains crisp and firm for up to a week.

SPOILAGE

Unattended or neglected fish lose their firmness, natural odours, colours and textures. Whether your outlet purchases finfish drawn, in fillets or fillets their own, it's the handlers' responsibility to check the condition of all seafood upon arrival and to preserve the seafood at temperatures congruent with the standards set to maintain the quality and freshness of the fish.

Spoilage is also caused by normal bacterial growth. This is primarily influenced by temperature. Between 4°C and 60°C bacteria can rapidly multiply and quickly spoil a good product. Any quality seafood program must be built around the proper storage and handling temperatures of all seafood.

60 degrees C	Most bacteria killed
4 degrees C	DANGER ZONE FOR SEAFOOD 4 to 60 degrees C
0 degrees C	IDEAL TEMPERATURE TO HANDLE ALL FORMS OF SEAFOOD -1 to 4 degrees C
	Frozen foods should be stored at -20 to -25 degrees C

Note: For further details on Bacterial growth & Safe Meat Handling see the thermometer guides, appendix pages 746-747.

Receiving Seafood

FRESH & FROZEN SEAFOOD

- Delivery should be made in refrigerated truck.
- Check temperature with a probe thermometer for agreed on delivery temperature.
- Inspect condition of cases for damaged or worn containers.
- Look for temperature abuse (moisture points or dried moisture indicating thawing and re-freezing of product).
- Check general quality of product for off odours and that all species are separated for allergen concerns.
- Use random weight checks.
- Use code information from supplier to assure receipt of new product.
- Check to see if you received what you ordered.

GENERAL SEAFOOD HANDLING PRACTICES

- Keep all varieties of seafood separate to avoid any cross-contamination with respect to possible allergens.
- If filleting drawn or dressed finfish, handling seafood (all species), traying or display seafood etc., the fish must be kept separate from other meats to avoid cross-contamination; seafood should have no contact with red meats, poultry, or finished cooked, marinated or processed food items.
- Bulk products in waxed cardboard cartons should be thoroughly re-iced before transfer to the cooler.
- Tray-packed items should be stacked below the load line in the display case allowing space between for circulation.
- Place only one layer on display with sufficient flaked ice for sufficient cooling.
- Rotate fresh product every few hours back to the cooler to maintain temperature only using the minimum number for eye appeal.
- Placing fillets on paper on the ice or in metal pans will protect water-soluble nutrients loss.
- Fresh fillets and steaks delivered in tubs or cans requiring excess liquid need to be drained and rinsed with a cold saltwater solution.
- Shellfish have a tendency to become dehydrated under mechanical refrigeration; perpetual misting is desired.

- Sand and grit on oyster and clamshells may be removed by wiping each shell with a wet cloth before displaying.
- Live lobsters and crabs must be kept moist and cool. If there is no tank, store them in the shipping container surrounded by damp towels placed on ice. Sell weakest specimens first.
- If you are fortunate enough to have a tank: keep it clean. Supply clean water, don't overstock and keep the glass clean.
- Scallops in bulk containers sold by the pound keep best on display nestled on ice, exposed scallops tend to become sticky; therefore, retain the natural liquid present.
- Oysters, clams and crabmeat in containers must be kept resting on slush ice with a minimum of handling to prolong shelf life.
- Smoked, salted and marinated seafood is perishable. Smoking only provides additional flavour. Refrigeration is necessary and the saleable timetable is a maximum of only seven days.
- Check for deterioration daily avoiding direct contact with ice on salted fish. They need protection from humidity, but do not require refrigeration.
- Marinated fish products not frozen or heat-sterilized need refrigeration.
- Unfrozen cooked seafood must be kept under refrigeration. If displayed, keep separated from raw seafood to prevent contamination.

Displaying the Product

- Put a fresh layer of crushed ice in the bed of the case.
- Keep species separate to avoid any cross-contamination with respect to allergens; this means care must be taken when handling one species of seafood to another as with finfish fillets to shellfish (see *Allergens* below).
- Remove any discoloured fillets or steaks and examine the whole fish for freshness and market appeal.
- Dress the fish counter with the freshest fish, on clean platters, in the front of the case, with yesterday's fish on top and at the back of the case.
- Fillet or steak any whole fish if it is unattractive or has not been selling in its present state.

Seafood displayed on ice in a show case
Credit: Save on Foods

- Be sure that the glass, scales and tops of the counters are scrupulously clean and sparkling. If the top of the counter is used for allied products make sure that they are arranged neatly.
- Always keep the display price tickets clean.
- Decorate the fish display with parsley and cut lemons (lemons are antibacterial).
- Make the most of the colour factors of different varieties by placing the extremes together.
- Sprinkle some ice on the skin of the whole fish. Do not put ice on the fresh-cut face of fish fillets or on smoked fish as it will draw the colour and flavour from the flesh.
- Keep the trays neat and tidy throughout the day.
- If items are moving slowly, it may be due to an unattractive display case. Go to the front of the display case and view it from the customer's position. Fillets and cuts may be disarranged, discoloured, ragged or just lying in their own juices in the trays.
- Fill up displays as often as necessary but avoid cutting fillets or steaks towards the end of the day.

Consumer Information

Allergens in Canada are recognized to be nuts (all varieties), seeds, grains, dairy products and seafood. Some people have allergens toward dust, grass, pollen, and even medications. Allergic reactions are severe adverse reactions that occur when the body's immune system overreacts to a particular allergen. So why do we mention allergens in this chapter and not elsewhere? The answer is: seafood allergens are more common than that of bovine, ovine, porcine or poultry, and therefore seafood allergens deserve a special notation with respect to the handling, storing and displaying of seafood and seafood items.

Not everyone is allergic to all seafood, some may be allergic to finfish or a specific species of fish while others may only be allergic to shellfish (a very common allergen) and able to eat all other varieties. Regardless of the seafood allergen, it is imperative that seafood handlers and retailers pass on to consumers the importance of keeping seafood species separate, should any of their family or guests have allergies toward seafood.

Fresh Fish spoils rapidly and therefore care should be taken to serve it as soon as possible after purchase. Handling fish properly will help to maintain its quality if it must be held for short periods of time.

When fresh fish is received from the market, remove the wrapper and wipe the fish with a clean, damp cloth. Wrap it in wax paper, place it in a tightly-covered container to prevent transfer of odours and store it in the refrigerator. If the fish is whole, eviscerate it immediately and store in the same way.

Freshly-caught fish may be frozen and stored in the home freezer. Fish should be eviscerated and washed soon after it is caught. If there is to be any delay before freezing, it should be packed in ice and stored in the refrigerator.

Fish may be packed whole, filleted or cut into steaks. Before packing, fish should be rinsed in cold water. To prevent deterioration as a result of drying or oxidation, fish should be wrapped in moisture/vapour-proof material and packed tightly to exclude air. Heavy aluminum foil, vapour-proof cellophane, pliofilm, polyethylene or laminated freezer paper make satisfactory packaging materials.

The packaged fish should be frozen quickly at a low temperature to maintain the quality and be stored at a constant temperature of -20° to -25°C. Lean fish will keep well if properly frozen for three or four months. Fatty fish should not be kept for more than two months.

The Quality of Fish is largely determined by its freshness. Fresh whole or drawn finfish should have the characteristics outlined as follows:

- The skin should be shiny and bright and the scales should cling tightly.
- The gills should be clear, bright red and free from slime. In time the colour fades to a light pink, then grey, and finally to a brownish or greenish colour.
- The eyes should be bright, clear and full. As a fish loses it freshness the eyes become faded and cloudy and tend to become sunken.
- The flesh should be firm and elastic to the touch and should not separate easily from the bone.
- Fresh fish has a mild characteristic odour, not a strong or fishy odour.

FISH FILLETS AND STEAKS

- The flesh of finfish should be fresh-cut in appearance; the colour resembling that of freshly-dressed fish. Textures should be firm. There should be no traces of browning about the eyes or drying of the flesh.
- The fish should have a fresh mild odour.
- Wrapped steaks and fillets should be in moisture-proof material with little or no air space between the fish and the wrapping.

Frozen Fish properly handled maintains its quality. Frozen fish should be kept frozen at temperatures of -20° to -25°C until time of use. The thawing of fish and fish fillets should take place in the fridge the night before it is to be cooked. Changes in this storage temperature during transport or in retail storage cabinets and home refrigerators affect the product negatively. Of course temperature fluctuation is not always avoidable but should be kept to a minimum. Let your consumers know to check their selection for quality by providing them with the information here directly below:

- Flesh should be frozen solid when purchased.
- The flesh should have a firm, glossy appearance with no evidence of drying out, such as white spots or papery corners or edges.
- There should be no dark spots or discolouration in the flesh and no fading of naturally-coloured flesh; as with salmon.
- If wrapped, frozen fillets and steaks should be wrapped in moisture-proof material. There should be little or no air space between fish and wrappings. A thick layer of

frost on the inside of transparent wrappers is evidence of long storage or poor condition or both.

- The majority of frozen fillets on the market are packaged in waxed cardboard boxes wrapped with waxed paper and machine sealed. The consumer must rely on established brand names and the reputation of the retail outlet as an assurance of quality.

- Whole fish, frozen in whole, drawn or dressed, are frequently not wrapped. When such is the case, they should be coated with a glaze to prevent desiccation and discolouration.

Remind your consumer after frozen fish has been brought home it should be kept frozen solid in the unopened package. A very low temperature is required to maintain quality in frozen fish. A constant temperature of -20° to -25°C is recommended and, since this low temperature is hard to maintain in household freezer units, it is advisable to keep supplies of frozen fish for relatively short periods. Consumers should be told that once the fish has been thawed it must be used quickly since it will spoil as readily as fresh fish. It is not advisable to re-freeze fish that has been thawed. The flesh of fish once frozen is more susceptible to spoilage than fresh fish; consequently, fish that has been frozen will not absorb the juices it loses again. The re-frozen product will be tough (dry), feel rubbery and lose its flavour.

Smoked Fish should be handled and stored in the same way as fresh fish. The smoking process is used only to enhance the flavour. It is not sufficient to preserve the fish but merely retards spoilage.

The Cooking of Fish

Fish is naturally tender and, unlike any bovine species, doesn't need to be aged. Fish has very little connective tissue, an important difference between seafood and muscle meats. What this means to consumers is fish cooks quickly and falls apart easily; it's delicate and should be prepared as such. We know the tenderness and flavour of meats depends on age of the product but with fish that isn't always the case. Younger fish do have more flavour than older fish of the same species, but both are handled in a similar manner when cooking as they both react to heat the same way.

Temperature Guidelines For Seafood Products

Product	Holding Temperature Range in Celsius
Fresh Finfish	0°C
Live Shellfish	Between 0°–2°C; on a bed of ice, not covering them
Shucked Shellfish	As per instructions on original container
Pasteurized Crab	As per instructions on original container
Fresh Cooked	0°C
Fresh Smoked	0°C ; avoid contact with ice
Fresh Prepared	0°C
Salted Finfish	0°C ; avoid contact with ice
Marinated Finfish	0°C
Live Lobster/Crab	In live tank or in fridge at 0°C (can't keep long)
Dried	Refrigeration not required
Canned Seafood	Room temperature

Seafood Inspection & Grading

Overseen by the CFIA, which sets stringent standards for seafood products and for seafood handling and processing, Canada has one of the world's' most rigorous seafood inspection and control systems. All establishments that harvest and prepare Canadian seafood designated for inter-provincial travel or export must be federally-registered and must comply strictly with international HACCP principles.

The CFIA also inspects our seafood for contaminants and ensures that ongoing testing falls within the guidelines established by Health Canada. These guidelines meet the standards of both the American Food and Drug Administration (FDA) and the World Health Organization (WHO).

While fish have no specific grade designation similar to that of bovine and ovine animals, all seafood in Canada is graded and must meet grade specifications set out by the CFIA in the Canadian Grade Compendium, Volume 8: Fish. This document is readily available on the following Canadian government website: www.inspection.gc.ca .

Due to the nature and length of the document, it is not repeated here. However, it is recommended that the reader become familiar with the content of the document to further their understanding of common names associated with grades of seafood.

CFIA Nomenclature Requirements for Seafood

When seafood is sold in Canada, fish and fish products are also subject to the labelling requirements under the Food and Drugs Act (FDA) and the Consumer Packaging and Labelling Act (CPLA). These are summarized in the core labelling, claims and statements, and food-specific labelling requirement pages of the Industry Labelling Tool provided by the CFIA. It is located on the www.inspection.gc.ca website under "Food, Labelling, Food Labelling for Industry, Fish and Fish Products" page.

RETAIL LABELLING
REQUIREMENTS FOR SEAFOOD

The labelling requirements that the CFIA put forth are extensive, cover a wide variety of fish products, are conclusive, have merit and are important to all involved in the catching, handling, selling and retailing of fish and fish products. At no time are these regulations and requirements meant to frustrate anyone. They are there for clarity so as to avoid any misinterpretation regarding the naming of fish and fish products. With that in mind we herein below record for your reading pleasure and information the more common concerns with respect to the regulations and requirements governing the labelling of fish and fish products at the retail level.

Essential Requirement

Every fish, can of fish, or the wrapper or label thereon shall be correctly and legibly marked with the common name of the fish.

The common name of a fish product is [B.01.001, B.01.006(1), Food and Drug Regulations]:

- the name prescribed by the Fish Inspection Regulations (or other applicable Canadian legislation) [38-40, 51, 52, 72, FIR] or
- the name identified by boldface type in the *Food and Drug Regulations*; or
- if the name is not prescribed in legislation, the name by which the food is generally known.

The CFIA Fish List provides regulatory guidance regarding the common names of fish. The names on the CFIA Fish List are considered acceptable common names and the use of these is recommended. The use of common names that are not on the CFIA Fish List can be assessed against the requirement that no person shall package or label fish in a manner that is false, misleading or deceptive [27, FIR; 5(1), FDA; 7(1), CPLA].

Generic Common Names

Unless outlined in the *Fish Inspection Regulations*, the use of generic names such as "fish fillets" or "fish portions" is not permitted. A name of the species should be incorporated into the common name, for example: "haddock fillets" or " cod portions".

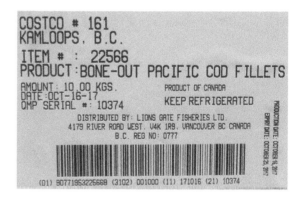

Pacific Cod fillets
Credit: Costco

Labelling of Pacific Salmon in Canada

The name "Pacific Salmon" is not included as an acceptable common name in the CFIA Fish List due to the different market values of species of Pacific salmon. As described above, the common name must always include the name of the species, for example "chum salmon fillets" or "sockeye salmon portions." The statement "Pacific salmon" is permitted on a label only as additional information, but may not replace the common name.

Chinook Salmon fillets.
Credit: Costco

Indication of Geographic Origin

The geographic location where the fish has been harvested may be added to the common name, however this is optional.

Tuna (smoked) Product of Vietnam.
Credit: Fisherman's market

Surimi

Fish products that are made from Surimi (a paste made from highly-refined minced fish) must use the name by which the food is generally known, as there is no prescribed common name in the *Fish Inspection Regulations* not identified in boldface type in the *Food and Drug Regulations*. Therefore, such products may use the term "Surimi" in the common name, and should include additional descriptors as appropriate (e.g. surimi roll, surimi cakes).

In some instances, surimi-based products closely resemble more expensive seafood products such as crab legs, shrimps, or scallops through flavouring and shaping. Surimi-based products that resemble these foods should be labelled and/or advertised to clearly show that they are imitations.

For example:

Imitation Snow crab made
from flavoured Alaska Pollock
Credit: Save on Foods

- The common name identifies the term "artificial" or "simulated" or "imitation", (such as "artificial crab legs" and "imitation lobster meat"); or
- The common name identifies the name of the species used in the product, (such as, "Crab- flavoured Alaskan Pollock" and "Lobster-flavoured seafood made from whiting");, or

- If various species were used, the common name refers to a generic name (such as, "Crab- flavoured seafood" and "Lobster- flavoured Kamaboko").

Whitefish

Each container of whitefish (*Coregonus clupeaformis*) must be marked in English or French with the name of the lake of origin of the whitefish, including the name of the province, and the words "dressed whitefish" or "round whitefish" or "whitefish fillets", as the case may be.

Net Quantity

The net quantity declaration on prepackaged fish is mandatory unless the container or label states that the contents are to be weighed at the time of retail sale (referred to as catch weight) [25(1)(b), 26(1)(b), FIR].

The words "net weight" or "drained weight" can be used only on fish products that contain only edible parts. If the product also contains inedible parts such as shells, the word "weight" alone must be used.

Weight declarations such as "made from X kg or lb" (e.g. for peeled shrimp) or "net weight when packed" (e.g. live mussels) are unacceptable.

Previously Frozen fish and Fish Products

Any fish [B.21.003, FDR] or the meat of any marine or freshwater animal [B.21.004. FDR] that has been frozen and thawed prior to sale must declare the words "previously frozen" on their principle display panel or on a sign displayed close to the food in letters that are legible and discernible. This includes both prepackaged and non-prepackaged products. When declared on the principal display panel, these words must either be close to the common name of the food in letters that are the same size as those used for the common name or anywhere on the principal display panel in letters that are at least 6.4 millimeteres in height [B.01.080, FDR].

If part of one of these foods has been frozen and thawed prior to sale, the words "Made from fresh and frozen portions" or "Made from fresh and frozen (naming the food)" must be declared [B.o1.080, FDR].

As per the FDR, "frozen" means preserved by freezing temperatures and does not include any surface freezing that may occur during holding and transportation [B.01.080, FDR].

SUMMARY

DISCUSSION QUESTIONS

1. The text talks about "whitefish" in two very different contexts. Discuss the differences and what they mean.

2. What role does aquaculture fill and what is its overall contribution to fisheries worldwide?

3. What is the difference between a "drawn" fish and a "dressed" fish?

4. What is Kamaboko?

5. In which year was the Fisheries Prices Support Board established? Why was it established?

6. Which fishing method is least sustainable? Why?

7. Which category of classification does "octopus" belong to?

8. How many legs do "crab" have?

9. If a "mussel" is found to be open and will not close at time of cooking, is it still safe to eat? Why?

10. Which species of "tuna" do Canadian vessels not harvest? Why?

11. Explain what "Pacific salmon" are?

12. Do fish have or carry parasites and, if so, are they harmful to humans?

13. Generally and ideally, at what temperature should seafood be kept at?

14. Why is it said of all fish "fish is tender"?

15. What is "red tide" and how does it affect shellfish?

Chapter 10

Charcuterie

Over the centuries charcuterie (sausage making) has developed into an art and with the demand for artisanal products on the rise has seen a renewed interest.

This chapter provides information on the five classifications of sausages, a clear succinct description of each, their production and some manufacturing basics. Included is the importance of raw product and material selection, meat, flavourings and spices. The subject of restricted ingredients is defined, and their usage is explained. Other non-meat ingredients used in the production and processing of sausage and sausage items are also listed and described. Briefly discussed is the role of water activity, the grinding of meats, the mixing of meat blocks and seasonings, and the making of emulsions.

Important to all charcuterie operations are the regulations governing the production, processing, storage and handling, and labelling of products. The chapter has an appendix emphasizing these regulations.

Highlighting this chapter are practical applications in the formulation of brines, fat calculations, restricted ingredients calculations and recipes for each of the five classifications of sausage.

Charcuterie

History

If you look up the definition of "charcuterie" you'll discover it has a dual meaning. One definition has charcuterie relating to a store that sells deli products such as hams, sausages and pâtés. Another has charcuterie as a branch of culinary devoted to prepared meats, such as bacon, terrines and galantines. There is very little difference between the two as the products are the same: hams, pâtés, sausages, etc. Charcuterie is about sausage and cured meats in the category of fresh sausage, cooked and cured meats, smoked, cured and cooked sausage and meats, uncooked cured and smoked sausage and meats, and/or dry and fermented sausage and meats.

Charcuterie (pronounced shahr-koo-tuh-ree) and sausage making are synonymous with each other and in this chapter we use them interchangeably. The difference, as we see it, is the use of the word "charcuterie," which gives the art of sausage making a distinct flare that diehard artisans enjoy with respect to artisanal meat products like those covered further on in the chapter.

The origin of charcuterie is lost in antiquity but probably began when someone learned that salt is an effective preservative. Sausage making evolved as an effort to economize and preserve meat that couldn't be consumed fresh at slaughter; this includes parts like the liver, heart, kidneys and tongue, not to mention any trimmings collected by the process of further fabricating the carcass.

Sausage and cured dried meats are the oldest forms of processed foods. It was known by the ancient cultures of Greece and the later Roman Empire, originating over a thousand years before the Common Era (CE). The word "sausage" is derived from the Roman word "salsus" which means salted or preserved meat. This was later translated into "sala" meaning "sausage."

Commercial sausage making began in the Middle Ages. Areas and towns developed their own specialties and very often their products took on the name of their origin for example, Genoa salami from Genoa, Italy, Prague ham from Prague, Czechoslovakia, and Lyoner sausage from Lyon, France.

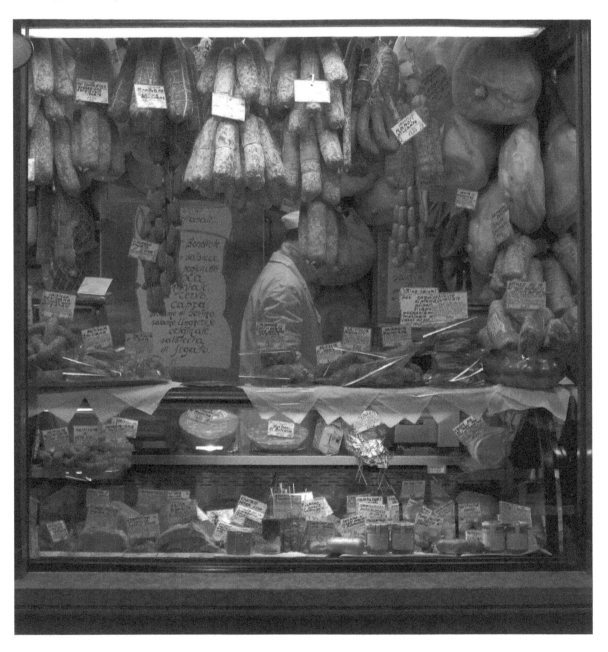

Old Italian sausage store
Credit: ©istock.com / Credit to jchambers

Old aging cellar with meat and barrels
Credit: ©istock.com / Credit to Peter TG

Over the centuries sausage making has developed into an art. Since the first sausage making endeavors, better and more effective processing equipment has been developed, very defined and exotic flavourings have been discovered, and new ingredients to overcome manufacturing troubles and allergen sensitivities came into use to improve quality, reduce shrinkage and enhance profits. However, the basic idea still exists: meat shops that fabricate sausage and cured meats have a better and much more profitable utilization of their trimmings; they can produce a significantly better trimmed fresh meat product and finally, they have a much greater variety of products to brand themselves by and offer their customers.

As time and science continues to advance so does the quality of our sausage, our understanding of processes and the production of sausage. Building on the successes of past and present master sausage makers, this chapter submits proven practices and procedures used in the production of charcuterie items. It is in no way exhaustive as there is much to know about the subject matter. Nevertheless, our intention is to support individual efforts in the practice of charcuterie.

Charcuterie Production

Sausages can be classified in a variety of ways, but probably the most useful is by how they are processed. Processing methods give sausage their recognized characteristics.

Types of Sausage

A selection of cured-smoked sausage & ham
Credit: ©istock.com / Credit to JannHuizenga

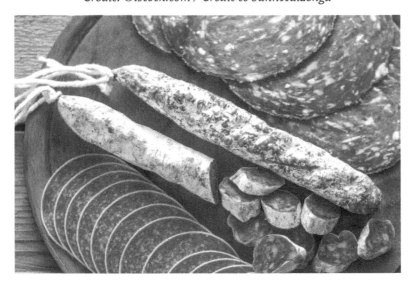

A selection of Salamis
Credit: ©istock.com / Credit to AlexPro9500

Sausage Classifications	
Classification	**Examples**
Fresh Sausage	Mild or Hot Italian, Beef and Onion, Chorizo, Bratwurst, Maple Breakfast Sausages, etc.
Cured Cooked Deli Meats	Head Cheese, Varieties of Meat Loaves, Tongue Sausage, Corned Beef, etc.
Cured Smoked/ Cooked Sausage and Deli Meats	Wieners, Smokies, Garlic Coil, Hams, Bacon, Pastrami, Smoked & Cooked Turkey Drumsticks, Wings Smoked Chickens, etc.
Uncooked Cured and Smoked Sausage	Farmer Sausage, European Mettwurst, Rookworst etc.
Dry and Semi- Dry Fermented Sausage	Genoa Salami, Landjaeger, Prosciutto, Soppressata, etc.

Along with sausage classification is the consideration we give to:

- the degree of chopping or grinding;
- the amount of water added and needed for the desired texture;
- moisture and flavour distribution;
- the addition and use of curing agents;
- the amount of smoking for colour and flavour;
- the amount of cooking or doneness for product stability;
- and the amount of fermentation and drying.

FRESH SAUSAGE

The definition of sausage is minced (comminuted) pork, beef, or other meats, stuffed into a prepared natural or artificial casing (natural: intestine; artificial: collagen or synthetic-based). They are often combined together with various added ingredients and seasonings and regularly made in links or placed in molds (patties or loaves).

By Canadian Food Inspection Agency's (CFIA) standard, the act of making a sausage involves a comminuting process, one that may include either mechanical separation, flaking and grinding or any combination thereof.

Fresh sausage as a processed meat originated to utilize the trim left over from meat cutting operations. The European concept of a butcher store involved both meat cutting and sausage making. Any suitable trim from pork and beef while preparing meat cuts for retail purpose went when usable (fresh) into the making of fresh sausages. The raw material was, and still is, mainly pork. Beef and veal were also used to a lesser degree, the latter for binding purpose only, since veal has little colour value. Lamb trimmings used for fresh sausages is a stand-alone source as lamb adds a distinct flavour not easily masked or blended with other meat like that of bison, beef and veal. About 70% of processed meats in Canada such as sausages or cold cuts, are made with pork.

A selection of fresh sausage Fresh Sausage
Credit: Save on Foods

Fresh sausages are commonly not cured, smoked or cooked. The taste of the sausage will depend on its flavour profile, which generally determines the name associated with it. For example if you wanted to make a fresh Italian sausage you would use a combination of spices such as fennel and anise. To make a hot version you would add peppers or cayenne. The Internet is literally loaded with recipes for fresh sausage posted by creative people with heritage and ethnic backgrounds from all around the globe. The problem is not all of them

are professional sausage makers, and not all recipes live up to their hype.

CURED COOKED DELI MEATS

Sausage items like loaves (Bavarian meat-loaf and liver sausage) are meats that are precooked and ready to eat. These items are comminuted, seasoned, cured, cooked and cooled for storage and sold whole, by the piece or sliced, depending on the size of casing, mold or form used to contain them. This category includes cured, ground, pressed and formed turkey rolls and chicken rolls. Hams are also part of this category, including tinned hams and other non-smoked but cooked deli meats like Lyoner, tongue sausage, blood sausage, corned beef, all baked loaves, galantines and terrines, pâtés and head cheeses (or any variety of meat jellies).

The majority of cooked deli meats are also comminuted pork, beef, veal or other meats often combined together with various added ingredients and seasonings. They too are usually stuffed into a prepared natural or artificial casing (intestine, collagen or synthetic-based) or placed in molds (patties or loaves). Most cooked deli meats contain curing salts (with the exception of roast beef and BBQ chickens). Curing salt is an important ingredient used for colour, bind and control of spoilage organisms and pathogens. The cooking process of cooked deli meats improves palatability

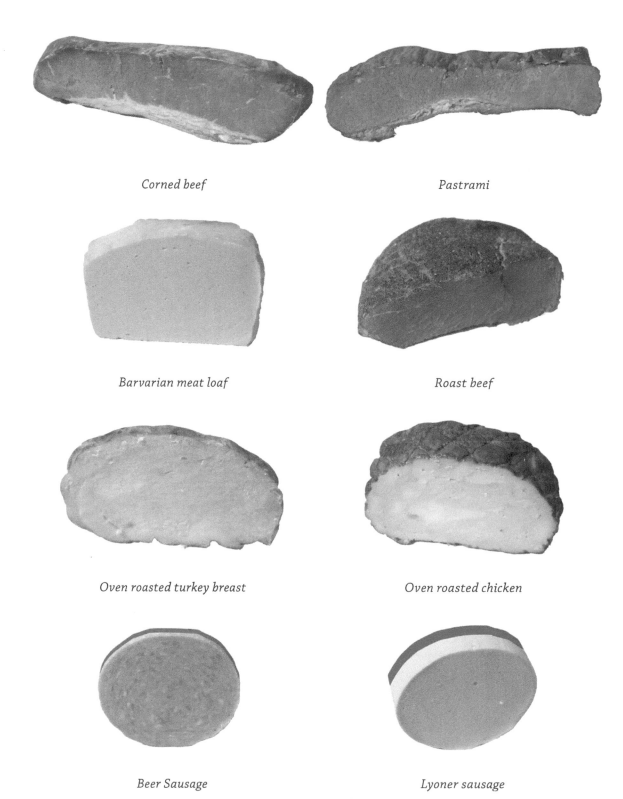

Corned beef

Pastrami

Barvarian meat loaf

Roast beef

Oven roasted turkey breast

Oven roasted chicken

Beer Sausage

Lyoner sausage

Credit: Save on Foods

by intensifying the flavour and altering the texture, it helps develop colour, bonds the water in the meat and lowers the water activity (the amount of water available within the muscle cells of the meat) making it easier to remove the end product from its mold or casing.

Cured cooked deli meats can be cooked or finished in a variety of ways. Some sausage makers or processors use the cook function of their smokehouse, others use kettles, pressure cookers, or ovens. There are those who use rational ovens, which have the versatility of functions like steaming, browning and holding products at a specific temperature. The cooking method used to finish products depends on the product type, its form and volume, and the functionality and capacity of the appliance. Once cooked, sausages are cooled down in showers or dipped in slush tanks (tanks filled with ice and water) to solidify the fats; this keeps the end product moist, flavourful and preventing the casing from wrinkling.

Due to volume, large processors that deal with larger batches of product will cook and chill their deli meats in the smoker; smaller, independent establishments that make smaller batches may use an oven or kettle. Either way the quality of the end product is managed by each process employed in its making.

Note: BBQ chickens are an in-house product and processed on site, on premise, according to supply and demand. Not all meat shops, delicatessens, or larger box stores have capacity to make and carry this product but it should be noted that it is a deli item sold as a finished product, seasoned and cooked.

CURED SMOKED AND COOKED SAUSAGE AND DELI MEATS

Sausage and meats in this category have the same attributes as those of cooked sausage and deli meats with the addition of smoking. Smoking and cooking are generally combined except when recipes call for other instructions (as with just cooking or just smoking).

Smoking the product adds flavour and a layer of protection. The smoke filament that adheres to the casing or product inhibits bacterial growth while adding a distinct flavour profile to the finished product. Smoke flavour can be imparted by liquid smoke or smoke generated from smouldering wood or wood chips/sawdust. The type of smoke flavour depends on the smoke application, duration, cycle(s) and the type of wood used. Meat that is exposed to the smoke or liquid smoke for longer periods of time will have a heavier, stronger smoke aroma and deeper, richer smoke flavour and colour. Some products carry the claim of "double smoked," asserting it has had twice the amount of exposure to the smoke process than other similar products.

The smoke for cured smoked and cooked sausage and deli meats is generated by means of friction or smouldering of a hardwood, most commonly hickory, beech or maple. For more on smoking, see *"Smoking and Cooking".*

UNCOOKED CURED AND SMOKED SAUSAGE

This category includes products that have a tangy, acidic taste or smooth texture, they are cured, smoked but not cooked. If the product requires cooking before consumption (like some Farmer, Mennonite and Rookworst sausages, etc.), the cooking of it is left to the consumer. Ingredients vary and can consist of finely or coarsely-ground, chopped or emulsified and seasoned meats. Depending on the product, often a cure accelerator or a bacterial culture has been added. The cure accelerator controls and accelerates the nitrite curing reaction and maintains colour brightness while the bacterial culture produces and gives the product its distinct flavour. In both cases their use is to help preserve an uncooked product by speeding up the curing process and warding off unwanted bacteria by lowering the pH value of the meat, making it more acidic.

Blood sausage ring
Credit: ©Christian Jung- Dreamstime

Turkey Kolbassa coil
Credit: Summit Gourmet meats

DRY AND SEMI-DRY FERMENTED SAUSAGE ITEMS

This category has another sub-category called "Semi-Dry Fermented Sausage." The drying and fermentation of sausages and meat(s) is a traditional method of preserving meat for later use. In times lost to history drying was the only way of assuring a consistent year-round supply of animal protein—and then came refrigeration. Today dry and fermented meats and sausages are a luxury and have become a sought-after artisanal product by sausage connoisseurs and foodies around the globe.

Fermented sausages are sausages that have aged slowly under a watchful eye. These items usually have a sour tang to them; Genoa, Cervelat, Soppressata and Calabrese salami are all types of fermented sausages. Traditionally fermented meat items had a bacterial culture introduced to them by natural means. The meats were prepared at a specific time of year, in a specific location, under specific conditions resulting in a consistent end product.

Teewurst
Credit: ©Grafvision/Dreamstime

Today with the use of bacterial cultures and modern equipment we can replicate those old-fashioned results year-round.

This particular classification of sausage is heavily regulated with respect to processing. Old world production methods of hanging product in the root cellar, basement or shed are no longer acceptable for food safety reasons. Today this type of sausage is made under very strict conditions where documentation and due diligence play a primary role. Important to the industry and consumers alike are the stability of the product, the temperature, the pH level and the moisture content (degree of dryness).

Hot Genoa Salami   *Cervelat Salami*   *Hot Calabrese*   *Swiss farmers sausage*

Credit: Save on Foods

Health and Wellness

Food safety is a collective responsibility of government, industry and consumers. All food operators are responsible under Canadian law for the safety of the food they produce and distribute. The *Guide to Food Safety* found on the Canadian Food Inspection Agency (CFIA) website is a voluntary tool that provides the Canadian food industry with generic guidance on how to design, develop and implement effective preventive food safety control systems. This will help to enhance food safety and prevent foodborne illness, foodborne injury and food spoilage. Also, Health Canada works with governments, industry and consumers to establish policies, regulations and standards related to the safety and nutritional quality of all food sold in Canada. Health Canada is responsible for assessing the CFIA's activities related to food safety. The CFIA is responsible for enforcing the food safety policies and standards that Health Canada sets.

The CFIA recognizes that various food safety programs and codes of practice have been implemented by the provinces and territories, and federally-registered sectors like meat and fish processing sectors. The *Guide to Food Safety* is not designed or intended to supersede or replace any existing requirements of federal, provincial and territorial governments. The *Guide to Food Safety* covers all aspects of food safety from the construction of buildings, facilities and food contact surfaces to the controls of operation and record keeping.

Traceability

Found on the CFIA website under "Traceability," is a factsheet concerning a proposed *Safe Food For Canadians Regulations* (SFCR) document. This document is not yet in effect but it soon will be. Once implemented the SFCR requires you, as a food retailer and producer of made in-house products or processed meats, to prepare and keep documentation that records the following:

1. **Identify the food indicating the:**
   - common name of the food
   - lot code to allow for the food to be traced
   - the name and principal place of business **by whom** the food was prepared
   - the name and principal place of business **for whom** the food was prepared (retail outlet or consumers)

2. **Identify any food commodity you incorporate into the food or from which you derive the food indicating the:**
   - name of any food commodity that was incorporated into the food
   - name of any food commodity from which the food was derived
3. **Trace the food commodity one step back. If someone else provided you with the food commodity that you incorporate into the food or from which you derive the food indicating the:**
   - name and address of the person who provided you with the food commodity
   - date you were provided with the food commodity
4. **Trace the food one step back. If someone else provided you with the food indicating the:**
   - name and address of the person who provided you with the food
   - date you were provided the food
5. **Trace the movement of the food or food commodity. If you move the food or food commodity to another place before you either sell it at retail or incorporate it into the food indicating the:**
   - address of each place you move the food or food commodity
   - name of an individual who is responsible for each place and date of each movement

Tools of the Craft

Equipment used in the production of sausage and other deli-type meats varies. The type of finished product characteristically determines the equipment needed to achieve desired outcomes, whether that be stuffed and linked, mixed and molded, or fermented and dried, etc. Most of the larger pieces of equipment used in the production of sausage can be found in Chapter 3 with the exception of some specialty items related specifically to charcuterie covered here in this chapter.

BASIC STEPS FOR SAUSAGE PRODUCTION
- Grinding
- Mixing
- Chopping
- Emulsifying
- Stuffing
- Linking and Tying
- Fermenting
- Smoking
- Cooking
- Chilling
- Drying or Aging

These eleven steps are used to varying degrees depending upon the type of product being processed. For example, producing fresh breakfast sausages utilizes: grinding, mixing, stuffing, linking and chilling, whereas the preparation of making an emulsified product such as Lyoner, involves grinding, mixing, emulsifying, stuffing, linking and tying and cooking.

Basics of Manufacturing Sausage

Before beginning the process of making a product, ensure that the right recipe is being used, and be aware of the desired batch size (in certain cases batch indications will have to be reduced or increased, never guess!). Weigh all the ingredients, and check the scale for the right setting for necessary tares. Use good quality fresh or frozen meats, as the recipe requires. Never use older, off-coloured, smelly meats or trimmings as these may be unsafe for consumption and will adversely affect your product (doubtful materials must be discarded).

Ensure that trimmings or parts are sorted to recipe and grading specifications. Meat should be free of bone chips and other hard particles, and not exceed limits of gristle or fat. Be sure to stock all the necessary ingredients (spices and additives); should an item be unavailable, try to determine whether it can be replaced by a substitute—never ever use unknown ingredients. If using premixed spice blend units, check for expiry dates and read the manufacturer's specifications on the label before proceeding. Remember, the finished product reflects the process and the quality of ingredients used. If poor quality meats (sour, old, discoloured, etc.) or outdated ingredients are used to make sausage, what comes out is poor quality sausage. Therefore, think twice before proceeding.

Sorting of Materials

In the production of exceptional products, one major concern is the choice of meat. Next is knowing the facts about the meat used to produce various charcuterie items. Not every cut of meat is suitable for every sausage or deli meat product. The choice of meat for a particular product depends upon the desired or traditional appearance the finished product should have. It is possible to choose between such characteristics as low bind ability with long shelf life (as with dry fermented items) and high bind ability with limited shelf life and higher weight retention (as with smoked and cooked items), resulting in higher profit margins.

Bind ability is influenced most by the pH value of the meat. Measuring the pH can be done using a simple pH meter with a digital readout. The following illustrates the pH scale.

One of the most important facts in any form of life is the pH value. It measures the acidity or alkalinity found in every life element. It is measured on a scale ranging from 0 to 14, where 0 is acid, 7 is neutral and 14 is alkaline.

In meat processing the pH scale presents the following picture:

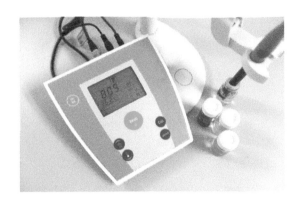

pH meter
Credit: © Korakot Khayankarnnavee / Dreamstime

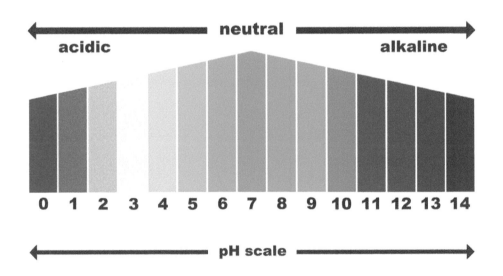

pH scale
Credit: © Roberto Atzeni- Dreamstime

Common characteristics of two groups of products

Semi-dry, cured, smoked and/or dried products.	Fresh, smoked/cured and/or cooked meat products.
Group #1 low **pH** of 5.3 minimum	**Group #2** high **pH** of 8 maximum
lower binding ability	higher binding ability
fast moisture release	better moisture retention
lower bacteria count	higher bacteria count
distinct taste	neutral taste
increased shelf life	decreased shelf life

A good sausage starts with the right selection of meat materials. Knowing this, the processing industry developed specific sorting systems for meat trimmings in order to assure consistent quality products and batch formulations. The three most common kinds of meat for sausage are: pork, beef and veal. Lamb and poultry play a somewhat limited role in sausage making and are used mostly by the larger (commercial) sausage manufacturing plants or specialty shops (independent retail meat shops or deli operations).

Special care should be taken with the sorting of different types of meats mentioned hereafter; meeting the specifications for fat and gristle content lays the foundation for a product. Fat content is necessary for product flavour and is important to formulate proper ratios per batch for different types of finished product. Pork can be visibly lean but could still contain up to 8% fat. Lean "A" grade beef will only be a maximum of 94% lean; other grades could be a maximum of 97% lean (*see fat usage and its calculation in this Chapter*). These are very important facts when calculating the fat content of processed meat products. The following number scale and explanations illustrate the sorting system for trimmings.

> **Note:** Well-sorted fresh trimmings are the only warranty for consistent quality and happy customers. Therefore, sorting trimmings is the most important charcuterie task one can perform and should always be done with special care and accuracy.

It is important to understand that the following system of ratios, i.e. 90/10 etc., is a system that explains the lean meat per fat content based on a chemical analysis of the meat. For example, if the fat content of the pork trimmings was found to be 20%, the meat might be described as "pork trimmings, 80% lean" (100 - 20 = 80), or "80% chemical lean." Of course this "lean" in turn contains protein and moisture. Also, important to note is that not all suppliers of trimmings (packing plants, for example) provide all of the ratios listed below. There are also those establishments that collect and sort their own trimmings gathered from operational day-to-day fabrication of retail items from carcasses, primal cuts etc., of beef, pork and veal.

BEEF TRIMMINGS

- 95/05 - absolute lean with no connective tissue and no visible fat
- 85/15 - 85% lean with no more than 15% fat and very little connective tissue
- 80/20 - 80% lean with no more than 20% of fat and connective tissue (a maximum of 5%)
- 50/50 - 50% lean, mostly flank and plate trim with a maximum of 50% of fat and connective tissue (a maximum of 15%)
- 25/75 - fatty beef trim with up to 25% of lean content and relatively fat with a higher percentage content of connective tissue

PORK TRIMMINGS

- 95/05 - 95% lean with no visible fat, collagen (gristle) or glands
- 90/10 - 90% lean with a maximum of 10% fat, but no gristle or glands
- 80/20 - 80% lean with a maximum of 17% fat and no more than 3% gristle, but no glands
- 70/30 - belly trim, 70% lean with no more than 30% fat
- 25/75 - seedy (soft part of belly trim) belly trim, with 25% lean content and 75% fat
- 40/60 - jowls with 40% lean and 60% fat content
- 05/95 - back fat and other pork fat with no visible content of lean meat and 95% fat

VEAL TRIMMINGS

Veal is valuable meat and therefore trimmings are limited. However, some products require veal meat for its flavour, bind ability and colour contribution. The suggested veal sorts are:

- 90/10 - absolute 90% lean with no connective tissue or visible fat
- 80/20 - 80% lean with a maximum of 20% fat and limited content of connective tissue (a maximum of 5%)

POULTRY TRIMMINGS

Poultry trim is also used in sausage manufacturing and the suggested sorting are:

- 95/05 - lean white meat with no visible fat or connective tissue
- 90/10 - darker red meat with a maximum of 10% visible fat and some connective tissue (a maximum of 5%)
- 20/80 - mostly skin with some lean and fat content

LAMB TRIMMINGS

Lamb trim is used in some specialty items and is also usable in meat mixtures at a concentration not higher than 10% (to keep taste neutral). Because lamb naturally has a higher fat content, it is necessary to monitor the fat total.

- 90/10 - lean trim with a maximum of 10% fat and connective tissue (a maximum of 5%)
- 50/50 - trimmings with a maximum of 50% of fat and connective tissue (a maximum of 10%)

Fresh meats that have been cooler-aged and darkened (due to oxidization) can be used in combination with fresh trimmings (recommended for use in cured items only, never in fresh sausage), but only in a concentration of approximately 25% of any recipe's meat block (total amount of meat used in a given recipe). The rest (75%) should consist of fresh materials only so as to prevent bad colour developing, off taste or texture inconsistencies and a decreased shelf life.

Note: All trimmings should be absolutely free of skin (chicken or pork rind unless called for), bone chips, glands or elastin (such as the back strap) material. Depending on the type of sausage there are limits to the amount of collagen (gristle) and connective tissue one can use. It is always best to refer to your recipe, which should outline the types of meats, their ratio of lean to fat, and their quantities. It should be clear that any foreign objects (nonedible debris) like metal, wood, plastic or paper or any such items are not accidently incorporated into your raw materials at any stage of processing.

Whole-Muscle Products

Whole-muscle products also play a major role in charcuterie. Many gourmet meats and famous regional specialties are derived from different whole-muscle parts of the animal. The following are examples and an illustration of proven possibilities of whole-muscle charcuterie products.

PORK LOIN

Bone-in smoked and cooked:

- Kassler loin
- Smoked pork chops

Boneless cured and smoked and/or cooked

- Back bacon
- Cornmeal bacon or
- Marinated B.B.Q. pork.
- Lonza

Canadian peameal bacon
Credit: ©Michael Gray/Dreamstime

Boneless with side pork attached and partly defatted:

- Italian porchetta
- Stuffed belly roll

Boneless with half side pork attached, skinned and lightly defatted:

- Irish bacon
- Danish bacon
- Yorkshire bacon

Porchetta roast stuffed
Credit: ©Bhofack2/Dreamstime

Top sirloin:

- Schinkenspeck
- Dry-cured ham
- Marinated pork

Back fat, skinless:

- Lardo

PORK LEG

Whole, bone-in, partly-skinned:

- RTE or RTS smoked and cooked (Easter or Christmas ham)
- Prosciutto ham
- Parma ham

Boneless, skinless or whole:

- Cooked ham
- Toupie ham

Tip: (knuckle)

- Nugget hams
- Old-fashioned
- Black Forest

Schinkenspeck
©istock.com / Credit to wirbnbrinf

Prosciutto Ham
Credit: Costco

Honey smoked ham
Credit: Save on Foods

Black forest ham – packaged
Credit: Costco

Inside and/or outside rounds,
skinned, defatted and trimmed:

- Black Forest ham
- Old-fashioned ham
- Westphalian ham
- Canadian-pressed ham

SIDE PORK

Skin on, trimmed:

- Side bacon

Skinless, trimmed:

- Westphalian bacon dry cured
- Pancetta
- A variety of Canadian flavours and cures (used in cooking recipes, mostly breakfast plates)

Skin on, pocketed:

- Stuffed belly.

PORK SHOULDER BLADE

Bone-in, skinless:

- Smoked blade roast
- Smoked blade chops

Boneless:

- Cottage roll
- Speck

Old fashioned ham
Credit: Save on Foods

Side bacon
Credit: Summit Gourmet meats

Pancette
Credit: Save on Foods

Cottage roll
Credit: TRU Retail Meat Processing Program

Boneless neck part off:

- Italian Capicola ham
- Coppa
- Smoked neck chops, boneless

PORK SHOULDER PICNIC

Bone-in, skin on or off:

- Smoked shoulder picnic

Boneless, skinless:

- Jellied pork
- Sausage meat
- Pork loaves

HOCKS

- Smoked hocks
- Jellied pork (headcheese)

PORK JOWL

Skin on:

- Cooked for pâtés
- Dry cured

Skinless:

- Guanciale
- Sausage meat—excellent use! (used in rings)

PORK HEAD

- Sausage meat
- Headcheese.

Capicola ham
Credit: Save on Foods

Shoulder picnic smoked
Credit: TRU Retail Meat Processing Program

Smoked hock
©istock.com / Credit to olgamarc

Head cheese
Credit: Save on Foods

PORK FEET AND SKIN

- Headcheese
- Jellied meat

BEEF INSIDE ROUND

Boneless, trimmed, cap removed:

- Cooked roast beef
- Smoked beef
- Cure- dried beef or
- Jerky (cut with the grain).

OUTSIDE ROUND (EYE REMOVED)

- Montreal beef
- Jerky
- Pastrami
- Smoked beef and/or
- Canadian corned beef

SIRLOIN TIP

- Smoked beef
- Cure-dried beef

EYE OF ROUND

- Smoked beef
- Cure-dried beef
- Beef jerky cut with grain

BRISKET

Boneless, partly defatted:

- Pastrami
- Corned beef
- Smoked brisket

Cooked roast beef
Credit: Save on Foods

Beef jerky
Credit: TRU Retail Meat Processing Program

Pastrami
Credit: © Shariff Che\' Lah/Dreamstime

Corned beef un-cooked
Credit: Summit Gourmet Meats

VEAL SHOULDER

Veal breast, veal flank and veal neck, partly defatted:

- Danish Rullepolse (a traditional Danish cold cut, can also be made from the pork belly or from the lamb shoulder)

VEAL TRIM

- Used for fresh, cured and smoked, cured/smoked and cooked sausage.

VEAL LEG

- Cured veal roasts or corned veal.

LAMB TRIM

Used for fresh sausage:

- In Australia and New Zealand (and some parts of Canada), lamb ham made from the lamb leg is popular.
- For the most part, lamb trim is used for fresh sausage and in larger processing plants where batch size and seasonings mask the flavour.

Oven roasted turkey breast
Credit: Save on Foods

POULTRY BREAST

Boneless and/or skinless:

- Smoked breast (duck, chicken and turkey)
- Cooked breast loaves or rolls

WHITE AND DARK TRIM USED FOR SAUSAGE

- Skin can be used for chicken skin emulsions, a valuable product that is used for further processing and binding

Cooked chicken
Credit: Save on Foods

Flavourings and Spices

Our ability to sense the five accepted categories of taste—sweet, bitter, sour, salty and umami (savoury)—comes from receptors on our taste buds. These tiny sensory organs appear mostly on the tongue, the roof of the mouth and in the back of the throat. The sense of touch also plays a role in experiencing taste, as evidenced by the strong opinions on crunchy versus smooth as with peanut butter. Smell also impacts our tasting abilities; when a food smells good we anticipate it will taste good. So too when we are ill, have a cold, the flu or a stuffy nose, things smell and taste different than when we aren't suffering from symptoms affecting our taste.

You might wonder what this has to do with spices. Well, bitter foods are generally found to be unpleasant, while sour, salty, and sweet-tasting foods provide a more pleasant eating experience. Sausage is formulated with flavourings and spices—sweet, bitter, sour and salty—giving them their extraordinary flavour. Therefore, it is necessary to select flavourings and spices that complement each other. It is not a single spice or flavouring that makes an excellent product, rather it is a selected combination of them. Remember, not every spice or flavouring combines with other spices or flavourings perfectly.

Consequently, it is necessary to select combinations carefully.

It is also necessary to consider the kind of product being made, the procedures being used, the required pH level, and the desired cooking yields in order to make the right selection of "non-meat ingredients" to achieve a perfect result.

Don't forget: there are legal limits to the amounts of non-meat ingredients added to a product, so watch for manufacturers' specifications regarding addition limits. Limits are usually found on the product label. It is also essential to remember that not every ingredient works in combination with other ingredients; in fact, sometimes they work against each other. Make absolutely sure such items are not combined.

Spices were discovered early in the Stone Age when hunters preparing their game or catch of the day wrapped their meats in certain kinds of leaves to prevent them from burning. These hunters began to realize that particular kinds of leaves gave their meats very distinct flavours. Spices grew in popularity over the centuries of the Greek and Roman Empires, and by the Middle Ages spices had developed into an important factor of trade between nations. Many of the richest people in those days were dealing in spices. Wars were fought over spices and their countries of origin. In many powerful countries spices were widely accepted as hard currency in place of gold.

Today spices still play a major role in our daily intake of food. Spices help speed up digestion, which is beneficial for our health and well being..

The smell and flavour of spices is determined by the content of etheric (essential aromatic) oils, the percentage of that content determining strength and quality. The higher the content of essential oils the higher the quality of a spice. Higher oil content also decreases spice usage per kilogram of product to be flavoured. Therefore, the most expensive spice, because of its high content of essential oils and thus extremely low usage, is usually the least costly. Spices are diversified into five different groups: seeds, roots, leaves, fruits and flowers and stems.

In order to assure maximum quality, spice producers are very careful in choosing grinding and packaging procedures. Essential oils tend to evaporate into the air under the influence of warmth, bright light and open-air flow (excessive humidity is also a negative factor). Because of this, spices should be ground with refrigerated grinding machines (below -30°C).

The best packaging is aluminum foil vacuum packaging, which protects against the influence of light and prevents any loss of essential oil. Manufacturers following these guidelines will always offer the best quality of spices. If high-quality spices are desired, look for producers following the above-mentioned criteria.

Note: All spices should be stored in a separate room or cabinet, in sealed food-grade containers, clearly labelled and away from light and heat.

Common Spices and Usage

ANISE SEED

Anise seed is derived from a flowering plant native to the eastern Mediterranean region and southwest Asia. Used in either whole or ground, anise seed is mainly found in Italian products. Maximum addition is 2 grams per kilogram of meat block.

Anise seed
©istock.com - Credit emer1940

CARAWAY SEED

Caraway seed comes from a flowering plant native to western Asia and Europe. It is used mainly in Italian, Polish, Hungarian and Bavarian products. Maximum addition of 2 grams per kilogram of meat block works best.

Caraway seed
©istock.com - Credit eyewave

CELERY SEED

Celery seed is grown locally and in most parts of the world familiar with celery. It is used whole or ground in most common products. Addition of up to 3 grams per kilogram of meat block is appropriate.

Celery seed
©istock.com - Credit Alina555

CARDAMOM SEED

Cardamom is native to Indonesia and Nepal. It's used in several high-quality processed products, but in limited quantities because of its strong aroma power. Maximum addition is 0.5 grams per kilogram of meat block.

Cardamom seed
©istock.com - Credit Toltek

CLOVES (FLOWER)

Also native to Indonesia, cloves have a strong aroma therefore they're used very carefully, mainly in pâtés or blood sausages. Maximum addition is 0.5 grams per kilogram of meat block.

Cloves flower
©istock.com - Credit Tinieder

CORIANDER SEED

Coriander is the seed of the cilantro plant and is common to southern Europe. Used in most common meat products and has a mild flavour that rounds off nicely. Maximum addition is 5 grams per kilogram of meat block.

Coriander seed
©istock.com - Credit kitzcorner

CINNAMON

Cinnamon comes from the inner bark of a cinnamon tree mainly grown in Sri Lanka. It is very sweet, but has a strong flavour, therefore it is used in very low quantities. Use a maximum of 0.2 grams per kilogram of meat block.

Cinnamon ground & sticks
©Anton Starikov - Dreamstime

ALLSPICE SEED

Grown mainly in Mexico; allspice tastes and smells somewhat similar to cloves but is less powerful. It's used mainly in beef products. Maximum addition is 0.8 grams per kilogram of meat block.

Allspice seed
©istock.com - Credit Handmadepictures

CUMIN SEED

Used mainly in Portuguese products, cumin is native to the Mediterranean and southern Asia. It is also the main flavour character in chili spice mixes. Maximum addition is 3 grams per kilogram of meat block.

Cumin seed
©istock.com / Credit to Suzifoo

CHILI PEPPER

Originating in Mexico and derived from red jalapeno peppers, chili pepper is available as crushed chilies containing the seeds or ground as cayenne pepper without seeds. It is used in all southern and Cajun food as well as in northern hot specialties. Maximum addition is 7 grams per kilogram of meat block.

Chili pepper
©istock.com - Credit theJIPEN

CURRY POWDER

Originating in south Asia, curry powder is mixture of up to nine different spices with the main character being turmeric. It is added to a few specialty items. Maximum addition is 7 grams per kilogram of meat block.

Curry powder
©istock.com - Credit vikif

DILL SEED

Grown in all parts of Europe and Asia, dill is used mainly in salads; use in meats is limited. Maximum addition is 2 grams per kilogram of meat block.

Dill seed
©istock.com - Credit PeterHermesFurian

FENNEL SEED

Origins of fennel are found in the Mediterranean and are now found in many parts of the world. It is a major flavouring of Italian products and is similar in taste and smell to anise; it is also contained in licorice. Maximum addition is 3 grams per kilogram of meat block.

Fennel seed
©istock.com - Credit FotografiaBasica

MUSTARD SEED

Grown in many parts of the world and in Canada, mustard seed is mainly used in whole form for its appearance in cold cuts. Maximum addition is 5 grams per kilogram of meat block.

Mustard seed
©istock.com - Credit bdspn

NUTMEG FRUIT

Nutmeg comes from the inner part or "stone" of a tropical fruit found in Indonesia, Malaysia, the Caribbean and Grenada. The tree is an evergreen with dark leaves. It is commonly used in a large number of processed meat products. Maximum addition is 1.5 grams per kilogram of meat block.

Nutmeg fruit
©Andrii Hrytsenko - Dreamstime

MACE FRUIT

Mace is the outer covering of the nutmeg fruit. It has a very particular flavour and is used mainly in emulsions, pâtés and salamis. Maximum addition is 2 grams per kilogram of meat block.

Mace fruit
©istock.com - Credit empire331

GINGER ROOT

Ginger is native to Asia and it is now grown in Japan, China, India, Jamaica and Africa. It is produced from herb-like plants with leaves similar to reeds. The food part comes from the rhizome (root). The flavour is pungent and spicy. It is used whole and most commonly found in Asian food or ground in several processed meats. Maximum addition is 2 grams per kilogram of meat block.

Ginger root
©istock.com - Credit Toltek

PAPRIKA FRUIT

Made out of dried red pepper fruits, paprika is available in "noble sweet," medium or hot. The most popular types are: Hungarian, which is bright red, and Spanish, in a darker red colour. This spice is also available in green or yellow. Maximum addition is 5 grams per kilogram of meat block.

Paprika fruit
©istock.com - Credit margouillatphotos

PEPPERS (BELL FRUIT)

Like paprika, pepper is made out of green, yellow, or red peppers, which are dried and chopped. It is used more for decoration than flavour. Maximum addition is 5 grams per kilogram of meat block.

Peppers
©Sally Scott / Dreamstime

PEPPER SEED

Is available in: "green," which is harvested unripe, marinated in a light, salty brine and either canned or vacuum sealed; "black," which is also harvested unripe and goes through a heat-drying process in which it lightly ferments and turns from a green into a black colour outside (not throughout the whole peppercorn); and "white," which is harvested ripe and has a red outer skin which is peeled off before drying and grinding. Pepper is used in almost every meat product, either whole, coarse medium ground, or fine ground. Maximum addition is 6-7 grams per kilogram of meat block.

Pepper seed - green
©Olga Popova / Dreamstime

Pepper seed - black
©Lenka Prusova / Dreamstime

Pepper seed – white
©istock.com / Credit
Ekaterina_Lin

Pepper seed - red
©istock.com / Credit Sjo

Pepper seed – red, black, green
& white
©istock.com / Credit Floortje

GARLIC

Garlic belongs to the onion family. Each bulb consists of several cloves enclosed in a membrane. Its most distinctive characteristic is its odour. Garlic is used extensively in sausage manufacturing. Recommended usage is 3-7 grams per kilogram of meat block.

Garlic bulbs
©istock.com / Credit Elovich

Garlic spice – granular
©Handmadepictures /
Dreamstime

Liquid garlic
Credit: Stuffers Supply Company

MARJORAM LEAVES

Marjoram belongs to herb family and is mainly used in eastern European country specialties. As a ground product and a relative to oregano, it is used extensively in sausage manufacturing. Maximum addition is 3 grams per kilogram of meat block.

Marjoram leaves
©istock.com / Credit lindavostrovska

OREGANO LEAVES

Related to marjoram, oregano is the wild form of the same plant, whereas marjoram is the cultured form. It is used in exotic dishes as well as in certain mainly-Mediterranean meat specialties. Maximum addition is 2 grams per kilogram of meat block (also comes in ground form).

Oregano leaves
©istock.com / Credit lunanaranja

Note: Marjoram and oregano are the most common herbs used in meat processing. The herb family is large and mainly used in combinations, therefore detailed specifications are not given here. Herbs commonly used in meat processing are: thyme, basil, tarragon, dill, savory, sage, rosemary and mint. The maximum addition of herbs is generally 1-5 grams per kilogram of meat block.

Dill weed
©istock.com / Credit
PeterHermesFurian

Rosemary
©istock.com / Credit Volosina

Sage
©istock.com / Credit hiklio

Thyme
©istock.com / Credit
IPGGutenburgUKLtd

Basil flakes
©istock.com / Credit rimglow

Tarragon
©istock.com / Credit Sebalos

Mint
©istock.com / Credit mashuk

PARSLEY

Parsley grows throughout the world and is a common garden herb. Its characteristic odour is due to the presence of volatile oils in the stems and leaves. General usage is 1-5 grams per kilogram of meat block.

Parsley
©istock.com / rimglow

TURMERIC

Turmeric spice is very intense and is bright yellow in colour. It is mainly used in East Indian and Pakistani dishes. Used only in very few processed meats, it is also the major flavour component in curry powder. Maximum addition is 0.2 grams per kilogram of meat block.

Turmeric
©istock.com / Kenishirotie

Spice Units are a blended formulation of spice mixtures and seasoning combined for specific batch sizes of jerky, sausage, brines, marinades or rubs. These units are made for convenience and consistency of product. Each premixed unit is labelled and provides usage instructions for preparation, handling and storage. Particular attention has to be paid to the labels of these products as some premixes come with salt and curing agents, while others do not.

After taking the cost of labour into consideration, premix units are a cost-effective way to make a consistent product by eliminating human error in the formulation of spices-per-batch recipe. When the directions on the label are followed the result should be a product that turns out the same way each time it is made, providing the same raw ingredients, quantities and processes are also identical for each batch.

There are spice units for all classification of sausages, hams and bacons. The variety seems endless and spice-blending companies keep coming up with innovative solutions to the fabrication of sausage and cured meats. Charcuterie is on the rise especially with artisanal products like those of salamis and other dry-cured meats.

Note: Total spice formulation cannot exceed 2% of total meat block. Any formulation greater than 2% needs to be identified on the product label ingredient list.

Non-Meat Ingredients

Something more than just meat and spices is needed in order to be competitive, create a consistent product, give products a certain required firmness or softness, the capability to ferment, or to increase or drop pH as desired. This is where additives come in. Such additives are referred to as non-meat ingredients. When adding non-meat ingredients, the operator must always be sure he/she knows what the non-meat ingredient is and how it is to be used. They should also know what limits are imposed by nature and what limits are imposed by law. Therefore, every time a certain ingredient is added, the manufacturer's label on the product must be read and recommended procedures must be followed exactly (Food and Drug Regulations B.14.008; B.14.030).

Note: All non-meat ingredients used in the production of charcuterie items should be stored in a separate room or cabinet, in food-grade containers, clearly labelled complete with usage instructions/ restrictions, and away from light and heat.

Below are some of the common non-meat ingredients used in charcuterie.

Salt (Sodium Chloride, NaCL) is a flavour enhancer and protein extractor. It is also the world's oldest food additive. Salt is important in the production of sausage products and charcuterie meats. It consists of 39.3% sodium and 60.7% chloride. Salt is produced by mining rock salt or evaporation (sea salt). Salt is an essential nutrient; insufficient supply of sodium in the body is a threat to the nerve and muscular system. An over supply of salt in the body leads to high blood pressure and other negative factors.

Historically salt was used as a preservative in high doses making it unpalatable to modern consumers. Today salt is used as a flavour enhancer and together with phosphate solubilizes protein, binds water and emulsified fat. The interaction of salt influences actin and myosin, which are salt soluble proteins. The lowest limit used to activate these proteins is approximately 12 grams per kilogram of meat block. Salt also helps lower the water activity (aw) value of sausage and meats and destroys or stops the growth of unwanted bacteria by creating an electrolyte imbalance in the cell. Salt simply reduces the amount of water available to bacteria and as we know, bacteria thrive in moisture. When the water inside the cells of the meat is bound by salt, bacteria begin to die off because their source of food is no longer available to them.

Salt in fresh sausages will have an ionic effect on the protein-heme configuration, causing molecules to experience physical changes, resulting in oxidation and followed by discolouration of the product into brown or grey tones. Salt may also contain pro-oxidants which could make the aforementioned scenario even worse. A small amount of ascorbic acid, namely "sodium ascorbate" or "sodium erythorbate," will temporarily slow oxidation but will not prevent it. Though 12 grams per kilogram is the lowest limit, our recommended salt usage for fresh sausage is 18 grams per kilogram of meat block.

Note: Iodized table salt should not be used in the production of sausage or charcuterie meats as it alters the taste of products. Sea salts or kosher salts are ideal as they blend well, are clean tasting and contain no additives that influence taste. Professional sausage makers do not use iodized table salt!

Sea salt
©istock.com / Floortje

Kosher salt
©Michelle Arnold / Dreamstime

SALT LEVELS IN SOME PRODUCTS

- Whole bone in hams may contain an average of 2–3% salt
- Bacon may contain an average of 1.25–2% salt
- Fresh pork sausages may contain an average of 1.5–2 % salt

- Dry fermented meats may contain an average of 2.6–4% salt (having a minimum of 2.5%)
- Country hams may contain an average of 5–8% salt content

Nitrites are added to sausage as inhibitors to bacterial growth and provide the product with the cured colour and flavour most people have become accustomed to seeing in all cured meats. Sodium nitrites (referred to as nitrites) used for charcuterie are incorporated in different products more commonly known as Sure Cure, Unicure, and Prague powder. These products have 93.75% salt as their base and 6.25% nitrite content. Great care should be taken not to confuse them with other all-purpose curing salts or regular salt as each of these also contain different levels of nitrite. Different levels of nitrite produce different effects: too much sodium nitrite is poisonous, and too little does not bring out the desired affect that creates colour, flavour and food safety.

> **Note:** The legal limit for nitrite use is 200 ppm (parts per million) in hams, corned beef, cooked sausage and cured meats (or 2 grams for every 10 kilograms of product), with a limit of 120 ppm in bacon. All spice suppliers recommend usage levels in cured/cooked sausage between 150–180 ppm with European masters recommending a level of 156 ppm.

NITRATE

The change from sodium nitrate (referred to as nitrate) to nitrite is due to bacterial action and the acidity of meat. The bacterial action alters the chemical formula by simply taking one atom of oxygen away (new formula: $NaNO_2$). Within the first 24 hours after processing, nitrite converts into nitrous oxide gas (NO_2), which is harmless. The nitrous oxide permeates through the meat mass, combining with the red muscle pigment (hemoglobin) to produce the typical cured colour of pink. The addition of ascorbic acid will speed up this process. It will also contribute to the maintenance of a large pool of nitric oxide in the finished product, which is necessary for product stability and for the control of bacterial activity (particularly the dangerous *Clostridium botulism* bacteria, preventing it from producing its deadly toxin).

There could be a residue of sodium nitrite in the finished product, especially in cure pockets or in the fat, which is not penetrated by the nitric oxide. Another possibility is the reformation of some nitrite in the finished product. Neither of these possibilities are cause for concern because both items (residue or reformed) are inactivated.

Surprisingly, an addition of only 120 ppm of sodium nitrite will produce all the unique features like stable colour (reddish to pink), unique flavour, improved texture, inhibition of bacterial activity and inhibition of oxidation. The addition of nitrate/nitrite produces a stable product with an extremely good shelf life.

NITROSAMINES

Nitrosamines occur when nitrite is broken down to nitrous acid (HNO_2), which react with proteins in meat. These are known to be carcinogenic and found mainly in fried bacon. A combination of cure and high heat is needed to produce or form nitrosamines. The cooking of bacon is not hazardous when an even medium-high heat is used (at or below 204°C). The benefits of nitrite uses far outweigh the hazards. Nitrosamines are also naturally common to other food groups such as cheese, fish and fish byproducts, pickles and beer.

Curing Salt, commercially premixed, may contain anywhere from 0.85-0.98% nitrites with a salt base in the range of 97-99%. These all-purpose curing salts are used in the production of brine, in cooked and smoked sausage and meats such as pastrami, garlic coil and Bavarian meat loaf, etc. Usage directions for such products are found on the label of the product container (see Appendix: *Data Sheets*). All-purpose curing salts come in bulk, need to be stored in a noncorrosive container and occasionally dry mixed to

ensure the even distribution of nitrite to salt is maintained.

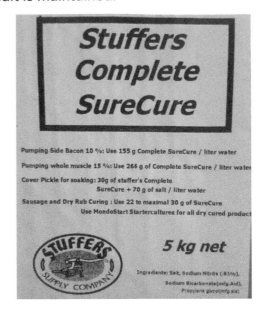

All-purpose curing salt
Credit: Stuffers Supply Company

Prague Powder comes in two forms, Prague powder number 1 (pink) contains 6.25% sodium nitrite with the remainder consisting of 93.75% salt, and Prague powder number 2 (also pink) contains 6.25% sodium nitrite, 4% sodium nitrate with the remainder consisting of 89.75% salt. These products are also known as:

- Insta-Cure
- Pink curing salt
- Tinted curing mixture
- TCM
- Tinted cure
- Curing salt

Prague powder is tinted pink to prevent it from being mistaken for other ingredients such as all-purpose curing salt or ordinary salt. Prague powder number 1 is not to be confused with Prague powder number 2, which is used in the fabrication of dry and semi-dry fermented sausage and meats. Both Prague powder number 1 and 2 are to be used in small quantities in accordance with regulations governing restricted ingredients. Like the vast selection of curing salts, Prague powder is used to add colour, flavour, and to inhibit unwanted bacterial growth (like *Clostridium botulinum).*

Our recommended usage for Prague powder number 1 is 2.5 grams per kilogram of meat block in the fabrication of cured sausages and per kilogram of water in the formulation of brine used for the curing of side pork and boneless pork loins in the production of bacons.

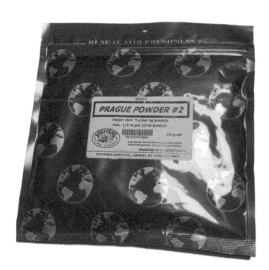

Prague powder 2 (pink)
Credit: Stuffers Supply Company

CURE ACCELERATORS

Cure accelerators have a legal limit of 550 ppm (0.055% or 0.55 grams per kilogram of product or brine) and react with nitrite to streamline the curing process. They block nitrosamine formation and improve colour fixation. Approved forms of cure accelerators are: sodium erythorbate, sodium ascorbate, ascorbic acid, erythorbic acid, sodium citrate, and citric acid. The two most common accelerators used in processing cured products are: sodium erythorbate and sodium ascorbate. Our recommended usage is 0.5 grams per kilogram of meat block.

SODIUM ERYTHORBATE

Sodium erythorbate is an antioxidant inhibiting the influence of oxygen on food and acts as a preservative. Starch is the main component; it is produced by microbial fermentation of food grade starch. Sodium erythorbate maintains colour and flavour in cured meats and extends shelf life. Sodium erythorbate accelerates curing by breaking nitrites for quicker distribution and stabilizes colour. When using this product always follow product usage recommendations found on the label, which will have taken into consideration legal limit usage.

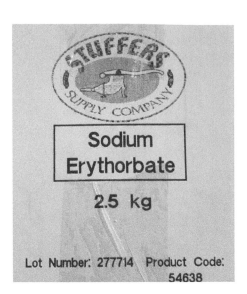

Sodium Erythorbate
Credit: Stuffers Supply Company

SODIUM ASCORBATE

Sodium ascorbate is an antioxidant produced in like manner to that of sodium erythorbate with the addition of vitamin C (ascorbic acid). It is mainly used for colour retention in fresh and cured products. When using this product always follow product usage recommendations found on the label, which will have taken into consideration legal limit usage.

FOOD GRADE PHOSPHATES

Phosphates act to increase the water-holding capacity of meat by forcing the proteins apart, which in turn allows water to move in between protein molecules. Food-grade phosphates are used in meat products for preservation of natural flavours and for binding. They are common to other food sources such as bakery products, milk, cheese, breakfast cereal, dehydrated potatoes and toothpaste (trisodium phosphate). The two food-grade phosphates more commonly used in the processed meats are sodium tripolyphosphate and tetrasodium pyrophosphate. Sodium tripolyphosphates have a higher solubility and are less prone to form insoluble precipitates. Other names for sodium tripolyphosphate are pentasodium triphosphate, pentasodium tripolyphosphate and sodium triphosphate. The generally accepted common name for this product is triphosphate.

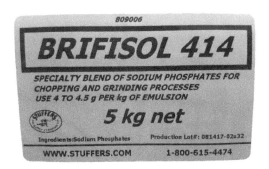 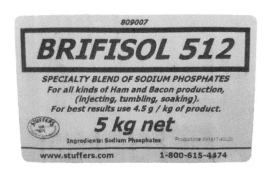

Food grade phosphates for Sausage & emulsions (Bristol 414) and Brines (Bristol 512)
Credit: Stuffers Supply Company

The permissible maximum concentration of residual phosphates in meat products is set at 0.5 % (500 grams per 100 kilograms or 5 grams per kilogram), which equates to 5,000 ppm (Food and Drug Regulations B.14.009 [S].(f)).

Keep in mind there are approximately 500 to 1,000 ppm naturally occurring in red meats. To stay within the legal limits our recommendation is a usage of 3–3.5 grams per kilogram of product.

BINDERS

Any ingredient that forms a gel or glue when combined with water acts as a binder. This binding effect is similar to, but different than, the binding effect of the proteins that are extracted from meats. Binders can be used either to bind water into the product or to bind meats together, so they do not fall apart after processing and cooking. Some binders add protein that encapsulates the fat and aids in retaining water bound in meats while others are fillers extending the volume of product. Most binders have a legal limit of 2% of total meat block.

Most commercial binders are sold as seasoned having any combination of salt, sweetening agents, spices or other seasonings (except tomato), egg, egg albumen, and may contain any of ascorbic acid, calcium ascorbate, erythorbic acid, iso-ascorbic acid, potassium nitrate or nitrite, sodium ascorbate, sodium nitrite or nitrate, provided that these nitrates and nitrites, if any, are packaged separately from any spice or seasoning (Food and Drug Regulations B.14.007[S].(a)).

WHEY POWDER

Whey powder is a high protein dry milk product. Whey powder proteins are being widely used in meat and poultry products as binding, extending and texture modifying agents. The legal limit of this product is 2% of the meat block.

Whey powder premium binder
Credit: Stuffers Supply Company

DE-HEATED MUSTARD (AIM)

De-heated mustard is made by a process of controlled manufacturing whereby the mustard heat enzyme (myrosinase) is inactivated, producing a mild-flavoured mustard product. De-heated mustard has antimicrobial properties and consists mainly of starch and has excellent natural binding quality. This product aids in the peel-ability of wieners (removing the plastic outer skins).

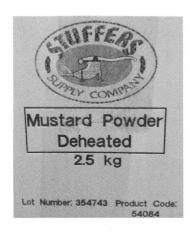

De-heated mustard
Credit: Stuffers Supply Company

SODIUM CASEINATE OR MILK PROTEIN

Adds more protein count to contained meat proteins, and combines with them. This is a dairy product and works as an excellent water and fat encapsulant in any processed meat product. It allows for a much higher addition of water and fat in the form of water fat pre-emulsifying; within the limits imposed by regulations governing the addition of water, restricted to 15%, and the use of fat to 40% maximum in ready-to-eat products. Regarding the addition of water and fat we recommend the levels of 10% water and 35% fat to remain well within the restrictions.

SOYA PROTEIN

Similar to milk protein, but different processing procedures are used, therefore watch for manufacturer's specifications.

This product works in conjunction with salt only if certain processing sequences are strictly followed.

Soya protein concentrate
Credit: Stuffers Supply Company

ISOLATED SOY PROTEIN (ISP)

ISP is 90% protein and very expensive. This product imparts a soya flavour that may not be desired. The legal limit of this product is 2% of the total meat block.

EXTENDERS

Extenders add starch to products acting as fillers that soak up moisture. In most cases the legal limit of extenders is 3.5% of the total meat block.

FLOUR BINDERS (STARCH)

The disadvantage of using flour-based binders is that excessive use will change the taste of the product and not necessarily for the better. It is not recommended that they be used unless a floury taste to meat products is preferred.

POTATO OR RICE STARCH

These starches have excellent binding ability resulting in better water retention in finished products.

MODIFIED CORN STARCH

This product also has excellent binding properties that activate at 71°C and replaces carrageenan in a lot of products. The use of modified corn starch in processed meats improves yields and reduces purge for a more moist and flavourful product.

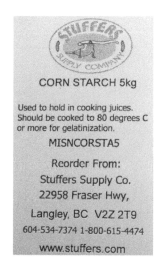

Modified corn starch
Credit: Stuffers Supply Company

CARRAGEENAN (GUM) (HIGH GEL)

This product can be used as a tumbler aid, which gels proteins and water to firm meat (a gelling agent), thus contributing to greater water retention and improved cooking yields. The Canadian Food Inspection Agency allows a maximum usage of 0.25 % of a product's weight or 2.5 grams per kilogram of product added to the tumbler. Carrageenan is not to be used as part of the injection cure but can be used as an ingredient in sausage or sausage emulsions. Read the manufacturer's specifications found on the product label before use.

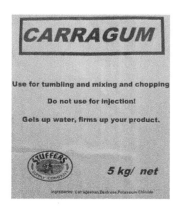

Carrageenan (high gel) Garragum
Credit: Stuffers Supply Company

BREADCRUMBS

Breadcrumbs represent a relatively inexpensive filler or extender with excellent water-retaining capabilities. It is advisable to use toasted breadcrumbs only as they will hardly alter the flavour of the product. Breadcrumbs produced out of a mixture of bread or stale bread are not recommended for use in meat products because they are subject to bacterial activity such as moulds or fungi which could alter the taste of the product, or even spoil it. Therefore, only use crumbs designated for use in meat products.

Miscellaneous Ingredients

ANTIOXIDANTS

Antioxidants like rosemary extract are used to combat the occurrence of oxidative rancidity, which is when unsaturated fatty acids react with oxygen to form hydroperoxides that can produce off flavours. This process is relatively rapid and often occurring in one or two days after processing. Antioxidants are most commonly associated with fresh sausage. Examples of antioxidants and their legal limits are:

- BHA – Butylated hydroxyanisole, having a legal limit of 0.01% of fat content
- BHT – Butylated hydroxytoluene, having a legal limit of 0.01 % of fat content BHA and BHT can be used in combination with a legal limit of 0.02% of fat content
- TBHQ – Tertiary butylhydroquinone, with a legal limit of 0.03 % of fat content

Rosemary extract shows remarkable antioxidant properties and has outperformed the above antioxidants and has no legal limit.

LIQUID PAPRIKA

Highly-concentrated paprika extract is used as a colouring agent with a legal limit of 0.1% of total meat block.

WINE (SHERRY WINE)

Wine products are used mainly for flavouring. They also help to increase shelf life due to decreasing pH levels. Recommended usage level for wine as an ingredient is 1 millilitre per kilogram of meat block and are added last.

Wine or Sherry
Credit: CPMCA Image Collection

Liquid paprika
Credit: Stuffers Supply Company

DISTILLED FLUIDS

Excessive use of distilled fluids could lower pH to an unwanted level, resulting in a sour taste, and taking away valuable pH bind ability, with the consequence of lower cooking yields and decreased profitability.

LEMON JUICE AND VARIOUS VINEGARS

Sour products like lemon juice or vinegars are used mainly for flavouring. They will work the same way as wine and distilled fluids in lowering pH levels so the same precaution should to be taken. Recommended usage level for any acidic ingredient is 1 millilitre per kilogram of meat block and added last.

Lemon juice powder

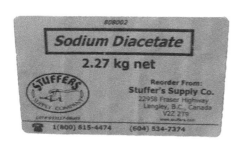

vinegars or Sodium diacetate a dry vinegar
Credit: Stuffers Supply Company

LIQUID SMOKE

Liquid smoke as a flavour agent is made from either caramelized smoked brown sugar, vegetable oil extract or as a product of natural smoke produced by the controlled pyrolysis of hickory, other hardwoods and mesquite.

Liquid smoke can be incorporated into the product or sprayed as a fine mist into the smoker to infuse a smoke flavour into meat products. Liquid smoke is available in water base (low pH) for use in curing, or oil base (high pH) for use in sausage meat and emulsions. It also gives companies that are not in possession of a smoker or smokehouse the opportunity of a simulated smoking procedure by adding the liquid smoke flavour in the cure or the sausage meat block recipe.

Our recommended usage level of this product is in the range of 1–4 grams per kilogram of product with the average being 2.5 grams or less per kilogram of product.

Liquid smoke

The most valuable sugars are the "multi sugars," which contain several different kinds of sugar and therefore have a much greater effect on pH of cured and fermented meat products. Dextrose sugars are a better nutrient source for lactobacteria used in the fabrication of fermented products. Single sugars like white and brown sugar are fine for use in fresh sausage and cured products, but not in fermented products. Syrups like corn syrup or maple syrup, honey and others can also be used as a sugar substitute in fresh and cooked sausage. However, honey poses risks of botulism contamination. Honey also solidifies when mixed with ice-crusted meats used in the fabrication of fresh and cooked sausage, making it harder to incorporate and blend into the product. If using honey as a sweetener it is best preheated and added to the meat block last so as to incorporate it thoroughly.

Sweeteners are not suitable for all products. Generally, sugars are used to improve flavour, take away the astringency (bitterness) of salt, enhance fermentation and improve the browning effect on meat products. Sweeteners used in combination with sodium ascorbate and curing salt containing sodium nitrite, stabilize the colour of cured products.

Usage levels of sugars are between 5–25 grams per kilo of meat.

Corn syrup solids are restricted to a limit of 2% (20g) per kilogram and corn syrup liquid is restricted to 2.5% (25g) per kilogram. Their usage can result in excessive charring of cured product that consumers fry, such as bacon.

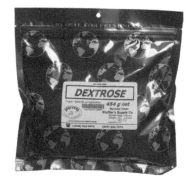

Corn syrup   Maple syrup   Honey   Dextrose

Credit: CPMCA image Collection

Credit: Stuffers Supply Company

HYDROLYZED VEGETABLE PLANT OR SOYA PROTEIN (HVP)

HVP proteins are flavour enhancers used in processed foods like soups, stews and meat products like hot dogs. HVP is produced by boiling foods such as corn, soy or wheat in hydrochloric acid and then neutralizing the solution with sodium hydroxide. The acid breaks down the protein in vegetables into their component amino acids. One of the components (amino acids) in the dark-coloured liquid that's left is glutamic acid (approximately 10% of it's total volume).

Liquid Attamate-Hydrolyzed vegetable plant protein (HVP)
Credit: UniPac Packaging Products Ltd

MSG

MSG, also known as sodium glutamate, is the sodium salt of glutamic acid, one of the most abundant naturally occurring non-essential amino acids found in tomatoes, cheese and other foods. MSG is used as a flavour enhancer that intensifies the meaty, savoury flavour of foods. MSG use in Canada is identified as an allergen and its use must be noted on all product labels.

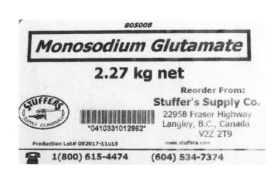

MSG
Credit: Stuffers Supply Company

Note: The afore-mentioned products are helpful in many ways; however, their use is regulated by law. All manufacturers' label instructions on such products must also comply with legal limit usage. Remember: the excessive use of one single ingredient will most likely result in a severe change of flavour and texture. Only a proportionate mixture of several items will keep products at a desired consistent taste and level of quality.

Casings and Molds (Forms)

Since meat product, as part of a recipe, is prepared with appropriate and well-selected raw meat ingredients, a balanced blend of spices and flavourings, the necessary non-meat items to achieve the product goal and the right sequence of production procedures and temperatures, there is one more task remaining: the right choice of casings.

There are four major groups of casings:

- Natural or intestine
- Collagen-based
- Synthetic fibrous
- Synthetic cellophane cellulose

When making a choice one cannot adopt an "I don't care" attitude regarding the use of casings. Casings hold the product making it presentable and by its nature suggest length of cooking and cooking style. Most recipes suggest casing usage, type, style and length of links as well as casing preparation. The handling and storage of casings can also be found on the product label or the manufacturer's specifications sheet. Make absolutely sure the right casing for the product is selected. Sometimes the same casing size comes with different modifications, such as colour, smoke adherence or varied cooking strengths, which make them suitable to specific products.

Before stuffing, take the necessary steps to prepare the casing, like presoaking, untangling and rinsing. By way of the recipe you'll need to inform yourself of processing steps, which in turn help decide how firm or soft the casing should be before and after stuffing. In the pages below, popular choices of casings and their particulars will be introduced.

NATURAL OR INTESTINAL

Natural or intestinal casings come from beef, pork or sheep intestines. They are edible, come in a variety of sizes (based on the animal) and are commonly used in the fabrication of a variety of sausage types. Natural casings have a distinct bite and give sausage the traditional curved appearance that customers like.

BEEF ROUNDS (MIDDLES)

Beef rounds come from beef intestine. Beef middles average 18 metres in length depending on the breed of cow. They are perfect for sausages that require a thicker, stronger natural casing, such as farmers sausage, liver and blood rings, kielbasa rings, Ukrainian rings, Lyoner rings and Bologna rings. They are edible but tough, and have excellent smoke ability. They are relatively inexpensive. They come bundled, salted and need to be refrigerated. They are to be used and treated like hog casings.

Beef rounds
Credit: Stuffers Supply Company

HOG CASINGS

Hog casings are pig intestines that are mechanically cleaned and sorted by machine. Intestinal casings known as "hog bungs" are in the range of one metre in length, while regular hog casings (the small intestine) range from 15-20 metres in length, depending on the breed of the animal. Hog bungs are used for traditional sausages such as soppressata, Calabrese or summer sausage salamis. Hog casings are commonly used on fresh, pre-cooked, smoked and/or cooked, semi-dry or dry-cured sausages. They have excellent edibility and they give the product a nice bite. These casings breathe, release moisture quickly, have excellent smoke ability and are still fairly inexpensive. They come in a variety of diameters, are bundled in 100-metre bundles or individual sleeves, packed in salt and refrigerated. Before using, bundles should be rinsed and presoaked overnight in cold water. When it is time to use the casings they will need to be rinsed again in lukewarm water. Before stuffing, some water should be run through the inside of the casing to make it slip on the stuffing horn easier and to locate possible holes (leaks). Leftover hog casings should be drained, salted carefully and kept refrigerated until further use to prevent spoilage and harmful bacteria growth, which could produce a dangerous toxin. Always remember these important safeguards, because stuffing meat into soured or rotten casings can result in an off-flavoured product or could create a food safety issue, a health hazard for customers.

Hog casings
Credit: Stuffers Supply Company

Hog casings on load sleeves
Credit: Stuffers Supply Company

SHEEP CASINGS

Sheep casings are processed from sheep intestine. The average harvest of sheep intestine ranges between 25-30 metres in length. They come tubed, sorted by diameter, with between eight and 12 pieces to each plastic vacuum-sealed bag. They are salted and need to be refrigerated. These are classic casings used for European wieners and pepperoni. They provide an excellent tender bite, have good smoke ability, appearance and colour. Disadvantages: they are costly, very labour intensive and easily breakable. Usage and storage procedures are identical to those for hog casings. Again, do not disregard the important safeguards for storage.

Sheep casings on load sleeves
Credit: Stuffers Supply Company

COLLAGEN CASINGS

Collagen casings are the most common casings used in the industry. They are made from an edible beef and pork hides, and bones and tendon collagen protein material. They are a popular choice when making snack sticks, fresh sausages such as bratwurst, breakfast and pork, as well as other fresh, smoked and/or cooked sausages. Collagen casings come in a large variety of diameters (13-35 mm) are edible and easily digestible.

There are two different kinds of collagen casings: one is for use with straight salt only (fresh sausage products), and the other is for use with curing salt (cured, smoked and/or cooked sausage products). Collagen casings come boxed (in caddies) from the factory with certain moisture content; moisture content should be maintained by replacing the original plastic cover seal over the box before storing it (the box should always be closed tight after using). The box also has a stuffing direction on it, which refers to the direction the casing is to be placed on the stuffing horn. Always make sure to stuff in that direction. Failing to do so makes the casing a lot harder to stuff (fill) and could result in breakage, which is costly and time consuming.

Usually the cost to produce sausages in collagen casings is significantly less than making sausages in natural intestinal casings due to ease of use during production. Collagen casings need less handling, no preparation and stuff quicker than natural intestinal casings, thus increasing production and lowering labour requirements.

Collagen casings should be kept dry and never soaked before using.

However, if hand linking, the casings will require a small amount of water sprayed on the surface to prevent drying and breakage.

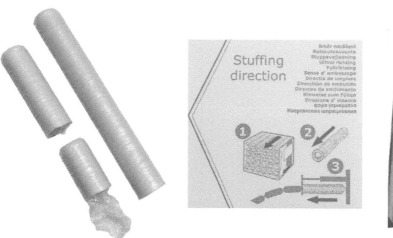

Collagen casing strands   Stuffing directions on Caddy   Collagen casings in Caddy

NATURIN CASINGS

These casings are used mainly in ring form for coil sausage, but are also available in chubs for smoked and cooked cold cuts and dry-cured salamis. They are collagen based, have good smoke adhesion and sold in edible and non-edible form. Naturin casings are tough and at times not easy to peel.

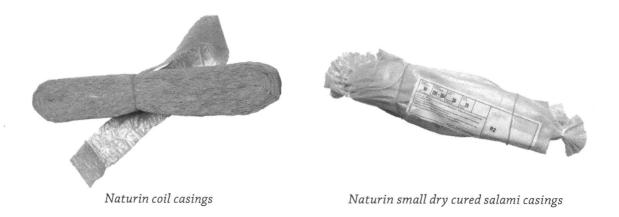

Naturin coil casings   Naturin small dry cured salami casings

Credit: Stuffers Supply Company

SYNTHETIC FIBROUS CASINGS

Synthetic fibrous casings have two categories: regular and moisture proof. They are made of a specially-processed paper and are coated with viscose, which means you can stuff them tight without worrying about breakage. Fibrous casings are the toughest casings produced and are used where maximum uniformity of the finished product diameter is desired. The uniformity these casings offer make them ideal for sliced luncheon meats destined for prepackaging. Fibrous casings come in a variety of colours and diameters, are pre-clipped, can have print and can come in straight or honeycomb shape.

Lyoner Sausage casing

REGULAR FIBROUS CASINGS

Regular fibrous casings can also be made with a mixture of vegetable and wood fibres, and/or proteins and/or gums. They are mainly used for salamis and particular smoked and/or cooked cold cuts. They can breathe and therefore allow the penetration of smoke flavour and release moisture easily. They are digestible but not necessarily edible. If you're going to use this type of casing it would be advised to inquire of your supplier best practices regarding types of products they could be used for, the pros and cons of the casing with cook and smoke applications, as well as handling and storage.

Synthetic fibrous casings

Regular fibrous casings (Brown with protein liner)

Summer sausage casing

Credit: Stuffers Supply Company

Regular fibrous casings (White -regular)

MOISTURE-PROOF FIBROUS CASINGS

Moisture-proof fibrous casings have the same ingredients as regular fibrous casings but with a plastic coating on the inside. This totally seals the product inside the casing, and after cooking keeps the product airtight. They are used for cooked deli meats and cold cuts that are not smoked as smoke does not adhere to nor penetrate this type of casing.

Moisture-Proof Fibrous Casings
Credit: Stuffers Supply Company

Note: After cooking a product in a moisture proof casing the sausage should be immediately cooled in a cold shower, **water slurry** or **slush tank** to an internal temperature of 15-20°C. Failing to cool the product properly may result in a splitting of the casing, destroying the appearance and product appeal; with the casing split the product will not be suitable for sale. After the recommended temperature has been reached, the product is to be kept refrigerated till sold.

SYNTHETIC CELLOPHANE CASINGS

Synthetic cellophane casings also have two categories: porous and moisture proof. Cellophane cellulose casings are multi-layer sausage casings produced on the same basis as cellulose film rolls. The casings are formed on special cylinder forms, the layers of which are joined together by food grade glue. They are also known or referred to as synthetic or artificial sausage casings.

CELLOPHANE POROUS CASINGS

Cellophane porous casings have limited smoke absorption and adherence and are not edible. They are mainly used for smoked pâtés.

CELLOPHANE MOISTURE-PROOF CASINGS

Cellophane moisture-proof casings are available clear and coloured and may also be marked with imprints. They are used for jellies (as with headcheese), blood sausage, ham products, roast beef and roast pork, etc. They have a high temperature cooking ability, they limit cooking losses, and they have excellent shelf life. They are not edible.

MOULDS (FORMS)

An alternative to the use of casings is cooking meat products in cooking containers, moulds or forms. This is probably a little bit less costly in the long run because these items are always reusable, although they do require cleaning and sanitizing after every use. Some moulds or forms need a paper or plastic liner so the product won't stick to the container. The use of a non-stick food-grade spray could also be used to avoid sticking.

Moulds and forms are mainly used in the production of pressed hams, corned beef, loaves, meat jellies and pâtés. Cooking losses will probably amount to the same level as with porous casings. The advantage of using moulds and forms are: to press items into a traditional shape and size, resulting in better slice-ability and even size of slices.

> **Note:** A clear disadvantage of using containers is that they must be cleaned thoroughly and sanitized after every use, making it labour intensive.

Aluminum & steel Moulds & forms
Credit: Jakes & Associates

NETTING OR NET TUBING

Netting is used extensively throughout the industry for both fresh and cured products. Roasts of beef, pork and lamb are commonly netted to keep and present them in a uniform shape. Cured, tumbled, and cooked meats such as turkey breasts, chicken breasts, and hams are also kept together by netting. These items are made of multiple parts squeezed and held together in a uniform shape by netting. Netting comes in a variety of diameters.

Netting or net tubing
Bunzl Processor Division/Koch Supplies

Advantages: Excellent smoke ability (netting and tubing). Very good peel-ability (tubing only). They create the possibility of forming one solid piece out of several small ones. These products provide for uniform shape and attractive appearance.

Disadvantages: Hard to peel and there is a danger of ripping or scaring the product thereby diminishing aesthetic appeal.

COLOURED STRING

Tying or clipping the ends of sausage casings and netted products is a common practice. The use of coloured string as a marker identifies the type of seasoning a particular product might have. For example, red string might be used to tie off the ends of sausage casings containing a spicy product; green string can represent a product containing a strong garlic flavour and white string for regular items such as liver sausage. Other colours are reserved for sausages made from specific species such as brown for moose sausage, purple for deer, and yellow for poultry sausage. Each establishment may designate a colour to a product.

Coloured string for tying larger casings
Credit: Stuffers Supply Company

Brines and Curing

Historical aspects of brines and curing involved the preservation of meat. Preservation of meat originally involved the adding of salt and the drying of meats. This process also added flavour, colour and tenderness. Some historical processed dry-cured products are still around today such as: prosciutto, Westphalia and Smithfield hams. Dry curing and the process used, take months to produce these hams.

Not all products are dry cured and with the modernization of the meat industry and in particular the processing portion, curing has become more efficient through development of faster processing methods and moister products and increasing yields. These methods and products have received widespread consumer acceptance.

Salometer
Bunzl Processor Division/Koch Supplies

Note: A salometer is a hydrometer for indicating the percentage of salt in a solution. Salometers are used to check the level of salt within brine or the density of the brine based on temperature of the solution. They are simply a glass or plastic hydrometer with a scale (0-100) that displays degrees of SAL (salt). They come with instructions on how to use them and a scale to correlate their readings. If the brine tests to be too weak, add salt, if the brine is too strong, add water.

There are five methods that can be used in the curing of meats: osmosis, stitch pumping, artery pumping, machine pumping, and dry curing, but first we'll talk about brines.

Brines are common to charcuterie. Brining is used to preserve or season meats as well as to flavour and tenderize them. For our purpose here, brining is the process of submerging product in a solution of salt, phosphate, nitrites, flavourings and water. Average water temperature for brine needs to be between -1° and 4°C.

Pickle brines are common to corned beef. Other brine recipes are formulated for hams, bacon, pastrami, pork hocks, jowls and even whole loins of pork, with each designed to produce a specific flavour profile, as well as a more moist and tender product.

Brines can be contained in food-grade buckets, pails, large wheeled containers or tubs and added to products in vacuum tumblers and sealed plastic or vacuum bags. Brines should be prepared in advance of using. They should be well blended, rested and checked to make sure the salt is at the correct level (using a salometer). Salt should be dissolved and evenly distributed, and then the brine refrigerated.

Products can also be injected with a brine solution so as to absorb the liquid, its flavourings and salt quicker, also resulting in a more flavourful, moist and tender product.

Brine solutions vary in their concentration of salt to water in the range of 3.5-25% salt; this is referred to as the "strength" of the brine. Brine strength differs from one product to another depending on the intended outcome. Brines designed for low salt products will have a lower percentage of salt-to-water solution (7% average), while regular brines used for bacon, hams and hocks etc., will have a 10-15% range of salt-to-water solution. Keep in mind that all brines have nitrite as an ingredient in the form of Prague powder 1 which contains 93.75% salt and 6.25% nitrites and this should be part of your calculation in the formulation of brine. Curing salts also have nitrite as an ingredient and its use needs to meet restricted ingredient limits (parts per million (ppm) calculation of which is covered in our topic of *Making a Brine*).

Note: All brines used for submerged product should ideally be used once and then discarded. There are those who, for economic reasons, use a brine solution more than once without realizing the solution could be seriously diluted of its salt, nitrites and flavourings from first use. This can potentially compromise the quality of products submerged on occasions of repeated use.

Curing is the combination of specific non-meat ingredients in or on meat and poultry items for: preservation, flavour, colour, tenderness and yield. Preservation is accomplished by adding nitrates, nitrites, salt and smoke, each providing properties that inhibit bacterial growth. Salts, nitrites and smoke that inhibit bacterial growth also contribute to flavour, colour, tenderness and yield.

Curing takes place when combined non-meat ingredients such as salts, all-purpose curing salts, and/or flavourings are either absorbed through osmosis, stitched (injected) into the product, artery pumped, machine pumped or rubbed onto the product.

The process of **osmosis** takes place when product is submerged in a curing brine solution (refer to *Brines* above). Osmosis is the diffusion of fluid (in this case brine) through a semi-permeable membrane, as with the wall of a living cell. This is a gradual process that takes place when you immerse meat items in a brine solution. The brine enters the meat cellular structure at a rate of two and a half centimeters per day at cooler temperatures of -2 to 4°C; providing the brine solution totally surrounds the item. This rate slows down with crowding of product (stacking products such as slabs of bacon) one on top of the other all in the same brine.

Injecting the product with brine (also referred to as **stitching**) is accomplished manually using a hand-held spray injection pump or an electric spray pump with single or multiple orifice needles. This action of spray pumping disperses the brine through the product. The curing process is accelerated in a more efficient manner through the pumping and manually controls the amount of brine the product should absorb. This method can be more profitable than using the osmosis method depending on the quality of the brine, the manual application of the brine, the quality of the meat and desired end product.

Used by large processors that harvest hogs, the most efficient method that distributes the brine uniformly and evenly throughout the product is **artery** pumping. Artery pumping is only used with the curing of pork legs (hams) while the legs are still warm after slaughter. The warm arterial system through which blood was carried has not yet collapsed or shrunk and becomes the pipeline for the brine, which cures the product. No part of the product is missed, not even the bone marrow as the brine travels through arteries to the remote capillaries and thereby evenly distributed throughout the ham.

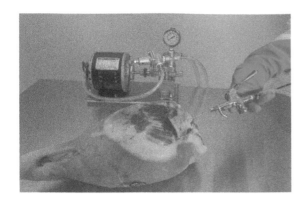

Stitch pumping a Pork leg (Ham)
Bunzl Processor Division/Koch Supplies

Auto brine pump pumping bacons
Credit: Professional image, industry approved

An automatic **machine pump** has a series of spring-loaded needles used to pump brine into meat items at high volumes. This machine uses multiple orifice needles to inject the brine by way of a pulsating pattern (up and down motion). An automatic brine injection machine is equipped with a conveyer belt, can be preprogrammed for speed and accuracy (thickness of product) that moves product through as a band of multiple orifice needles penetrate and inject precise quantities of brine.

Automatic brine pumping machine
Credit: ©istock.com / Credit IP Galanternik D.U.

Rubbing or **dry curing** is used to cure traditional hams and other products, mostly whole muscle items. It is also the most historical method in use. Dry curing involves rubbing a mixture of salt, cure and/or sugar and spices on the meat in a massaging manner. This application is repeated every two to four days for a period of forty days (approximately 10 to 20 times). Average salt rub per kilogram of product is in the range of 3-5% (30-50 g per kg).

> **Note:** All manual, electric and machine pump hoses and needles require a thorough hot water rinse up to 20 litres for smaller pumps and 40 litres for automatic pumping machines after each use to prevent salt buildup. Hoses and needle orifices are easily blocked or plugged with brine debris and salt. Precautions with filtering brines and rinsing equipment maintain proper function and even distribution of brine to product.

Tumbling

Vacuum tumblers assist in increasing meat yields by mechanically extracting salt-soluble proteins (actin and myosin). These extracted proteins coat the massaged muscle, acting as an adhesive that glue whole muscles together. In other words, the protein actin and myosin bind the massaged meat together. At the same time, using a tumbler accelerates the curing process by aiding brine dispersion through muscles by way of its massaging properties. It also improves uniformity of colour and texture of products.

Too much tumbling leads to excessive muscle destruction expanding the muscle surface to the extent that the binding properties (actin and myosin) can no longer coat the surface area. Too little tumbling results in poor protein extraction, poor colour development and poor dispersion of brine. The danger of poor brine dispersion leaves the product susceptible to bacterial growth or habitation (particularly botulism). Properly dispersed brine will spread the required bacterial inhibitors.

The tumbling of meats usually runs on a 3:1 ratio, meaning for every three hours of tumbling the product should rest for one hour. An example would be if we were to tumble whole muscle hams for a period of three hours, we would also need to rest those hams for one hour. People who use tumblers must be careful not to over tumble bone-in products because the tumbling action causes the bones to tear up the muscle, damaging the product.

Biro Table Top Vacuum Tumber-VTS42
Credit: Biro Model-VTS42 table top vacuum tumbler

Large commercial vacuum tumblers
Credit: Professional image, industry approved

Smoking and Cooking

Smoking is subjecting meat items, processed meat or other similar products like poultry to an environment of smoke for the purpose of adding flavour, colour and preservation. Smoke can be generated from hardwood, hardwood sawdust, corncobs and natural or artificial liquid. Smoke is transformed into a gaseous state by the application of direct heat. Smoke applications are either hot or cold, hot meaning at cooking temperatures to impart smoke and cooked flavours and colour, or cold at lower temperatures for the purpose of imparting flavour and colour only.

The factors that affect smoke deposition (smoke adhering to product) are:

- Smoke density
- Smokehouse air velocity (circulation)
- Smokehouse relative humidity
- State of product surface (type of casing, moisture content etc.)

The final internal temperature of smoked meats depends on the type of product being smoked (the desired or required internal temperature), the available functions of the smokehouse itself (whether programmable, automated, gravity fed or homemade) and the diameter of the product (whole muscle, casing or slices/patties as with jerky products). For the purpose of this text the following information about smoking refers to the use of a programmable smokehouse with functions such as, but not limited to: steaming, cooking, smoking, showering and chilling.

Hot smoking of whole muscle meats should be done at a maximum temperature of 90°C to avoid excess shrinkage. Sausage products in the range of 15-120 mm in diameter can be smoked and cooked at a lower temperature of 75°C to an internal temperature of 71°C with the exception of poultry products, which require an internal temperature of 75°C to combat the possible presence of salmonella.

Once cooked and chilled all charcuterie products should be stored at appropriate temperatures in the range of 0-2°C.

Cold smoking temperatures fluctuate and are generally less than 30°C and are strictly dependent on the end product. Cold smoking is done mainly to impart a smoke flavour and as a means of preserving the product without cooking it. Most dry-fermented items are cold smoked for these reasons.

Smoking and cooking are generally combined except when recipes call for other instructions like cold smoking verses liquid smoke or in the case of using pre- smoked casing, where steam cooking the finished item is all that would be required.

SMOKEHOUSE MANAGEMENT

The product quality and throughput of a smokehouse is determined by its loading capacity and function, how fast it can dry, smoke and cook. The basic working cycles of today's programmable smokehouses are: reddening and warming, drying, smoking, cooking and finishing, evacuation, and shower and cooling.

The cycles of reddening and warming, drying, smoking, and evacuation are timed cycles. The cycles of cooking and finishing, and cooling and chilling are temperature controlled. All cycles are based on size of load and density of product with the exception of the cooking and finishing cycle. The cooking and finishing cycle is dependent on product temperature (which will be probed). Let's have a quick look at each cycle.

Product ready to go into a smokehouse
Credit: NAIT Professional Meat Cutting &
Merchandising Program

Bank of commercial smokehouses -
cooked product exit doors
Credit: Professional image, Industry approved

Reddening and warming slowly warms the product to unify surface conditions before drying and smoking.

a) The smokehouse is loaded and the air velocity set to low with an open damper

b) Smokehouse temperature is set at 50°C with the length of time depending on volume, density, and/or casing of product

c) The combination of (a) and (b) begins the cured colour development, known as the reddening stage

Drying of product before smoking is important to smoke adherence and is affected by the amount of heat, humidity, air velocity, air exchange, product characteristics (outer surface; muscle meats or type of casing) and product density (thickness). A brief drying cycle helps the product form a coating of protein on the surface leaving it sticky to the touch. Once the tacky or sticky surface is achieved the product is ready for smoke.

a) Airflow is important to the drying cycle; this cycle has the dampers open, allowing product to dry

b) The temperature of this cycle should be set at 55°C

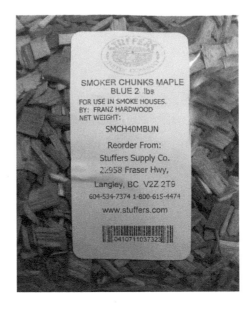

Smoking the product provides a layer of preservation. The amount of smoke that adheres to the surface of the product depends on the airflow and density of the smoke. The smoking cycle is used to develop product flavour and colour.

a) The dampers are closed

b) The temperature of this cycle should be set in the range of 60-65°C

A Maple wood chips
Credit: Stuffers Supply Company

c) Smoke is applied until the desired colour is obtained (a trial and error approach or by visual evaluation)

The main components of smoke are: phenols, organic acids and hydrocarbons. Phenols add flavour while organic acids make up the antibacterial agents (bacterial growth inhibitors). Hydrocarbons add colour to the product. Each component compliments the other and work together to produce the end result, flavour and preservation of product.

> **Note:** The smoke cycle can be repeated at different intervals with a drying and evacuation cycle set between them. The first cycle can be 15 minutes long set at a temperature of 60°C followed by a quick evacuation cycle (5 minutes) and a drying cycle (10 minutes). The next smoke cycle could be longer, 30 minutes with a temperature set at 65°C, followed by an evacuation cycle and another repeated 10 or 15 minute smoke cycle, etc. This pattern of smoking removes excess humidity, which provides an atmosphere for superior smoke adherence and absorption resulting in better colour and flavour.

Cooking and finishing is the transition period from raw and smoked to cooked and finished product. Cooking requires the application of heat and humidity at a temperature of 78°C. Finishing the product requires a set probe temperature of 70-75°C depending on the product. For example, beef, pork, lamb, and bison products have to have a finished internal temperature of 71°C and poultry products need to be 75°C.

a) Ready-to-eat products must reach an internal temperature of 71°C
b) Bacon and bone-in hams should have a minimum of 60°C internal temperature; anything higher results in greater weight loss

Evacuation is the cycle that clears the smoke and humidity out of the smoker preparing the internal atmosphere to match the external atmosphere and thereby avoids filling the building with residue smoke and humidity (steam) produced by the last cycle(s).

Shower and cooling is another cycle controlled by product temperature probe. This cycle should be set to an internal product temperature of 20°C, which will cool and chill the product significantly and enable it to be refrigerated.

Finished product showering & cooling
Credit: Professional image, Industry approved

Note: Cooling and chilling is important to the quality of the product as it helps to keep internal moisture and fats from escaping, producing a moist and flavourful end product. After the product is removed from the smoker it should be wheeled on its rack into the cooler to complete the chilling process.

Note: For further details on Bacterial growth & Safe Meat Handling see the thermometer guides, appendix pages 746-747.

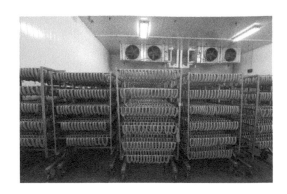

Cooked product going to cooler
Credit: Professional image, Industry approved

European weiners cooked and cooling
Credit: Professional image, Industry approved

Canadian Regulations and Nomenclature Requirements for Charcuterie Products

Requirements for processed meat products are governed by both the Meat Inspection Regulations, 1990 (MIR) and the Food and Drug Regulations (FDT). The operator must ensure, through the establishment's mandatory Prerequisite Programs and HACCP Plan (Control Programs) that these regulatory requirements are met.

Health Canada is responsible, under the Food and Drugs Act (FDA), for the establishment of policies and standards relating to the health, safety and nutritional quality of food sold in Canada.

The CFIA is responsible for the administration of food labelling policies related to misrepresentation and fraud in respect to food labelling, packaging and advertising and the general agri-food and fish labelling provisions respecting grade, quality and composition specified in the Meat Inspection Act (MIA) and the Fish Inspection Act (FIA). In addition, the CFIA has responsibility for the administration of the food-related provisions of the Consumer Packaging and Labelling Act (CPLA), including basic food label information, net quantity, metrication and bilingual labelling.

The CFIA is responsible for the enforcement of all of the above requirements.

Meat Inspection Regulations, 1990, states as follows:

9.(1) Subject to subsection (2) and section 121, no meat product shall be identified as edible unless

(c) the meat product (sausage or charcuterie product) must conform to the applicable standards prescribed by these Regulations and the Food and Drug Regulations

22.1 Every operator that prepares meat products must prepare them in accordance with the process control requirements specified in the Manual of Procedures

30.1 (1) Every operator of an establishment shall develop, implement and maintain

(a) the required prerequisite programs, HACCP plans and other control programs as set out in the Food Safety Enhancement Program (FSEP) Manual and the Manual of Procedures; and

(b) the procedures to ensure compliance with the performance requirements set out in the Manual of Procedures

57.2 Every operator shall carry out control programs in accordance with the FSEP Manual and the Manual of Procedures to ensure that

(c) the requirements of the Act and these Regulations are met in respect of the registered establishment, equipment, food animals, meat products, ingredients, food additives, chemical agents, packaging, and labelling materials, training and any other requirement of a control program set out in the FSEP Manual and the Manual of Procedures; and

(d) in all other respect, inspection programs or examination programs, as the case may be, are operated in accordance with the Act and these regulations.

As with other chapters of this book we try to provide an overview of regulations governing the specific topic. Here, with charcuterie products, the federal stance is rather rigid and not loose to interpretation by the average lay person. However, it is advisable to become acquainted with these acts and their regulations, investigating the do and don'ts of the craft as all territorial, provincial and municipal inspection offices are now in sync with the federal CFIA's Manual of Procedures and in particular Chapter 4 (*Meat Processing Controls and Procedures*), and Chapter 7 (*Packaging and Labelling*) regardless of whether or not you are a federally-registered establishment.

What the practitioner needs to understand is the essential obligation they have to document each process in the making of sausage, especially the hurdle strategy (see "Hurdle Technology" under the section *Making Fermented Sausage*) used in the production of charcuterie products, the use of restricted ingredients, thermo processing, temperature controls, and dates and times of each batch, etc. This must be done in the name of food safety, for potential recall purposes and ultimately for consumer protection.

Charcuterie Processing

The following supplies information, examples and procedures that all sausage making requires. The reading and understanding of this section goes a long way toward the successful application of the practices discussed in this chapter.

It is vitally important that the practitioner have a working knowledge of the information provided in this section which, when utilized fully, offers working examples as background to recipes and methods used in the formulation and processing of charcuterie items. We will cover:

- making a brine,
- pumping of product,
- calculating ppm of restricted ingredients,
- recipe formulation of both meat block and flavourings,
- batch fat calculation,
- the role of water activity,
- grinding of meats,
- mixing of ingredients,
- the making of emulsions, and
- a practical application of each of the five categories of sausage classification.

INTRODUCTION

Temperature during processing is a critical factor therefore it is necessary to watch for specifications in the recipe regarding temperatures. Exceeding the proper temperature will result in rendering the fat, thus creating an oily and mushy product. Insufficient heat will limit the coagulation of proteins resulting in lower cooking yields and decreased profits. In both cases the product is also less attractive, producing poor quality and sale-ability. Protein extraction occurs between -2 and 14°C with an optimum temperature of 7°C. This is crucial in extraction of myosin and actin the salt soluble proteins that bind fat and water.

Knowing that temperature plays an important role in the fabrication of quality products we now turn our focus to the practical aspects of charcuterie. Let us start with the basics.

We cannot over emphasize before starting any formulation, ensure that the right recipe is being used, and be aware of the desired batch size. Weigh all the ingredients, checking the scale for the right setting of necessary tares. Remember to use fresh or frozen quality meats, as the recipe requires. Should older meats (oxidized) or trimmings be used, make certain they are not smelly (sour) or totally discoloured and thus not safe for consumption (doubtful materials must be discarded).

Again, all trimmings or parts are assorted to recipe and grading specifications. Meat should be free of bone chips and other hard particles and not exceed limits of gristle or fat. Be sure to stock all the necessary ingredients; should an item be unavailable, try to determine whether it can be replaced by a substitute - never ever use unknown ingredients. When using premixed spice units, read the label specifications for quantities, limitations or needed additional ingredients (such as salts or nitrites). Remember, the intended outcome (final product) is determined by each step of processing. If poor quality ingredients (sour, old, discoloured meats or outdated premixed spices etc.) are put into sausage, what comes out is a poor-quality sausage.

MAKING A BRINE

Typical ingredient targets for a brine used to pump meat items or submerge them is 1.25-2% salt, 0.5–1.0 % for sugar, for phosphates 5,000 ppm or 0.5 %, for nitrites 120 ppm for bacon and 200 ppm or less for other cured meats (hams, for example) and for erythorbate (cure accelerators) 550 ppm. Below we have an example of how stitching (pump) percentages can be calculated for cured products.

Bacon Pump

First weigh all meat items (bellies) to be pumped.

Secondly, calculate the amount of water needed for the recipe (here we will use a 15% brine pump).

Take the weight of the meat item and use the following formula:

Kilogram of meat x 15% = "X" (X represents the amount of water needed).

For example: If you have 50 kilograms of meat, multiply that figure by 0.15 (50 x 0.15) = 7.5. So, using our example we would use 7.5 kilograms of water for 50 kilograms of product.

Typically there is need for an overrun of brine solution and in most cases this overrun is 25% of the total brine. To calculate this overrun use the following formula:

"X" x 25% = "Y" (Y represents the amount of overrun needed). Let's keep to the above example and use the figure of 7.5 kilograms of water: (7.5 x 0.25) = 1.875 kilograms of water for overrun.

Now we can add the water needed and the overrun to get the total amount of water content needed for our pump solution:

"X" + "Y" = kilograms of water. Again, keeping with the above example, we add 7.5 ("X") and 1.875 ("Y") for a total of 9.375 kilograms of water.

Once we have the amount of water we need for our pump solution, we also need the salt and spice content for flavour. Below we have a recipe commonly used in making brine solution. Knowing how to calculate the amount of water needed for a particular brine solution, we should also be able to adjust any brine flavour recipe to suit our needs. Below is an example of that based on the figures we used in our above examples for calculating the amount of water needed for a 15% pump solution for 50 kilograms of meat.

Note: Those using this method naturally vacuum tumble the product to accelerate the curing process thus saving time in the fabrication of the end product as with the case presented here, bacon.

Bacon Brine					
Product Weight:	50 kilograms			Kilograms of water: 9.375	
Recipe Ingredients	Amount		Water		Amount Needed
Salt	95.0 g	X	9.375	=	891.0 g
HVP	10.0 g	X	9.375	=	94.0 g
Liquid Smoke	20.5 g	X	9.375	=	192.0 g
Prague Powder 1	18.0 g	X	9.375	=	169.0 g
Dextrose	63.0 g	X	9.375	=	591.0 g
Maple Seasoning	06.0 g	X	9.375	=	56.0 g
Sodium Erythorbate	05.0 g	X	9.375	=	47.0 g
Phosphate	22.0 g	X	9.375	=	206.0 g
Total	Ingredients		=		2.246 kg
Water + Ingredients =	Total Brine		=		11.621 kg

Take the amount of water and mix the recipe ingredients with it in a container. Stir water until ingredients are dissolved (blend thoroughly). Using a weigh scale to measure percentage pump, stitch the solution into meat product until percentage weight is gained, For example: if a meat item weighs 10 kilograms, the stitched item should weigh 11.5 kilograms.

PARTS PER MILLION (PPM)

PPM is an expression that means 1 part of one million parts. It can be expressed mathematically in any of the following ways:

- 0.000001
- 0.0001% or
- 1 gram per 1,000 kilograms

Therefore 200 ppm can also be expressed in the following ways:

- 0.000200
- 0.0200%
- 200 grams per 1,000 kilograms
- 20 grams per 100 kilograms or
- 2 grams per 10 kilograms
- 0.2 grams per kilogram
- 200 milligrams per kilogram (or equal to 200 ppm)

RESTRICTED INGREDIENT CALCULATION

PPM Formula for Percentage Pump of Brine Solutions:

Parts Per Million = ((Restricted Ingredients x the percentage pump gain) / by total weight of brine) / by total weight of product including pump gain.

Once again, let's use the above recipe example with the restricted ingredients of nitrite, sodium erythorbate and phosphate.

Weight of product is 50 kilograms with an addition of 15% pump representing 7.5 kilograms (50 x 15%). New total weight of product after 15% pump is 50 + 7.5 gain equals 57.5 kilograms of product. The total weight of our brine including ingredients is 11.621 kilograms.

PPM Calculation

Nitrite is 6.26% of the total amount of Prague powder used in the recipe: 18 x 9.375 = 169 grams of Prague powder. Calculation of restricted ingredient is as follows:

a) 169 x 6.25% = 10.5 g of nitrite
b) (10.5 x 7.5) ÷ 11.621 = 6.8
c) 6.8 ÷ 57.5 = 0.118 g/kg
d) 0.118 g/kg = 118 mg/kg or 118 ppm

Our nitrite is within the restricted limits of 120 ppm for bacon at a 15% pump.

Sodium erythorbate is set at 5 grams per kilogram of water: 5 x 9.375 = 47 g

Erythorbate = 47 g x 7.5 (results of 15% pump solution) divided by 11.621 kg total brine solution = grams per kilogram, also represented by milligrams per kilogram = ppm of erythorbate in our product. Calculation of this restricted ingredient is as follows:

a) (47 x 7.5) ÷ 11.621 = 30.333
b) 30.333 ÷ 57.5 = 0.528 g/kg (or 528 mg/kg)
c) 528 mg/kg = 528 ppm

Our sodium erythorbate is within the restricted limit of 550 ppm at a 15% pump.

Phosphate usage is 22 grams per kilogram of water giving us an equation that looks like this: 22 x 9.375 = 206.25 grams of phosphate needed for the recipe.

Phosphate = 206.25 grams x 7.5 (results of 15% pump solution) divided by 11.621 total brine solution = grams per kilogram, also represented by milligrams per kilogram = ppm of phosphate in product.

a) (206.25 x 7.5) ÷ 11.621 = 133.11 g/kg
b) 133.11 ÷ 57.5 = 2.314 g/kg
   (or 2,314 mg/kg)
c) 2,314 mg/kg = 2,314 ppm

Our phosphate is well within the restricted limits of 5,000 ppm at a 15% pump.

BRINE SOAKING

There are those who rather soak meat items, like fresh hams and side pork for processing, and there are those who pump and soak them with a brine solution. To calculate the ppm of restricted ingredients for soaked, and for pumped and soaked items, you would have to record the known amount of water used for the brine and product weight before soaking. The product needs to be tracked and the soaked weight of it recorded. The difference between the soaked product weight and start weight provides us with the percentage brine solution absorbed.

The calculation is: subtract the original start weight from the soaked weight and divide the difference by the original weight, multiplied by 100. Once you know the percentage of brine solution absorbed you can calculate the ppm of restricted ingredients using the Restricted Ingredient Formula. Example:

Soaked weight of product = 54.5 kg
Start weight of product = 50.0 kg
Difference is gain = 4.5 kg

Percentage brine solution calculation
(4.5 ÷ 50.0) x 100 = 9% (pump)

Note: If not vacuum tumbling the product, regardless whether you cure meats via pumping or soaking in brine, you will need to ensure your product is totally submerged preventing drying or crusting of items exposed to circulating air. In addition to making a brine solution that covers pumping, you will need to make enough brine to cover the product until it is ready for smoking and cooking.

MIXING THE BRINE INGREDIENTS

There is a correct order of dissolving ingredients in what we call complex brines, those brines having more than just salt and cure. When adding ingredients to a brine such as phosphate or HVP there is an order to dissolving these ingredients into the required volume of water. Using our example bacon brine, the following sequence is commonly recommended for the successful preparation of this type of brine.

- Start with cold water (in the range of -1 to 4°C)
- Add phosphates first, stir and dissolve as they are less soluble than the other ingredients
- Add plant proteins (HVP and liquid smoke), stir and dissolve
- Add cure and salt (Prague powder), stir and dissolve
- Add sugars (dextrose and maple seasoning), stir and dissolve
- Add cure accelerators (erythorbate), stir and dissolve

Brine barrel and pumping machine
Credit: Bunzl Processor Division/Koch Supplies

Sausage Recipe Calculations

Recipe calculation is a process that enables one to formulate spice-to-meat ratios regardless of quantity of meat block. The following example outlines the grams per kilogram format used to determine a consistent end product and desired outcome concerning flavour and appearance.

To calculate this formulation simply take the chosen batch weight figure (20 kilograms batch size in our example) and multiply it by the percentage of identified sorted trimmings (80/20, etc.) of meat species (beef, pork or fat, etc.).

Example: Calculation used to formulate the following recipe at 20 kg of meat

MENNONITE SAUSAGE:

Total Meat Block	% Of Meat Block Formula	Totals Used
20 kg x	42.5% 80/20 Beef	= **8.5** kg 80/20 Beef
20 kg x	42.5% 80/20 Pork	= **8.5** kg 80/20 Pork
20 kg x	10% Pork Fat	= **2** kg Pork Fat
20 kg x	5% Ice	= **1** kg Ice

To calculate the amount of each spice for this recipe, simply multiply the meat weight (20 kg in our example) by the ingredient weight (18.0 g of salt as per our example).

SPICES (GRAMS PER KG OF MEAT)

Meat Block	Grams per Kilo Formula	Totals Used
20 kg x	18.0 g Sea Salt	= 400 grams
20 kg x	04.0 g Coarse Pepper	= 080 grams
20 kg x	00.5 g Liquid Smoke	= 010 grams
20 kg x	30.0 g Maggie	= 600 grams
20 kg x	00.5 g Sodium Ascorbate	= 010 grams
20 kg x	02.5 g Prague Powder 1	= 050 grams

FAT CALCULATION

Weight	Product	Ratio	Fat % Calculation	Net kg
08.5 kg	Beef Trim	80/20	8.5 kg x 20%	1.7 kg
08.5 kg	Pork Trim	80/20	8.5 kg x 20%	1.7 kg
02 kg	Pork fat	100	2 kg x 100%	2.0 kg
01 kg	Ice			0.0 kg
20 kg	**Totals**			**5.4 kg**

Using the above information of our 20-kilogram meat block (referred to as green weight) of Mennonite sausage, we can calculate the percentage of fat and lean of this product. Percentage of fat equals 5.4 kg divided by 20 kg (total meat block) multiplied by 100, and the percentage of lean is the sum of 100 minus the percentage of fat.

FAT AND LEAN PERCENTAGE FORMULATION:

a) (5.4 ÷ 20) x 100 = 27 % fat

b) 100 − 27 = 73 % lean

There is a need to control the amount of fat in a meat block because it can either dry your product or make it too greasy if you add too much. Fat helps profitability but endangers quality. The recommendation for fat content in sausage and deli meats is 30% (with the legal limit set at 40%) at the high end with 10% the absolute lowest. The average for fat content is in the range of 25–35% depending on the product and the process used.

While the calculation is not infallible, it does offer a more reliable guide to maintaining a reasonable percentage of fat. The formulas are intended to be a solid substitute for guesswork.

Ingredients of a Meat Block

- Moisture
- Fat
- Protein
- Collagen

Important to any formulation of meat block is the type of product desired versus the actual raw product used to obtain the intended outcome, the edible sausage. Example, if the desired outcome were Mennonite sausage, one would not use raw product high in collagen (like shank meat).

A certain amount of collagen is going to be found in any meat block. To control those amounts is vital to the quality of product with a recommended maximum use of 35% of the total meat block. Thermo processing is vital to the end product as overheating products high in collagen produces gelatin caps (pockets of gelatin within the product). If you are to use meats high in collagen (like meat from the shank) you need to determine which types of charcuterie items best suit that particular assortment of meat.

WATER ACTIVITY

Water activity (aw) of a food is the ratio between the vapour pressure of the food itself, when in a completely undisturbed balance with the surrounding air media, and the vapour pressure of distilled water under identical conditions. A water activity of 0.91 means the vapour pressure is 91% of that of pure water.

The water activity increases with temperature, thus the importance of keeping perishable items under refrigeration.

Most foods have a water activity above 0.95, which provides sufficient moisture to support microbial activity. The amount of available moisture in charcuterie items can be reduced to a level that inhibits harmful microbial action. If the water activity of food is controlled to 0.85 or less in the finished product, it is not considered to be subject to regulations governing refrigeration as with some fermented items that are deemed shelf stable.

With respect to sausage and in particular fermented meats, aw levels are an important measuring tool that indicate whether or not a product can support or inhibit microbial activity and in particular, *Clostridium botulinum* (botulism). Botulism will not grow in a product if it has a pH of 4.8 or less, or a water activity level of 0.91 or less, which helps determine the quality of the product with respect to microbial support. The higher water activity is in a product, the more likely the product will support microbial action. Bacteria usually require at least 0.91 level of aw and fungi at least 0.71.

The values of pH and aw below which the common bacteria to sausage will not grow are as follows:

Bacteria	pH	aw
Bacillus	4.3	0.91
Campylobacter	4.9	0.91
Clostridium Botulinum	4.8	0.91
E.Coli	4.4	0.91
Listeria	4.4	0.91
Salmonella	3.8	0.91
Shigella	4.0	0.91
Staphylococcus aureus	4.2	0.85

GRINDING OF MEATS

As we can't state enough, temperature plays an important role in the fabrication of sausage. The lower the temperature the better the particle definition will be. When grinding the meat block of a recipe the product should be chilled and crusted with a temperature in the range of -4 to 0°C. Low temperatures avoids fat smearing and provides good particle definition.

Fat smearing or smearing occurs whenever friction-heated mechanical parts such as grinder blades and plates, augers, mixing arms, etc., encounter fat particles that are not cold enough to maintain their particle consistency. The heat produced by the action of the equipment alters the fat, breaking it down and smearing it on the equipment or casing used to hold the product.

First, coarse grind the meat block using an 8 to 25 mm-size plate (depending on desired definition for mixing) to initially break the crusted meat for a uniform distribution of fat. Second, regrind using a plate size that best reflects the desired texture of the finished product (coarse for a fatter product or fine for a leaner product). If using a mixer/grinder, avoid over mixing as it leads to fat smearing and excessive extraction of salt soluble proteins; conditions that interfere with the drying process of fermented sausages.

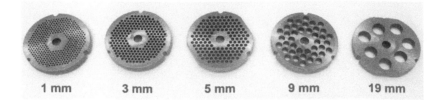

Grinder plate sizes
NAIT Professional Meat Cutting & Merchandising Program

Note: Rework materials (leftovers from former seasoned and mixed batches) can be used in the fabrication of sausage but must comply with regulations governing their use. For more on this see the CFIA website inspection.gc.ca in their Manual of Procedures, Chapter 4, "Meat Processing Controls and Procedures" (4.2.4).

MIXING OF MEAT BLOCK AND SEASONINGS

The mixing of meats after they have been ground to a specific particle definition is critical to the end product. Evenly mixed seasoning, salts, cures and other required ingredients make for a consistent quality throughout the product, from its first link or slice to its last. The meat needs to be cold (chill-crusted), ground and mixed with all ingredients evenly. This is best accomplished with mechanical devices designed to carry out this function effectively. Some establishments use bowl cutters (silent cutters), others large capacity mixers (from 25 to 100 kg batches and larger) or with the use of a mixer-grinder combination, and others by hand.

The problem with mixing sausage ingredients and spices by hand is you don't get an even distribution of spice and meat mixture. Mechanical equipment does a better job of dispersing the seasonings and meat mixture evenly, producing a more consistent end product.

The order of mixing non-meat ingredients with meats is just as important as the mixing process. The following is the recommended order for mixing non-meat ingredients to a ground meat block recipe, whether in a bowl cutter, grinder/mixer or by hand:

- Blend the salt with colour stabilizer (cures or sodium ascorbate, if required); keep separate
- Blend spices (dry seasonings) and keep separate
- Blend liquid flavourings (HVP or syrups) with the required called for amount of water
- Add chill-crusted ground meat block to the mixer; mix for 30 seconds
- Add 75% of salt and mix for 30 seconds

- Add 75% of the seasonings and mix for 30 seconds
- Add remainder of salt and seasonings, mix for 30 seconds
- Add the liquid and mix for 2 minutes
- Remove mixture and place in stuffer for stuffing, or in forms if making loaves

Note: If using premixed spice units, follow the directions on the label.

SAUSAGE EMULSIONS

The definition of a meat emulsion is: "A finely chopped batter composed of lean meat and water, in which small particles of fat are held in suspension by protein extraction."

This is created by mixing the two ingredients, lean meat and water, in a bowl cutter (silent cutter) to make a solid.

Emulsion in a cutter
Credit: Professional image, Industry approved

The optimum temperature range for the extraction of salt soluble proteins (actin and myosin) from the lean meat is between 7-10°C. Any temperature exceeding 14°C starts to extract collagen proteins, that runs the risk of product failure due to gelatin build up causing gelatin pockets in the finished product. The quick action of the blades and the rotation of the bowl heat the meat as it is being chopped. Keeping track of temperature fluctuation caused by this process is vitally important to the outcome of the finished product.

Four factors that effect the production of a stable emulsion in relation to time are:
- the amount of salt,
- the temperature of the meat,
- the mechanical aides used, and
- the degree of protein extraction desired.

Five factors that affect the development of an emulsion are:
- protein,
- fat,
- water,
- temperature and
- the amount of agitation (bowl rotation and the speed of the blades).

EMULSION DEVELOPMENT

The protein myosin is the primary muscle protein that suspends water and emulsified fat. The other is a salt soluble protein called actin. Salt is added to emulsions to release the myosin from the muscle fibre so the protein can encapsulate the fat and trap the water.

European sausage makers know that different components of a meat block (beef, pork, fat, skin, etc.) used in the fabrication of sausage exhibit distinct water holding capacities. Lean meat can hold more water than fat. Other meats, like that of pork snouts and organ meat such as heart, tripe and pork tongue, all have poor water-holding properties. The red meat of pork exhibits good water-holding properties, but the lean red meat of beef has the best water-holding properties.

Emulsified sausages are cooked sausages that have been finely comminuted to the consistency of a fine paste. Hot dogs, frankfurters, bologna, liver sausage and pâtés are typical examples. In most cases they are cured, smoked and/or cooked with moist heat (steamed or in hot water).

Combining various meats and/or poultry and additives is an important step in sausage making. In sausage preparation, the protein in the meat and/or poultry and added water are combined (through chopping or blending) to form a matrix that encapsulates fat, thus forming the emulsion.

There are two methods used in the making of emulsions: the shock method and the buildup method.

The Shock Method is used in the making of soft, spreadable deli meats such as liver sausage and pâtés. The shock method uses the following steps:

- Chop the chill-crusted fine pre-ground (5mm plate) lean meat in the bowl cutter, starting at low speed while adding 75% of the salt and cure of the meat block recipe for 30 seconds, gradually increasing speed to medium rotation; add 90% of the recipe's ice
- Chop in bowl cutter until temperature reaches 2°C and remove from cutter
- Chop the chill-crusted fine pre-ground (5mm plate) fat and 25% salt and cure for 30 seconds in bowl cutter; add the remainder of ice and chop to 14°C
- Add the chopped lean and seasonings; chop to 12°C.

The Buildup Method is used in the making of firmer cooked and/or smoked products like wieners and loaves. The buildup method uses the following steps:

- Starting at low speed chop the chill-crusted fine pre-ground (5mm plate) lean meat, salt in the bowl cutter, and cure for a few rounds for mixing purposes
- Add 50% of the ice, chop to 4°C (can reach 7°C if meat is extra lean)
- Add seasonings and fat; chop for 30 seconds
- Add balance of ice and chop at high speed to 12°C.

EMULSION DEFECTS IN FINISHED PRODUCTS:

- Fatting out fat caps (too much fat in the meat block)
- Gelatine pockets (too much collagen)
- Smearing (chopped at too high of a temperature)
- Separation of fat or fat on surface of product, caused by too much collagen extraction and overworking the emulsion

Note: For further details on Bacterial growth & Safe Meat Handling see the thermometer guides, appendix pages 746-747.

Recipes

Here we concentrate and provide a recipe for the making of fresh sausages complete with ingredients and procedure instructions. At the end of this chapter you will find other sausage and charcuterie recipes.

> **Note:** Whenever we refer to meat as "crusted" or "chill-crusted" we're referring to meat that has been slightly frozen but is still pliable, a meat grinder should be able to handle the grinding of the product with little difficulty. The important thing to remember is keeping the temperature low during initial fabrication of fresh sausage for food safety reasons and product quality.

Fresh Sausage Classification

PORK BREAKFAST SAUSAGE

This sausage is made with 70/30 pork trim. It is a mild sausage with great flavour and universal appeal. The salt usage varies with this item ranging between 16 and 20 grams per kilogram of meat block. Below we recommend 18 grams per kilogram of salt.

Determine the size of your meat block, which is the amount you want to make in kilograms. Ex: using a total of 5,10,15, 20 or 25 kilograms of meat; in this case all pork.

Pork breakfast sausage
Credit: Credit: Costco

Size of Meat block	% Of Meat Block Formula	Amount required
? kg x	100% 70/30 pork	= **?** kg of 70/30 pork
	Total Meat Block	**= ? kg**

Verify fat usage with a fat calculation and include the weight of your ingredients as part of the meat block total weight when doing so.

NON-MEAT INGREDIENTS:

Meat Block	Grams per Kilo Formula for Ingredients	Total Required
? kg x	18 g Sea Salt	= ? grams
? kg x	2 g Black Pepper	= ? grams
? kg x	2 g White Pepper	= ? grams
? kg x	2 g Ground Coriander	= ? grams
? kg x	3 g Onion Powder	= ? grams
? kg x	0.5 g Ground Sage	= ? grams
? kg x	1 g Marjoram	= ? grams
? kg x	150 g Crushed or Flaked Ice	= ? grams
	1 Raw Egg per kg of Meat Block	
	Total Weight of Ingredients =	

Procedure

- Crust the meat block in the freezer cutting it into 15 cm lengths with an approximate 2.5 cm square diameter
- Keep the salt in a separate bowl
- Combine the seasonings in a separate bowl
- Shell the eggs and blend lightly in a separate bowl
- Grind the meat block through 8 mm plate and place into mixer; mix for 30 seconds

- Add 75% of the salt; mix for 30 seconds
- Add 75% of the combined seasonings to the meat block and mix for 30 seconds
- Add the ice and mix for 30 seconds and the remaining salt mixture; mix for 30 seconds
- Add the remaining seasonings and eggs; mix for 60 seconds;
- Regrind the mixture through 5 mm plate
- Let mixture rest in fridge for 10 minutes
- Cook in frying pan a small patty to test the consistency and flavour distribution.
- Adjust seasoning if necessary, remix and rest for 5 minutes
- Put mixture into stuffer and stuff into 20–22 mm casing (sheep or artificial) using appropriate size stuffing horn
- Link and or cut into desired lengths
- Package and keep refrigerated (sell or cook and eat).

Cured Cooked Deli Meats Classification

With cooked deli meats it's important to remember that this category classification deals mostly with cure, a restricted non-meat ingredient. The calculation can be one of two methods depending on whether you use an all-purpose cure, in which case you would simply follow the label instructions, or use Prague powder 1.

Restricted ingredient calculation for green weight of meat block using an all-purpose cure is as follows:

Refer to the all-purpose cure label for percentage of nitrites and follow the instructions (see Appendix: *Data Sheet* for an example):

- Amount of cure required for the recipe x percentage of nitrite (as per label) = amount of nitrite usage.
- Amount of nitrite x 1,000,000 = parts in million of nitrite
- Divided by green weight of meat block in grams = ppm of meat block

Using an example of 20 kilograms of meat block and a percentage of 0.91 nitrite content in the all-purpose cure our calculation will be as follows:

a) 20 kg x 20 g of all-purpose cure = 400 g
b) 400 g x 0.91% nitrite in all-purpose cure = 3.64 g nitrite
c) 3.64 x 1,000,000 = 3,60,000 parts in million of nitrite
d) 3,640,000 ÷ 20,000 g (green weight of meat block in grams) = 182 ppm

If using Prague powder 1 as cure for our recipe the restricted ingredient calculation is as follows:

- Amount of Prague powder (2.5 g/kg) x 6.25% of nitrite = amount of nitrite usage
- Amount of nitrite x 1,000,000 = parts in million of nitrite
- Divided by green weight of meat block in grams = ppm of meat block

Using our example of 20 kilograms of meat block and a percentage of 6.25 nitrite content in Prague powder our calculation will be as follows:

a) 2.5 g x 20 kg = 50 g of Prague powder
b) 50 g x 6.25% nitrite content = 3.125 g nitrite
c) 3.125 g x 1,000,000 = 3,125,000 ppm of nitrite
d) 3,125,000 ÷ 20,000 g (green weight of meat block in grams) = 156.25 ppm

Both calculations demonstrate ppm of nitrite using different products for curing. Both product usage amounts are well within the restricted ingredient limits of 200 ppm.

> **Note:** The use of Prague powder 1 more accurately hits the target most European masters objectively obtain in their production of smoked cooked sausage and deli meats (156 ppm).

BAVARIAN MEAT LOAF

This recipe has great utility as you can make a variety of products using it as a base. If a finer product is desired, then chop the entire meat block to the same consistency in a bowl cutter or food processor. If looking for a mushroom loaf, simply add steamed (or canned) mushroom slices into the mixture just before panning into loaves. The same goes for mac and cheese loaves, where you will need to dice the cheese and precook the pasta, and again, mix the two into the batch just before panning the product. This also goes for pickle and pimento loaf.

Deli loaves are traditionally made with a bowl cutter starting with an emulsion, but can also be made with a food processor in smaller batches. In addition, these loaves can be made with the use of a grinder and mixer where the meat block should be ground in stages from coarse to fine using different size grinder plates, mixing in the ingredients as you proceed from one plate to the next.

Bavarian meat loaf
©istock.com / Credit: to sinankocaslan

Size of Meat block	% Of Meat Block Formula	Amount required
? kg x	15% 80/20 Lean Beef	= **?** kg of 80/20 Beef
? kg x	30% 80/20 Pork Shoulder	= **?** kg of 80/20 Pork
? kg x	15% Pork Jowl (no glands)	= **?** kg Jowl Meat
? kg x	25% Pork Belly	= **?** kg Belly Meat
? kg x	15% Flaked or Crushed Ice	= **?** kg Ice
Total Meat Block		= **? kg**

Meat Block	Grams per Kilo Formula for Ingredients	Total Required
? kg x	16 g Sea Salt	= ? grams
? kg x	2.5 g Prague Powder 1	= ? grams
? kg x	3 g Erythorbate	= ? grams
? kg x	1 g Dextrose	= ? grams
? kg x	2 g White Pepper	= ? grams
? kg x	0.5 g Ground Mace	= ? grams
? kg x	5 g Onion Powder	= ? grams
? kg x	0.5 g Coriander	= ? grams
? kg x	0.5 g Thyme	= ? grams
? kg x	0.5 g Ginger	= ? grams
? kg x	1 g Smoked Paprika	= ? grams
Total Weight of Ingredients =		

Procedure

- Crust the meat block in the freezer cutting it into 15 cm lengths with an approximate 2.5 cm square diameter, keeping each separate (beef, pork shoulder, pork jowl/belly)
- Combine the salt, Prague powder and erythorbate in a separate bowl
- Combine the seasonings in a separate bowl
- Grind each part of the meat block separately through 8 mm plate and regrind through 5 mm plate (keeping parts separate)
- Chop the lean beef meat first, adding the jowl and belly meat in stages using the **buildup** method (here the belly meat replaces the fat); chop to 12°C
- Mix the pork shoulder meat in thoroughly (or remove the meat from the cutting bowl and mix in the pork shoulder meat), keeping the 5 mm texture.
- Place mixture into loaf pans (size is optional)
- Let rest in fridge for 20 minutes (with option to freeze and cook when required)
- Cook loaves to an internal temperature of 71°C; cool and refrigerate overnight
- Remove from loaf pans and keep refrigerated.

This product can be sliced for luncheon meat, reheated as a warm entrée, or served warm.

Cured Smoked and Cooked Sausages and Meats

HAM RINGS

Ringed sausage is always a favourite. The size and weight of ring depends largely on the size of casing used and the amount of meat stuffed into the casing; this is where the skill of the person using the stuffer comes into play. Too much meat stuffed too tightly causes the rings to burst during the cook cycle while too little makes the product look gangly. The average ring weighs approximately 375 – 400 grams green weight with a finished weight in the range of 350 – 375 grams.

Ham rings
Credit: CPMCA image collection

Size of Meat Block	% Of Meat Block Formula	Amount Required
? kg x	50% 90/10 X-Lean Pork Leg	= **?** kg of Lean Pork Leg
? kg x	30% 70/30 Pork Shoulder	= **?** kg Pork Shoulder
? kg x	05% Pork Belly	= **?** kg Belly Meat
? kg x	15% Flaked or Crushed Ice	= **?** kg Ice
Total Meat Block		**= ? kg**

Meat Block	Grams per Kilo Formula for Ingredients	Total Required
? kg x	18 g Sea Salt	= ? grams
? kg x	2.5 g Prague Powder 1	= ? grams
? kg x	3 g Ascorbate or erythorbate	= ? grams
? kg x	1 g Dextrose	= ? grams
? kg x	2 g White Pepper	= ? grams
? kg x	1.5 g Cracked Black Pepper	= ? grams
? kg x	0.5 g Nutmeg	= ? grams
? kg x	3 g Onion Powder	= ? grams
? kg x	2 g Coriander	= ? grams
? kg x	0.25 g Cardamom	= ? grams
? kg x	5 g Granulated Garlic	= ? grams
Total Weight of Ingredients =		

Procedure

- Crust the meat block in the freezer cutting it into 15 cm lengths with an approximate 2.5 cm square diameter, keeping the leg meat separate
- Combine the salt, Prague powder and erythorbate in a separate bowl
- Combine the seasonings in a separate bowl
- Grind leg meat once through 25 mm coarse plate and place in mixer
- Grind the shoulder meat twice in 8 mm plate and add to mixer
- Grind the belly meat twice in 1–3 mm plate and add to mixer
- Add 75% of the salt and ascorbate mixture; mix for 30 seconds
- Add 75% of the combined seasonings to the meat block and mix for 30 seconds

- Add the ice and mix for 30 seconds and the remaining salt mixture; mix for 30 seconds
- Add the remaining spices and mix for 30 seconds
- Let mixture rest in fridge for 10 minutes
- Cook in frying pan a small patty to test the consistency and flavour distribution.
- Adjust seasoning if necessary (salt), remix, and rest for 5 minutes
- Put mixture into stuffer and stuff into 29-32 mm casing (hog or artificial) using appropriate size stuffing horn
- Cut into desired lengths for rings (usually 35-45 cm lengths)
- Space rings on smoke sticks, keeping them from touching each other
- Place sticks of rings on smoke rack and rinse them off with cold water
- Let rest 10 minutes
- Place product into smoker
- Smokehouse program as follows for 50 kilogram or more batch size
  - Reddening and warming at 50°C for 15 minutes
  - Drying at 55°C for 15 minutes
  - Smoking at 60°C for 15 minutes
  - Evacuation at 60°C for 5 minutes
  - Drying at 60°C for 10 minutes
  - Smoking at 65°C for 30 minutes
  - Evacuation at 65°C for 5 minutes
  - Drying at 65°C for 10 minutes
  - Smoking at 65 °C for 15 minutes
  - Evacuation at 65°C for 5 minutes
  - Drying at 60°C for 10 minutes
  - Cooking to an internal temperature of 71°C
  - Chilling and showering to an internal temperature of 20°C
- Move rack into refrigeration and cool till internal temperature is 2°C
- Remove product from rack and sticks; vacuum package and keep refrigerated.

Uncooked Cured and Smoked Sausage Classification

METTWURST (FINE)

This sausage is a European favourite. Made mostly from pork, it is cured and slowly smoked. It is a sausage spread with a smooth delicate texture and vibrant tangy flavour.

The meat for this product needs to be well trimmed of all glands and gristle, and free of bone chips and visible collagen. The meat is then cut into strips, frozen, coarsely ground and reground for good definition. The product is normally processed in a bowl cutter but can be made with a meat grinder equipped with a 1 mm fine plate or a food processor. The main concern with using a grinder or food processor is temperature and final texture. The meat should never exceed a temperature of 12°C near the end of the process (stuffed and hung on smoke sticks).

Mettwurst is traditionally stuffed into 40-45 mm beef middles, tied carefully, cold smoked and refrigerated. For cutter and grinding procedures refer to the appropriate sections of this chapter: *Grinding Meats and Sausage Emulsions*.

Mettwurst
©istock.com / Credit: to HandMadePictures

Size of Meat Block	% Of Meat Block Formula	Amount Required
? kg x	20% Trimmed Beef Plates	= **?** kg Plate Meat
? kg x	30% 70/30 Pork Shoulder	= **?** kg Pork Shoulder
? kg x	50% Pork Belly	= **?** kg Belly Meat
	Total Meat Block	**= ? kg**

Meat Block	Grams per Kilo Formula for Ingredients	Total Required
? kg x	23 g Sea Salt	= ? grams
? kg x	2.5 g Prague Powder 1	= ? grams
? kg x	3 g Sodium Erythorbate	= ? grams
? kg x	3 g Dextrose	= ? grams
? kg x	2 g White Pepper	= ? grams
? kg x	0.5 g Paprika	= ? grams
? kg x	1 g Nutmeg	= ? grams
? kg x	0.25 g Caraway	= ? grams
? kg x	1 g Ground Mustard	= ? grams
? kg x	0.5 g Ginger	= ? grams
? kg x	0.5 g Liquid Smoke	= ? grams
? kg x	5 ml Dark Rum	= ? ml
? kg x	0.12 g T-SPX Bactoferm Starter Culture	= ? grams
	Total Weight of Ingredients =	

Procedure

- Crust the meat block in the freezer cutting it into 15 cm lengths with an approximate 2.5 cm square diameter
- Combine the salt, Prague powder, erythorbate and dextrose in a separate bowl
- Combine the seasonings in a separate bowl
- Prepare the T-SPX using distilled room temperature water
- Grind the meat through an 8 mm plate and mix for 30 seconds
- Grind the meat twice through a 3 mm plate and add to bowl cutter
- Chop at low knife speed and slow to medium bowl speed to a fine creamy consistency, keeping temperature between 10-12°C
- Add seasonings, starter culture, and mix 30 seconds
- Add salt mixture and mix for 1 minute keeping temperature below 14°C
- Remove product from bowl and into stuffer with dry hands
- Keep stuffing table dry

- Stuff with no air pockets into 40-45 mm pre-soaked and well rinsed/ partially dry beef middles or fibrous casings
- Space on smoke sticks and hang on smoke rack
- Let cure and ferment at 18°C with humidity set at 75-80% for 48 hours.
- Cold smoke at 18-20°C at one-hour intervals for 12 hours (six smoke cycles of 1 hour, six rest cycles of 1 hour for a total of 12 hours)
- Move rack into refrigeration and cool until internal temperature is 2°C
- Remove product from rack and sticks; vacuum package and keep refrigerated.

Making Dry and Semi Dry Fermented Sausage Classification

Many assortments of fermented sausage are produced in Canada. These may be broadly classified into "dry" or "semi-dry" varieties, based on the moisture content of the finished product. Semi-dry sausages usually lose 10-20% of their moisture during processing, have a pH in the range of 4.6–5.2 with water activity (aw) at 0.91 or less, are generally smoked, usually cooked (thermo processed) to an internal temperature in the range of 46-63°C, and depending on the type, are ready in 14 to 21 days. Dry sausages on the other hand can take up to 120 days to be ready for use. They usually lose 20–50% of their moisture, have a pH in the range of 5-5.3 with a water activity (aw) of 0.85 or less, are generally not smoked with processing temperatures rarely above 30°C. The combination of low pH and moisture loss contribute to the shelf life of these products. Semi-dry sausage must be refrigerated whereas dry sausages, having lower water activity, are shelf-stable.

Fermented sausages are characterized by a higher acid content resulting from the conversion of existing and/or added carbohydrate to lactic acid by appropriate bacteria. The added acidity gives these products a flavour often described as tangy or sourly, provides for a firm texture, and contributes to microbiological stability and a longer shelf life.

Fermentation prevents spoilage bacteria from growing as the stronger lactic bacteria take over reducing the competition between other bacteria for food. There are additional factors at work, the amount of salt, nitrites, nitrates, cure accelerators, and other bacterial counts that may be naturally present. These non-meat ingredients help retard or eliminate most bacteria from growing whereas the friendlier lactic acid bacteria are more tolerant (less resistant) of these ingredients and continue to grow producing lactic acid, helping preserve the product.

Lactic acid bacteria naturally found in the meat or introduced with the use of starter cultures accomplish the fermentation of the meat. These bacteria feed on the natural sugars (carbohydrates) in meats, or added sugars, and go into a reproduction phase to produce the lactic acid needed for the fermentation process, increasing the acidity level of the meat, lowering the pH, which in turn inhibits the growth of unwanted spoilage bacteria. The rate at which lactic acid bacteria grow depends on the amount present in the meat, and/or the amount of starter culture used, as well as the amount and type of sugar naturally available or added.

STARTER CULTURES

Starter cultures are used to ensure pH drop will be rapid enough to inhibit the growth of unwanted microbial action. There are two basic types of starter cultures: "slow fermenting cultures" and "fast fermenting cultures." Slow fermenting cultures grow best in lower temperature settings in the range of 20–30°C, while fast fermenting cultures work best in warmer temperatures in the range of 30-46°C. Slow fermenting cultures are used for dry fermented items while fast fermenting cultures are used for semi-dry fermented sausages. Slow fermenting cultures provide a pH level of 5–5.3 while fast fermenting cultures provide a pH level of 4.8 or less.

Examples of slow fermenting cultures are:
- *Staphylococcus xylosus* and *sakei*
- *Pedicocus pentoseceus*
- *Lactobacillus curvatus*

Examples of fast fermenting cultures are:
- *Lactobacillius sakei*
- *Staphylococcus carnosus* and *sakei*
- *Pedicoccus pentosaceus*

One other type of bacteria needs to be mentioned: *Micrococcus*. *Micrococcus* is a salt tolerant, aerobic organism widely distributed in nature and a common contaminant of meat. They are capable of converting nitrate into nitrite, and thus play an important role when nitrate is included in the formulation. *Micrococcus* bacteria are also equipped with an enzyme system (catalase) that breaks down hydrogen peroxide produced by some strains of lactic acid bacteria.

As hydrogen peroxide accumulates in the sausage, it initiates oxidation reaction, which can lead to deterioration of flavour and colour. Therefore, although micrococcus does not produce lactic acid, it is included in some starter cultures to aid in the reduction of nitrate to nitrite and to protect flavour and colour by eliminating the presence of hydrogen peroxide.

Cultures are normally frozen and each requires special handling. All cultures should be stored frozen in the freezer and reconstituted in distilled water that is at room temperature.

STARTER MOULDS

In addition to starter cultures there are starter moulds used on sausage surfaces to both impact consumer appeal and product inoculation. Moulds used for various artesian products are carefully selected, having gone through multi-stage tests including several analytical and biochemical assessments. They are safe to use providing usage instructions are followed and are sprayed directly onto the sausage.

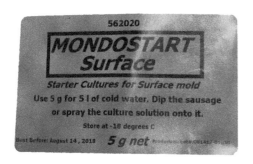

Starter culture for surface moulds

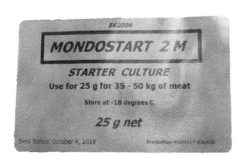

Starter culture for sausage

GDL (GLUCONO DELTA LACTONE)

In addition to starter cultures, some processors of fermented meats use approved chemical acidulants, such as GDL regarded as a safe additive and a natural food acid that contributes to the tangy/sourly flavour. GDL lowers pH and helps preserve the meat from deterioration. In meat GDL becomes hydrolyzed to gluconic acid under the influence of the meat's own water content, gradually decreasing the pH of the product. GDL reaches its lowest pH after approximately 60 minutes, depending on the type and temperature of the meat (species), and the concentration of GDL. The speed of hydrolysis and thus the speed of acidification can be accelerated by increasing temperature—the reason why GDL is commonly used with semi-dry fermented sausage.

GDL

Credit: Stuffers Supply Company

Note: The regulated use of GDL is 5 grams per kilogram of product.

DEXTROSE

The type of sugar added to help feed the lactic bacteria is definitely important to the success of the fermentation. Lactic acid bacteria require a readily available supply of sugar to convert to lactic acid. Although meat is an excellent source of essential nutrients required for microbial growth, it contains only a trace of sugar, stored in the form of glycogen. If fermentation is to proceed, a sugar source must be added to the sausage batter (batch).

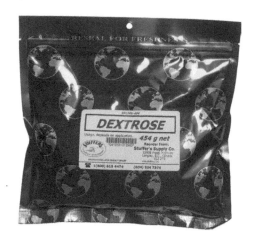

Dextrose
Credit: Stuffers Supply Company

All strains of lactic acid bacteria readily ferment simple sugars, and dextrose (glucose) is the carbohydrate of choice for fermented sausage in Canada. The amount of sugar added also affects the outcome of fermentation. Just as an automobile stops when it runs out of gas, likewise acid production by lactic acid bacteria in a sausage is halted when available sugar is exhausted. The extent of acid production can be somewhat controlled by the amount of available sugar added. Below is a table, which relates the amount of added dextrose to the expected final pH of the sausage, assuming the fermentation is allowed to go to completion.

Grams of Dextrose per Kg of Meat	Expected pH
4.0 g	5.2
5.0 g	5.0
6.0 g	4.8
7.5 g	4.6

TRADITIONAL METHOD OF FERMENTATION

The traditional process practiced by sausage makers in the making of salamis over the centuries relied solely on the naturally occurring lactic acid bacteria contained in the meat and surrounding environment. Today many do-it-yourself (untrained) sausage makers still rely on this method, trusting what has been handed down to them over decades is reliable and safe when it's really a matter of chance and circumstance.

The meat was mixed with salt, cure and spices and placed in a cooler for two to 10 days. Under the influence of the added salt and anaerobic conditions, the lactic acid bacteria acclimatize and develop more fully in the meat, in preference to the usual spoilage organisms (*Pseudomonas*), which require air and are sensitive to salt. This enrichment step supposedly increases numbers of lactic acid bacteria and establishes conditions within the batter for later growth and acid production under favourable fermenting.

Despite this enrichment step, it is not uncommon for the traditional process to result in fermentation failure (no acid production). Sometimes there simply aren't sufficient numbers of lactic acid bacteria contaminating the meat to support a successful fermentation. This is especially true in recent years, as improved sanitation at plant and retail levels has reduced the microbial load in the meat and on product contact surfaces. The lack of acid production is a detriment to flavour, and may allow undesirable bacteria to grow to high numbers and cause serious defects such as off-flavours, gas production or proteolysis (soft texture).

A technique of back-inoculation or "back-slopping" has been employed to help assure adequate numbers of lactic

Sausage curing in a root cellar
©istock.com / Credit: to slovegrove

acid bacteria in traditionally produced fermented sausage. This involves saving a small portion of batter (perhaps 3%) from a successfully fermented batch of sausage before its final heating, and blending this "seed" batter containing high numbers of lactic acid bacteria into a new batch. This technique has been used successfully to increase the load of lactic acid bacteria, but can also produce erratic results and carries with it some potential problems.

Since all the components of the sausage batter are back inoculated the possibility exists for transferring undesirable microorganisms, as well as the favored lactic acid bacteria. This could result in product defects in subsequent batches unless controls are maintained. It is unwise to add the back-inoculums to a new batch before the quality of the preceding batch has been evaluated.

If a starter culture is not used in the sausage, fermentation at temperatures below 23°C is strongly recommended. *Staphylococcus* exhibits optimum growth at 39°C, but does not compete well with other bacteria in the batter at low temperatures. Therefore, if the rate of acid production is uncertain (which is usually the case with the traditional method), a low fermentation temperature provides a measure of safety against outgrowth and toxin production by *Staphylococcus*. It is also wise to regularly monitor the pH level with a pH meter as *Staphylococcus aureus* growth can be controlled if the pH of the product is 5.3 or less.

THE USE OF PORK IN FERMENTED SAUSAGE

Trichinosis has been virtually eliminated in Canada and the Canadian inspection system, which is in fact one of the best in the world, is not conducting a search for it. Consequently, there could be the possibility of an isolated case here or there. In order to be safe, pork for dry cured products should be frozen, stacked at -29°C for at least six days or at -25°C for at least 10 days.

HURDLE TECHNOLOGY

The use of starter cultures, GDL, and thermo processing are parts of a method known as "hurdle technology," an approach to controlling or eliminating unwanted microbial action in food. This technology usually works best when combining such practices as: good personal hygiene; food safe surfaces; clean and sanitized equipment and utensils; temperature control of atmosphere and raw product; the use of cultures, sugars, salts, nitrites and nitrates; and thermo processing. Each step becomes a hurdle for unwanted microbial action producing a safer and more stable end product.

The processing of fermented products has three stages: the curing stage, where the salts and nitrites go into action; the incubation stage, where the onslaught of fermentation begins and ends; and the maturing stage, where the ripening and drying takes place.

The **curing stage** results with the addition of salts, nitrites and nitrates, and acidifiers. The frozen starter culture is prepared and activated in a half cup of lukewarm distilled water. The meat block should be chilled or crusted (partially frozen) and coarse ground producing uniform particle definition. Cold temperatures at this stage must be kept to avoid any fat smearing. Once the meat has been ground then mix in the non-meat ingredients at 30-second intervals beginning with the starter culture followed by the cures, cure accelerators, spice flavourings and lastly salt. Mixing time will be no more than one and a half to two minutes. Store in refrigerator overnight to complete the curing.

The **incubation stage** (fermentation) starts when the sausage batter is stuffed into its casing, allowed to reach room temperature to begin activating the lactic acid bacteria (2–6 hours depending on the diameter), and then placed in a warm fermentation chamber with a humidity level of 85-90% for the prescribed time. Once in the warm humid chamber the product is held at a consistent temperature, this allows the lactic acid bacteria (starter culture) to acclimatize to its host environment, feed off any natural or added carbohydrate (glucose) and reproduce, producing the lactic acid needed to ferment the product. Depending on the type of fermented sausage, dry or semi-dry, the incubation period will range between 17–150 hours and temperature will vary in the range of 20–46°C.

Large commercial fermentation chamber dry curing Landjaeger
Credit: Professional image, Industry approved

Landjaeger curing
©istock.com / Credit: to Martin Lang

Fermentation is complete when a pH level of 5.3 or less has been achieved within regulated time and temperature restrictions. (See Appendix: *Degree Hours*)

The **maturing stage** depends greatly on the water holding capacity and pH of the fermented product. At this phase the meat acquires flavour, looses moisture and develops its texture (firmness). Again, depending on the type of fermented product, dry or semi-dry, this takes place anywhere between 14–120 days at temperatures in the range of 12–16°C with the humidity set within a range of 75–80%. Our own practice has shown that increasing the incubation time, the concentration of starter culture, and the amount of dextrose, lowers the pH and decreases the water holding capacity of the product, which in turn aids the drying process.

Small fermentation chamber with product
NAIT Professional Meat Cutting &
Merchandising Program

THE PROCEDURE

Here, as always, time, temperature and the use of fresh products of the highest quality, are critical to the success of our end product due entirely to microbial concerns. The explanation for this is simple, dry and semi-dry fermented sausages and meats will be held at temperatures ideal for microbial growth, particularly E.coli 0157:H7 and *Listeria*—two reasons why our products will need to be heat treated.

> **Note:** CFIA regulations clearly state that any processed ready-to-eat product containing beef, or processed in a facility that also processes beef, must be subjected to a heat treatment control step. This requires heating the product to an internal temperature of 71°C for 15 seconds by means of a prescribed treatment such as thermo processing as outlined in the Manual of Procedures, Chapter 4: "Meat Processing Controls and Procedures," that achieve a 5D reduction for E.coli 0157:H7.

Regarding thermo processing of fermented items, the best practice is heating the product to an internal temperature of 54.4°C for 121 minutes. (Manual of Procedures, Chapter 4.16.2.2.1 Option 1)

STEPS FOR MAKING FERMENTED PRODUCTS

The nitrate usage level for dry fermented sausages is 200 ppm in addition to the 200 ppm of nitrites. The amount of nitrite for dry fermented sausage is two times higher than other cooked and smoked sausage because nitrite dissipates rapidly during the drying process. Salamis are air dried for periods up to 12 weeks. The high nitrite levels in dry fermented sausages contribute to colour stability and food safety. Once these items have reached a stable pH (5.3 or less) and water activity (aw) level of 0.9 or less, the bulk of these nitrites will have been spent and their assignment complete.

The order of adding non-meat ingredients is critical. Contrary to normal procedures where salt is added first for maximum protein extraction, with fermented items salt should be added toward the end of the mixing cycle. Temperatures must be cold. Anything above 4°C may cause fatting out and fat smearing. Temperatures should be in the range of -2 to 0°C while mixing and 1-2°C for stuffing. The process of making dry and semi-dry fermented products is as follows:

- Coarse grind all meats and crust in freezer
- Grind or chop in a bowl cutter meats to desired texture and consistency
- Mix in cure, spices and culture
- Blend thoroughly, add salt and mix
- Stuff mixture into casings
- Hang on sticks and racks, let product come to room temperature
- Place product in fermentation chamber (or smokehouse) at temperatures between 20-30°C for a period of 24 to 72 hours with a relative humidity setting of 85-95%
- Cold smoke if called for or desired
- Place in smokehouse and apply thermo process (see Appendix: *Degree Hours*)
- Cool product (shower) to 20°C allowing to stand at room temperature until dry
- Place product in aging chambers at appropriate temperature till product reaches the desired pH level and/or water activity measurement.

LAMB SALAMI

This item is one that is not that popular in Canada, at least not yet. As interest in the ovine species increases this may become a popular slow-fermented salami. It is made with spring lamb and beef, an item for those who for dietary reasons cannot eat pork. It's important to use only fresh lamb that is free of glands, fat, gristle, tendons and heavy collagen.

Salamis
©istock.com / Credit: to Magone

Size of Meat Block	% Of Meat Block Formula	Amount Required
? kg x	80% 90/10 X-Lean Lamb	= ? kg Lamb
? kg x	20% Beef Fat	= ? kg Beef Fat
Total Meat Block		**= ? kg**

Meat Block	Grams per Kilo Formula for Ingredients	Total Required
? kg x	23 g Sea Salt	= ? grams
? kg x	4 g Prague Powder 2	= ? grams
? kg x	3 g Ascorbate or Erythorbate	= ? grams
? kg x	5 g Dextrose	= ? grams
? kg x	1 g White Pepper	= ? grams
? kg x	2 g Cracked Black Pepper	= ? grams
? kg x	0.5 g Cardamom	= ? grams
? kg x	2 g Granulated Garlic	= ? grams
? kg x	0.5 g Smoked Paprika	= ? grams
? kg x	0.12 g T-SPX Slow Fermenting Culture	= ? grams

Total Weight of Ingredients =

Procedure

- Crust the meat block in the freezer cutting it into 15 cm lengths with an approximate 2.5 cm square diameter
- Prepare starter culture with distilled room temperature water (see directions on label)
- Combine the salt, Prague powder 2 and erythorbate in a separate bowl
- Combine the seasonings in a separate bowl
- Grind the meat and fat once through 25 mm coarse plate and mix
- Grind the meat through 8 mm plate and add to mixer
- Add the culture and mix for 30 seconds
- Add 75% of the combined seasonings to the meat block and mix for 30 seconds
- Add the remaining spices and mix for 30 seconds
- Add the salt, Prague powder 2 and ascorbate mixture; mix for 30 seconds
- Let mixture rest in fridge for 10 minutes
- Put mixture into stuffer and stuff into desired diameter casings (50 75 mm) using appropriate size stuffing horn
- Hang and space product on smoke sticks, keeping them from touching each other
- Place sticks of product on smoke rack and let product come to room temperature
- Place product into fermenting chamber for 48-72 hours at a temperature of 20°C with humidity set between 85–95% and an air exchange at 50%
- Cold smoke at 20°C for 6 hours
- Apply thermo process (see Appendix: *Degree Hours*), shower, and let dry and cool to room temperature
- Age in chamber at 14°C until desired pH level and water activity levels have been reached (when product has lost 30 -35% of its moisture)
- Move product into refrigeration and cool until internal temperature is 2°C
- Vacuum package and keep refrigerated.

SUMMARY

TERMS FOR REVIEW

Artificial Casing	Fermented Sausage	Phosphate
Bind	Fresh Sausage	PPM
Brine	GDL	Pumping
Buildup Method	Hurdle Technology	Restricted Ingredients
Charcuterie	HVP	Ripening
Chill/crusted	Incubation Stage	Shock Method
Collagen Casings	Jellied Meats	Smoking
Cultures	Maturing Stage	Tumbling
Cure Accelerators	Meat Block	Water Activity (aw)
Curing	Natural Casing	
Dextrose	Netting	
Emulsion	Non-meat Ingredients	
Extenders	Pâtés	
Fermentation Chamber	pH	

DISCUSSION QUESTIONS

1. In a group, discuss the five classifications of sausage and provide an example of each.

2. What constitutes a fresh sausage as "fresh"?

3. Explain traceability as it refers to charcuterie items and the making of sausages.

4. Why do we sort meat trimmings?

5. What does 80/20 pork trimmings mean? What does it refer to?

6. Provide three examples of whole muscle products commonly found in a deli.

7. What products could be processed from a beef brisket point?

8. Why is it noted that we should store spices and non-meat ingredients in a separate room, in non-corrosive containers and away from light?

9. Discuss the differences and similarities of non-meat ingredients and restricted ingredients.

10. What's the difference between Prague powder 1 and Prague powder 2?

11. What function do cure accelerators play in the fabrication of cured meats?

12. How does tumbling affect the proteins in meat?

13. What's the purpose for using binders and extenders?

14. Why and when do we use sugar in the making of sausage?

15. What are the pros and cons of pumping meats with brine vs. soaking meats in brine?

16. Most automated smokehouses have programmable operational cycles for the holding, smoking and cooking, etc. of meats. What purpose does the "reddening and warming" cycle have?

17. Why do we need to know how to calculate ppm of ingredients in the formulation of sausages?

18. What roles do pH and aw have in the making of fermented sausages and meats?

Appendix:

- Data Sheets
- Regulations References (www.inspection.ca)
  - CFIA Manual of Procedures, Chapter 4, Annex C, Curing of prepared meats
  - CFIA Degree Hours
  - CFIA Requirements for Shelf Stable Meat Products

- Extra Recipes
- Data Sheet: Premix Product Information

NEWLY WEDS FOODS CO.
CUSTOMIZED TASTE TECHNOLOGY

Edmonton, Alberta

Product Data Sheet

Customer: Unipac Packaging

Product: Unicure All Purpose   **Product Code:** C069D

Unit Weight: 25.00 kg (55.12 lb)

Usage: For pumping ham, use 0.57 kg to 4.546 kg water. Pump at 20%.
For pumping bacon, use 0.63 kg to 4.546 kg water. Pump at 12%.
For sausage cure, use 0.91 kg to 45.36 kg finished sausage. Add extra salt, if needed. Water for pickle should be 30-40°F.

Keep this product dry.

Ingredients: Salt, sodium nitrite, propylene glycol and silicon dioxide (manufacturing aids).

Typical Analysis

Chemical:			
	Protein	0	%
	Fat	0	%
	Moisture	0	%
	Salt	97.9	%
	Sodium Nitrite	0.91	%

Microbiological:		
	Total Plate Count	1 000 /g maximum
	Yeast & Mold	100 /g maximum
	Coliform	10 /g maximum
	Salmonella	Negative /25 g
	E. coli	< 3 /g

Packaging and Storage:

The product is packaged in a multiwalled bag and it should be stored in a cool dry place. Under these conditions, the expected shelf life is 6 months.

Date: **September 26, 2007** supersedes all previous versions.

The suggestions and data contained herein are based on information believed to be reliable and are given without guarantee or representation as to results. Because several factors may affect results, we recommend that customers conduct their own tests before using the product in full-scale production. We assume no liability or responsibility for the result of the customer's decision regarding usefulness of our ingredients. The suggestions offered here are not to infringe on existing patents.

C069D ~ 53722   Page 1 of 1

9110 - 23 Avenue • Edmonton, Alberta T6N 1H9 • 780-414-9500 • Fax 780-440-1628 • www.newlywedsfoods.com

1.0 CURING BY STANDARD METHOD

"Cured" (MIR) means, in respect of an edible meat product, that salt together with at least 100 ppm of sodium nitrite, potassium nitrite, sodium nitrate or potassium nitrate, or any combination thereof, was added to the meat product during its preparation.

The use of these nitrite or nitrates together with salt is therefore required when "cured" is listed as a mandatory process in Schedule 1 of the MIR. The nitrite and nitrate salts may also be used as preservatives where permitted in Schedule 1 of the MIR and in accordance with the *Food and Drug Regulations* Division 16, Table XI Part 1.

Meat products can be cured using a slow curing or a rapid curing method. The nitrate and/or nitrite salts are used in slow curing processes whereas the nitrites are used in rapid curing of meat products.

In the slow curing process the meat product is rubbed with a nitrate mixture, or soaked in a mixture of nitrate and water, for a period of several days or weeks. The nitrates are slowly converted by bacterial action to nitrite, which is the active curing agent. For example, dry cured hams are produced by coating hams with salt and nitrate.

The calculations for nitrate and /or nitrite in product(s) are made at the input level. For all curing methods (standard and alternative) the operator shall verify as part of the HACCP system that recipe and method of production will result in product compliant with the permitted level of use.

In products other than side bacon, the maximum input level of sodium nitrite salts is 20 g per 100 kg of meat product, i.e. 200 ppm. In the curing of side bacon, the maximum input level of sodium nitrite salts is 12 g per 100 kg of pork bellies, i.e. 120 ppm.

In the production of slow cured meat products, sodium nitrate salt at a maximum input level of 20 g per 100 kg of meat products, i.e. 200 ppm, may be used in addition to the nitrite salts. An exception to the maximum level of use is permitted for dry rub cured meat products on racks. The maximum level of use permitted is 62 g of sodium nitrite salts and 186 g of nitrate salts per 100 kg of meat product.

In the formulation of a cured meat product, the use of a previously cured meat product as ingredient in excess of 10% will necessitate recalculation of the nitrite/nitrate input to account for the contribution from those ingredients.

CFIA, Manual of Procedures, Chapter 4 – Meat Processing Controls and Procedures.

4.16.2.1 TIME AND TEMPERATURE FOR FERMENTED PRODUCTS

The operator is required to implement a control program based on 4.16.2.1.1, Fermentation Done at a Constant Temperature (Constant Temperature Process) and 4.16.2.1.2, Fermentation Done at Different Temperatures (Variable Temperature Processes) to control pathogens.

Certain strains of the bacteria *Staphylococcus aureus* are capable of producing a highly heat stable toxin that causes illness in humans. Above a critical temperature of 15.6°C, *Staphylococcus aureus* multiplication and toxin production can take place. Once a pH of 5.3 is reached, *Staphylococcus aureus* multiplication and toxin production are stopped.

Degree-hours are the product of time as measured in hours at a particular temperature multiplied by the "degrees" measured in excess of **15.6°C (the critical temperature for growth of *Staphylococcus aureus*).** Degree-hours are calculated for each temperature used in the process. The limitation of the number of degree-hours depends upon the highest temperature in the fermentation process prior to the time that a pH of 5.3 or less is attained.

The operator is encouraged to measure temperatures at the surface of the product. Where this is not possible, the operator should utilize fermentation room temperatures. The degree hour calculations are based on fermentation room temperatures. Temperature and humidity should be uniform throughout the fermentation room.

A process can be judged as acceptable provided the product consistently reaches a pH of 5.3 using:

- fewer than 665 degree-hours when the highest fermentation temperature is less than 33°C;
- fewer than 555 degree-hours when the highest fermentation temperature is between 33° and 37°C; and
- fewer than 500 degree-hours when the highest fermentation temperature is greater than 37°C.

4.16.2.1.1 FERMENTATION DONE AT A CONSTANT TEMPERATURE (CONSTANT TEMPERATURE PROCESS)

When fermentation is done at a constant temperature, operators can either use the following table or the calculation method (see examples below) for determining degree-hours limits and maximum time for fermentation at a given room temperature.

Fermentation Done at a Constant Temperature (Constant Temperature Process)		
Degree-hours limit for the corresponding temperature	Fermentation room temperature (°C)	Maximum allowed hours to achieve a pH of 5.3 (based on guideline)
665	20	150.0
665	22	103.4
665	24	78.9
665	26	63.8
665	28	53.6
665	30	46.2
665	32	40.5
555	33	31.8
555	34	30.1
555	35	28.6
555	36	27.2
555	37	25.9
500	38	22.3
500	40	20.5
500	42	18.9
500	44	17.6
500	46	16.4
500	48	15.4
500	50	14.5

Examples of how to use the calculation method for constant temperature processes:

Example 1:

Fermentation room temperature is a constant 26°C. It takes 55 hours for the pH to reach 5.3.

Degrees above 15.6°C: 26°C - 15.6°C = 10.4°C
Hours to reach pH of 5.3: 55
Degree-hours calculation: (10.4°C) x (55) = 572 degree-hours

The corresponding degree-hours limit (less than 33°C) is 665 degree-hours.

Conclusion: Example 1 meets the guideline because its degree-hours are less than the limit.

Example 2:

Fermentation room temperature is a constant 35°C. It takes 40 hours for the pH to reach 5.3.

Degrees above 15.6°C: 35°C - 15.6°C = 19.4°C
Hours to reach pH of 5.3: 40
Degree-hours calculation: (19.4°C) x (40) = 776 degree-hours

The corresponding degree-hours limit (between 33 and 37°C) is 555 degree-hours.

Conclusion: Example 2 **does not meet the guideline** because its degree-hours exceed the limit - hold the product and refer to sub-section 4.16.2.1.3.

4.16.3 REQUIREMENTS FOR SHELF STABLE FERMENTED MEAT PRODUCTS

For all fermented meat products, in order to minimize the danger of outgrowth of *Clostridium botulinum* spores and development of the botulinal toxin in fermented product, nitrite/nitrate shall be added at a minimum level of 100 ppm along with a minimum of 2.5% of salt.

In order to be considered "shelf-stable" and not require refrigeration, a fermented meat product must have a minimum of 100 ppm nitrite/nitrate, a minimum of 2.5% of salt, meet degree hours requirements (4.16.2.1) and meet one of the following sets of specific requirements.

- The pH of the finished product is of 4.6 or less, regardless to its final aw.
- The aw of the finished product is 0.85 or less, regardless of its final pH.
- The pH is 5.3 or lower at the end of the fermentation period and the end product has an aw of 0.90 or lower.

The level of nitrate-nitrite should not interfere with the process of fermentation.

Fermented products, which do not meet these requirements must be labeled with a refrigeration statement.

Operators of registered establishments who wish to market a meat product without a refrigeration declaration which does not meet the "shelf stable" criteria set out above, must submit a request for the acceptance of their proposal to the Inspector in Charge. The submission must be accompanied by detailed recipe, formulation and processing information for the product. Submissions will be sent to the Area Program Specialist for review with a Food Safety Microbiology Specialist and Health Canada.

REGULATIONS REFERENCES

- CFIA, Annex C: Use of Phosphate Salts and Nitrites in the Preparation of Meat Products
- CFIA, Manual of Procedures, Chapter 4 – Meat Processing Controls and Procedures. Main topics are as follows:
    - Handling of Meat Products
    - Fresh Meat Control Programs
    - Cooking
    - Cooling of Heat Processed Meat Products
    - Edible rendering
    - Canning
    - Casings
    - Emulsification
    - Aging and tenderizing
    - Drying Treatments
    - Formulation
    - Preservation
    - Tumbling
    - Smoking
    - Fermentation
    - Post Processing Lethality Procedures and
    - Packaging
- CFIA, Food Labelling for Industry, Meat and Poultry Products, Labelling Requirements for Meat and Poultry Products, Food Labelling for Industry.
- CFIA, Meat and Poultry Products, Manual of Procedures, Chapter 7, Packaging and Labelling.

Extra Recipes: Fresh Sausage

BREAKFAST SAUSAGE

This sausage is made with both beef and pork. The beef and pork meat trim ratios are 70/30 with a 50/50 mix (half pork and half beef). The regular breakfast sausage tends to be a bit drier than the regular pork breakfast sausage. The recipe can also be used to make a pork maple sausage, where you would use all pork trim with a ratio of 70/30 and add a maple flavouring (which will vary on amount added depending on type of flavouring used).

Determine the size of your meat block, which is the amount you want to make in kilograms. Example: Using a total of 5,10,15, 20 or 25 kilograms of meat; in this case half beef and half pork.

Breakfast sausage
Credit: CPMCA image collection

Size of Meat Block	% Of Meat Block Formula	Amount Required
? kg x	50% 70/30 Beef	= ? kg 70/30 Beef
? kg x	50% 70/30 Pork	= ? kg 70/30 Pork
? kg x	15% Flaked or Crushed Ice	= ? kg Ice
	Total Meat Block	**= ? kg**

Meat Block	Grams per Kilo Formula for Ingredients	Total Required
? kg x	18 g Sea Salt	= ? grams
? kg x	2 g Black Pepper	= ? grams
? kg x	2 g White Pepper	= ? grams
? kg x	2 g Ground Coriander	= ? grams
? kg x	3 g Onion Powder	= ? grams
? kg x	0.5 g Ground Sage	= ? grams
? kg x	1 g Marjoram	= ? grams
? kg x	150 g Crushed or Flaked Ice	= ? grams
	1 Raw Egg per kg of Meat Block	
	Total Weight of Ingredients =	

Procedure

- Crust the meat block in the freezer cutting it into 15 cm lengths with an approximate 2.5 cm square diameter
- Keep the salt in a separate bowl
- Combine the seasonings in a separate bowl
- Shell the eggs and blend lightly in a separate bowl
- Grind the meat block through 8 mm plate and place into mixer; mix for 30 seconds
- Add 75% of the salt; mix for 30 seconds
- Add 75% of the combined seasonings to the meat block and mix for 30 seconds
- Add the ice and mix for 30 seconds and the remaining salt mixture; mix for 30 seconds
- Add the remaining seasonings and eggs; mix for 60 seconds;
- Regrind the mixture through 5 mm plate
- Let mixture rest in fridge for 10 minutes
- Cook in frying pan a small patty to test the consistency and flavour distribution.
- Adjust seasoning if necessary, remix, and rest for 5 minutes
- Put mixture into stuffer and stuff into 20–22 mm casing (sheep or artificial) using appropriate size stuffing horn
- Link and cut into desired lengths
- Package and keep refrigerated (sell or cook and eat).

MILD ITALIAN SAUSAGE

Italian sausage is most often seasoned with fennel and/or anise and has become one of the favoured flavours of fresh sausages. The sausage is made with 70/30 pork trim, stuffed into 28-32 mm hog casings and linked in lengths of approximately 15 cm. Italian sausage is made with the use of a meat grinder using an 8 mm plate and ground twice.

Mild Italian sausage
Credit: CPMCA image collection

Determine the size of your meat block, which is the amount you want to make in kilograms. Ex: using a total of 5,10,15, 20, or 25 kilograms of meat.

Size of Meat Block	% Of Meat Block Formula	Amount Required
? kg x	85% 70/30 Pork	= ? kg 70/30 Pork
? kg x	15% Flaked or Crushed Ice	= ? kg Ice
Total Meat Block		**= ? kg**

Meat Block in kg	Grams per Kilogram Formula	Totals Used
? kg x	18 g Sea Salt	= ? grams
? kg x	1.5 g Black Pepper	= ? grams
? kg x	1.5 g White Pepper	= ? grams
? kg x	4 g Ground Coriander	= ? grams
? kg x	2 g Onion Powder	= ? grams
? kg x	1 g Basil	= ? grams
? kg x	3 g Anise	= ? grams
? kg x	3 g Ground Fennel	= ? grams
? kg x	2 g Cayenne	= ? grams
? kg x	2 g Caraway	= ? grams

1 Raw Egg per kg of Meat Block

Procedure

- Crust the meat block in the freezer cutting it into 15 cm lengths with an approximate 2.5 cm square diameter
- Keep the salt in a separate bowl
- Combine the seasonings in a separate bowl
- Shell the eggs and blend lightly in a separate bowl
- Grind the meat block through 8 mm plate and place into mixer; mix for 30 seconds
- Add 75% of the salt; mix for 30 seconds
- Add 75% of the combined seasonings to the meat block and mix for 30 seconds
- Add the ice and mix for 30 seconds and the remaining salt mixture; mix for 30 seconds
- Add the remaining seasonings and eggs; mix for 60 seconds;
- Regrind the mixture through 5 mm plate
- Let mixture rest in fridge for 10 minutes
- Cook in frying pan a small patty to test the consistency and flavour distribution
- Adjust seasoning if necessary, remix, and rest for 5 minutes
- Put mixture into stuffer and stuff into 28–32 mm casing using appropriate size stuffing horn
- Link and cut into desired lengths
- Package and keep refrigerated (sell or cook and eat).

FRESH BRATWURST SAUSAGE

Bratwurst is an all-time favourite sausage among consumers of sausages. Originating in Germany there are as many varieties of this sausage as there are villages in Germany, each claiming their own genuine version. Here we present a common generic formula with no distinct label designation. Bratwurst has the known distinction of having mace as it's distinguishing trademark. The sausage is made with 70/30 pork trim, stuffed into 28-32 mm hog casings and linked in lengths of approximately 15 cm. The sausage is made with the use of a meat grinder using an 8 mm plate for the first grind and a 3 mm plate for the second and final grind.

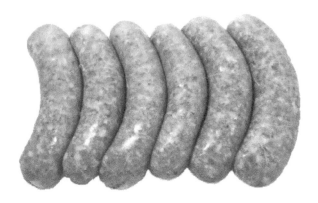

Fresh Bratwurst sausage
Credit: NAIT Professional Meat Cutting & Merchandising Program

Determine the size of your meat block, which is the amount you want to make in kilograms. Ex: using a total of 5,10,15, 20, or 25 kilograms of meat.

Size of Meat Block	% Of Meat Block Formula	Amount Required
? kg x	85% 70/30 Pork	= **?** kg 70/30 Pork
? kg x	15% Flaked or Crushed Ice	= **?** kg Ice
	Total Meat Block	= ? kg

Meat Block in kg	Grams per Kilogram Formula	Totals Used
? kg x	16 g Sea Salt	= ? grams
? kg x	3 g Mace	= ? grams
? kg x	2.5 g White Pepper	= ? grams
? kg x	3 g Ground Coriander	= ? grams
? kg x	3 g Onion Powder	= ? grams
? kg x	3 g Caraway	= ? grams
? kg x	3 g Anise	= ? grams
? kg x	3 g Ground Fennel	= ? grams
? kg x	2 g Cayenne	= ? grams
? kg x	2 g Caraway	= ? grams

1 Raw Egg per kg of Meat Block

Procedure

- Crust the meat block in the freezer cutting it into 15 cm lengths with an approximate 2.5 cm square diameter
- Keep the salt in a separate bowl
- Combine the seasonings in a separate bowl
- Shell the eggs and blend lightly in a separate bowl
- Grind the meat block through 8 mm plate and place into mixer; mix for 30 seconds
- Add 75% of the salt; mix for 30 seconds
- Add 75% of the combined seasonings to the meat block and mix for 30 seconds
- Add the ice and mix for 30 seconds and the remaining salt mixture; mix for 30 seconds
- Add the remaining seasonings and eggs; mix for 60 seconds
- Regrind the mixture through 5 mm plate
- Let mixture rest in fridge for 10 minutes
- Cook in frying pan a small patty to test the consistency and flavour distribution
- Adjust seasoning if necessary, remix, and rest for 5 minutes
- Put mixture into stuffer and stuff into 28–32 mm casing using appropriate size stuffing horn
- Link and cut into desired lengths
- Package and keep refrigerated (sell or cook and eat).

Cured Smoked and Cooked Sausages

GARLIC RINGS

Ringed sausage is always a favourite. The size and weight of ring depends largely on the size of casing used and the amount of meat stuffed into the casing; this is where the skill of the person using the stuffer comes into play. Too much meat stuffed too tightly causes the rings to burst during the cook cycle while too little makes the product look gangly. The average ring weighs approximately 375–400 grams green weight with a finished weight in the range of 350–375 grams.

Garlic rings
Credit: CPMCA image collection

Size of Meat Block	% Of Meat Block Formula	Amount Required
? kg x	30% 80/20 Pork Trim	= **?** kg Lean Pork Leg
? kg x	40% 70/30 Pork Shoulder	= **?** kg Pork Shoulder
? kg x	15% Pork Belly	= **?** kg Belly Meat
? kg x	15% Flaked or Crushed Ice	= **?** kg Ice
Total Meat Block		**= ? kg**

Meat Block	Grams per Kilogram Formula	Total Required
? kg x	18 g Sea Salt	= ? grams
? kg x	2.5 g Prague Powder 1	= ? grams
? kg x	3 g Ascorbate or Erythorbate	= ? grams
? kg x	2 g Dextrose	= ? grams
? kg x	1.5 g White Pepper	= ? grams
? kg x	2.5 g Ground Black Pepper	= ? grams
? kg x	2 g Mace	= ? grams
? kg x	3 g Onion Powder	= ? grams
? kg x	2 g Coriander	= ? grams
? kg x	6 g Granulated Garlic	= ? grams

Total Weight of Ingredients =

Procedure

- Crust the meat block in the freezer cutting it into 15 cm lengths with an approximate 2.5 cm square diameter, keeping the leg meat separate
- Combine the salt, Prague powder and erythorbate in a separate bowl
- Combine the seasonings in a separate bowl
- Grind 80/20 lean pork trim once through 8 mm coarse plate and place in mixer
- Grind the shoulder meat twice in 3 mm plate and add to mixer
- Grind the belly meat twice in 1–3 mm plate and add to mixer
- Add 75% of the salt and ascorbate mixture; mix for 30 seconds
- Add 75% of the combined seasonings to the meat block and mix for 30 seconds
- Add the ice and mix for 30 seconds and then add the remaining salt mixture; mix for 30 seconds
- Add the remaining spices and mix for 30 seconds
- Let mixture rest in fridge for 10 minutes
- Cook in frying pan a small patty to test the consistency and flavour distribution.
- Adjust seasoning if necessary (salt), remix, and rest for 5 minutes
- Put mixture into stuffer and stuff into 32–36 mm casing (hog or artificial) using appropriate size stuffing horn
- Cut into desired lengths for rings (usually 35-45 cm lengths)
- Space rings on smoke sticks, keeping them from touching each other
- Place sticks of rings on smoke rack and rinse them off with cold water
- Let rest 10 minutes
- Place product into smoker
- Smokehouse program as follows for 50 kilogram or more batch size
  - Reddening and warming at 50°C for 15 minutes
  - Drying at 55°C for 15 minutes
  - Smoking at 60°C for 15 minutes
  - Evacuation at 60°C for 5 minutes
  - Drying at 60°C for 10 minutes
  - Smoking at 65°C for 30 minutes
  - Evacuation at 65°C for 5 minutes
  - Drying at 65°C for 10 minutes
  - Smoking at 65 °C for 15 minutes
  - Evacuation at 65°C for 5 minutes
  - Drying at 60°C for 10 minutes
  - Cooking to an internal temperature of 71°C
  - Chilling and showering to an internal temperature of 20°C
- Move rack into refrigeration and cool till internal temperature is 2°C
- Remove product from rack and sticks; vacuum package and keep refrigerated.

Fermented Sausage

BASIC SALAMI

This item is very popular among artisanal practitioners and connoisseurs. The recipe we provide can prosper into many varieties by changing the texture or particle definition of the meat, the addition of one or more seasoning ingredient, and the type and size of casing. Example: Genoa Salami has whole black peppercorns (1.5g per kilo) and granulated garlic (0.5g per kilo) added to the ingredient list.

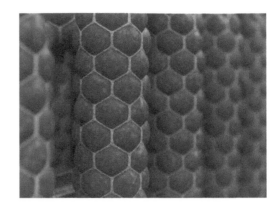

Salami
©istock.com / Credit: to IP Galanternik D.U.

It's important to use only freshly frozen pork trim that is free of glands, excess fat and gristle, tendons and heavy collagen (see "The Use of Pork in Fermented Sausage")

Size of Meat Block	% Of Meat Block Formula	Amount Required
? kg x	80% 80/20 Pork Shoulder	= **?** kg
? kg x	20% Back Fat	= **?** kg
	Total Meat Block	= **?** kg

Meat Block	Grams per Kilogram Formula	Total Required
? kg x	25 g Sea Salt	= ? grams
? kg x	3.5 g Prague Powder 2	= ? grams
? kg x	5 g Erythorbate	= ? grams
? kg x	5 g Dextrose	= ? grams
? kg x	2 g Cracked Black Pepper	= ? grams
	Total Weight of Ingredients =	

Procedure

- Prepare the starter culture (slow fermenting) according to manufacturer's label specifications
- Crust the meat block in the freezer cutting it into 15 cm lengths with an approximate 2.5 cm square diameter
- Combine the salt, Prague powder 2 and erythorbate in a separate bowl
- Combine the seasonings in a separate bowl
- Grind the meat and fat once through 25 mm coarse plate and mix for 30 seconds
- Grind the meat mixture through 8–9 mm plate and mix for 30 seconds
- Add the culture and mix for 30 seconds
- Add 75% of the combined seasonings to the meat block and mix for 30 seconds
- Add the remaining spices and mix for 30 seconds
- Add the salt, Prague powder 2 and erythorbate mixture; mix for 30 seconds
- Regrind through 8 mm plate
- Let mixture rest in fridge for 10 minutes
- Put mixture into stuffer and stuff into desired diameter casings (50-75 mm) and lengths using appropriate size stuffing horn
- Hang and space product on smoke sticks, keeping them from touching each other
- Place sticks of product on smoke rack and let product come to room temperature
- Place product into fermenting chamber for 48-72 hours at a temperature of 20°C with humidity set between 85–95% and an air exchange at 50%
- Check pH (should be in the range of 5–5.3)
- Cold smoke at 20°C for 6 hours (optional)
- Apply thermo process (see Appendix: *Degree Hours*), shower, and let dry and cool to room temperature
- Age in chamber at 14°C until desired pH level and water activity levels have been reached (when product has lost 30-35% of its moisture)
- Move product into refrigeration and cool till internal temperature is 2°C
- Vacuum package and keep refrigerated.

Example of Sausage Processing in a larger plant setting

Sequence is as follows:

- Place the selected trim into the silent bowl cutter and cut raw product to desired texture and consistency
- Add seasonings and mix
- Remove and stuff
- Link by automation or smaller batches by hand
- Check quality of casing and links

Adding pork trim to an emulsion
Credit: Professional image, Industry approved

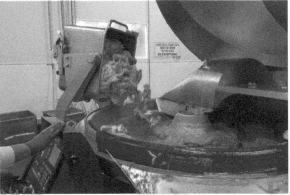

Adding pork fat to an emulsion
Credit: Professional image, Industry approved

Adding beef trim to an emulsion
Credit: Professional image, Industry approved

Cutting & mixing in beef trim
Credit: Professional image, Industry approved

Ejector wheel about to remove product from cutter
Credit: Professional image, Industry approved

Ejector wheel removing product from cutter
©istock.com / Credit: fmajor

Product ready to load into auto linker-stuffer
Credit: Professional image, Industry approved

Auto linker in action
Credit: Professional image, Industry approved

Stuffing Sausage by hand from a vacuum stuffer
©istock.com / Credit: tomch

Stuffing & hand linking sausage
Credit: ©istock.com / Credit: branex

Sausage pricker for releasing air in casings
Credit: Stuffers Supply Company

Chapter 11

Marketing and Merchandising

This chapter is designed to educate the reader on the subject of marketing and merchandising in the retail sectors of the meat industry. Discussed is the business view of the meat industry, government regulations, managing products, employees and customers.

As the bottom line is important to the survival of any business, a portion of this chapter is dedicated to math practices common to the day-to-day operation of a retail outlet.

Also discussed is information about packaging, labelling and customer service. Topics include the forms of communication, personal appearance, teamwork and integrity.

CHAPTER 11

Marketing & Merchandising

This chapter is designed to assist those interested in either working within the meat industry, exploring opportunities of self-employment and/or for a general understanding of how marketing and merchandising is used in the retail sales sector of the meat industry. The information we provide is the basis of what marketing and merchandising in our industry is about. What we have to offer by no means exhausts our topic, and though we talk about marketing and merchandising, our main focus is price point, meaning value for goods received or better still a reasonable return on our investment in all areas. However, if it weren't for our customers who buy and consume our products, we wouldn't have an industry or a need to implement marketing and merchandising strategies. So, understanding customer service is integral to marketing and merchandising as we continue to follow and examine consumer trends. Having said that, the marketing and merchandising information herein is just a starting point, something you can expand to suit your own needs whatever they may be considering

the topic. Keep in mind that no amount of literature can substitute practical experience and training.

Marketing is a commercial activity whereby goods and services are exchanged. A marketplace without competition is called a monopoly, meaning whatever the establishment is it will be the only game in town; what you see is what you get, so to speak. Markets with competitors have other considerations when identifying the needs, wants and trends of consumers willing to purchase products they perceive provides satisfaction and receiving value for their money.

From a societal point of view, marketing provides the link between a society's material requirements, in our case meat products, and its economic patterns of response, meaning consumer habits, wants and needs. This way marketing satisfies these needs and wants through the development of exchange processes and the building of long-term relationships, a following or customer base. It's an exchange of goods for money in a relational environment between seller and buyer.

Marketing considers:

- What goods and services will be exchanged (product or type of business, direct shopping and/or online shopping, etc.), with knowledge of
- Location
- Competition, an understanding of consumer needs and the economic response
- Monthly costs associated with the running of a venue (private or corporate)

Marketing is about how an establishment advertises itself and how it brands itself within the community it serves. It considers the type of products and services offered, the cost or price of those products and the type of promotion used to sell or attract attention to products being offered or promoted. In short, marketing is all about the cost of doing business.

Operational Considerations for Marketing in the Retail Meat Industry

a) **Identify the Market**
- know your consumer's economic status
- know their ethnic background and particular needs
- know their average age and marital status
- know their average income status (dual or single)

b) **Location**
- high profile, whether in a strip mall or shopping centre, etc.
- easy access, walk-in traffic, parking, etc.
- recognized area - city, town, street, concerns, demographics, etc.
- - why this particular location? (a gut feeling doesn't cut it)

c) **Competition**
- know who the competition is (similar outlets)
- know what makes your competitor competitive (goods and services offered)
- know why the consumer will choose you over your competition

d) **Monthly Costs associated with running a venue**
- rent and common fees
- hydro
- telephone

- water, heat and air conditioning
- taxes
- insurance
- employee benefit packages (workers' compensation)
- salaries
- bank charges, loans and interest
- licensing
- vehicles
- office supplies
- operational supplies: uniforms, wrapping and cleaning supplies
- advertising (marketing)
- budget for repairs

If you are a manager or merchandiser in a large corporate setting, some of what we talked about above doesn't apply because these things will already have been taken care of. However, regardless of if you are or are not in that situation, we feel it is wise to apprise yourself of this information. In other words, we think anyone who aspires to a career in this industry needs to realize what type of decisions are to be considered and the expenses related to the everyday business of "doing business."

Necessity of control over these costs (the cost of doing business) and maximizing profits (a product of merchandising) to ensure your budget has been met will realize a fair return for your employer or company (or yourself) and possibly a successful career. The flip side of controlling costs is being able to forecast potential in the following areas:

- sales
- gross profits
- salary costs
- supply costs
- inventory costs
- repair costs

These figures should be projected weekly, monthly and yearly for budgetary reasons. They should also be tracked for future consideration and projections.

Merchandising is a commercial activity employed with marketing in optimizing a consumer's perception of value. The ultimate goal of all merchandising activity is to increase sales and profits while enticing and satisfying the needs of consumers at the retail level. To accomplish this, one needs not only to look at the facilities and in particular the retail layout or counter display space, but also the promotion and utility of the product or products being offered.

So with merchandising we'll look at the following: 1) maximizing sales through product utility, 2) gross profit, 3) customer satisfaction, and 4) counter displays.

Maximizing Sales

If you're designing the retail space, you'll need to consider the flow of traffic. If you're looking to improve on an existing space, you'll need to observe the flow of traffic. Either way flow of traffic is important to product presentation because flow dictates consumer patterns.

Once this flow has been identified, you can set the display. Displays are usually set so the customer sees high volume and high gross items first (items having greater profit potential, profit returns or quick turnover). The utility of the product is determined by its value whether or not it can be fabricated into a like or similar product being offered but at a higher return on investment.

Customers enter the store or department knowing the nature of your business (retail). Upon doing so, they already have a purchase in mind, but they are not positive on the form their purchase may take. So this is where good merchandising comes in. It will be your experience to supply the customer with what they want, what they need and what you would like to sell them. For example, on sale is ground beef displayed with seasoned meatballs or meatloaf at a better price point (also known as cross-merchandising).

Cross merchandising display
Credit: Save on Foods

Gross Profit

Gross profit is the difference between revenue and the costs of making a product or providing a service. In other words, gross profit is the profit a retail outlet makes after deducting the costs associated with making and selling its products. Merchandising is employed to increase that profit picture. Another example of how we can increase or improve the gross profit picture in the retail sales area would be to build different types of displays in our display counters and small end bunkers or what are known as "merchandisers" (small independent refrigeration units). Bunkers or merchandising units are best utilized by displaying high profit or quick turnover items used to entice impulse buying. However, we need to use these units wisely. They best serve their purpose during seasonal fluctuations like during summer months or holiday seasons such as Thanksgiving, Christmas and Easter. During these times, we should concentrate on merchandising items associated with them or common to them. It would also be advantageous to consider the local demographics, current trends and other events in the community, like hot dogs during local baseball tournaments. Based on demographics the retailer can also take into consideration dietary restrictions imposed by religious practices or holidays.

Maintaining potential profits and customer satisfaction is providing goods and services for your customers during all hours of operation. To do this you will need to ensure full counter displays with a good variety of cuts. Whether the customer enters your department or store at 9:00 am or 5:50 pm, they should have the same advantage regarding opportunity of selection. In this regard, there are a few standard concerns for your consideration:

1. Small counters limit the variety you could offer.
2. Large counters are a challenge to keep full.
3. With large counter displays you run the risk of that "old" look where meats dry-out.

Cleanliness plays an important role. Keeping the counters neat and tidy, with rewraps removed and excess meat purge cleared should be a standard. Continuous cleaning is required throughout the day to remove fingerprints and moisture from the stainless steel, glass and mirrors. Customers will appreciate your department or store if cleanliness is a standard, as esthetics are important to appeal and keeping the customer's interest.

Customer Satisfaction

Customer satisfaction is a term frequently used in marketing. It is a measure of how products and services supplied by a retailer meet or exceed customer expectation.

The basic product is not enough; just meeting product or service requirements has never been enough. Customers expect additional service to support the products or services they use, and the meat industry is no exception. Customer satisfaction will be in direct proportion to how closely they feel connected, how well their expectations are met or are not met. Customer expectations are elastic or variable because their expectations change according to trends, price or service. It invariably includes what the competition offers, the customers' prior experience with other meat or food, retail or wholesale operations, personal values and a host of other criteria and factors.

Counter Displays

RETAILING OF MEATS - DIVERSITY OF PRODUCTS

Retailers usually look to recover anywhere from 800 to 1,000 dollars' worth of sales per linear foot of counter space. To get that, the following suggestions will help guide you as many counters are arranged in the following order (this may vary depending on, location, customer base and different ethnic groups):

- beef, because it has a large variety of fresh items
- veal, optional, located next to beef, usually an impulse item
- pork, associated with better gross profits (often cheaper than beef)
- lamb, optional, located next to pork, which is becoming a more attractive item
- sausage, freshly made or as a fresh item is a high gross profit product
- poultry, because it's a very common commodity and has a high per capita consumption and is traditionally less costly than beef

Looking at the variety of species, we should also consider the average or common counter line-up of each starting with the following:

Beef

Most common to beef displays are:

- Top Sirloin Grilling Steaks
- Porterhouse, T-Bone and Wing Grilling Steaks
- Strip Loin Grilling Steaks
- Rib Grilling Steaks
- Round Steaks Marinating Steaks
- Beef Stew
- Ground Beef
- Roast Beef, both pot & oven

There are many other items produced from beef, but the variety of items displayed depends on the linear footage available, and the above is the basis for building better and bigger displays. Value-added products such as kabobs, rouladen, stir-fry and pepper steaks may take more time to produce (labour intensive), but such items add to the flavour or colour of displays and can be interspersed between the common items listed.

Top sirloin grilling steaks

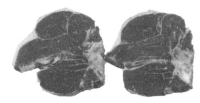

Porterhouse grilling steaks

T-Bone grilling steaks

Wing grilling steaks

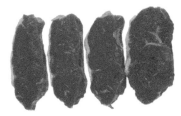

Striploin grilling steaks

Rib & Prime rib grilling steaks

Inside round marinating steaks

Beef stew
Credit: ©Erik Lam / Dreamstime

Ground beef
Credit: ©Le Thuy Do/Dreamstime

Cross rib pot roast

Outside round oven roast

Veal

Most common to veal displays are:

- Veal Cutlets
- Veal Scallopini
- Veal Steakettes
- Veal Chops
- Veal Roasts
- Veal Stew
- Ground Veal

Veal is an item that you must keep constant control of as it is not a major volume item and does lose its colour and moisture very quickly. Veal is appealing to a particular clientele as it is delicate in colour and flavour, and its texture characteristics are a little more attractive and pleasant to some culinary palates than others.

Veal cutlets
Credit: ©istock.com- credit to
yvdavyd

Veal oven roast
Credit: ©istock.com- credit to
sinankocaslan

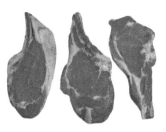

Veal chops
Credit: ©Swissmargrit /
Dreamstime

Pork

Most common to pork displays are

- Pork Loin Centre Chops Butterflied
- Pork Loin Centre Chops (regular or boneless)
- Pork Shoulder Blade Steaks
- Pork Leg Steaks
- Pork Sirloin Chops
- Pork Leg Inside Schnitzel, (breaded)

- Pork Back Ribs
- Pork Side Ribs
- Pork Tenderloin
- Ground Pork
- Pork Bones
- Pork Hocks
- Pork Liver

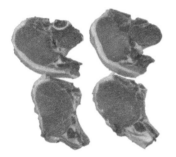

Pork loin center chops bone in

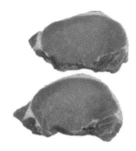

Pork loin center chops Boneless

Pork shoulder blade steaks

Pork sirloin chops

Pork back ribs

Pork side ribs

Pork hocks front & hind

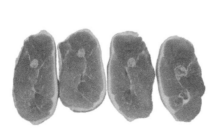

Pork leg center steaks

Pork liver
Canada Pork International

Pork is an item that is easy to cut and display, and it has a very low price cost per package, making it attractive to customers. Pork is a product that traditionally has a low investment and high return because of its versatility. Pork value-added items include fresh sausage and stuffed items like chops. A good variety of pork items assist with bringing gross profits in line. Pork is also very popular in North American and Asian diets.

Lamb

Most common to lamb displays are
- Lamb Loin Chops
- Lamb Shoulder
- Lamb Shoulder Arm or Blade Chops
- Lamb Roasts,
- Lamb Legs
- Lamb Racks
- Ground Lamb
- Lamb Stew

Lamb is an item requiring close surveillance as it is not high volume and will discolour more quickly than other meats. Lamb is available in greater quantities as a frozen product than a fresh product. Most lamb in Canada sold in supermarkets comes from foreign markets such as New Zealand and Australia. Becoming popular among smaller meat and specialty shops is local Canadian lamb.

Lamb loin & rib chops

Lamb rack

Lamb shoulder blade chops bone in

Lamb shoulder arm chops bone in

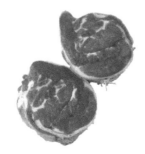

Lamb shoulder roast boneless

Lamb leg outside

Sausage

Most common to fresh sausage displays are

- Mild Italian
- Hot Italian
- Honey Garlic
- Bratwurst
- Oktoberfest
- Breakfast sausages

Sausage greatly increases the bottom line and increases gross profit margins. Material used to produce fresh or processed sausages must be of high-grade and high-quality (see chapter on sausage). When developing a sausage program, start with the basics such as fresh sausage and expand to include cooked, cured and fermented as volume and space allows. As well depending on the type of market you manage, one might consider fabrication of in-store or in-house home-style items.

Mild Italian sausage
Credit: Save on Foods

Hot Italian sausage
Credit: Save on Foods

Hot Chorizo Sausage
Credit: CPMCA image collection

Pork Breakfast Sausage
Credit: Costco

Poultry

Most common to poultry displays are

- Chicken Breasts (Bone- in)
- Chicken Breasts (Boneless, and/or skinless)
- Chicken Legs
- Chicken Drumsticks
- Chicken Thighs
- Chicken Wings, wing drumettes & winglets
- Roasting Chickens
- Frying Chickens
- Chicken backs & Necks
- Fresh Turkey

Poultry is most often put at the end of the meat counter display or in a separate display counter (case), as this item needs to be kept separate for health and safety concerns. Poultry is popular with almost everyone. Putting poultry at the end of your display forces customers to view the entire display looking for what they may want. This type of marketing produces interest in other similar items. Poultry like pork is an item that assists greatly with gross profit margins. As with pork, poultry sales are enhanced with value-added items such as vacuum tumbled or marinated breasts, seasoned drums or wings and boneless items like thighs and breasts. Most counters are set up to maximize sales and profit.

Chicken breast boneless
Credit: Jakes & Associates

Chicken breast boneless -
skinless – portions
Credit:CPMCA Image collection

Chicken legs
Credit:CPMCA Image collection

Chicken Drumsticks
Credit:CPMCA Image collection

Chicken thighs
Credit:CPMCA Image collection

Chicken Wings
Credit:CPMCA Image collection

Chicken wing drumettes
Credit:CPMCA Image collection

Chicken winglets
Credit:CPMCA Image collection

Roasting chicken packaged
Credit: Save on Food

Fresh Turkey
Credit: ©istock.com/credit to Paul Cowan

DELI

The cold cut counter space in larger retail outlets will probably be the same size as all of the fresh meat combined. The variety carried depends on the locale or demographics we spoke of earlier. The deli counter is a very large portion of the meat business and should not be neglected. All expired dates and shopworn products should be removed and discarded. Regular facing of products needs to be done as most processed items discolour when exposed to light. It's important to keep that fresh cut look for customer appeal.

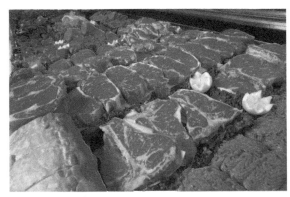

Retail beef display in case
Credit: Canada Beef

Retail chicken display in case
Credit: Summit Gourmet Meats

Retail pork & beef display
Credit: Save on Foods

Retail seafood display in case
Credit: Save on Foods

Well-stocked delicatessen case
Credit: Save on Foods

Cross-Merchandising

Cross-merchandising takes place when you are promoting an in-house or external special like chicken fryers, whole, three per bag, with a restriction of one bag per customer. The cutters would then cross-merchandise other fryers into segments, drumsticks, thighs, wings and boneless and/or skinless breasts and surround the SPECIAL with the higher priced and more profitable segmented items and condiments. This is a very proactive way to move the more profitable items while still offering a great deal on whole fryers. The fryer special draws the customer to the selected target sales zone in your store/department or meat counter display.

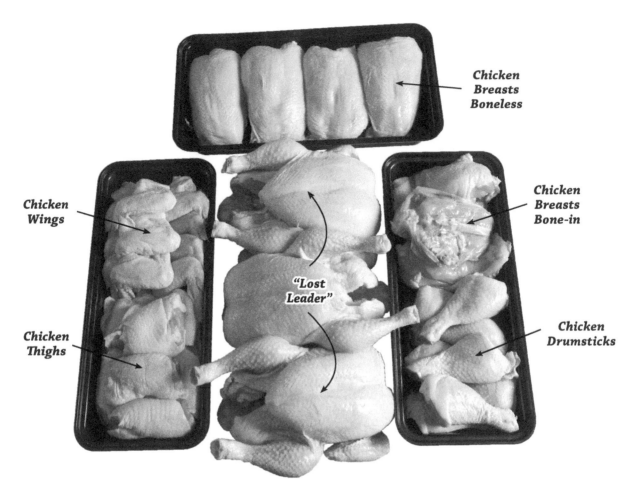

Lost leader item surrounded by
cross merchandised items
Credit: CPMCA Image Collection

Loss Leaders is a term used to identify a strategy whereby a product is sold below or at cost to stimulate other more profitable sales. The whole fryer would then be considered a LOSS LEADER as the product is traditionally sold at or near cost price to attract new customers and bargain hunters to your client base, with the expectation that many of them would purchase some of the "cross merchandised" products, thus ensuring your business maintains its projected profit margin. Larger outlets use this strategy as a means of attracting customers especially during seasonal times like Thanksgiving, Christmas and Easter. They may offer whole turkeys below cost in anticipation that customers coming in for turkeys will also stop to pick up other complimentary or essentials like meats for stuffing, seasonings, foil roasting pans, etc.

Social Media and Advertising

Social media has different forms, Twitter, Pinterest, Instagram, Youtube, Linkedin and Facebook etc. The more common social media forms used by business to market or advertise are twitter and Facebook (though at times we find Youtube videos embedded in the Facebook page). Twitter is used to announce current offerings with other twitter followers such as special of the day. Facebook on the other hand has proven to be a powerful way to communicate with customers and potential customers. It allows people to visit your establishment without physically being there through videos, photos, testimonials and an overview of what the business has to offer and how it has branded itself. With Facebook potential customers can get to meet the owner(s), staff and tour the facility before actually visiting or patronizing the business.

CFIA Advertising Regulations: To safeguard the general public and retailer, the Canadian Food Inspection Agency (CFIA) provides regulations to protect both parties from unfair business practices. An example would be our bagged chicken special offered at an attractive price, perhaps at cost. The retailer limits the quantity per purchase, assuring enough supply for their customers in compliance with advertising regulations, and customers are not misled with the knowledge that supply is as advertised. This prevents one customer clearing out the item (as per our example of the bagged chicken) so that the retailer can continue to offer the special to others.

The regulations require that the seller must inform the general public in their advertisement what they have to offer for sale and the conditions for the sale such as:

1. Name, phone number, email address and social media contact information of establishment
2. Product price per kg
3. Correct name of product: (frying chickens, whole)
4. Weight range of product(s)
5. Grade of product
6. Number or items (three whole chickens) in the package or bag
7. State if there are limits (one bag per customer) or other options such as: We reserve the right to limit quantities, or 30 day limit on all returns, returns must have a receipt, or all sales are final.
8. Applicable service charges (if any)
9. Sale dates (from/ to)
10. Are rain checks available or not

ADVERTISEMENTS FOR BULK BEEF, VEAL, PORK AND LAMB

[B.14.018, B.14.019]

The *Food and Drug Regulations* of Canada apply to the advertising of beef, veal, pork and lamb carcasses. Where a carcass or a portion weighing over seven kilograms is advertised for sale, the advertisement must include an **indication of the grade** assigned to the carcass by a Canadian or foreign grading authority. If no grade has been assigned, the advertisement must indicate that the carcass or portion has not been graded.

Further requirements apply when that same meat advertisement states a **selling price**.

B.14.019

(1) Where a carcass of beef, veal, pork or lamb or a portion thereof that weighs 7 kg or more is advertised for sale and a selling price is stated in the advertisement, the advertisement shall

(a) contain the words "price per kilogram is based on carcass weight before cutting, boning and trimming" or the words price per kilogram is based on the weight of the meat after cutting, boning and trimming", whichever words are applicable; and

(b) where in addition to the selling price a charge is payable for cutting, boning, trimming, wrapping or freezing the carcass or portion thereof, indicate

(i)   the amount of the additional charge, and

(ii) where the additional charge is payable on a price per unit weight basis, whether the additional charge is based on the weight of the carcass or portion thereof before or after the carcass has been cut, boned and trimmed.

(2) Any information required by subsection (1) to appear in an advertisement shall be located therein immediately adjacent to the selling price stated therein, without any intervening written, printed or graphic matter.

Packaging

Packaging plays an important role in the marketing and merchandising of product. Often consumers buy a product based on looks (appeal). Packaging protects the product on display from contaminants and is designed to attract customers. Packaging ensures the volatile aromatic and flavour components of a product are safely sealed.

Today's marketplace has a variety of packaging options, each designed for a specific purpose. We package meats to avoid contamination and product damage, for ease of distribution and display, but most assuredly for our retail consumers, who look to packaging to inform them of the contents, the product name, type, nutritional value, handling and storage and even perhaps cooking instructions.

For the most part, packaging materials provide

Wax coated wrapping paper roll
Credit: Bunzl Processor Division/Koch Supplies

- **Low permeability to oxygen**: Off-flavours in meats and fish that develop during storage (or display) are caused by oxidation of the fat, particularly those of red meats and fish, making it important that such foods be protected by wrapping material with low permeability to oxygen.
- **Protection**: Deterioration of meats in storage results from either dehydration or rancidity or a combination of the two. For protection of meat products (fresh and/or frozen), the packaging material should keep moisture in and air out.

Double roll paper dispenser & cutter
Credit: Bunzl Processor Division/Koch Supplies

- **Strength** (wet or dry): For cuts of meat that are irregular in shape and size or that have sharp corners, strength of packaging material is essential.
- **Wrap-ability**: The packaging material must be flexible enough for wrapping and moldable enough to tightly wrap odd shapes. The material shouldn't be brittle or sensitive to temperature fluctuations, should not crack or deteriorate in storage.
- **Resistance (**to water and grease): The material used to package should withstand condensation due to temperature changes (freezing, thawing, defrost cycles. etc.) and/or grease from markers or labels, etc.
- **Identification**: Packaging material must have good surface for labelling.

Packaging can be paper-based, brown wrap, wax coated freezer wrap, cartons and cardboard, etc. Packaging can be tin, ceramic or glass-based as with canned products. Packaging can be vacuum based (including gas flushed), shrink wrap based or plastic film based. Again, the nature and operation of an outlet determines the type of packaging used for handling, storage or display of product.

Something to consider is the packaging material themselves. The safety of all materials used for packaging foods is controlled under Division 23 of the Food and Drugs Act and Regulations, section B.23.001, which prohibits the sale of foods in packages that may impart any substance to the contents that may be harmful to the consumer of the food. For more information on this visit www.hc-sc.gc.ca and look under the topic of food safety.

Regardless of the type of packaging or packaging machines used for protecting products, persons using the equipment should be trained to do so in accordance with OHS standards and regulations as well as the needs of the establishment.

Vacuum packaging involves eliminating air and sealing a product in an impermeable plastic bag. Vacuum packaging is the simplest form of modified atmosphere packaging (MAP) or controlled atmosphere packaging (CAP). This type of packaging is commonly used for ham rings, garlic rings, cold cuts, corned beef, etc.

Double chambered vacuum machine.
NAIT - Professional Meat Cutting &
Merchandising Program

Gas flushing is a variation of vacuum packaging where air is removed, and carbon dioxide is flushed into the package and sealed. The carbon dioxide helps preserve the product inside the bag.

Packaging cooked sausages
through a gas flush system
Credit: Professional image, Industry approved

Shrink packaging is another variation of vacuum packaging where air is removed and the bag heat shrunk (moulded) to fit tightly around the shape of the product. This offers maximum protection against moisture loss while highlighting product conformation. Shrink wrap is used with packaging wieners, hams, rings and other processed meat items.

Ham product - shrink wrapped
Credit: Costco

Pork loin boneless - shrink wrapped
Credit: Costco

Heat seal wrapping is common to most supermarkets and independent outlets. The product is arranged on polystyrene trays and vita-film wrapped either manually or automatically by a programmed machine and sealed via a hotplate.

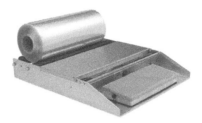

Manual single roll wrapping machine
Credit: Bunzl Processor Division/Koch Supplies

2 Manual double roll wrapping machine
TRU-Retail Meat Processing Program

Automatic wrapping machine
Credit: Costco

Labelling

Information on packaging, including words, pictures, claims, vignettes and logos will contribute to the overall impression created about the product inside, including "best before" date or "packaged on" dates indicating freshness and quality. Therefore, all labelling information on packaging, as required by legislation, must be accurate, truthful and not misleading. For example,

- Ingredient lists must accurately reflect the contents and their relative proportions in a food.
- Nutrition fact tables must accurately reflect the amount of nutrition present in a food.
- Net quantity declarations must accurately reflect the amount of food in the package.

Nutrition Label – lean ground beef
Credit: Costco

Best before & packaged on dates on label -Pork rib chops
Credit: Costco

Best before date on Meat package – Prime rib grilling steak
Credit: Canada Beef

Cooking logo for ground meats
Credit: Costco

Mechanically tenderized meat cooking guide for steaks
Credit: Costco

Mechanically tenderized meat cooking guide for roasts
Credit: Costco

Label indicating product is locally raised
Credit: TRU-Retail Meat Processing Program

In general, claims may be made about various aspects of a food, providing they are truthful, not misleading nor likely to create an erroneous impression, and that they are in compliance with any specific requirements that exist for a given type of claim. Certain claims, such as those relating to nutrient content, organic, kosher, halal and certain disease-risk reduction claims are subject to specific regulatory requirements in addition to the prohibitions in the Food and Drug Act (FDA) and the Consumer Packaging and Labelling Act (CPLA).

Quality Customer Service

These are exciting times in the meat industry. Interest in food and meat is growing in popularity. Consumers are more and more conscious of the food they eat and where that food comes from, how it is handled, grown and put to market. This can also be seen in the restaurant trade where chefs and owners are sourcing local products, organic products and fabricating in-house made products. The key to success is understanding marketing and merchandising as they apply to good customer service. Customer service as a means of consumer awareness of the image you want the public to have is important to repeat business. We feel this to be crucial to building a positive rewarding business operation.

Definitions of quality customer service vary and will continue to vary because customers demand changes, and this is what causes customer service to be continually redefined. For our context, customer service is the provision of service to customers before, during and after a purchase. **Customers, in most cases, can get the same quality of meat products or any commodity products from numerous companies; however, the quality of service aspect is what makes the difference.** Major food chains market the same top-quality meats. Many purchase from the same packing plants. The difference between them is in the personal dimension, where attitudes, behaviours and verbal skills of servers are vital to the quality of customer service.

Communication is a process by which information is exchanged between individuals through a common system of signs, symbols and behaviours. It involves both mind and body, where the spoken word ends up being a small part of total communication. Along with the language we use, gestures, facial expressions and voice tone can change the intended meaning of the message. As a result, people may not always hear and understand the intended meaning of the communication. As a practitioner of communication, having a good understanding of the following five principles can positively shape our communication with others:

- Understand and interpret verbal and non-verbal messages
- Use positive body language and voice tone
- Use language others will understand
- Actively listen to what the other is saying
- Communicate effectively and clearly when using forms of media, including the telephone

VERBAL COMMUNICATION

Communication is more than just spoken words. It is the way that we say things and not so much what we say when we communicate with others. Experts identify face-to-face communication as conveying only 20% of your message through words and 45% of your message by the quality of your voice tone and inflection. The remainder of the message is transmitted through body language or the non-verbal form of communication.

NON-VERBAL COMMUNICATION

Before we get too carried away, you need to understand that non-verbal communication comes in many forms. It can be in the form of either written and unwritten words. As you progress through this material, you will see the focus is concentrated more on body language than the written word. However, it is the medium of the written word we use to convey that message to you.

Body language is an interesting topic that fascinates many people particularly when one is passing time watching people. When people are unaware of others, they are more relaxed and revealing. Some observations are the way they stand, sit, use their hands and their facial expressions. Each facet of a person's body language can be a clue to what he or she is thinking or feeling and may contrast directly with what is being said (verbalized).

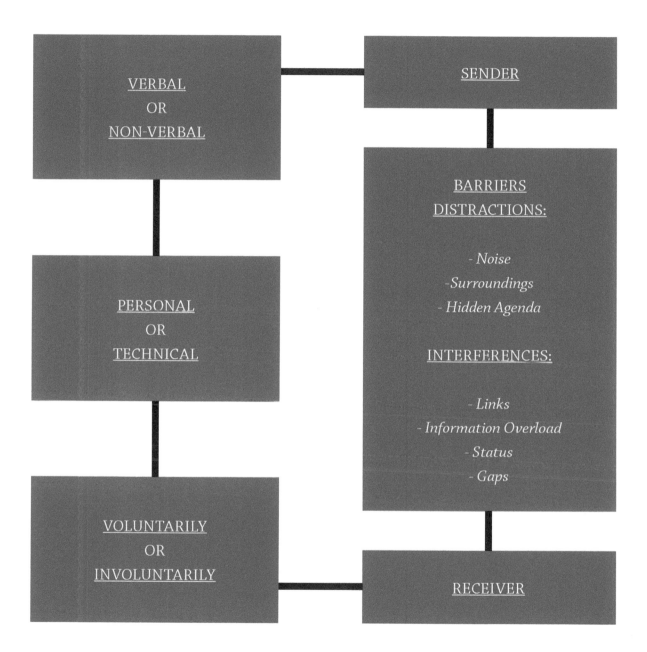

An illustration outlining the flow of information through a common system of signs, symbols and behaviours and how problems can arise while communicating with others!

Dan Westgeest, 1992

Customer Service

The following is information that applies directly to all facets of the food service industry. Here we've decided to illustrate more the retail viewpoint, and we do so without discrimination of other service disciplines that can also benefit from the content of this chapter. After graduating from a meat training program, you can follow the basic framework we outline and apply it as a meat cutter, server or retailer. The information we provide herein is a nutshell of what anyone in the service industry should know or at least have an awareness of, and that being the basic aspects of customer service. We also supply a few exercises on how to apply the basic principles of quality customer service within the text.

Customer service is the assistance and advice you provide to those consumers who buy or use your products or services.

If you are going to be successful either on a personal or business level, it is important you have a good basic knowledge of interpersonal communication. The public, as customers, expect you to attend to their needs and/or demands; if you don't, they'll find someone who will, even if it means finding another venue or outlet.

For most people protein is a necessary staple of their daily diet, motivating them to purchase meat products. Although customers are unique, there are certain concerns and demands common to them all.

First, is the desire to be treated with courtesy and respect.

Second, customers are concerned with getting value and quality; meat is expensive and people want to feel they have spent their money wisely.

Thirdly, people are concerned primarily with themselves and with their families. Make customers feel important, as they **are** important to you; your job is dependent upon them. Recognize individuals, if possible, and be friendly. Smile!

Integrated and driving the above three points are: having knowledge of your product(s), your personal appearance, your honesty and your product presentation.

KNOW YOUR PRODUCT WELL

One of the most important requirements for meat cutters is to know the product well and be able to communicate that knowledge to the customer. As previously stated, this includes knowing the origin of the meat products, their ingredients, their care, harvesting practices and whether or not the product is hormone and antibiotic free, free-range and/or organic. Having a good fundamental knowledge of cooking methods also helps, especially for meat products, so as to advise the customer on the appropriate preparation and storage, carving methods, number of servings and possible food accompaniments that can be important to customers. Sharing ideas and advice with customers fosters an "association" between seller and customer, encouraging repeat business - an important part of marketing, something that can't be stressed enough.

PERSONAL APPEARANCE

Your appearance is also extremely important, as you never get a second chance at making a first impression. Meat cutters must be neat and practice appropriate personal hygiene as part of both food safety and public safety. As noted in the chapter on sanitation, your skin and hair must be scrupulously clean, if male. This includes being clean-shaven or well trimmed and maintained facial hair and/ or wearing a chin net guard and for both sexes having their hair under control. In addition, pay attention to the mouth area, including teeth, which should receive frequent attention. Clothing must also be kept clean, which means regular changes and laundering of clothes.

HONESTY

One of the most important characteristics a person needs is integrity. If you have integrity, you have everything you need to be successful both individually and professionally. With integrity comes honesty, something a meat cutter should have. Genuineness is also a part of honesty. Let the customer know what you can do

Staff in uniform in a meat store
Credit: Summit Gourmet Meats

for them and not what you can't do. Avoid flattery, false promises or exaggerations. These will be quickly detected and will ultimately create a lack of confidence in both the seller and in the company. For example, customers should be given the facts on their purchases in a straightforward manner. Say, "nine hundred grams at $9.18 a kilogram comes to..." rather than vague phrases such as "That's about 1 kg...." Check your scales frequently to make sure they are accurate (a legal requirement). Always confirm the purchase before proceeding.

ATTRACTIVE PRESENTATION

Connected directly to personal appearance is the presentation of your product. Meat that is imaginatively displayed will be more attractive to the customer than meat laid out in a disorderly or sloppy manner, having no aesthetic (eye) appeal. A display case may appeal to a wide range of tastes and pocketbooks featuring a variety of items from tenderloin grilling steaks to ground meat items. At the risk of sounding repetitive, customers are becoming more and more concerned with the handling of meat and meat items from a health and wellness point of view. It is up to you to make sure you pose no health risk to them or their families. Wear disposable gloves when handling meats or different species in the presence of customers, changing them as often as needed to avoid cross-contamination. The use of tongs or other suitable utensils is also acceptable. A clean working area under safe conditions and good personal hygienic practices by staff are of vital importance to customers. Customers need to know that you are following government regulation standards.

Finally, the meat cutter who is helpful and sincere, with a cheerful disposition and a desire to please, will foster a good personal reputation and instill customer confidence. You need to enjoy your work and perform your tasks skillfully with pride. Your interaction with customers must be genuine and pleasing to reflect a continued effort of doing a good job in the eyes of the customer. Remember, service and satisfaction will bring customers back, and that is the best marketing tool available to you, "word of mouth."

SOME HELPFUL TIPS FOR QUALITY CUSTOMER SERVICE

Handle meat carefully both in public and in private. Remember, you're handling product that people will be eating.

1. Call out the weight and prices of the product when serving the customer.
2. Don't try to oversell.
3. Wrap meat purchases carefully.
4. Accept cheques graciously as some senior customers still use them. Remember to ask politely for ID from customers that are not established with your business.
5. Never talk about one customer to another. People will assume that you will treat them in the same manner.
6. Do not criticize competitors.
7. Do not say things that give a negative overtone like, "We do not have that product." and leave it at that. Offer a substitute or acquire the item for your customer at a later date. Make a note of requested items not currently stocked and consider carrying them.
8. If you have a very busy shop or counter, consider establishing a priority number system.
9. Be patient with senior customers. They may make small purchases, but they can be invaluable in sending new customers your way, such as their families.
10. Serve children as customers with the same courtesy you extend to adults. They influence others as well.
11. Regardless of whether it is 5 minutes after opening time or 5 minutes to closing, the service to the customer should always be the same.
12. Finish off the sale with a courteous, "Will there be anything else for you today?" and always remember to say "Thank you" as the customer prepares to leave.

Do not be disappointed if customers seem not to appreciate the fact that you have tried to make their shopping experience easier and more enjoyable. The results may not be immediate. In any case, you will get far more enjoyment and satisfaction from your work if you interact pleasantly with people. Remember, your customers are the reason that you have a career.

CHOOSING APPROPRIATE WORDS

A service provider's choice of words can make a difference. The English language is made up of thousands of words. There are several words known as synonyms, which carry or convey the same message. As a simple exercise list as many words as you can think of that mean the same thing as the word, **"customer."** Example: consumer or shopper.

EXTERNAL AND INTERNAL CUSTOMER

Keep it clear and simple – An important concept to remember and exercise is to keep the language simple, clear, positive and enthusiastic. Avoid jargon, technical terms and abbreviations with external customers. (However, if it applies to internal customers or people in your organization, it may be appropriate.) But keep in mind that referring to your customers as "end users" or "bargain hunters" isn't positive.

Emphasize the positive – To be good at your craft you need to like what you do and want to do it well. Being serious about the quality of your work doesn't mean you can't enjoy it. The importance of a positive attitude begins even before you start your first day at the job. It begins with the job interview. Dress and behave not for the group you belong to, but for the group you want to join. The meat industry requires physical and mental stamina, good health and a willingness to work. At times the pressure can be intense, gruelling or monotonous. Overcoming these hurdles requires a sense of responsibility and a dedication to your craft, to your coworkers and most importantly to your customers.

This positive attitude flows over into the service you provide and the interaction you have with customers. Acknowledge customers as they walk in, greeting them with a good morning, good afternoon or good evening. Let those who are waiting know you will attend to them as soon as humanly possible. Offer customers choices and take on the responsibility for them. For example, if a customer is waiting in line, make sure that he/she is waiting for assistance in the correct line, area or department, if any. This is done by asking the appropriate questions instead of telling them when they reach the front of a long line of people.

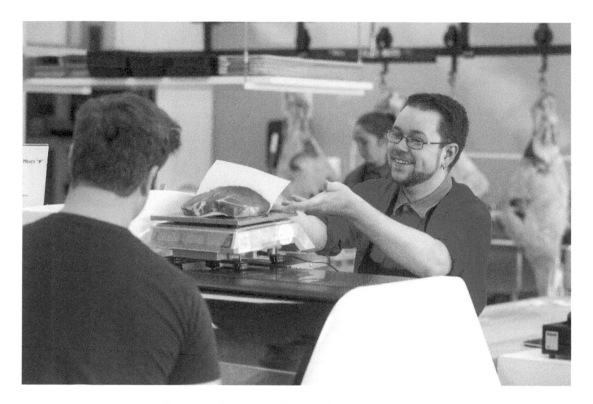

Customer Service - Scaling product for a customer
Credit: Summit Gourmet Meats

Exercise

Rephrase the following negative statements with responses that emphasize the positive attitude customers deserve by offering choices that demonstrate responsibility.

1. Negative: That's not my department.

    Positive: _____

    _____

    _____

2. Negative: There's not enough demand for that item.

    Positive: _____

    _____

    _____

3. Negative: I only work here.

   Positive: _____

   _____

   _____

4. Negative: It's over there in the freezer.

   Positive: _____

   _____

   _____

5. Negative: I need your photo ID.

   Positive: _____

   _____

   _____

Dealing with People

One must also understand that no matter where you are in an organization, you will deal with difficult people as customers both internally and externally, meaning those that frequent your establishment and those who work within the establishment. External customers can be difficult to satisfy, but the toughest people to deal with are often people in your own organization. An effective attitude to customer satisfaction would be to approach them professionally and not personally. Being professional means keeping the spotlight on the issue under discussion and away from you or them personally. If you have unsolved difficulties with peers, it will not take long for these unsolved matters to spill over onto the external customers. Seeking new customers is always an objective; however, equally important is to retain the customers that you currently have. The key is repeat business! Think about it; if you think it is tough getting customers, try getting them back.

THE CUSTOMER IS ALWAYS RIGHT.

A servicer needs to learn not to get embroiled in an argument with a customer, deciding who is right or wrong! The core issue or purpose here is to provide the customer with the best possible service for what they want and need. The servicer needs to handle the issue as a sale, not be concerned about who is right.

THE CUSTOMER IS "NOT" ALWAYS RIGHT

The customer is always the customer, who may or may not be right. When a customer has an issue, the servicer needs to seek out remedies such as solving the problem without laying blame on anyone such as a co-worker, the customer or themselves. Stick to the facts and don't get flustered by the customer's response. Focus on the result you want, customer satisfaction. If the customer responds in anger, know that this is just a defense mechanism alerting you they are not pleased. It doesn't have to be a personal attack. Take charge of your reaction(s).

SOLVE ISSUE(S)/ PROBLEM(S) WITHOUT BLAME.

Blaming yourself or blaming others is unproductive. It wastes time and hurts relationships. Blaming creates negative energy, which does not provide any remedies for solving problems. Remember, focus on what you can do, not on what you can't do. You

Retail store cutting team all working together
Credit: Summit Gourmet Meats

Wrapping product in a retail meat store.
Credit: Summit Gourmet Meats

Wrapping meat in a larger meat retailer
Credit: Costco

can't control a customer's feelings of right or wrong. They are who they are, and it is up to you to serve them as kindly and quickly as possible, putting aside your personal prejudice about the matter. When the customer purchases the product and you put the money in the cash register, you've won because at that point the customer is obviously satisfied enough to make the purchase and have you serve them. Think of the end goal!

Teamwork

We now take a quick look at teamwork as it applies to our internal customers (fellow workers) and how effective teamwork adds to the customer satisfaction component of our business.

Teamwork is the process of working collaboratively with a group of people in order to achieve a goal. It means we try to cooperate using our individual skills toward a common goal or outcome. Teamwork is an important part of our business, as often we don't work alone. There are literally volumes of literature written about teamwork, and for the most part this literature focuses on team performance, seen as a cyclical series of input-process/output-process episodes. Plainly put, this means people within a team will cooperate using their skills and provide constructive feedback, despite any personal conflict between them while evaluating the results of their efforts and making any changes they collectively deem necessary. The team is supposed to be a safe environment where each member can express their opinions, make suggestions and offer feedback without prejudice, fear of reprisal or ridicule.

The principles involved with teamwork are very good, but it is the application of teamwork by the people involved that decides its usefulness. Within teamwork people have the opportunity and commitment of finding the best possible solution rather than imposing a solution from one person. Agreed-upon ideas and possible solutions should be challenged by team players in order to test the significance and validity of solving a particular problem. Team players need to monitor the effect of the new solutions once they have been accepted, to determine whether new problems will arise as a result of the solutions.

When the teamwork isn't functioning effectively, the result may be due to the people within the team, and this in turn becomes problematic. This can lead to difficult situations happening in the workplace. Workers within a team need to be flexible and resilient to spontaneous situations, particularly in retail orientated businesses.

Team relationships may and can become more harmonious when members understand what is expected of them individually as well as from each other. Team players are required to participate in authentically learning how to contribute toward the objectives and benefits involved. Members learn to deal effectively with conflict resolution of issues, where fact-based problem-solving approaches need to be utilized in producing positive resolutions from everyone's perspective. The central concept of teamwork is the activity of all members sharing information and responsibilities, which allows individuals to maximize their potential and develop strong customer relationships. Teamwork is facilitated by effective team leaders, who assign roles and are responsible for maintaining consistency of effort and knowledge of the team. An effective team leader will recognize that problem-solving strategies become one of the most important activities for teamwork processes. All members must have the same focus and methods in place in order to effectively deal with specific agendas.

Team players need to build their professional characters. The following are warning signs that indicate you are beginning to take customer interactions personally.

1. It is not that easy!
2. No one appreciates the things I do!
3. You don't know the "bimbos" I have to work with!
4. You can't soar with eagles when you are cooped up with turkeys.
5. Do you want to know what he/she said about. . .
6. I don't get paid enough to be professional.
7. They never do anything around here!
8. They always do things like that!

Superlative words like "biggest, largest, never, always, etc." are not held as being very descriptive for professional conversation or writing. People often use these types of words to over or under exaggerate situations that they are describing. If you hear your inner voice saying any of the above, the answer is clear. You're taking things personally. In order to reduce stress at work, we suggest you build your skills toward becoming more professional when responding to situations instead of blowing steam and giving customers the cold shoulder.

According to the professional research authors of quality service, you may find that the people inside your store or organization are tougher to deal with than the outside customers. Some people have excellent skills in handling outside customers while being totally insensitive to their peers on the inside.

POSSIBLE TECHNIQUES FOR KEEPING THE SPOTLIGHT ON THE ISSUE

Things your inner voice should NOT say!

- I'm being accused of making a mistake.
- No one can talk to me that way.
- You make mistakes too! You're not perfect!
- Well, here is a replacement item, but next time, bring your receipt with you.

Things your inner voice CAN say!

- How can I solve this issue?
- Can you please tell me what needs to be done?
- This is not the way we normally provide service. I would like to correct the mistake and provide the quality you have paid for.
- For your inconvenience, I'd like you to try some samples of processed meat products that we make here at store level.

CHECKPOINT:

- Some of the biggest challenges centre on the people part of my job.
- Many of the difficult or tough situations stem from people on the inside.
- The most effective way to handle difficult situations is to handle them professionally and not personally.

REINFORCEMENT WOULD BE TO SAY TO YOURSELF:

I like my job. It is not easy to deal with difficult people; however, I've chosen a people business industry, and I'm making things better for myself by interacting with people professionally.

It has been demonstrated that taking things professionally and not personally pays off; however, it takes a lot of energy and concentration. We are faced with rapid change and constant demands of today's competitive market place, and if we do not heed what our bodies and minds are telling us, we can easily slip into a burnt-out state.

BURNOUT CUES & SIGNALS

- Decreased concentration
- A short fuse
- Suspension of joy
- Complaining
- Use of stimulants
- Substance abuse

Exercise

Rewrite these statements in a proactive and positive manner.

1. You'll have to come back tomorrow when the manager is here.

   _____

   _____

2. You can't return any goods without a receipt. It's company policy!

   _____

   _____

3. I'm sorry, but you will have to wait another twenty minutes!

   _____

   _____

4. You must have neglected to follow up on our request.

   _____

   _____

5. You'll have to stand in line just like everyone else!

   _____

   _____

6. Give us a call and see if we can't set up an appointment for you.

   _____

   _____

7. Unfortunately, we can't accept your explanation.

   _____

   _____

8. We never set up our schedule that far in advance.

_____

_____

9. You failed to call us far enough in advance for that arrangement to be made.

_____

_____

10. The least you could have done was to provide us with complete information.

_____

_____

11. You must not have understood me correctly; I was very clear in what I said!

_____

_____

12. I'll check with the manager, but I don't think he/she will approve something like this!

_____

_____

13. If I were you, I would forget about all this. You're wasting your time over something so small.

_____

_____

14. The smart thing for you to do would have been to return this product immediately.

_____

_____

15. If you had looked closer, you would have noticed that you bought this six months ago, not two weeks ago!

_____

_____

16. If you were smart you would have noticed that you did not buy this product here. We don't handle this brand!

_____

_____

Many who write about customer service talk about "beyond customer service" or "service beyond expectations." The main reason for providing service beyond what is expected is to create repeat business, to have customers return on a regular basis. The following points suggest ways to provide superior service and the retention of customers:

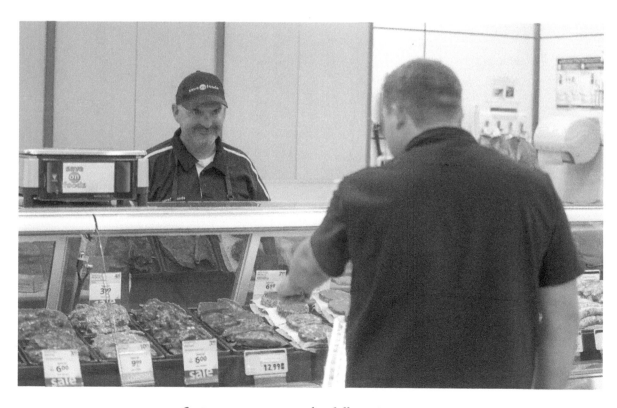

Customer at a supermarket full service counter
Credit: Save on Foods

Customer at a supermarket self service meat counter
Credit: Canada Beef

1. Customers are the most important people in the company.
2. The customer is independent. When it comes to grocery purchases, it is you, the the server, manager or store owner, who are dependent upon people shopping at your establishment.
3. You work for customers. They are the lifeblood of your job or your business. Without customers you would not have a job, and the business would not exist.
4. Customers are not people who you want to argue with or match wits with; it is not conducive to the environment of "service."
5. Consumers are people with feelings and emotions just as you are. They are not a cold statistic.
6. Consumers are the purpose of your work. They are not an interruption of your work!
7. Consumers are as much a part of your business as other aspects of your business, including employees, the building, equipment and inventory.
8. Consumers deserve the most attentive, courteous and professional treatment that service providers can give.
9. Call your customers by name and listen to what they have to say.
10. Get to know your customers' buying habits and show concern for each customer as an individual.
11. Ask your customers for advice and suggestions. Involve them in your business.
12. Take sufficient time with customers making them feel important by giving them compliments.

Ways of Establishing Customer Retention

1. **Unique Personalized Service Philosophy**: Your business would benefit from creating a service philosophy or mission statement, which would complement the overall service aspects of your business. A mission statement would describe exactly how customers would be treated when purchasing products and services from your business with a list of preferred outcomes.

2. **Customer Feedback**: It is crucial to have feedback from your customers. They will tell you how to improve your service and/or products. You can set up focus groups, hand out surveys, mail out surveys, conduct personal interviews and continually ask for their feedback. Listen to what they have to say, evaluate what they say and then act on the suggestions that would benefit everyone involved.

3. **Meet and Exceed Expectations**: All customers have expectations when they spend money on service and product, and you should meet these expectations to achieve customer satisfaction. Furthermore, if you exceed their expectations, you have the potential of ensuring their loyalty. Exceeding customer expectations is the key to repeat and steady business.

4. **Customer Reward Programs**: Many types of rewards are aimed at customers, such as demonstration food displays, frequent buyer prizes, complimentary tickets to hockey games, gift certificates and any kind of referral program. Rewards will make customers feel special, and they will likely return to do more business with you.

5. **Community Service**: Your community service will help customers feel good about doing business with you, providing your business is involved with school team sponsorships, charity tie-ins and environmental issues. Make sure that your customers know of your efforts in these areas.

6. **Convenient, Accessible, User Friendly Service Systems:** Make sure that your services and products are accessible and readily available when the customer needs them – especially the following:
   - New available products
   - Refunds
   - Rain checks
   - Solutions to complaints

Much of customer service involves common sense. You give customers what they want and make sure that they are happy with it. And if you manage complaints appropriately, offer refunds and smile at customers, then you're providing a small part of excellent customer service. Excellent customer service also means going out of your way for customers and doing everything possible to satisfy customers. You need to make decisions that benefit the customer, sometimes even at the expense of the business. In today's competitive market, you need to provide superior service. The payoff is *long-term customer retention*.

You may think some of this information is stuff for management. Well, this information is also valuable for those who are training because it demonstrates the value of understanding all aspects of the meat or food business. Employees in each area need to be aware of what is going on around them. Students and trainees can gain an appreciation for people who demonstrate good management principles.

Value-added service means giving the customers more than they expect. Sometimes you can charge more for value-added products/service. You can do your own customer service marketing program to increase customer retention by going beyond customer service through the following:

Frequent buyer programs - Reward those customers who buy from you regularly to show them that you appreciate their business. You could have a card punch system that after the tenth or twelfth purchase, customers get something free or a significant discount. Repeat purchase cards can be an excellent way to retain customers, and they are an excellent marketing tool.

Frequent referral programs - When the same customer refers potential customers, do something special for the referring customer in a way that recognizes their valued contribution.

Thank you cards - A simple and effective customer retention technique for customer groups such as community league sports teams, church groups, schools and business associations, etc. If you operate a small specialty meat business, food store or any food outlet, you can send out referral thank you cards and at the same time record information and dates of when the cards were sent out, which you can then track (by a database program, etc.).

Customer reward and recognition programs - Recognizing and rewarding your customers should be a regular business practice. It informs customers that you understand their contribution to your business success. It is important to learn and use their names. They will appreciate your interest in them. Sending out thank you cards and giving gifts for referrals, mentioned earlier, are all part of rewarding and recognizing customers.

Employee Recognition and Reward programs - Employees as well as customers need to be recognized for their contributions. After all they interact directly with customers all the time. Customers also like to see familiar faces where they shop, as it is taken as a sign of stability and good morale.

An important part of customer service is ensuring that the products your customers are purchasing are safe to eat and that they are quality products. You just can't have one without the other; the two go hand-in-hand. It makes no sense at all to have great customer service that promotes an inferior product. Customers determine the success of the operation through their purchases. Without customer retention, there is no real quality service to be offered.

Regulations and Standards are directly and indirectly linked to customer service. Food Safe programs and the hazard analysis critical control point (HACCP) have established codes specifically for the food industry. In Canada, the meat industry is scrutinized and policed by the CFIA, which is specified in Communiqué 16 (1977) that all meat species, primal and retail cuts will follow a standardized nomenclature system. Communiqué 16 also provides guidelines that personnel in the meat industry must follow. According to the Quality Management Institute (QMI), it is the customer who defines quality through product and communication consistency.

Marketing & Merchandising Customer Service Math

METRIC & IMPERIAL CONVERSION

It is important for workers in the meat industry to know how to do metric conversions. Even though Canada is supposed to be entirely on the metric system, there are still many people who think in terms of the imperial system (pounds and ounces). Converting from metric to imperial and back to metric is a daily occurrence in the meat industry, and is a skill that is easily mastered.

Metric to Imperial / Imperial to Metric

Kilograms to pounds / pounds to kilograms

Actual Conversion Ratio:

1 kg = 2.2046 lbs   *or*   2.2046 lbs = 1 kg

*** HELPFUL THINGS TO KEEP ON TOP OF ***

What is your weight? _____ lbs *or* _____ kg

Your weight is roughly twice as much in _____

Your weight is roughly half as much in _____

For your weight which is the larger figure? lbs _____ *or* kg _____

For your weight which is the smaller figure? lbs _____ *or* kg _____

The following weights should be used as a guide, and they should also be memorized:

8	Oz.	=	227	grams	
1	lb	=	454	grams	
2	lbs	=	908	grams	
10	lbs	=	4.5	kg	(4.54 kg)
100	lbs	=	45	kg	(45.40 kg)
1	kg	=	2.2	lbs	(2.2046 lbs)
10	kgs	=	22	lbs	(22.046 lbs)
100	kgs	=	220	lbs	(220.46 lbs)

Note: There are 1,000 grams in one kilogram.

In the meat industry meat cutters and meat processors will be expected to make conversions with, 1) weights, of pounds to kilograms and vice versa, 2) cost of pounds to kilograms and vice versa, and 3) price per kilogram to price per pound and vice versa. In more specialized operations such as sausage manufacturing, the conversion of: 1) temperatures, Centigrade and Fahrenheit, and 2) volume, litres and gallons may also be required.

How are kilograms converted to pounds and back again? The example below will illustrate:

> 1 kg = 2.2046 lbs, meaning there are 2.2046 lbs in every kilogram.
> So 10 kg = 10 X 2.2046 *or* 22.046 lbs
>
> Let's try another one...8 kg = 17.64 lbs How do we know?

In every kilogram there are 2.2046 lbs. If the item in question weighs 8 kg (metric), the weight is simply multiplied by 2.2046 to convert it to imperial weight measurement (pounds):

> 8 (kg) X 2.2046 = 17.64 lbs

To convert from imperial to metric, simply divide the number of pounds by the actual conversion factor (2.2046).

> Example: 17.64 ÷ 2.2046 = 8.00 kg

When doing these conversions, a calculator will not always be available. The following is an exercise to assist in the mental calculation of conversion from metric to imperial.

Example: A meat cutter in a supermarket is filling the display freezer with turkeys. A customer comes along and picks out one weighing 12 kilograms and turns to the meat cutter for assistance in converting the weight to imperial (pounds). The meat cutter does not have a calculator handy, so what now?

Here is an easy and effective way to make the calculation:

> - take the weight of the turkey (12 kg) and multiply
> it by two and then add ten percent of the answer:
>
> (12 X 2) + 10% = 24 + 2.4 which = 26.4 lbs

Let's break this down one step at a time so that we fully understand it!

The turkey weighs 12 kg. Multiply that by two, which equals 24. Then take ten percent of 24 (which is 2.4) and add it to the answer to get 26.4, which is the weight in pounds.

Converting Price per Kilogram to Price per Pound. Now that metric units can be comfortably converted to imperial units and back again, let's take it a step further. What about the conversion of price per kilogram to price per pound and the other way around, price per pound to price per kilogram?

*** NOTICE! THIS IS IMPORTANT ***

If the sign above the Eye of Round steaks indicates the price per kilogram to be eleven dollars and ninety-eight cents ($11.98), then to convert this to price per pound it is necessary to do the opposite of weight conversion and divide 2.2046 into the price per kilogram. Why? Because it is known that in every kilogram, there are 2.2046 pounds. Therefore to find the cost per pound it is necessary to divide (not multiply) the 2.2046 figure into the per kilogram price. The objective is not to find the weight in pounds, but rather the cost per pound. And remember, we're dealing with currency, so we round off to the nearest cent, meaning the second decimal place.

Knowing that it is necessary to divide the 2.2046 into the cost per kilogram ($11.98), the result is:

> 11.98 ÷ 2.2046 = $5.43 (per pound)

Converting price per kilogram to price per pound: divide the price per kilogram by the actual conversion ratio.

Example: To find the price per pound on an advertised price per kilogram item, the following equation would be used:

$$\boxed{\text{price per kg} \quad \div \quad \text{actual conversion ratio} \quad = \quad \text{price per pound}}$$

Advertised price: $5.05 kg for Outside Roast

   We know that one kilogram is equal to 2.2046 pounds. To determine price per pound for the above item, it is necessary to divide the price per kilogram by the actual conversion ratio:

$$\boxed{\$5.05 \quad \div \quad 2.2046 \quad = \quad \$2.2906649 \text{ or } \$2.29 \text{ per pound (rounded to the nearest cent)}}$$

Converting price per pound to price per kilogram. Above we have a working formula that converts price per kilogram to price per pound, and now we try some conversions of price per pound to price per kilogram.

   How? Simply do the opposite. Instead of dividing the price per kilogram by 2.2046, multiply the price per pound by 2.2046.

Converting per pound to price per kilogram: multiply the price per pound by the actual conversion ratio.

Example: To find the price per kilogram on an advertised price per pound item, use the following equation:

$$\boxed{\begin{array}{c} \text{price per pound} \quad X \quad 2.2046 \quad = \quad \text{price per kilogram} \\[2mm] \text{Advertised price: \$2.29 lb for outside steak or roast.} \end{array}}$$

We know that one kilogram is equal to 2.2046 pounds. To determine price per kilogram for the above item, multiply the price per pound by the actual conversion ratio:

$$\boxed{\$2.29 \quad X \quad 2.2046 \quad = \quad \$5.048534 \text{ or } \$5.05 \text{ per kilogram}}$$

PRICE PER 100 GRAMS

Converting price per pound to price per 100 Grams and vice versa.

   First and before proceeding, remember there are 1,000 grams in every kilogram or ten 100-gram units in every kilogram (10X100=1,000).

There are many times when products received are priced at a cost per pound and must be sold or advertised at a cost per 100 gram units. Examples are higher priced products often sold in meat counters, the deli or seafood sections of a market. To do this conversion, follow the steps below.

Example: A product costs $2.45 per pound, and it is to be sold per 100 g.

> **Step one:** convert from pounds (imperial) to kilograms (metric)
>
> $2.45 (price per lb)   X   2.2046   = $5.40 (price per kg)
>
> **Step two:** convert from price per kg to price per 100 grams
>
> $5.40 (price per kg)   ÷   10   =   54 cents per 100 grams

When the products received are priced at a cost per kilogram, then determining the cost per 100 grams is much easier because it eliminates the need to first convert from cost per pound to cost per kilogram.

There are many times when a customer wants to know the price per pound when the product is sold by 100 grams. Examples are products often sold in the deli or seafood sections of a meat market. To do this follow these steps:

Example: A product sells for 79 cents per 100 grams. What is the price per pound?

> **Step one:** convert from price per 100 grams to price per kilogram
>
> .79   X   10   = $7.90 (price per kg)
>
> **Step two:** convert from price per kg to price per pound
>
> $ 7.90 (price per kg)   ÷   2.2046   = $3.58 (price per pound)

Note: For further details on Bacterial growth & Safe Meat Handling see the Appendix temperture guides on pages 746-47.

Temperatures

The use of temperature controls are common in all meat industry settings, including supermarkets, smaller retail outlets, custom processing operations, sausage processing operations, slaughter or animal harvesting facilities and other fabrication plants for animal species sold in the food chain.

Some examples would be a supermarket that sells ready to eat foods such as BBQ chickens and other cooked deli food items, items that must be kept at the proper holding temperatures either cold (below 4° C) or hot (above 60°C). Manufactured products like cooked and smoked sausages are also subject to rigid temperature control during fabrication and at various holding stages. Though most modern equipment sold and operated in Canada is equipped with controls that read and calculate in metric, there still exists equipment that only reads in imperial. As well, problematic to the industry is recipe formulation, which can appear in either metric or imperial. Furthermore, many customers we deal with on a day-to-day basis are not fully familiar with the Celsius scale.

CONVERTING CELSIUS TO FAHRENHEIT

When converting the temperature from Celsius to Fahrenheit, multiply the Celsius degrees by 1.8 and add 32. Example:

$$(\text{Celsius temperature} \times 1.8) + 32 = \text{Fahrenheit or}$$

$$(68°C \times 1.8) + 32 = 154° \text{ Fahrenheit}$$

And when you need to convert Fahrenheit to Celsius, you simply reverse the calculation. To convert Fahrenheit to Celsius subtract 32 from the degrees in Fahrenheit and divide by 1.8. Example:

$$(\text{Fahrenheit temperature} - 32) \div 1.8 = \text{Celsius or}$$

$$(154° F - 32) \div 1.8 = 68°C$$

Note: For further details on Bacterial growth & Safe Meat Handling see the Appendix temperture guides on pages 746-47.

Volume:

Volume measurement is used extensively in the meat industry where liquids are used and required for processing and fabrication, processes such as tumbling, making of brines, cooking or sausage making, etc. In this regard, metric volume measurements and calculations are much easier to use compared to imperial or US volume, gallons, quarts, pints and ounces.

> 1 litre is equal to: 1,000 millilitres
> 1,000 grams
> 1 kilogram
>
> That means one litre of water is equal to: 1 kilogram
> 1,000 grams
> 1,000 millilitres

This means ingredients with approximately the same density as water can be measured by weight rather than by calibrated measuring devices such as gallon pails, cups or spoons (tablespoon, teaspoon).

Most recipes in the Canadian meat industry are formulated by grams of spice or millilitres of liquid per kilogram of product (meat), which makes calculating amounts easier, whereas the formulation of a recipe in imperial requires you to have a working understanding of the following:

> 1 US gallon   =   4 quarts
> 4 quarts   =   8 pints
> 1 quart   =   2 pints
> 1 pint   =   16 fluid ounces (oz.) *or* ½ quart
> 16 oz.   =   1 pound

Converting imperial volume to Metric

1 US gallon	=	3.786 litres		
		1 quart	=	0.946 litres
		1 pint	=	0.473 litres
		1 pound	=	454 grams
		1 ounce	=	28.35 grams

As you can see, the conversion of imperial volume to metric volume can be complicated and could lead to serious miscalculations. Miscalculation can produce inaccuracies, and so we recommend you stick to the metric volume measurement when and where the need arises.

SUMMARY

Breakeven	Customer Satisfaction	Marketing
Communication	Customer Service	Mark-up
Cost	Gross Profit	Merchandising
Cross- Merchandising	Honesty	Metric Conversion
Customer Retention	Loss Leader	Teamwork

DISCUSSION QUESTIONS:

1. What is the difference between Marketing and Merchandising?

2. What are some of the operational considerations of Marketing?

3. Explain how you could maximize sales by merchandising Inside Rounds of Beef.

4. What term is used to describe the exercise of question number 3?

5. What is the meaning of the term Gross Profit?

6. What do we mean when we talk about a Loss Leader?

7. Define communication and draw a diagram explaining the process.

8. Define customer service and explain what it means to any business.

9. Reflect on what it means to work in groups and how a member contributes to the overall success or failure of a team.

10. Within a team setting, develop a customer retention program.

11. Why is it important for you to know how to convert metric measurements to imperial measurements and vice versa?

12. Determine when a product should be advertised at a cost per 100 gram rather than at a cost per pound or at cost per kilogram.

Appendix

MATH

An important part of marketing is determining what we call your real cost or costs, costs incurred as part of doing business on an ongoing basis (see monthly costs associated with running a venue). Here in this appendix we demonstrate how to calculate real cost per kilogram for a random weight meat item. The cost per kilogram is commonly derived from variable costs and fixed costs incurred by the production process, the invoice cost per kilogram of product, the delivery or freight charges (if any), shrink, purge, or waste and overhead before retailing. Once you know or realize the cost per kilogram of your product, you can quickly calculate the selling price, providing you know what margin of profit (markup) you need or would like to get for that product. These quick functions we have here for you do not take into consideration your overall costs like salaries, etc., as they may vary from location to location. We just concentrate on the products individually, their actual or real cost, and then we offer a formula that helps to determine the amount or percentage you might want for a particular product.

Establishing Breakeven and Calculating Selling Prices

As stated, to determine true, real or actual cost of retail meat products, managers and meat cutters must know the invoice cost per kg of the product and, if applicable, the cost of delivery or freight per kg (see example 1 step 1). To establish selling prices of retail meat products, the shrink loss due to transportation, dry aging of carcass meats, vacuum packaged meat drip (or purge), fat, bone and trim loss from boning, cutting and trimming of products needs to be taken into consideration. This process we call determining breakeven. Breakeven is the amount we need to recover the cost of the product.

Mark-up or the margin you want for the product, can usually be calculated using the invoice cost price, including freight or delivery charges (if any), provided there is NO known shrink or waste loss from the product.

In the case of products that have known shrink and/ or waste loss due to trimming or moisture loss from the aging process, these are taken into account and determined as part of our cost. This process formulates our break even calculated prior to determining our mark-up or margin of profit. Our break even then becomes the starting cost price per kilogram (see example 1 step 2).

Example # 1 – step 1 *Calculate Total Cost.*

Product Name	Product Weight (PW)	Invoice Cost per kg	Cost of Freight per kg	Cost of Product + Freight per kg	Total Cost
Boneless Sirloin Butts	8 kg in bag	$ 12.00 kg	$ 00.22 kg	$ 12.22 kg	$ 97.76

Above we have a bag of Boneless Sirloin Butts weighing 8 kilograms at an invoice cost of $12.00 per kg. We have an additional freight charge for delivery of 22 cents per kg, giving us a more accurate cost per kg of $12.22 ($12.00 + 0.22 cent = $12.22). We then take the cost of $12.22 per kg to determine the total cost of the 8 kilograms of Boneless Sirloin Butts: 8 X $12.22 kg and we see the total cost of this product is $97.76.

Shrink and/or waste loss due to trimming or moisture loss from the aging process are taken into account and determined as part of our cost.

Example # 1 – step 2 *Calculate Breakeven.*

Product Name	Product weight	Cost per kg	Total Cost of Product (TCP)	Saleable meat weight (SMW)	Breakeven
Boneless Sirloin Butt	8 kg	$12.22 kg	$ 97.76	6 kg	$ 16.29 kg

Step 2 of our example shows how we formulate our break even cost per kilogram. We factor in all our shrinkage, the purge, the waste, etc., and end up with a saleable product weighing 6 kg. Those 6 kilograms have to minimally get back our initial cost of $97.76. To do this we have to charge $16.29 kg. We get this sum by taking the total cost of product and dividing it by the saleable weight: $97.76 ÷ 6 = $16.29. Our breakeven now becomes the starting point in determining selling price per kilogram for our Boneless Sirloin Butts.

Important factors to remember

1. Freight must always be included in the cost price of the product where applicable (refer to example 1 step 1).
2. Subtract your saleable meat weight (SMW = 6 kg) from your original carcass weight (OCW = 8 kg) – this equals your shrink weight (SW = 2 kg).
3. Divide the shrink weight (SW) by the original carcass weight (OCW) and multiply it by 100: (2 kg ÷ 8 kg) x 100 = shrink (25 %) This is an important factor to record.

Example #1 – step 3   *Calculate Shrink %.*

Original Carcass Weight (OCW)	Saleable Meat Weight (SMW)	Shrink Weight (SW) OCW – SMW = SW	Shrink Percentage SW ÷ OW x 100 = S %
8 kg	6 kg	2 kg	25 %

Below we show how to calculate mark-up or a selling price based on a percentage of expected return. The example shows an expected mark-up of 30% on the Boneless Sirloin Butts we already determined have a breakeven cost of $16.29 kg (also represented as 70 in our formula). Selling Price is based on 100 and the mark-up we want is 30, so our product represents 70 (100-30). The 30 is the unknown, and below we show you how to get that figure.

Example #1 – step 4   *Calculate expected Mark-up.*

Fast Formula	Full Formula

Fast Formula

Break even $16.29 kg (100 – 30 = 70)

Therefore: $16.29 ÷ 0.70 = $ 23.27 = SP

SP = Selling Price

Full Formula

%		$
70	CP	16.29
30	MU	6.98
100	SP	23.27

Blue boxed numbers are given, or formula start figures

Red boxed number = ANSWER

The above example can be used for any boxed meat product or beef, pork or lamb sub-primal from a fresh carcass. However, when whole carcass sub-primal cuts are processed, it is important to establish a break even for all the sub-primal cuts, based on the total saleable meat weight from each of the different species. After which, reworking of each sub-primal into retail cuts can proceed. Each of these cuts will usually require a different (greater or lesser) selling price depending on the market value of each sub-primal and the seller's profit expectations. Furthermore, the expected selling price must be balanced against what the current market price and client expectations can bare.

Mark-up on Selling Price

HOW TO ARRIVE AT A SELLING PRICE WITH A KNOWN MARK-UP %

Use this simple accounting formula and follow the procedure listed below.

> **Note:** Mark-up can be calculated using a Cost Price including freight provided there is NO known shrink or waste losses from the product. In the case of products that have known shrink and/ or waste losses due to trimming or moisture losses from the aging process, breakeven must be calculated prior to calculating MARK UP. BREAK EVEN Price then becomes the starting Cost Price for the formula below.

An item Costs $4.95kg and must be marked up 32%. What is the New Selling Price?

Formula set up:	
%	$
CP	
MU	
SP	

COMPLETE THE FOLLOWING PROCEDURES:

1. In the % column opposite SP write 100 down
2. In the % column opposite MU write 32 down
3. Subtract 100 − 32 = 68... write 68 in the % column opposite CP
4. In the dollar column opposite CP write down $4.95
5. Now cross multiply $4.95 x 32 ÷ 68 = $2.33 (Make sure you have rounded off)
6. Write down $2.33 in the $ column opposite MU
7. Add $2.33 to $4.95 = $7.28 (This is your NEW SELLING PRICE)
8. Write your answer in the $ column opposite SP
9. Or $4.95 marked up 32% = (100 − 32 = 68)
10. Therefore $4.95 / Divide .68 = $7.28

Chapter 12

Harvesting

History shows that humankind has always attached importance to the source of their food including the handling of a meat supply. As time progressed inspection began to play an important role in determining whether or not the meat they harvested was fit for human consumption.

This chapter covers harvesting, or the slaughter of domestic animals designated for the food chain, bovine, porcine, ovine, and poultry. Topics include but are not limited to the humane stunning of animals, bleeding, scalping, skinning, and evisceration.

Other topics include the proper handling of animals prior to and during harvesting, specified risk materials (SRMs), as well as inspection and grading of the common species.

Harvesting

History

Since antiquity man has attached importance to the source of his food including the handling of the meat supply. Laws, called the Florentine Laws, were developed in Medieval Europe. The Butchers Guild arose out of the Florentine Laws. New laws were developed that prohibited unsanitary practices such as improper disposal of offal and other practices considered to be fraudulent. Looking back to medieval times responsibility for meat hygiene passed from the church, which looked to the education of the populous, to the artisans of the Guilds and eventually to municipal governments.

The first Public Health Laws in North America relating to meat hygiene were passed in New France in 1707, which lead to the Act of 1805 entitled, *An Act to Regulate the Curing, Packing and Inspection of Beef and Pork.* This legislation made provisions for the appointment of one or more beef and pork inspectors in each district of Lower Canada. Inspectors were required to file an annual report in June of each year, stating the amount of pork and beef inspected during the past 12 months. These inspectors were required to take an oath that they would perform their duties to the best of their ability and that they did not have any financial interest in the product being inspected. Providing the inspector was not sick, he was required to inspect all beef and pork no later than two days after receiving a request to do so. Failure to perform the inspections within the allotted time of two days led to a fine of forty shillings, a severe fine considering inspectors were only paid approximately 1 shilling for every barrel of beef or pork they inspected.

In the United States, as early as 1890, laws for the inspection of meat for export were passed. These laws did little to assure food safety because they made no provision for ante mortem or postmortem inspections (before and after slaughter). They only required a superficial inspection of the pieces of meat intended for export, which said and did nothing about the domestic product sold in local markets.

In the early 1900s Upton Sinclair wrote a book called, "The Jungle". This book highlighted the deplorable and primitive conditions that existed in the meat industry at that time. For example, open latrines were located right off the killing and processing areas. In most instances only a stud wall separated the latrine from the kill floor. Worse yet, in some plants, these toilet areas also served as the lunchrooms for the workers. Basic hygiene measures such as hand washing facilities were primitive to non-existent. Sinclair's book prompted the United States government to establish a full-scale veterinary meat inspection Act in 1906. The laws of this Act only provided for compulsory inspection of meat destined for export or interstate movement and still said or did nothing about product headed for local markets.

No doubt prompted by developments in the United States, the first Canadian meat Inspection Laws were passed in 1907. Similar to those in the United States, these laws only applied to meat moving interprovincially and internationally.

Various amendments to the Act and Regulations have been made from time to time. The current federal Meat Inspection Act was passed on May 16, 1985. It is defined as an Act respecting the import and export of meats as well as the interprovincial trade of meat products, the registration of establishments, the inspection of animals and meat products in registered establishments, and the standards for those establishments regarding animals slaughtered and meat products prepared in those establishments. The current federal Meat Inspection Regulations were passed in 1990, making federal inspection mandatory for plants wishing to export or market meat products internationally and/or interprovincially and its enforcement is the responsibility of the Canadian Food Inspection Agency (CFIA).

In addition to the federal Meat Inspection Regulations each Canadian province and territory now has regulations governing the harvesting of domestic animals by way of an Act specific to meat inspection, animal livestock and livestock products or food handling and safety under the jurisdiction of a food inspection branch of the provincial or local Health Department authority. Prior to having any specific Acts or Health Department authority, meat inspection at provincial abattoirs was purely voluntarily. Municipalities and their provincial counterparts continue to make amendments to bylaws regarding food and meat inspection as the need arises.

Provincial Meat Inspection Acts and Regulations/Programs are quite similar to federal meat inspection legislation. All meat intended for public sale come from animals that receive an *ante mortem* and a *postmortem* inspection. Adoption of federal standards in the provincial system provides Canadian consumers with the same degree of protection as that provided by plants under federal inspection. Even though the provincial system is based on the same principles as the federal system, meat from provincial abattoirs cannot be sold outside of the province's jurisdiction. Inspection of meat destined for interprovincial or international trade remains under the exclusive jurisdiction of the federal system.

The meat slaughter and processing industry is a pillar in Canada's Agri-food economy, representing the largest food-processing sector in Canada. The Canadian meat processing industry also represents significant job creation, accounting for 67,000 people, 28% of the Canadian food industry's workforce, with combined (pork, beef, veal, lamb and poultry) sales of 20.5 billion annually (Agriculture and Agri-Food Canada, economic Publications www.agr.gc.ca).

Inspection

ANTE MORTEM INSPECTION

All animals are individually observed for evidence of disease or other condition which would render their carcasses unfit for human consumption, referred to as a pre-slaughter inspection. The animal is observed at rest and in motion. The meat inspector inspects all animals in holding pens looking for abnormal behaviour and evidence of a medical condition (glassy eyes, running nose, difficulty breathing etc.) If any is found, a veterinarian is called in to further examine the animal. They also are looking for the following conditions:

- Suspected presence of a disease that may result in condemnation
- Broken bones or crippling but not serious enough for immediate condemnation
- Animals known to have reacted positively to tuberculin tests
- Advance stages of pregnancy
- Fever

POST MORTEM

During post-slaughter a qualified inspector inspects the harvested carcasses. A careful inspection of lymph nodes, glands, internal organs and other tissues of each slaughtered animal are carried out simultaneously with the slaughter operations. A carcass or any part of the carcass can be found to be unfit for consumption.

Examining a gland near the hanging tender (diaphram) (Posterior Mediastinal)
Credit: CPMCA image collection

PRODUCT INSPECTION

Inspection of products produced by further processing such as sausages, smoked meats or canned meats are termed product inspection. Such inspection includes formulas used and procedures employed. This type of inspection also extends to the normal cutting, handling, packaging and storing procedures used in fresh, frozen or processed meats.

Harvesting (Slaughter)

We've all heard the horror stories of inhumane practices with respect to the handling of animals designated for the food chain (which thankfully are far and few between) but hopefully you'll never become the author of one of them. The animals we use for our nourishment deserve humane handling not just because they are living animals but also because they become our food. Who among you treats their food with a disconcerted and abusive attitude? Chefs and cooks around the world strife to create meals that are presentable, flavourful and appealing to the consumer. No one we know likes to eat food that has been mishandled.

STUNNING THE ANIMAL

Stunning an animal humanly is not only morally ethical it is essential to meat quality. Humane stunning when properly executed results in immediate insensibility (brain death), which is maintained until the animal is bled out.

There are four approved methods of humane stunning in Canada:

- Gunshot – the use of a bullet to enter the brain and render the animal insensible (used mainly on cattle and bison)
- Captive bolt – also known as Percussive Stunning is the use of a retractable bolt to enter the brain and render the animal insensible (used mainly on cattle)
- Electrocution – the use of a high voltage electric charge to the brain that renders the animal insensible (used mainly on sheep, goats, poultry, and with smaller operations, hogs)
- Gas – the use of carbon dioxide within an enclosed chamber that produces unconsciousness or death through hypoxia or asphyxia rendering the animal insensible (used mainly with hogs)

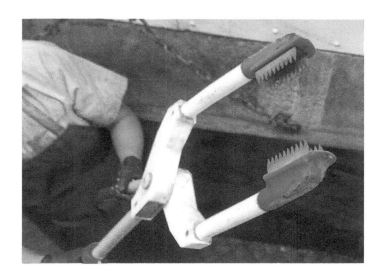

Electrical stunning device for hogs
Credit:Provincial licensed & inspected harvesting facility.

Jarvis Type P PAS stunner
Credit: Jarvis Products Corporation

Jarvis Type C PAS stunner
Credit: Jarvis Products Corporation

Jarvis compressed air stunner-USSS-1
Credit: Jarvis Products Corporation

Jarvis stunner-USSSS2A
Credit: Jarvis Products Corporation

Bovine Harvesting

Harvesting facilities require bovine animals to be rested for a minimum of two to four hours before slaughter, depending on the duration of hauling before processing. The purpose of resting the animals is primarily to relax them from their journey and to somewhat acquaint them to their new environment.

PSS (DFD, PSE)

Pre-slaughter stress syndrome (PSS) results in two different types of meat discolouration referred to as dark firm and dry (DFD) and pale soft and exudative (PSE). DFD is more common in bovine animals and PSE is more common in porcine animals. Nevertheless, stress can alter the pH of an animal (see chapter 4 under the topic of Harvesting).

Separate Holding pens for cattle at a Federal processing plant
Credit: Canada Beef

The amount of stress animals suffer depends on how they are handled before harvesting. For example, when animals are selected for harvesting, they may be separated from the herd, rested overnight and then loaded on a truck to be driven to the harvesting plant (Abattoir). Sometimes the animals have to be transported long distances, especially in Canada. Once unloaded at the plant, they are rested, hopefully with the same group of animals they have been transported with. All these sudden changes are stressful to the animals, and each step of the process must be carefully handled. Excessive heat, dehydration, cramped conditions, and strange surroundings have a negative effect on most animals, with some finding the process more arduous than others.

Holding pens for cattle at a Provincial harvesting plant
Credit: CPMCA image collection

At the time of slaughter, animals are moved from their holding pens into a specially designed S-shaped approach chute that helps to keep the animals calm. Cattle as herd animals are naturally curious, so when the animal in front of them moves ahead through the S-shaped chute their curiosity forces them to follow the animal in front of them, keeping them calm till they reach their final destination. The chute leads cattle one by one into a tight holding box where the animal is stunned, shackled and raised, bled, then winched up for skinning, eviscerating, splitting, and washing followed by rapid cooling in a special holding cooler.

For more on livestock handling visit: *http://www.grandinlivestock handlingsystems.com/about.html*

Beef animal in an S chute
Credit: CPMCA image collection

USING THE CAPTIVE BOLT

As with gunshot, to produce instantaneous unconsciousness, the bolt must penetrate the brain with a high concussive impact. There are two types of Captive bolt stunners (also referred to as Captive Bolt Pistols), pneumatic (air) and cartridge fired.

The bolt consists of a stainless spring-loaded rod held inside a barrel of the stunner. It is activated by a trigger pull and is propelled forward by compressed air or by the discharge of a blank round ignited by a firing pin. The bolt strikes the animal on the forehead and recoils back into the pistol barrel.

Beef cattle in an S chute –Large Harvesting plant
Credit: emesilva ©istock.com

Note: A good stunner operator learns not to chase the animal's head. Take the time and aim for one good shot. The stunner must be placed squarely on the animal's head. All equipment manufacturers' recommendations and instructions must be followed. Training is advised.

Poor maintenance of bolt stunners is a major cause of misfires and bad stunning. Pneumatic stunners must have an adequate air supply with good pressure. Low pressure is one cause of poor stunning.

For cattle, the stunner is placed on the middle of the forehead on an "X" formed between the eyes going up 3 cm to the soft spot between them. There should be no concern regarding damage to the brain, due to concerns about BSE (Bovine Spongiform Encephalopathy), as saving brains is not recommended. Brain and spinal cord tissue from cattle should be discarded and not used as food for either people or animals.

Hand held stunner and stun area with cross
Credit: CPMCA image collection

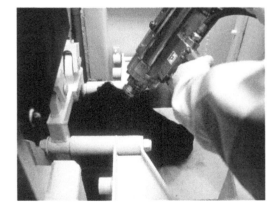

Head control unit & Compressed air stunner
Credit: Jarvis Products Corporation

INSENSIBILITY

To determine if the animal is insensible eye reflexes should be checked often to ensure that stunning is making the cattle unconscious. When the eyelid or cornea is touched there should be no response. An animal that blinks is not insensible and not properly stunned. Breathing should have stopped and there should be no indication of a righting reflex when the animal is hanging on the rail. Reflexes may cause a stunned animal's legs to move, but the head should hang straight down and be limp and the tongue and tail should be hanging loosely.

BLEEDING

Bleeding is accomplished when the animal is suspended in the air and a traverse cut is made in the neck, severing the carotid artery and the jugular vein.

- The animal suspended upside down is then bled by making an incision about 40 cm long down the middle of the neck starting at just below the brisket.
- Insert your knife at about a 45-degree angle toward the head starting just below the brisket and make a cut in one movement severing the carotid artery and jugular vein causing the animal to bleed out. About two-thirds of the total blood capacity will come out of the carcass.
- Make sure that you sanitize your knife after you open the hide and before you bleed the animal to prevent contamination.

Animal on winch after stunning & bleeding
Credit: CPMCA image collection

Note: Leg movements and twitching after stunning and bleeding (also referred to as sticking) are muscle reflex action initiated by synapses coming from the spinal cord, not the brain which is rendered dead with stunning.

SCALPING

Scalping is the process of skinning out the head and preparing to salvage the cheek meat, tongue, and exposing the lymph nodes that the meat inspector needs to examine as part of the inspection process.

- Extend the cut from the brisket down to the bottom of the lip.
- Make an incision from one ear to the other as tight to the pole of the skull as possible.
- Sever the spinal cord and loosen the meat around the atlas joint.
- Skin down the skull's face from the pole cut, through the eye, down to the nostril.
- Skin the face around to your lip line, cut staying below the ear; be careful around the teeth as hitting them will dull your knife.

- Once you have skinned the entire side of the face to the lip line, cut up through the ear cartilage and cut the remaining muscle from the atlas joint.
- Start at the lip line and skin the other side of the face staying under the ear. When this is completed, cut up through the ear and sever the muscle from the atlas joint.
- To remove the head, cut through the atlas joint (the joint between the skull and the first vertebrae).
- Drop the head from the carcass by cutting through the esophagus and the windpipe (trachea).

PREPARING THE HEAD FOR INSPECTION

The head must be free of contaminants, hair and fecal matter. Tonsils have to be removed and the lymph nodes have to be exposed before the head can be inspected. The following lymph nodes have to be inspected: parotids, sub-maxillary and the retropharyngeal.

- Hang the head by the jaw on the inspection hook
- Trim all the contaminants (hair etc.)
- Wash head and blow out nostrils
- Trim out all tonsil tissue
- Expose lymph nodes in throat for inspection
- Perform final wash and present the head for inspection

Beef head cleaned & prepared for inspection
Credit: CPMCA image collection

Tape worm inspection on cheek muscles
Credit: CPMCA image collection

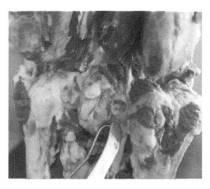

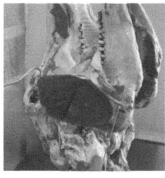

Examining parotid glands
at base of tongue
Credit: CPMCA image collection

Examining jaw muscles
for tape worms
Credit: CPMCA image collection

Removing tongue & leaving
contaminated underside
with the head
Credit: CPMCA image collection

PRE-SKINNING

Pre-skinning of the carcass involves laying the carcass on the skinning cradle and removing the legs then skinning the insides of the legs as preparation for removing the hide.

- Lay the carcass in the skinning cradle
- Remove the front feet at the knee by cutting between the metacarpals and carpals, if done correctly it should be a smooth joint

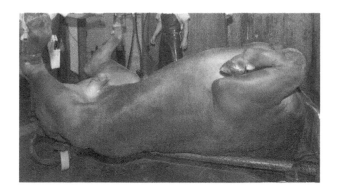

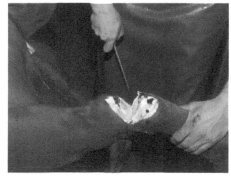

Beef animal on a skinning cradle
Credit: CPMCA image collection

Removing the front foot
Credit: CPMCA image collection

- Remove the hind feet by severing the tendon between the hoof and dewclaws to release tension on the hoof
- Open the hide down the center of the hind leg over the Achilles tendon to the center of the pelvic area
- Skin the hind leg down both sides from the bottom of the Achilles tendon to the dewclaws
- Remove the leg by cutting between the metatarsals and tarsals and prying the leg out sideways exposing the joint; finish by cutting the cartilage at the joint.

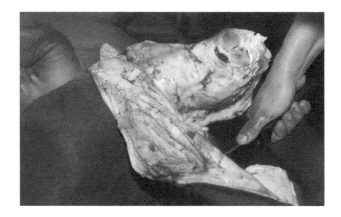

Hind foot removed
Credit: CPMCA image collection

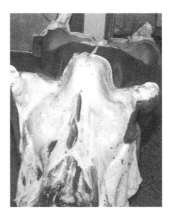

Carcass ready to skin out
Credit: CPMCA image collection

SKINNING

Skinning is the process of removing the hide from the carcass. This should be accomplished in such a way as to protect the carcass from contamination from the outer hide and damage (to the meat). Remember to sanitize your knife whenever you open the hide as the hide contains contaminants such as fecal matter.

- Open the hide down the center of the animal carcass from the brisket to the pelvic cut made at the pre-skinning preparation
- Start skinning out the hide by grasping the corner of the hide in the pelvic area and skinning back towards the flank until you have exposed the flank meat
- Skinning the carcass from the shoulder to the flank
- Skin the carcass in as long strokes as possible, starting your stroke at the shoulder and ending at the hip. Continue down to the cradle
- Skin the front shoulder down to the knee of the front leg, cut through the skin to the knee
- Open the hide of the front leg, skin the rest of the shoulder leaving the rosette intact

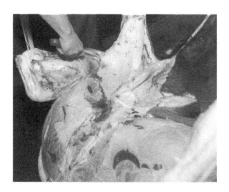

Skinning out pelvic area
Credit: CPMCA image collection

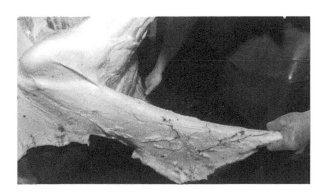

Skinning out the foreshank & shoulder
Credit: CPMCA image collection

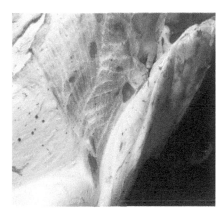

Skinning the sides down to the support cradle
Credit: CPMCA image collection

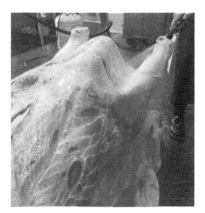

Hide skinned down to the cradle & washing
carcass prior to evisceration
Credit: CPMCA image collection

PRE-EVISCERATION

This is the process of opening the brisket and bunging the animal before the hide is removed in such a way as to avoid contamination from the anus and esophagus.

- Saw open the brisket from the neck to the end of the sternum
- Loosen and separate the windpipe and esophagus from the throat area and tie the esophagus closed. Loosen them as far up into the shoulder cavity as possible taking care not to nick or puncture the esophagus as it may (will) contaminate the carcass with stomach contents.
- Hang the carcass by the Achilles tendon using a spreader jamb
- Raise the hind of the carcass to a comfortable height

- With the rump of the carcass raised to a comfortable height, skin down under the tail
- Skin a strip off the tail and pull the hide off the tail and continue to skin down and around the rumps
- Bung the animal by cutting around the anus and pull it out away from the carcass, bag it and tie it to prevent contamination, and then push it back into the cavity.

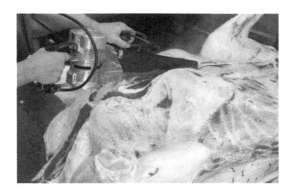

Opening the brisket bone with a well saw
Credit: CPMCA image collection

Carcass on spreader hook
Credit: CPMCA image collection

Placing a protective covering on separated anus
Credit: CPMCA image collection

SKINNING THE BACKSIDE OF THE CARCASS

This is the process of harvesting the tail, skinning off the hips of the carcass and pulling the hide down the backside from the hips to the neck.

- Remove the skinned tail from the carcass between the coccygeal and sacral vertebrae
- Hang the carcass on the rail and finish dropping (skinning) the hide

Skin the tail by pulling down on the hide
Credit: CPMCA image collection

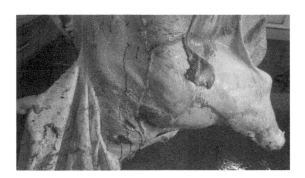

Skinning the hide off at the neck & shoulder
Credit: CPMCA image collection

Preparing to skin the tail & the beginning of evisceration
Credit: CPMCA image collection

EVISCERATION

This is the process of removing the digestive tract from the carcass in such a way as not to contaminate the carcass. Care and attention must be given to the opening of the stomach wall.

- Open the stomach wall just below the pelvic region, careful not to cut to far down and poke the intestines. Open just enough to get your fist in.
- Put your fist into the cavity and point the knife straight out, open the stomach wall down to the brisket cut you made earlier with the saw

- Pull the bung down and to the right outside of the carcass; be careful not to pull the kidney fat with the bung; there are several connective tissues holding the bung that you will have to break
- Push down on the big paunch until it is outside the carcass
- Scoop the intestinal tract out exposing the connection to the diaphragm and the liver
- Cut the diaphragm, reach in and pull out the tied esophagus and the guts will fall forward into a receiving bin to be presented for inspection

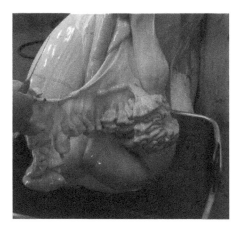

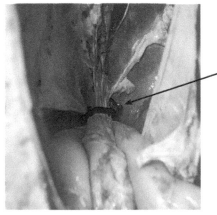

Paunch &
intestine removal
Credit: CPMCA
image collection

Removing the small
intestine (Distilelium)
Credit: CPMCA image collection

Esophagus & trachia clamped prior to
removal of the liver
Credit: CPMCA image collection

OFFAL REMOVAL

Offal removal is the process of harvesting the liver, heart and kidneys as consumables along with the lungs for inspection. The steps for this process is as follows:

- Reach up and over the liver and cut and remove the bile sac
- With the bile sac removed, reach up and over the liver and pull it down; you will find a finger hold (artery) that allows you to carry the liver to the inspection tray
- Cut the diaphragm adjacent to the skirt meat on both sides of the carcass exposing the heart sack; cut the heart sack and remove the heart

- Just below the kidneys, cut underneath the hanging tender and slide the knife down the backbone cutting the rest of the windpipe loose, while doing this grasp the lungs pulling them outside the carcass cavity
- Grab the windpipe between the lungs and trim the blood vessels on either side of the carcass
- Place the lungs in the inspection tray with the windpipe hanging out
- Cut the kidney fat and pop out the kidneys, placing them on the inspection tray
- After inspection hang the offal in the cooler on an offal tree hook to wait further processing.

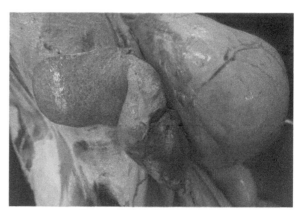

Stomach & spleen removal
Credit: CPMCA image collection

Stomach & intestines in drop tub
Credit: CPMCA image collection

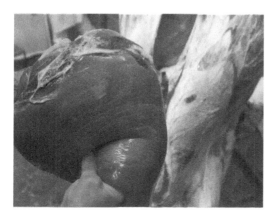

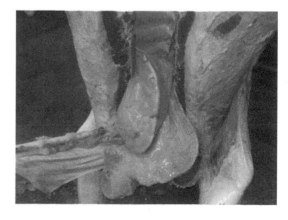

Liver removed
Credit: CPMCA image collection

Lungs & trachia out
Credit: CPMCA image collection

THE DROP

Meat is not the only product that can be attained from a slaughtered animal. There are many industrial, pharmaceutical and household products manufactured from salvaged animal parts by larger slaughter plants. Small provincial plants don't operate on a scale to make salvaging these products feasible and pay to have them removed and disposed of.

These inedible animal by-products are commonly referred to as the Drop. By-products manufactured from the drop result in approximately 99% utilization of every animal harvested in larger plants. The primary raw commodities by volume are hides, fat and bone, blood and meat meal. (or protein meal)

Some examples of how other industries utilize the inedible animal byproducts of harvested domestic species are household products made from fats/fatty acids and protein meal, such as candles, crayons, toothpaste, detergents, shaving cream, deodorants, mouthwash, cosmetics, etc. From the hide we have luggage, clothing, gloves, belts, purses, wallets, shoes, etc. The pharmaceutical industry utilizes the pancreas to make insulin, the liver for vitamin B-12 and the soft bone cartilage for manufacturing plastic surgery components.

SPECIFIED RISK MATERIAL (SRM)

Health Canada and the CFIA have identified, through changes to the Food and Drug Regulations and the Health of Animals Regulations, that SRMs are excluded from the human food chain as a precautionary measure to further enhance public health protection. SRMs are tissues that will typically contain prions associated with bovine spongiform encephalopathy (BSE) in an affected animal. SRMs will include the skull, brain, eyes, tonsils, trigeminal ganglia, spinal cord, and dorsal root ganglia of all cattle over 30 months of age (OTM), and the distal ilium (portion of the small intestine) from cattle of all ages. Implementation of this regulation began in August of 2003.

OTM side with blue identification dye on the back bone
Credit:Canada Beef

While the presumed prevalence of BSE is very low, implementation of the ban on SRMs is also presumed to result in a 99% reduction in the infectivity of a BSE positive animal through the elimination of specific parts known to be potentially infectious risk material.

An inspector when encountering an OTM animal will paint the backbone blue to ensure that all of the SRMs get accounted for. The butcher or cutter deboning an OTM animal has the responsibility to retain the boned material, the backbone, complete with the SRM tag, until the inspector has verified that all SRMs are accounted for. Care must be taken when boning these animals as to do so means the butcher or

Note: More information on SRMs is available in the Appendix of this chapter.

meat cutter must stay at least 2.5 cm from each side of the backbone of the entire animal; which incurs quite a bit of waste in avoiding the Dorsa Root Ganglion.

Start splitting the carcass from the tail & pelvis
Credit: CPMCA image collection

SPLITTING THE CARCASS

Splitting is the process of breaking the carcass in half or separating the sides by sawing down the center of the backbone.

- Spread the legs and remove the spreader jamb
- Place the saw at a 45 degree upward angle between the legs on the inside of the carcass to split the aitch bone (pelvic bone)
- As you cut through the aitchbone with the heel of the saw blade, the tip should reach and cut through the center of

Splitting the carcass at the neck
Credit: CPMCA image collection

the tailbone before finishing your cut through the aitchbone thereby stabilizing the saw

- Saw down the center of the carcass leaving equal portions of feather bones on each side
- Keep the saw on an upward angle until you reach the shoulder and then reversing the angle in a downward motion through the neck

TRIMMING AND WASHING THE CARCASS

This process involves removing any contaminants that might be present on the carcass with removing the hide and by evisceration. This step is always done in preparation of inspection.

- Trim all visible contamination, blood clots and any other imperfections such as bruising before washing
- Pump the front legs up and down to expose any blood clots, and remove any that appear on the shoulder
- Trim excess fat in the udder region and kidney area taking care not to score or cut into the tenderloin
- Wash the carcass from top to bottom and present for inspection
- After the carcass has passed inspection, weigh and tag each side

Remove spinal cord with tool
Credit: TRU Retail Meat Processing Program

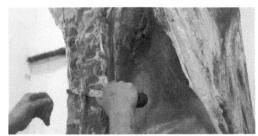

Spinal cord removal with knife
Credit: CPMCA image collection

Washing the carcass
Credit: CPMCA image collection

The split carcass that just passed inspection, weighed and tagged must be chilled to an internal temperature of 4°C within 48 hours. The purpose of chilling is to remove heat from the sides of the split carcass. This is important because the temperature of the carcass, the time it takes for the carcass to chill and the rate of pH decline must all be taken into consideration as these factors play a significant role in the quality and tenderness of the meat. In addition, chilling the meat creates an environment that is unfavourable to microbial growth, a temperature dependent process.

Chilling not only slows or stops the development of surface microbial growth but also reduces weight loss and discolouration of the exposed surface of the carcass by way of hemoglobin oxidation (see chapter 4 Meat Science). The coolers where chilling takes place must have a low air temperature, good refrigerating capacity, high volume air circulation and high humidity. The air temperature of these coolers should be in the range of 0°C to minus 1°C.

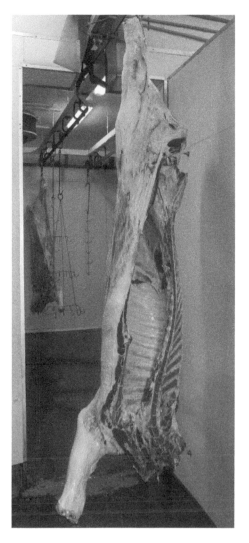

Carcass ready to go to the chill down cooler
Credit: CPMCA image collection

The sides of each carcass should be spaced to allow air to circulate freely between and around them, overcrowding slows the chilling process.

During post-slaughter a qualified inspector inspects the harvested carcasses. A careful inspection of lymph nodes, gland, internal organs and other tissues of each slaughtered animal are carried out simultaneously with the slaughter operations. A carcass or any part of the carcass can be found to be unfit for consumption.

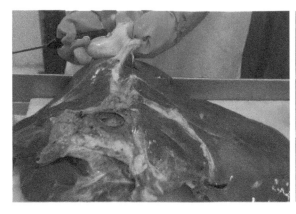

Liver inspection-removing bile duct

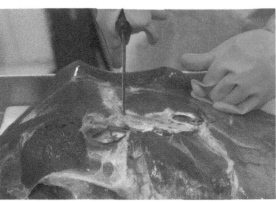

Liver inspection- looking for liver flukes

Palpating liver for cysts & lumps

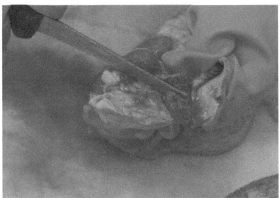

Kidney inspection

Lung inspection

Lung & bronchial lymph node inspection

Credit: CPMCA image collection

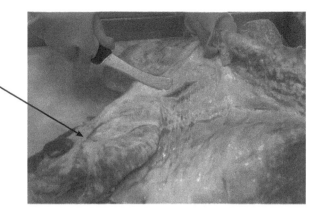

Inspection off posterior mediastinal gland. The diaphragm, hanging tender is to the left (arrow)

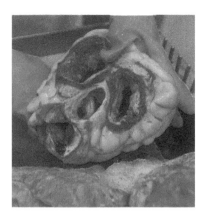

Heart inspection showing ventricles

Heart floating bone removed

Internal exam of heart looking for pericarditis (internally sliced open 5 times)

Credit: CPMCA image collection

PRODUCT

Inspection of products produced by further processing such as sausages, smoked meats or canned meats are termed product inspection. Such inspection includes formulas used and procedures employed. This type of inspection also extends to the normal cutting, handling, packaging and storing procedures used in fresh, frozen or processed meats.

The Grading of Bovine Animals

The CFIA regulates grading in both federally and provincially inspected plants. The delivery of beef, veal and bison grading is the responsibility of the Canadian Beef Grading Agency, accredited by the CFIA to deliver grading services.

A good understanding of the general characteristics, dressing and chilling practices, and presentation as they pertain to a bovine carcass is necessary if the Grading Regulations are to be correctly applied. The grader is entrusted with the classification of a carcass. Every carcass bears value based on its quality and yield as assessed by the grader. Therefore, it is imperative that each carcass assessment be accurate and consistent with the Regulations. A grader is trained in their duty to:

- Understand factors and characteristics that determine carcass quality and yield
- Be knowledgeable and capable of readily identifying the different grades as defined in the Regulations, and
- Be capable of applying the grade standards using sound judgment

A carcass may only be graded after it has been inspected and approved for health and safety standards and bears a federal or provincial meat inspection legend or stamp. A grader assesses a carcass based on several visual factors that determine carcass quality and yield. These factors are directly related to the tenderness, juiciness, consumer acceptability, shelf life and yield of a carcass and vary between the bovine species. Table 1 below highlights the characteristics and factors of quality a grader assess with each carcass that is graded.

Characteristics	Factors of Quality
Maturity (age)	The age of an animal affects tenderness
Sex (Male or Female)	Pronounced masculinity in animals affects meat colour and palatability (texture & taste)
Conformation (muscling)	Meat yield is influenced by the degree of muscling
Fat (colour, texture, & cover)	Fat colour and texture influence consumer acceptability whereas fat cover affects yield
Meat (colour, texture, & marbling)	Meat marbling affects eating quality for juiciness and tenderness. Colour and texture influence consumer acceptability.

Table 1: Grading Factors and Characteristics

Below are tables highlighting the grades and factors that support their grade designation for each of the following bovine species, beef, veal and bison based on meat quality and meat yield. Meat quality is concerned with the maturity of the animal, the colour of the meat, and the amount of marbling. Meat yield is concerned with outer fat measure and muscle score (see Yield Ruler).

BEEF GRADES

The Canadian Beef Grading Agency is a private non-profit corporation accredited by the CFIA to deliver grading services for beef in Canada. The grade standards are set by the federal government based on recommendations from the Industry/Government Consultative Committee on Beef Grading. It should be noted that beef grading is not mandatory.

Grade	Maturity (Age)	Muscling	Rib Eye Muscle	Marbling	Fat Colour & Texture	Fat Measure
Canada Prime	Youthful	good to excellent with some deficiencies	firm, bright red	slightly abundant	firm, white or amber	2 mm or more
Canada A, AA, AAA	Youthful	good to excellent with some deficiencies	firm, bright red	A - trace AA - slight AAA - small	firm, white or amber	2 mm or more
B1	Youthful	good to excellent with some deficiencies	firm, bright red	devoid	firm, white or amber	less than 2 mm
B2	Youthful	deficient to excellent	bright red	no requirement	yellow	no requirement
B3	Youthful	deficient to excellent	bright red	no requirement	white or amber	no requirement
B4	Youthful	deficient to excellent	dark red	no requirement	no requirement	no requirement
D1	Mature	excellent	no requirement	no requirement	firm, white or amber	less than 15 mm
D2	Mature	medium to excellent	no requirement	no requirement	white to yellow	less than 15 mm
D3	Mature	deficient	no requirement	no requirement	no requirement	less that 15 mm
D4	Mature	deficient to excellent	no requirement	no requirement	no requirement	15 mm or more
E	Youthful or Mature	pronounced masculinity				

Canada A grade   *Canada AA grade*   *Canada AAA grade*   *Canada Prime*

Credit: Canada Beef

BEEF YIELDS

The yield reported by the grader is an estimation of the percentage of the carcass that is red meat. The method the grader uses to estimate lean yield was developed by Lacombe Research Station and implemented in April of 1992. The ruler was revised in 2001 to accommodate changes to the regulations for a reduction in minimum back cover fat thickness. Yield measurement is taken from between the 12th and 13th rib of the carcass. Yield designations are Canada 1, Canada 2, and Canada 3.

Prime and A grade Yields	
Canada 1	59 % or more lean useable meat
Canada 2	54-58% lean useable meat
Canada 3	53% or less lean useable meat

Yield stamp 1   *Yield stamp 2*   *Yield stamp 3*

Credit: Canada Beef Grading Agency

THE YIELD RULER

In order to assist the grader in determining the proper grade for a carcass of beef, a Yield Ruler has been developed. This yield ruler allows the prediction of lean meat yield based on the graded fat measure and muscle score. The ruler allows for an improvement of accuracy in the range of 7 - 8% over predictions based on fat measurements only.

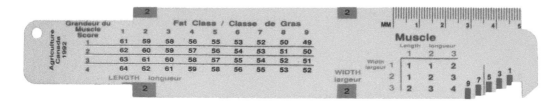

Beef yield ruler
Credit: CPMCA image collection

1. *The correct fat class is established by placing the ruler point at the minimum of the fat thickness in the fourth quarter of the loin-eye on the left side of the carcass. The nine fat classes span the fat thickness range of 4 to 20 mm for grade carcasses.*
2. *Here we measure loin-eye length and width. Both measurements are scored 1 (small), 2 (medium), or 3 (large) depending on how they compare to the "width" and "length" boxes. Anything between the ruler point and the box is a 1, in the box is a 2, and beyond the box is a 3. Next, the muscle grid is used to determine the final muscle score.*
3. *The ruler is used to measure the fat depth and rib-eye length and width. These measures of fat and lean are then used to predict an overall carcass lean yield.*

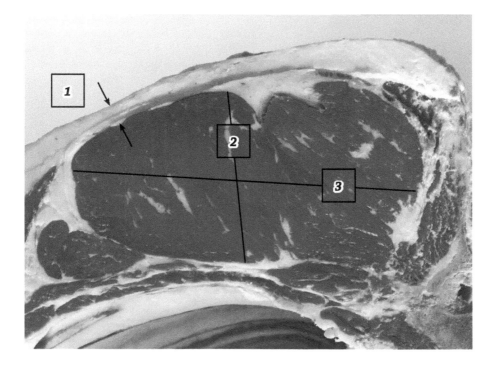

Credit: Canadian beef grading agency

Note: Marbling assessment is based on the average amount, size and distribution of fat particles or deposits in the rib eye. Canadian beef carcass grading utilizes only four (highlighted) of the nine recognized levels of marbling from USDA marbling standards. Listed in order of increased marbling content the nine levels are: **Traces, Slight, Small**, Modest, Moderate, **Slightly Abundant**, Moderately Abundant, Abundant and Very Abundant.

CANADA	MARBLING SCORE	
Canada Prime	Abundant	
	Moderately Abundant	
	Slightly Abundant†	
Canada AAA	Moderate	
	Modest	
	Small†	
Canada AA	**Slight†**	
Canada A	**Trace**	
	Practically Devoid	

† The above illustrations are reduced reproductions of the official USDA Marbling photographs prepared for the U.S. Department of Agriculture by and available from the National Cattlemen's Beef Association.
Donated by Canada Beef

GRADE LABELLING

When beef is fabricated into wholesale and/or retail cuts, the grade label on the box or package must correspond to the carcass grad stamp. Although the expression "or higher" is also allowed if the box contains more than one of the Canada A, Canada AA, Canada AAA, and Canada Prime grades.

Note: The Canadian beef industry also makes use of computer vision grading. This technology produces digital photographs of the rib-eye and performs objective analysis of these images for yield and quality grade assessment, thereby enhancing the accuracy and consistency of beef grading.

VEAL GRADES

There are ten (10) grades of veal carcasses with the grade names Canada A1, Canada A2, Canada A3, or Canada A4; Canada B1, Canada B2, Canada B3, Canada B4, Canada C1 and Canada C2. For a Dressed Veal Carcass to be graded it must fall into the weight range of 80 -180 kilograms.

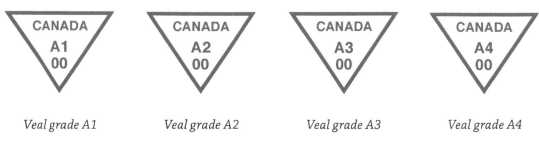

| Veal grade A1 | Veal grade A2 | Veal grade A3 | Veal grade A4 |

Credit: Canadian Beef Grading Agency

The vast majority of veal grades applied to veal carcasses are in the province of Quebec as Quebec is the largest producer of veal for market.

Colour Criteria for Canada Veal Grades

Grade	Colour of Flesh
Canada A1/B1	Flesh that is bright pink or lighter in colour and has a colour reading of 50 or more
Canada A2/B2	Flesh that is pink in colour and has a colour reading of 40 - 49
Canada A3/B3	Flesh that is pale red in colour and has a colour reading of 30 to 39
Canada A4/B4	Flesh that is red in colour and has a colour reading of 0 to 29
Canada C1	Flesh that is pink or lighter in colour and has a colour reading of 40 or more
Canada C2	Flesh that is pale red or dark red in colour and has a colour reading of 39 or less

Veal colour criteria is established using the following method

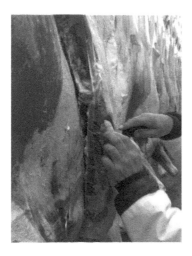  

A fresh cut is made on the brisket to evaluate colour   *The colour-meter is placed on the fresh cut to assess brilliance*   *The information is captured in the establishment data system*

Credit:Canadian Beef Grading Agency

MATURITY CHARACTERISTICS FOR VEAL CARCASSES

- Bones that are soft and reddish in colour
- Ribs that are narrow and slightly rounded
- A sternum that shows distinct divisions
- An aitchbone that is covered by cartilage

BISON GRADES

Official grading of bison began on February 28, 1995 and regulations were implemented March 1, 1995 and amended on May 16, 2007.

Grading evaluates carcass quality. There are 10 grades of bison with the grade names Canada A1, Canada A2, Canada A3, Canada A4, Canada B1, Canada B2, Canada B3, Canada D1, Canada D2 and Canada D3, with each indicated by a blue stamp. All graded bison from a federally or provincially inspected plant must have the grade clearly marked on the carcass. Grades are stamped in three places on the hind quarter (flank, loin & hip) and two places on the front quarter (shoulder & rib).

The grading of bison is voluntary and is a service for fee by the Canadian Beef Grading Agency. The government of Canada maintains the regulations and grade standards. Only carcasses that pass health and safety inspection may be graded. A certified grader assesses a carcass based on maturity characteristics muscling, fat, and meat quality.

MATURITY CHARACTERISTICS

The age of a bison is an important factor in the classifying of bison into the various grades since there is a direct relationship between tenderness and maturity.

Maturity Class I for bison carcasses graded with Canada A and Canada B designations:

- Cartilaginous caps on the 9th, 10th and 11th thoracic vertebrae immediately anterior to the knife rib site (between the 12th and 13th rib) are no more than 80% ossified.

Maturity Class II for bison carcasses graded with a Canada D designation:

- Cartilaginous caps on the 9th, 10th and 11th thoracic vertebrae immediately anterior to the knife rib site (between the 12th and 13th rib) are more than 80% ossified.

MUSCLING

Muscle is related to meat yield. Muscling, as considered in meat grading, refers to the proportionate development of the various parts of the carcass or wholesale cuts and to the ratio of meat to bone. The muscling of a bison carcass is determined in the same manner as that of beef. However, a grader takes into consideration that a bison carcass is more heavily muscled in the front and less muscled in the hind than beef when making the final muscling determination.

FAT COVER

Fat cover refers to the degree of fat covering on the outside of the carcass, its thickness, colour, firmness and distribution. Fat colour, thickness and firmness affect consumer acceptance and meat yield. The best fat covering is a uniform distribution of fat over the entire carcass on the outside.

MEAT QUALITY

Meat colour and texture affect consumer acceptance and shelf life. Bison meat quality is assessed by colour (bright red and firm). Unlike beef, the assessment of marbling is not part of the grading regulations for bison because bison meat comes from animals that have little or no marbling in their muscle structure.

Bison A Grades					
		Grades			
	Quality Factors	A1	A2	A3	A4
Age Maturity Class I	Muscling	Excellent to Good			
	Fat Colour	White to Amber & Firm			
	Meat Colour	Bright Red & Firm			
	Millimeter of Fat Cover	2-6	7-12	12-18	>18

Bison grade A1   Bison grade A2   Bison grade A3   Bison grade A4

Credit: Canadian Beef Grading Agency

Bison B Grades		
B1		
	Muscling	Excellent to Good
	Fat Colour	White to Amber & Firm
	Meat Colour	Bright Red & Firm
	Fat Cover	<2 mm
B2		
	Muscling	Excellent to Medium
	Fat Colour	White to Yellow
	Meat Colour	Bright to Dark Red
	Fat Cover	<2mm
B3		
	Muscling	Deficient to point of Emaciation
	Fat Colour	No Requirements
	Meat Colour	No Requirements
	Fat Cover	No Requirements

(Age Maturity Class I applies to the Bison B Grades table.)

Bison D Grades	
D1	
Muscling	Excellent to Medium
Fat Colour	No Requirements
Meat Colour	No Requirements
Fat Cover	2-6 mm
D2	
Muscling	Excellent to Medium
Fat Colour	No Requirements
Meat Colour	No Requirements
Fat Cover	6+ mm
D3	
Muscling	< Medium
Fat Colour	No Requirements
Meat Colour	No Requirements
Fat Cover	<1 mm

(Left side spanning label: Age Maturity Class II)

Bison/Beef Grading Comparison

Bison	Beef
10 grades	13 Grades
Ribbed between 11 & 12th ribs	Ribbed between the 12 & 13th ribs
2 mm minimum fat cover for A grades	2 mm minimum fat cover for A grades
Heavily muscled fronts	Heavily muscled hinds
2 maturity divisions	2 maturity divisions
More age in A grades than beef	Less age in A grades than bison
Grade stamped in blue ink	Grade stamp in red ink
5 stamps per side	2 stamps per side
Not ribbon branded	Ribbon branded
No marbling assessment	Marbling assessment
3 meat yield grades	3 meat yield % for A grades

Harvesting of Porcine Animals

As with all animals designated for slaughter, harvesting facilities, local abattoirs or large plants, require hogs to be rested for a minimum of two to four hours before slaughter, depending on the duration of hauling before processing. In federal and provincial inspected facilities, there is a pre-slaughter and post-slaughter inspection. As with bovine animals, part of the pre-slaughter inspection may involve a veterinarian performing an ante mortem inspection of all animals in holding pens, while during post-mortem meat inspectors inspect the harvested carcasses.

STUNNING THE ANIMAL

Stunning can be successfully accomplished using one of the four approved methods. For larger hog processing plants this would be gas. Small abattoirs use electrical or a captive bolt pistol. Either way the animal must be rendered insensible.

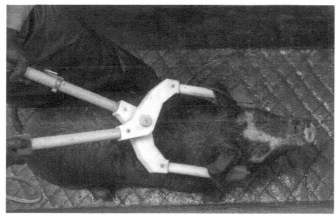

Electric stunning of hogs
Credit: CPMCA image collection

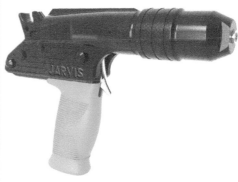

Captive bolt gun
Credit: Jarvis Products Corporation

Once stunning has taken place and insensibility has been determined the following procedure is followed.

- A shackle is placed around one hind leg between the dewclaws and the hock and the animal is then hoisted and suspended.
- The suspended hog is then bled by inserting a knife midway between the tip of the sternum and the throat latch (where the head and the windpipe meet)
- With the tip of the knife pointed directly to the tail of the hog, and squarely in the middle of the ventral aspect (center of the throat area), give an upward thrust to the hilt of the knife blade (length of the blade), striking the backbone, and withdraw making sure not to slit the incision wider, keeping it the size of the width of your blade.
- Sterilize your knife before sticking the next animal

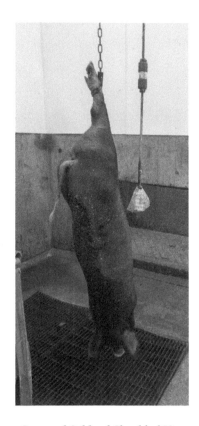

Stunned & bleed Shackled Hog
Credit: CPMCA image collection

SCALDING AND DEHAIRING

Not all abattoirs scald and de-hair their hogs in the following manner but we supply the information, as there are some who still do. Scalding is the process of loosening the hair from the carcass by using a hot water vat set at a temperature of approximately 60 - 65ºC. When using the water vat caution must be taken not to over scald the hog making it more difficult to remove the hair. Dehairing is the process of mechanically removing the hog hair, then manually checking for accuracy and removing any remaining hair. Scalding and Dehairing commonly involve the following:

- Lower the hog carcass into the scalding vat and keep the carcass moving as to avoid any formation of hot and cold spots, at about the 3 minute mark begin to test dehairing by pulling a small tuff of hair off the carcass

- The dewclaws should slip off the hind legs
- When the hair slips off the flank area and the dewclaws slip off the hind legs, remove the carcass from the vat and place in the dehairing machine
- Spray the hog with warm water while it is turning in the dehairing machine. This keeps the hair lubricated for ease of removal.

Note: In larger plants this process is automated and the carcasses are shackled coming out of the stunning chamber, hosted and bled, moved along a rail through the vat, to the hair removal, to the propane torches lining the walls of a tunnel or chamber that singe the remaining hair as the carcass progresses through.

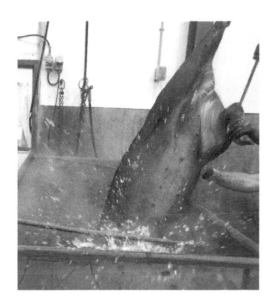

Scolding a hog to get ready for de-hairing

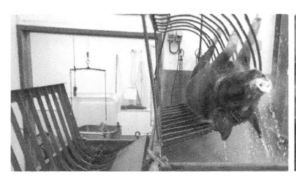

Transferring hog from hot water tank to de-hairer

De-hairing machine .

Credit: CPMCA image collection

CLEANING THE HEAD, FEET AND GAMBRELS

The legs, ears, face and jowls are regions of the carcass where it is difficult to remove hair with a dehairing machine. Greater effort is needed to remove hair from these areas. If not using an automated system of hair removal manual application will need to be employed. In the case of a manual system the following steps apply to the completion of hair removal from the hog carcass.

- Using a bell scraper remove any remaining hair on the legs
- Special care must be given to areas of skin fold, beneath the shackle crease, on the lower feet and around the snout and lips. The use of a sharp knife acting as a razorblade may be necessary taking care not to cut or slash the skin.
- Remove the dewclaws and toenails from the feet with a hook by inserting the hook into the tip of the toenail and pulling it off and away from the feet
- Cut away the soles and between the toes
- Expose the gambrel (upper part of the hock referred to as the foot in retail) tendons by cutting 2 parallel incisions through the skin on the backs of each hind leg from the dewclaws to the hock. With the incision made squarely in the center, the tendons will be exposed and the gambrel inserted for subsequent suspension on the rail.

Note: Gambrel has two meanings here, one referring to the hock's leg of the animal the other referring to the framework or spreader jamb butchers use to hang carcasses by the legs for evisceration of the animal.

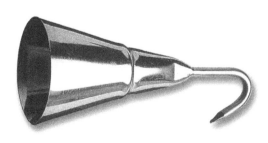

Hog bell scraper
Credit: Friedr.Dick- Germany

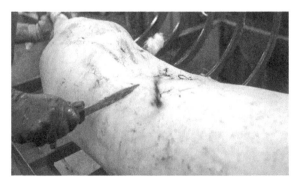

Shaving remaining hair with a knife
Credit: CPMCA image collection

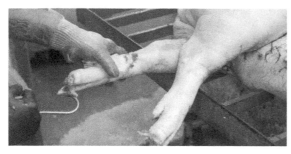

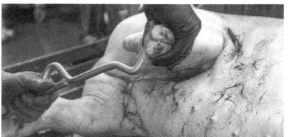

Removing dewclaws & toenails with hook
Credit: CPMCA image collection

Placing the gambrel on the hind feet
Credit: CPMCA image collection

MANUAL SINGEING AND SHAVING

Singeing and shaving are the last manual steps in hair removal. Once completed, the hog carcass should be totally devoid of hair. The process is as follows:

- Using a gas flame directly applied to the skin surface (like that of a propane torch), singe off any visible hair; this process makes visible that hair which wasn't visible before starting the process
- Keep the flame moving to avoid any burning of the skin surface
- Shave the remaining hair from the carcass with a sharp knife using razor motions
- Wash the carcass skin to remove any foreign material before moving on to evisceration.

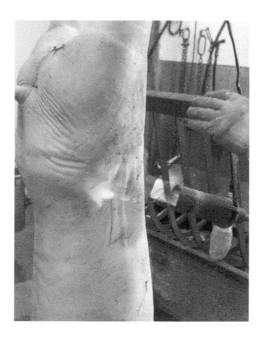

Singe off remaining hair
Credit: CPMCA image collection

EVISCERATION

The process of evisceration is the removing of the digestive tract from the carcass in such a way as not to contaminate the carcass. If the hog is a barrow, the pizzle (penis) and sheath should be dissected free and removed. If a barrow is found to be a ridgling (having an ingrown testicle), the carcass is set aside for further examination.

Begin the evisceration process by loosening the bung, and then dividing the pelvic bone finishing with opening the carcass. Take care to just break the skin, cutting through and toward the sternum and then apply the following steps:

- With the backside of the hog facing you, bung the hog pointing the tip of the knife downward and around the anus (and vulva in gilts).
- Spin the hog and have the belly facing you and divide the hams down the center of their medial juncture following the cartilaginous seam to the pelvic bone. Split the pelvic bone with the point of the knife.
- Make a short incision in the upper belly wall, grasp the knife with the thumb on the back of the blade and insert the fist into the body cavity with the blade pointed outward. Push downward cutting through the belly wall to your sternum and cut the sternum. With the severance of the abdominal wall, the viscera will fall forward and out.
- Pull the anus down being careful to separate the kidney from the anus. Grasp the viscera with the free hand, supporting the intestines with your forearm. Sever the blood vessel near the top of the liver on the right side to release the liver. Insert the free hand behind the stomach and roll it forward and out.
- Sever the gullet (esophagus) to release the viscera
- Cut around the juncture of the skirts and pillars of the diaphragm with the diaphragm membrane. Lift the hanging tender (pillar) to expose the dorsal aorta, cut across and then behind the aorta next to the backbone. Pull downward on the pluck and make two cuts, one on either side of the first ribs to free the pluck.
- Cut the jowls loose and make an incision down the inside of the jaw to remove the tongue and lymph nodes
- Remove the leaf fat by inserting the fingers beneath the layer of fat adhering to the abdominal wall near its juncture with the skirt at the center edge of the belly. Pull the fat upward slowly until the fist can be inserted, then fist the leaf fat to remove it from the belly pocket and ham base.
- The kidney is removed at the same time and is placed with the viscera for inspection

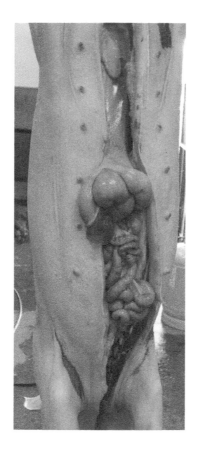

Evisceration preparation

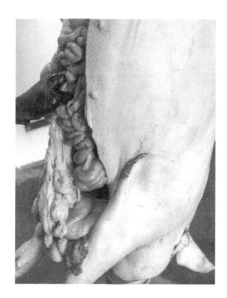

*Remove the intestines and pluck
(heart, lungs & liver)*

*Lift & peel the leaf lard
(internal belly fat lining)*

Credit: CPMCA image collection

SPLITTING THE HOG CARCASS

Splitting the hog carcass in preparation for inspection and chilling involves a degree of skill, eye and hand coordination. The butcher that splits hogs cuts them in half separating the sides by sawing down the middle centerline leaving equal portions of feather bones on each side producing two equal halves. The following steps are guidelines for splitting the carcass in preparation for inspection and chilling.

- Remove the head at the atlas joint and set aside for inspection
- Split the carcass through the centerline of the vertebral column and down the midline with a hand or power saw
- Prepare the sides for inspection by visually checking each side for traces of hair or other foreign matter and remove it
- Wash each side to remove traces of blood and bone dust from the splitting operation
- Tag, weigh and record each side moving them forward for inspection
- After inspection move the sides of pork into the chill cooler for overnight chilling

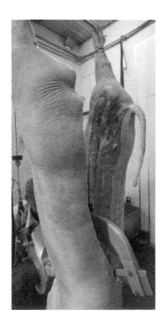

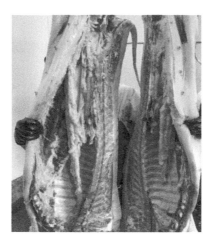

A split hog showing leaf lard & kidney location

Splitting the hog

A split hog head off, jowls on, washed & ready for the cooler

Credit: CPMCA image collection

Note: In automated plants this process is run on a continual basis with the hogs moving along a processing rail line where at each station a trained butcher performs a specific task i.e. sticking, bleeding, scalding, dehairing, evisceration, splitting, washing, weighing, etc.

GRADING OF PORCINE CARCASSES

The Canadian pork grading system was developed to facilitate the trade of carcasses by describing the commercially important attributes of pork carcass conformation. This system of grading ensures producers receive a fair, impartial, and equitable return based on the lean yield of their carcasses.

Quality Evaluation of the composition, amount of lean, and the weight of a carcass are three important criteria used to determine the value of a pork carcass to the packer. Objective instrumentation based on **light reflectance** (probe), **ultrasound**, or **electromagnetic conductivity** can be used to measure composition and carcass value. The need to increase lean value continues to be emphasized as external fat and seam fat deposits have little value and are both costly to produce and process. Pork, to be competitive with other sources of animal protein, must have desirable lean colour and acceptable water-holding capacity, and when cooked must be tender, juicy and flavourful.

Pork quality is assessed by the evaluation of the longissimus muscle (loin eye) and the back fat in the same general area. Colour, wetness, firmness, texture and marbling content of the exposed loin eye, are the primary lean quality traits. In addition, overall carcass quality assessment includes evaluation of belly thickness and the colour and firmness of the fat. Fat should be white in colour; variations from white hinder consumer acceptance. Soft, oily fat is not desirable.

Light Reflectance Probe is used to establish objective measurements. The probe needle is an objective way to previous subjective assessments and manual measurements. The probe needle is inserted between the 3rd and 4th rib of the carcass. The eye of the needle has a light sensor that measures the thickness of meat and fat levels as the probe is pulled out from each carcass by a government grader. A computer that is electrically connected to the probe then calculates the measurement of meat and fat. The computer generates a yield class, which estimates the percentage lean meat in each carcass (see Fig 1, page 695).

Ultrasound allows carcass composition to be evaluated more accurately. The ultrasound data form a 3 dimensional image describing the carcass composition of fat thickness and loin eye muscle thickness.

Electromagnetic conductivity refers to a method used to estimate carcass composition and in particular carcass fat. This method called a bioelectrical impedance, calculates the electrical opposition to the flow of an electrical current through muscle tissues producing a measurement of muscle water holding capacity, which is used to estimate fat-free muscle tissue mass and, by difference with carcass weight, carcass fat.

The factors used to evaluate pork carcasses also include rib-cage feathering, colour of lean and fat, firmness of lean and fat, and belly thickness. Feathering refers to the diagonally oriented streaks of fat bridging the lean between the ribs. Feathering is assumed to be a useful predictor of marbling within the muscle.

Carcass grading is based on a warm carcass weight, lean yield and fat cover. Lean yield is estimated from fat thickness and muscle depth, measured at the 3rd and 4th last ribs, 7 cm off the mid-line with either a Hennessy HGP-2 or Destron PG-100 probe. Yield is governed by a mathematical formula based on extensive carcass cutouts. The equation has two variables, fat thickness and lean depth measured by the probe. Probed fat measurements account for 90% of the variation in the lean yield percentage calculation while the lean measurement only provides a small modifying influence, in the formula. Generally, the lower the fat measurement, the higher the estimated percent lean yield.

The recorded warm carcass weight and the probe measurements are then placed on a grading grid.

The intersection of the dressed warm carcass weight and the calculated probe results of estimated percent lean yield within the grid, establishes the grade index for a carcass. 'The highest grade indexes within the grid determine best carcass value and pork meat yield (see Table 1).

Yield Class Number	Estimated Lean Yield Percentage	0 - 67.9 kg	68 - 72.9 kg	73 - 77.9 kg	78 - 82.9 kg	83 - 87.9 kg	88 - 92.9 kg	93 - 97.9 kg	98 - 102.9 kg	103 - 107.9 kg	108 - 111.9 kg	112 - 116.9 kg	117 - 999 kg
1	64.3 - 100	10	10	50	75	95	95	100	100	100	100	100	50
2	63 - 64.29	10	10	50	75	95	103	109	109	107	105	100	50
3	61.8 - 62.99	10	10	50	75	95	108	113	113	111	107	100	50
4	60.7 - 61.79	10	10	50	75	95	110	116	116	113	109	100	50
5	59.6 - 60.69	10	10	50	75	95	110	116	116	113	109	100	50
6	58.6 - 59.59	10	10	50	75	95	109	114	114	111	108	95	50
7	57.7 - 58.59	10	10	50	75	95	103	109	109	107	105	90	50
8	56.9 - 57.69	10	10	50	60	85	95	104	104	95	90	80	50
9	56.1 - 56.89	10	10	50	60	70	90	95	95	90	80	70	50
10	0 - 56.09	10	10	50	60	60	70	70	70	70	60	60	50

Table 1: Pork Grading Grid
Credit: Western hog Exchange

The probe needle is inserted between the 3rd and 4th ribs of the carcass.

The grader probe 7cm off the mid-line or split edge at 90 degrees to the outside surface of the skin

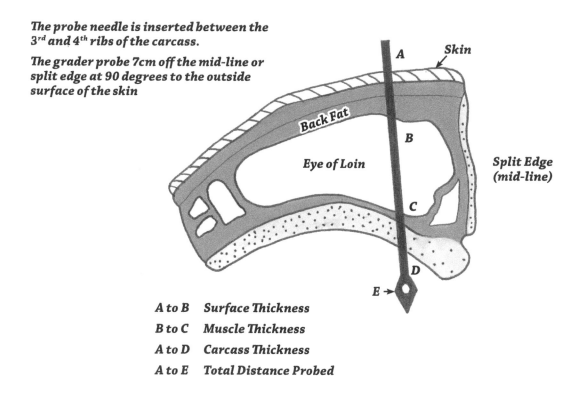

A to B	Surface Thickness
B to C	Muscle Thickness
A to D	Carcass Thickness
A to E	Total Distance Probed

Figure 1: Hog carcass fat & muscle probe

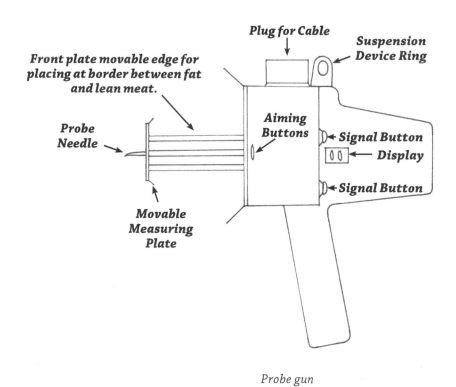

Probe gun

Harvesting of Ovine Carcasses

As with other domestic animals designated for the food chain, sheep should be rest overnight before being brought forward to the stunning area. The rest period allows for injured and victimized animals to be identified and for sick animals to be quarantined. When ready for slaughter, animals should be herded to the stunning area in a quiet and orderly manner without undue fuss and noise so as to keep them calm and not placing on them any undue stress. Animals should never be beaten nor have their tails twisted. Most sheep are passive creatures and need little encouragement to move forward.

STUNNING, SHACKLING AND STICKING

The process of harvesting sheep starts with gently herding the sheep one at a time into the stunning box. If a stunning box is not available or if only harvesting one animal, the nature of most sheep allows the butcher to manually restrain the animal by standing over it and holding it firmly between the legs (much like getting onto a horse but of course much smaller).

The common practice for stunning sheep is by electrocution using a two prong tong place strategically on the head and applying a high voltage current to render the animal insensible. The process of stunning, shackling and sticking is as follows:

- Gently herd the sheep into the stunning box
- Immobilize and make insensible by administering an electrical current to both temples, or to the center of the forehead, or by applying a mechanical stunning device to the poll (top or back of the head) or center of the forehead
- Shackle and suspend the animal, grasp the ear and insert the knife posterior to the mandible at its juncture with the base of the ear
- Insert the blade of the knife completely through the neck. The animal is bled by severing the carotid arteries and jugular veins
- Allow the carcass to remain suspended over a bleeding pit for about 8 minutes before initiating pelt removal.

REMOVING THE PELT

Removing the pelt or skin of ovine animals is initiated around the free hind leg exposing and loosening the tendon of the hock in preparation of hanging the carcass. This process is called legging. The second step is call pelting, the removal of the entire pelt in preparation for evisceration. Pelting (or skinning in the case of goats) can be performed with the carcass suspended or in a horizontal position (depending on the size of the operation or abattoir).

The pelts of sheep are most often contaminated with fecal matter. Important to the butcher skinning the animal is keeping the knife sanitized and keeping the outside of the pelt from touching the inside of the carcass during the skinning process. The steps to remove the pelt or skin of an ovine animal is as follows:

- Remove the skin around the hock and work toward the toes. This exposes the tendon on the back leg and the smooth joint just above the toes.
- Cut the foot off at this joint between the dewclaws and hooves and loosen the tendon for hanging. Hang the carcass by the leg.
- Remove the shackle and repeat the above steps.
- Open the pelt from the exposed leg region down along the posterior side and continue toward the anus; do both sides.
- Using either a knife or your fist, open the pelt to expose the leg and continue down the leg and over the rump region.
- Free the pelt at the front legs, score the joint at the lower end of the metacarpus and break it back and sideways. With sheep, the joint is a cartilaginous suture that can be broken apart. This break joint is the widest bulge at the end of the foreleg or just above the true spool or mutton joint.
- Make a cut through the pelt starting at the break/spool joint and continue up to the elbow pocket toward the jaw.
- Open the mid-line of the pelt by scoring a cut (taking care that you do not penetrate the abdominal cavity) from the crotch region to the throatlatch.
- Using a knife, the brisket is skinned back and up until the flanks are exposed.
- At this stage the knife is not normally used. This is to protect the fell, a fine membrane occurring between the skin and the carcass.
- Using your fist, separate the pelt from the carcass starting over the flanks and working up toward the legs, rump and around the sirloin region until it is loosened except at the point of attachment at the dock (tail). Work down the ribs, over the loin and rack and down the shoulders.

- The carcass should now be turned so to pull the pelt loose as close to the bung and dock as possible before a knife is used to cut this attachment loose.
- The pelt should be dropped to hang from the carcass with only the neck and fore legs being attached
- Make a knife cut from the cut made in the pelt on the fore leg through the elbow pocket to the breast region. The pelt can now be pulled down off of the neck and fore legs with knife cuts being made to loosen the feet attachment at the break/spool joint.
- This should leave the pelt attached at the head.
- A 10 -15 cm knife cut made longitudinally down the neck above the throatlatch (where the head and windpipe meet) will expose the trachea. Find the gullet (esophagus) and tie it off near attachment to the head.
- Cut the gullet and windpipe between the tied area and the head
- Remove the pelt with the head by cutting the head loose between the occipital condyles and the atlas vertebrae.
- Move the carcass to the first wash area.
- Thoroughly wash the carcass before evisceration

EVISCERATION

With the external coverings and parts removed, the pelt, feet and head, and with the esophagus tied off, the next step is to open the carcass cavity to dislodge and remove the contents. To avoid contamination of the carcass through accidental cuts or punctures of the stomach or intestines, we offer the following simple steps:

- First cut around the anus bung (about 25-30 cm) and tie it shut, and cover with a plastic bag preventing any fecal matter from contaminating the carcass. Cut it free and drop it in the pelvic cavity.
- If the animal was a wether (castrated ram), the pizzle should be disclosed free as near the base as possible
- Make a short incision in the upper abdominal wall, grasp the knife with the thumb on the back of the blade and insert the fist into the body cavity with the blade facing out.
- Push downward cutting the belly wall continuing the cut to the sternum. With the severance of the abdominal wall, the viscera will fall forward and out.
- Grasp the viscera with the opposite hand, supporting the intestines with the forearm.
- Sever the blood vessel near the top of the liver on the right side to release the liver, and inserting the hand behind the stomach, roll it forward and continue to hold it up

- Cut across and then behind the dorsal aorta next to the backbone.
- Pull outward on the pluck and make two cuts, one on either side of the first ribs, to free the thoracic contents
- Place the viscera and the pluck with the proper animal identification tags on the inspection table.
- Remove the kidneys and the kidney pelvic fat from the abdominal cavity. Expose the kidneys and place them with the viscera and the pluck for inspection.
- Saw through the sternum with a handsaw.

PREPARATION FOR CHILLING

To reduce and prevent deterioration of the carcass it must be chilled quickly in a cooler or chill chamber at a temperature in the range of minus 2 - 0°C.

- Bend the trotters back and pin them under the Fore shank tendons (cut through the back of the muscular portion of the fore shank about ½ cm deep and pull the narrow white tendon out and around the trotter).
- Carefully trim and remove any pieces of adhering pelt or skin, wool, bruises, hair and fecal matter. Wash the carcass with water being certain to clean the pelvic anal, throat region and areas beneath the fore shanks.
- Weigh and tag the carcass and present it for inspection.
- Chill the carcass.

Primary chilling is completed when the warmest point of the carcass has reached a temperature of about 4°C.. Providing there is good air circulation in the chilling cooler, this temperature can take between 12 – 24 hours but most certainly not longer than 48 hours to reach. Remember not to overcrowd the carcasses, leaving enough room between them for cooling purposes.

GRADING OF OVINE CARCASSES

There are 5 grades of ovine carcasses with the grade names of Canada AAA, Canada C1, Canada C2, Canada D1 and Canada D4, with 4 yield classifications of Canada 1, Canada 2, Canada 3 and Canada 4.

The maturity of the carcass is determined by examining its dentition or by determining the presence of a break joint or spool joint and examining the colour and distribution of blood deposits in the joint; or by way of an ear tag registering the animals date of birth.

Newborn lambs have no teeth and at 3 months of age have a full set of temporary teeth. In the range of 12 – 15 months, lambs have two permanent incisors. If the lamb has more than 2 permanent teeth it is then classified as mutton and graded accordingly.

GRADE STANDARDS FOR LAMB

A grader determines the average muscle score of an ovine carcass by evaluating the muscling of each primal cut. Each muscle from each primal is assigned a score ranging from a minimum of 1 to a maximum of 5 (meaning from poor, fair, good, very good, to excellent). The sum of the total score derived from each primal cut is then divided by 3 producing an average muscle score for the carcass.

The standards for an ovine animal carcass of the grade Canada AAA are as follows:

- The maturity characteristics,
  - fewer than 2 permanent incisors
  - 2 breaker joints with 4 intact and well-defined ridges with at least a slightly red and slightly damp surface
  - Ribs that are no more than slightly wide, tend to be rounded rather than flat and are reddish in colour

- A minimum muscling score of 2 for each primal cut and a minimum average muscling score of 2.6
- Flank muscles that are pink to light red in colour

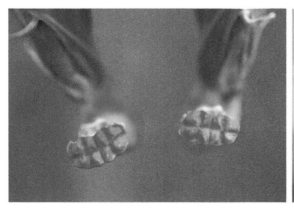

Break joints with 4 red intact ridges each
Credit: Summit Gourmet meat

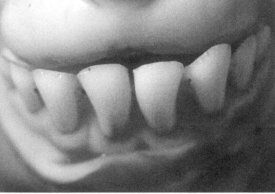

Under 12 months Lamb teeth
Credit: CPMCA image collection

- A fat covering that
  - is firm and white or slightly tinged with a reddish or amber colour
  - is not less than 4 mm in thickness at the measurement site, and
  - extends to provide at least a thin cover over the top of the shoulders, the back and the outside of the center part of the legs; and

- A minimum of traces of fat streaking(s) on the inside of the flank muscles.

The grader determines the fat level of an ovine carcass by measuring the fat with a ruler over the 12th rib and 11 cm off the midline of the carcass. This fat measurement determines the yield class. Yield class is only assigned to ovine carcasses graded as Canada AAA.

Yield Class for Lamb Carcasses Graded Canada AAA	
Fat Measurement (mm)	Yield Class
Less than 13	Canada 1
13 to 18.9	Canada 2
19 to 24.9	Canada 3
25 or more	Canada 4

MATURITY CHARACTERISTICS FOR MUTTON CARCASSES

- 2 or more permanent incisors
- 2 spool joints or, in the case of a carcass with one break joint and one spool joint, the break joint has a dry and mainly white surface with rounded or spooled ridges
- Ribs that are wide, flat and white.

The grading of lamb is voluntary and is seldom done except in larger processing facilities. The main objective of lamb grading is to set obvious standards of quality that can be readily recognized by those purchasing and selling ovine carcasses. The grading standards were developed to facilitate trade, establish equitable producer settlement, for consumer acceptance and as data for herd improvement.

For more on ovine carcass grading visit the Justice Laws Website, Livestock and Poultry Carcass Grading Regulations, SOR/92-541.

Spooled joints on a over 12-month carcass   *Images of teeth for 1-2 year old sheep*

Credit: CPMCA image collection

Harvesting Poultry

The system employed for the harvesting of poultry depends greatly on the poultry operation. For the most part, birds are caught, carried and placed in cages by hand. These cages are then loaded onto transport trucks and delivered to poultry plants for harvesting. Most all this takes place in the dark, keeping the birds calm.

Large Poultry automated plant
Credit: ©istock.com/credit to roibu

In large scale operations the birds are rested, individually loaded onto shackles by the legs and moved along a conveyer rail into the plant. From there the birds are rendered insensible by electrocution, throats slit, bled, have their heads removed, scalded, de-feathered, eviscerated and air or ice chilled all by automation, except for the inspection which is carried out by an inspector on the line.

Small-scale operations carry out the harvesting of birds manually, using simple equipment as follows:

- Stunned birds are held in a bleeding cone, with the head and neck pulled downward through the opening of the cone.
- The birds are dipped into a scalding tank, removed, placed in a de-feathering machine (a rudimentary tumbler with short rotating rubber fingers that strike the bird to remove the feathers).

- Pinfeathers are removed by hand and those that can't be removed by hand are singed off using a propane torch.
- The body cavity is opened, viscera removed, washed and inspected.
- The bird carcass is rinsed clean and ice packed in cold water for chilling.
- After chilling, the bird carcass is packaged and refrigerated for further processing and marketing.

GRADING OF POULTRY

Like red meats, poultry is subject to inspection and grading by the CFIA or a provincial counterpart. Inspection of poultry ensures poultry products are produced under strict sanitary guidelines and are wholesome and fit for human consumption. Inspection of poultry products destined for the food chain is required by Canadian law and is mandatory. No retail outlet may sell poultry that is not inspected or which does not carry a provincial or federal stamp of approval.

There are three grades assigned to poultry carcasses with the grade names Canada A, Canada Utility, and Canada C. These grades have no bearing on tenderness or flavour. Birds are graded according to their overall quality based on the following criteria:

- Shape of the carcass
- Amount of flesh
- Amount of fat
- Amount of pinfeathers present
- Skin tears, cuts, broken bones
- Blemishes and bruises

GRADE STANDARDS FOR CANADA A POULTRY

A poultry carcass of the grade Canada A shall meet the requirements set out in the Livestock and Poultry Carcass Grading Regulations and in accordance with the following standards:

Canada A grade poultry stamp
Credit: CPMCA image collection

- In the case of a chicken, chicken capon, Rock Cornish hen, mature chicken, old rooster, young turkey and mature turkey, not more than the wing tips and the tail have been removed;

- In the case of a young duck, mature duck, young goose, mature goose, young guinea and mature guinea, not more that the wing tips and the flat wings have been removed from the carcass;

- The carcass is not deformed except for a slightly crooked keel bone that does not interfere with the normal placement of the meat;

- The carcass is moderately plump breasted on both sides of the keel bone at the anterior end, with a moderate tapering of flesh towards the posterior end, and the keel bone at the anterior end does not project more that 3 mm beyond the flesh;

- In the case of poultry, other than a turkey, the breast, thighs and back show evidence of fat cover;

- In the case of turkey, the carcass has deposits of fat in the main feather tract on each side of the breast as indicated by a pronounced thickening at the centre of each such area;

- The carcass has no prominent discolourations exceeding an area of 1.6 cm squared in the aggregate of the breast, and an area of 6.5 cm squared in the aggregate elsewhere on the carcass (meaning overall);

- Where the carcass weighs less than 5.5 kilograms, the skin on the breast is not torn in excess of 6 mm in length and any tears on the skin elsewhere on the carcass do not exceed 2.5 cm in length in the aggregate;

- Where the carcass weighs 5.5 kilograms or more, the skin of the breast is not torn in excess of 1.2 cm in length and any tears on the skin elsewhere on the carcass do not exceed 3.5 cm in length in the aggregate;

- The carcass has no broken or dislocated bones; and

- The carcass does not have more than 3 cm of exposed flesh at the posterior end of the keel bone.

GRADE STANDARDS FOR CANADA UTILITY POULTRY

A poultry carcass of the grade Canada Utility shall meet the requirements set out in the Livestock and Poultry Carcass Grading Regulations and in accordance with the following standards:

- The carcass is not missing more than
  - the wings, or
  - one leg including the thigh or both drumsticks, or
  - the tail, or
  - small areas of the flesh, and
  - skin not exceeding an area equivalent to one half of the area of the breast;
- Where no skin has been removed, the carcass breast has sufficient fullness of flesh on both sides of the keel bone to prevent a sharp falling away of flesh from the anterior to the posterior end and the keel bone does not project more than 3 mm beyond the flesh;
- The carcass has at least a minimum fat cover to prevent the flesh from appearing prominently through the skin;
- The carcass has no prominent discolourations exceeding
  - An area of 6.5 cm squared in the aggregate on the breast, and
  - An area of 8 cm squared in the aggregate elsewhere on the carcass;
- The carcass has no dislocated bones other than in the wings or legs; and
- The carcass has no broken bones

A Poultry carcass may not be graded Canada Utility if the wings or any part of them has been removed elsewhere than at a joint; and only part of the drumstick has been removed (both being indications of broken bones).

A poultry carcass may not be graded Canada Utility if it meets the standards for grade Canada A. Poultry graded Canada Utility must bear the marks of poultry designated as Canada Utility, meeting the standards of Canada Utility. However, a mature chicken may be graded Canada Utility if the carcass weighs less than 1.8 kilograms.

Canada Utility grade poultry stamp
Credit: CPMCA image collection

A poultry carcass of the grade Canada C shall meet the requirements set out in the Livestock and Poultry Carcass Grading Regulations and in accordance with the following standards:

- The poultry carcass is the carcass of a mature chicken;
- The carcass breast has sufficient fullness of flesh on both sides of the keel bone to prevent an extremely sharp falling away of flesh from the anterior to the posterior end and the keel bone does not project more than 5 mm beyond the flesh; and
- The carcass has no prominent discolourations exceeding an area of 14.5 cm squared in the aggregate
- Mature chickens may not be graded Canada C if the carcass meets the standards for Canada A or the grade Canada Utility.

The colours of grade stamps for poultry are: Red for Grade A, Blue for Utility Grade, and Brown for Grade C.

Canada C grade poultry stamp
Credit: CPMCA image collection

SUMMARY

There are other forms of harvesting of animals not covered herein this chapter, game hunting and field dressing, mobile slaughtering, farm kills, and ethic or religious influences such as those of Halal and Kosher (see note below). What we have presented is the order and importance of inspection regarding the health and welfare of the animal, humane handling, the importance of inspection and cleanliness, and the condition, quality and processing of carcasses destined for the sole purpose of human consumption.

> **Note:** Halal meats are derived from the Islamic form of harvesting animals or poultry known as dhabiha, which involves slaughtering an animal by cutting through the jugular vein, carotid artery and windpipe. Animals must be alive and healthy at the time of slaughter and all blood is drained from the carcass. This process adheres to Islamic law as defined in the Koran.
>
> Kosher meats are harvested in accordance with the laws of the Torah. To be eaten, kosher animals must be slaughtered by a "Schochet," a ritual slaughter. Jewish Law permits the consumption of species that both chew their cud and have split hooves such as cattle, sheep, goats, bison and deer etc., though beef and lamb are generally the most common meats harvested in the kosher style of slaughtering.

TERMS FOR REVIEW

Abattoir	Gilt	Scalding
Abundant	Marbling	Shackle
Ante mortem	Muscling	Slight
Barrow	OTM	Small
Bung	Pizzle	SRM
Captive Bolt	Pluck	Stunner
Chilling	Postmortem	The Drop
DFD	Probe	Trace
Evisceration	PSE	Yield Ruler
Feather Bones	PSS	
Gambrel	Punch	

DISCUSSION QUESTIONS

1. Why do we require animals to be inspected before slaughter?

2. What are the four approved methods of humane stunning used in Canada?

3. Which of the above methods is most commonly used and why?

4. What might one repercussion be of low air pressure in a pneumatic pistol?

5. When bleeding an animal, which artery and which vein are severed?

6. What main sanitary precaution should a person skinning a carcass be concerned with?

7. Explain what the Drop refers to.

8. Why do we scald a porcine carcass after sticking it?

9. Pelts are associated with which species of animal we harvest?

10. Explain SRMs and list them.

11. Why do we grade meats?

12. Is grading mandatory for all species?

13. What is the meaning of the beef grade yield Canada 1?

14. Why does the colour of flesh play an important role in determining grades of veal?

15. How are porcine carcasses graded?

16. Explain the role of chilling?

17. Birds are graded according to their overall quality. List the criteria used to determine the quality of birds.

Appendix:

- SRMs
- References and Resources
    - Harvesting
    - Grading
    - Poultry
    - Seafood

SRMs

Legislation

The Food and Drug Regulations
Section B.01.047.1:

1. The following definitions apply to this section.
    "BSE" means bovine spongiform encephalopathy
    "Specified risk material" means:
    a) the skull, brain, trigeminal ganglia, eyes, tonsils, spinal cord and dorsal root ganglia of cattle aged 30 months or older; and
    b) the distal ileum of cattle of all ages.
2. No person shall sell or import for sale food that contains specified risk material.
3. Subsection (2) does not apply in respect of food that originates from a country that is designated as being free from BSE in accordance with section 7 of the Health of Animals Regulations.
4. Subsection (2) does not apply in respect to food that is packaged for sale or imported for sale before the day on which subsection comes into force.

The Health of Animals Regulations
Part 1.1: Specified Risk Material

6.1   In this part, "specified risk material" means:
      a) the skull, brain, trigeminal ganglia, eyes, tonsils, spinal cord and dorsal root ganglia of cattle aged 30 months or older; and
      b) the distal ileum of cattle of all ages.

6.2   Every person who slaughters, cuts up or debones cattle for human consumption, as food shall ensure that the specified risk material has been removed from the cattle.

6.3   No person shall use or export for human consumption as food specified risk material in any form, whether or not incorporated into another thing, where the specified risk material was removed from cattle slaughtered in Canada.

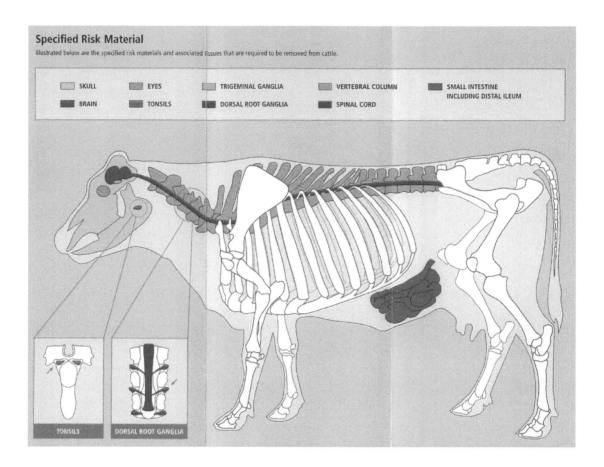

Specified Risk Material

Illustrated below are the specified risk materials and associated tissues that are required to be removed from cattle.

SKULL	EYES	TRIGEMINAL GANGLIA	VERTEBRAL COLUMN	SMALL INTESTINE INCLUDING DISTAL ILEUM
BRAIN	TONSILS	DORSAL ROOT GANGLIA	SPINAL CORD	

TONSILS   DORSAL ROOT GANGLIA

SRM HANDLING AND DISPOSITION

Because of structural differences between establishments, procedures for separating and isolating the various SRMs may vary. Generally, separation of SRMs should occur as soon as possible and care should be taken to avoid contamination of meat products and the established environment of SRMs. SRMs should be separated from carcasses at the earliest opportunity during the dressing process. SRM should be placed in inedible containers without delay and regularly moved to the inedible products area. This must include all SRMs separated from the carcass, equipment and debris from the floor.

Systems for containing debris from SRMs and operational cleaning of areas where SRMs are removed from OTM carcasses is important to the control of SRMs and food safety. SRMs debris shoveled from the kill floor or other areas where they may be, such as, drain channels, covers and traps, should all be deposited into an inedible container that is clearly marked as inedible. Use of squeegees is recommended. Drain covers and traps should be lifted and all matter collected from these sources shall be deposited into an inedible container, at the very least at the end of each day.

DETERMINING AGE FOR BEEF CATTLE

For the purposes of these regulations regarding SRMs, the CFIA has determined that cattle will be aged by dentition (eruption of permanent teeth). Cattle are considered to be aged 30 months or older when they have more than 2 permanent incisor teeth erupted (i.e. the first pair of permanent incisors and as least 1 tooth erupted from the second pair of permanent incisors). Illustrated below are the ranges of age in comparison to the eruption of permanent incisor teeth in cattle.

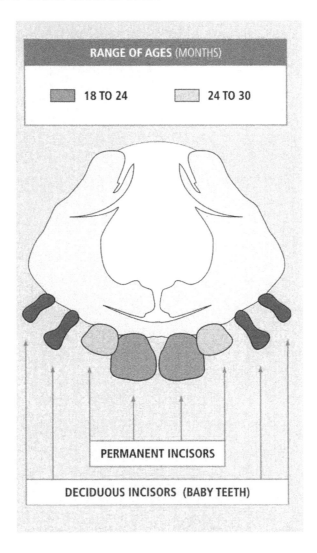

References and Resources:

GRADING OF DOMESTIC SPECIES

Justice Laws Website
Livestock and Poultry Carcass Grading Regulations
SOR/92-541
Canada Agricultural Products Act
Regulations Respecting The Grading of Livestock and Poultry Carcasses

POULTRY

CFIA, Meat and Poultry Products, Manual of Procedures, Program Changes, Inspection
Manual for Graded Poultry (www.inspection.ca)

Canadian Carcass Poultry Grading Program – Inspection Manual for Graded Poultry

Table of Contents

SEAFOOD

See chapter 9 and the CFIA website www.inspection.ca
Canadian Grade Compendium

Volume 8 – Fish
Fish Grade Requirements

Indices

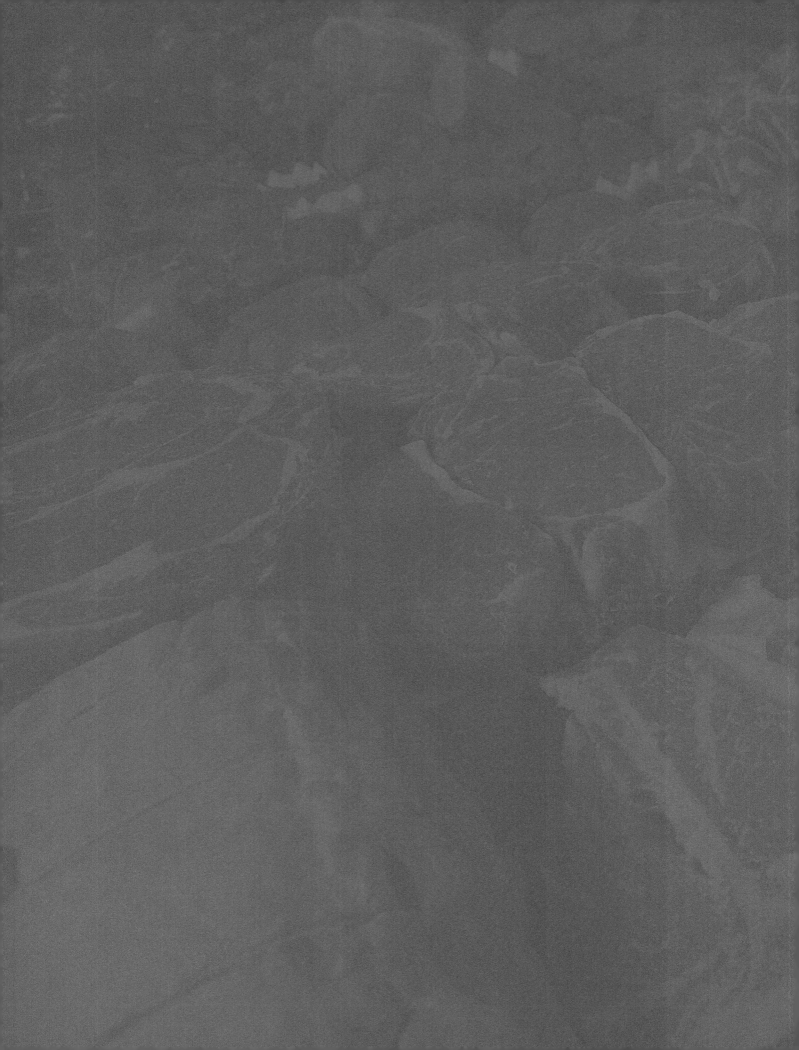

Key Words Index

This keyword index is sorted in alphabetic order and categorized by species, beef, bison, lamb, pork, poultry, veal etc., listed by primal, sub primal and retail options. When searching for a specific word you refer to the alphabetic order.

When searching for a specific primal, sub primal or retail option you would refer to the categorized order of species first and then the primal, sub primal or retail option.

Example: Looking for Lamb leg sirloin you would search under "L" for Lamb, continue to Lamb primal, ``leg`` and sub primal, ``sirloin.'' (351, 367, 368)

Example: when looking for equipment you would search under the name of the piece of the equipment, such as the Power saw under (P) and find there the pages referring to the power saw (94-103).

Image Key Index

This image index is sorted in alphabetic order and categorized by species, beef, bison, lamb, pork, poultry, veal etc., listed by primal, sub primal and retail options. When searching for a specific word you refer to the alphabetic order.

Example: when looking for images of knives you would search under "K" and find there the page reference (83).

When searching for an image of a specific primal, sub primal or retail option you would refer to the categorized order of species first and then the primal, sub primal or retail option.

Example: Looking for an image of a beef inside round you would search under "B" for beef and continue till you come to "Beef sub primal, inside round." (280)

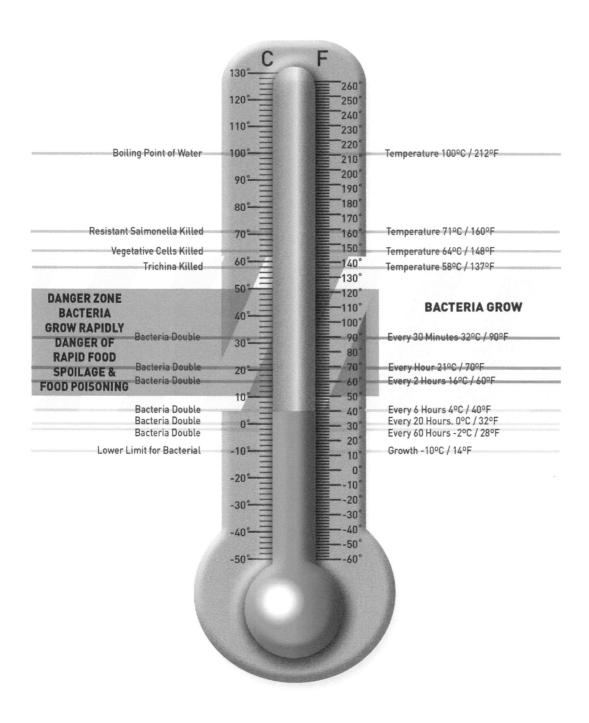

Appendix: Bacterial Growth Temperature Guide
Credit: Canada Pork International

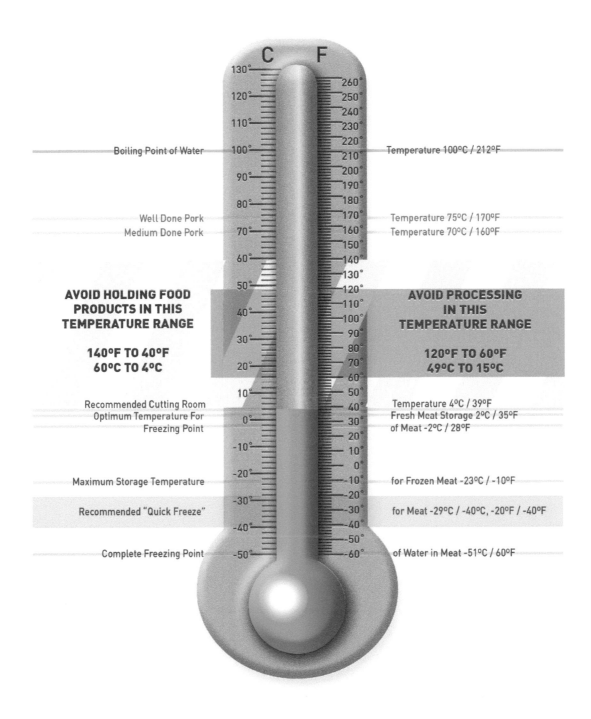

Boiling Point of Water — 100° — Temperature 100°C / 212°F

Well Done Pork — — Temperature 75°C / 170°F
Medium Done Pork — — Temperature 70°C / 160°F

**AVOID HOLDING FOOD
PRODUCTS IN THIS
TEMPERATURE RANGE**

**140°F TO 40°F
60°C TO 4°C**

**AVOID PROCESSING
IN THIS
TEMPERATURE RANGE**

**120°F TO 60°F
49°C TO 15°C**

Recommended Cutting Room — — Temperature 4°C / 39°F
Optimum Temperature For — — Fresh Meat Storage 2°C / 35°F
Freezing Point — — of Meat -2°C / 28°F

Maximum Storage Temperature — — for Frozen Meat -23°C / -10°F

Recommended "Quick Freeze" — — for Meat -29°C / -40°C, -20°F / -40°F

Complete Freezing Point — — of Water in Meat -51°C / 60°F

*Appendix: Safe Meat handling Temperature Guide
Credit: Canada Pork International*